Cassian the Monk

OXFORD STUDIES IN HISTORICAL THEOLOGY

PRIMITIVISM, RADICALISM, AND THE LAMB'S WAR
The Baptist-Quaker Conflict in Seventeenth-Century England
T. L. Underwood

THE GOSPEL OF JOHN IN THE SIXTEENTH CENTURY
The Johannine Exegesis of Wolfgang Musculus
Craig S. Farmer

CASSIAN THE MONK
Columba Stewart

Cassian the Monk

Lawrence S. Cunningham
Notre Dame — 1998

Columba Stewart

New York   Oxford
OXFORD UNIVERSITY PRESS
1998

Oxford University Press

Oxford   New York
Athens   Auckland   Bangkok   Bogota   Bombay   Buenos Aires
Calcutta   Cape Town   Dar es Salaam   Delhi   Florence   Hong Kong
Istanbul   Karachi   Kuala Lumpur   Madras   Madrid   Melbourne
Mexico City   Nairobi   Paris   Singapore   Taipei   Tokyo   Toronto   Warsaw

and associated companies in
Berlin   Ibadan

Published by Oxford University Press, Inc.
198 Madison Avenue, New York, New York 10016

Oxford is a registered trademark of Oxford University Press

Library of Congress Cataloging-in-Publication Data
Stewart, Columba.
Cassian the monk / Columba Stewart.
p. cm. — (Oxford studies in historical theology)
Includes bibliographical references and index.
ISBN 0-19-511366-7
1. Cassian, John, ca. 360–ca. 435.   2. Monastic and religious
life — History of doctrines — Early church, ca. 30–600.   I. Title.
II. Series.
BR65.C33S74 1998
271'.0092 — dc21   97-12127
[B]

1   3   5   7   9   8   6   4   2
Printed in the United States of America
on acid-free paper

*For my parents,
and in memory of my grandparents.*

Preface

I WRITE AS A MONK ABOUT A MONK. But it is not that simple. John Cassian was a monk of his own time and place, shaped by cultures and encounters we can never know as he did. My affinity with him lies not in shared experience but in a shared commitment to the monastic life. I find Cassian's teaching to be often stunningly relevant for modern monastic Christians who take monasticism seriously as a way of life for the world and not against it, but simply to repristinate his understanding of the monastic life would be to deny the very Spirit which gave it birth. I am most intrigued not by the details of monastic observance Cassian describes, but by his fundamental convictions. Only they can explain the daring scope of his project: a comprehensive monastic theology. His achievement is unique.

It is impossible in one book to explore the vast landscape of Cassian's monastic writings. I focus primarily on the issues to which my monastic experience and interest naturally lead me. Even so I have had to choose, and therefore have selected what I have judged to be the most central and distinctive aspects of Cassian's monastic theology. As a result, important topics such as the discernment of thoughts, Cassian's consideration of the traditional eight principal faults and many other aspects of his ascetical theology receive little direct attention in this study. Cassian's teaching on those topics, accessible to us elsewhere in the literature of early monasticism, requires comparatively little exploration here.

This book begins with an overview of Cassian's life and work. Cassian is elusive, yet establishing what we know about him allows us to relate his writings to his own experiences and to the places and events that shaped what he wrote. He was a man of many lands and roles; the constant in his extraordinary life was a monastic vocation lived in service to the church. "Cassian the Monk," the title of chapter 1, appropriately serves as the title for the whole book.

Chapter 2, "Cassian the Writer," explores the nature and scope of Cassian's monastic writings, the *Institutes* and *Conferences*. There I suggest that one must recognize the various (and concurrent) intentions and meanings those texts bear so as to avoid reductionist interpretations of them.

Chapter 3, "Cassian the Theologian," sketches Cassian's fundamental theology of the monastic life. He described a trajectory toward a proximate goal of "purity of heart" and an ultimate destination of the "reign of God." His eschato-logical orientation was central to his intention and therefore must be so to our understanding of his theology. His goal of purity of heart meant a contemplative stance toward all human experience, including human experience of God. His teaching on the interplay of contemplation and action speaks directly to a peren-nial challenge in the monastic life. Finally, there is the question of the end: is heavenly beatitude somehow possible in this life, or is it a purely eschatological reality?

Chapter 4, "Flesh and Spirit, Continence and Chastity," probes Cassian's ascetical teaching as given to us in his writings about lust and chastity. Given that I could not adequately explore all eight principal faults and their corresponding virtues, I chose the theme that most fully integrates and represents Cassian's un-derstanding of human development. Because he always presented his controver-sial teaching on grace and free will within discussions about chastity, I shall study it where he did.

Chapters 5 and 6, "The Bible and Prayer" and "Unceasing Prayer," explore the interplay of the Bible and prayer in Cassian's theology. Because Bible and prayer converge in the monastic encounter with Christ, Cassian's reading of the Bible and his teaching on imageless prayer were inseparable from his Christology (chapter 5). His ways of prayer, especially his method of unceasing prayer, were all based on biblical models and texts (chapter 6). Cassian's teaching on prayer is faithful to earlier monastic tradition but distinctive in scope and depth: his presen-tation of a method of prayer based on a continually repeated biblical phrase is the most thorough in early monastic literature.

Chapter 7, "Experience of Prayer," considers the most intriguing aspect of Cassian's theology of prayer, his emphasis on experiences of ecstasy and tears. Here Cassian's teaching has remarkable affinities with that of Diadochus of Pho-tike, who, like Cassian, integrated the spiritual theology of Evagrius Ponticus with the kataphatic spiritual tradition exemplified by the writings of Pseudo-Macarius. Cassian may, then, have been the bridge to the Latin West not only for Evagrian spirituality but also for the affective, experiential mysticism typical of the Syrian tradition. His creative synthesis would bear great fruit in the spirituality of Greg-ory the Great and the medieval theologians inspired, in turn, by Gregory.

This book has been written for two audiences that partly overlap: on the one hand, monastic men and women and those who are drawn to monastic spiritual-ity; on the other, scholars and students of the early Christian era. As I wrote I always kept in mind those who regard Cassian primarily as a teacher in the mo-nastic life. They may wish to concentrate on chapters 3–7. Despite the heavy burden of notes in this book, its narrative line does not depend on the notes, and they may safely be left aside by those uninterested in the details. I have, however, included abundant references both to Cassian's writings and to other early monas-tic texts so that a reader's interests can be pursued in the sources themselves. Cassian has long deserved thorough study. I hope that my colleagues in the study of early Christian monasticism will find the details as intriguing and enriching as I have.

A detailed list of acknowledgments appears elsewhere. Here I must acknowledge two debts. My confreres of Saint John's Abbey sustain me daily with their love and their prayers. With and from them I have learned what I know about the monastic life, and they have given me the opportunity to teach and to write. I owe a scholarly debt to previous students of early monastic history and spirituality. I feel obliged to recognize particularly the great French scholars of this century whose names are so evident in the notes and bibliography. Their work has been a constant source of inspiration and edification.

I dedicate this book to my parents, especially my mother, Lorraine Mackay Stewart, for her seventieth birthday; and to the memory of my grandparents, especially Frances Isabella Stewart, whose generosity supported my undergraduate education.

Columba Stewart OSB   Saint John's Abbey and University
                                        Collegeville, Minnesota
                                        Gaudete Sunday 1996

Acknowledgments

THE RESEARCH FOR THIS BOOK was made possible by a sabbatical leave from Saint John's University, a fellowship from the National Endowment for the Humanities, and the generosity of Abbot Timothy Kelly and the monks of Saint John's Abbey.

The following individuals read and commented on portions of this book: Dr. William Cahoy, Dr. Sarah Coakley, Br. Joseph Feders OSB, Fr. Alexander Golitzin, Mr. Daniel Gullo, Fr. Terrence Kardong OSB, Fr. Edmund Little, Fr. Kilian McDonnell OSB, Fr. Rene McGraw OSB, Br. Gregory Perron OSB, Dr. Philip Rousseau, Fr. David Scotchie, Mr. A. W. Richard Sipe, Mrs. Lorraine Mackay Stewart, Fr. Adalbert de Vogüé OSB, Sr. Susan Wood SCL, and an anonymous reader for Oxford University Press. Portions of this book were shared with the theology faculty of Saint John's University and the College of Saint Benedict; members of the Master Theme on Monasticism at the Twelfth International Conference on Patristic Studies (Oxford, 1995); the junior monks of Saint John's Abbey and their formation director, Fr. John Klassen OSB; the members of the American Benedictine Academy; the students of the Saint John's University School of Theology seminar on "The Bible and Prayer" (fall 1996).

I have received support of various kinds from the faculty, staff, and student workers of the department and School of Theology, Saint John's University; the staff of the Alcuin Library at Saint John's University, especially Ms. Anne Schluender and Ms. Beverly Ehresmann; the staff and faculty of the École Biblique et Archéologique Française de Jérusalem, where much of the first draft of this book was written; Dr. and Mrs. John S. Kendall. Fr. Mark Sheridan OSB allowed me to use his invaluable electronic index of Cassian's monastic works; Fr. Boniface Ramsey OP allowed me to consult the manuscript of his then unpublished commentary on the *Conferences*; Dr. Steven Driver allowed me to read his unpublished thesis on Cassian. Ms. Mary Schaffer of Arca Artium, Saint John's University, found the eleventh-century drawing used on the cover; I thank the Historisches Archiv in Cologne for permission to use it. Br. David Manahan OSB helped with technical matters and prepared the map. Br. Boniface Jacobs OSB checked the hundreds of references to Cassian's works. I thank all of these people and all my long-suffering confreres and friends.

Contents

Note on Citations

A list of abbreviations and full references to works cited may be found in the bibliography.

Citations of Cassian's works are from the edition edited by Michael Petschenig in CSEL 13 and 17. For the *Institutes*, book, chapter, and section are cited: for example, *Inst.* 4.39.2. The *Conferences* are cited by the number of the Conference, chapter, and section: for example, *Conf.* 16.3.1. For the treatise *The Incarnation of the Lord*, book, chapter, and section are cited: for example, *De Inc.* 7.31.4–7. In the interest of economy I have omitted page references to Petschenig's edition. His divisions and numbering of the text are followed in the various modern translations of Cassian's works.

Quotations from Cassian follow the orthography of Petschenig's edition, with the exception of consonantal *u*, which I have changed to *v*.

Cassian the Monk

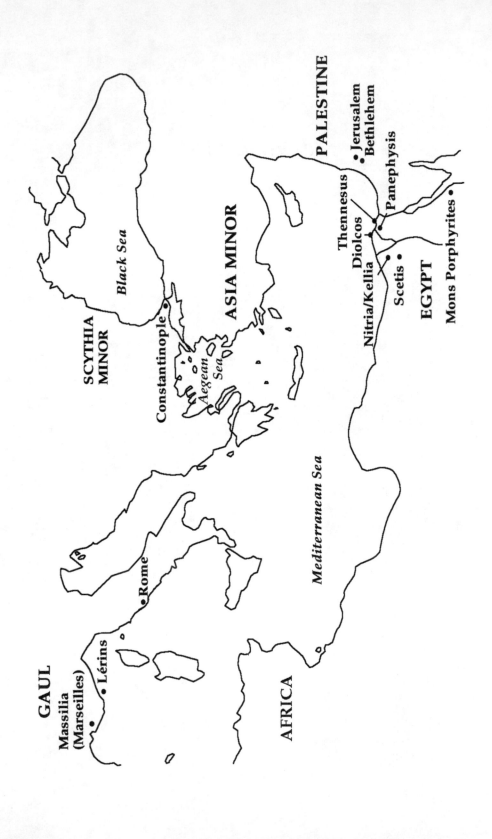

CHAPTER ONE

Cassian the Monk

What is most striking in Cassian's work are his silences.

—Cappuyns, "Cassien"

Elusiveness

JOHN CASSIAN, LIKE OTHER EARLY MONKS, eludes his modern readers. His discursive writing style, his evocations of incredible degrees of ascetical and contemplative perfection, his antique (and male-centered) understanding of sexuality dissuade even the hardy from threading their way through his thicket of words. More fundamentally, the religious assumptions and imperatives that underlie and empower his works can be unfamiliar or misunderstood. Monastic readers, and those who share their interests, continue to find much of Cassian's teaching helpful, though his work is increasingly opaque even to them. The aim of this study is to bring us to Cassian and him to us, to catch his voice as well as I can while knowing that whatever he says requires both translation and interpretation.

Cassian offers his *Conferences* as a way for the new monks of Gaul to overhear the great monks of Egypt speaking as they did back home (though now, of course, in Latin).[1] His pose of faithful reporting and neutral translation is just that, for his audience in Gaul looms large in both the *Institutes* and *Conferences*. Any effort to understand and interpret Cassian for readers today will be equally subjective and will surely betray interests besides his. But as Cassian himself found, the imperative to interpret finally overcomes the fear of betrayal.

Cassian's elusiveness is central to his story.[2] Extraordinarily self-effacing, he resists our efforts to know and understand him. There are clues but no *Vita Cassiani*. He had no contemporary biographer, and the brief sketch by Gennadius a few decades after Cassian's death has generated more controversy than certainty. We do not know where or when he was born, and even his name is not certain. The chronology of major events in his life or of his writings rests on deduction rather than solid evidence.

Had we only Cassian's *Institutes* and *Conferences*, which are the major focus of this study, our sense of him as a monk very much involved in the larger church would be vastly diminished. A handful of references in contemporary documents reveal that this great advocate of the monastic life had served in the episcopal retinue of John Chrysostom in Constantinople and helped to carry the deposed Chrysostom's appeal to Rome. All this ecclesiastical activity was *after* his experience of the anchoritic life in Egypt that became his monastic ideal. His little-read treatise on Christology, *The Incarnation of the Lord*, proves that his last public act was to write a work of polemical theology aimed not at monks but at the doctrinal challenge posed by Nestorianism. Crucial scholarly discoveries of the twentieth century have uncovered his carefully (and necessarily) concealed dependence on his unnamed master, Evagrius Ponticus, and on their common inspiration, Origen.

Although there are many things he does not tell us about himself, Cassian does not seem to have been embarassed by his extensive (and sometimes "unmonastic") *curriculum vitae*. His personal reticence can be explained only by his own sense that he was a monk with a mission. His mission was simply this: to provide the best foundation for the emerging monasticism of southern Gaul. Having seen his monastic ideal in Egypt shattered by politics and sheer spite, Cassian was given the unexpected chance to craft another. He did so with remarkably little self-advertisement beyond what he judged necessary to establish his monastic credentials.[3] As Karl Suso Frank has noted, Cassian's information on himself "merges with his presentation and is absorbed by it."[4] His humility, however virtuous, is his biographer's first challenge.

Birthplace and Childhood

Cassian's thorough self-effacement begins at the beginning: he never tells us where he was born. This gap in our knowledge has generated a subindustry within Cassian studies. Whatever evidence Cassian himself provides is stunningly neutral, and can be made to fit either of the two major contenders: Gaul and the region between the Danube and the Black Sea known in late antiquity as Scythia Minor and more recently as the Dobrudja, a part of modern-day Romania. The arguments made for these and other putative birthplaces swirl dizzyingly about the meager evidence.[5]

First, his name: he is always called "Cassianus" by his contemporaries and near contemporaries. In his own works, the name "Iohannes" appears only twice, and "Cassianus" never.[6] It may be that Cassian was his given name and John a monastic one.[7] Cassianus was a common enough name, derived from the even more common Cassius; both were found throughout eastern and western regions of the Mediterranean world.[8] The name itself tells us nothing about his birthplace.[9]

Cassian was probably born sometime in the early 360s.[10] One learns from his own writings that the family landholdings were wooded and fruitful (*Conf.* 24.1.3)[11] and that the weather was cold (*Conf.* 24.8.5).[12] The region was also "bound by the cold of great infidelity" (*Conf.* 24.8.5)[13] and without many monks (*Conf.* 24.18).[14] As a young man Cassian had a tutor and learned classical literature (*Conf.* 14.12). Of family members he mentions only a sister who remained somehow a part of his monastic life (*Inst.* 11.18); she may have ended up with him in Marseilles, perhaps at the monastery for women he is reputed by Gennadius to have founded.[15] For him to travel to Palestine and Egypt meant passing through "many lands" (*Conf.* 1.2.3, 3.2.1).

Cassian's most direct statement about his *patria* is the one least to be credited. In *The Incarnation of the Lord*, when appealing to the church of Constantinople to avoid the heresy of Nestorius, he calls them his "fellow-citizens through love of the homeland" (*patria, De Inc.* 7.31.3). This rhetorical tribute to the work of his dead master, John Chrysostom, was not meant to be read literally. Our only other clue, another rhetorical flourish, occurs in the preface to the *Institutes.* Cassian compares himself to Hiram of Tyre, who although a poor man and a foreigner was called to advise Solomon on the building of the Temple (3 Kgs. 7:13–14). Cassian has been invited by Bishop Castor of Apta Julia, north of Marseilles, to advise on the construction of the true temple of monastic life (*Inst. Pref.* 1–2). When he completes the parallel and speaks of himself as "in want of all things and among the very poorest," he omits the descriptor of foreigner; to some this omission has indicated that he was no stranger to Gaul.[16] Yet the power of the biblical type itself, to which Hiram's alien status is integral, may well supply what Cassian fails to state explicitly about himself: that he, like Hiram, was a foreigner.

The only near contemporary who remarks on Cassian's nationality is Gennadius, also of Marseilles, who opens his biographical sketch with the note that Cassian is "of the Scythian people" (*natione Scytha*).[17] This apparently straightforward remark has become the most thoroughly plowed patch of scholarly investigation. Those inclined to place Cassian's homeland in Gaul have suggested that the phrase *natione Scytha* refers to Scetis, Cassian's *monastic* homeland, while others have read Gennadius in the more obvious sense of locating Cassian's birthplace in Scythia Minor.[18] Other nominees have been Athens, Palestine, and Sert, a town near Bitlis in Kurdistan.[19] Gaul and the Dobrudja are the main contenders, with the weight of modern scholarly opinion favoring the latter. There is no consensus and probably never will be.

Photius, the ninth-century bishop of Constantinople whose notes on the contents of the patriarchal library provide precious information about many ancient writings that no longer survive, referred to Cassian, whom he had read in a Greek abridgement, as "a Roman"; he probably meant simply that Cassian was a Latin.[20] The reference does not help us locate Cassian's birthplace, but Photius' notes on a Greek version of Cassian's works alert us to an important fact: Cassian was recognized by Greek monks as somehow one of their own. Their translation of his works into Greek was a rare compliment; even more remarkably, some of his stories were included in the great *Alphabetical Collection* of the *Apophthegmata*, the sayings of the desert monks. He is the only Latin so honored within that vastness of monastic wisdom.[21]

Cassian professed to be bringing the eastern monastic tradition to the West. His reception by the East provides at least some validation of his claim, for one sees him moving between eastern and western Christianity with ease.[22] The medium was his bilingualism, and his entire achievement was built on that simple fact. While Cassian's mastery of Latin suggests that he was a native speaker and writer,[23] he used Greek daily for at least twenty-five years in Bethlehem, Egypt, and Constantinople. One can judge his Greek only on the indications he gives within his Latin writings, but these suggest that he both spoke and read the language well.[24] He knew his Bible in Greek and could cite Greek Christian authors.[25] This bilingualism makes the most compelling argument for the Balkan hypothesis: in Cassian's day Scythia Minor was a bilingual region where he could have received a classical Latin education in an environment where Greek had a strong presence.[26] A century later a Scythian living in Rome, Dionysius Exiguus, would draw on such a background to translate Greek theological, monastic, and canonical texts into Latin.[27] Of course, an educated young man in Gaul could certainly have studied Greek; Marseilles, where he spent his final years, was a city with Greek roots and a brisk sea trade with the East.[28] Cassian could also have learned Greek when he arrived in Palestine. Whatever his background, he made his way comfortably in the Christian East, where he learned the monastic life and, later, worked in the church of Constantinople. Though his destiny lay in the Latin West, he was very much at home in the Greek East.

Monastic Beginnings in Bethlehem

Around 380 Cassian went to Palestine,[29] travelling with an older friend, Germanus, who was to be his constant companion for at least the next twenty-five years.[30] Cassian writes warmly of Germanus, using the beautiful, though unoriginal, image of their being as "one heart and soul in two bodies" (Conf. 1.1). Germanus serves as the interlocutor in the Conferences; in one of them, Abba Nesteros addresses Cassian as the younger (Conf. 14.9.4). External evidence from the time they later spent in Constantinople confirms both that Germanus actually existed and that he was the elder.[31]

We do not know why Cassian settled in Bethlehem, a small town dominated by the Constantinian basilica built over the Cave of the Nativity of Jesus. He and Germanus came to the Holy Land at a time when both pilgrimage and the monastic life were booming, and their intentions surely pertained to both. A couple of asides indicate a familiarity with the geography of Palestine; surprisingly, however, Cassian never mentions the Jerusalem of his day or its holy places.[32] His focus remains on Bethlehem, where he and Germanus became monks.

The cenobium in which they lived seems to have been near the basilica, for Cassian describes it as "our monastery where our Lord Jesus Christ was born of a Virgin" (Inst. 3.4). He notes that they were not far from the Cave of the Nativity (Inst. 4.31) and that the fateful promise to make only a brief visit to Egypt was sworn in the cave itself (Conf. 17.5). Theirs was perhaps the monastery at the Shepherds' Field where Palladius would later spend a year.[33] Although Cassian used and recommended Jerome's writings,[34] he makes no mention of Jerome's monastery in Bethlehem founded in 386.[35] Because of this omission, it is commonly assumed that Cassian and Germanus had arrived in Bethlehem before Jerome and thus were not monks of his community.[36] The language of Jerome's community was Latin (though there were some easterners in it[37]); Cassian seems to have been formed in an entirely Greek monastic milieu.[38]

Cassian's depiction of the Bethlehem community is skewed by his exaltation of all things Egyptian. He shows us a cenobium struggling somewhat with disciplinary matters. The monks liked to go back to bed after the night office, and a way had to be devised to keep them awake (thus, suggests Cassian, the origins of a new morning liturgical office);[39] at the same time, they tended to be rather inflexible about rules of fasting and unlikely to accommodate their discipline to the demands of hospitality (*Inst.* 5.24). These sleepy but dutiful cenobites could not match the real monastic perfection of the Egyptian desert; although Cassian and Germanus were nourished appropriately for their "infancy" (*Inst.* 3.4.1), Bethlehem came to represent a stage to be left behind.[40] Once in Egypt, Cassian claimed, they were told to forego all they had been taught previously and to follow only the Egyptian ways: perhaps this statement was a signal to the monks of Gaul to do the same (*Conf.* 18.3.1).

Cassian's comments about Bethlehem suggest that he entered the monastery young and was not there for more than a few years.[41] Inspired by the lore of an old Egyptian fellow named Pinufius who was put up in their cell, Cassian and Germanus were dazzled when he was revealed to be a famous cenobitic abbot who had fled his monastery in the Nile Delta in order to preserve his humility. His monks tracked him down and then hauled him home, as they had already done once before.[42] This Abba Pinufius left his young friends with a thirst for the monasticism to be found only in Egypt. Despite their youth, Germanus and Cassian secured permission to visit Egypt for a short tour of the monasteries.[43] Their journey took place not long after meeting Abba Pinufius;[44] while in Egypt Cassian could still be described as "young," suggesting that they left Bethlehem in the mid-380s for what was to become a new monastic home.[45]

Egypt

A Trustworthy Witness?

For Cassian's early life we have only picked-over scraps of evidence, but his experiences in Egypt produced a bewildering array of information. His intention to give the monks of Gaul a vivid picture of Egyptian monastic life meant that he laced the *Institutes* and *Conferences* with a good deal of geographical, biographical, anecdotal material. He was not, however, writing a gazetteer of Egyptian monasticism, and the goal of monastic instruction determined both the structure and the content of his writings. Details about landscape and people are primarily illustrative, included to lend both atmosphere and authority to his own synthesis of monastic theology.[46]

When one moves from incidental remarks about Egypt to the narrative level, Cassian's theological intentions predominate: for him, history is in the details, and the bigger picture is theological. His account of the origins and evolution of monasticism, for example, is historically worthless, but it serves his pedagogical task well.[47] His report on the Anthropomorphite controversy in Scetis is only a vignette, so narrow in its view that it can easily mislead the reader into thinking that his side won the day (*Conf.* 10.2–3). When interpreted theologically, however, the story becomes central to his teaching on prayer.[48]

Both the determinative role of Cassian's larger purpose and the problem of his tendentious narratives about monastic life in Egypt are real issues that inevitably shape one's interpretation of his writings. Nonetheless, these concerns are at least somewhat distinct from the issue of the *reliability* of his geographical and biographical asides. Although there is disagreement about how much time he actually spent in Egypt, no one doubts that he was there. Close study reveals that there is more autobiographical and historical data to be gleaned from his writings than has sometimes been allowed.[49] In his monastic writings Cassian interweaves his direct knowledge with the literary sources available to him. Much of the information contained in the *Institutes* and *Conferences* is unique to him and is based evidently on his own experiences. What he tells us about places and people can often be collated with other texts[50] to indicate that by and large he is a useful, trustworthy and important witness to the late-fourth-century monastic scene in Lower Egypt.[51] Such evidence of his familiarity with the principal places and people of that extraordinary monastic world supports his oft-repeated claim to teach from experience rather than hearsay.

Early Days: Monasticism in the Nile Delta

Cassian and Germanus probably left for Egypt in the mid-380s and stayed until 399–400. There is only one datable incident mentioned in his writings about the stay in Egypt: we can date Theophilus' controversial letter about Anthropomorphism (*Conf.* 10.2) to early 399. We know from external evidence that the controversy must have occurred near the end of Cassian's stay. Dating the departure for Egypt depends on conjectures about Cassian's cenobitic life in Bethlehem. The only other clue is a reference at the end of *Conference* 17 to a brief visit to Bethlehem after seven years in Egypt, followed by a return to Scetis. This timeframe has been accepted by most scholars even though the passage is not found in at least one early manuscript.[52] While the argument for excluding that reference is hardly conclusive, it is nonetheless true that the chronology of Cassian's stay in Egypt must be inferred largely from circumstantial evidence and from the significance he himself attaches to his experiences there. The normative role of Egyptian monasticism in Cassian's imagination and teaching suggests that his sojourn in Egypt was deeply formative and therefore must have been at least several years long.

Cassian never lays out a complete itinerary for the fifteen or so years he and Germanus spent in Egypt. We know they spent time in the Nile Delta, in Scetis, and at Kellia. They never went farther south despite their original hope to do so (*Conf.* 11.1).[53] From *Conferences* 11–17 we can construct a coherent picture of their visit to Lower Egyptian monasteries.[54] Arriving by boat at the port of Thennesus,[55] they met a former anchorite named Archebius[56] who was now bishop of the nearby city of Panephysis.[57] Elected bishop after what he reckoned to have been thirty-seven years of anchoritic failure, Archebius maintained a monastic discipline even after his election (*Conf.* 11.2.1). To do so may not have been difficult, for Cassian notes the destruction of the surrounding area by the encroaching sea and the subsequent abandonment of the region by all but monks.[58]

As Cassian tells it, Archebius was in Thennesus for the election of a new bishop. He offers to take Cassian and Germanus with him to Panephysis, visiting anchorites along the way (*Conf.* 11.3). *Conferences* 11–17 are attributed to three of these anchorites, Chaeremon, Nesteros and Joseph (see *Conf. Pref.* 2 2). Joseph, says Cassian, came from an illustrious family in Thmuis and had himself been a leading figure in the town. Cassian notes that unlike most Egyptian monks, Joseph spoke Greek, allowing him to converse directly with his visitors (*Conf.* 16.1).[59] Near Panephysis, Cassian and Germanus visit their old friend Pinufius (*Conf.* 20), the runaway abbot, who repays their hospitality by housing them in his own cell (*Inst.* 4.30–31, *Conf.* 20.1–2). Panephysis may also be the location of the cenobium of Abba Paul, the setting of *Conference* 19.[60]

They continued on to Diolcos,[61] a monastic center already mentioned in the *Institutes*.[62] Cassian contrasted the heroism of its anchorites, toiling against encroaching sand and sea and hauling fresh water three miles from the river to the salty wasteland in which they live, with the respectable but unimpressive regimen of the cenobites nearer to town (*Inst.* 5.36). At Diolcos they meet another monk named Archebius, whom Cassian describes as the most famous anchorite of the area. His detachment from possessions is evident in a charitable deception by which he will yield his cell and furniture to newcomers under the pretense of leaving the area, only to return a few days later with the materials to build a new cell for himself (*Inst.* 5.37). Despite Archebius' succession of cells, Cassian presents him as a model of monastic stability because he spent his entire monastic life of fifty years in the monastery[63] without returning to Diolcos, which was his hometown (*Inst.* 5.38).[64]

Cassian attributes *Conference* 18 to Abba Piamun and *Conference* 19 to Abba John, both monks of Diolcos; each had extensive anchoritic experience, though John returned to the cenobium later in life.[65] Piamun, the senior anchorite of Diolcos, laid things on the line for his visitors.[66] Anticipating Saint Benedict's detestation of gyrovagues,[67] Piamun observes that he had seen many come "from your country" in search of comfort rather than conversion, unwilling to change their mode of prayer, fasting, or dress (*Conf.* 18.2). Piamun did not have the measure of his guests: they were in Egypt for the real thing, which they were soon to find in Scetis.

Scetis

Doubtless inspired by stories of the monastic heroism to be found there, Cassian and Germanus went to the desert of Scetis, located west of the Nile in the area now known as Wadi al-Natrun. This isolated and renowned monastic center, source of the core elements of the *Apophthegmata Patrum*, was to become their Egyptian home.[68] There is no doubt that Cassian actually spent time in Scetis, and so his, along with Palladius' *Lausiac History*, is one of the first (and few) eyewitness accounts we have of this famous but little visited monastic center.[69] Cassian's love for Scetis was more than nostalgic, for throughout his works he presents Scetis as the pinnacle of monastic perfection.[70] In the original plan of his monastic writings, Scetis typified culmination of monastic progress. The *Institutes* were to present cenobitic rules; the *Conferences*, attributed to monks of Scetis, were to emphasize the contemplative dedication that surpassed the disciplinary focus of cenobitic life.[71] Normally Cassian means by "Scetis" the monastic settlement of Wadi al-Natrun itself, especially when he writes of his own experience there. Sometimes he uses the name in a broader generic sense encompassing the similar monastic settlement of Kellia,[72] which was actually an outpost of Nitria.[73]

Cassian obviously loved the monastic life he found at Scetis. He and Germanus joined a group of monks led by Paphnutius, who was sympathetic to Origen's theology and presbyter of one of the four "churches" of Scetis.[74] This group became "our community" (*nostra congregatio*); the phrase suggests a degree of membership that could be paralleled only by the cenobium at Bethlehem.[75] Returning to Bethlehem for a reconciliation with their first community after seven years in Egypt, they seem to have left from and returned to Scetis,[76] which had become their Egyptian monastic base.

Of all the monks mentioned in his writings, Cassian reserves his most effusive praise for the "remarkable and incomparable" Nubian monk Abba Moses, a former brigand and murderer who had been a disciple of Isidore and Macarius the Egyptian (*Conf.* 7.27).[77] "Chief of all the saints" (*Inst.* 10.25), Moses had the "sweetest fragrance among the distinguished flowers" of Scetis (*Conf.* 1.1).[78] When listing the four greatest anchorites, Cassian places Moses first, followed by Paphnutius and the two Macarii (*Conf.* 19.9.1). Cassian visited Moses in an area of Scetis known as "Calamus" ("Reed"),[79] probably another name for the "Petra" mentioned in the *Apophthegmata*.[80] As the first speaker in the *Conferences*, Moses sketches out the basic map of the monastic journey to purity of heart and then outlines the primary means, discernment of thoughts (*Conf.* 1–2).

Paphnutius, to whom Cassian attributes *Conference* 3, is the very type of the Egyptian monk of the old school.[81] Paphnutius' name occurs more frequently than that of any other monk.[82] A lover of solitude who withdrew into the deep desert near Scetis (whence his nickname "the Antelope"[83]), Paphnutius was famous for his humility (*Conf.* 18.15.2–7). He was physically tough (*Conf.* 3.1.1) and stern with those he thought to be in error (*Conf.* 2.5.4, *Conf.* 10.3). Succeeding Isidore as presbyter of one of the groups of hermits in Scetis (*Conf.* 18.15.2), Paphnutius (according to other sources) became "Father of Scetis" after Macarius the Great.[84]

As a leader of the Origenist minority in Scetis, Paphnutius welcomed Theophilus of Alexandria's condemnation of Anthropomorphism in 399, the only one of the four presbyters of Scetis to do so (*Conf.* 10.2–3).[85] Paphnutius' correction of the Anthropomorphite monk Sarapion in the opening pages of *Conference* 10, as Cuthbert Butler noted, is one of the more vivid narratives in the *Conferences*.[86] Cassian's account of this event is a theological illustration rather than a historical record; nonetheless, Paphnutius' stance is plausible, given what we know of him from other sources, and Cassian probably constructed his account from actual events of those difficult years.

According to Palladius, Paphnutius had the charism of interpreting the Bible without resort to commentaries. Cassian embodies the same virtue in Abba Theodore (*Inst.* 5.34) and explores its significance in *Conference* 14. Both Paphnutius and Theodore remind us that the "Origenism" of Cassian's circle in Scetis was not speculative; Cassian insists repeatedly (as I will show in chapter 5) that "spiritual knowledge" of the Bible depends on purity of heart, not sophistication of learning. Paphnutius, a tough old man of the desert, embodied the interplay of ascetical rigor and contemplative insight that Cassian thought ideal.

Cassian presents *Conferences* attributed to five other monks of Scetis: Daniel (*Conf.* 4), Sarapion (*Conf.* 5), Serenus (*Conf.* 7–8), Isaac (*Conf.* 9–10) and Theonas (*Conf.* 21–23).[87] Cassian also relates several stories about the founder of Scetis,[88] Macarius the Great or "the Egyptian,"[89] though Cassian never claims to have met him. Macarius' association with Scetis and links with both Antony the Great and Evagrius assured his significance for Cassian.[90] No *Conference* is attributed to Macarius, even though he was probably still alive when Cassian and Germanus arrived in Scetis.[91]

Kellia and Nitria

Distressed by news they received of murder and mayhem in Palestine, Cassian and Germanus went to Kellia (the "Cells") to see Abba Theodore (*Conf.* 6.1).[92] This outpost of Nitria had an ascetical reputation equal to that of Scetis.[93] According to *Conference* 6, they went to seek advice from Abba Theodore, to whom the *Conference* is attributed. Cassian describes Theodore as "unique in the practical life" of monastic asceticism and discernment; he is probably Abba Theodore of the *Institutes*, who was possessed of the "greatest holiness and knowledge . . . not only in the practical life, but also in understanding the scriptures."[94] By including Theodore's among the *Conferences* attributed to monks of Scetis, Cassian follows the convention of referring to all monastic settlements of the inner desert west of the Nile as "Scetis."[95]

Cassian describes Kellia as eighty miles from Scetis and five from Nitria. The first figure is far too high and the second too low, probably an effect of the passage of time on Cassian's memory (*Conf.* 6.1.3).[96] He mentions Nitria, the monastic settlement from which Kellia was founded, only when describing Kellia (*Conf.* 6.1.3). A visit to Kellia without calling at Nitria is conceivable, though perhaps unlikely, given their close links and proximity.[97] Nowhere else does Cassian refer to Kellia or Nitria,[98] and he never mentions any of the famous monks of either place: not Amoun, Macarius the Alexandrian,[99] or Evagrius Ponticus.[100] Compared to Cassian's eloquence about Scetis, this reticence is stunning.

Origenism, and more particularly, Evagrius, was the reason for the silence. The rest of this study will indicate that Evagrius was the single most important influence on Cassian's monastic theology, although Cassian never mentions him by name.[101] After the condemnation of Origenism by Theophilus of Alexandria in 400 and the subsequent success of the anti-Origenist cause, it became politically inexpedient to advertise connections with Evagrius, the great theoretician of monastic Origenism. Even after twenty-five years, with the fiercest of the anti-

Origenists dead and doctrinal controversy now focused on other issues, Cassian felt constrained to downplay his links with the Evagrian Origenism of Nitria and Kellia.

Cassian systematically effaces obviously incriminating evidence of his association with Evagrius, either by selective narration (his reporting of the Anthropomorphite controversy in *Conference* 10) or by changing controversial terminology (e.g., *apatheia* becomes "purity of heart"). The impossibility of openly repaying his debt to his master must have been deeply painful to Cassian, who identified monastic tradition so closely with those who embodied it.

Leaving Egypt

The only historically datable event among Cassian's stories of Egypt is the arrival in Scetis of a letter from Theophilus, patriarch of Alexandria, condemning those who conceived of God as having human form (the Anthropomorphites). It is generally thought that Theophilus wrote in winter of 399.[102] Cassian states that the letter was received joyfully by Paphnutius' congregation; their sympathies for Origen's theology made them hostile to Anthropomorphite views. On the basis of the letter, Cassian claims, they challenged the Anthropomorphism of a certain Abba Sarapion. Cassian's account is primarily about the theological grounds for this challenge. He says nothing about the next phase of the controversy, with its turn against the Origenists. That change of tide probably swept Cassian and Germanus from their monastic home and into exile.

The veil of silence, though frustrating to the historian, is a mute memorial to the devastation of Origenist monasticism in Egypt, the monasticism to which Cassian and Germanus wanted to devote their lives. Besides the merely frustrating silences in Cassian's writings, such as that about his birthplace, there are many poignant ones as well. His silence about Evagrius and Origenism is the most significant, for it conceals the reasons why Cassian and Germanus left the monastic Egypt they loved so much. Similarly, Cassian tells us nothing of later painful experiences such as the exile and suffering of his mentor, John Chrysostom, or the death of his close friend Germanus. At times tactical, his reticence is often equally explicable as the privacy of grief.

It is generally thought that Cassian and Germanus left Egypt along with other Origenist exiles such as the "Tall Brothers" of Nitria. Cassian's devotion to Evagrian spiritual theology, so evident in the *Institutes* and *Conferences*, would have made an increasingly anti-Origenist Egypt an uncomfortable home. There is every reason to think that he would have contentedly remained in Egypt had it been possible; his praise for the monastic life he experienced in Scetis is surely more than nostalgia or a rhetorical device. The Origenist exodus, noted by Theophilus himself,[103] brought many monks to Palestine and to Constantinople.[104] We know that Cassian and Germanus found their way to Constantinople, and that they must have been there well before 403–4. By that time they had become trusted clergy of John Chrysostom, who had welcomed many Egyptian monastic refugees.

Constantinople and Rome

Refuge with John Chrysostom

During the fifteen or so years between leaving Egypt with Germanus and settling in Gaul, Cassian earned the ecclesiastical credibility that would enable him to undertake his greatest work. As I will show, Cassian's monastic writings were not in-house documents for use only in his monastery at Marseilles. He dedicates the *Institutes* and *Conferences* to a broad network of bishops and monks. This array of contacts, both impressive and quickly established, suggests that he must have arrived in Gaul as something of a recognized authority on monastic and ecclesiastical matters. Much of this stature can be explained by his association with a great hero of the early fifth century, the bishop of Constantinople, John Chrysostom.

Like other Origenist refugees from Egypt who sought refuge with Chrysostom, Germanus and Cassian could have enjoyed his patronage only until Chrysostom was deposed and exiled in 403–4. Therefore, the two monks must have arrived in Constantinople fairly soon after the Origenist uproar of 399–400, for they became close enough to Chrysostom to serve as his envoys during his own crisis only a few years later. Cassian says nothing in the monastic writings of his time in Constantinople. He ruefully admits that he had been unable to avoid "a bishop's hands," failing to note that the ordaining hands were Chrysostom's and the place was Constantinople (*Inst.* 11.18).

Only in *The Incarnation of the Lord* does he admit what Gennadius found so significant.[105] However much Cassian disguised his former ecclesiastical life in the *Institutes* and *Conferences*, it is the foreground of this treatise. He concludes with an encomium of Chrysostom and the church of Constantinople, contrasting their fidelity with the perfidy of Nestorius. These last surviving words of Cassian, among his most moving, claim Chrysostom as his teacher and the people of Constantinople as "my fellow-citizens through love of the homeland (*patria*)[106] and my brothers through the unity of the faith" (*De Inc.* 7.31.3).

Mission to Rome

Once again, however, Cassian would lose a venerated teacher and be forced to take to the road. The political and theological drama that found Chrysostom at odds with both Theophilus of Alexandria and his own erstwhile imperial supporters inevitably drew in followers such as Cassian and Germanus, who were by then members of his clergy (Cassian a deacon, Germanus a priest). We do not know the positions they held before the crisis, but two extant documents refer to their work on Chrysostom's behalf: Palladius' *Dialogue on the Life of John Chrysostom* and a letter from Pope Innocent I. The *Dialogue* and the letter mention *both* Germanus and Cassian, and therefore almost certainly refer to the displaced monks. These first historical references to Cassian—written some twenty years before his own works—place him and his friend amidst well-known ecclesiastical events.[107] Germanus, the elder of the pair and now a priest, figures more prominently in these accounts than Cassian (as is also the case in the *Confer-ences*, where Germanus is cast in the leading role appropriate to his seniority). Only later, after his friend's death, would Cassian emerge to make his own mark.

Palladius' testimony is the most valuable. He lists "the presbyter, Germanus" among the brave loyalists who brought Chrysostom's response to the notorious Synod of the Oak in 403 (at which Theophilus of Alexandria was presiding).[108] From Palladius we also learn that Cassian and Germanus were among those who travelled from Constantinople to Rome after Chrysostom's second and definitive exile in 404: "there were the presbyter Germanus and the deacon Cassian, pious men, who brought a letter from all of John's clergy in which they wrote about the violence and tyranny to which their church had been subjected."[109] Their arrival in Rome has been dated to the autumn of 404.[110] Presumably their facility in Latin made them likely candidates for this important (and sensitive) appeal to the papacy, just as Cassian's knowledge of Greek would later recommend him as a critic of Nestorius.

The two monks brought with them an inventory of the patriarchal treasures that had been deposited by the clergy with the civil authorities. The act of deposit itself and the delivery of the inventory to Pope Innocent were meant to vindicate Chrysostom of the charges of financial malfeasance that had been brought against him.[111] Some have inferred from this commission that Cassian and Germanus had been in charge of the cathedral treasury in Constantinople;[112] Palladius' text, however, is not so specific.[113]

Pope Innocent's reply to Chrysostom acknowledges the letter sent from Con-stantinople "by the priest Germanus and the deacon Cassian."[114] The pope's re-sponse was probably sent to Constantinople toward the end of 405 or the begin-ning of 406 with a delegation carrying letters from Pope Innocent to Chrysostom and from the western emperor Honorius to his counterpart in the East, Arcad-ius.[115] It is possible that Cassian and Germanus returned to Constantinople with this delegation,[116] which was brutalized by hostile authorities and could remain in Constantinople only briefly. Palladius' description of the mission mentions nei-ther Germanus nor Cassian.[117] It has also been suggested that Cassian returned to Bethlehem, his first monastic home.[118] John, bishop of Jerusalem, was a sup-porter of Chrysostom and favorably disposed toward Origenists. However, the ra-bidly anti-Origenist Jerome had fought John and Origenism from Bethlehem. One wonders if Cassian would have found his former home a safe haven, even with the protection of his monastic brothers. Cassian and Germanus may simply have remained in Rome, and it is perhaps there that Cassian was ordained to the priesthood;[119] during that dozen years or so he may also have befriended the young Leo, later archdeacon and pope, of whom he writes warmly in the preface to *The Incarnation of the Lord* and at whose behest he would write that final treatise.[120]

An alternative scenario is suggested by two letters sent by Pope Innocent to Alexander, bishop of Antioch (413–21), which mention a presbyter named Cas-sianus. Alexander was trying to heal a schism resulting from the Chrysostom af-fair; before his election, the see of Antioch had been unfavorably disposed toward partisans of Chrysostom. Alexander restored Chrysostom's name to liturgical com-memoration in Antioch and then sought to reconcile the clergy belonging to the various parties.[121] "Cassianus" was the pope's consultant on these faraway matters. In this century Elie Griffe revived a suggestion made almost three hundred years earlier by Louis-Sébastien le Nain de Tillemont[122] and seconded by Pierre Cous-tant[123] that the Cassianus mentioned in these two letters might be John Cassian. Griffe argued that after Alexander's election as bishop in 413 and the resultant change in climate toward supporters of Chrysostom's cause, Cassian found his way to Antioch and was ordained there to the priesthood.[124] Even were this hy-pothesis true, it would leave the years between 405 and 413 unexplained; as a fervent supporter of Chrysostom's cause, Cassian could hardly have found Anti-och an inviting place before Alexander's episcopate.

Pope Innocent's letters, the only evidence for this theory, resist precise inter-pretation. The "Cassianus" mentioned in them seems to be a priest who has counseled the pope on matters pertaining to the Antiochene schism; nothing conclusively identifies him as a priest of Antioch itself.[125] The link with John Cassian also remains uncertain.[126] A passage from *The Incarnation of the Lord* in which Cassian praises the church of Antioch, read by Rousseau as corroboration that Cassian had been one of its clergy,[127] is more likely only a rhetorical device used against Nestorius.[128] Pope Innocent's earlier letter and Palladius' *Dialogue on the Life of Chrysostom*, with their references to both "Germanus" and "Cas-sianus," are surer ground.

Among the many uncertainties about Cassian's movements and work be-tween 404 and ca. 415 is the fate of Germanus. After 405 we hear no more of Cassian's friend, who presumably died during those years before Cassian went to Gaul.[129] The *Conferences*, in which Germanus plays a prominent role, serve as Cassian's tribute to his older companion and monastic confrere; of this very pri-vate man's grief we hear nothing.

Gaul

A Monastic Haven

In Gaul Cassian was to fulfill his first vocation, to the monastic life, by establish-ing monasteries. But he was also to discover a second vocation, to monastic theol-ogy, by undertaking the literary work for which he is now remembered. We do not know why or when he came to Massilia, the port city on the south coast of Gaul now known as Marseilles. Massilia, founded as a Greek city in the seventh century BCE and a principal city of the Roman province of *Gallia Narbo-nensis*,[130] was a center of trade and port of call for travellers from the eastern Mediterranean; it was located in a region that remained comparatively stable while the European social order to the east, north, and west was reshaped by the invading Germanic tribes.[131]

If Cassian indeed stayed in Rome after his mission for Chrysostom, it may be that he eventually left because of Alaric's sack of the city in 410. It has been suggested that Cassian's somewhat uninformed remarks about Pelagius and Pelagianism indicate that he had already left Rome when the controversy reached there in 417–18.[132] Some have followed Marrou's theory that Cassian arrived in Gaul from Palestine, travelling with Lazarus, the bishop of Aix, who had been exiled from Gaul in 412 but was allowed to return ca. 416 with a promise of sanctuary from Proculus, bishop of Massilia.[133] This hypothesis, of course, requires that Cassian had returned to Palestine after his Roman mission.

It is safer to argue from clues in Cassian's own writings. He dedicates the *Institutes* to Castor, bishop of Apta Julia from at least 419.[134] The *Institutes* were followed closely by the first set of *Conferences*, written in the early to middle 420s. Allowing Cassian time to have become settled and known in Gaul—that is, long enough to have his monastic authority recognized by Castor and others—before beginning his literary work, an arrival in Marseilles in the middle to late 410s fits the evidence well.

Cassian's Network and Monastic Situation

Marseilles was a natural haven for someone like Cassian.[135] Its monastically inclined bishop, Proculus (who served from 381 to after 418),[136] was praised by Jerome in a letter to the monk Rusticus (later bishop of Narbonne) in 411/12.[137] Epigraphical evidence indicates that Rusticus lived at a monastery in Marseilles along with Venerius, Proculus' successor as bishop; it was probably a community for clerics along the lines of Augustine's in Hippo.[138]

Cassian did not come to Marseilles to retire. According to both Gennadius and subsequent tradition, he founded two monasteries, one for men and one for women.[139] The first and more famous, Saint Victor, was named for a third-century martyr of Marseilles. Built on the high rocks above the port, across from the city, the monastery was adjacent to the martyr's shrine.[140] Cassian himself was buried in the crypt and his tomb venerated until it was despoiled in the French Revolution.[141] The site of the monastery of women remains uncertain; tradition has associated it with the monastery in the city later dedicated to Saint Savior. Recently it has been suggested that the original patron may have been Saint Cyricus and later Saint Cassian.[142] It may be that Cassian founded this monastery for his sister (*Inst.* 11.18). A century later Caesarius would send his sister there to be "a disciple before being a teacher," preparing her for leadership of the new monastery at Arles.[143]

Cassian's writings show him in lively contact with the monasticism of his time and place. His involvement with the ecclesiastical and monastic establishments (incredibly intertwined as they were) is mapped by the dedications in his prefaces, the asides in the *Institutes* and *Conferences*, the forays into controversy over Pelagianism (*Conference* 13) and Nestorianism (*The Incarnation of the Lord*).[144] As Philip Rousseau notes, "Cassian was to assist, in other words, a program already under way."[145] His own monastic agenda emerges as one reads his prefaces. The *Institutes* are dedicated to Castor, bishop of Julia Apta, a town northwest of Marseilles.[146] Castor, according to Cassian, hopes to establish a cenobium in his region which as yet is without monasteries. He has turned to Cassian for help. The prescription is simple: follow the ways of the East and, especially, of Egypt (*Inst. Pref.* 3). Cassian offers to be the conduit, supplementing what can be found in the writings of Basil and Jerome (*Inst. Pref.* 5).[147]

Castor's diocese may have lacked cenobia, but there were monasteries elsewhere in Gaul and even in Marseilles (Proculus' community). Cassian at first gives the impression that he was working in a monastic vacuum (he never mentions Martin, Paulinus of Nola, or their chronicler Sulpitius Severus). But as the first preface continues, Cassian acknowledges the existence of other monasteries in Gaul, while criticizing them for following the whims of their founders rather than the model established by the (Egyptian) elders. Cassian's premise is that nothing "the western parts of Gaul" have to offer monastically can compare with the apostolic foundations of the East (*Inst. Pref.* 8). Whether the phrase *in occiduis Galliarum partibus* meant Gaulish monasticism generally or, more specifically, western Gaul and monastic movements such as Martin's,[148] Cassian's principle was always *ex oriente lux*: "light from the East."[149] Even in this first installment of his literary project, Cassian sets his sights beyond Castor's territory, seeking to reform existing monastic movements as well as to help establish new communities.

The *Institutes* are inescapably a critique of the native monastic tradition associated especially with Martin of Tours.[150] Cassian's proposal to concentrate on traditional teaching on the amendment of faults and the attainment of perfection rather than on miraculous stories (*Inst. Pref.* 8) can be read as a counterpoint to Sulpitius' *Life of Martin* and *Dialogues*, in which tales of Martin's wondrous deeds abound.[151] Even worse, Sulpitius reports such wonders about Egyptian monks;[152] Cassian will write *Conference* 15, set of course in Egypt, on the dangers of emphasizing miraculous powers over goodness of life. Cassian sees monasticism in Gaul as a poorly organized and undisciplined way of life that substitutes individual preference for traditional rules (*Inst.* 2.3.4–5, 4.16.3), and he relates with horror that a young monk "in this region" openly rebelled against the commands of his senior (*Inst.* 12.28). Cassian finds anarchy in the liturgy: there is no universal system of psalmody (*Inst.* 2.1–3.1),[153] the monks are sloppy and indecorous when praying in common (*Inst.* 2.7.1 and 3), and they go back to bed after the morning office (*Inst.* 3.5.1). He parodies the Gaulish monks who keep their valuables under lock and key, wear signet rings, and need whole wardrobes in which to store their possessions (*Inst.* 4.14.–15).

Cassian's charge that these monks rely on the financial support of others rather than on their own earnings from manual labor (*Inst.* 10.23), though a frequent theme in monastic literature generally,[154] strengthens the impression that he is opposing his eastern, regulated model of the monastic life to the more free-form indigenous monastic movements whose members were not as convinced of the necessity of manual labor. Martin's followers at Marmoutier, for example, undertook no work except the copying of manuscripts, and even that work was done only by the young; the seniors devoted themselves entirely to prayer. Cassian's objection to the ostentatious wearing of clothing made from animal hair (*Inst.* 1.3) may also be another critique of Martin's monks, many of whom, reports Sulpitius, wore camel-hair garments.[155]

Cassian's scornful description of the Sarabaites in *Conference* 18, though inspired by Jerome's portrayal of the monks he calls *remnuoth*,[156] serves as a reprise of his own remarks in the *Institutes* about those who lack any rule or guidance from the elders and devalue manual labor; in this case, however, the sarabaites overwork to satisfy their avarice (*Conf.* 18.7). Despite the Egyptian setting for *Conference* 18, Cassian is, of course, writing for Gaul. In *Conference* 24, Germanus asks Abraham why he and Cassian shouldn't return to their native country, where they can be financially supported by relatives and devote themselves entirely to reading and contemplation. Abraham replies that it is safer to toil for subsistence than to risk affluence with its "idle meditation of the scriptures and unfruitful application to prayer" (*Conf.* 24.12.1). Without manual labor, says Cassian, spiritual practices lose their efficacy: so much for Martin's monks and their graduation beyond work.[157]

Cassian's interactions with both bishops and "approved" monastic figures in Gaul become more evident in the prefaces to the three sets of *Conferences*. The first ten are dedicated to Leontius, bishop of Fréjus (ca. 400–ca. 432–33), and to the "holy brother" Helladius, a monk of anchoritic inclination and instinct (*Conf. Pref.* 1 2–3, *Conf.* 9.1). Leontius was Castor's brother;[158] within his diocese of Fréjus lay the the extremely important island monastic center of Lérins, whose first abbot, Honoratus, he had ordained.[159] Adalbert de Vogüé has suggested that Leontius might even have been one of the "four fathers" who wrote the first Lerinian rule.[160] Helladius himself became a bishop almost immediately after Cassian's dedication was written; in the preface to the next set of *Conferences* Cassian notes Helladius' elevation to the episcopate.[161]

With the next set of *Conferences* the link with Lérins, the monastic powerhouse of southern Gaul, is even more direct.[162] Cassian dedicates them to Honoratus, still superior of the "enormous" cenobium at Lérins,[163] and to Eucherius, monk of Lérins and author of the treatises *In Praise of the Desert* and *On Contempt for the World*, who later became bishop of Lyons.[164] Cassian provides Honoratus the teaching of the Egyptian anchorites for use in the cenobium at Lérins. Eucherius, writes Cassian, strongly desired to leave the harsh chill of Gaul by flying "like the chastest of turtledoves" to Egypt, "the land where the sun of righteousness" brings forth the fruit of the virtues. Cassian writes in order to spare Eucherius the perils of the journey (*Conf. Pref.* 2 1–2).[165] Eucherius would later repay his debt to Cassian by preparing an epitome of the *Institutes*.[166]

Cassian addresses the third set of *Conferences* to four monks living on the Stoechadic islands near Massilia.[167] The first three, Jovinian, Minervius, and Leontius (all otherwise unknown to us) are praised for their encouragement of both the cenobitic and anchoritic ways of life on the islands.[168] Cassian singles out the the fourth, Theodore, for having established cenobitic life in Gaul along traditional lines. Theodore later became bishop of Fréjus, succeeding Leontius (ca. 432–33).[169]

These prefaces with their impressive range of addressees show Cassian to be a monastic authority very much involved with the direction and expansion of monasticism in southern Gaul. He came to know all of the key players in the growing eastern-oriented monastic movements and influenced their work through his writings. But his impact was felt beyond monasteries, for again Cassian found himself in the midst of controversy. This time the issue was grace, and at stake was the value of ascetical discipline. Although he spoke from his monastic concerns, the conversation into which he entered was much broader in scope, involving the greatest Latin theologian of the day, Augustine of Hippo.

Grace and Free Will

Cassian's fame—to some, his notoriety—has largely to do with his role in the debates over grace, free will, and asceticism that began in the 420s and continued sporadically for a century until the Council of Orange in 529. These debates were aftershocks of Augustine's fierce resistance to the overly optimistic anthropology of the British monk Pelagius.[170] After Pelagius' formal condemnation at the Council of Carthage (418), arguments shifted to Augustine's hardline anti-Pelagian doctrines and their relationship to traditional theological anthropology. The problem was particularly acute for monks, whose anthropology, essentially eastern Christian in inspiration, was more open to natural possibility than Augustine's. Thus the issue was not really Pelagianism but Augustinianism: these monks were no Pelagians.

My concern here is with Cassian's historical role in what has been known since the seventeenth century as the Semi-Pelagian controversy.[171] His actual teaching will be considered in Chapter 4 with his theology of chastity, where he himself situates it. Here it can be noted that throughout his monastic writings Cassian highlights the danger of confusing ascetical means (and thus human effort) with their theological end, achievable only with the constant help of God. Cassian was very much aware that one of the great monastic dangers is focusing too intently on structures and practices, losing sight of both dependence on God and the obligations of charity toward others.

At the same time, Cassian and other monks thought that Augustine's denial of any *initium fidei* ("initiative of faith") to human beings and his concomitant doctrine of predestination effectively excluded human responsibility from the process of salvation. This made little sense in a monastic context where the interplay of ascetical discipline, prayer and the support of other human beings created the context for growth toward Christian perfection. In terms of the *practice* of the Christian life, Augustine and Cassian may scarcely have differed:[172] Augustine, after all, was a monastic founder himself.[173] But in theological reflection on experience (and in controversy) Augustine and the monks of Gaul moved in opposite directions.

The monastic reaction to Augustine's anti-Pelagian teaching is understood to have begun about 426 when monks at Hadrumentum (in modern-day Tunisia) initiated an exchange with Augustine that generated his treatises *Grace and Free Will* and *Rebuke and Grace*, commonly known by their Latin titles *De gratia et libero arbitrio* and *De correptione et gratia* (both dating from ca. 426–27). The initial African phase has left no further historical traces; new questions were emerging in southern Gaul, and our interest lies there with Cassian and his monks.

In Gaul, as in Africa, the locus of controversy was predominantly monastic, and later monastic-episcopal, as bishops from the monasteries assumed major roles in the church. In Gaul there had been signs of official concern about lingering Pelagianism; in 425 the bishops of southern Gaul were commanded by imperial decree to profess their anti-Pelagian views to Patroclus, the bishop of Arles later assassinated for his political involvements.[174] We do not know if or how this crackdown related to the questions emerging in Marseilles about hardline Augustinianism. Soon Cassian was writing *Conference* 13, and concern spread to other monastic centers such as Lérins.[175]

Neither the exact shape of Cassian's involvement in the monastic reaction nor the events surrounding his famous *Conference* 13, "On Divine Protection," can be readily discerned. We know from the dedication of *Conferences* 11–17 that Cassian wrote them before Honoratus' move to Arles as bishop. Thus *Conference* 13 was finished before copies of Augustine's addresses to the monks of Hadrumentum could have found their way to Gaul.[176] Cassian was not writing a rebuttal of those treatises. Because *Conference* 13 fits so well into the overall scheme of the *Conferences* it is better seen as a general response to aspects of Augustine's thought—already well known in Gaul—than as a tactical move in response to Augustine's latest works.[177] Like so many of the *Conferences*, *Conference* 13 develops themes already introduced in the *Institutes*, in this case the link between chastity and grace.[178] It is the culmination of Cassian's teaching on grace and free will, not an initial foray.

About the time Cassian wrote *Conference* 13, a lay enthusiast of Augustine's views living in Marseilles, Prosper of Aquitaine, wrote to Rufinus, another layman, about those who were undermining Augustine's teaching by their "many conferences."[179] Later Prosper wrote to Augustine himself, claiming that the "servants of Christ living in the city of Marseilles" had become hardened in their error by reading Augustine's *De correptione et gratia*.[180] Prosper notes their fame and outstanding virtue—he even refers to them as *sancti*—despite their attraction to Pelagian views.[181] These "servants of Christ" were surely Cassian and his monks. A similar letter sent to Augustine by an otherwise unknown disciple named Hilary describes the anti-Augustinian ideas circulating among those "in Marseilles and other places in Gaul."[182] A layman like Prosper, Hilary notes that the ecclesiastical rank of some of these people calls for a certain deference on his part.[183]

All three letters point to Cassian and the monks of Saint Victor (and their episcopal allies).[184] Cassian's stance on free will, as expressed throughout the *Institutes* and *Conferences*, joined with Prosper's later attack on *Conference* 13 confirm the hints. One cannot say, however, whether Prosper or Hilary had read *Conference* 13 when they wrote to Augustine. Although the *Conference* had been written, the two Augustinians may not have read it yet.[185] Prosper was to read it soon eough.

Augustine addressed two of his last works to Prosper and Hilary in reply to their letters: *The Predestination of the Saints* (*De praedestinatione sanctorum*) and *The Gift of Perseverance* (*De dono perseverantiae*, both dated to 429–30). Shortly after Augustine's death in August 430, the two zealots sought a papal condemnation of their opponents but found themselves in the awkward position of trying to

secure a condemnation of someone (Cassian) who had just written the anti- ⎫
Nestorian treatise *The Incarnation of the Lord* at the behest of Leo, archdeacon ⎰
of Rome. Cassian had, surely not coincidentally, linked Nestorius to Pelagius and
attacked both vigorously. His stock was high in Rome.[186]

Pope Celestine handled the matter by writing to the bishops of southeastern
Gaul. He praised the zeal of Prosper and Hilary and asked the bishops to silence
those presbyters causing trouble with their "novel" ideas. The letter concludes
with a plea to respect the memory of the recently deceased Augustine.[187] No
doctrines are specified, no names or places given. The letter must have been
something of a disappointment to Prosper and Hilary.[188] Nonetheless Prosper
plunged ahead, publishing in 432 his critique of *Conference* 13, entitled *Against
the Conferencer (Contra collatorem)*.[189] The "conferencer," of course, was Cassian. Prosper never uses Cassian's name, just as Cassian had avoided naming
Nestorius in *The Incarnation of the Lord*, but his tone toward the "conferencer"
himself is fairly respectful.[190]

Prosper's attack on the teaching of *Conference* 13 focuses on Cassian's concur-
rence with the traditional eastern teaching that stirrings of good remain possible
even to fallen humankind;[191] Prosper sidesteps Cassian's arguments against predestination.[192] The assault is relentless and unfair.[193] After writing the *Contra
collatorem*, Prosper left the contentious atmosphere of Marseilles and settled in
Rome, where Leo's friendship (as well as affection for Cassian) seems gradually
to have mellowed his views.[194] Prosper's treatise is the last contemporary witness   ✗
to Cassian or his teaching that we have.

Controversy sputtered on, with new contenders, until 529, when the Council
of Orange (later affirmed by Rome) condemned the Massilian teaching that allowed some initiative, however feeble, of the human will (the *initium fidei*). The
council did so without embracing Augustine's later views on predestination.[195]
Included among its canons were opinions sent from Rome at the request of Caesarius, bishop of Arles, as well as items drafted by Caesarius himself. The decisive
rejection of the anthropology of Cassian and his followers was, therefore, engineered by a monk-bishop who had sent his own sister to Marseilles to be trained
in a monastery founded by Cassian.

Cassian's role in the monastic response to Augustine's views has denied him
liturgical and devotional recognition as a saint of the western church.[196] In this
respect he resembles his mentors Origen and Evagrius: he has been widely read,
respected for his psychological realism and his teaching on higher forms of contemplation and prayer, but in the minds of some he has remained doctrinally
suspect. The late-fifth and early-sixth-century list of "Books To Be Received and
Not To Be Received" attributed (falsely) to Pope Gelasius I (461–96) includes
Cassian's works among those considered suspect, surely because of *Conference* 13.
Although this widely copied but spurious document did not prevent Cassian from
being read, it did contribute to the prejudice against him.[197]

The judgment against Cassian is perhaps even less just than those against
Origen and Evagrius, whose esoteric speculations did carry them near or beyond
the borders of what is normally understood by orthodoxy. The link with them, of
course, is forged of more than coincidence of condemnation. Cassian shared their

belief (the tradition of the Great Church) that human beings retain some vestige of their created goodness and can learn to walk again as God intended. He taught the necessity of grace, but it was a liberal grace pervading a creation still rich in possibility. In his view, monasticism, like the Christianity of which it is a trope, educates and develops the human person called forth by God from sin into freedom.

Against Nestorius

Before Prosper's attack on *Conference* 13 Cassian had already turned to his final literary project, the lengthy and rather wearying treatise entitled *The Incarnation of the Lord.*[198] In the preface he tells us that he is writing at the request of Leo, then archdeacon of Rome and later pope (440–61). Cassian addresses Leo warmly, but it is not easy to ascertain the degree of their acquaintance. If Cassian spent the decade between leaving Constantinople and coming to Gaul in Rome, he could have known Leo as a young cleric of the Roman church. If Cassian left Rome after completing his mission for John Chrysostom, he could have known Leo only as a boy.[199] Whatever their relationship, there is no reason to doubt Cassian's claim that Leo had invited him to join what was shaping up as a campaign against Nestorius; the preface to Cassian's treatise refers several times to Leo's "command" that Cassian write.[200] We do not possess Leo's actual request, and therefore cannot know exactly what Cassian was asked to do or why he was chosen for the job. It may have been because of his knowledge of Greek[201] and his familiarity with the church in Constantinople.[202]

Cassian wrote on the basis of documents made available to him in late 429 or early 430. Because he still refers to Nestorius as bishop (though without actually using his name), he must have been was writing before the Roman synod convened by Pope Celestine in August 430 condemned and deposed Nestorius.[203] Cassian provides a campaign piece rather than a theological assessment.[204] The most distinctive aspect of his defense of the divinity of Christ is a connection he makes between Pelagianism and Nestorianism. This odd linkage may arise from the fact that Julian of Eclanum and Pelagius' disciple Celestius had sought refuge in Constantinople, and Nestorius had asked Rome about them in the same letters in which he denied the *Theotokos.*[205]

The link between Pelagianism and Christology can also be explained on other grounds. Cassian describes the case of Leporius, a monk of Gaul who had recently, under Augustine's tutelage, recanted his dyophysite Christology.[206] Cassian seems to have got Leporius wrong, attacking him for adoptionism rather than for his actual errors about the union of the two natures in Christ. Amann has suggested that Cassian's hypervigilance about Pelagianism led him to interpret what he thought was Leporius' teaching on the moral perfectibility of the human nature assumed by Christ in terms of Pelagian tenets.[207] It may also be that Cassian used the example of Leporius as an opportunity not only to certify his anti-Pelagian credentials in Rome but to do so in association with Augustine. Cassian suggests that he himself played some part in Leporius' return to orthodoxy;[208] by claiming that he was an agent of Leporius' change of heart in Gaul, Cassian steals some of Augustine's credit by leaving to his African adversary only the mopping-up of the case once Leporius had gone to Africa.

A great work of Christology this is not.[209] As Marie-Anne Vannier observes, "instead of arguing, Cassian proceeds by accumulation," piling up evidence from the Bible and the work of venerable theologians.[210] The first book establishes the parallel between the putative Pelagianism of the recently reformed monk-priest Leporius and Nestorius' Christology.[211] Books 2–5 contain the biblical argumentation in favor of the title *Theotokos* and the full divinity of Christ, with a return to the Pelagian theme in book 5. Vannier has noted that Cassian's set of prooftexts on the divinity of Christ can be traced to John Chrysostom, who emerges at the end of the treatise as its supreme authority.[212] Book 6 presents the creed of Antioch, home church of both Nestorius and Chrysostom, as a model of orthodoxy. Finally, in both Books 6 and 7, Cassian recapitulates the basic arguments, concluding with patristic witnesses of both West (Hilary of Poitiers, Ambrose, Jerome, Rufinus, Augustine) and East (Gregory Nazianzen, Athanasius, John Chrysostom).

The tilt toward western authorities reminds one that Cassian was writing for a Latin audience, though his highest praise is reserved for Chrysostom. Along the way, Cassian's own dogmatic statements veer between Nestorian and Cyrilline formulations; his grasp of the fine points of controversy was, to put it kindly, imprecise.[213] As we have noted, his purpose was not investigative so much as polemical. Émile Amann remarks, with some exasperation:

> the polemical part—alas, polemic is everywhere!—is completely spoiled by the fact that Cassian has not bothered to reconstruct the thought of the author he intends to combat. . . . He fences against a phantom and all of his thrusts, or nearly all, fall away into nothing.[214]

If the *Institutes* and *Conferences* had been lost, and Cassian were judged solely on the basis of this treatise, he would be dismissed as a second-rate theologian. But to assess *The Incarnation of the Lord* purely on doctrinal grounds is to miss what it tells about Cassian's monastic life. As Rousseau notes, "its chief significance is its very existence."[215] The treatise shows Cassian actively at work in the church of his time and place. Invited by highest authority to respond to a problem of great doctrinal and diplomatic import, he did not disdain the task as unworthy of a monk. After the obligatory sighs of regret for being called out of the refuge of silence (*De Inc. Pref.* 1),[216] he dutifully ground out his seven books, combing the scriptures and invoking theologians of East and West to support his spirited defense of the full divinity of Christ. From his monastic base in Marseilles Cassian involved himself in more than monastic formation or even monastically influenced anti-Augustinianism; his pastoral concern is manifest.[217]

Despite its lack of sparkle, *The Incarnation of the Lord* fills in some of the blank canvas of Cassian's self-portrait. Only here does he himself mention his association with John Chrysostom or actually use Augustine's name (albeit tepidly). Amidst the array of prooftexts there are flashes of his own deep faith in the divine and glorified Christ, echoes of the high Christology that pervades the *Institutes* and *Conferences* (as I will show in chapter 5).[218] *The Incarnation of the Lord* is the last we hear from Cassian himself. The shortcomings of the text may be attributable to his age and perhaps to poor health. By this time he must have been at least sixty-five, and probably closer to seventy, a far more advanced age in his time than it is now.

Cassian's Death

One infers from Prosper's *Against the Conferencer* that Cassian was still alive in 432; perhaps Prosper's respectful allusions to the author of the text that he attacks so vigorously come at least partly from recognition that Cassian's days as a controversialist were numbered. After Prosper's rebuttal of *Conference* 13 we have no further reference to Cassian in contemporary literature until Gennadius' brief sketch of his life and writings a few decades later.[219] Gennadius tells us only that he died in Marseilles in the reigns of Theodosius and Valentinian; the *terminus ad quem* of 450 provided by those dates would take us far beyond his actual death, which must have occurred in the mid-430s.

Legacy

Cassian's influence on western monasticism has been incalculable.[220] Unlike the works of many of his contemporaries and successors, Cassian's writings continue to be read by monks and scholars alike. His practical orientation and ability to write accessibly about asceticism, prayer, contemplation, eschatology — really the whole range of the monastic life — has meant a prodigious fulfillment of his original intention to help monks base their lives on the great traditions of the East.

We know that Cassian was highly regarded by the monks of Lérins; Eucherius borrowed from *Conference* 14 in his *Formulas for Spiritual Understanding*[221] (ca. 440) and made an epitome of Cassian's writings, now lost.[222] Cassian's contemporary Vincent, another monk of Lérins, was deeply influenced by Cassian's emphasis on tradition; the *Commonitory* with its famous "Vincentian Canon" makes the measure of orthodoxy what has been believed "everywhere, always, and by everyone."[223] Faustus, abbot of Lérins (433–57) and later bishop of Riez (457–90/95) took up the struggle against hardline Augustinianism; Cassian's influence on him would have been great.[224] But even someone on the other side, the fiercely Augustinian Fulgentius, bishop of Riez (507–32), shared Faustus' admiration for Cassian's monastic writings. Fulgentius, converted to the monastic life by reading Augustine, was aflame with desire to visit Egypt after reading (the unnamed) Cassian's *Institutes* and *Conferences*.[225]

Gennadius' entry on Cassian lists the title of each of his writings (including each of the twenty-four *Conferences*).[226] An African bishop, Victor of Mattara, produced an edition of Cassian's monastic writings sanitized of problematic statements about free will. Cassiodorus (ca. 485/90–580) noted that Victor did so "with the Lord's help" but also, he adds, "we believe under the direction of others from African regions."[227] A "Rule of Cassian" was developed from books 1–4 of the

Institutes[228] and included by Benedict of Aniane in his *Codex regularum* of the ninth century.

A century after his death, Cassian earned the epithet "most eloquent" from Cassiodorus, another bilingual monk with extensive eastern experience who perhaps recognized in Cassian a monastic and stylistic soulmate.[229] Cassiodorus evidences genuine familiarity with Cassian's monastic writings, citing them naturally in the course of his own work with a particular emphasis on Cassian's teaching on prayer.[230] Cassiodorus duly notes Prosper's judgment about Cassian's position on free will and warns the reader to exercise caution when reading about such a controversial topic.[231]

The greatest impact of Cassian on later tradition came through his influence on the emerging Latin monastic rules. In the early sixth century one sees his mark on Caesarius' monastic legislation; the first section of the *Rule for Nuns* manifestly depends on book 4 of the *Institutes*,[232] and other indications show Caesarius' familiarity with Cassian's monastic writings.[233] Even more significant for the Middle Ages and beyond was Cassian's influence on the anonymous legislator known as the Master and his wise heir, Benedict of Nursia.

The Master's debt to Cassian, especially in ascetical doctrine, is tremendous. To the Master goes the credit for the creative elaboration of Cassian's ten marks of humility (*Inst.* 4.39) into twelve degrees of humility.[234] Benedict inherited Cassian's teaching from the Master, and also added his own deep knowledge of both *Institutes* and *Conferences*.[235] Benedict's understanding of prayer, for example, is traceable directly to Cassian.[236]

Gregory the Great used Cassian's mediation of the Egyptian tradition of the eight principal faults as the basis for his teaching on the seven deadly sins and, as I will show in chapter 7, developed Cassian's teaching on the theology of compunction and prayer. Gregory, like many others, elaborated Cassian's teaching on the active and contemplative aspects of life.[237]

We know there were Greek versions of Cassian's works circulating in the East; portions of a Greek epitome of the *Institutes* and *Conferences* are still extant.[238] Material from the *Institutes* found its way into the Alphabetical Collection of the *Apophthegmata*;[239] Cassian is the only Latin so honored by inclusion among the great fathers and mothers of the desert tradition.[240] Sometimes his work even circulated under the name of a famous eastern monk. Thus the passage in book 4 of the *Institutes* (*Inst.* 4.39) that inspired the "ladder of humility" of the *Rule of the Master* was included among works of Evagrius, and a section of the Greek epitome on the eight principal faults was attributed to Nilus.[241] It is ironic, given Cassian's silence about Evagrius, that his own words came to be attributed to his teacher. Derwas Chitty detected reminiscences of Cassian in letters of Barsanuphius,[242] as did Lucien Regnault and Jacques de Préville in Dorotheus' *Instructions*;[243] while these are as likely to be attributable to sources shared with Cassian, they at least bear witness to Cassian's resonances with the eastern monastic spirit. With John Climacus we are on surer ground: he knew Cassian's work, referring to him by name and quoting the title of *Conference* 2.[244] John Damascene in the early eighth century—or a contemporary—quoted Cassian's teaching on sadness and accidie from the Greek epitome of the *Institutes*.[245]

A Monk for Others

We know that Cassian's contemporaries saw him as a monastic authority and leader; the tradition in Marseilles names him founder of Saint Victor and at least one other monastery. But what sort of monastic life did Cassian actually lead after so many years of migration and ecclesiastical involvement?[246] His own effort to retain his monastic integrity in the midst of a full and varied life would have been the same challenge faced by his many brothers called out of monasteries in Gaul to serve the local church in the episcopate and other ministries. His writings can be read as encouragement for them to make the effort to live as monks "in the world."[247] Certainly he wrote for those who would spend their life within the monastery, but as I will show, his teaching on contemplation, chastity, and prayer is eminently portable, constituting a kind of ascetical breviary compiled with the conviction that charity must always prevail over personal preference, even preference for solitude and contemplation.

The corollary of such a conviction is that service of others in hospitality and teaching are a real work of the monk: after all, these are the virtues modelled by the monks to whom he attributes the *Conferences*. Cassian's emphasis on experience rather than rhetoric, and the profundity and realism of his monastic theology, persuade at least this reader that in the many places he lived and in the many things he did, he was always Cassian the Monk.

CHAPTER TWO

Cassian the Writer

*We will show them to you embodied in their teachings and, better yet,
explaining them in Latin.*

—*Conf. Pref.* 1 6

Ways of Reading

IN THE MONASTIC WRITINGS ONE MEETS SEVERAL JOHN CASSIANS: a young monk
dazzled by monastic Egypt and an old man relating youthful experiences; an
advisor of church leaders in Gaul and an apologist scarred by battle; a monastic
founder concerned that new monasteries learn the right kind of monasticism; a
spiritual writer integrating earlier traditions into a theology of the monastic life.
These authorial personae coexist in the texts, generating an array of purposes and
meanings. Like the Bible so central to his life and thought, Cassian's own works
must be read through several interpretative lenses.

For Cassian and the tradition that formed him, moving from the literal to the
spiritual meaning of a text was a natural step. His monastic theology continually
pierces the apparent to find what is hidden, advances from the provisional to the
ultimate. In beginning the *Institutes* with a spiritual interpretation of monastic
clothing, he establishes the agenda he will follow right through to the very last
Conference. The physical aspect of some monastic practice or the literal sense of
a text may be "true," but other tracks of meaning, equally "true," have a much
greater bearing on spiritual growth.

In *Conference* 14, following the lead of Origen, Cassian sketches four kinds of
contemplative knowledge to be found in the Bible: historical (past and evident),
allegorical (prefigured and enduring), tropological (moral and practical), and anagogical (foreshadowing and heavenly).[1] One can apply Cassian's schema of four
kinds of meaning to his own writings as a way to understand his personae and
intentions.

Cassian's historical intention was to describe his own experiences as a young
monk living in Palestine and Egypt (see *Inst. Pref.* 7–8). He writes about places
he visited and people he met, informing his readers about monastic structures
and practices. These "historical" elements create the framework for his writings.
Although he was writing neither travelogue or history, he grounded his teaching
in a tradition he sought to present faithfully even as he adapted and developed it.

I have already discussed the impressive range of monks and bishops to whom Cassian dedicated the various phases of his project (see chapter 1). His stance of helpfulness was surely more than just a pose,[2] though the determination with which he undertook his project indicates his conviction that monasticism in southern Gaul should be of a very specific kind. For example, his stated reason for augmenting his original plan of only ten *Conferences* is to support Honoratus' efforts to base his community on the teachings of the Egyptian fathers and to spare Eucherius the "dangerous" journey to Egypt (*Conf. Pref.* 2 1). These are suspiciously ingenuous motivations. To support Honoratus' program, of course, means to advance his own. In telling Eucherius why he himself went to Egypt and what he found there, Cassian substitutes his own synthesis of the Egyptian tradition for whatever Eucherius might have found there himself. By this time, the monasticism Cassian had known in Egypt had been dramatically affected by both the Origenist Controversy in 399–400 and the barbarian devastations of Scetis in 407–8; Cassian wrote the *Gone with the Wind* of early Egyptian monasticism.

Therefore, although the great Egyptian monks to whom Cassian attributes the *Conferences* were historical figures, he uses them and the literary structure he creates for them as a monastic allegory designed to lead his readers to true doctrine and traditional monasticism. By presenting his own theological synthesis as their teaching, Cassian uses the Egyptian monks as validating authorities. The Egyptian guise also permitted him to teach controversial ideas without directly engaging in polemics. He advances his theological arguments in the *Institutes* and *Conferences* without naming his opponents or even admitting that his views are partisan.[3]

Few of Cassian's readers would have perceived the allegorical dimension of his writings. They would have accepted the attribution of the *Conferences* and been unaware that in them he was responding to critics or advancing contested ideas. This deception was not malicious. Cassian's intention was to focus attention on the teachings themselves, understood traditionally and practically, rather than on the controversies that distorted or abused them. It really mattered little to his readers that Cassian's "purity of heart" was Evagrius' *apatheia*, or that the story of Sarapion's "Anthropomorphism" in *Conference* 10 was a very partial view of that controversy that devastated Egyptian monasticism, or that *Conference* 14 outlined the Origenist approach to Scripture that was part of that same controversy, or that *Conferences* 13 and 23 can be read as responses to Augustine and Jerome, respectively.[4] Cassian had his agenda, certainly, but it was not in service of self. He sought to preserve and to propagate the teaching he himself had found life-giving.

Another example of monastic allegory was Cassian's use of labels such as "cenobitic" and "anchoritic". The words have obvious meanings based on common usage, but they also denote developmental stages within any form of the monastic life. As noted later, his labels of "cenobitic" for the *Institutes* and "anchoritic" for the *Conferences* are incoherent if interpreted literally. Similarly, as I will show in Chapter 4, sexual "continence" is a metonymy for the whole ascetical aspect of monastic life (*vita actualis*), and "chastity" becomes synonymous with "purity of heart" as a way to describe the monastic goal.

Cassian crafted his monastic works to facilitate moral and spiritual instruction. His tropological intention was to give the monks of southern Gaul (and their bishops, many of them monks as well) an overview of the monastic life, explaining where to begin, what to do, what to expect along the way, and where it all leads. These writings have proved incalculably helpful throughout the many centuries of western monastic life. The tropological aspect of monastic formation will be a particular focus of this chapter as I consider Cassian's own statements about the genesis and plan of his works, as well as the pedagogical significance of the sources, structure, and literary style of his monastic writings.

Finally, Cassian's anagogical perspective directed his own life and deeply influenced the nature of his monastic theology. Most important to him was not monastic history or even monastic instruction, but his conviction that monastic life is meant to bring one to the vision of God in heaven. As I will show in chapter 3, Cassian's love of God and neighbor for the sake of the reign of God still to come energized his writing and shaped his teaching, providing the fundamental unity of his thought and much of his originality as a teacher.

Cassian's Monastic Writings

The Evolution of the Project

According to what Cassian states in the prefaces to his monastic writings, they developed in the following way[5]:

PHASE I A:	*Institutes* Bks. 1–4
	Institutes Bks. 5–12
PHASE I B:	*Conferences* 1–10
PHASE II:	*Conferences* 11–17
PHASE III:	*Conferences* 18–24

The original plan was twelve books of *Institutes*, pertaining both to monastic "rules" (*Inst.* 1–4) and the origins, causes, and cures of the eight principal faults (*Inst.* 5–12). The Latin word *instituta* is the plural of *institutum*, a noun formed from *instituere*, "to establish" or "to lay down." These words have both a constructive and an instructive sense, evident even in the English usage of "institute" for an establishment of learning. Cassian always uses *instituta* in the plural as a collective term for the teachings, customs, and structures of the monastic life.[6] The word is not restricted to cenobites, for he refers to the "institutes" of anchorites[7] and attributes some of his *Conferences* to cenobites.[8]

Cassian uses *instituta* much like words such as *regula*,[9] *disciplina*[10] and *praecepta*[11] which at this time were becoming technical terms in Latin monasticism.[12] Referring to the *Institutes* in the *Conferences*, he occasionally uses *institutio*, a word with a stronger pedagogical nuance closer to what would today be called "monastic formation."[13] The *Institutes* are a foundational work designed to guide and instruct and thus are more than simply a collection of customs and rules.[14] As I will show, the teaching of the *Conferences* is often to be found in germ among the *Institutes*.

Cassian planned to complement the *Institutes* with ten *Conferences* attributed to anchorites of Scetis (*Conf.* 1–10). Responding to demand for more, Cassian produced two further installments (*Conf.* 11–17 and 18–24). The Latin word for "conference" is *conlatio*, which essentially means "a gathering together," whether of objects or of persons. Cassian uses it in both ways. For example, he refers to the *conlatio* of money mentioned by Paul in the Letter to the Romans.[15] Usually, however, Cassian employs *conlatio* in the human and social sense of a gathering of people for consultation or discussion,[16] normally a monastic elder speaking to a group of monks;[17] the discourse itself assumes the name for the gathering, as in modern monastic practice.

All twenty-four *Conferences* are presented as conversations between a specific elder and the young John and Germanus. The format is generally that of the classical dialogue or *erotapokriseis* (question and answer session),[18] which had already been used by Sulpitius Severus to teach (his version of) Egyptian monasticism.[19] Cassian is the narrator, an Egyptian monk is the speaker, Germanus is the interlocutor.[20] Most of the *Conferences* begin simply with a question or topic submitted by the young monks to the elder,[21] the classic opening for a monastic story,[22] though some also have a brief introduction setting the scene or introducing the elder.[23]

Relationships between the Institutes and the Conferences

Cassian had the *Conferences* in view even as he wrote the *Institutes*. The preface to the *Institutes* contains no mention of the *Conferences*, but the work itself has many. In book 1 Cassian alludes to a subsequent phase,[24] and in both books 2 and 5 he postpones certain topics until the "conferences of the elders."[25] It is more difficult to determine how he actually understood the relationship between the two parts of his monastic writings. The complex interconnections between the two parts immediately present one of the major problems facing any interpretation of Cassian's monastic theology, the relationship between the "cenobitic" and "anchoritic" forms of monastic life. The preface of the *Institutes* indicates that he offers his work for the assistance of cenobites in a newly founded monastery. His stated distinction between the "cenobitic" teaching of the *Institutes* and the "anchoritic" teaching of the *Conferences* led Julien Leroy to conclude that Cassian was at a loss as to what to advise cenobites and had to include material of limited relevance to them (that is, *Inst.* 5–12) or "manifestly made for anchorites and of only indirect interest to cenobites" (that is, *Conf.* 1–10).[26] Leroy's characterizations are unsustainable, however, in view of Cassian's own stated plans for the *Institutes* and *Conferences*.

As Cassian described his project, the *Institutes* were to be devoted to the "institutes or rules of the monasteries, and especially the origins, causes, and cures of the principal faults, which they reckon as eight"(*Inst. Pref.* 7).[27] The focus was on cenobitic life, which Cassian understands as primarily concerned with the "outer person",[28] that is, the emendation of faults.[29] The *Conferences* have an anchoritic veneer[30] but are more accurately understood as directed toward the concerns of the "inner person" striving for perfection.[31] Despite the anchoritic rhetoric of the *Conferences*—including Cassian's stated desire to stay among the anchorites of Scetis rather than return to his cenobium in Bethlehem—Cassian discourages invidious comparisons between the two forms of monastic life.[32] He posits a common ideal pursued in different ways,[33] and his terminology of "anchorite" and "cenobite" is not so much a taxonomy of forms of monastic life as a way to describe the experiences of every monk aiming for perfection.

The best illustration of the essential unity of *Institutes* and *Conferences* is their teaching on the most fundamental monastic practice, prayer. Cassian claims in the *Institutes* to be concerned with the structure and measure *(modus)* of the "canonical" prayer celebrated at regular times of day and night;[34] again, this concern pertains to the "outer person" (*Inst.* 2.9.1). The *Conferences*, on the other hand, deal with the inner disposition of the one who prays and the nature of prayer itself,[35] especially as unceasing.[36] Clearly one cannot divide cenobites from anchorites by distinguishing *Institutes* from *Conferences*. Anchorites are obliged by the "canonical" prayers of the appointed psalmody, and cenobites pray inwardly and seek to pray unceasingly. In the *Institutes* Cassian mentions the custom of suspending both fasting and kneeling on Sundays and during the Fifty Days of Easter, but defers the reason for this "relaxation" to the *Conferences*.[37] Cenobites who ate and stood would have sought, one presumes, some explanation for why they did so. In the *Institutes* Cassian does, in fact, address the inner experience of prayer, both in case an untimely death should intervene before he is able to complete his project and also to help those in the future who may not have access to the *Conferences* (*Inst.* 2.9.3).

Even the first four books of the *Institutes*, the most explicitly "cenobitic," have close links with the *Conferences*.[38] The description of ecstatic prayer in Book 2 of the *Institutes* (*Inst.* 2.10.1) anticipates those found throughout the *Conferences*.[39] The homily closing book 4 of the *Institutes*, attributed to the cenobitic abbot Pinufius, ends exactly where *Conference* 1, attributed to the anchorite Abba Moses, begins: "purity of heart and apostolic love." The same themes are treated more fully in *Conferences* 11 and 12, and recur later.[40]

The second part of the *Institutes* (books 5–12) has its own thematic affinities with the *Conferences*, for the topic of the eight principal faults is taken up again in *Conference* 5.[41] Indeed, throughout the second part of the *Institutes* Cassian introduces many elements of his overall vision of the monastic life that will be developed further in the *Conferences*. Book 5 of the *Institutes*, the seedbed for the *Conferences*,[42] is packed with such foreshadowings.[43]

The *Institutes* and *Conferences*, then, are two sides of one coin. They are more than complementary: both were essential reading for Cassian's entire audience, cenobites and anchorites alike. The cenobitic momentum in the Latin world, and perhaps especially in southern Gaul, meant however that Cassian's audience was probably almost entirely cenobitic from the outset, as it certainly was by the time of Benedict's recommendation of Cassian's writings. Cassian's concern that anchorites receive a thorough grounding in the monastic life in a cenobium before proceeding to solitude,[44] as well as his own ecclesiastical situation in Marseilles, suggest that Cassian's anchorites are best understood as figures for the contemplative monks even cenobites hope to become. Both at the outset of the *Institutes* and at the end of the *Conferences,* his purpose is the same: not to dazzle his readers with tales of wonder-working monks, but to support them in the emendation of their own faults and the pursuit of monastic perfection.[45]

Relationships among the Conferences

Cassian wrote three sets of *Conferences.* The first (*Conf.* 1–10) was part of the initial plan for the monastic writings. It is apparent from both structural and thematic evidence that those first *Conferences* form a coherent unit and complete the project begun in the *Institutes.* Nonetheless, there are topics explicitly deferred to the *Conferences* that are not addressed in the first ten.[46] As he wrote the first set of *Conferences* he must have already recognized the need for more; by the time he wrote the far more; preface to the second set (*Conf.* 11–17), he was ready to announce the third (*Conf. Pref.* 2 3).

In order to understand the interrelationships among the *Conferences,* one needs an overview, beginning with the first set.

Conferences   1–2
SPEAKER: Moses of Scetis
TOPICS: goal/end of monastic life
              discernment

Conference   3
SPEAKER: Paphnutius of Scetis
TOPICS: progressive renunciations, perfection, free will

Conference   4
SPEAKER: Daniel of Scetis
TOPICS: spiritual combat, free will

Conference   5
SPEAKER: Sarapion of Scetis
TOPICS: eight principal faults

Conference   6
SPEAKER: Theodore of Kellia
TOPICS: trials, free will, perseverance

Conferences   7–8
SPEAKER: Serenus of Scetis
TOPICS: anthropology, free will, temptation
              interpretation of the Bible, demons

Conferences   9–10
SPEAKER: Isaac of Scetis
TOPICS: disposition for, kinds of, and experiences in prayer
              unceasing prayer, biblical interpretation, distractions

All the speakers are anchorites, and all except Theodore are from Scetis; the anchoritic setting balances the cenobitic milieu of books 1–4 of the *Institutes*. The set is dominated by the pairs at beginning and end. Both pairs contain statements of the monastic goal (*Conf.* 1, purity of heart; *Conf.* 9–10, unceasing prayer) and a discussion of how to attain it (*Conf.* 2, discernment; *Conf.* 10, the method of unceasing prayer). After a restatement in *Conference* 3 of the entire monastic trajectory, *Conferences* 4–8 are devoted to difficulties in the monastic life. These are not esoteric treatises or of interest only to anchorites. *Conferences* 9–10, as will be seen later, are catechetical treatises on prayer, biblical interpretation, and Christology that range from the most basic to the most sublime levels of instruction.

In the second set of *Conferences* Cassian turns somewhat more to matters of disposition and intention, though the ascetical emphasis of much of *Conferences* 1–10 by no means disappears. These *Conferences* are set at a time prior to the first ten and purport to describe Cassian's visit to anchorites in the Nile Delta shortly after his arrival in Egypt. Their content, of course, depends on neither geographical nor chronological setting.

Conferences 11–13
SPEAKER: Chaeremon, anchorite near Panephysis
TOPICS: perfection, love, chastity
             chastity, patience
             chastity, grace

Conferences 14–15
SPEAKER: Nesteros, anchorite near Panephysis
TOPICS: ascetical and contemplative aspects of monastic life, spiritual
                interpretation of the Bible
             miraculous powers, perfection, humility

Conferences 16–17
SPEAKER: Joseph, anchorite near Panephysis
TOPICS: true friendship; love, patience, anger
             promises, lying, acts and intentions

In the first three *Conferences* of the second set, Cassian again sketches the monastic trajectory through its various stages. The dominant topics of love, chastity, and free will are interwoven throughout; *Conferences* 11–13 may be seen as a development of the themes introduced in *Conference* 6. (The significance of chastity for Cassian as a metaphor for monastic perfection is considered in chapter 4.) Then in *Conferences* 14–15, Cassian presents his classic exposition of the interplay between progress in the monastic life and the ability to understand the Bible, emphasizing spiritual growth and humility rather than intellectual ability (*Conf.* 14) or miraculous powers such as the gift of healing (*Conf.* 15). The final two *Conferences* in this set contain the musings that are both Cassian's most personal and his most philosophical. Both arise from situations in his own life: his friendship with Germanus prompts the reflection on true friendship in *Conference* 16; their anxiety about the promise to return home to Bethlehem after only a brief visit to Egypt sets the stage for the discussion of act and intention in *Conference* 17. Despite their particular circumstances, both *Conferences* support Cassian's larger project. When writing about friendship (as about chastity in *Conf.* 12), he returns to the fundamental theme of patience and anger. Considering the grounds for breaking a promise, he deepens the reflections on ends and means begun in *Conference* 1.

Conferences 18–24 feature cenobitic as well as anchoritic speakers. As a set this third group seems more random than the first two; the mix of speakers, the variety of locales (both the Delta and Scetis), and the lack of an obvious structure contribute to the impression of a hodgepodge:

Conference 18
SPEAKER: Piamun, anchorite (former cenobite) of Diolcos
TOPICS: the three types of monks, patience

Conference 19
SPEAKER: John, cenobite (former anchorite)of Diolcos
TOPICS: cenobites and anchorites compared, dangers of solitude, lust

Conference 20
SPEAKER: Pinufius, cenobite of Panephysis
TOPICS: sorrow for sins, assurance of forgiveness

Conferences 21–23
SPEAKER: Theonas, anchorite of Scetis
TOPICS: law versus freedom and perfection, fasting and chastity, Lent
        and Easter
        nocturnal emissions, grace, impossibility of sinlessness
        impossibility of sinlessness

Conference 24
SPEAKER: Abraham, anchorite of Diolcos
TOPICS: renunciation and separation, thoughts, love for others

A closer look, however, suggests that because *Conferences* 18 and 19 are both about monastic taxonomy and the dangers of solitude, they form a unit despite their attribution to different monks. In them one can see Cassian's use of the terms "cenobite" and "anchorite" operating on both the literal level of different forms of monastic life and the allegorical level of different aspects or phases of every monastic vocation. These two *Conferences* return to the theme of a monastic goal (with stages of progress toward it) that opens each set of the *Conferences*. *Conference* 20 is as much about the danger of morbid obsession with personal sinfulness as about monastic perfection. In the next three *Conferences* Cassian returns again to ends and means in order to correct misunderstandings about his claims for conquest of the passions and achievement of chastity (i.e., he is not equating these with "sinlessness"). The focus on chastity and grace makes these *Conferences* a counterpart to *Conferences* 11–13 and, therefore, a last excursus on the themes of *Conference 6. Conference 24* is a final exhortation to renounce both premonastic and nonmonastic entanglements while yet remaining open to the legitimate demands of charity toward others. The *Conferences* end where they began, balancing the disciplines of monastic life against the ultimate goal of love (see *Conf.* 1.6–7).

Language and Style

Cassian's sentences are long, and his vocabulary is vivid and tending toward the superlative. Cassiodorus admired Cassian's style, twice describing him as "most eloquent."[47] Modern readers are less effusive, though noting the correctness of Cassian's grammar[48] and his deliberate effort to craft an accessible Christian style avoiding classical references and remaining focused on the subject matter.[49] He peppers his monastic writings with Greek (and, occasionally, Coptic) words, sometimes in Greek letters and sometimes in transcription.[50] Because his principal sources are Greek, the effort of translating their spiritual vocabulary into Latin sometimes requires him to cite the original Greek before venturing a translation. Thus one finds the Evagrian vocabulary of *praktikē* and *theōrētikē* (*Conf.* 14), Greek names for four of the eight principal faults,[51] Greek words for "goal" and "end" (*Conf.* 1), Platonic anthropology explained via the Greek terminology (*Conf.* 24.15 and 17), the Greek *nous* for the Latin *mens*, "mind."[52] Several transliterations or translations of Greek are original to Cassian, a further witness to his role as a bridge between eastern and western monasticism.

Cassian's love of both Latin and Greek is evident in his biblical quotation and interpretation. He compares Old Latin versions to Jerome's Vulgate[53] or remarks on textual variants in Latin manuscripts.[54] He quotes the Septuagint or the Greek New Testament for nuances unparalleled in the Latin.[55] Some of his interpretations depend on the Greek or on a comparison between the Greek and Latin versions.[56]

Editors of Cassian's works since Ciaconnius in 1588 have noticed that his biblical quotations frequently seem to be his own Latin translation of the Septuagint, portions of which he had probably memorized as a young monk in Palestine and Egypt. When he cites Proverbs and Ecclesiastes, two books particularly beloved by monks, nearly all his quotations are based on the Septuagint.[57] On the other hand, he almost always cites the Psalms in the so-called Gallican Latin version of Jerome, reflecting his liturgical experience of that translation at the monastery in Marseilles. Other texts from the Wisdom literature, however, used for his private *meditatio*, retained their Greek character.[58]

Cassian's Sources

Cassian's primary source, of course, is the Bible. But he also read widely in both classical and Christian texts. He states—ruefully—that he had received a good education with ample attention to epics and poetry (*Conf.* 14.10). He demonstrates a basic knowledge of Greek philosophy and quotes a few Greek aphorisms and bits of Latin literature.[59] He alludes to Cicero in the *Institutes* (12.19), and *Conference* 16, entitled "On Friendship" *(De amicitia)*, echoes Cicero's treatise of the same name.[60] However, he mutes his classical background, and the biblical and Christian texts that shaped his theology dominate his writings.

Cassian's reading was broader than normal because of his bilingualism. He shows a familiarity with standard theological works in both Latin and Greek, though our sense of the full range of his reading is incomplete. Despite significant studies of his use of sources, much work remains to be done.[61] I have already discussed the complexity of his relationship to historical sources about Egyptian monasticism (see chapter 1 and the appendix); his synthesis of theological sources and his own experience will concern the rest of this study.

Cassian's most explicit use of theological sources is in *The Incarnation of the Lord*. There he cites several Greek and Latin theologians (especially John Chrysostom) within a dossier of anti-Nestorian Christological texts.[62] In the monastic writings he is more circumspect, citing only Basil and Jerome by name *(Inst. Pref.* 5).[63] Cassian notes that Jerome was both a writer and a translator, and Cassian certainly knew Jerome's translation of the Pachomian materials, as well as Jerome's letters.[64] As one would expect, Cassian had also read Jerome's *Life of Paul the First Hermit* and probably the *Lives* of Hilarion and Malchus as well.[65]

In Cassian's monastic writings there are quotations from the *Shepherd* of Hermas, possible traces of Irenaeus, the influence of fundamental Latin writers such as Tertullian and Cyprian, and material from the Latin translation of Eusebius' *Ecclesiastical History*.[66] Cassian knew the *Life of Antony*, evidently in Evagrius of Antioch's Latin translation,[67] and perhaps Antony's letters. He read and used Rufinus' translation of the *History of the Monks in Egypt*.[68] Vogüé has noted that Cassian may also have known the Greek original text of both the Basilian and Pachomian materials;[69] he seems also to have read Palladius' *Lausiac History*.[70] He depended on, and took issue with, both Sulpitius Severus and Augustine; he knew Sulpitius' *Dialogues*,[71] several works by Augustine, and also the Augustinian *Ordo monasterii*.[72] He had access to the traditions behind the later collections of *Apophthegmata*, though the evolving state of those texts and collections in Cassian's day makes it difficult to know his exact relationship to them.[73]

Since Salvatore Marsili's groundbreaking study in the 1930s, it has been accepted that Evagrius Ponticus was the single greatest inspiration for Cassian's spiritual theology. Cassian relied heavily on Evagrius' writings and on those of their common master, Origen, though he does not credit either by name. The reason for this omission was political, as explained in chapter 1. Cassian seems to have read Clement of Alexandria's writings, though the extent of his dependence is unclear; the mediation of Clement's thought by Origen and Evagrius may explain many of the parallels that have been adduced between Clement and Cassian.[74]

Cassian was certainly much more than "merely the Latin translator" or popularizer of Evagrian spiritual theology.[75] His development and departure from Evagrian thought is often as notable as his dependence on it. His pastoral and practical orientation determined how he used all of his sources, and this orientation is most evident in the way he handles the Origenist tradition and Evagrian theology.

The unique matrix of his life experience, which both shaped and was shaped by the matrix of his literary sources, generated his spiritual theology.

The most controversial and puzzling question about Cassian's sources was first posed by Alfons Kemmer, writing like Marsili in the 1930s. Kemmer sought to demonstrate affinities between Cassian's writings and literature associated with the "Messalian" movement such as the *Liber graduum* and the works of Pseudo-Macarius.[76] Scholars have conceded that there are aspects of Cassian's teaching that seem explicable only by some sort of contact with the milieu that produced such texts, though Kemmer's evidence has not been widely accepted. In chapter 7 of this study the question will be revisited from a new perspective. It will be suggested there that Cassian's teaching on prayer was shaped not only by Evagrian spirituality but also by the affective mysticism typified by Pseudo-Macarius and Cassian's near contemporary, Diadochus of Photike.

Cassian's Pedagogy

Repetition

The sheer mass of the *Institutes* and *Conferences* daunts those who approach them. It is little wonder that Cassian's readers have sought to tame the wildness of his monastic writings. Within a few years of his death, abridgements provided the basic elements of his theology in a manageable package for both Latin and Greek readers.[77] Both the variety and the extent of Cassian's writings were motivated by pedagogical concerns. He knew that a teacher must keep returning to basic themes but must also keep them fresh and appealing.

His basic method was to postulate an ideal and then to consider practical considerations that make the ideal only imperfectly or fleetingly attainable. In this way he was anticipating Benedict's counsel: "[the Abbot] must so arrange everything that the strong have something to yearn for and the weak nothing to run from," a text itself perhaps inspired by Cassian.[78] Cassian revisits fundamental topics again and again, nuancing and developing his approaches. He had a penchant for maxims and illustration, and his spiritual vocabulary was always being redeveloped and refined.[79] He was partial to schemata, though he was not a systematic thinker; his talent for variation and development means that whatever model he presents will probably be replaced later by another. Affixing his ideas to schematic or thematic grids degrades his kaleidoscopic vision to a single optic or exaggerates his dependence on sources.

I have shown that Cassian uses the *Conferences* to develop themes introduced in the *Institutes*. He draws and redraws his maps of the monastic journey, punctuating the *Conferences* with redefinitions of the monastic goal: purity of heart and continual contemplation in *Conference* 1, unceasing prayer in *Conferences* 9–10, perfection of chastity in *Conference* 12, incessant rumination of Scripture in *Conference* 14, different goals for cenobites and anchorites in *Conference* 19, the "remembrance of God" in *Conference* 24. Each of these themes unfolds his conception of monastic perfection. The result is neither incoherent nor ultimately contradictory, though certainly not the work of someone with an overriding concern for perfect consistency.[80]

An Illustration: Goals in Monastic Life

The way that Cassian gradually develops his notion that monastic life has a goal illustrates the way his metaphors and vocabulary evolve throughout his works. In book 5 of the *Institutes*, the inspiration for much of what Cassian later elaborated in the *Conferences*, he compares the monk's focus on heaven to an athlete's concentration on targets and finish lines. He begins with the "mark" *(indicium)* at which javelins are thrown *(Inst.* 5.15) and then shifts metaphors to the runner's finish line *(destinatum)* evoked by Paul in Philippians 3:13–14 *(Inst.* 5.17).

In the *Conferences*, Cassian's love of Scripture, his philological curiosity, and his creative imagination transform the metaphor. He opens *Conference* 1 with the image of monastic life as travel toward a goal *(scopos,* a Latin transliteration of the Greek σκοπός) *(Conf.* 1.4.4). Then he reverts to the athletic metaphors of the *Institutes:* a thrower's eyes must be fixed on the target lest shots be wasted *(Conf.* 1.5.1; see 1.13.1); he again cites the text from Philippians about the race and the finish line. As in the *Institutes,* he quotes the Vulgate text but then adds the original Greek of the phrase about the finish line, claiming that the Greek word *skopos* makes plainer the idea of a goal than does the Latin *destinatum.*

The real reason he prefers the Greek to the Latin at this point is that *skopos* is a key word in the opening chapters of *Conference* 1. He argues there that monastic life has both a proximate goal ("purity of heart") and an ultimate end ("the reign of heaven"). To distinguish the proximate from the ultimate, he uses the Stoic distinction between *skopos* ("goal") and *telos* ("end"), which had been adapted for Christian purposes by Clement of Alexandria to *(Conf.* 1.2–5).[81] Cassian was familiar with Evagrius' use of *telos* to define the ultimate end of monastic life; indeed, Cassian's definition of the monk's *telos* is based on Evagrius. The Stoic distinction, which Cassian probably knew from Clement, must have seemed a useful complementary device.[82] Cassian found biblical support for the Stoic term in the Greek original of the Pauline text he had used earlier in the *Institutes.* This kind of pedantic reference to the Greek Bible is a device Cassian employs on several other occasions in the *Conferences.*[83] Although his use of the Greek is not essential to his argument, it shows the evolution of Cassian's thought since the earlier treatment of the same theme in the *Institutes.* Incidentally, the comparison of Latin and Greek versions assures us that the voice one hears in this *Conference* is that of Cassian and not Abba Moses.[84]

Within *Conference* 1, Cassian then moves from the Greek *skopos* and *telos* to the Latin *destinatio* and *finis,* preserving the distinction between proximate goal and ultimate end.[85] In subsequent *Conferences,* however, *finis* becomes synonymous with *destinatio* and largely replaces it,[86] joining more common words like *propositum*[87] ("purpose"), *intentio,* or *professio* to describe the earthly aim or purpose of monastic life. Despite the shifting terminology, the two fundamental themes of "purity of heart" and the "reign of heaven" continue to underlie the whole of his theology.[88]

Cassian did not abandon focal metaphors. In *Conference* 24, he turns the image outside-in so that the distant mark or target of the earlier texts becomes an architect's compass point.[89] Around that central point a perfect arch can be traced, beautiful in itself and also serving a structural purpose. For the monk, the still point around which all else turns is the love of God. Working from that mark, a spiritual temple of God can be designed and built in the heart (*Conf.* 24.6). Moving from thrower's target to runner's finish line to architect's reference point, Cassian's lively mind refuses restriction to a single image.

Cassian the Teacher

Cassian's whole life prepared him for the task he undertook in Gaul. Deeply rooted in the Christian and monastic traditions he knew from experience and from wide reading, he shaped his monastic theology according to the needs he perceived in his own time and place. There are many things going on in Cassian's monastic writings. He portrayed a lost golden age of Egyptian monasticism, wanted to salvage and to propagate Origenist theology, and had definite ideas about the direction of monasticism in southern Gaul. Through all these agenda ran his fundamental concern for instruction, his "tropological level" of intention. The rest of this study is devoted to Cassian's teaching itself. As I will show, for Cassian tropology was inseparable from anagogy. The lively and restless intelligence one meets in his writings had a definite orientation toward the heaven on which Christians stake their hope. His map of the monastic journey to that heavenly hope is my next concern.

CHAPTER THREE

Cassian the Theologian

The end of our profession is the reign of God or the reign of heaven; but the nearer goal, or aim, is purity of heart, without which it is impossible for anyone to arrive at that end.

—*Conf.* 1.4.3

Journeying toward Goal and End: Mapping the Monastic Life

JOHN CASSIAN WAS BOTH A VISIONARY AND A PRAGMATIST. He urged his readers to look beyond their mundane tasks and preoccupations, yet acknowledged the fragmenting pressures of the present life. In his mind, the purpose of the monastic life was to prepare for citizenship in heaven and to anticipate, however fleetingly and imperfectly, the joy to be fully realized there. He is often read as a "spiritual-izer" of the monastic life, caricatured as a neo-Platonist who exalted eternal and spiritual goals at the expense of the present and material aspects of human existence. The philosophical influences on his thought are certainly profound, but it is more accurate to characterize his approach as consistently eschatological rather than spiritualizing. He explores the temporal and experiential disjunction between present experience and future hope, and he places the monk on the frontier between them.

The significance of Cassian's eschatological orientation, a perspective he and his mentors simply took for granted, cannot be overemphasized. His belief in heaven and his attendant conviction that monastic life is entirely oriented toward preparing for heaven shape everything he writes. What he seems to declare absolutely about the necessity of ascetical discipline, contemplation, prayer, chastity and everything else must be nuanced against that enormous backdrop of eternity that we today are far more likely to neglect than were Cassian's earlier readers.

The tension between the demands of this world and the peace when "God will be all in all"[1] energizes the *Conferences*. Speaking through each abba, Cassian shuttles us between present experience and future ideal, tracing and retracing the paths that connect them. Indeed, the *Conferences* are perhaps best seen as maps of the spiritual life. Each is based on a particular projection and characterized by distinctive emphases and scale. They are not a scientific atlas, but a collection of pilgrim's maps: everything on them is oriented to a destination. In these maps one sees Cassian, that great traveler, charting various ways to travel across the temporal and spiritual vastness between earth and heaven.

Cassian's spiritual theology is also profoundly Christocentric. This aspect too is not always immediately apparent to modern readers. His original readers shared his Christological instincts just as they were attuned to his eschatological presuppositions (even if they, like him, argued about Christological formulations). Christ pervades Cassian's teaching on contemplation, chastity, prayer, and spiritual knowledge. The eschatological and Christological foundations of his work are so firm that it should be unnecessary to draw particular attention to them. However, precisely because they are foundations they are not always apparent to those who do not know to look for them.

This chapter explores three recurring paths found on Cassian's maps of the monastic life: the quest for purity of heart; dedication to contemplation; and anticipation of the heavenly beatitude of seeing God. The three paths often run in parallel and their destinations, though described in particular terms, are not always clearly distinguishable.

Cassian's basic map in *Conference* 1 is drawn on the assumption that monastic life, like any art or science, has both a near "goal" (Gk. *skopos*, Lat. *destinatio*) and an ultimate "end" (Gk. *telos*, Lat. *finis*).[2] He illustrates the difference between them with examples drawn from his fifth-century world. A farmer works day in and day out, through all weathers and seasons, pursuing the "goal" of a field kept clear and tilled so as to attain the "end" of a good harvest. The prospect of harvest makes even heavy labor endurable, for every turn of the spade brings the farmer closer to both goal and end. So too the merchant travels and the soldier fights: each way of life is shaped by disciplines that will lead to future reward. Such analogies between monasticism and other disciplines reappear whenever Cassian turns to fundamental monastic ideals and the means of achieving them.[3] Thus the monk practices the fundamental disciplines of the "the practical life" (*vita actualis*)—fasting, vigils, reading and meditation of Scripture, various kinds of self-denial, the barrenness of the desert, and the loss of home and family—for the sake of a goal (*Conf.* 1.2).

What possible goal and end could induce a monk to endure and even to cherish such harsh disciplines? The obvious Christian answer is the "reign of heaven" or the "reign of God."[4] The answer would have been even more patent to any student of Evagrius, whose map of the monastic life led to the "reign of heaven" and then to the "reign of God," each defined in quite precise terms.[5] Cassian makes no distinction between the two reigns, but he shared Evagrius' conviction that the Christian end is the beatitude (Gk. *makariotēs*, Lat. *beatitudo*) consisting of the vision of God.[6]

Heaven, however, is a faraway destination. Cassian was pragmatic enough to know that for all its theological and imaginative significance for his readers, eternal beatitude can seem unreal and distant from the essential elements of daily monastic life. Because heaven lies beyond the horizon it can seem to have little practical effect in directing the monk's life here and now. Cassian suggests that monks need a closer "target" or "goal" as a navigational bearing. This nearer destination, says Cassian, is "purity of heart" (*Conf.* 1.4.3–4). Purity of heart is the centerpiece of Cassian's monastic theology, the term he uses to describe monastic perfection. As a generic and inclusive concept, purity of heart embraces Cassian's many other metaphors of perfection such as "tranquillity," "contemplation," "unceasing prayer," "chastity," and "spiritual knowledge."

The Quest for Purity of Heart

Background

Rooted in biblical tradition, the concept of purity of heart (*puritas cordis*) was not new to Cassian. Nor was its introduction in *Conference* 1 an innovation; the long homily on renunciation in book 4 of the *Institutes* ends with the theme.[7] By Cassian's time "purity of heart" had already become a privileged term that Christian and monastic writers used to describe moral and spiritual integrity.[8] Originating in Old Testament concerns for ritual purity, the concept came in Christian texts to focus on the avoidance of evil thoughts. Since Plato, "purity" had signified clarity of purpose, freedom from distraction or needless disturbance, a simplicity hard-won through experience, for both pre-Christian and Christian writers. A fruit of philosophical or ascetical discipline, purity was not a trait of the untested. As the American author Flannery O'Connor remarked, "I think the phrase 'naive purity' is a contradiction in terms. I don't think purity is mere innocence; I don't think babies and idiots possess it. I take it to be something that comes with experience or with Grace so that it can never be naive."[9] She, like Cassian and his predecessors, saw purity not as a pristine state to be protected from corruption but as the trait of human beings become fully alive despite—and because of—the scars inevitably left by this life.

The theme of purity, then, is even more pervasive in Cassian's writings than purity of heart. While *puritas cordis* is undoubtedly Cassian's favorite way of characterizing monastic perfection,[10] the addition of synonymous expressions such as purity of mind (*puritas mentis*) and purity of soul (*puritas animae*),[11] and of similar concepts like purity of body or pure prayer, quadruples the total number of such phrases. I will consider some of these corollary uses of *puritas* and *purus* in the discussions of chastity and unceasing prayer in chapters 4–6.

Evagrius had defined the goal of the "practical life" to be the "purified mind."[12] Following the Christian Platonist tradition, he read "heart" as the biblical equivalent to "mind" (Gk. *nous*, Lat. *mens*), understood to be the superior and integrating faculty of the soul.[13] Cassian's understanding of *puritas cordis* as "tranquillity" or "stability" of heart points to another element of the Evagrian model of the monastic life, the controversial doctrine of *apatheia*, "passionlessness," which Evagrius inherited from the Stoics and Clement of Alexandria and reinterpreted for his spiritual theology.[14]

Cassian's complete avoidance of the word *apatheia*—despite borrowings of other Evagrian terminology—signifies more than prudence about controversial aspects of his mentor's theology. Evagrius' term *apatheia* was prone to misinterpretation. Jerome, for example, caricatured *apatheia* as sinlessness and condemned the audacity of such a claim.[15] Cassian's choice of "purity of heart" also avoids the awkwardness of an obviously technical and philosophical term.

The biblical anchor for Cassian's doctrine of purity of heart is "blessed are the pure in heart, for they shall see God" (Matt. 5:8). By linking purity of heart to the vision of God, the beatitude connects "goal" to "end." At the same time, Cassian's infrequent quotation of this particular text[16] reminds us that his understanding of purity of heart does not depend on one biblical text alone but is rooted in a rich biblical and post-biblical tradition.[17]

In *Conference* 1 he quotes the beatitude only in his summary statement, following the Latin versions which use *mundus* ("clean") instead of *purus* (*Conf.* 1.10.5). That rich early Christian teaching on purity of heart may explain Cassian's use of the phrase *puritas cordis* rather than *munditia cordis*, which would have been closer to the Latin text of Matthew 5:8.[18] Cassian's *puritas* may be seen as an attempt to preserve the nuances of the Greek *katharotēs*, which since Plato had been used to describe physical, moral, and spiritual purity.[19] Cassian evidently thought that *puritas*, based on the adjective *purus*, bears those overtones more readily than does *mundus/munditia*.[20] The Greek original of the beatitude immediately lends itself to connection with that tradition because it uses the word *katharos*. Cassian's infrequent quotation of Matthew 5:8 may, therefore, be attributable at least in part to the shortcomings of its common Latin translation.

The Place of Purity of Heart in Cassian's Monastic Theology

Cassian was surely wise to opt for biblical ambiguity of purity of heart rather than risk the misunderstanding possible with Evagrius' term *apatheia*, but he was left with the task of explaining just what purity of heart meant in a monastic context.[21] Despite the shift of language, Cassian is faithful to Evagrius' teaching on *apatheia* in considering purity of heart to be both a goal and a means to something greater.[22] Sometimes Cassian emphasizes purity of heart as a goal in itself,[23] while at other times he emphasizes the experiences that purity of heart makes possible, such as love, contemplation, spiritual knowledge, unceasing prayer, chastity, union with God, the beatitude of heaven.[24] Again like Evagrius, Cassian thought of purity of heart as progressive and consisting of degrees of achievement. He writes of perfect, or perpetual, or most sublime purity of heart,[25] recognizes the possibility of diminishment or loss of purity of heart,[26] and measures it by the contemplative possibilities it opens and the potential trials that threaten it.[27] He does not define the different degrees of purity of heart as exactly as Evagrius did the stages of *apatheia*.[28] As I will show later with respect to kinds of contemplation, Cassian tends to simplify Evagrius' schemata and to avoid his highly technical vocabulary.

PURITY OF HEART, ASCETICISM, AND LOVE

Cassian's teaching on purity of heart has three main aspects: ascetical purification, a theological equation of purity of heart with love, and the experience of liberation from sin in tranquillity of heart. In *Conference* 1 he uses three biblical texts to elucidate *puritas cordis*. He anchors both goal and end biblically with Romans 6:22, "having then your fruit in sanctification, the end *(finis)* is eternal life." Sanctification is purity of heart, eternal life is the reign of God.

Cassian then underscores the developmental aspect of purity of heart by citing Philippians 3:13–14 ("forgetting what lies behind, stretching toward what lies ahead, I pursue the goal, the prize of the heavenly call of the Lord").[29] Time and disciplined effort are required to restrain the human mind's natural attraction to the stimuli that come at us from all directions *(Conf.* 1.5.2–3). The contrast between the destabilizing challenges of human existence and the goal of purity of heart is the existential dilemma before anyone who tries the monastic life, and Cassian devotes considerable attention to it in the *Conferences.* Acknowledging this dilemma—and presenting the means of resolving it—is the central *practical* issue for Cassian's monastic theology, arising in a variety of contexts such as prayer, chastity, interpreting the Bible, and the forms of monastic life.

Cassian defines purity of heart theologically by pointing beyond process to achievement: purity of heart is love. Quoting Paul's ode to love in 1 Corinthians 13.4–13, Cassian follows both Origen, who closely associated love and contemplation,[30] and Evagrius, who saw *apatheia* as the gateway to love *(agapē)*[31] and love as the portal to knowledge *(gnōsis).*[32] For Cassian, love is the very definition of eternal life with God, as we shall see in his teaching on contemplation.[33]

Cassian's equation of purity of heart with love is part of his strategy to forestall misunderstandings about the proper place of ascetical discipline or works of ministry in the monastic life. Ascetical deprivations help to purify the heart, but they are not themselves the goal *(Conf.* 1.5.3).[34] Cassian knew that obsession with "perfect" monastic observance can lead to despair and abandonment of the monastic life, or to anger (a most fatal passion for the monk), or to a judgmental stance toward others. Mistaking the means for the goal can arouse the very "passions" the monk is meant to shun, creating resentment toward those who disrupt one's daily routine or anger over the borrowing or disappearance of trivial items.[35] A monk who has abandoned a great fortune in the world can become fanatically protective of even an insignificant possession like a pen or a knife. Cassian echoes Paul: not even total destitution can assure perfection unless there is also the love that "consists of purity of heart alone" *(Conf.* 1.6.3).[36]

In the *Institutes* Cassian praises the willingness of Egyptian monks to suspend their fasts for the sake of hospitality, an accommodation to charity he claims was unknown in the evidently more priggish monasteries of Palestine. The principle of placing hospitality over personal discipline is a strong theme in the Egyptian desert tradition of the *Apophthegmata,*[37] and Cassian found the lesson important enough to mention four more times in the *Conferences.*[38]

Cassian revisits the distinction between means and goal throughout the *Conferences,*[39] for it is emblematic of his continual effort to shift the monk's outlook from earth to heaven, from the literal meaning of the Bible to the spiritual one, from image-filled to imageless prayer, from ascetical continence to graced chastity. Cassian develops his theology of love most fully in *Conference* 11, entitled "On Perfection." That *Conference* is a pendant to *Conference* 3, for both of them trace the maturing of monastic motivation from fear of punishment through hope of heavenly reward and finally to love of virtue in itself, which is equated with love of God.[40]

The speaker in *Conference* 11 is Abba Chaeremon, so old and feeble, and also so holy, that he has passed beyond both the need (and the possibility) of rigorous asceticism to a kind of second childhood. Cassian's vivid picture of the aged monk sketched at the beginning of the *Conference* is an icon of monastic transformation. The central claim is that perfect love means attaining the "image and likeness of God" evident in purity of heart. Like God, the monk is to extend a "calm love *(placida . . . caritas)* from the heart" toward all, both good and bad alike (*Conf.* 11.9–10, 14). This love builds on "perfect purity" manifest in "full tranquillity of heart" (*Conf.* 11.9.2).[41] In *Conference* 12, Chaeremon teaches that chastity is the perfect expression of such love. (The theme of chastity is so central to Cassian's theology that it merits special treatment in the next chapter.)

Cassian's theological rationale for his distinction between means and goal comes in *Conference* 17. The *mise en scène* for the *Conference* is a crisis faced by Cassian and Germanus after their arrival in Egypt. Having promised their superiors in Bethlehem that they would visit monasteries and then return home to their own cenobium, they have found in Scetis the monastic ideal they have been seeking. A return to Palestine, they fear, would be fatal to their monastic aspirations. Cassian, speaking through Chaeremon, makes a distinction between "bodily exercises," which can never be absolutes, and "fundamental obligations," which are to be observed at all costs (*Conf.* 17.28–30).[42] These obligations pertain to basic virtues and become imperative when necessary for the "preservation of love" (*Conf.* 17.28.2). The obligation of hospitality, for example, can justify lying, one ✗ of the points on which Cassian and Augustine disagree (*Conf.* 17.15–20).[43]

In defining purity of heart as love, Cassian relativizes a monk's personal discipline by subordinating it to the ultimate goal. He hopes to short-circuit obsessions about ascetical practices and to make his readers more open to the needs of others. At the same time, he warns against the equal danger of becoming overly involved with works of service. He knew that hospitality and pastoral care can provide the most seductive of excuses for neglecting monastic duties and collude with the workings of accidie and vainglory.[44] The relationship between action and contemplation is a classic monastic issue. As I will show, Cassian addresses it in his interpretation of the story of Martha and Mary in *Conference* 1, as well as in his frequent return to the problem of distraction in contemplation and prayer throughout the *Conferences*. Cassian's great contribution to monastic theology, evident here as in so many aspects of his teaching, is a relentless insistence on the long view. He finds the reason for every action and aspect of the monastic life in the striving to reach its goal and end.

TRANQUILLITY OF HEART

In experiential terms, purity of heart means freedom from domination by sin and the possession of a deep inner peace. These traits, fundamental to Cassian's teaching on monastic perfection, appear early on in his works in a homily on renunciation and mortification attributed to Abba Pinufius, the Egyptian monk Cassian and Germanus had known in Bethlehem. Pinufius' address, which anticipates the format of the *Conferences*, is delivered to his cenobitic community on the occasion of admitting a novice to the cenobium. Pinufius describes the ideal monk as one who has become "fastened to the wood of the cross." Having crucified all wrongful desires, with no concern for the present, no thought about personal likings, no anxiety about the future, he remains undisturbed by avarice, pride, contentiousness, envy, or remembrance of wrongs. While still in the body, he is dead to all material and earthly elements, and he turns the "eyes of the soul" to heaven (*Inst.* 4.35). These ideals inform all Cassian's descriptions of monastic perfection.

In *Conference* 1, Cassian defines purity of heart as "the purity and tranquillity of the mind" (*Conf.* 1.7.4). Like Evagrius and his predecessors, Cassian uses "mind" (*mens*) synonymously with "heart" (*cor*).[45] Tranquillity (*tranquillitas*) is the principal manifestation of purity of heart and often functions as a metonymy for it,[46] as do similar concepts like stability (*stabilitas*)[47] and steadfastness (*firmitas*).[48] All these qualities are reminiscent of the Evagrian *apatheia*, an emphasis confirmed by Cassian's other descriptions of monastic perfection as patience (*patientia*),[49] constancy (*constantia*)[50] or stillness (*immobilitas*).[51] Integrity (*integritas*)[52] indicates the wholeness and stability of chastity achieved by grace.

All Cassian's experiential descriptions of perfection suggest a focusing of fragmented energies on what is truly important. In *Conference* 3, he interweaves the themes of "three calls," perhaps based on a letter of Antony the Great, and "three renunciations," a theme evidently borrowed from Evagrius' *Chapters on Knowledge*.[53] The renunciations begin with external attachments, move to passions and internal attachments of any kind, and end with transcendence of any hindrance to contemplation. With God's grace, the monk can attain an even higher level, "the completion and perfection of purity" (*consummatio perfectionis ac puritatis*), free of the "thorns and thistles of sins" even while still in the body.[54] Though "walking in the flesh," one serves the Lord "not according to the flesh" (*Conf.* 3.6.4).[55]

In subsequent *Conferences* Cassian will develop the social and personal implications of his teaching on focused tranquillity and freedom from upheaval by the passions. In *Conference* 12, immediately following the analysis of love in *Conference* 11, Cassian describes perfect chastity as the "firm and lasting peace" of freedom from anger (*Conf.* 12.6–7). His teaching on monastic friendship in *Conference* 16 emphasizes the corrosive effects of anger and the need to cultivate patience. In *Conferences* 18 and 19, in which he returns to the goals of the monastic life, he emphasizes the tranquillity, gentleness (*lenitas*), calm (*placiditas*), and mildness (*mansuetudo*) of the monk who is no longer captive to anger (*Conf.* 18.12–13). Cenobites, freed from the anchorite's anxieties about material necessities and constant disturbance by visitors, attain "tranquillity of soul and heart" and "quiet stability of mind" (*Conf.* 19.6.5). The cenobium becomes the training ground where monks develop "the constancy of an imperturbable mind and immovable firmness of patience" (*Conf.* 19.11.1). With such preparation, the ancho-

[margin note: Vocabulary]

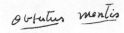 *obtutus mentis*

rite then seeks to have the "mind freed from all earthly things, and to unite it, as far as human frailty allows, with Christ" (*Conf.* 19.8.4). Asceticism and contemplation meet, as always, in purity of heart.

Abba Pinufius returns in the final set of *Conferences*, where Cassian has him describing the transformation of heart after all attraction to or desire for sin has been "expelled" and no "image" (i.e., mental picture) of former or prospective sins haunts the memory or imagination.[56] As fantasies fade away, the pangs of guilt that accompany them are eased as the "thorns of conscience" are lifted away from the heart (*Conf.* 20.7.2). In the next *Conference*, Cassian claims that those who have passed from service under the Law to life under the grace of Christ have been transfused with "divine love" and no longer desire what is sinful (*Conf.* 21.33). He sets a standard of purity of heart that seems impossibly lofty. Before probing his teaching about human perfectibility, however, one needs to understand why purity of heart is not an end in itself: the point really is to see God, an endeavor that begins in contemplation.

Contemplation

Cassian places the quest for the vision of God at the heart of his monastic theology. Any possibility of approaching God now in contemplation depends on "quality of life and purity of heart" (*Conf.* 1.15.3). Contemplation is purity of heart in action, the present mode of the vision of God promised to the pure of heart. Contemplation is the ground between the present "goal" and the heavenly "end," and it is always centered on Christ. In *Conference* 10, the Christocentrism of Cassian's teaching on contemplation becomes quite explicit,[57] though even in *Conference* 1 Cassian's model of contemplative devotion, Mary of Bethany, focuses her attention entirely on Jesus.

In book 5 of the *Institutes* Cassian states his basic thesis: contemplation is a transcending of mortal, earthly limitation and a foretaste of heaven. Someone who regards all things in the present as perishable and fixes the "mind's gaze" (*mentis obtutus*) unswervingly on what is immovable and eternal contemplates the beatitude of future existence even while still in the flesh (*Inst.* 5.14.4). In *Conference* 1, Cassian develops the following rationale for placing contemplation rather than action at the center of his theology:

1. Practical works of asceticism and of service are an essential part of the Christian life, but they are provisional, necessary now because of the sinful reality of human existence. Their necessity ends with death.
2. Contemplation is part of both the present life and the life beyond death because its object (Christ) and its basis (love) are enduring.
3. The "beatitude" of the saints in heaven consists of their "contemplation" of God (i.e., the "beatific vision").
4. Contemplation in this life can anticipate and participate in that heavenly contemplation.

5. Although constant contemplation is impossible "while still in the flesh," every effort must nonetheless be made to maintain a contemplative focus.

The rest of this chapter will explore these premises as Cassian sketches them in *Conference* 1 and develops them throughout the *Conferences*.

Seeing and Knowing

Cassian's theology of contemplation in *Conference* 1 opens with his first re-statement of the monastic goal: for the heart to be "joined always to divine things and to God" (*Conf.* 1.8.1). Another indication of Cassian's Christocentric under-standing of contemplation is that he writes interchangeably of union with "God" and with "Christ."[58] Such inherence in God comes via contemplation.[59] Cassian uses the Greek loanword *theōria* and, more commonly, the Latin equivalent *contemplatio* and its verb *contemplari*.[60] These words are essentially visual, and Cassian's other ways of describing contemplation are equally so: nouns meaning "regard" or "gaze" (e.g., *intuitus, obtutus, conspectus*) and verbs of sight or insight (e.g., *intueor, conspicere, videre*). The vision, of course, is spiritual.

Visual metaphors pervade Cassian's writings, and his use of the Greek termi-nology is surely attributable to the paramount role of *theōria* as a means of union with the divine in the Platonic tradition of Origen and Evagrius from which Cassian draws.[61] In Cassian's theology, monastic asceticism develops keenness of vision in the "eyes of the soul."[62] The pure of heart become able to see the "divine," "heavenly," "spiritual," "invisible," "future," and "hidden" things that are all the more real for their elusiveness to ordinary means of perception.[63] The monk seeks to become a child of Israel, a name that Cassian, like Philo and Origen, understood to mean "the one who sees God."[64]

For Cassian the ultimate stage of contemplation is "feeding on the beauty and knowledge of God alone" (*Conf.* 1.8.3). Again he is in the Alexandrian Pla-tonic ambit of Clement, Origen, and their heir Evagrius. For them contemplation (*theōria*) was closely tied to knowledge (*gnōsis*).[65] For Clement, the perfect Chris-tian was the *gnōstikos*, the "knowing one"; Clement sought to rescue the title from its use in Gnostic circles. Because of those heterodox associations, Origen avoided the adjective while retaining an emphasis on *gnōsis* itself; Evagrius re-trieves Clement's name of *gnōstikos* for the perfect Christian and applies it to the advanced monk able to teach others.[66] Cassian uses the word *scientia*, "knowl-edge," dozens of times, usually referring to a spiritual gift or ability. For him, as for his predecessors, "knowledge" is as much faculty as object, more like "wis-dom" than "learning." A matter of insight or perceptiveness rather than literary education,[67] knowledge is inseparable from contemplation.

For Cassian *scientia* is but one among many ways of describing perfection. "Knowledge" characterizes the process of contemplation, just as contemplation is a dynamic way of describing purity of heart. Later in *Conference* 1, he writes: "The reign of God is possessed by means of the exercise of the virtues in purity of heart and spiritual knowledge" (*Conf.* 1.14.1). As will be seen later, he keys this spiritual knowledge to biblical texts kept close to the heart through *meditatio* and prayer.

Philosophy and the Bible: Cassian on Martha and Mary

Cassian uses a Hellenistic conceptual tradition for his teaching on contemplation but anchors his teaching in biblical texts. The first is the story of Martha and Mary of Bethany (Luke 10:38–42). Since Origen, the story had been read as an allegory of the active versus the contemplative way of life.[68] Cassian uses the story twice, at the beginning and end of the *Conferences* (*Conf.* 1 and 23). He echoes Origen's interpretation of the story by seeing Mary as the type of the contemplative disciple who sits at Jesus' feet "intent on spiritual instruction" (*Conf.* 1.8.1). She has chosen the "supreme" and "principal" good[69] of "contemplation alone" (*theoria sola, Conf.* 1.8.2).[70] The latter phrase is also used for "virtue" (*Conf.* 6.3.1 and 7) and in the comparison (*Conf.* 21.13–17) between salutary observances and absolute obligations. Contemplation is superior to action because it is "simple and one," in contrast to practical work (*actualis opus*), which bears many fruits but which in its inherent variety and diffuseness cannot compare with the single focus of contemplation.[71]

Behind Cassian's reading of "many" and "one" is a Christian version of the Platonic movement from the mutable (the many) to the immutable (the One).[72] Contemplation was the means of return and, as the eschatological experience of the beatific vision, also its goal. For Origen and Evagrius the cosmological saga of the soul's pilgrimage through this material and complex world to union with God was tremendously significant and accordingly prominent in their writings.[73] Cassian shared their emphasis on contemplation but was more interested in exegesis of monastic experience than in cosmological schemata. For him the dominant issue was gathering fractured intentions and scattered energies into the singleness of purpose manifest in "contemplation alone." For the monk, as for Mary of Bethany, this meant contemplation of Christ. Cassian's relentless teleology galvanizes all effort toward the goal of purity of heart. Purity of heart means clarified and sharpened contemplative insight, the way in this life to anticipate the end of the "reign of God."

Cassian's reading of the story of Martha and Mary allows him to make three very important points. First, he divides human existence into two fundamental aspects, active and contemplative. In relating these aspects to the monk's ongoing ascetical discipline and growing dedication to contemplative prayer, he applies a venerable philosophical model of human existence to his monastic theology. Second, he sketches a continuum of contemplations ranging from the acts of God *Origen* manifest in visible creation to the divine mysteries perceptible only by the spiritual senses. By doing so, he is able to demonstrate how contemplation bridges the temporal and experiential divide between this life and the eternal beatitude of heaven. Both of these points about contemplation came to him with a long philosophical and theological lineage. Third, he works out the relationship between present action and both present and future contemplation. Cassian clarifies this fundamental problem of the monastic life by reminding his readers of both the realities of the present and the hope of the future.

PRACTICAL LIFE AND CONTEMPLATIVE LIFE

Cassian's distinction between ascetical discipline and the contemplation for which it prepares is based on a Platonic and Aristotelian model that had a great influence on early Christian theologians. It described two aspects of philosophy, the "active life" *(praktikos bios)* and the "knowing" or "contemplative life" *(gnōstikos* or *theōrētikos bios)*.[74] A later Stoic version featured three aspects: moral *(ēthikos)*, "natural" (Gk. *physikos*, Lat. *naturalis*), and "logical" (Gk. *logikos*, Lat. *rationalis*).[75] Classical, Jewish, and Christian writers adapted this language to their own purposes. For most of the early philosophers (and indeed for Gregory of Nazianzus), the distinctions were taxonomic and exclusive and were related to the object of endeavor: one could be either active or contemplative. For others, including later Stoic thinkers as well as theologians and philosophers such as Philo, Clement, Plotinus, Origen, Porphyry and Evagrius, the distinctions had a pedagogical and progressive interaction, and each aspect was dedicated to the pursuit of truth. In other words, "action" preceded and enabled contemplation but was never left entirely behind.[76]

Origen and Evagrius were Cassian's precursors. Origen followed the threefold Stoic division with its moral, "natural" and "insightful" (Gk. *epoptikos*, Lat. *inspectivus*) elements of life. He correlated these with the biblical books of Proverbs, Ecclesiastes, and Song of Songs.[77] Evagrius used both a twofold and a threefold model. In the simpler schema, the monk who initially was *praktikos* was to become *gnōstikos*, "knowing."[78] Evagrius generally used "knowing" *(gnōstikos)* rather than "contemplative" *(theōrētikos)*, though both words can be found in his works. His preferred tripartite scheme echoes Origen's, distinguishing two kinds of contemplative knowing: first the *praktikos* monk becomes *physikos*, that is, knowledgeable through contemplation of created nature, and then *theologikos*, gifted with insight into divine and uncreated realities.[79] Evagrius used these divisions to describe the monastic life itself and also as a hermeneutical device for interpreting the Bible.[80] (I will return to the threefold model later.)

Evagrius understood the "practical life" to be monastic asceticism. It was not a passing phase: a monk never finishes with asceticism in this life.[81] However, because ascetical disciplines were a primary focus at the beginning of the monastic life, *praktikos* could serve as a label for that initial phase.[82] Evagrius defined the "practical life" as "a spiritual method that purifies the impassioned part of the soul."[83] Gradually, he taught, the monk's energy and attention would shift more and more to "knowledge," that is, contemplation.

Cassian adopted the general Evagrian system for understanding the relationship between "active" and "contemplative" life. He prefers the simpler, twofold distinction of practical and contemplative to the tripartite schema, though (as I will show later) he knew and used the Evagrian model, which included "natural contemplation" as a middle term.[84] The twofold division is generally implicit in Cassian's writings rather than explicit, though in *Conference* 14 he applies the terminology of *praktikos* and *theōrētikos* to the process of biblical interpretation. There he explains that the "discipline and profession" of the Christian life consists of a twofold knowledge, practical and contemplative. The first is fundamental, "perfected by amendment of life and purging of the vices."[85] Cassian equates this way of knowing with "ethical" training, as earlier writers had done.[86] His later translation and definition of the Greek noun *praktikē* is simpler: it is "practical discipline" (*actualis disciplina, Conf.* 21.34.4).[87] "Practical knowledge" (*scientia actualis*), then, has to do with understanding the working of the principal faults and their amendment.[88] This kind of knowledge was the *actualis opus* of Martha (*Conf.* 1.8.3).

The Latin adjective *actualis*, unlike its Greek counterpart *praktikos*, did not have a nominal form.[89] Therefore Cassian paired it with nouns anchoring it in the monastic context: discipline (*disciplina*),[90] life (*vita*),[91] manner of life (*conver-* [Vocab] *satio*),[92] work (*opus, operatio*),[93] engagement (*congressio*).[94] The word also characterizes particular aspects of the life: discernment (*discretio*),[95] experience (*experientia*),[96] results (*fructus*),[97] teaching (*instructio*),[98] perfection (*perfectio*),[99] virtue (*virtus*).[100] The *praktikē* is characterized by its multiple expressions, being found equally among anchorites, cenobites, and those who do apostolic work.[101]

The second form of knowledge, "spiritual knowledge" or "true knowledge" (*scientia spiritalis*[102] or *vera scientia*[103]), follows the acquisition of the practical. This knowledge is what the philosophers had called the "contemplative" (*theōrē-tikos*) aspect of life. Although Cassian uses the Greek terminology a few times, he prefers the Latin equivalent *contemplatio* or, in *Conference* 14, the phrase "spiritual knowledge."[104] That knowledge consists of "contemplation of divine things and awareness of most sacred meanings," that is, of the biblical text.[105]

Cassian's subdivisions of the contemplative life refer to the various "senses" of scripture, the levels of increasingly more profound insight reached by those growing in purity of heart. Spiritual knowledge is not esoteric *gnōsis* but the ability to see more deeply into the biblical material that constitutes a monk's daily prayer. In *Conference* 1 he claims that the highest form of contemplation is "feeding on the beauty and knowledge of God (*scientia dei*) alone";[106] in *Conference* 10 he describes the illumination given to one able to understand the "higher and more sacred mysteries" of scripture and to graze on the high mountains of the prophets and apostles (*Conf.* 10.11.2–4).[107] Feeding on contemplation and knowledge of God was a theme prized both by Origen and Evagrius.[108] As I will show later, Cassian's elaboration of the kinds of spiritual knowledge in *Conference* 14 unites his insistence on ascetical discipline with his teaching on contemplation and unceasing prayer.

A CONTINUUM OF CONTEMPLATIONS   •

As Cassian interprets the story of Martha and Mary in *Conference* 1, he outlines a progression of objects of contemplation. The continuum he describes bridges the distance between the visible traces of divine agency in the world and the invisible and immaterial God responsible for them. The same principle underlies his teaching on contemplation of Christ as both human and divine (*Conf.* 10.6) and on interpreting the Bible in literal and progressively spiritual senses (*Conf.* 14.8–

11). His claim that the experience of contemplation deepens with progress in the monastic life provides the rationale for perseverance in the formative ascetical disciplines.

Cassian's teaching on the continuum of contemplations was based on Evagrius' threefold understanding of human life as *praktikos, physikos* and *theologikos.* I have already noted that among the Stoic divisions of philosophy was "natural" philosophy (Gk. *physikē*), the study of the nature and workings of the cosmos.[109] Clement, Origen, and Evagrius linked such "natural knowledge" to understanding or "seeing" God.[110] Encountering material things through the mediation of the physical senses was one end of a continuum of contemplations that reached all the way to contemplation of the invisible and immaterial by the spiritual senses. The doctrine itself had biblical justification (e.g., Rom. 1:20), though the language later used by theologians to articulate it owed much to philosophy.

Origen had developed a doctrine of the "spiritual senses," especially in the extraordinarily influential prologue to his *Commentary on Song of Songs,*[111] and also wrote of the soul's contemplative progress after death as it acquires new and deeper insight into various things and beings.[112] Evagrius followed Origen's lead about spiritual senses, elaborating stages of "natural contemplation" (*theōria physikē* or *theōria tōn gegonotōn*) leading to the contemplation of God alone, which he called "theology."[113]

Evagrius compresses Origen's time-frame while complicating his schema. Evagrius understands the monastic life to include a contemplative discernment of the "raisons d'être" (*logoi*)[114] of corporeal and incorporeal beings. This discernment brings insight into God's structuring of the Universe, preparing one for unmediated contemplation of God ("theology"). Evagrius described natural creation as "letters" written to human beings by God.[115] He relates a story about Antony's encounter with a visiting philosopher who marvels that the famous hermit lives without books. Antony responds, "My book, O philosopher, is the nature of things that exist (*tōn gegonotōn*), and it is there whenever I want to read the words (*tous logous*)of God."[116]

Evagrius presented his teaching about natural contemplation in both schematic and narrative form. He presents the basic premise when commenting on Ecclesiastes 3:10–13:

> I have seen, [the Ecclesiast] says, the sensory matters occupying human understanding (*dianoia*) that God gave to human beings to keep them occupied before purification. . . . It is one thing for the mind to be affected by applying itself in a sensual manner through the senses to sensory things; the mind's situation is quite different, however, when it contemplates the raisons d'être (*tous logous*) placed within sensory things. This knowledge comes only to the pure, while the encounter with things through the senses belongs to both the pure and the impure.[117]

Evagrius elaborated his series of contemplations most notably in the *Chapters on Knowledge,* but the idea pervades his exegetical writings as well. Typically he posits five stages, almost always given in descending order: contemplation of the Trinity, of the incorporeal, of the corporeal, of judgment, and of providence.[118]

The "incorporeal" are rational beings (angels, human beings, and demons) under-stood in their original, immaterial condition. The "corporeal" includes the same understood in their "fallen," "material," "bodily" state but also includes other parts of the physical universe. By "judgment" Evagrius means God's arrangement of the cosmos into its various orders, and by "providence" he describes God's provi-sion of ways by which human beings (and other fallen rational beings) can come to virtue and knowledge.[119] Because these stages are progressive, there is always the danger of getting stuck in one of them and not moving on.[120]

Cassian preserves the outlines of Evagrius' model but sets aside the more esoteric aspects of Evagrius' hierarchy of contemplations. He does not include the concept of the *logoi* within created things, though elsewhere he maintains a similar doctrine of the "seeds of virtue" implanted in human nature (compare the Stoic concept of *logoi spermatikoi*).[121] Nor does he maintain Evagrius' distinction between corporeality and incorporeality, which rested on an Origenist cosmology of "double creation."[122] Cassian taught that God alone is incorporeal, using this approach as a way to resolve the metaphysical problem of distinguishing between God and other "spiritual" beings such as angels or the human soul.[123]

Cassian bases his exposition on a version of the story of Martha and Mary found in some significant Greek manuscripts and also in Origen's homily on the story, though not in the extant Latin biblical translations. As Cassian preserves this tradition, Jesus' reply to Martha reads: "Martha, Martha, you are concerned and disturbed about many things: there is need of only *a few things*, or even one: Mary has chosen the good part, which will not be taken away from her" (*Conf.* 1.8.2–4).[124] The practical life is characterized by "many things," while the contem-plative life has "few" and then only "one." The few and the one become markers for a progressive *theōria* that moves from contemplation of the lives and deeds of the saints (the "few") to "regarding God alone" and "feeding on the beauty and knowledge of God alone" (the "one").[125]

Cassian echoes and amplifies this theme later in *Conference* 1 when he corre-lates "character of life and purity of heart" with the various kinds of contempla-tion by which "God is seen or held with pure gazes" (*Conf.* 1.15.2–3).[126] The ultimate form of contemplation is wonder at God's "incomprehensible substance" (Evagrius' theology or knowledge of the Trinity), but this contemplation is "hid-den in the promise." Now, however, we can contemplate God's creation and gov-ernance of the universe (Evagrius' judgment), God's patient provision of "occa-sions of salvation" such as the Incarnation and the sacraments (Evagrius' providence),[127] the things done through the saints in each generation (Evagrius' corporeal and incorporeal beings; see *Conf.* 1.8.3). When he returns to the story of Martha and Mary in *Conference* 23, Cassian makes the point more simply: the fabric of the universe and the existence of all things in it are means of contem-plating the "power and divinity" of the one who made them (see Rom. 1:20).[128] Their significance, however, lies only in their orientation to the Creator: as al-ways, the "many" must lead to the "One" (*Conf.* 23.3.1–4).

The important commonality between Cassian's teaching and that of his mas-ter Evagrius is the belief that all of creation, like the Bible, provides ordered opportunities for seeing and learning the things of God. The various contemplations, like the levels of spiritual interpretation of the Bible and the progressively simpler forms of prayer, mark the stages of the monk's journey to the "invisible and incomprehensible God" (*Conf.* 1.12). At their summit, the monk can begin to experience a foretaste of the "beatitude" that awaits in heaven.

THE NECESSITY OF ACTION

Cassian allows that ascetical and charitable works are important for reaching purity of heart or preparing for contemplation. In the larger scheme of things, however, meritorius deeds are manifestly secondary[129] to the incomparable worth of contemplation.[130] Do Cassian's strong statements about the inferior role of even charitable actions subvert the simple imperative of humble service found in the New Testament?[131] Is Cassian (and indeed the greater number of early monastic theologians) at odds with the Gospel?

These are serious questions. If the perfection of the monastic life does not include loving care for other human beings, then one would have to conclude that the evangelical heart has been removed from the body of Cassian's monastic spirituality. Cassian does not, however, oppose the "practical" and "contemplative" aspects of the monastic life. Monastic life is *always* both "practical" and "contemplative"; contemplation includes and situates action without eliminating its necessity. Cassian is very realistic about the limits of perfectability and contemplation in this life (especially in *Conference* 23). His teaching on hospitality strongly affirms the imperative of practical charity. Even the most perfect anchorites, "afire with perfect love of the Lord," must respond to the many people who will see and be drawn by that love: "never to be visited by others is an indication of unreasonable and thoughtless strictness, or indeed of the greatest coldness" (*Conf.* 24.19.1).[132] Laying out his model distinguishing between "practical life" and "contemplative life," he urges perseverance in whichever form of practical life one has undertaken, whether it be primarily ascetical or ministerial (*Conf.* 14.4–5).[133] Each way can train one for contemplation.

Only on the eschatological level can we resolve the apparent contradiction between Cassian's exaltation of contemplation and his insistence on love for others. Practical charity and contemplation are not mutually exclusive. We have now the urgent necessity of compassion. In the future lies the possibility of continual contemplation. Now, all are called to the "mixed life" of *both* action and contemplation as a provisional accommodation to the circumstances of human existence in a fallen creation. Like Plato's escaped cave-dwellers who finally see true reality but must return to help their former companions, even the greatest anchorites must be available to those who need their skills.[134] Such was Antony's way, and also that of Cassian's Abba John who returns to the cenobium after twenty years of solitude and teaches young John and Germanus about the goals of the monastic life (*Conf.* 19.1–2).[135]

Cassian's final and most important point about the story of Martha and Mary, therefore, is that Mary's "intentness" (*studium*) on God—which shall not be taken from her—is an icon of eternal happiness. Martha's corporal ministry will come to its inevitable end with her death (*Conf.* 1.8.4). Cassian works through a series of other biblical texts[136] to argue that works are useful but cannot produce the perfection of love that is God's promise of life now and forever. Although the brutality of human selfishness makes works of mercy necessary, they are not essential to human nature as God intended it to be (*Conf.* 1.10.4). In the age to come, when all people are brought to the security and equality meant for them, the need for ministry to others (and to oneself in asceticism) will be over. Then "all people will pass from this multiple, that is practical, work to love of God and contemplation of divine things in perpetual purity of heart" (*Conf.* 1.10.5). Only love never fails (1 Cor. 13:8). Paul's corollary that all other things, even gifts of the Holy Spirit, will pass away underscores Cassian's reminder about the provisional character of works.[137] After bodily necessity has been cast off, only love will endure, becoming stronger as "perpetual incorruption" allows an even more ardent and intense clinging to God (*Conf.* 1.11.2).

Concerned that dazzling displays of healing power not distract from the more important agenda of growth in holiness, Cassian returns to the theme of works and love in *Conference* 15, "On Divine Gifts." Abba Nesteros urges his listeners to weigh supposed powers of healing against the same person's progress in "driving out sins" and "improving morals," that is, the *actualis scientia* that leads to purity of heart and love.[138] True perfection will be measured by "purity of love" rather than by marvelous deeds that vanish and perish. Love and love alone endures (*Conf.* 15.2.2–3).

Heavenly Beatitude and the Vision of God

"Blessed Are the Pure in Heart, for They Shall See God"

The eschatological orientation of Cassian's theology obliges one to consider the theme of heavenly beatitude that runs through the whole of his monastic writings. Purity of heart is a goal for this life, oriented toward contemplation. Contemplation prepares for—and anticipates—the fullness of the reign of God, the monk's "end," which Cassian calls "beatitude" (Lat. *beatitudo*, Gk. *makariotēs*). One must understand his theology of beatitude in order to appreciate his views on the efficacy of asceticism and on the possibility of realizing at least some degree of heavenly beatitude in the monastic life.

Greek philosophical and theological writers used the word *makariotēs* to describe the utter bliss of human fulfillment.[139] In the theological tradition that formed Cassian, *makariotēs* had a specifically contemplative content traceable to Plato through a series of Classical, Jewish, and Christian writers.[140] As the Jewish exegete Philo of Alexandria wrote, "the beginning and end of happiness is to be able to see God."[141] This spiritual vision, whether in present contemplation or in the fullness of heavenly beatitude, was explicated in Christian appropriation of Platonic themes.[142]

"Beatitude" has strong biblical resonances, most famously from the Sermon on the Mount.[143] Irenaeus had recognized the aptness of Matthew 5:8 ("Blessed are the pure in heart, for they shall see God") for his own emphasis on the eschatological vision of God, which he proclaimed to be "life for the human person."[144] That particular beatitude became a favorite of later writers, especially those in or influenced by the Alexandrian tradition who sought to integrate Christian mystical experience and eschatological hope with their philosophical heritage.[145]

Cassian uses the word *beatitudo* more than sixty times in the monastic writings, almost always with the meaning of "ultimate reward" or "highest happiness."[146] The Matthean "Blessed are the pure in heart" epitomizes the monastic goal in *Conference* 1, and other beatitudes anchor Cassian's major teachings. The monk who has simplified prayer to the "poverty" of a single psalm verse repeated over and over has become "poor in spirit" and worthy of the "reign of heaven" (Matt. 5:3 as in *Conf.* 10.11.1). Perfect chastity is the "meekness" of those who shall inherit the earth of a body at peace with the spirit (Matt. 5:4 as in *Conf.* 12.6.1–3).

Cassian's emphasis on beatitude may be particularly attributable to the influence of Evagrius. The phrase "blessed is the one who . . ." appears frequently in Evagrius' writings.[147] Like other writers, Evagrius used *makariotēs* as a technical term for the fullness of Christian life: "the end of the human person is beatitude."[148] He understood blessedness to consist of *theōria* or *gnōsis* of God, quoting Matthew 5:8 several times in his extant writings[149] and alluding to the text on many other occasions.[150] Commenting on Proverbs 14:9 ("The dwellings of the senseless will have to be purified, while the dwellings of the righteous will be acceptable"), Evagrius observed: "so that, having become pure, they might see God: this is the blessed end that is reserved for each rational nature."[151] This scholion from the desert could have been written by Origen or, gospel allusion aside, Philo: surely Plato would recognize a kindred spirit.

In Cassian's monastic theology—as for the Sermon on the Mount—beatitude has an eschatological orientation. His interpretation of the biblical Beatitudes is explicitly eschatological (*Conf.* 11.12.1–3). He orients his major themes eschatologically by linking them with beatitude: "purity of love"/"purity of life and of heart,"[152] chastity,[153] the anchorite's angelic solitude and tranquillity.[154] Such happiness can begin now but comes to fulfillment only in heaven. Thus his comparison between the "beginnings of beatitude" produced by consideration of divine justice and the "summit of beatitude" experienced in unceasing meditation (*Conf.* 11.12.6 and 11.15) echoes what he says about the stages of purity of heart or of contemplation. Perfect beatitude is to be continually in the presence of the Teacher with all thoughts caught up in ceaseless rumination of the divine Law (*Conf.* 14.13.7). Such constant devotion can be evoked, but not fully achieved, in the present life.

Cassian sometimes blurs the line between the heavenly beatitude of the life to come and the contemplative bliss attainable in this life. The experience of saints and angels in heaven is "beatitude";[155] monastic contemplation can be a window onto beatitude or even itself "true beatitude."[156] More precisely, contemplation in this life is a "likeness"[157] of the perfect and enduring bliss of heaven.[158] As noted earlier, monks can imitate the angelic life through their contemplation.

Ambiguity about present possibility runs throughout Cassian's monastic writings. In that part of book 5 of the *Institutes* that provides the basic themes for *Conference* 1, Cassian suggests that someone who fixes the mind's gaze on the eternal already begins to contemplate the "beatitude" of heavenly existence (*Inst.* 5.14.4). He concludes in *Conference* 1 that through purity of heart and spiritual knowledge a monk can obtain even now the salvation promised in Matthew 5:8 (*Conf.* 1.10.5).[159] In the late (and more cautious) *Conference* 23, he notes the present impossibility of total focus on the "beatitude on high" while attending to necessary tasks but also calls contemplation "true beatitude."[160] The ambiguity runs deeper than these passages indicate: to explore it, I must turn to Cassian's teaching about heaven itself.

"The Reign of God Is within You"

Cassian writes about the promise of beatitude and its anticipation by purity of heart and contemplation, but he actually says little about the "end" of monastic life, which is the reign of God or reign of heaven. Basically, heaven is the antithesis of the mortal, material, visible things we know in this age.[161] Heaven is elsewhere than here, a "higher" place to which the soul (or its prayers and thoughts) can ascend when freed from the constraints of the body.[162] Cassian quotes various biblical texts about heaven but engages in little imaginative description of paradise; such reticence locates him in the mainstream of the early Christian tradition. As much as early theologians assert that heaven is the ultimate human hope, typically they refrain from speculating about what it will be like.[163]

In *Conference* 1 Cassian works with two biblical texts to explain the monastic "end": Jesus' dictum "the reign of God is within you" (Luke 17:21) and Paul's definition of the reign of God as "righteousness and peace and joy in the Holy Spirit" (Rom. 14:17). Cassian's choice of texts might initially suggest that he intends to erode further the distinction between "goal" and "end." In fact, he dramatizes the gap between professed intention and actual experience. Although the reign of God is meant to be manifest within the human heart, the monk's self-awareness is of chaos and confusion rather than righteousness, peace, and joy. The contrast between aspiration and disappointment introduced in *Conference* 1 will find its most poignant expression in *Conference* 23.

Cassian begins his foundational discourse on heaven by noting (as he will again in *Conf.* 23) that continual contemplation is impossible for those "still in this fragile flesh" (*Conf.* 1.13.1). Nonetheless, the reign of God can be established in mind and heart after the reign of sin and the devil has ceased.[164] The alternatives are stark: within the soul knowledge and ignorance cannot coexist, nor can virtue and vice (*Conf.* 1.13.2–3).[165] These oppositions derived from Origen's ascetical theology also occur throughout Evagrius' exegetical works.[166] The reign of the devil, marked by signs of hell and death, contrasts with the reign of God, which is recognizable by the "continual tranquillity and everlasting joy" of heavenly powers already in the reign of God (*Conf.* 1.13.2–3).[167]

Only when he returns to Luke 17:21 in *Conference* 18 does Cassian draw out the ascetical significance of the text. Warning that external safeguards alone cannot safeguard monastic identity, Cassian reminds his readers that the real struggle, for patience, is fought within the heart.[168] Simply closing the door of one's cell, or retreating to the deepest desert, or relying on the support and protection of a band of holy hermits provide false security, for the reign of God is acquired in "tranquillity of mind" (*Conf.* 18.16.1–4). Such teaching on the insufficiency of physical asceticisms, of course, is one of Cassian's standard themes. Here, however, his point is akin to Antony's observation that Greeks must cross the seas "to learn letters" while the monk can find both virtue and the reign of heaven without leaving home, for "the reign of heaven is within you."[169] Antony urges a return to the original perfection of the soul,[170] but Cassian looks ahead rather than back. The reign of virtue within the soul anticipates the full realization of the reign of heaven.

Cassian's interpretation of Luke 17:21 illustrates his willingness to depart from Evagrius' systems. Whenever Evagrius quoted the Lucan text (at least in his extant works), he followed Origen in changing "reign of God" to "reign of heaven."[171] Evagrius developed Origen's suggestion into a distinction he makes in the *Praktikos* and follows throughout his other writings. The "reign of heaven" consists of *apatheia* and knowledge of created things, while the "reign of God" is knowledge of the Trinity.[172] The biblical text is adjusted to his understanding of the knowledge possible "within" human experience. Just as Cassian simplifies and freely adapts the Evagrian hierarchy of contemplations, so here he jettisons the distinction between the two reigns.

The most crucial point in Cassian's teaching about heaven is that progress toward or away from the "goal" of purity of heart bears directly on hopes for attaining the "end" of the reign of God. Even now one can be "counted in" (*deputandus*) for heaven; what is now service of God will later be transformed into partnership with Christ (*Conf.* 1.14.1; see John 12.26). This theme of preparation runs throughout the *Institutes* and *Conferences*. In the *Institutes*, Abba Pinufius exhorts a novice to send the thoughts of his heart on ahead to heaven while mortifying earthly desires (*Inst.* 4.35). Commenting in *Conference* 7 on another saying from the Gospels, "the reign of heaven suffers violence and the violent seize it" (Matt. 11:12), Cassian explains that monastic disciplines, however imperfectly followed, prepare the monk for the "fullness of the measure of Christ."[173] In his final exhortation in the very last chapter of *Conference* 24, Cassian uses the same text to praise cenobites who "do violence" to themselves by mortifying their will in obedient submission to an abbot (*Conf.* 24.26.12–14). Progress is slow and difficult, but it is real: "the reign of God is attained through the practice of the virtues in purity of heart and spiritual knowledge" (*Conf.* 1.14.1).

Heaven on Earth?

As I have shown, Cassian allows that a monk can anticipate something of heavenly beatitude in contemplation. How far can he be pressed on the possibility of a "realized" eschatology? His descriptions of monastic possibility are of three kinds: those that typify a maximalist perspective; those that allow for fleeting experiences of bliss even now; those that downplay expectations. This range of opinions opens Cassian to charges of inconsistency and even incoherence. Such ambiguity assisted his anti-Pelagian critics in the past and can still frustrate the systematically inclined reader of today.

Cassian's most optimistic statements about personal transformation are found in his writings on chastity. Unafraid to enter this most intimate arena of human experience, he displays there both his greatest realism and his most provocative idealism. The claims he makes are truly impressive: even now one can go "beyond nature," no longer feeling the "stings of the flesh" (*Inst.* 6.6). Sexual desire can be "extinguished" (*Conf.* 12.3.1); sexual fantasies, even when sleeping, can be eliminated (*Conf.* 12.8.5, 22.6.10). There can be even a further state for those (males) in whom the "natural movement of the flesh" is "deadened." Their bodies no longer produce seminal fluid, and they no longer suffer the nocturnal emissions so problematic for ancient monks (*Conf.* 12.7.6). Abba Serenus was said to have attained this extraordinary condition.[174]

Cassian's claims are remarkable. There is no question that he regards chastity as a powerful emblem of purity of heart. But chastity is even more powerfully the greatest experiential proof of God's grace, which alone can accomplish what is humanly impossible and unthinkable. As I will show in chapter 4, Cassian's treatises on chastity (*Inst.* 6, *Conf.* 12 and 22) are odes to the divine power of transformation. The high ideal makes the ache of experience more, not less, acute: nowhere does Cassian suggest that perfect chastity is easily or commonly attained. Each declaration about chaste perfection comes with the proviso that such a marvel is God's work, not the product of ascetical determination. *Conference* 12 on chastity segues into *Conference* 13, on "Protection by God," Cassian's study of grace and free will. *Conference* 22, on the "Illusions of the Night," leads to the definitive statements on the limits of ascetical possibility made in *Conference* 23, "On Sinlessness." These two late *Conferences* sharply distinguish even perfect purity of heart from "sinlessness." The holiest are not immune from sin and are considered to be holy even while still "in sin."[175] Whatever perfection is possible in this life remains contingent on human frailty and always dependent on God's grace.

One can apply the same qualification to Cassian's other maximalist statements about perfection. In his schema of three "calls" and three "renunciations," he allows for a rare fourth degree of renunciation in which the monk while still in the body enters the promised land free of the "thorns and thistles" of sin (*Conf.* 3.10.5). Even the third renunciation, detachment from all that is "present and visible," was for the few (*Conf.* 3.10.3); the fourth is exceptional, beyond the scope of human effort. In *Conference* 13 Cassian employs a different map of the monastic life, charting three stages of grace. Those in the last stage have persevered in virtue to the point that surrendering again to the bondage of sin is unthinkable (*Conf.* 13.18.4). Like the icons of perfect chastity, however, these are exceptional cases.

More typically Cassian provides a realistic assessment of what monastic growth really involves. He observes that progress in purity of heart brings deeper insight not only into the things of God but also into one's own sinfulness and unworthiness.[176] His anthropology requires him to acknowledge that because the need and desire for food never leave us, neither can the danger of gluttony (*Conf.*

5.19.1). Perfect concentration on contemplation is impossible while in this life with its many and necessary demands and with ever-roving minds ready to hive off after every distraction. Even as Cassian evokes the ideal, he will qualify it with "as much as human frailty allows" or a reminder of the instability of the mind.[177] Even the holiest of monks inevitably commit small sins, even if they can withstand more serious temptations;[178] the greatest remain vulnerable to sudden catastrophe.[179] Cassian establishes the border between present perfection and future beatitude along the frontier of human physical and psychological reality (see *Conf.* 23.16). I will explore that frontier more fully in chapter 4.

There remain suggestions in Cassian's writings that monastic life can be a purchase on heaven. In *Conference* 1 he claims that those who make it their task (*cura*) to pursue knowledge and the purification of their mind while still in the "corruptible flesh" have already in some sense assumed the place (*officium*) destined for them when they will have "laid aside corruption" (*Conf.* 1.10.5). The ethereal Abba Serenus in *Conference* 7 urges his listeners to possess "now, in the present, as a pledge (*subarratum*), that which is said of the blessed life of the saints in the future, that 'God may be all in all' [1 Cor. 15:28]" (*Conf.* 7.6.4). The same idea (and biblical quotation) reappears in *Conference* 10, when Abba Isaac urges John and Germanus to aim for a "likeness" or "image" of future beatitude even now.[180]

Cassian employs two unusual words in those passages of *Conferences* 7 and 10, *subarratum* and *arras*,[181] which echo Paul's use of a word of Aramaic origin, *arrabōn*, "pledge."[182] Paul transposed *arrabōn* from its usual financial or legal context to an eschatological frame of reference. Cassian does not cite the Pauline texts, but his introduction of *arras* and *subarratum* suggests their influence. Few other writers in Latin Christian tradition used these unusual words,[183] though one finds *arrabōn* used by Greek authors who knew it via the Greek text of Paul.[184] These words provide Cassian with a theological vocabulary for his claim that contemplation and prayer are a kind of participation in heavenly beatitude, a foretaste of what lies ahead. Using another Pauline metaphor to complete his thought, he writes that a monk can be designated a "precious limb" of Christ, receiving the *arras* of union with the Body of Christ.[185] The sacramental, and specifically eucharistic, connotations of this description would not have been lost on Cassian's readers. Cassian brings to his eschatology a liturgical (and, as we shall see later, a mystical) consciousness.

Monks for the World

Cassian maps the monastic life on a grand scale. He wants his readers to appreciate the vastness of the Christian landscape and to understand their monastic lives as a pilgrimage across it. He also recognizes the practical challenges of the journey, assuring his monks that their charity toward others is integral to their monastic vocation and demanded by the lot they share with all human beings in a fractured world. While asserting the inestimable worth of heavenly beatitude and the joy of anticipating it in contemplation, he knows that total devotion to prayer is impossible on both practical and psychological grounds. To monks in any age Cassian's evocation of their ideal and realism about its attainment form a powerful charter for the monastic life. For monks in Gaul working out their relationship with a church that needed their prayers and their ministry, Cassian's teaching would have contributed to their effort to be monks for the world while being ever mindful that their "end," that of all Christians, lies beyond.

CHAPTER FOUR

Flesh and Spirit, Continence and Chastity

> Arriving at that condition in which he is found to be the same at night as in the day, the same in bed as at prayer, the same alone as when surrounded by a crowd of people, he sees nothing in himself in private that he would be embarrassed for others to see, nor wants anything detected by the omnipresent Eye [of God] to be concealed from human sight.
>
> —*Conf.* 12.8.5

Chastity and Asceticism in Cassian's Works

BOTH THE THEORY AND THE PRACTICE OF MONASTIC ASCETICISM pervade Cassian's *Institutes* and *Conferences*. One needs a way through the vastness, a paradigm for asceticism that can help to understand Cassian's perspective and contribution. Fortunately Cassian gives us precisely the focus that is needed, for he made the pursuit of chastity the centerpiece of his ascetical theology. The intentional celibacy of the monastic life is the principal marker of its social distinctiveness, as celibacy has often been for both Christian and non-Christian ascetics. Although the renunciation of possessions and withdrawal from normal social responsibilities signify a break from conventional norms, they are parameters for the interior transformation experienced most intimately at the relational/sexual core of the human person.

For Cassian, the physical and psychological processes of growth into chastity become a privileged language expressing the monk's relationship to God and to other human beings.[1] Cassian's major analyses of grace and human possibility are always in the context of teaching about chastity. The murkiness and apparent intractability of human sexuality call the question of human potential most vividly: how much progress can be made by ascetical effort alone? Cassian's answer could not be more forceful. The horizon of human effort can be only discipline, and even that can be only imperfect. Ascetical discipline can battle lust to a truce, but only grace can bring freedom. The "peace" of chastity, with its ever deeper contemplative possibilities and reordering of desires, lies entirely in the gift of God.

Cassian's first extended discussion of the necessity of grace is in book 12 of the *Institutes*, where he focuses on chastity under its synonyms of "integrity" and "purity" (*Inst.* 12.9–23). *Conference* 13, his major treatise on grace and free will, follows *Conference* 12 on chastity and opens with the speaker's ascription of the "perfection of chastity" to God's mercy rather than to a monk's "dedication and work." In *Conference* 23 Cassian nuances claims for monastic achievement by cautioning that perseverance in virtue by the saints is entirely sustained by grace and does not represent "sinlessness" *(anamartēton)*. The preceding *Conference* 22 had been devoted to "nocturnal illusions," that is, orgasmic dreams.

Cassian's chastity was also a social virtue, for with the growth of chastity comes the possibility of human relationships founded truly on love rather than selfish desire or vainglorious manipulation. In his teaching on chastity Cassian joins his defense of the transformative possibilities of monastic asceticism to his task of providing a spiritual theology for monks who must be prepared for a variety of circumstances. Cassian, a monk formed by the Christian East, brings the tradition into focus for his confreres in southern Gaul facing both hardline Augustinianism and the call to serve a church in need of their gifts.

Cassian's three major treatises on sexual issues (*Inst.* 6, *Conf.* 12 and 22) form a coherent program of instruction second in overall length only to his treatises on prayer (*Inst.* 2–3, *Conf.* 9–10). When the corollary *Conferences* on grace and human possibility (*Conf.* 13 and 23) and the several discussions of chastity scattered throughout the *Institutes* and *Conferences*[2] are added to them, Cassian's pages on sexual and directly related issues exceed even those on prayer. This substantial collection of material on male monastic sexuality is unique in early monastic literature.

Cassian's teaching on the process of chastity is profoundly connected to the rest of his spiritual theology. Most obviously it closely parallels his approach to biblical interpretation. The monk's body is multivalent like the biblical text. The body is an anchor in the human condition of physical necessity and mortality (historical/literal meaning) as well as the monk's vehicle for spiritual progress (spiritual meanings). Like the biblical text, which must be read and understood beyond its literal or historical meaning, the body too must be drawn into the journey from mortality to immortality and read in progressively more spiritual ways.[3] Cassian establishes a "natural" baseline of sexual disposition and physical manifestations and then advances through stages of "continence" and "chastity."

Cassian's sexual version of spiritual progress becomes complicated by the interplay of body and soul. Although the body can be seen as the "text" of the soul, the medium for reading the inner workings of the human person, there are also thoughts, fantasies, and dreams that may not have physical expressions but must nonetheless be read and interpreted. Cassian devotes so much attention to the phenomenon of orgasmic dreams because he was aware that the interdependence of soul and body eluded dualistic analysis: in this phenomenon the relationship between soul (memory and will) and body is most elusive and intriguing.

When Cassian outlines his teaching on levels of spiritual knowledge to be found in the Bible (see *Conf.* 14.16), he insists on the parallel relationship between spiritual insight and the pursuit of the virtues. Without the "practical life" of ascetical discipline, spiritual knowledge of the Bible is impossible. Chastity is the paradigm of the Christian good life, a paradigm he opposes to non-Christian philosophical ethics. The sexual restraint of the philosophers, he claims, must never be confused with the divine gift of chastity, which enables contemplation and "true knowledge."[4] Their celibacy, like their pseudoknowledge, was a superficially impressive human achievement without the enduring theological significance that only grace can ensure.[5]

Like that other great paradigm of perfection, "purity of heart," chastity means for Cassian an abiding tranquillity in anticipation of heaven. Chastity, like purity of heart, is finally and forever about love; and love, in Cassian's view, is always about God rather than about secular "wisdom."[6] Cassian founds his teaching about chastity on the eschatological assumptions that still remain the theological basis for monastic celibacy. His starting point, as always, was a conviction that the true homeland of believers lies beyond the horizons of this world. The longing for that homeland where humankind will be free from the constraints of mortality, and turn unhesitatingly to the infinite vistas of the glory of God, inspired monks to their otherwise inexplicable renunciations.

This chapter begins with Cassian's anthropology and his understanding of the power of lust. His teaching coalesces on the role of lust in marriage, a way to assert that human sexuality has become so distorted since the Fall that lust haunts even the "lawful" sphere of marriage. His portrayal of marriage is grim to the point of apparent denigration, but his intention is to shatter any illusion held by his monks that marriage is the easier path to sexual integrity. I then turn to Cassian's understanding of the body, both physiological and psychological. On that basis one can explore his teaching on the difference between sexual continence and chastity and the process of ascetical discipline that tames unruly passions. At the limits of ascetical accomplishment one finds Cassian's theology of grace and human possibility where he presents it, in the context of chastity. Finally there is Cassian's interpretation of the experience of nocturnal emissions, a recurring concern in early literature about monastic men. Simultaneously the most private aspect of male sexuality and the least subject to control by the will, the "problem" of orgasmic dreams gave Cassian an opportunity to explore once more the interplay of inmost thoughts with external (in this case, physical) factors.[7] This "problem" was both a practical issue that disturbed monastic consciences and a demonstration that the ascetical struggle extended into the realm of sleep and the unconscious, where only God could bring peace.

Lust

Lust and Nature: Cassian's Anthropology

Cassian uses the word *concupiscentia*, "lust," for an array of desires.[8] He is following the tripartite Platonic anthropology he learned from Evagrius in which the soul consists of "rational," "irascible," and "desiring" faculties. Each is necessary for the proper functioning of the human person, but the two irrational faculties must always be subordinated to the guidance of reason, Plato's "charioteer," which regulates the potentially unruly steeds of repulsion and attraction.[9] Evagrius makes ample use of this model,[10] and Cassian presumes it, though he cites it explicitly only in the very last *Conference* as a way to classify the vices.[11]

Cassian's understanding of human desire has two perspectives: that which is *original* nature, that is, as God intended for us to be, and that which has *become* natural as a result of the Fall (*post ruinam, Conf.* 4.7.1). Most of his descriptions of the body and its natural needs fall somewhere between these two poles. He realized that nature is not easily discerned and that appeals to the natural can be an excuse for shirking the difficult process of returning to the original condition of body and soul (see *Conf.* 12.8.2). In *Conference* 23 Germanus argues that old habit (*antiqua consuetudo*) acts like a "natural law" carrying those of "tender chastity" off to vice, but Theonas replies that such an excuse is valid only for minor sins inherent in the human condition. It does not apply to major sins such as those against chastity, for in Christ we have been set free from the law of sin and death.[12] In the next *Conference* Abraham claims that good habit can ingrain even apparently impossible disciplines into one's very nature.[13]

These two perspectives explain the apparent dichotomy in Cassian's anthropology: sometimes, as in his discussions of grace and free will, he shares the optimism characteristic of much eastern Christian theology.[14] It is natural for us to desire the good, and we have been given a natural knowledge of God's moral ordering of the universe.[15] We seek God's assistance to recover this goodness, so that we can once more live virtuously "as if naturally" (*velut naturaliter*).[16] Cassian compares the soul's "natural blessing of purity" to a feather's airy lightness; when the soul is purified from sin, it recovers its own "natural lightness" (*subtilitas naturalis*) and can be lifted to God by the "light breath of spiritual meditation" (*Conf.* 9.4.1–3).

When the focus is primarily on the ascetical agenda and the power of the vices, Cassian takes a more pessimistic tone. What has *become* natural is the war between flesh and spirit, each with its own lust (*concupiscentia*) utterly opposed to that of the other. Cassian devotes *Conference* 4, "On the Lust (*concupiscentia*) of the Flesh and the Spirit," to this aspect of human experience and returns to it in *Conference* 23, "On Sinlessness." The human condition is fragile, prone to sin,[17] and dependent on the power of grace to rise above (fallen) nature.[18] The real struggle is in the heart, where the "ingrained" tendency toward fleshly lusts is to be found. Thus it is the heart that must be cleansed.[19] Cassian follows Augustine and others in identifying a sinfulness "in the flesh" because human beings are born "from intercourse of the two sexes" distorted by problematic desire.[20] Christ, although he assumed the "full substance" (*integra substantia*) of human flesh, did not inherit the sinfulness of the flesh because he was born of a virgin.[21] Thus he bears the "likeness of sin in the assumption of true flesh" (*Conf.* 22.12.1) but did not feel the "stings of carnal concupiscence."[22] Only a miracle of grace can restore compromised human nature to its original condition exemplified by Christ.

Lust and Other Faults

When Cassian writes about *concupiscentia* he normally means the "carnal lusts" of gluttony and fornication, either singly or together. These are the first two of the eight principal faults in the systems of both Evagrius and Cassian.[23] Gluttony and fornication are so closely linked in Cassian's thought that it is sometimes impossible to determine how precisely he is using *concupiscentia*.[24] Occasionally avarice, another fault of the "desiring" faculty, gets lumped with gluttony and fornication (*Conf.* 24.15.4) or is described as a "lust"[25] although it is not a fault involving the body and its cause lies outside of human nature.[26] In contrast, gluttony and fornication are maladies of both body and soul,[27] arising from "natural" impulses inappropriately used (*Inst.* 7.3–4). Gluttony is dangerous because it tends toward fornication: "No one will be able to inhibit the stimuli of burning lust *(concupiscentia)* who will not restrain the desires *(desideria)* of the stomach."[28] When Cassian writes of "fleshly lusts," even of the stomach, the sexual implications are not far to seek. His teaching is unexceptionably traditional; Basil described asceticism *(enkrateia)* as the mother of chastity,[29] Evagrius named gluttony as the mother of lust.[30] I will discuss later the physiological assumptions behind their linkage of gluttony and lust.

Because sexual desire is a matter of both body and soul, it can become intertwined or involved in faults that are not physical. The most significant link is with anger, a passion similar to sexual lust in its "fiery" spirit: "where the virus of anger is found, inevitably the fire of the libido intrudes" (*Inst.* 6.23).[31] Anger is a "movement of the soul" *(animi motus)* analogous to sexual "fire of the body"; more precisely, the conquest of wrathfulness by mercy plays a direct part in the securing of bodily purity (*Conf.* 12.6.1–6). In Cassian's tripartite anthropology, anger and lust represent the most vivid disorders of the irascible and desiring faculties, respectively, and play off of one another. Purity of heart, tranquillity, patience, and chastity converge in Cassian's story in *Conference* 12 about a paragon of chastity living in Alexandria. When unbelievers harassed him about his Christian faith, demanding to know what miracles Christ had performed for him, he said simply, "No matter what injuries you inflict, I will remain unmoved and take no offense" (*Conf.* 12.13.3).

Sexual desire has a distinctive relationship with the most serious of the eight principal faults, vainglory and pride. Lust cannot coexist with vainglory, and in fact vainglorious fantasies about priesthood and the good opinion of others can hold impure thoughts at bay. There is a trade-off, however. Even though vainglory is an easier burden to carry, once established it is more difficult to uproot.[32]

Pride poses a far more insidious and complex danger to the one making progress against domination by lust. To place confidence in ascetical discipline alone without acknowledging the need for grace can forfeit whatever progress has been made.[33] The arrogance of those unafflicted by lust and judgmental toward those who are afflicted will eventually bring the proud to their knees, as in the story of the old monk who berates a brother humble enough to confess his struggle against fornication. The old man ends up worse off than the junior (*Conf.* 2.13.4–12). Equally humbled, though in a different manner, was Abba Paul, whose overly harsh asceticism and pathological fear of women drove him to a breakdown and the ironic consequence of needing to be nursed by nuns (*Conf.* 7.26.2–4). Even the great Paphnutius thought he was free of sexual desires until he found himself troubled by "carnal motions" despite his strict discipline and success against obvious forms of temptation (*Conf.* 15.10).

The Power of Lust

Cassian warns in the *Institutes* that the "savage war" *(inmane bellum)* against the "spirit of fornication" is more protracted than the other ascetical struggles and rarely completely successful; it continues even after the other vices have been conquered *(Inst.* 6.1). Even for the married, the "fire" of sexual desire can flare out of control, and unless held firmly in check it tends "habitually" to adultery.[34] For monks, the memory of former sexual experiences or temptations poses an ongoing threat to the "contemplation of purity." Compunction for sins or sorrow for other sinners can lead all too quickly to morbid delight in fantasy and finally to a "filthy and harmful conclusion," by which Cassian presumably means masturbation *(Conf.* 20.9.5). Someone who chooses to stand over a sewer *(cloaca)* or to stir its filth, Cassian cautions, is bound to suffocate from the fumes *(Conf.* 20.10).

Cassian cites all the expected Pauline texts about sexuality, especially when defining his subject.[35] He outlines three varieties of "fornication"—a late Latin word derived not from *fornax,* "furnace," as one might think, but from *fornix,* "arch" or "vault," also used for "cellar" and especially for subterranean brothels.[36] The word *fornicatio* suggests illicit sexual activity (i.e., outside of marriage) and thus describes any sexual activity by monks. Cassian's three kinds of fornication are: sexual intercourse *(conmixtio sexus utriusque);* masturbation and nocturnal emission, euphemistically described as "[fornication] without touching a woman," also termed "uncleanness" *(inmunditia;* see Col. 3:5);[37] and fornication in heart and mind (Matt. 5:28).[38]

Ascetical disciplines such as drinking less water[39] can harmonize the "law of the flesh" and the "law of the soul" by reconciling opposites, "igniting a cold fire" like the burning bush or kindling a "dewy flame" like that of the Babylonian furnace *(Conf.* 12.11.5). But only God can so chill the fire of lust that what was believed to be "natural and inextinguishable" no longer produces even the "simple motion" of the body *(Conf.* 12.12.3). The rule of grace replaces that of law when the fire of divine love burns up the thorns of lust and one fire consumes another.[40]

Marriage

Because Cassian seems to foreclose any possibility of healthy sexual activity, his stories about marriage are a stumbling block to modern readers. The married people who appear in his writings either commit to celibacy within marriage or decide to separate from a spouse in order to undertake the monastic life.[41] Abba John marvels at the exorcistic power of a visiting layman and discovers that while the man has many virtues, his supreme claim to sanctity is marital virginity. Compelled by his parents to marry, he had lived twelve years with his wife as if she were his sister *(Conf.* 14.7.4–5).[42] Abba John regards this proximity to temptation as a particularly heroic form of chastity and does not recommend it to others, echoing repeated ecclesiastical condemnation of such practices.[43] Abba Joseph argues that the allowance of marriage for the sake of populating the world has been superseded by "evangelical perfection"; what was previously a blessing for the synagogue must yield to virginity and celibacy for the church (*Conf.* 17.19.1–2). In the final *Conference*, Abba Abraham, himself once married, notes the "brief and fragile" ties of the "carnal love" joining spouses to one another and parents to children. Subject to sickness and death, to divorce and disinheritance, such relationships cannot approach the hundredfold sweetness of "conjugal continence" or cenobitic community.[44] The wife Abba Abraham once had in the "lascivious passion of desire" is now his "in the honor of holiness and the true love of Christ": "the woman is one and the same, but the reward of love has grown a hundredfold" (*Conf.* 24.26.6).

We hear nothing more of Abraham's story, though Cassian presents a similar tale, in greater detail, about Abba Theonas. The story echoes those of both Abba Abraham and the celibate married man depicted in *Conference* 14, though it has enough divergences from both to suggest originality or, at least, literary independence.[45] Theonas, a married man, visited a monastery to offer the firstfruits of his harvest. While there, he heard an exhortation on the superiority of grace over Law encouraging the voluntary renunciation of lawful goods for the sake of divine love.[46] Although the address refers only briefly to marriage and virginity (*Conf.* 21.4.2), its general theme of renunciation and perfection inspires Theonas to follow the Gospel through chastity. He returns home, where he undertakes to persuade his wife "day and night, and with tears" to join him in this undertaking.[47] She is not interested, retorting that if he abandons her, forcing her to turn to another man, the blame for her adultery will rest on Theonas for having broken the marital bond. He counters with the argument that the call to virtue, once heard, must be obeyed: it would not be right (*non licere*) to do otherwise (*Conf.* 21.9.1). Divorce becomes the only option, a perhaps unexpected application of the principle of grace over Law. Theonas suggests that if Moses permitted divorce for hardness of heart, why shouldn't Christ allow it because of desire for chastity? His wife must conspire in virtue if she is truly his partner and companion (*adiutrix*) in marriage. Since she will not, Theonas concludes, "it is safer for me to be divorced from a human being than from God." He flees to the monastery (*Conf.* 21.9.3–7).

This story typifies an attitude toward marriage and celibacy found in many forms in early Christian (and later) literature, which is reducible to the basic contention that virginity is the most perfect form of Christian life. The practice of celibacy by those who are not virgins comes a close second, with sexual activity in marriage ranked lower as a "lawful" compromise, and other sexual activity, whether heterosexual or homosexual, beyond the pale. The development of this hierarchy of sexualities involved many factors, and its history lies beyond the present purpose of this study.[48] The question to ask here is why Cassian uses stories like those of Abraham and Theonas in a work addressed to monks.

Cassian's intention does not seem disciplinary, as appears to be the case in many of the antisexual and misogynistic references to be found in monastic literature.[49] He has an important theological argument to make. However, for modern readers the early monastic use of stories about sexuality can obscure rather than reveal any theological intention. Cassian and other writers focused on sexuality and stories about sexuality because the topic galvanized interest and spoke to the most intimate aspects of human life. This approach is perhaps best seen in the stories of reformed prostitutes like Mary of Egypt or Pelagia of Antioch.[50] Were Cassian writing today, he would not—and should not—use such stories: they would likely be read too literally and then either rejected or misapplied. As even many monastic texts illustrate, these possibilities were real in Cassian's day, too.[51]

Although Cassian's own perspective was surely not entirely free of an exaggerated suspicion toward the body and its functions, the consistency between his views on sexuality and his teaching on other subjects—such as the renunciation of possessions, the tyranny of the other "principal faults," the move from wordy to wordless prayer, the progression from the literal to the spiritual meanings of biblical texts—suggests that his comparison between marriage and monastic chastity should be understood in the same way. His concern, like that of Evagrius, was to contrast the multiple cares of marriage with the single focus and freedom from worldly distraction of his ideal of chastity.[52] The challenge for modern monastic writers is to evoke the distinctive qualities of celibate chastity without doing so at the expense of other ways toward holiness. The challenge for all of us might be to match Cassian's realism in working out a renewed understanding of sexuality and spirituality.

The Body

Cassian's anthropology is a complex and not always consistent interplay of physiological, moral/psychological, and theological factors. At times he deals with sexuality on a more or less purely physical level, referring to the natural "stirring of the flesh/body" *(motus carnalis* or *motus corporalis)*. By this phrase he means male sexual excitement manifest in penile erection, a phenomenon found even among children and infants.[53] Cassian recognizes this "natural stirring" to be God's provision for human reproduction *(Inst.* 7.3.1–2) while noting that on the purely physiological level penile erection can also be caused by the pressure of a full bladder.[54]

Cassian sees nocturnal seminal emissions as a "natural necessity" for relieving the "humors" produced from the consumption of food and drink.[55] According to the medical wisdom of Cassian's day, these humors accumulate in the spinal "marrow"[56] and must be "expelled" on a regular basis.[57] Cassian gives various estimates for the frequency of "natural" nocturnal emissions, ranging from three times a year *(Conf.* 2.23) to every two months (thought by the elders to be too frequent, *Inst.* 6.20) or more prudently, "some months" *(Conf.* 22.6.4). When these "stirrings" or "emissions" occur without associated fantasies and passions, Cassian describes them as *simplex,* "simple."[58]

Therefore, every monk should expect arousal and emissions, except for those spared them by physical infirmity or age *(Conf.* 22.3.2) and the very few who by grace are no longer bothered by the "natural incentives" and "simple and natural movements" *(Conf.* 7.1–2). This condition "above nature," in which not only is the "natural movement" dead, but even the "shameful fluid" *(obscenus liquor)* of semen is no longer produced, is a particular and rare divine gift granted to people such as Abba Serenus and the few who are like him. Cassian therefore excludes this unusual state from his schema of stages in the development of chastity (*Conf.* 12.7.6). He notes later that only grace can destroy *(interimit)* the natural movement of the body and dry up "the most impure mess" that collects in the "marrow" (*Conf.* 22.6.7).[59]

Cassian generally does not isolate physiology from moral and theological factors. His insistence that corporal discipline alone cannot attain the peaceful integrity of chastity means that a monk must enter the moral arena of the heart.[60] Cassian quotes an otherwise unknown saying of Basil the Great to underscore the moral dimension: "I know not woman and yet I am not a virgin" (*Inst.* 6.19; see Matt. 5:27–28). Even the mundane realities of male sexuality can play a formative role as moral invigilators in a monk's life. Sexual arousals are like "whips" punishing overindulgence in food and drink (*Conf.* 4.15.1); males, says Cassian, are fortunate to have such a bodily "signal of carelessness" *(index negligentiae)* as an incentive toward perfection (*Conf.* 4.16). Any responsiveness of the flesh to deliberately induced fantasy signals that chastity is not yet perfect; for obvious reasons, this test is not recommended for beginners (*Conf.* 19.16.4). In this respect the virile male is more fortunate than the eunuch, who lacks the physical spur to chastity. The eunuch has to fight solely within the heart, a battle more easily avoided because it is not manifested physically.[61]

The body has its own rules but takes its orders primarily from the mind or heart, the "fount and spring of sin" (*Conf.* 23.1.5) as well as of virtue. Cassian's use of Matt. 15:19 ("from the heart proceed evil thoughts")[62] inevitably would suggest to biblically informed ancient readers a preceding verse: "Do you not see that everything that enters the mouth goes into the stomach, and is emitted in seclusion?" (Matt. 15:17). The Vulgate's *in secessum*, "in seclusion," is more ambiguous and euphemistic than the Greek *eis aphedrona*, which means specifically "toilet." Cassian's male monastic readers would have made an association with nocturnal emissions.

Cassian notes that the body is the best counterweight to a prideful exaltation of personal ascetical achievement. His repeated insistence that chastity is a divine gift, and that even "continence" is possible only with divine protection, carries with it warnings about trusting in one's own discipline as the safeguard of chastity. Those who conclude from a lack of nocturnal emissions that they have been freed from the realities of life in the flesh (and, therefore, from the need to be vigilant) are reminded by an emission *(fluxus)* that they are indeed human, dependent on God's grace for even brief respites from reminders of mortality.[63] Cassian claims that blasphemous attitudes engendered by overweening confidence in ascetical prowess can also result in temptations to "unnatural acts" and delivery to "shameful passions." In one of his examples, a monk's obsessive desire to be the passive partner in anal intercourse is traced to an "impious thought" about Christ. Cassian suggests that spurning the One who offers the gifts of purity deprives the monk of perfect integrity and chaste holiness (*Inst.* 12.20).[64] It is an odd illustration of what becomes one of Cassian's major preoccupations in the

Conferences: the monk's utter need for grace to advance from tenuous discipline to abiding security.

distinction

Continence and Chastity
ἐυκρατὴς

The Divide between Asceticism and Grace

In book 6 of the *Institutes* Cassian introduces the fundamental distinction that guides his discussions of sexuality: a monk can be "continent" *(continens)* or "chaste" *(castus)*.[65] The first is equivalent to the Greek *enkratēs*, which in this context could be translated "celibate."[66] Beyond continence there is the state of "chastity,"[67] a "quality of integrity and incorruption," describable by the Greek adjective *hagnos*, "pure."[68] Typologically Cassian ascribes continence to cenobites and chastity to anchorites *(Inst.* 6.3–4), another instance of his allegorical use of monastic categories. All monks are called to the passage from continence to chastity, just as all monks are called to both renunciation and contemplation. The real difference between continence and chastity is that between human discipline and divine grace.

I have already noted Cassian's warnings against confusing ascetical means with contemplative ends (see chapter 3). Any page of *Conferences* 12, 13, or 22 drives home the point: sheer determination might battle sexual desire to a truce but can never produce the inner purification effected by grace. Fear can motivate discipline, but only love can ensure the peace of chastity *(Conf.* 11.8.4). In the midst of the battle against lust, a human struggle engaged by free will and fought with the ascetical disciplines of the monastic life, one hopes for the lasting end to war made possible only by grace (see *Conf.* 12.4.1–2). Continence entails constant police action over a restive body, while chastity brings the tranquillity and freedom Cassian prizes as the hallmarks of monastic perfection. Thus Cassian contrasts the continual risk of defeat in the "struggle of continence" with the abiding peace that is chastity *(Conf.* 12.11.1 and 4). The "place of God" is the "place of peace,"[69] which is found in Israel, who is "the one who sees God."[70] From the place of peace where carnal passions are extinct, the chaste monk ascends to the "spiritual Zion," the watchtower and dwelling place of God *(Conf.* 12.2–4).[71]

Just as sexual desire has links with other vices, so continence and chastity are associated with other virtues. As lust and anger are related, so too are chastity and patience *(Conf.* 12.6.1–6). Because pride is the major cause of defeat in the pursuit of chastity, it is no surprise that Cassian emphasizes humility as foundational for progress against lust.[72] Similarly, "contrition of heart" *(contritio cordis)* is another essential attitude.[73] The key to progress in chastity, as indeed in all virtues, is realism, a quality associated in monastic theology with humility and compunction. It is precisely this realism that excludes Pelagian overoptimism about ascetical possibility. Cassian observes that the sign of "approaching purity" is the surrender of any hope that it can be attained by one's own efforts *(Conf.* 12.15.3). The paradox of loss and gain, the paradox of the Cross itself, lies at the heart of the sexual struggle even more vividly than anywhere else. Every aspect of the monk's being is called up for a battle which cannot be won unaided.

Disciplines of Continence

BODY AND SOUL

Because sexual desire is rooted in both body and soul, the war against it is fought both with physical and spiritual disciplines. There is no doubt, however, that for Cassian the spiritual means are both fundamental and ultimate, for they alone can reach into the heart. At the end of *Conference* 21, preparing for his analysis of nocturnal emissions in *Conference* 22, he notes that a visible "continence of the flesh" cannot contain the fullness of perfection, which belongs only to hidden and invisible purity of heart. The first may be gained by constraint or under false pretences even by unbelievers (such as the philosophers of *Conf.* 13.5), but true chastity lies not in the realm of constraint but in the freedom that comes only by grace (*Conf.* 21.36.1). By quoting Paul's insistence that one move beyond the fleshly, literal definition of who is a Jew or what is circumcision to the hidden, spiritual meaning of those categories, Cassian recalls his own hermeneutic of human experience (Rom. 2:28–29 as in *Conf.* 21.36.2). To deal only with the physical aspects of monastic asceticism is to miss the heart of the early monastic endeavor, which was to take human potential to its limits in order to show those limits to the God who alone could surpass them.

The disciplines of bodily constraint are the familiar ones of fasting, work, and keeping vigil, that is, deprivation of sleep.[74] Cassian intones the litany of these observances throughout his writings, for they are the basis for all monastic asceticism. In his discussion of sexuality he refers to them in both a generic and a quite specific manner. In *Conferences* 12 and 13 he suggests a dietary regimen of two *paxamatia* (dried bread loaves) per day, taken with minimal water, and three–four hours of sleep.[75] I have already discussed Cassian's medical assumptions about food and drink in relation to sexual arousal and nocturnal emissions[76] and his linking of gluttony to fornication.[77] He praises the austere Egyptian monastic diet consisting largely of dried and uncooked foods (*Inst.* 4.21–22).[78] The emphasis on dried food and restricted intake of water derives from the ancient classification of foods and their effects according to categories of "dry" or "moist"; drier foods were thought to cool the body and reduce the production of semen.[79] Evagrius was noted by Palladius for his renunciation of fresh vegetables and fruits[80] and was prone in his own writings to emphasize the danger of drinking too much water. Thirst, he claimed, was a remedy for lust.[81]

Cassian states his principle simply: "the chastity of the inner person is discerned by the perfection of this virtue [of dietary restraint]" (*Inst.* 5.11.1). Such perfect restraint is itself a matter of discernment, not meant to be regulated by rigid times of fasting or regulations about kinds of food. "Conscience" is the standard, determining what is truly necessary for the body's legitimate needs and ruling out what is superfluous.[82] Cassian is wary of the physical and psychological enervation that comes from alternating severe fasts with excessive eating and therefore recommends a regular and moderate diet.[83] Cassian's treatise on discernment (*Conf.* 2) is largely devoted to the dangers of overly strict asceticism.[84]

Some modern scholars have seen the dietary recommendations of Cassian (and other desert monks) as a means of reducing sexual energy through near starvation.[85] There is little in Cassian's writings to suggest that diet, however important as a component or indicator of chastity, was seen as its guarantor. Sexual desire seems to have remained a vivid aspect of monastic experience, meriting the extended treatment Cassian gives it. In any case, one should question how literally Cassian's descriptions of desert meals were meant to be taken: writing for monks in southern Gaul where both foods and climate were different from Egypt, these certainly were not sample menus.[86] Cassian admits that nocturnal emissions continue even for disciplined monks, that the real battle is in the heart, and that chastity is attained within a process sustained by grace rather than by ascetical effort.

Cassian's famous program in *Conference* 12 for testing in six months whether or not someone has potential for staying the course to chastity (*Conf.* 12.15.1) is quoted by Aline Rousselle in support of the theory that severe undernutrition was the key to sexual peace.[87] Cassian does prescribe a spare diet and little sleep but not as a quick path to chastity. His test was to determine the *possibility* of chastity, not to provide a timeline for attaining it. Before even getting down to the dietary regimen or the mention of a six-month trial, he establishes as preconditions separation from all unnecessary human contact and an end to all anger and worldly cares.[88] These ascetical prerequisites are already beyond a novice's scope. By following the prescribed alimentary and sleeping guidelines, after six months the monk can know "if such perfection is not impossible for him," hardly a guarantee of successful achievement.[89] Uneasy about laying down such a guideline, Cassian hedges his regulations with comments about the variety of human temperaments and, more important, with his typical insistence that divine grace rather than human effort guarantees progress. That fundamental insight—and, much more, chastity itself—eludes beginners (*Conf.* 12.16.1). Cassian is providing a tool to discern entry into a process, not a plan for crossing the finish line.

Cassian suggests no additional physical asceticisms. He is suspicious of the sackcloth Evagrius recommends,[90] as indeed he is of all practices he considers excessive. Although Cassian refers to athletic training that includes the application of lead foil to the genital region to "cool" the flesh, he does so as an analogy rather than as a prescription.[91] He is comparing the athletic disciplines of nonbelievers to the tested asceticisms of the monastic life, which begin with purifying the heart (*Inst.* 6.9). He does not recommend dramatic techniques such as Evagrius' own remedy of standing naked in a well throughout a winter's night.[92] The exceptional disciplines of the great are dangerous temptations for the ordinary monk: the normal disciplines are hard enough.

More important than physical disciplines are the spiritual ones of reading, *meditatio*, and unceasing prayer.[93] The practices of *meditatio* of the scriptures and unceasing prayer constitute the hinge between the ascetical and contemplative aspects of human life, filling the mind and heart with good material while blocking the intrusion of destructive thoughts.[94] They also are the constant companions of the chaste monk, for the very point of chastity is to permit greater insight into biblical texts and to further contemplative possibility. These aspects of "care of the soul" (*cura animae*)[95] or "focusing of the heart" (*directio cordis*)[96] are associated particularly with keeping vigil during the night, thus joining spiritual practices to the asceticism of remaining awake. The night was the time most vulnerable to demonic suggestion, whether waking or sleeping, and Cassian, like other monastic writers, sought to extend the range of ascetical vigilance as far into the night as possible.[97] Cassian praises the Egyptian cenobitic custom of remaining awake in prayer and manual labor after the night office lest a return to sleep provide occasion for erotic dreams and a "pollution."[98] Those who guard themselves at night will be readied for the day, for nothing establishes purity, Cassian claims, as well as nocturnal vigilance (*Inst.* 6.23).

SOLITUDE AND ENCOUNTER

Among the disciplines of continence, Cassian places a particular emphasis on the value of solitude or a "remote" location.[99] The prescription of solitude sets fornication apart from other faults, which are best treated in the company of others.[100] The reason is not far to seek: other people provide sexual temptation, and the anxieties and stresses of social interaction can encourage escape into sexual fantasy. Faces and bodies (*effigies et materia*) are the stuff of this desire and should be "withdrawn";[101] even the recollection of them, their "forms" (*figurae*) that intrude on the mind when at prayer, are a danger.[102] Thus the numerous warnings in monastic literature to avoid women and boys, and anxieties about sexual attraction between monks.[103] Even eating with female relatives was thought to pose dangers.[104] Cassian follows Evagrius here, as he does for most of his more psychological teaching about chastity.[105] Evagrius had warned against excessive socializing in the early stages of the monastic life, lest the mind be filled with fantasies.[106]

Cassian's awareness of the perdurance of memories, especially in the subconscious, will be noted later with respect to dreams. But fantasy works even in the full light of day, drawing on memory, suggestion, and desire. At the very outset of the *Conferences*, Cassian locates the roots of obsessive thoughts in inappropriate behavior (*Conf.* 1.17–19). Later, he cautions that pious remembrance of holy women can transmogrify into a dangerous excitement, as can the racier portions of the Old Testament.[107] As a balance to such hypervigilance, he also recognized that a pathological fear of women can lead to a breakdown rather than to genuine chastity (*Conf.* 7.26.4).[108]

Cassian suggests as the culmination of the process of chastity that the monk respond to mentions of sexual matters with the same indifferent attention that would be paid to the topic of brickmaking (*Conf.* 12.7.3). The image may seem absurd, but Cassian's point is not: if every encounter with anything even vaguely sexual sends tremors through the psyche, one is far from the focused tranquillity of purity of heart. The distance from that goal is proportional to the monk's ability to receive others as Christ and to meet them on the ground of their needs rather

than of the monk's own. The goal is not isolation, even if the process of growing
into chastity may require some degree of separation.[109] Such therapeutic solitude,
however, was not absolute. The harshest words in Cassian's monastic writings are
addressed to fraudulent anchorites who claim to seek perfection by fleeing human
company, when the truth is that they simply cannot cope with other people.[110]
Their flight from others signifies an even more dangerous evasiveness, from the
slow and painful labor of discernment of thoughts. This work could not be undertaken alone: it required companionship, but of the constructive kind based on
shared purpose and the experience of a wise elder.[111] The false anchorites were
those who shunned all human relations, including—or especially—those with a
spiritual guide.

It is by no means incidental, then, that Cassian writes about friendship (Conf.
16). He spent much of his life in the constant company of his boyhood friend
Germanus and in Conference 16 offers us his mature reflection on the value of
human partnership in the monastic quest.[112] It may seem odd that Cassian devotes much of this Conference to the problem of anger,[113] but I have already
shown the link he establishes between anger and lust: the social consequence of
unresolved sexual issues is rage directed at other people. He traces the corrosive
effects of anger and division on friendship (Conf. 16.6–9) and then transposes the
issue into a communal setting (Conf. 16.15–27). The bridge between the two sections is his reminder that monastic friendship is never the private concern of two
people but always lived in relationships of discernment with other monks (Conf.
16.10–11).

Friendship and chastity are meant to be social virtues grounded in love.[114]
Only love can allow the monk "to say with the prophet: 'I have run the way of
your commandments, for you have enlarged my heart'" (Ps. 118[119]:32, in Conf.
16.27.5). That enlarged heart embraces all whom it meets and becomes the emblem of the patient and loving monk. Cassian depicts the perfect monk, "afire
with perfect love of our Lord," as surrounded by those who seek that same love:
"To the extent that the fire of divine love draws you closer to God, so too will a
greater multitude of holy brothers flock to you." Refusing to receive visitors would
be a sign of "irrational" strictness and of spiritual "lukewarmness" (Conf. 24.19.1)
In Cassian's theology these are damning criticisms. As Evagrius noted, "flee lust
but pursue hospitality."[115] One of the traits of Evagrius' "Gnostic," the advanced
monk who has become a teacher, is hospitality.[116] What may at times be experienced as a threat to virtue can also be an opportunity for love. We know from
Cassian and other monastic writers that many of the most perfect anchorites
ended up in community, where they could be more available to the needs of
others.[117]

Stages of Chastity

Cassian outlines the process of psychological, physical, and spiritual transformation in six stages, though he notes that the actual progress occurs almost invisibly
from day to day, as in physical growth. The journey into chastity begins with the
cessation of deliberate sexual activity: "when awake the monk is not overcome

(*elidatur*) by an attack of the flesh" (*Conf.* 12.7.2).[118] Presumably Cassian means resisting fantasy, sexual arousal,[119] and the accompanying temptation to masturbate.[120] The next two degrees of progress mark freedom from thoughts and desires, first obsessive thoughts and then occasional ones prompted by seeing or remembering a woman's face.[121] Fourth is the imperviousness of the body when awake even to "simple" stirrings of the flesh, that is, spontaneous sexual arousal without deliberately savored fantasy.[122] The next degree is utter detachment of the mind when presented with the fact of human reproduction in a reading or a conference. The monk is to be "tranquil and pure," serenely regarding sexual intercourse as no more inherently stimulating than brickmaking or other crafts. Finally, in the last stage, chastity reaches into the far country of dreams, stilling erotic fantasies even in sleep.[123] At this point, the body has been restored to its "natural" condition of moderate intake of food and periodic nocturnal emissions caused by purely physiological necessity. Heart and mind are able to focus completely on contemplation, discernment, the Bible, the needs of others.

As noted earlier, Cassian claims that for the rare few, there is a state beyond restored nature in which even "natural" physical processes are stilled. In *Conference* 12, he names Abba Serenus as someone who has been raised above the natural order; in *Conference* 7 he narrated how this happened. Serenus' extraordinary gift *follows* the grace of perfect inner purity. Serenus prays that God might give him the additional, though less theologically significant, gift of bodily purity. Noting that surgery or drugs can artificially accomplish a cessation of "simple and natural movement" of the genitals, he asks that such mortification be given him by God. In a vision by night, he sees an angel come to him, reach into his groin, and remove the "fiery fleshly mass" responsible for sexual arousal (*Conf.* 7.2.1– 2).[124] In this most dramatic example of Cassian's teaching on the role of grace in attaining chastity, Serenus, having first secured that which is granted *only* by grace (inner purity), additionally seeks by grace what he could obtain by medical means. In a rebuke to the temporary continence of athletes and the pseudochastity of the philosophers, Cassian's Abba Serenus exemplifies the power of the Christian God who alone can master both body and soul.

Divine Grace and Human Will

Frontiers of Flesh and Spirit

Cassian records that both the "teaching of the fathers" (*patrum sententia*) and general experience of the process itself indicate that divine help is particularly necessary for the attainment of chastity (*Inst.* 6.6).[125] Therefore he positions his analyses of grace and free will within his discussions of chastity. With some understanding of his teaching on continence and chastity, one can then turn to his intricate and controversial views on human ascetical and moral potential. He insists on the need for grace so that he can extend the scope of chastity beyond the reaches of the human will. Chastity is a state of the entire person, body and spirit, all the time. Cassian focuses on the problem of nocturnal emissions because they can indicate the progress of chastity in the life of the (male) monk. Only grace can cross the border between waking and sleeping, between conscious and unconscious states. The chaste monk can safely commend himself to sleep, for the disposition of chastity (*castitatis affectus*) has been assimilated "in the bones" (*medullitus*). Such a depth of transformation is impossible for mere continence (*Conf.* 12.10.2–3).

The border between waking and sleeping signifies another, far more significant divide that again only divine grace can cross: the frontier between the desires of "flesh" and of "spirit" (see *Conf.* 4 *passim*).[126] Human beings are an uneasy union of both, experiencing a perpetual state of potential or actual warfare. Astride the borders (*confinia*) between flesh and spirit sits the human will (*voluntas*), immobilized by the conflict between them. The fearful energy of the desires of the flesh and the prospect of losing the "delight of purity" inhibit the will from yielding fully to either; at the same time, bodily weakness checks zealous pursuit of ascetical virtue (*Conf.* 4.11–12). The conflict functions like a "most diligent schoolmaster" (*paedagogus*) to remind the monk that only by grace can the "gift of purity" be attained (*Conf.* 4.15.1–2).

Cassian returns to the "frontiers" of flesh and spirit in *Conference* 12, where he describes the transformed, chaste monk as no longer trapped by these opposing forces but serenely presiding over the relations between them. Formerly the conflict between flesh and spirit established the balance of power in the "scale of the body" (*in statera . . . corporis, Conf.* 4.12.3). Now the monk freed from the pressures of both internal discord and external constraint stands at the frontiers of flesh and spirit determining matters of purity with the "sure scale" of experience (*certa experientiae suae libra, Conf.* 12.8.2).[127] Without God's help, the will is severely crippled; acknowledging the need for divine assistance opens the heart to liberating grace. This understanding is surely why Cassian makes the opening verses of Psalm 69(70) his formula for unceasing prayer: "God, come to my assistance; Lord, make haste to help me" (*Conf.* 10.10.2–15). In *Conference* 13, his most controversial work, he turns his full attention to the interplay of human effort and divine grace.

Cassian and Semi-Pelagianism

Cassian's thirteenth *Conference*, entitled "On Protection by God," like the two previous ones, "On Perfection" and "On Chastity," is attributed to Abba Chaeremon. A focus of controversy since its first circulation,[128] the text has generally been approached through the Semi-Pelagian controversy and in terms of Prosper of Aquitaine's spirited attacks on Cassian's critique of hardline Augustinian views on grace and free will.[129] Prosper wrenched passages from *Conference* 13 to create a virtual parody of Cassian's teaching; one needs to situate *Conference* 13 and Cassian's other work on this topic within his ascetical theology. Cassian himself introduces *Conference* 13 as an explanation of why chastity depends on grace rather than on ascetical effort. His suggestions that ascetical discipline develops the possibility remaining to a weakened but not utterly crippled human will and that human beings need a special gift of grace to guide such "beginnings of willings of the good" to the "perfection of virtues"[130] were seen by Prosper as insufficiently insistent on the absolute necessity of grace.

Cassian was no Pelagian, as his ascetical theology illustrates and his Christological treatise *The Incarnation of the Lord* boldly asserts.[131] As Owen Chadwick concludes, "Cassian upon the central fact of dependence [on grace] still aligned himself with Augustine."[132] At the same time, however, Cassian sought a theology of grace that took ascetical effort seriously while avoiding the fatal extreme of total reliance on ascetical means.[133] The focus on chastity is understandable, for it is the ascetical crucible par excellence. Cassian's perspective was very much that of the eastern Christian and monastic traditions that formed him.[134] These traditions granted more scope to human possibility and conceived of grace more broadly, and perhaps less precisely, than did the western theologians whose tools had been sharpened by the Pelagian controversy.[135]

Cassian's First Treatise on Grace: Book 12 of the Institutes

Conference 13 develops themes introduced initially in book 12 of the *Institutes*.[136] The larger part of this book about the vice of pride is a study of the limitations of human possibility and the necessity of grace. The focal point, as in *Conference* 13, is the attainment of chastity. Cassian starts with the human experience of the "warfare between flesh and spirit" (later to be the topic of *Conference* 4).[137] Only divine mercy can deliver human beings from the paralysis of this conflict and bring them to the "palm of integrity and purity" (*Inst.* 12.10). Although human efforts, namely the ascetical disciplines prescribed for the "battle of continence," are essential for progress, they cannot bring one to perfection.[138] Offered to God in the right spirit, however, they can provide the opportunity for God to confer the grace needed to complete human effort (*Inst.* 12.14.2). This point, certainly open to misinterpretation, is later nuanced in the *Conferences*.[139] It must be understood in the context of Cassian's essentially optimistic anthropology and strong assertion of continual providence, which is capable not only of assisting human effort but also of overcoming resistance to grace (*Inst.* 12.18).

Cassian claims to present "the very words" of the fathers (*Inst.* 12.13), the "constant teaching of the elders" (*Inst.* 12.14.1), the "genuine faith of the most ancient fathers" (*Inst.* 12.19). As Chadwick has observed, Cassian and his allies in this controversy viewed themselves as conservators of traditional theology.[140] Cassian also insists that this theology rests on experience rather than on the empty words of dreamers, on the simple faith of the apostles rather than on the syllogisms of Ciceronian dialectic.[141] This point is key. While Cassian may be bolstering his presentation by appealing to tradition, he is also indicating the location from which he does theology. He writes as a participant in a process of spiritual growth that is a mysterious interplay of human and divine elements. He describes rather than prescribes, teaches rather than defines. Because experience is the baseline, he is more interested in the monk's growing awareness of weakness and dependence on grace[142] than in an airtight argument that foresees and deflects all objections.[143] His practical orientation will get him into trouble with theologians who position themselves differently, preferring the polemical dialectic he eschews.[144] His allusions to other perspectives indicate that he was aware of the hardline views of the Augustinian party,[145] which he clearly found unhelpful for his own pedagogical purposes.[146]

Cassian's Conference 13, "On Divine Protection"

Conference 13 is a reprise of Cassian's earlier arguments, with more extended biblical illustration. He addresses the shortcomings of the earlier presentation (with respect to "prevenient" grace) but creates new possibilities for misinterpretation. Continuing from Conference 12, the discussion opens with Germanus' objection that it is absurd not to credit the perfection of chastity to the monk who works so hard to attain it.[147] Both John and Germanus are confused by Abba Chaeremon's repeated emphasis on divine gift, which seems to diminish the significance of ascetical effort (Conf. 13.1–2). Chaeremon unequivocally states the theological principle: "the beginning of not only [good] acts, but even of good thoughts, is from God, who inspires in us the beginnings of a holy will and gives us the strength as well as opportunity for attaining those things we rightly (recte) desire."[148] He asserts that human beings can attain nothing pertaining to salvation without God's help, a fact of existence nowhere so plainly evident as in the "acquisition and guarding of chastity" (Conf. 13.6). All the disciplines of the battle for continence, namely the solitude and the fasts, the vigils and the reading, require grace to sustain them. Human frailty inevitably inhibits even ardent desire and a "perfect will" for good unless divine mercy confers the strength (virtus) to complete them.[149] Thus the pagan philosophers and their "continence," a fragile and provisional discipline that cannot be compared with the "perfect purity" of chastity, God's gift alone (Conf. 13.4–5).[150]

The problem for Prosper and his followers lay with Cassian's claims for human potential even after the Fall. The human heart, originally created good by God, still remains capable of a "spark," however small, of that good will. The spark is really God's work, of course, so it is as if God had actually struck the spark from the "hard flint of our heart" (Conf. 13.7.1).[151] In effect, divine providence both precedes and accompanies human effort,[152] a point Cassian has made earlier.[153] The ground of possibility is the "excellence of nature granted by the goodness of the Creator" (Conf. 13.9.5). The spark of good will prompts "impulses" (motus) toward virtue, which require God's guidance for completion.[154] These "impulses" are the "opportunity" for God's grace described in the Institutes (Inst. 12.14.2). Cassian is describing the trajectory observable in monastic life, which begins with an experience of divine call and radical renunciation. He is writing in medias res: for the monks, grace has already prevened.[155]

Cassian situates the will in the complex reality of a human nature primordially good but presently inhibited: thus the will pinned down on the "frontiers of flesh and spirit" as in Conference 4. The will can still be attracted to virtue, though because of the "flesh" it cannot move very far toward it (Conf. 4.12.3) and must be rescued and assisted by grace (Conf. 13.9.5). This understanding leads Cassian to reject an exclusive opposition between what could be called, in Augustine's terms, operative and cooperative grace.[156] To Cassian's mind, such a simplistic approach underrepresents a complex process, neglecting the larger anthropological issue of the graced status of human nature itself (*Conf.* 13.11–12).[157] Having strongly asserted the prevenience of grace, Cassian is really more interested in how things play out.

Cassian has the Bible on his side, for it provides him with various scenarios of how grace and free will interact.[158] He begins with texts like Paul's assertion of natural law in Romans 2 as evidence for an enduring human awareness of the good (*Conf.* 13.12.1–6). There are "seeds of virtue" planted by God in human souls and still there even after the Fall. Though the seeds can germinate even in the poor soil of fallen human nature, they cannot grow to fullness without the help *(opitulatio)* of God (*Conf.* 13.12.7).[159] The anthropology is very much like Basil's classic exposition in the *Asceticon* of the neo-Platonic/Stoic perspective determinative for Hellenistic Christian theology.[160]

The key point for Cassian is that both grace and human will must be "free" and cooperating, even though the scope of free will is necessarily limited.[161] The biblical examples[162] suggest that sometimes God requires or looks for *(vel exigat vel expectet)* some effort *(conatus)* of good will before conferring special gifts of grace (*Conf.* 13.13.1). This possibility of the "initiative of good will" or "deed" *(initium bonae voluntatis/operis)* is Cassian's emblematic assertion.[163] Paul strives yet relies on grace for success,[164] Job and other patriarchs endure trials and receive subsequent vindication (*Conf.* 13.14.1–6). Grace can be seen as a response to faith, as in the healing stories of the Gospels (*Conf.* 13.15.2–5). Nonetheless, grace is not a reward calculated according to human merit. That is a "profane view": "we completely and clearly declare that the grace of God abounds and sometimes surpasses the limits of human unbelief."[165] Thus, grace can overcome resistance and unbelief, as it did for Paul and does for those whom God calls; Cassian had made the same point in book 12 of the *Institutes*.[166] He preserves the freedom of the will by distinguishing between an unwillingness that is nonetheless susceptible to grace and a stubborn, persistent refusal.[167]

A series of biblical examples of the ways in which God tests human intention lead up to Cassian's own image of God as a nursemaid watching us grow from infancy to adulthood, occasionally stepping back to test our ability to resist temptation.[168] Cassian outlined this process in his discussion of chastity (*Conf.* 12.6.6–9). The metaphor of the nursemaid (*Conf.* 13.14.9) resembles that in one of the Pseudo-Macarian *Homilies*,[169] reflecting the optimistic anthropology of Cassian's eastern formation. The same phenomenon of an apparent withdrawal of grace for the sake of testing is illustrated vividly in the *Life of Antony*,[170] and Cassian's view of the cooperation of grace and free will is similar to that of Gregory of Nyssa.[171]

The perspective is monastic, rooted in experience and grappling with a mysterious redemptive process that began long before any particular human life. God is primordially the creator, but also, as Cassian notes, the protector and savior in the early stages of Christian growth and helper, sponsor, and refuge in the course of the journey.[172] As Lauren Pristas has argued, Cassian claims that God plays all these roles for all people, for everyone needs both "operative" and "cooperative" grace. The biblical examples suggest the suppleness of God's work in human and are not meant to suggest that some people have less need for grace and others more.[173]

   Conference 13 concludes with a three-point summary of the economy of grace attributed to "all the Catholic Fathers" who have taught not by "useless disputation of words" but by "fact and deed" *(re et opere)*. This appeal to experience, one of Cassian's refrains throughout his work, acquires a particular urgency here because it reminds one that debates about grace and free will rarely found the disputants arguing directly with one another. One reads Cassian, and then Prosper's critique, and realizes they inhabited different theological worlds. Cassian's summary is unexceptionable. Grace initiates the desire for good, makes possible the practice of virtue, and sustains goodness. God works throughout the process, but in such a way that the freedom of the will, itself God's gift, is not taken away *(Conf.* 13.18.4–5). Finally Cassian counsels that his readers not be sidetracked by any subtler argumentation, for "how God works all things in us and yet all of it can be ascribed to free will cannot be fully comprehended by human understanding and reason" *(Conf.* 13.18.5).

   For the monks of Gaul seeking theological understanding of their monastic experience the middle path of what later historians call Semi-Pelagianism was the prudent one to take.[174] As Chadwick notes, Cassian's "system was an ethical system, not a metaphysical [one]."[175] Pristas concludes, "When Cassian is understood on his own terms, and when the limits he puts on his discussion are fully respected, he cannot be said to err—even by the standards of later orthodoxy."[176] A monk and teacher of the Great Church, he remained faithful to the legacy of his own teachers in the monastic life.

Nocturnal Emissions

Cassian studies the interplay of body and morality via the male phenomenon of "nocturnal emissions."[177] The experience was part of the monk's physical environment, especially for the young, looming larger in significance (and perhaps occurring more frequently) for monks than for nonmonks because of a lack of other sexual release.[178] Cassian wrote as a male primarily for other males, and it is no surprise that he took up a topic that was a commonplace of monastic literature. He was not alone among monastic authors in addressing this issue; such experiences evidently caused anxiety for young monks unsure of their vocations and for older monks despairing of their progress toward perfect chastity.

   The issue was not exclusively or originally a monastic one. Classical writers had pondered the moral implications of orgasmic dreams,[179] and early Christian writers regularly commented on the question of whether nocturnal ejaculation barred one from receiving the eucharist.[180] Writing as bishop, Athanasius sent a letter to a monastic superior urging him to reassure the scrupulous among his flock.[181] The monastic writers, like Cassian, were typically interested in in assessing moral responsibility for dreams and emissions,[182] while nonmonastic writers were typically more concerned with avoiding scrupulosity about worthiness for communion.[183]

Cassian goes beyond the usual discussion of whether or not erotic dreams and/or emissions are morally culpable. He uses them as a way into the subconscious and unconscious mind to measure the permeation of the grace of chastity. He is less interested in the phenomenon of nocturnal orgasm itself than in the psychodynamics thought to lie behind it. These provide Cassian with yet another example of the hindrances to perfect intention he explores elsewhere with respect to waking thoughts, images in prayer, and misinterpretation of the Bible.

According to Cassian's teaching, the erotic dreams that are often associated with nocturnal emissions replay experiences and images from past and present encounters and therefore have a moral significance.[184] In linking dreams to waking experiences, Cassian is following classical and Christian predecessors;[185] Evagrius had provided a typically acute analysis of dreams and their relationship to larger psychological and ascetical issues.[186] Cassian notes that although sexually inexperienced monks have dreams of a "simpler" kind than those of monks who have experienced intercourse, such dreams are nonetheless disturbing (*Conf.* 12.7.4). Even certain biblical texts can fuel the juniors' fantasies and are best avoided—a concern also voiced by other monastic writers.[187] For more advanced monks, dreams can indicate a perdurance in the unconscious of passions that are no longer active when the monk is awake.[188] The proof of real progress in purity, then, is the absence of "illicit images" even in sleep.[189]

In turn, the link between dreams and nocturnal emissions (for men and, surprisingly, for women) was a commonplace of ancient medical literature.[190] Cassian admits that there is disagreement about the relationship between the "deceit of dreams" (*fallacia somniorum*) and nocturnal emissions. While positing that the actual emissions are typically prompted by dreams, he notes that the dreams themselves can be stimulated by the "abundance" of "humor" seeking release in ejaculation.[191] Cassian reflects the divergence between, on the one side, Hippocratic and similar schools that claimed that the "humor" produces the dream, and, on the other side, the tendency of some authors to emphasize the role of somnolent fantasy.[192] The ambiguity affects Cassian's use of the word *inlusio*, which means "illusion" when he applies it to fantasies and "trick" or "humiliation" when he refers to the emission itself.[193] Cassian notes that the difference between "natural" and morally culpable emissions can become a point of contention, with some people prone to plead nature when it is actually their own negligence that is to blame for their frequent emissions (*Conf.* 12.8.2). Even what is "natural" from the standpoint of sinful human nature can be contrary to chastity (*Inst.* 5.14.3).[194]

Augustine had written in the *Confessions* about the ineradicable nature of sexual memories and their ability to compel consent and ejaculation in dreams.[195] Cassian argues, however, that even these "ingrained habits" of memory can be lifted from the heart by God's grace. Thus, for the truly chaste, emissions will occur for purely physiological reasons, without the nocturnal fantasies that signalled unresolved passions.[196] For them even the experience of penile erection, inevitable while one is asleep, cannot be attributed to concupiscence.[197] One has left the scope of physical discipline far behind; only God, through grace, can stand the night watch in the heart (*Conf.* 12.9–10).

Later, in both *Conference* 22 and its companion, *Conference* 23 ("On Sinlessness"), Cassian tries to maintain his ideal of chastity while backing off from the potentially misleading picture of *Conferences* 12 and 13. The reason for this accommodation is probably the pastoral one of helping young monks prone to anxiety and despair. Physical, moral, and ascetical perspectives converge in *Conference* 22 as Cassian analyzes the trap of shame and guilt into which even a well-behaved monk can fall after an emission. The *Conference* was set up by Germanus' cri de coeur at the end of *Conference* 21 that ascetical discipline sometimes seems to increase rather than decrease the frequency of emissions.[198] Cassian invokes a traditional explanation for emissions and "illusions": the devil uses these physical and psychological experiences to discourage the zealous. Cassian attributes to "the Elders" the view that most emissions are attributable not to excessive consumption of food or lack of moral vigilance but to demonic deception.[199] He then suggests that the demons use "simple" emissions (i.e., those without erotic dreams) to make a monk believe that there was in fact complicity of the will and consequently that he is not worthy to approach the eucharist (*Conf.* 22.6.4).[200] The point made in *Conference* 1 about the diabolical origin of certain kinds of thoughts now gets connected to sexual behavior (*Conf.* 1.19.3).

The case study Cassian presents in *Conference* 22, of a zealous monk who has an emission on the eve of every Sunday's eucharist, becomes a parable of monastic transparency. The troubled monk presents his situation to his seniors for discernment, answers their questions fully, and is found morally blameless. When the diagnosis of demonic instigation is made and he returns to regular communion, the "attacks" cease (*Conf.* 22.6.1–4).

The story is interesting for its psychological tension between shame and reward, but for Cassian the point is twofold. There is the monk's obedience to discernment, especially notable in such a private and embarassing realm. Even more, there is his complete openness, for this monk illustrates the ideal Cassian had evoked in *Conference* 12:

> He is found to be the same at night as in the day, the same in bed as at prayer, the same alone as when surrounded by a crowd of people, he sees nothing in himself in private that he would be embarassed for others to see, nor wants anything detected by the omnipresent Eye [of God] to be concealed from human sight. (*Conf.* 12.8.5)[201]

The night, formerly so fearsome, has become like day; God has so profoundly transformed both body and spirit that even the kidneys, identified by ancient writers as the source of sexual potency, have been "possessed" by God (Ps. 138[139]:11–13).[202] This condition, "beyond the natural condition" of human beings, can only be the work of grace (*Conf.* 12.8.6). Such integrity and consistency of life is another form of the ideal evoked in *Conference* 9, where Cassian notes that because prayer follows from what precedes it, we should strive for a unified life of virtue (*Conf.* 9.3.4).

Frankness and Freedom

For Cassian, chastity was the defining virtue of the perfect monk. It was the ground of contemplative insight,[203] ecstatic prayer[204] and spiritual knowledge of the Bible.[205] Only the perfection of chastity, he claimed, can lead to the heights of love, and only from there can we hope to ascend to the image and likeness of God that is one's birthright (*Conf.* 11.14). Cassian models the transparency he praises by his willingness to speak freely about topics that "we 'other' Victorians"[206] find embarassing, relegate to clinical analysis, or trivialize. Many of his assumptions and answers are not suited to the modern situation. However, his attempt to interpret human sexual experience within a theological framework challenges modern Christians to summon the faith and candor that made his work possible and fruitful.

CHAPTER FIVE

The Bible and Prayer

Why do you hold me back, O sun, by rising now? Why do you draw me away from the radiance of this true light?

—Antony the Great, in *Conf.* 9.31

Oh, how I am miserable! They have taken my God from me, and I do not have anyone to hold on to. I do not know whom to adore or implore!

—Abba Sarapion, in *Conf.* 10.3.4

ANTONY, AFRAID TO LOSE THE SPIRITUAL LIGHT[1] OF CONTEMPLATION,[2] and his antitype Sarapion, bereft without his mental picture of God, stand at either horizon of Cassian's map of prayer. Their stories illustrate the urgency of moving beyond the cramped parameters of human imagination to the divine glory of Christ accessible in contemplation, spiritual interpretation of the Bible, and prayer.

Whatever the mode, the ideal lies beyond superficial appearance or experience. The progress in contemplation is from the divine purpose manifest in creation to a more direct encounter with the uncreated and immaterial God who is invisible but wishes to be seen. For interpretation of the Bible, the imperative is to probe beyond letter and history to the spiritual mysteries (*sacramenta*) within, to get under the skin of text and live inside it so that the biblical words become one's own spiritual bones, sinews, and flesh. For prayer, the move is from words to wordlessness, from complex form to utter simplicity, from material preoccupations to ecstatic transcendence of all thoughts. Antony reproached the sun for holding him back from such a move; Sarapion despaired at having to make it. In another saying Cassian attributes to Antony, the saint declares, "It is not perfect prayer when monks are aware of themselves or even that they are praying" (*Conf.* 9.31).[3]

Prayer and spiritual knowledge converge most obviously in Cassian's method of unceasing prayer, which is rooted in the continual meditation of a phrase from the Psalms. Cassian suggests in *Conference* 10 that to surrender all but those few biblical words will make it possible to navigate the rest of the Bible with keener insight into its meanings. This insight can grow so profound that the monk becomes the "author" of the text, apprehending its meaning even before the words are formed by the tongue. In *Conference* 14 he calls this insight "spiritual knowledge" (*spiritalis scientia*). It is not acquired learning but the experience of monastic life brought to the monk's principal contemplative medium, the text of the Bible. Cassian's biblically based method of unceasing prayer requires one to study his teaching on prayer and his approach to biblical interpretation jointly. Both prayer and spiritual knowledge bring one to the glorified Christ, and through him into the love between the Father and the Son. At the center of Cassian's teaching on prayer and spiritual knowledge is his Christology.

Occasional and ephemeral experiences of ecstatic, wordless prayer are foretastes of the monk's end, the reign of God or of heaven. Cassian's descriptions of ecstatic experience are among the most distinctive elements of his spiritual teaching. They manifest his affinities to the non-Evagrian milieu of Syrian mysticism that produced writers like Pseudo-Macarius, author of the *Homilies* beloved of eastern Christian traditions. Cassian's synthesis of Evagrian and Syrian spiritualities anticipates the similar work of Diadochus of Photike a couple of decades later, Maximus the Confessor two hundred years later, and Symeon the New Theologian at the turn of the millenium. This extraordinary achievement has remained virtually unremarked by modern scholars.

To understand Cassian's teaching on prayer one cannot simply follow its unfolding throughout the *Institutes* and *Conferences*. Instead one must begin with the spiritual interpretation of the Bible as it bears on the experience of prayer and then move to the Christological focal point of Cassian's teaching on prayer. This chapter introduces his theology of prayer and spiritual knowledge of the Bible. Chapter 6 studies practices and forms of unceasing prayer, and chapter 7 explores Cassian's interest in spiritual experience as expressed in his descriptions of ecstatic prayer, "compunction," and tears.

Exemplars of Prayer and Biblical Interpretation

The Story of Sarapion

My starting point is Sarapion, the old monk whose cry of spiritual bereavement haunts the beginning of *Conference* 10. This extraordinary scene, presented in Cassian's own voice, interrupts the gradual unfolding of Abba Isaac's teaching on unceasing prayer. Cuthbert Butler thought Cassian's story of Abba Sarapion too vivid to be false,[4] though we would better ask if it is too vivid to be true. Cassian's version of the Origenist controversy is so partial as to be misleading about its eventual outcome (see chapter 1). Furthermore, the story he tells about Sarapion consists of elements drawn from passages in the *Institutes* about correct interpretation of the Bible. That concern for proper understanding of biblical texts is focused in *Conference* 10 on the tendency of "Anthropomorphites" to conceive of God in human form. The issue there is the role of human imagination in prayer, and one must consider the theological and spiritual reasons that led Cassian to develop and include the story at a critical point in his two *Conferences* on prayer.

Cassian was well aware that in the twenty-five years since he had left Egypt a fault line had opened up between those who acknowledged their debt to Origen's allegorizing interpretation of the Bible and those who rejected his approach (or denied practicing it even as they continued to do so). The victory of the anti-Origenist party led to violent persecution of those sympathetic to Origen's biblical interpretation and its theological consequences.[5] Cassian himself had suffered the consequences of the anti-Origenist campaign in both Egypt and Constantinople. Although his own thinking had been shaped by the sophisticated monasticism of Evagrius, heavily indebted to Origen, Cassian knew that most monks are not scholars. In any case, the monks of southern Gaul were not being formed in Origenist circles like those that had existed in the previous century in Nitria, Kellia, or Scetis. Cassian must, therefore, exclude any suggestion that interpreting the Bible properly or praying correctly depends on intellectual sophistication. Whether he succeeds or not can be determined only by a closer look at the story of Sarapion and its antecedents.

Abba Sarapion is an old man who typifies monastic antiquity (fifty years in Scetis, *Conf.* 10.4.1), ascetical rigor (*Conf.* 10.3.1), and "rustic simplicity" (*Conf.* 10.3.4). According to Cassian's narrative, when the first letter of Archbishop Theophilus (399) was read to the monks of Scetis, condemning anthropomorphism and supporting Origenist spiritual interpretation of the Bible, Sarapion found himself torn between his lifelong habit of imaginative prayer and his loyalty to episcopal authority. Sarapion's virtue is that he is open to persuasion despite the great pain that change would cause him. In this he is unlike the monks of the other three congregations of Scetis, whom Cassian describes as utterly resistant to the letter.

Paphnutius, as leader of Cassian's non-Anthropomorphite group, turns to the deacon Photinus, recently arrived from Cappadocia, for help in persuading Sarapion of his error. The contrast between Sarapion and Photinus could not be greater. Sarapion's very name is redolent of pagan antiquity (derived as it is from Serapis),[6] while Photinus, whose name means "shining,"[7] stands ready to dispel the darkness of Sarapion's error. Cassian takes every opportunity to emphasize both Sarapion's venerable age and his (theological) "inexperience" or "simplicity"; this juxtaposition finally modulates into a comparison of his ignorance with the demonic idolatry of paganism.[8] Photinus comes not from Egypt with its highly visible pagan heritage but from Christian Cappadocia with its new repute for theological erudition (which, of course, produced Evagrius). Although Cassian never mentions Photinus' age, he is clearly younger than Sarapion, well-versed in theology and able to expatiate on the way the "Catholic churches of the entire East" and "all the leaders of the churches" would interpret the key passage from Genesis. Cassian spares his readers the many examples adduced by Photinus in what he describes as a lengthy refutation of anthropomorphism (*Conf.* 10.3.3).

Sarapion is intellectually convinced by Photinus' arguments, and the monks rejoice. But when the old man tries to pray, he discovers that without the familiar picture of God, now "abolished from his heart," he is unable to do so. Devastated and "confused in mind," he collapses in despair.[9] In a cry reminiscent of Mary Magdalene's at the empty tomb of Jesus, Sarapion wails: "Oh, how I am miserable! They have taken my God from me, and now I have no one to hold on to, and I do not know whom to adore or beseech."[10] The story ends with this great monk of the desert thoroughly broken in spirit.[11]

From Cassian's perspective, although Sarapion may be pathetic, he is certainly wrong. The parallel drawn between his anthropomorphic conception of God and pagan idolatry is interesting, but peripheral to Cassian's argument.[12] The crux of the saga is the biblical text " 'Let us make humankind in our image, after our likeness' " (Gen. 1:26). The text can be read in either a descending or ascending manner, that is, moving from God to human beings (somehow "like" God), or leading from human beings to God (somehow "like" humans). Both readings were at issue in the Origenist controversy.[13] The first approach was prominent in complaints against Origen and "Origenists," who were suspected of denying the perdurance of the divine image in human beings after the Fall.[14] Such a suggestion by Theophilus of Alexandria, evidently in the same festal letter to which Cassian refers (*Conf.* 10.2), prompted the rustic monk Aphou to go to Alexandria to persuade the archbishop to modify his position.[15]

Cassian's concern in *Conference* 10, however, is with the alternative reading, associated with a group which he calls the Anthropomorphites.[16] Cassian's account of Sarapion's anthropomorphism does not state explicitly whether the object of his prayer is God the Father conceived anthropomorphically or God the Son venerated solely in his incarnate humanity. Cassian writes simply of *divinitas* or *deitas*, "divinity" or "Godhead." There are indications, however, that Cassian is thinking of anthropomorphic prayer to Christ. As noted, Sarapion's cry of abandonment echoes that of Mary Magdalene when she discovers the empty tomb (John 20:13), and Cassian follows the story of Sarapion with various ways to encounter Christ, beginning with the earthly ministry of Jesus and leading to the divine glory of the Transfiguration. These elements suggest a Christological orientation for Cassian's narrative.[17] We must not forget that Cassian wrote an entire treatise on Christology critiquing what he perceived to be overemphasis on the humanity of Christ by Nestorius and his followers.

The soteriological consequences of an anthropomorphic, literalist reading of Genesis 1:26 and a correspondingly ascending Christology worried Cassian greatly. Anthropomorphic prayer brought the Arian controversy into the realm of spirituality: if the human mind conceives of God in human form, God is thereby reduced to the human level. If Christ is contemplated only in his earthly, pre-Resurrection humanity, he is not encountered in his glorified, heavenly state. If prayer never passes beyond words directed to a mental image of God, the one who prays does not experience the pure or true prayer that transcends language and self-awareness, as defined by Antony's dictum, "It is not perfect prayer when monks are aware *(intellegit)* of themselves or even that they are praying" (*Conf.* 9.31).

For Cassian and the theological tradition that shaped him,[18] God became human to experience and to overcome death, in order to take human beings beyond their fleshly mortality. Jesus' earthly ministry and teachings were meant to point beyond themselves to a larger and ultimate reality. The life of Jesus was not simply a pattern relevant for this world only but a starting point for contemplation, the way to begin the passage from the mortal and the material to the longed-for beatitude. I will explore this point more fully in the final section of this chapter.

Cassian uses the story of Abba Sarapion because of its soteriological lesson: it was fatal for Sarapion to foreclose, even through ignorance, the possibility of knowing something now of the reality of heaven. For Cassian that possibility was the whole point of the monastic life. Anthropomorphism, as presented in *Conference* 10, was not simply an issue of piety. Such imaginative prayer was not a less sophisticated or less desirable way to pray; it was a "terrible blasphemy and detriment to the Catholic faith" (*Conf.* 10.1) and, as Sarapion learned, practically impossible to change once it had become habitual. Although Sarapion was perfect in the *actualis disciplina*, the ascetical life, he had not advanced to contemplating spiritual realities. The abolition of the anthropomorphic image of God from his heart was the critical spiritual renunciation required to make such contemplation possible, the analogue to the basic monastic program of uprooting vice, setting aside wordly cares, and forgetting former ties and affections. Sarapion had accomplished those basic renunciations but there he had stopped. The whole weight of Cassian's monastic teaching is brought to bear at this critical juncture of theology and spirituality; hence both the pathos of the scene and the unsparing judgment on Sarapion's error.

The Sources for the Story

The saga of Sarapion seems like an odd and unexpected intrusion into Cassian's two *Conferences* on prayer. However, he had already written about similar problems in book 8 of the *Institutes*, though without such dramatic touches or the connection to prayer. Then the major issue had been the attribution to God of the human passion of anger, an error arising from reading biblical texts "anthropopathically" *(anthrōpopathōs)*, as if they referred to human feelings.[19] The problem of anthropomorphism was described in language anticipating that of *Conference* 10, though the word "anthropomorphite" was not used. In his critiques of both anthropopathic and anthropomorphic biblical interpretation, Cassian locates the problem in reading the biblical text "according to the base sound of the letter"[20] rather than "figuratively" *(figuraliter)*[21] or "spiritually" *(spiritaliter)*.[22] In both book 8 of the *Institutes* and in *Conference* 10, he underscores the absurdity of attributing to God either human "features" *(liniamenta)* or form.[23] In both he warns that a literal reading of biblical descriptions of God can result in an "abominable statement" *(dictu nefas)* about the divine nature,[24] tantamount to blasphemy[25] and meriting punishment by eternal death.[26] The two texts contain similar lists of divine attributes, used to refute the absurd limitation of God to human passions or physical shape.[27]

The players in the Sarapion story, however, are traceable to that seedbed of the *Conferences*, book 5 of the *Institutes*. There Cassian had written about Abba Theodore, who embodied the virtues later to be apportioned between Sarapion and Photinus in order to construct the story in *Conference* 10 (*Inst.* 5.33–34).[28] Theodore is an exemplary interpreter of the Bible, accomplished both in the practical life and in his knowledge of scripture.[29] His wisdom came not from secular learning (Cassian remarks that he knew scarcely any Greek) but from "purity of heart alone," which gave him the "light of knowledge." Like Sarapion, Theodore is skilled in the ascetical life *(actualis disciplina)*[30] but uneducated by worldly standards.[31] Like Photinus, he is a man of "supreme knowledge" *(summa scientia)*,[32] concerned to interpret the Bible according to the faith of the church.[33]

Theodore's emphasis on purity of heart—as the way to "true knowledge" *(vera scientia)* and contemplation of the "mysteries" *(sacramenta)* of Scripture—applies Cassian's teaching from *Conference* 1 on the goal of the monastic life to the monk's daily encounter with the Bible.[34] Sarapion, however, negatively illustrates another strand of Cassian's thought from the same *Conference*, for by his literalism he confuses means with goal *(Conf. 1.7.3–4)*. In *Conference* 14 Cassian develops his teaching on the spiritual knowledge discoverable through proper interpretation of the Bible and the prerequisites for it. Before returning to *Conference* 10, one must look ahead to *Conference* 14 to appreciate the significance of Sarapion's error.

Spiritual Knowledge

Worldly Knowledge and Spiritual Knowledge

In *Conference* 14, Cassian explains the interdependence of ascetical rigor and interpretative insight that he had personified in Abba Theodore. *Conference* 14, with its teaching on "spiritual knowledge," must be understood in context. It follows *Conferences* 12–13, with their basic theme that divine grace, rather than human effort, brings a monk to perfect chastity (see *Inst.* 12.19). *Conference* 13 had opened with a comparison between the alleged continence of the philosophers and the secure chastity of those to whom such grace has been granted by God *(Conf. 13.4–5)*. The teaching of *Conference* 14 rests on an analogous claim. On the one hand, there is the pseudoknowledge of those who have mastered the content of the Bible but cannot advance to true spiritual knowledge because of inexperience, heresy, or sin. On the other hand, there is the keen insight into the Bible given to those who have advanced in virtue, even if they be unsophisticated and uneducated *(Conf. 14.9, 14–19)*.

Cassian will continue the polemic against secular erudition in *Conference* 15, which, like *Conference* 14, is attributed to Abba Nesteros. There he adds a critique of overconfidence in miraculous works. Neither philosophy nor dazzling accomplishment, then, can compensate for deficiencies in the practical life. The link between *Conferences* 12–13 and 14–15 is chastity. Like *Conferences* 12–13, both *Conferences* 14 and 15 contain object lessons intended to rebut suggestions that monastic virtue, exemplified by chastity, can be obtained without perseverance enabled by grace.[35]

The contrast between philosophical learning and Christian wisdom based on the Bible was a commonplace of theological literature since Paul (see 1 Cor. 1–2) and of monastic writings in particular. Athanasius portrays Antony refuting visiting philosophers,[36] and Evagrius contrasted such "exterior," mediated knowledge with that given directly by grace.[37] Evagrius quotes Basil as saying that while exterior knowledge can be taught and inculcated by study and effort, divine knowledge comes only through progress in virtue. Those still in the throes of the passions can learn the former, but only those beyond passion, the *apatheis*, are ready and worthy *(dektikoi)* of knowledge by grace.[38] This is equally Cassian's view.

Cassian's insistence that purity of heart is the prerequisite for true insight into the Bible (*Conf.* 14.9.3 and 7) brings us back to Abba Theodore, who gained his insight into the Bible not by education or even by sheer effort but by "purity of heart alone" (*Inst.* 5.33). He admonished his visitors to labor not at reading the "books of the commentators" but at cleansing themselves of vices, so that with the help of the Holy Spirit the "eyes of the heart" could contemplate the mysteries of the Bible *naturaliter*, "naturally" (*Inst.* 5.34). Cassian reports that Theodore once came upon an obscure passage of the Bible and prayed for seven days and nights until the solution came to him by divine revelation (*Inst.* 5.33). Cassian himself, of course, read and profited from the "books of commentators." His argument is not so much that book learning is wrong, as that it cannot be a shortcut or substitute for the knowledge gained by monastic experience. As one grows in experience and insight, the commentaries, like the Bible itself, will unfold their meaning.

In *Conference* 14, Cassian calls the kind of understanding given to Theodore "spiritual knowledge" (*spiritalis scientia*).[39] Only in this *Conference* is the phrase a technical term for insight into the Bible; the theme of knowledge, of course, is common in Cassian's writings, though usually less precisely keyed to the Bible.[40] Cassian's identification of spiritual knowledge with deeper understanding of the Bible rests on his conviction that Christ, the Word of God, is discoverable in the books of both the Old and New Testaments.[41] The unity of the scriptures and the pervasiveness of Christ in them were the starting points for early Christian exegetes. Difficulties or obscurities in the text were thought by some commentators to protect the deeper meanings from those unprepared to receive them. The veil over spiritual meaning would become transparent to insight trained through ascetical discipline. Cassian follows this tradition, which is associated especially with the Alexandrian school of Clement and Origen.[42]

Abba Theodore's prayer over mysterious passages was acknowledgment that the difficulty of interpretation lay with him, not with the text. Thus Cassian insists on progress in the ascetical life as both prerequisite and companion for progress in prayer and spiritual knowledge: "as the renewal of our mind proceeds through this effort, the face of the scriptures also begins to be renewed, and the beauty of the holier meanings will grow as we grow" (*Conf.* 14.11.1). Meeting Christ in the text was the goal of the monk who read, meditated, and prayed over the Bible. To know the text properly was to see it transfigured and revelatory of its deepest meaning. As Cassian suggests in *Conference* 10, reading the Bible spiritually meant climbing to the mountaintop with Jesus, there to see him transfigured.

Practical Knowledge and Spiritual Knowledge

Cassian builds *Conference* 14 on three demonstrations that "practical" and "contemplative" or "spiritual" knowledge are inseparable.[43] The significance of their connection is twofold: without practical knowledge one cannot advance to spiritual knowledge; without spiritual knowledge, one cannot comprehend the biblical texts that are the monk's constant companion day and night.

Although *Conference* 14 seems to describe a template for reading the Bible on various spiritual levels, it is not really a treatise on biblical interpretation. To concentrate on Cassian's presentation of the "four senses of Scripture" is to miss his main point. His real concern is the reminder that growth in virtue is the key to acquiring insight into the Bible. As a corollary to that main point, he rebukes those who would claim spiritual knowledge, or even worse, presume to teach it, on the basis of their own cleverness rather than as a gift of grace. In all these concerns, of course, Cassian represents the patristic tradition, for which biblical interpretation was a way of life rather than an academic exercise based on purely human learning.

As I have shown in chapter 3, Cassian inherits a long tradition of distinguishing the active or practical from the contemplative aspects of life, and he makes that distinction a basic element of his teaching in *Conference* 1. Evagrius used such a model throughout his writings, though he generally preferred a tripartite version that included natural contemplation as a middle term between "practical" and "theological" knowledge.[44] That threefold schema, which was a constant part of Evagrius' theological landscape, and to which his monastic theology was always keyed, also shaped Cassian's thought while being far less explicitly prominent in his writings. Cassian inherited and taught Evagrius' doctrine of stages of contemplation. Although he never refers to natural contemplation as *theōria physikē* or writes about contemplation of the *logoi* or raisons d'être within created things, he describes a process of natural contemplation that is clearly similar to that of Evagrius.[45]

When Cassian finally introduces the Evagrian vocabulary of *praktikē* and *theōrētikē* in *Conference* 14, he does so specifically and deliberately to characterize the monk's encounter with the fundamental medium of contemplation, the Bible. His conception of spiritual knowledge as insight into the Bible was in accord with the Alexandrian tradition that considered the Bible to be the source of all theological knowledge. Evagrius' theological application of the philosophical distinction between the practical life and the contemplative life must always be understood in relation to the Bible. As Jeremy Driscoll notes, "*Praktikē*, natural contemplation, and theology were a sort of framework with which Evagrius received the scriptures. . . . Through assiduous meditation and study of the scriptures he suffuses the framework with what can be legitimately considered a profoundly biblical content."[46]

Cassian presents the *praktikē* and *theōrētikē* as two aspects of the *scientia* proper to monastic life. Both are essential for monastic perfection (*Conf.* 14.1.3). The *praktikē* is accomplished by improvement of morals and purging of faults;[47] the *theōrētikē* consists of "contemplation of divine things and awareness of most sacred meanings *(sensuum)*," that is, of the biblical text (*Conf.* 14.1.3). Although one can be proficient in asceticism without acquiring spiritual or contemplative knowledge, as Sarapion was, the reverse is impossible: "Vainly does one who does not turn away from involvements with the vices strive for the vision *(conspectum)* of God."[48]

The "professions and pursuits"[49] of the practical life are many, embracing both monastic and lay forms of life. This view is a significant indication that Cassian's typical exaltation of the anchoritic life is not to be taken literally or exclusively (see *Conf.* 24.8.3). Here he notes that Macarius the Hosteler, who ran a guest house in Alexandria, was considered inferior to none who had withdrawn into solitude (*Conf.* 14.4.2). The important point is perseverance in the way one has chosen (*Conf.* 14.5–6). Cassian then turns to the kinds of contemplative knowledge of the Bible. None of these is restricted to a particular way of life. Distinctions between anchorites and cenobites, indeed between monastic and lay Christians, are left behind. All who are intent on practical knowledge, that is, on attaining purity of heart, have access to contemplative knowledge of the Bible by perseverance in their chosen way of life.

Kinds of Spiritual Knowledge: the Senses of Scripture

Cassian divides contemplative knowledge into two parts. Their names immediately indicate their biblical object: "historical/literal" and "spiritual." The spiritual, in turn, is subdivided into three kinds, which become accessible—he quotes Proverbs—"on the basis of the breadth of your heart" (Prov. 22:20 [LXX]).[50] These are: tropology, to do with morality and the ascetical life; allegory, indicating spiritual mysteries prefigured or signified by the literal meaning; and anagogy, "the higher and more sacred mysteries of heaven," which are "future and invisible" (*Conf.* 14.8.2–5). These categories derive from earlier exegetical tradition, especially from Origen.[51] By including both allegory and anagogy, Cassian produces a fourfold[52] scheme that would have a rich development in the Middle Ages.[53] Here he departs from Evagrius, who followed a simple division between literal and allegorical meanings. Both the literal and the allegorical meaning of a text would pertain to one of the three aspects of monastic life, namely, *praktikē, theōria physikē, theologia.*[54]

There are ambiguities and inconsistencies in Cassian's presentation of the kinds of spiritual knowledge. He uses the fourfold scheme to indicate the richness of the Bible rather than to order its meaning systematically. He does not claim that all four kinds of knowledge are to be found in every text. In *Conference* 8, following the simpler distinction between letter and spirit, he suggests that some texts can profitably be read either literally or allegorically and some can be read in both ways. There are passages with an accessible and helpful meaning at the literal level, which can be especially beneficial for unsophisticated hearers.[55] Other texts, however, are indigestible when read literally and must be "cooked" by interpretation before they can yield spiritual nourishment for the more advanced. Some texts can benefit both the beginner and the proficient (*Conf.* 8.3). Cassian goes no further on this question. Not particularly concerned with the problem of multiple signification of the same text, he allows the possibility but does not insist on it. More important for him is the pursuit of a spiritual meaning of some kind beyond the letter of the text. In this respect he stands in an intermediate position between Origen, who was ingenious in probing texts for multiple meanings, and Evagrius, who tended to assign a single signification to a text and was wary of interpretative bravado.[56]

For the sake of illustration, Cassian does manage to wring all four kinds of spiritual knowledge from Galatians 4:22–27 (*Conf.* 14.8.2–4). He is helped by Paul himself, who had already allegorized the two sons of Abraham into the two covenants. To Paul's already awkward interpretation Cassian adds the encumbrance of descriptive labels and a tropological reading not found in the original.[57] The other examples Cassian offers follow the simpler Evagrian approach, using texts appropriate to each kind of spiritual meaning (*Conf.* 14.8.5–7). It is curious that Cassian chooses texts mostly from the New Testament, especially those that are self-interpreting like the allegory in Galatians. It may be that he wants to include biblical justification for the very notion of allegorical interpretation. It is also obvious that his heart is not in demonstrating how to apply the fourfold system.[58] Within the one chapter he devotes to the four kinds of spiritual knowledge, he presents them in three different sequences before finally abandoning them.[59]

A study of Cassian's own use of the Bible in his monastic writings would be a book in itself.[60] The best example of spiritual interpretation in *Conference* 14 comes after Cassian has abandoned the fourfold system. Writing more freely than earlier in the *Conference*, Cassian explores various ways to interpret the biblical prohibition against adultery (Exod. 20:14). Beginning with the literal sense, that of forbidding illicit sexual acts, he works through the spiritual "fornications" of idolatry, Judaism, heresy, and finally wandering thoughts (*Conf.* 14.11.2–5). The last is the most important, returning to one of Cassian's fundamental themes (in *Conf.* 1.13.1 he had drawn the same parallel between distraction and fornication) and preparing for the final section of the *Conference*, which is about true and false knowledge.

Cassian confesses that the classical literature he had learned as a child remains ineradicably in his memory. Images of heroes and battles return to him when he tries to pray, deflecting him from "higher insights" (*Conf.* 14.12). Just as in *Conference* 9 the wrong sort of thoughts distract from prayer and in *Conference* 10 the wrong understanding of God blocks prayer, here in *Conference* 14 it is the wrong kind of knowledge that preoccupies the mind. Abba Nesteros advises that young John (this is the only time he is called by this name) give himself to biblical instruction with the fervor he once devoted to secular learning. What cannot be unlearned must be replaced. As he acquires wisdom from his monastic teachers and his own experience, his wandering imagination will become "a holy and unceasing rumination of the divine law" (*Conf.* 14.13.7). The intimate awareness of the Bible that belongs to one advanced in spiritual knowledge, the constant presence of the Word in meditation, the revelation of meaning even in sleep, the probing into the very marrow of the text—all these claims for spiritual knowledge echo the fruits of unceasing prayer described in *Conference* 10.[61] As I will show in chapter 6, for Cassian asceticism, unceasing prayer, and spiritual knowledge converge.

Cassian's emphasis on the necessity of the practical life for the acquisition of spiritual knowledge leads to a series of counsels for those who teach. *Conference* 14 thus becomes a manual for monastic teachers, like Evagrius' *Gnostikos*.[62] One of Cassian's principal themes throughout his writings is the contrast between real familiarity with the monastic life and superficial acquaintance with it.[63] Monasticism rests on experience and practice *(experientia ususque)*, not idle theorizing and verbal instruction.[64] Cassian bases his own authority on his experience of the monastic life in Egypt.[65] In *Conference* 14, he underscores the necessity of experience in a series of admonitions directed by Abba Nesteros to Cassian's own young self, then still in the first fervor of the monastic life. In this charming though disingenuous conceit, Nesteros suggests that John may someday be called on to teach others what he is learning in the desert. He repeats his earlier warnings against presuming to teach while still preoccupied with worldly matters and one's own sins.[66] Attempting to give others what one does not have[67] or to pose as an expert out of vainglorious motives[68] are equally dangerous.[69] The focus then shifts from teacher to prospective students, who also must have some experiential basis for learning the "mysteries of the spiritual meanings" *(spiritalium sensuum . . . sacramenta)* of biblical texts.[70] Cassian's point by now is quite plain, and the *Conference* can end on a humble note as Nesteros, speaking for the author, concedes that God sometimes grants even the unworthy the "grace of spiritual teaching" for the sake of others *(Conf. 14.19)*.[71]

Seeing and Knowing Christ

In the light of Cassian's teaching on spiritual knowledge in *Conference* 14, one can return to Abba Sarapion and why his inability to move beyond the practical life, and thereby beyond the literal sense of the fateful text from Genesis, was so calamitous. Cassian condemns not the desire of the Anthropomorphites to see God but their misunderstanding of what that means. They have reduced an encounter with a divine person to an imaginative depiction, which for Cassian means replacing Someone with something. He will later attack Nestorius on the same point, for reducing Christ to creaturely status and making him an image of God, like Adam:[72] "you have turned the God of all power and majesty into inanimate matter and insensate devisings."[73] As Victor Codina demonstrates, Cassian's spirituality rests on the doctrinal presuppositions he later articulated in his polemical treatise *The Incarnation of the Lord*. Likewise, his Christocentric spirituality is the key to understanding his doctrinal preoccupations.[74]

The section of *Conference* 10 which follows the story of Sarapion demonstrates that Cassian believed that in prayer one is meant to "see" God in the glorified Christ. "Pure prayer" is not an escape into anaesthesia or nothingness; it is the awakening of the real (i.e., "spiritual") senses in the contemplation of the divine nature of Christ.[75] Toward the end of his life, Cassian wrote, "I see the

ineffable illumination, I see the unexplainable brilliance, I see the splendor unbearable for human weakness and beyond what mortal eyes can bear, the majesty
of God shining in unimaginable light" (*De Inc.* 3.6.3). In *Conference* 10 he had
already located this brilliance in the transfigured Christ. Cassian's explicit and
accessible Christology, and his use of vivid, experiential language in his descriptions of prayer preclude the possibility latent in Evagrius' writings of misunderstanding true prayer to be some sort of intellectualized blankness.

In *Conference* 10, Cassian describes two kinds of contemplations of Jesus;
both depend on "the measure of one's purity," just as the various contemplations
of God sketched in *Conference* 1 are accessible according to our "character of life
and purity of heart."[76] There are those who see the "humble and fleshly" Jesus
among the ordinary people in towns and villages. Exclusively occupied with the
practical life (*actualis conversatio*) and its works, these people are prevented[77]
from seeing Jesus "coming in his glory." The pure of heart, on the other hand,
"freed from all earthly thoughts or tumult of disturbances and separated from the
admixture of any vice," ascend the "high mountain of solitude." There they see
the glorified Jesus of the Transfiguration, "coming in the glory of his majesty"
and showing the "glory of his face and the image (*imago*)[78] of his splendor"
(*Conf.* 10.6.1–3).[79] The vision of Christ's glory granted to them is "the likeness
(*similitudo*) of that beatitude that in the future is promised to the saints," when
"God is all in all" (*Conf.* 10.6.4). In *Conference* 14 a similar contrast is made
between the "earthly" meaning of a biblical text read by "carnal" people and the
"divine" meaning accessible to "spiritual" people. All depends, once more, on the
"capacity of human understanding" developed through the practical life and constant *meditatio* (*Conf.* 14.11.1).

Cassian's exegesis of the Transfiguration is strikingly like that of Origen, who
compared those who remain below in an "earthly way of life" to those who ascend the mountain of wisdom.[80] To the latter, Jesus is known no longer according
to the flesh but "in the form of God." Origen bases his interpretation on the
claim that "the Word of God has many forms, appearing to each person [in a
form] he knows to be profitable to the seer, and appearing to no one [in a form]
beyond what the seer can bear."[81] Cassian agrees. Like Origen, he urges that
seers develop their ability to climb the mountain and see more fully.[82] Sarapion
was unwilling, and then unable, to do so. Such teaching was not confined to the
expressly Origenist and Evagrian monastic tradition; even the *Bohairic Life of
Pachomius*, describing Pachomius' vision of the fate of souls after death, notes:

> [W]hoever are negligent in their practices have not deserved to see God in the
> glory of his godhead, because their purity of heart is not perfect. Nevertheless if
> they deserve simply life, they see the flesh of the Son of God, that is, his human-
> ity, which is one with his divinity.[83]

According to Cassian's high Christology—remembering that he later wrote a
treatise refuting Nestorius' emphasis on the humanity of Jesus—Jesus' earthly
ministry was exemplary, providing a model for approaching God with a "pure
and whole (*integro*) disposition of heart" (*Conf.* 10.6.4). Simply following Jesus'
instructions on prayer (summarized by Cassian in *Conference* 9) or his example

of going off to pray alone, however necessary and praiseworthy these actions may be, does not comprise the fullness of relationship with him. Cassian wants to move his readers beyond imitation of the earthly life of Jesus to real participation in the glorified Christ. In his treatise *The Incarnation of the Lord*, he attacks the Pelagians for suggesting that *imitatio Christi* is sufficient for salvation.[84] For Cassian, imitation of Christ is the way to recover the full image and likeness of God in the perfection of love.[85] Then one is able to climb the mountain to see Christ transfigured.

Cassian's narration of Sarapion's tragedy seems difficult to reconcile with his description of the "splendor" seen by the monk who advances beyond the practical life alone. His emphasis on "seeing" Christ, even at the highest stages of prayer, also appears to contradict Evagrius' teaching, which can seem to suggest that perfect prayer is a complete blankness: "Blessed is the mind that at the time of prayer experiences perfect anaesthesia."[86] This dictum is very much like that of Antony quoted approvingly by Cassian in *Conference* 9: "It is not perfect prayer when monks are aware of *(intellegit)* themselves or even that they are praying (*Conf.* 9.31). In fact, Evagrius followed the Alexandrian tradition in identifying the goal of the Christian life as "seeing God" (see chapter 3).[87] In the highest state of prayer one "sees" something, though such "seeing" is beyond the ordinary faculty of sight.[88] Evagrius cautions against desiring to see angels, powers, or Christ "with the senses" *(aisthētōs)*,[89] but they are contemplated in a nonsensory way.[90] What one does "see" is the "light of the mind" or even the "light of the Trinity."[91] The superficial anaesthesia gives the far more acute, but easily stifled, senses of the soul a chance to come to life.

Neither Evagrius nor Cassian suggest that the pure of heart see an "image" of Christ in the sense of a limiting "picture." For Evagrius, to speak of an "image" in prayer meant something created, and something created was neither God nor a proper object of prayer. He was always suspicious of the boundless energy of the passions, which could cast up thoughts and images even of a deceptively spiritual nature.[92] He also taught that the lower stages of contemplation, filled with holy thoughts,[93] were to be left behind just as their pernicious antitypes were. With respect to the specific problem of imagining God in prayer (Cassian's "anthropomorphism"), Evagrius noted both the danger of demonic deception[94] and the failure to move beyond material limitations.[95]

Gabriel Bunge has argued that Evagrius' spiritual theology was shaped by a coherent and sophisticated trinitarianism.[96] The same cannot be said of Cassian. His understanding of prayer is both more explicitly and more accessibly Christocentric than Evagrius', but he should not be pressed on finer points of trinitarian theology.[97] For Cassian, to know the glorified Christ is to know God, and to be with Christ is to be with him and the Father.[98] He does not posit contemplation of Christ as a stage in the ascent to union with God, as Evagrius can seem to do with his emphasis on the move from multiplicity to unity in the mind's ascent to the Father. Cassian's Christology was shaped by his pedagogical situation,[99] but also surely by the controversies that had developed in the quarter century since Evagrius' death and that led Cassian to write his refutation of Nestorius.

Evagrius' Christology is complex, and the exposition of it from work to work is not always consistent.[100] Both his Christology and his trinitarian mysticism are directed toward eschatological unification with God the Father, a process Evagrius conceived on a vast cosmological scale in a manner akin to Origen's.[101] This ultimate union was possible only by means of Son and Spirit, but the Father is the unifying source and goal of all being;[102] hence Evagrius' distinction between the "reign of heaven," which he also calls the "reign of Christ," and the "reign of God," which is the "reign of the Father." The first consists of knowledge of material things, the second of knowledge of the immaterial Trinity.[103] While this teaching could be interpreted in an orthodox manner by understanding the comparative inferiority of the "reign of Christ" in terms of the economic role of his human nature rather than as a lessening of the significance of Christ as Son of God,[104] nonetheless such language is prone to a subordinationist interpretation, as indeed happened in the sixth-century phase of the Origenist controversy.[105] It also gave rise to manifestly unorthodox development, as in the writings of the Syrian Origenist monk Stephen Bar Sudaili, who in a kind of annihilationist eschatology wrote of the merger of the "perfect mind" with God.[106]

Cassian's borrowings from Evagrius' theology avoid its risks while sacrificing some of its precisions. As noted in chapter 3, Cassian does not make a theological distinction between "reign of heaven" and "reign of God." Nor does he have a two-track Christology as Evagrius does.[107] Cassian's Christ is experienced more deeply and truly (that is, in his divinity) as one develops the ability to see. Christ can be seen at work in the towns, but not with the brilliance he shows his chosen disciples on the mountain. The radiant Christ of the Transfiguration is not a floodlit human Jesus, still bound by form and time, but the divine transcendence of all limits; he is Christ contemplated "according to the spiritual sense."[108] Sarapion, bound too long by his anthropomorphic imagination, could not ascend the mountain to see the divine nature of Christ with the eyes of his heart. For Cassian, the goal of "seeing God" of Conference 1 means to see Christ (*Conf.* 10.6) and to be drawn into the love between Father and Son that he describes so beautifully in Conference 10 (*Conf.* 10.7).[109]

In that love, one dwells in the intimacy with God that Cassian evokes in his interpretation of the Lord's Prayer (*Conf.* 9.18.1–2). The description of eschatological union builds on the "perfect prayer" of Jesus at the Last Supper that "all might be one" in the love between himself and his Father (John 17.21–24).[110] Cassian frames his vision of perfect unity with hauntingly rhythmic cadences:

when all love,	*cum omnis amor,*
all desire,	*omne desiderium,*
all effort,	*omne studium,*
all inclination,	*omnis conatus,*
all our thought,	*omnis cogitatio nostra,*
all that we live,	*omne quod vivimus,*
that we speak,	*quod loquimur,*
that we breathe,	*quod spiramus,*
will be God,	*deus erit,*
and that unity that now is	*illaque unitas quae nunc*
the Father's with the Son	*est patris cum filio*

and the Son's with the Father	*et filii cum patre*
will be poured into our	*in nostrum fuerit sensum*
perception and our mind,	*mentemque transfusa,*
so that just as God loves us	*id est ut quemadmodum nos*
with sincere and pure and	*ille sincera et pura atque*
indissoluble love	*indissolubili diligit caritate,*
we may be bound to God	*nos quoque ei perpetua*
with perpetual and	*et inseparabili dilectione*
inseparable love,	*iungamur,*
joined to him in such a way	*ita scilicet eidem copulati,*
that whatever we breathe,	*ut quidquid spiramus,*
whatever we know,	*quidquid intellegimus,*
whatever we speak	*quidquid loquimur,*
would be God.	*deus sit.*

(*Conf.* 10.7.2)

Cassian has added another Johannine theme, the love with which God "first loved us" (1 John 4:10),[111] and Paul's prayer "that God may be all in all" (1 Cor. 15:28) to the matrix provided by the prayer from the Last Supper.[112] Cassian may well have been inspired by Origen's moving meditation on Paul's text in book 3 of *On First Principles*. The text was a favorite of Origen's because of its suggestion of *apokatastasis*, that restoration of all things that was central to his eschatology.[113] Cassian had quoted 1 Corinthians 15:28 in the seminal book 5 of the *Institutes*, in *Conference* 1, and in an important passage in *Conference* 7 about the "foretaste" of beatitude.[114] For him, as for Origen, it was a key text.

Cassian's theology of prayer rests on the same assumptions as his teaching on contemplation and spiritual interpretation of the Bible. All three are presumed to be progressive, becoming more acutely attuned to the presence of God as they move away from surface appearances to what is, for Cassian, the place of true encounter with God. That place is the transcendence of things seen and thought by ordinary means, the place where a monk can taste the sweetness of longed-for heaven, even if only briefly. In the next chapter I turn to the ways of prayer that lead there.

CHAPTER SIX

Unceasing Prayer

For the monk every goal and perfection of heart is directed toward constant and uninterrupted prayer.

—*Conf.* 9.2.1

The Interplay of Bible and Prayer

EARLY CHRISTIANS TOOK THE BIBLICAL COMMAND TO "PRAY ALWAYS" very seriously. Jesus used the parable of the importunate widow to teach perseverance in prayer (Luke 18:1; see 21:36); Paul urged the Thessalonians to pray "without ceasing" (1 Thess. 5:17; see Eph. 6:18). The practical application of these commands was variously understood, but the imperative was accepted as a defining trait of the Christian life,[1] especially that of monks. Whether alone or in community, whether chanting the official psalmody of the offices or pondering texts in the reflective recitation known as *meditatio,* the basic work of monks was to give voice to the Bible and to respond to it with the prayer of their hearts.[2] All prayer arose within a continual encounter with the biblical word.

The relationship between the Bible and prayer took many forms, and Cassian uses several words with overlapping meanings to describe them. For him, as for many monastic writers, "prayer" *(oratio)* was both a generic and a particular term. It was used inclusively for all forms of human communication with God, communal or individual, audible or silent, verbal or wordless, petitionary or doxological. Cassian uses *oratio* in such an inclusive sense for the "canonical prayer"[3] of the hours, consisting of psalmody, intervals of silence for personal response in prayer, and readings. This communal pondering of the Bible was a way for monks to remember God and to reflect on divine providence at work in their lives. Such official prayer, which Cassian also called *sollemnitas* or *synaxis*[4] (the Greek term used in Egypt), was observed both by cenobites and anchorites, though the latter would often or usually do it alone.[5] The presence or absence of other people made no difference to the fundamentally ecclesial nature of the canonical prayer.

In the monastic milieu, "prayer" also had a more specific meaning. Cassian follows earlier monastic tradition by locating *oratio* particularly in the reflective pause following each psalm of the canonical office. Although the Bible itself consists of many prayers, preeminently in the Book of Psalms, Cassian would not have thought the recitation of psalms or other texts to be wholly in itself "prayer."

The biblical word was essential preparation for *oratio* and could provide language for it, but *oratio* in this narrower sense happened when the flow of recited or sung text paused and the heart spoke from its own appropriation of the texts.[6] Offered by each monk in silence and then communally in a prayer by the leader, such prayer arises from, and responds to, the biblical words that have been vocalized.[7] For Cassian this interval for prayer was to be of brief duration;[8] the monks would then return to the biblical texts. The Bible and prayer, though not identical, were inseparable.

Cassian notes that Egyptian cenobites observed only two communal offices, before dawn and in the evening, leaving the time in between to be filled with *meditatio* and *oratio* while the monks undertook necessary tasks (see *Inst.* 3.2). The monks of Palestine, Mesopotamia, "and all the East," however, gathered for the "day hours" of Terce, Sext, and None as a way to keep prayer going throughout the workday.[9] This approach, justified most famously by Basil, became normative for the later monastic traditions of both East and West.[10] The monks of southern Gaul followed the model of several "day hours" of prayer; Cassian accepted this practice even though the Egyptian model occupies pride of place in his exposition.[11]

The differences really did not matter, for whether alone or in community, all monastic prayer was rooted in *meditatio*. The Bible both established the ground of possibility for unceasing prayer and provided its method. The interplay of Bible and prayer in individual observance paralleled that of psalmody and prayer in the *synaxis*. Cassian describes the Egyptian monks who prolonged the communal office of prayers (*orationum officium*) into the watches of the night by reciting, working, and praying in their cells.[12] The line between liturgical prayer and individual prayer blurs, especially for the anchorites, who observed even the canonical prayers alone. As they prayed in solitude, their postures would not be so formally prescribed, the rhythm of psalm and silence could vary, and the choice between vocal or silent response would be ad libitum. The difference between the canonical prayer of anchorite and cenobite would be of formality and ambience, not of essential elements.[13]

In later monastic practice, the liturgical psalmody itself came to be understood as prayer, and the periods of silent reflection between the psalms were omitted.[14] The communal and ecclesial dimensions came more and more to be emphasized, thereby sharpening the distinction between liturgical and personal prayer.[15] Cassian speaks from the earlier perspective, and to understand his view of the Bible and prayer, one must go, like him, to Egypt.

Bible and Prayer in Egypt

Meletē *and* Meditatio

Early monks kept the biblical text constantly before them by reciting memorized texts in the communal *synaxis* and when alone. In both anchoritic and cenobitic Egyptian monasticism, this recitation of memorized biblical texts was generally μελεῖη

called *meletē*; in the Latin monasticism influenced by Egyptian traditions, the Greek *meletē* was typically translated *meditatio*.[16] *Meletē* means "study" or "exercise" and in classical usage was often applied to rhetorical declamation.[17] In Stoic practice, *meletē* was the continual remembrance of philosophical dicta, one of the "spiritual exercises" that cultivated attentiveness *(prosochē)* to the universal realm beyond one's own life. Fundamental "rules" could be easily memorized and continually remembered as a technique of philosophical mindfulness.[18] The monastic use of the words *meletē* and *meletaō* for the chanting or recitation of biblical texts is perhaps traceable to the use in the Septuagint of *meletaō* to describe the pondering of God's word or the Law.[19]

Monks concretized the reflective assiduousness of *meletē/meletaō* in the practice of reciting memorized biblical texts. It was more than simply an exercise of the memory: the texts were recited aloud, just as they would be read aloud in these cultures where silent reading was unknown.[20] The purpose of monastic *meletē* was to create an atmosphere conducive to prayer. As Heinrich Bacht writes, "The unceasing recitation of the Holy Words should bring the soul into a climate, into a disposition, from which its own prayer can arise spontaneously."[21] In the *Apophthegmata* one finds *meletē/meletaō* used technically to mean recitation[22] and also more broadly to describe "reflecting on" or "considering" themes such as one's own sinfulness or the need for divine mercy.[23] In the narrower usage *meletē* can be distinguished from the prayer *(euchē)* to which it gives rise.[24] *Meletē* and its kindred practice of psalmody are sometimes synonymous, while at other times psalmody's liturgical role singles it out for special emphasis.[25] Abba Lot described his anchoritic regimen in this way: "As I am able, I do my little synaxis, and my little fast, and prayer *(euchē)*, and meditation *(meletē)* and quiet, and as I am able, I purify [my] thoughts."[26] The foundations of the monastic life, according to another saying, are "meditation *(meletē)*, psalmody, and manual labor."[27]

In the *Life of Antony* and other literature of the Egyptian monastic movement, the accent often falls on the memorization of texts, a practice characterized by the verb *apostēthizō*, "to learn by heart."[28] Antony was noted for his memorization of the Bible; in the *History of the Monks in Egypt*, such an ability was regarded as a divine gift.[29] Ammonius, one of the Origenist "Tall Brothers," was noted for memorizing *(apostēthisas)* both the Old and New Testaments, as well as astonishing quantities of the writings of Origen, Didymus, and others.[30] Evagrius' teaching about psalmody corresponds to the way other sources describe *meletē*.[31] In his system, psalmody mediated between the practical life, of which it was one of the disciplines, and the lower stages of contemplation, for which it provided the medium.[32] Cassian attributes such a bridging role to *meditatio*, especially in *Conferences* 10 and 14.

For the most vivid illustrations of the practice of *meletē/meditatio* and to discover the Latin vocabulary that influenced Cassian and others in the West, one must go to the Pachomian literature.[33] Jerome's translation of a dossier of Pachomian texts made this tradition accessible to emerging western monastic movements. As in his first revision of the Latin Psalter (based on the Septuagint),[34] he translated *meletē* and *meletaō* with *meditatio* and *meditari*.[35]

The "Rules of Pachomius" depict *meditatio* as a pervasive and unifying element of the monastic life.[36] Monks were expected to recite *(meditari)* biblical texts on the way to and from the communal liturgical assembly,[37] while working,[38] and while performing community tasks such as sounding the signal for meals or handing out desserts.[39] In the liturgical gatherings soloists recited psalms (or other texts) from memory while the other monks listened and probably did simple manual tasks like weaving baskets.[40] Newcomers to the monastery were required to memorize at least the Psalms and the New Testament.[41] Another text translated by Jerome, the *Testament of Horsiesios*, exhorted, "Let us devote ourselves to reading and learning the Scriptures, reciting them continually *(in earum semper meditatione versemur)*."[42] Through Jerome's translations of both biblical and monastic texts (which Cassian knew and recommended: see *Inst. Pref.* 5), and surely because of Cassian's own use of the *meditatio/meditari* terminology, the words became increasingly prominent in Latin monastic texts.[43]

The Pachomian texts present an elaborate choreography for *oratio* in the communal liturgical gatherings. After a soloist had finished reciting, the brothers would rise from their seated position and make the sign of the Cross. They would then kneel and prostrate for silent prayer, standing after a signal from the superior and again making the sign of the Cross. Together they would pray the Lord's Prayer (probably with their arms outstretched in the *orans* position), followed by another sign of the Cross. Then they would sit for another text recited by the soloist.[44] Cassian admired the decorous stateliness of these Egyptian cenobites; he reproaches the lazy monks of Gaul who threw themselves down on the ground even before a psalm was finished and yawned while prostrate in prayer.[45]

Pachomian monks, like their anchoritic cousins, spent time in *meditatio* and prayer when alone. Theodore sat in his cell plaiting ropes and reciting memorized texts; he "would get up and pray every time his heart urged him to do so."[46] Theodore's practice mirrors that of the angelic visitor sent to help Antony the Great in his struggle against the monastic listlessness known as accidie. The angel models for Antony how he should stay constructively occupied throughout the day, sitting at the steady work of weaving palm branches, rising now and again to pray, and then returning to work. The angel says simply, "Do this, and you will be saved."[47] The story does not mention *meditatio*, but it can be presumed as the normal accompaniment to manual labor. Palladius' references to the "prayers" offered by Macarius the Alexandrian and Evagrius represent the same tradition.[48] Pachomius' liturgical choreography gives us a more ritualized form of the standard combination of work, *meditatio*, and prayer that he had learned from his teacher, Palamon the anchorite.[49]

Monologistic and Antirrhetic Prayer

Many of the *Apophthegmata* depict a form of prayer consisting of a verse from the Bible or a brief phrase used as a plea for divine help or as a weapon directed against temptation. Such prayers are generally prescribed for particular situations or for limited periods of time.[50] One saying notes that biblical words have power against demons even when their power is not appreciated by the one who prays them.[51] Evagrius, following this tradition, recommended "short, intense prayer" in time of trials.[52] His *Antirrhetikos* ("Refutation") provides hundreds of biblical phrases that were to be used to combat specific passions or temptations.[53] Approximately half of the suggested phrases are from the Psalms. Antirrhetic prayer was a highly targeted form of *meditatio*, not a leisurely pondering of biblical texts. It was a therapeutic practice designed to counter particular thoughts with brief and particularly appropriate phrases.

There was also a more sustained practice of using brief formulae of prayer, called monologistic prayer by Cassian's contemporary Mark the Monk because it relies on a formula of only a few words. This method of prayer arose in the desert monasticism of Egypt and was destined to shape Byzantine and, later, Russian monastic spirituality in the shape of the Jesus Prayer.[54] Particular formulas were associated with or taught by certain elders.[55] Diadochus taught that the name of Jesus "meditated unceasingly in the heart," even when asleep, would cultivate remembrance of God, a theme important in the Cappadocian spirituality of Basil and Gregory Nazianzen, among others.[56] Diadochus claimed that this practice could bring one to the stage of seeing "the light of the mind," a description of the contemplative goal inherited from Evagrius.[57] In the sixth century Dorotheus taught his disciple Dositheus the unceasing repetition of the phrases "Lord Jesus Christ, have mercy on me" and "Son of God, help me," anticipating the later tradition of the Jesus Prayer.[58] A hundred years later, John Climacus shows the influence of both Diadochus and Dorotheus; the eastern tradition was well on its way toward the doctrine and practice of the Jesus Prayer associated with the Hesychast movement.[59]

Cassian's Appropriation of the Tradition

Cassian places biblical *meditatio* at the center of both his ascetical and contemplative agendas.[60] He includes it among the basic practices of the monastic life such as fasting, vigils, and manual labor,[61] for there is an ascetical boon in employing the mind constructively with biblical material (see *Conf.* 1.18). Vocalizing the text in *meditatio* was meant to fill body, heart, and mind with nourishing matter even as it blocked dangerous thoughts.[62] Saying the text aloud was a key part of the exercise; by engaging body as well as mind in holy occupation, the intrusion of destructive thoughts was less likely.[63] Cassian often mentions reading (*lectio*) and *meditatio* together,[64] for both were oral exercises, though the basis of *meditatio* in memory and its repetitive aspect distinguish it from *lectio*.[65] The sheer effort of memorization was in itself an ascetical task (*Inst.* 2.6). For Cassian, *meditatio* was a test and a sign of perseverance[66] as well as a means (along with vigils and prayer) of stabilizing the wandering mind (*Conf.* 10.14.1).[67] He has particular praise for the Egyptian monks whose *meditatio* during the night[68] fought off sleep and its danger of erotic dreams.[69]

He identifies two problematic areas in the ascesis of *meditatio*. The first is distraction, a failure to engage the words being recited or a misuse of the opportunity provided by the silence following each psalm of the canonical prayers. The distractions are the perennial ones of tasks to be done, worries, and so on.[70] Because of the dual risk of sleepiness and distraction while prostrate in prayer, Cassian recommends what he claims is the Egyptian custom of fairly brief intervals between psalms.[71] Cassian addresses the struggle against distraction repeatedly in his writings and devotes the whole of Conference 7 to the general issue of inconstancy of mind. As I will show, the method of unceasing prayer suggested in Conference 10 is, at least in part, a focusing technique.

Cassian also notes that the Bible itself can be a particularly seductive source of distraction. While pondering the meaning of one text, the mind may discover a thematic link to another text, and then to another, wandering from psalm to psalm, gospel to epistle, prophecy to history "touching and tasting" spiritual meanings without really owning them (Conf. 10.13). Such intellectual vagabondage by the "the mobile and wandering mind"[72] is the antithesis of Cassian's goal of complete interiorization of the text. The intervals meant for oratio could also be occasions for the mind to think ahead to what comes next rather than to remain in prayer about the last psalm (Conf. 23.6.2). More sinister, pious psalmodizing can mask or be an escape from feelings of anger (Conf. 16.15). Cassian knew that focus and purification come hard to the human heart.

More important to Cassian than the ascetical use of meditatio, however, is the growth in understanding of the Bible as its various meanings gradually unfold through continual encounter with the words.[73] Psalmody and meditatio stir the desire for understanding, for acquiring "spiritual knowledge": thus the opening of Conference 14, in which Cassian and Germanus ask Abba Nesteros for deeper comprehension of the biblical texts they had so assiduously memorized (Conf. 14.1.1).[74] Constant meditatio brings the biblical text closer and closer to the monk's own life and serves as the springboard to the ecstatic experiences that Cassian so highly prized.[75] Through the practice of meditatio spiritual knowledge begins to deepen and the Bible becomes so internalized that the recited words can become genuine prayer.[76] The distinction between meditatio/psalmody and "prayer" then loses any meaning; the Bible is no longer a text external to the monk. The progression from the ascetical use of the Bible as a means of combating vice and cultivating virtue to the full interiorization of the text, which Cassian describes as being "shaped into its likeness" (Conf. 14.10.2), is akin to the transformation from continence into chastity. Both processes are lifetime projects perfected by grace.

Ways of Unceasing Prayer

Everything Cassian teaches about prayer depends on the Bible. One finds both the interplay of meditatio and oratio and the link between imageless prayer and the spiritual interpretation of Scripture. In Cassian's world prayer simply could not exist outside of a biblical environment. His map of progress in prayer leads from multiple forms and words to simpler forms and fewer words and finally to wordless ecstatic prayer. At each stage, however, the basis of prayer is biblical. He prescribes particular words for prayer even as he urges his readers toward wordless prayer. Only the Bible can sustain the paradox of the human need for words and the divine imperative to transcend them. The biblical text, which like Christ is both historical and spiritual, mediates between the ascetical realities of human frailty and the theological promise of intimate communion with God.

Cassian begins his theology of prayer in *Conference* 9 as Origen did in his great treatise *On Prayer*, by interpreting the four varieties of prayer listed in 1 Timothy 2:1 (supplication, prayer, intercession, thanksgiving). For Cassian these four kinds of prayer are not "forms" (*modus*) of prayer like those outlined in books 2–3 of the *Institutes*; rather than structures or models for prayer, they are attitudes or stances. On that basis he then turns to actual models of prayer, first the Lord's Prayer and then, in *Conference* 10, his method of unceasing monologistic prayer. His catechesis on prayer, therefore, begins with a biblical description of the nature of prayer (interpreted monastically by him) and then proceeds to biblical formulae of prayer.

Asceticism and Prayer

Before turning to kinds and forms of prayer, Cassian enunciates his central assumption about life and prayer: "The way we want to find ourselves when praying is the way we ought to be preparing ourselves before praying" (*Conf.* 9.3.3).[77] Here Cassian's debt to Origen's *On Prayer* is first apparent, for, like Origen, Cassian begins with the proper disposition for prayer before turning to the four kinds of prayer listed in 1 Timothy 2:1 and then to the Lord's Prayer.[78] Cassian's maxim is analogous to his other claims about the continuity between the present life and the next. If this life is meant to be a foretaste of heaven,[79] and if prayer is a monk's best opportunity for real communication with God, then daily life and prayer are inseparable, bound together in moral and spiritual kinship.

The ideal of "pure" prayer, that is, prayer beyond distractions and their manifestation in mental images, rests on the same ascetical presuppositions as Cassian's teaching on purity of heart and chastity.[80] He links Paul's "pray without ceasing" (1 Thess. 5:17) to the instruction to pray by "lifting up holy hands without wrath or disputing" (1 Tim. 2:8).[81] To "lift up holy hands" in prayer means to pray in purity of heart. The mind must be purified of faults and established in virtue so that it can "feed unceasingly on contemplation of almighty God" (*Conf.* 9.3.4).[82] When Cassian describes the "purest and most sincere prayer" arising from thoughts that have been refashioned into a "spiritual and angelic likeness,"[83] he emphasizes the integration of unceasing prayer with purity of heart.[84] The gradual easing of the heavy load of sin allows the soul and its prayers to reach "the heights of heaven . . . beyond the sky" (*Conf.* 9.4.1 and 3).[85] One becomes able to climb the mountain to see the transfigured Jesus (*Conf.* 10.6.2) or to graze with the "reasoning deer" on the highest pastures of biblical understanding (*Conf.* 10.11.2–4).

Purification in prayer also means the elimination of distracting thoughts and preoccupations. For one to pray in purity of heart means forbidding all distracting thoughts entry to the "shrine" of the heart.[86] Besetting passions such as anger, sadness, or lust accompany the monk into prayer and produce images that dance before the eyes even as one tries to pray.[87] Good thoughts—those arising from "gazing on heavenly mysteries"[88]—tend to pass away quickly, yielding their place to less salubrious ones (*Conf.* 9.7.1–2). In *Conference* 10, Cassian also considers another aspect of purity of prayer: freedom from the constraint of all images, even good ones, which can prevent the mind's encounter with the immateriality of God.[89] The concern about distraction runs throughout the first set of *Conferences*[90] and returns in *Conferences* 23–24.[91] The question of focus is the single most important practical problem Cassian addresses in his monastic theology.

The practical work by which one prepares for prayer is of the familiar kind: clearing away faults, laying a foundation of simplicity and humility, building a "spiritual tower" of virtues raised to heaven (*Conf.* 9.2.2–3).[92] The remedy against distraction proposed at the end of *Conference* 10 is the standard monastic one found in the *Apophthegmata*, in Evagrius' *Praktikos*, and in other monastic sources: vigils, *meditatio*, and prayer (*Conf.* 10.14.1).[93] Prayer is a discipline as well as the fruit of a disciplined life. Cassian also includes manual labor among the fundamental disciplines of the ascetical life, a traditional attitude based on the view that prayer and manual labor are natural partners.[94]

Cassian cautions that prayer varies with the circumstances in which it is offered; indeed, there are really as many kinds of prayer as there are situations of prayer. More fundamentally, the condition (*status*)[95] of the soul affects the quality of a monk's prayer. For prayer to be unceasing, the soul must be pure and focused (*Conf.* 9.8.2).[96] Cassian suggests three kinds of circumstances that affect prayer: moods, states of conscience, and stages of spiritual progress.[97] The last is the bridge to his spiritual theology, enabling him to recapitulate the stages of monastic progress outlined in *Conference* 1 and elsewhere. Those preoccupied with worldly cares will pray differently from those established in "security and tranquillity" or those "enlightened by revelations of heavenly mysteries (*sacramenta*)." Cassian recognizes the vicissitudes of spiritual experience, and he includes spiritual aridity among possible conditions (*Conf.* 9.8.3). His concern for different spiritual states will return in the analysis of compunction and tears later in *Conference* 9 and again in *Conference* 10 when he reviews the variety of contexts in which the formula of unceasing prayer can serve.

The Four Kinds of Prayer

Following Origen's example, later theologians applied their own ingenuity to the text of 1 Timothy 2:1: "First of all, I urge that supplications (*obsecrationes*), prayers (*orationes*), intercessions (*postulationes*), thanksgivings (*gratiarum actiones*) be made on behalf of all people." Transforming this list into a taxonomy of prayer gave commentators an opportunity to dress it with a theology of prayer.[98] Cassian, like Origen, did not view the four varieties as simple alternatives.[99] He linked them to stages of progress in monastic life and prayer. Although some of his interpretations were based on those of Evagrius, the greater part of this section does not appear to be based on Evagrian material.[100] Cassian defines "supplication" as prayer for pardon from sins,[101] "prayer" as a "vow" of dedication to the monastic goal,[102] "intercession" as prayer for others undertaken by the spiritually

1 Tim 2:1 [margin note]

advanced,[103] and "thanksgiving" as contemplation of God's work in past, present, and future. This quite precise schema clearly tells more about Cassian's understanding of the monastic trajectory than it does about the biblical text he is interpreting. The theme is always progress: and with progress comes change in prayer. The ascetical focus on the self in supplication and prayer yields gradually to the other-centeredness of intercession and thanksgiving.

The sections on "prayer" and "thanksgiving" connect the discussion on the four kinds of prayer to Cassian's broader monastic theology. Following Origen's lead in reinterpreting "prayer" to mean "vow" opens the door to Cassian's distinctive ways of describing monastic perseverance and perfection (*Conf.* 9.12). Within a few lines, several characteristic phrases occur: "all intention of the heart," "clinging to the Lord," "most pure chastity of body," and "immovable patience" (the goal elucidated in *Conference* 12).[104]

Cassian understands "thanksgiving" as contemplation and its reward: one contemplates "with the purest eyes" the works of God in every age, offering "ineffable transports *(excessus)*" and "ineffable thanks" in "immense joy" (*Conf.* 9.14). The ecstatic language becomes more marked as *Conferences* 9–10 proceed, signalling Cassian's most significant departure from Evagrius' teaching on prayer. Evagrius shies away from any suggestion that the mind somehow surpasses itself when fully possessed of knowledge. For Evagrius, knowledge is the mind's full realization of its proper condition, a "going deeper in" rather than a "going out or beyond." As one reads through *Conferences* 9–10 and encounters Cassian's ecstatic and experiential vocabulary, with its language of *excessus mentis*, "transports" or "ecstasies" of mind, the difference between Cassian's language of experience and Evagrius' becomes more evident. (I shall explore this point further in chapter 7.)

Cassian allows that each of the four kinds of prayer can be the occasion for "most fervent and fiery prayers," "pure and most fervent petitions," "pure and intent prayers" (*Conf.* 9.15–16).[105] Pure prayer here seems to be more a matter of intensity ("fervor") and character (wordlessness) than of level of perfection.[106] Even beginners can experience a "keenness" *(alacritas)* of spirit as intense as that experienced by the pure in heart, though their fervor results from contrite fear rather than contemplation of divine generosity (*Conf.* 9.15.3). Cassian urges his readers to advance from the prayer suitable to the *vita actualis* of eliminating faults and cultivating virtues to the prayer that arises either from the fervor of love or from the "contemplation of the good things of the future." "Little by little" *(gradatim)* one advances to the higher, ineffable prayer (*Conf.* 9.16).

Here, as at other key points in his theology of prayer, Cassian anchors his teaching Christologically. Both the progression of methods[107] and the descriptions of highest prayer[108] chart a deepening encounter with Christ. In *Conference* 9, Cassian presents Jesus as an example and teacher who practiced the four kinds of prayer and was able to gather them into one as in his "high priestly" prayer at the Last Supper (John 17; *Conf.* 9.17). Jesus taught his disciples the "Our Father" so that through the familiarity with God signified by those words they might advance toward the "higher" and "more exalted" state of "contemplation of God alone" (*Conf.* 9.18.1). Cassian suggests that Jesus' own prayer in solitude was of the silent and ecstatic kind Cassian describes as the highest form of prayer (*Conf.*

9.25). As one progresses, Christ becomes the object of contemplation rather than the teacher of prayer, drawing the monk into the very center of the "indissoluble love" between Father and Son (*Conf.* 10.6–7). For Cassian, the form, disposition, and goal of prayer meet in Christ himself. This should be no surprise when one recalls Cassian's other great theological project, *The Incarnation of the Lord*. Although that work is for the most part a fairly dull example of polemical Christology, it reminds one that a firm faith in the divinity of Christ was at the heart of Cassian's own life and prayer.

The Lord's Prayer

Cassian followed what had become established custom by commenting on the Lord's Prayer. His commentary exhibits some affinities with a commentary by Evagrius, now extant only in a Coptic summary.[109] Because of the partial state of Evagrius' commentary it is impossible to know the full extent of its influence on Cassian. The elements in Cassian's commentary characteristic of his own teaching suggest that he has adapted the Evagrian material as he typically did, amplifying and modifying aspects of it while integrating it into his own exposition.

For Cassian the Lord's Prayer is valuable not only because Christ himself taught it but also for its intrinsic merits. Because it includes no petitions for material needs (Cassian interprets "daily bread" spiritually), the prayer transcends earthly concerns; even more important, the intimacy of the words *Pater noster* anticipates the "higher prayer" that transcends all verbal forms and consists entirely of divine love (*Conf.* 9.18.1). Because Cassian understands the Lord's Prayer to point beyond itself to higher prayer, he interprets its opening words to be about passing through earthly life as safely and speedily as possible in order to reach the heavenly reality signified by calling God "Father" (*Conf.* 9.18.2).[110] In *Conference* 10, in his most developed and beautiful description of higher prayer, Cassian writes of being drawn so fully into the indissoluble love that unites the Father and Son that "all love, all desire, all endeavor, all effort, all our thoughts; all that we live, that we speak, that we breathe will be God" (*Conf.* 10.7.2). The intimacy of *Pater noster*, for Cassian, is anticipatory participation in the very heart of God.

The eschatological orientation shapes Cassian's interpretation of the petition "your kingdom come," in which he recalls his teaching in *Conference* 1 on the reign of heaven. He interprets *regnum* in two ways, both meant, he says, for those of the "purest mind." The first approach is a form of realized eschatology contrasting Christ's reign in the heart with the devil's. Virtue supplants vice, chastity overcomes lust, tranquillity triumphs over fury, and humility tramples down pride (*Conf.* 9.19; cf. *Conf.* 1.13.2–3). Alternatively, he presents "reign" as a future prospect, the hope of the perfect.[111] The monk keeps "intent and fixed gazes" on the future promise, thereby bridging present and future in contemplation. This dual view of present situation and future hope continues throughout the commentary on the remaining petitions.

Cassian's commentary ends as it began, with a reminder that the worthiness of this prayer lies in its orientation to the eternal and immaterial. By praying it one has already left behind temporal and earthly concerns (*Conf.* 9.24).[112] This conclusion, which perhaps would have surprised the disciples who learned the prayer from Jesus, is consistent with Cassian's approach to prayer and will reappear later (cf. *Conf.* 9.34.9).

Words and beyond Words: The Method of Unceasing Prayer

Germanus had asked for a method of unceasing prayer at the beginning of *Conference* 9 (*Conf.* 9.7.4) but received instead a basic catechesis on monastic prayer[113] and the saga of Abba Sarapion's misinterpretation of biblical texts about imaging God which opens *Conference* 10. After those preliminaries, Cassian finally reveals the monologistic method of prayer taught in the Egyptian desert, simple in itself though difficult to practice faithfully. It consists of continually repeating a brief verse from the Psalms, which becomes a leitmotif running through everything a monk does, including other prayer-related practices such as psalmody and *meditatio*.

Cassian begins his teaching on monologistic prayer as he began *Conference* 1, by describing the monastic life as an art or discipline with its own methods[114] directed toward the goal of clinging to God continually.[115] Germanus has asked for help in maintaining focus of heart (*cordis intentio*), finding that his attention wanders easily from his spiritual contemplations.[116] He therefore asks for some material (*materia*), formula (*formula*),[117] or theme (*propositum*) "by which God can be conceived in the mind and perpetually held there."[118]

Germanus' request comes immediately after the tragic story of Abba Sarapion's inability to pray without a mental image of Christ. In appraising Sarapion's error, Cassian defined the "highest quality of prayer" to be the exclusion of any picture (*effigies*) of God, any recollection of things said, things done, or anything of any kind (*Conf.* 10.5.3).[119] Now Germanus wants something to hold on to. His request is met neither with the horrified silence nor sharp rebuke that one might expect, for he is asking for a technique to keep his attention on God, not for an "image," "composition," "form," or "figure" of God. It is really Germanus' own mind, rather than the illimitable God, that needs to be held. Cassian accepted that however formless and wordless perfect prayer should be, the human mind and heart normally subsist on thoughts and words. While pointing beyond normal experience to an ideal of wordless prayer, he makes provision for ordinary experience. The crucial point is not that thoughts, forms, and words subvert pure prayer but that certain kinds of thoughts, forms, and words do so. Anything that distracts from the monastic goal is subversive: obsessions, vices, secular involvements undertaken for unholy purposes. Mental pictures that limit one's encounter with the divine are subversive, such as pagan idols or the well-intended but equally dangerous piety he attributes to the Anthropomorphites. A monk needs matter for prayer that neither distracts nor subverts and that furthers progress toward the goal.

After acknowledging Germanus' readiness for the method,[120] Abba Isaac reveals what has been handed on to him by "a few of the oldest fathers" (*Conf.* 10.10.2). The suggestion of long custom anchors this way of prayer in the tradition. Sarapion represented one kind of old school, associated by Cassian with pagan religion and Jewish literalism (*Conf.* 10.5–6), while Isaac claims a venerable antiquity of Christian and monastic practice. The formula Isaac gives to Germanus for his *meditatio* is a single verse from Psalm 69(70): "God, come to my assistance; Lord, make haste to help me."[121]

Although Cassian had suggested that this way of prayer is for the advanced few (*Conf.* 10.10.2), his overview of circumstances embraces the whole of the monastic life. His inclusion of references to ecstatic prayer links the method of unceasing prayer with the catechetical overview in *Conference* 9 and parallels Diadochus' understanding of monologistic prayer centered on the name of Jesus. For both Cassian and Diadochus the constant repetition of the biblical "formula" or the name of Jesus is not only a protection against demonic assault or other kinds of distraction but also a means of unceasing prayer and a way to some kind of "higher prayer." Antirrhetic and monologistic prayer meet in the formula.

Cassian's method is a means of ascetical discipline as well as of prayer; the constant turning over (*volutatio*) of this verse in the heart keeps one firmly in "remembrance of God" (*memoria dei, Conf.* 10.10.2),[122] a remembrance that is fundamentally Christological, for the prayer can be understood as addressed to Christ.[123] The challenge of focusing on this one verse epitomizes the broader struggle for dedication and perseverance in the monastic life. The formula also provides the pastorally involved monks of southern Gaul with a form of *meditatio* and unceasing prayer that is traditional and "approved" while being portable and compatible with a variety of circumstances.[124] Cassian himself would have tested the advantages of this form of prayer in his own many years of living outside a purely monastic setting. It is also accessible to everyone, even the illiterate and rustic like Abba Sarapion (*Conf.* 10.14.3).

Cassian claims that the particular phrase he has suggested for prayer is "necessary and useful to each one of us, in whatever state (*qualitas*) we may be" (*Conf.* 10.10.5).[125] As an antirrhetic prayer it is effective against demons and the eight principal faults.[126] A support during trials,[127] the formula puts the mind back on track when distracted and dry[128] and can help draw those who use it into ecstatic prayer.[129] This verse begs for what alone can bring someone to the fullness of prayer: God's help. As in his teaching on chastity, Cassian will not bank here on the success of ascetical discipline alone.[130] The plea for divine assistance makes the formula the monk's vade mecum from the outset of the monastic life to its fulfillment. Cassian presents the formula as a monastic equivalent to Israel's *Shema*, a phrase to be meditated " 'sitting at home and walking on a journey, when asleep or awake' [Deut. 6:7]. This 'you shall write on the threshold and doors' of your mouth, this you shall set on the walls of your house and in the recesses of your heart [see Deut. 6:9]" (*Conf.* 10.10.15). The simplification of thoughts to the single verse enacts the dependence on God expressed in its words. Through "unceasing use and constant meditation," the comfort and illusory satisfaction of other thoughts are "cast off" (*Conf.* 10.11.1).

The great paradox Cassian evokes is that renunciation leads not to destitution and abandonment but to beatitude: "Blessed are the poor in spirit, for theirs is the reign of heaven" (Matt. 5:3, as in *Conf.* 10.11.1). Cassian had used another beatitude in *Conference* 1 for his "goal" of purity of heart in relation to contemplation (Matt. 5:8); now he returns to the definition of the "end" of the monastic life, the "reign of heaven." Radical renunciation, which includes ultimately the inner possessions of distorted thoughts and fantasies, brings one to the threshold of real possibility. The monk who claims nothing for the self can receive, by divine enlightenment, the "variform knowledge (scientia) of God,"[131] that is, spiritual insight into the Bible. Purged of self, the purified heart with its imageless prayer can be filled with God.

The key to understanding Cassian's insistence on the formula is to realize that although prayer is *anchored* in this single verse, psalms are still chanted in the "canonical" prayer of the hours, biblical lessons are read at the liturgy, and *meditatio* of other biblical texts continues. The formula is an undercurrent in the river of words that carries both anchorites and cenobites through day and night, coming to the surface in the interstices of other forms of prayer or in times of particular need. On the basis of total intimacy with the one verse, the monk can navigate the rest of the Bible with ever greater delight and ease.

Cassian describes familiarity with the Bible in two ways. First, he quaintly compares the "spiritual hedgehog" (the monastic beginner) with the more agile "reasoning deer" (the advanced monk). The hedgehog seeks protection from a hostile world by hiding behind the rock of the Gospel, while the deer roams the high pastures of the Bible, feeding[132] freely on the "mountains of the prophets and apostles, that is, on their highest and most sublime mysteries (*sacramenta*)."[133] The hedgehog has the "simplicity of innocence," but the deer has learned discernment and quickness of mind. A monk can acquire both qualities by praying the formula (*Conf.* 10.11.2–4). The metaphor of the hedgehog and the deer gives way to a less picturesque but more profound description. The daily psalmody can become not just something read or sung but one's very own composition and prayer, offered with "profound compunction of heart."[134] Cassian ascribes a particular intensity to compunction in *Conferences* 9–10, where *conpunctio* describes the experience of pure and ecstatic prayer. He means more than sympathy with the text; the words become known from within themselves, in their very "veins and marrow." The monk now experiences not the words of the Psalms, but the very "feeling of heart" (*cordis affectus*) that generated them (*Conf.* 10.11.5):

> We find all those feelings expressed in the Psalms,
>> but because we see the things that happen [in them] as in the purest mirror,
>>> we understand them more easily.
>> As [our] feelings become [our] teachers,[135] we touch the [words] not as things
>>> which are heard, but rather as things perceived;
>> we give birth [to them] in feeling from within our heart,not like things
>>> committed to memory, but as if they were grafted into the very nature of
>>> things,
> and we penetrate their meaning (*sensus*) not by reading the text
> but by our previous experience. (*Conf.* 10.11.6)

Having passed from the outward forms of the words by this extraordinary insight so much like Evagrius' *theōria physikē* (compare "the very nature of things"), one may attain the fiery prayer described in *Conference* 9. In this prayer without images, sounds, or words, but with "fiery intention of mind," "ineffable

ecstasy of heart," and "inexpressible keenness of spirit" one can offer only "unutterable groans and sighs" (*Conf.* 10.11.6). In Cassian's original plan for his monastic writings, this passage was to be his final description of ecstatic prayer. The
biblical text dissolves into direct apprehension of its spiritual meaning, and finally
even that meaning yields to the realities it signifies. This pinnacle of the spiritual
life is an extraordinary gift, but the gift is not capricious. It is the fruit of the well-
tilled earth of the monk's heart (*Conf.* 1.22.2), worked by the daily labor of *meditatio* and prayer sustained by grace.

Cassian has given us the fullest exposition of monologistic prayer to be found
in the early monastic sources. His synthesis of biblical *meditatio* and both antirrhetic and monologistic prayer, describes a method of unceasing prayer paralleled
later by Diadochus and the Sinai tradition of the Jesus Prayer, which became so
central to later Byzantine mysticism. Through Cassian the monastic West gains
access to the eastern monastic traditions of unceasing prayer to Christ, long before
the Russian "Pilgrim" whose writings on the Jesus Prayer so captured the western
religious imagination in the twentieth century.[136] Benedict adopted Cassian's formula, introducing it into both the the daily liturgy of the hours and the weekly
blessing of table servers, perhaps the greatest tribute to Cassian's transmission of
this tradition.[137] Cassian's method never attained the dominance in the West that
the Jesus Prayer gained in the East, though the influence of monologistic prayer
on the author of the *Cloud of Unknowing* and on the development of the Rosary
is readily apparent.

Cassian's greatest influence on the Latin tradition is to be found elsewhere.
In his theology of prayer and his complementary teaching on spiritual knowledge
one sees the beginnings of the western monastic tradition of *lectio divina*.[138] To
understand *lectio divina* one must understand Cassian's teaching on *meditatio,
oratio*, and unceasing prayer: Benedict's recommendation of communal and private reading from the *Institutes* and *Conferences* was integral to the formation of
his monks.[139] As Cassian admits at the end of *Conference* 10, Isaac's method of
unceasing prayer proved harder to practice than expected, harder even than the
discursive prayer to which Cassian and Germanus had been accustomed (*Conf.*
10.14.3). Cassian does not resolve the problem of unceasing prayer: the challenge
of focus simply remains part of monastic experience in this life. The only relief
comes from the momentary experiences of ecstatic prayer that intrigued Cassian,
to which I now turn.

CHAPTER SEVEN

Experience of Prayer

That still higher condition . . . that fiery prayer known and experienced by very few, and which properly speaking is ineffable, transcending all human thought, marked not by any sound of the voice, nor movement of the tongue, nor speaking of words. The mind enlightened by the infusion of that heavenly light speaks not with human and limited language but richly pours forth [its prayer] with a mass of feelings, as if from a copious fountain, ineffably uttering such great things to God in the shortest possible space of time that when it returns to its normal state it cannot easily express or relate them.

—*Conf.* 9.25

CASSIAN'S DESCRIPTIONS OF ECSTATIC PRAYER are one of the most compelling and attractive features of his monastic writings. These evocations of wordless and "fiery" prayer are central to his teaching on prayer.[1] Cassian's understanding of "pure" or "higher" prayer has been noted by commentators but little explored.[2] There are reasons for their hesitation. Writing about ecstatic prayer is difficult: definitions are elusive and ambiguous, Cassian's vocabulary of ecstatic experience is unusual, and the source of his teaching is unknown. The study begun here can be only tentative, suggesting paths for further exploration.

In *Conference* 9, Cassian quotes Antony the Great as declaring, "it is not perfect prayer when the monks are aware *(intellegit)* of themselves or even that they are praying" (*Conf.* 9.31). Cassian's use of this saying—unknown from any other source[3]—suggests that "perfect prayer" is an encounter of the intellect with a divine reality beyond the world of ordinary thought and word, and even beyond self-awareness. As Evagrius writes: "just as when we are asleep we do not know that we sleep, so neither when we are contemplating do we know that we have passed into contemplation *(theoria)*."[4]

Cassian also depicts Antony as praying in "transport of mind" (*in excessu mentis, Conf.* 9.31). The phrase links the portrait of the great monk to Cassian's many evocations of ecstatic and "fiery prayer," a sudden, intense, and dramatic (though brief) transcendence of normal experience. The atmosphere is no longer purely Evagrian. To Cassian one can compare the fifth-century Greek writer Diadochus of Photike (ca. 400–before 486),[5] who like Cassian modifies Evagrian

compunctio
not
compunctio?

spirituality in significant ways. Diadochus offers this definition: "knowledge: not to know oneself while with God in ecstasy."[6]

Cassian's iconic descriptions of Antony at prayer occur in a key section of *Conference* 9 dedicated the ways that the mind can suddenly be "inflamed and set afire, prompted to pure and most fervent prayers" (*Conf.* 9.26). There Cassian examines the causes and manifestations of the intense spiritual experiences he calls "compunctions."[7] By moving it beyond its usual meaning of penitential sorrow, Cassian makes *conpunctio* in those chapters a label for all kinds of extraordinary experiences in prayer. The analysis of tears that accompanies his teaching on *conpunctio* understands tears to signify more than simply repentance and sorrow; tears, too, are marks of ecstatic prayer. By working with the themes of compunction and tears Cassian anchors himself in a familiar part of the monastic spiritual tradition. He then stretches their normal significations to include the spiritual exhilarations he evidently experienced and treasured.

As chapters 5 and 6 have indicated, Cassian certainly prized the Evagrian contemplative tradition of "pure" (or imageless) prayer. But his emphasis on *conpunctio* indicates that he was also drawn to a more affective and ecstatic mysticism akin to that of the Syrian tradition of the Pseudo-Macarian writings and kindred texts such as the Syriac *Book of Steps (Liber graduum).*[8] Cassian's teaching on prayer draws from both approaches. Although modern scholars have suspected a link between Cassian and the Pseudo-Macarian tradition, efforts to prove the connection on the basis of direct literary dependence have failed, and thematic arguments have proven unconvincing.[9] There has also been resistance because of concerns about the the relationship between the Pseudo-Macarian texts and the Messalian controversy of the fourth and fifth centuries.[10] Some scholars have sought to protect Cassian from association with the Messalian "movement," which was anathematized with some regularity from the late fourth century onward.[11] Writing in the 1930s, Michel Olphe-Galliard observed cautiously that "Cassian has without doubt drawn from sources common to the author of the *Liber Graduum,* Pseudo-Macarius and a lot of others. He is a witness to a period that was gradually elaborating doctrines that the Church would gradually make more precise."[12]

More recent perspectives on the issue of Messalianism—as on Evagrius' orthodoxy—make such caution unnecessary. Given Cassian's deep interest in the spiritual life, and his knowledge of Greek, he could naturally have been drawn to the popular and attractive spirituality that had already left its mark on Gregory of Nyssa, as it would on many later spiritual theologians. But did Cassian have direct contact with these writings and their distinctive themes? Had he perhaps read these or similar texts during the years he spent in Constantinople working with John Chrysostom, a monk of Syrian origin? Or had the texts reached him elsewhere, either before or after his sojourn in the Byzantine capital?

Such questions, as intriguing as they are, elude historical or literary solution. The answer may not lie with history or texts at all, for Cassian's own experience of prayer could have been his source. For my purposes the significant point is that Cassian complemented the Evagrian tradition with a vivid understanding of prayer that spoke comfortably about ecstasy, fire and tears. The closest literary

Excessus = εκστασις

parallel we have to such an understanding is found in the Pseudo-Macarian *Homilies* and related texts. Surprisingly, even scholars arguing for Cassian's dependence on Pseudo-Macarius have paid little attention to the practice and experience of prayer.[13]

In this chapter I will explore Cassian's teaching on ecstatic prayer and tears, situating it in the tradition and exploring parallels with the teaching of Pseudo-Macarius and also of Diadochus. Diadochus, like Cassian, was heir to the Egyptian monastic tradition. Evagrius' influence on Diadochus' thought is manifest,[14] but his work is also permeated by Pseudo-Macarian language and themes.[15] While it is impossible chronologically for Cassian to depend on Diadochus' work, and equally impossible to prove that Diadochus knew Cassian's writings,[16] they achieved a surprisingly similar integration of two traditions of spirituality, and both were key sources for the work of later writers. Diadochus' synthesis of Evagrius and Pseudo-Macarius, continued by theological heirs such as Maximus the Confessor and Symeon the New Theologian, was vitally important for the development of eastern Christian spirituality. Cassian's integrative effort, somewhat earlier and admittedly less thorough than Diadochus', influenced the western spiritual tradition through both Benedict and Gregory the Great. In chapter 6 I showed that Diadochus' teaching on the ceaseless repetition of the name of Jesus in prayer has strong affinities with Cassian's teaching on the monologistic "formula" of unceasing prayer. Once more one finds their teaching converging.

Ecstasy

The word "ecstasy" (Greek *ekstasis*) literally means "standing outside" of familiar circumstances or even of the normal experience of the self. When applied to experiences of prayer, it can denote heightened spiritual awareness or a radical departure or removal from ordinary experience, normal faculties of perception, and self-awareness. The very nature of ecstatic prayer hinders attempts to describe or define it, though many attempts have been made. To transcend ordinary means of perception and articulation, to leave words behind, means that the return to words in an attempt to characterize the experience can be only provisionally successful. The variety of experiences described as "ecstatic" and the numerous phenomenological, sociological, psychological, neurological and theological methodologies used to study these experiences are a vast subject far beyond the scope of this study of Cassian's teaching on prayer.[17] However, because Cassian describes an experience of prayer which he calls *excessus*, a Latin translation of *ekstasis*, we need to reckon with this phenomenon as he presents it.

The ambiguity of the experiences and of the word used to describe them, an ambiguity which could encompass visionary experiences, prophetic utterances, mystical states, and Bacchic frenzies, meant that early Christian writers often avoided any positive use of the term *ekstasis* even though they described, with approval, experiences of prayer that can be labelled "ecstatic."[18] Even modern scholars, especially those who shared the doctrinal anxieties of their early Christian predecessors, have shown a similar reluctance to apply the term to descriptions of prayer by "orthodox" writers.[19] The challenge of studying early Christian experiences is complicated by the tendency especially in modern typologies of mysticism to regard later spiritual writers such as Teresa of Avila as normative, to the neglect of earlier writers.[20] Cassian's teaching is rarely mentioned, despite his contribution to the western tradition through Benedict and Gregory the Great. The starting point here must be Cassian's own descriptions of ecstatic prayer, which can then be placed in the context of the traditions which preceded and helped to shape his language of experience in prayer.

Cassian on Ecstasy: Excessus Mentis and Fiery Prayer

Like all attempts to verbalize intense religious experience, Cassian's descriptions of ecstatic prayer are fascinating but difficult to interpret.[21] In both the *Institutes* and *Conferences* he describes a kind of prayer[22] that is fiery, fervent, pure, ready, intent, lively, light, and incorrupt.[23] Within these descriptions one finds Evagrian terminology such as "pure prayer,"[24] which is "spiritual" and "invisible"[25] and associated with *theoria*, *meditatio*, and *contemplatio*.[26] However, other elements of Cassian's spiritual vocabulary and his overarching emphasis on ecstatic experience mark a divergence from Evagrius' approach.

Cassian himself notes that the highest form of prayer is ineffable and indescribable. He writes in *Conference* 10,

> Our mind arrives at that incorruption of prayer . . .
> that is not concerned with considering any image, and indeed is not
>   distinguished by any accompaniment of voice or of words,
> but with the intention of the mind on fire *(ignita)*
> [this prayer] is produced through an inexpressible ecstasy of heart *(per
>   ineffabilem cordis excessum)*, by an unexplainable keenness of spirit
>   *(inexplebili spiritus alacritate)*;
> and so the mind altered beyond sense or visible matter pours forth [prayer] to
>   God with unutterable groans and sighs. *(Conf.* 10.11.6)

Cassian describes such prayer as a "departure of/from the mind or heart" *(excessus mentis* or *cordis).*[27] The phrase is as ambiguous as the Greek *ekstasis* that it translates in Latin biblical and postbiblical Christian texts. For Cassian, *excessus* signifies a blissful experience in which one is "rapt"[28] or "awestruck" *(adtonitus).*[29] Many of Cassian's descriptions suggest the "departure of the mind or heart" from bodily constraint and ordinary experience to encounter spiritual realities by the higher faculties of perception known as the "spiritual senses."[30] But there are also suggestions of another kind of ecstasy, also a "departure from the mind or heart" when the "mind on fire" cannot contain the prayers inspired in it by grace. This seems to be a kind of spiritual ravishment, in which the resulting prayers burst the limits of human understanding and expression.[31] Sometimes Cassian seems to suggest both kinds of ecstasy, as the mind overflows in prayer from its experience of heavenly realities.[32]

The distinctive marks of Cassian's ecstatic prayer are a sudden "keenness" *(alacritas),*[33] "exuberance" *(exuberantia)*[34] and great joy *(gaudium).*[35] The prayer is beyond words,[36] expressible only in sighs *(gemitus)*;[37] it is ineffable *(ineffabilis)*,[38] unutterable *(inenarrabilis)*,[39] unexplainable *(inexplebilis)*.[40] It is beyond form and image, which of course was the principal criterion for pure prayer in *Conference* 10 and also a central element of Evagrius' teaching.[41] The particular intensity of ecstatic prayer is underscored by words connoting fire and light. The "fire" words are the more plentiful: *ardor, fervor, flamma/inflammatus, ignis/igneus, succensus*.[42] Cassian, like other monastic writers, often uses such words negatively to characterize demonic assault or temptation. When applied to ecstatic prayer, however, such language is so distinctive that commentators remark on Cassian's teaching on "fiery prayer."[43] Accompanying the "fire" language are evocations of "light" *(inluminatio, inlustratio/inlustratus, lumen)*.[44] These words are common throughout Cassian's works, as are their Greek counterparts in eastern theological and spiritual writings generally.[45]

According to Cassian, ecstatic prayer is rare[46] and of brief duration,[47] except in truly exceptional cases such as that of Abba John, who was so caught up in contemplation that he forgot to eat.[48] This highest form of prayer is not a matter of human attainment but a gift of grace like chastity. The heartfelt singing of psalms or the method of unceasing prayer taught in *Conference* 10 can dispose one to receive a divine gift of ecstatic prayer but cannot guarantee it.[49]

Cassian's Teaching in Context

Cassian's teaching was shaped by the biblical texts and earlier theological writings that gave him a language of spiritual experience. Their influence is evident not in direct quotation but in affinity of experience and expression. To study his teaching on ecstatic prayer requires one to survey the earlier tradition, consult the formative texts, and note the descriptions of ecstatic experience most similar to his both in content and articulation. The interconnectedness of Christian theological traditions and texts is extremely complex, making the task of discerning strands of thought or expression an impressionistic exercise rather than an exact science. The result of such study is more likely to be "Hmm" than "Eureka!"

The role of ecstasy in the religious milieu of ancient Israel is a complex and even controversial topic, drawing one into questions about how to characterize prophetic and visionary experiences.[50] There are, of course, texts in the Old Testament that clearly describe ecstatic experience, of a kind perhaps best called possessional trance.[51] The most obvious of these are the descriptions of Samson's sudden bursts of strength, in which the Spirit of the Lord "falls" upon him,[52] the prophetic frenzies of Saul just after his anointing as king[53] and then of both Saul's agents and himself when in pursuit of David.[54] To these one could add the visionary experiences of Isaiah, Ezekiel, and Daniel.[55] In the Septuagint *ekstasis* and related words translate at least a dozen Hebrew verbs[56] that describe intense emotional experience.[57] None of these is an obvious source of Cassian's understanding of ecstatic prayer, for which one must look to the New Testament.

In the New Testament, *ekstasis* is the reaction of amazement to a miracle worked by Jesus or an apostle.[58] It is used for Peter's vision at Joppa (Acts 10:10, 11:5) and Paul's vision of Jesus warning him not to return to Jerusalem after his conversion (Acts 22:17). One can also add the visionary experiences of the author of the Book of Revelation when "in the spirit," though these are more akin to the visionary trances of the Old Testament with their vivid descriptive content.[59] In the Vulgate, Peter's experience is described as an *excessus mentis*; Paul's *ekstasis* is a *stupor mentis*, a "stunning" of the mind.

The richest lode of ecstatic language in the New Testament is found in Paul's Second Letter to the Corinthians. Paul's remark that "when we are outside of ourselves[60] we are with God; when we are of right mind we are with you" (2 Cor. 5:13) is perhaps an allusion to ecstatic experience. His experience of being "caught up to the third heaven," described in the same letter (2 Cor. 12:2–4), has certainly been interpreted in that way and became the template for later descriptions of ecstasy in Christian spiritual writings.[61] Its influence on Cassian is readily discernible. Paul writes,

I know someone in Christ who, fourteen years ago,
whether in the body or outside of the body, I don't know, God knows,
was caught up[62] to the third heaven.
And I know that such a person,
whether in the body or beyond the body, I don't know, God knows,
was caught up[63] into paradise,
and heard unutterable words[64] which it is not possible for a human being to
    speak. (2 Cor. 12:2–4)

Cassian, like other Christian authors, drew upon Paul's description to articulate his own experiences, while adding imagery such as fire and light. Cassian parallels Paul in significant ways: feeling oneself somehow "outside the body," "seized" or "taken up," and hearing words that are "unutterable" and beyond the capacity of human speech. Paul's influence is evident, even though Cassian's one actual quotation of the text from 2 Corinthians serves a very different argument.[65]

Both Greek and Latin Christian writers drew from the biblical sources within a framework also shaped by Platonic (and Plotinian) mysticism, which featured ecstatic encounter with spiritual realities.[66] Although Philo had worked with the Old Testament ecstatic texts in a Platonic ambient,[67] writers such as Clement and Origen were reluctant to emphasize the theme of ecstasy as such, doubtless wishing to avoid confusion with either pagan or heterodox Christian groups. Origen has more to say about ecstatic experiences than does Clement; Origen was clearly deply interested in describing spiritual experience despite his ambivalences toward "ecstasy" per se.[68] On the basis of Origen's tentative suggestions Greek writers such as Gregory of Nyssa, and later Dionysius the Pseudo-Areopagite, felt able to develop their distinctive theologies of ecstatic encounter with God.[69] Later writers, preeminently Maximus the Confessor and Symeon the New Theologian, drew from these apophatic theologies while infusing them with the more kataphatic approach characteristic of Pseudo-Macarius.[70]

Tertullian used the Latinized *ecstasis* to mean "dream"; the word occurs in his version of Genesis 2:21, "God sent *ecstasin* to Adam, and he slept."[71] Both Ambrose and Augustine in the West described ecstatic experience, Augustine most famously in the *Confessions*, when he and his mother had a shared encounter with the "eternal wisdom above all things."[72] Augustine was intrigued by ecstasy (for which he used the Greek word, transliterated as *exstasis*) and explored the theme several times.[73] Commenting on Paul's experience of the third heaven, Augustine described it as an ecstatic experience of seeing God "face to face."[74] Augustine's fascinating analysis with its exquisite Plotinian overtones was not, however, Cassian's inspiration. Nor was any other Latin author. One must look instead to the Egyptian monastic tradition and also to the writings of Pseudo-Macarius.

Egyptian monastic texts often refer to "ecstasy" and to visionary or "raptured" states.[75] Several sayings and stories are about monks so rapt in prayer that they forget their surroundings or the passage of time.[76] There are descriptions of specific visions seen while in an ecstatic state;[77] often these contained warnings of some kind and were related for admonitory purposes.[78] "Ecstasy" could also be synonymous with insanity, indicating a disastrous loss of discernment through departure from one's senses.[79] The imagery of fire is often used negatively to characterize the effects of the passions or of demonic assaults, but there are numerous examples of wholly positive spiritual experiences described in fiery terms. Indeed, "fiery" metaphors for prayer similar to Cassian's are common enough in the Egyptian desert tradition to have drawn scholarly attention.[80] Some monks were reputed to become visibly like fire while at prayer,[81] while others were seen to have fire coming from their mouths or surrounding them as they prayed.[82] Prayer itself is described as fire and, in a reversal of typical imagery, could burn demons like fire.[83] Fire and fervor are metaphors for all-consuming dedication to the monastic life and for the experience of divine grace.[84] The first saying attributed to Syncletica speaks of enkindling divine fire with tears and effort, noting that after the struggles of the ascetical life comes "ineffable joy."[85]

Evagrius, formed by earlier philosophical and theological texts as well as by the desert monastic tradition, followed Clement (and to a lesser extent Origen) in downplaying the theme of ecstasy and its attendant terminology.[86] Although he had a rich understanding of the practice and experience of prayer, his descriptions of being taken up into, or going forth toward, knowledge or God[87] are better characterized as the mind realizing its true condition *(katastasis)* than transcending itself in *ekstasis*.[88] He typically understood *ekstasis* to be a pathological insanity resulting from domination by the passions or surrender to evil.[89] As Bunge notes, "Mystical experience of self and of God is for [Evagrius] not 'ecstatic' but 'contemplative', or *seeing-knowing*, in which the accent falls on personal, unmediated encounter with the Seen and Known."[90] Although Evagrius occasionally described the keen longing for migration to the infinite in vivid terms reminiscent of Plotinian mysticism,[91] such language was not his typical idiom. Two texts from the Syriac versions of Evagrius formerly cited by scholars as evidence that Evagrius recognized a form of ecstatic prayer were later found to be misinterpretations of the Greek originals.[92]

Evagrius does, however, use light imagery, especially in his claim that the intellect *(nous)* "sees its own light" at the highest stages of prayer.[93] Guillaumont has noted Evagrius' reliance on Plotinian language in his development of this theme.[94] Like other writers of the desert tradition, Evagrius describes demonic torment as "fire."[95] Only occasionally does he use fiery metaphors positively. The mind at prayer can be a "censer," its converse with God can occur "fierily," prayer itself can be "fiery" (empurōs).[96] One of these texts describes a state of "fiery" prayer lasting for two weeks;[97] although Cassian in Conference 19 mentions similarly prolonged "ecstasies" (Conf. 19.4–5), there he does not use the "fire" language that he reserves for his descriptions of (brief) experiences of higher prayer. In Conference 19 Cassian is making another point, more definitely Evagrian, about transcending earthly, material things in the encounter with heavenly mysteries.[98] In his teaching on excessus mentis and fiery prayer, Cassian goes beyond the tentative suggestions of his great mentor.[99] Evagrius' hesitation about "ecstasy," a mark of his fidelity to the Alexandrian tradition, and the rare occurrence of "fiery prayer" in his writings suggest that one must look elsewhere to find Cassian's inspiration.

The Greek Pseudo-Macarian writings and the Syriac Book of Steps[100] contain frequent references to the rapture or dwelling of the mind "on high," far removed from earthly considerations.[101] The Pseudo-Macarian texts depict an unnamed monk's ecstatic prayer (probably that of Pseudo-Macarius himself); again one notes the influence of and development from Paul's description (2 Cor. 12):

> The inner self is caught up (harpazetai) into prayer, into the limitless depths of that age [102] in much sweetness, such that the mind (nous) is entirely removed on high and caught up there;
> during that time there is forgetfulness with respect to thoughts of the earthly understanding, because the thoughts are filled with and captivated by divine and heavenly things, by limitless and unutterable matters, by certain marvels that the human mouth cannot describe,
> so in that hour one prays and says, "would that [my] soul could depart together with [my] prayer!" [103]

The writer cautions that such an experience is neither assured nor permanent. Grace—the indwelling Holy Spirit—is compared to a fire always present within the human person by virtue of creation by God:

> At times the fire burns greatly kindled, [while at other] times more gently and calmly. For a while the light flares out and shines, and then it draws in and dims.
> The lamp itself always burns and shines; and whenever it brightens greatly, it flares out intoxicated by the love of God.
> But sometimes, according to the dispensation of God, it happens that the light is dim, though it is still there.[104]

The divine fire of grace or the Holy Spirit shining out from the human person is a frequent theme in the Homilies;[105] one also finds mention of a "fiery" desire or love for God.[106] The next paragraph of the same homily describes various forms of spiritual experience; three are visionary, but the fourth reminds us of Cassian's descriptions of ecstatic prayer:

> The light shining in the heart opened the inner, deeper and hidden light, in such a way that the whole person was swallowed up by that sweetness and contemplation (theōria), no longer having a grip on the self, but being like a fool and a barbarian to this world because of the surpassing love and sweetness, the

hidden mysteries, so that during that time one was set free to anticipate the full measures (teleia metra) and to be pure and free from sin.[107]

Such language seems far from the world of Evagrius, though not from that of Cassian. Is there in fact a link between Pseudo-Macarius and Cassian? Might Cassian's divergence from Evagrius on the issue of ecstatic experience be explained by Cassian's greater fidelity to the non-Evagrian desert tradition? Cassian's teaching on ecstatic prayer does bear a greater resemblance to that of the Apophthegmata and related texts than to Evagrius'. But are those parallels as strong as the affinities between Cassian's descriptions and those of the tradition represented by Pseudo-Macarius and his heirs? Without the exact proof of direct textual dependence, the judgments cannot be final. But when one turns to the work of Diadochus, the great synthesizer of Evagrian and Pseudo-Macarian spirituality, it is difficult to resist the strong impression that the common ground between Cassian and Diadochus is not only their debt to Evagrius but also their shared interest in religious experience of the kind described by Pseudo-Macarius.

The exploration of Cassian's similarities with Diadochus and of their common divergence from Evagrian teaching on this topic will lead me to Cassian's analysis of compunction and tears. As a preliminary indication, however, I can note Diadochus' synthesis of Evagrian and Pseudo-Macarian themes in this text from his Chapters on Knowledge:

> One who loves God in feeling of heart[108] is known by God.
> Inasmuch as someone in feeling of soul receives the love of God, such a person
>   is in the love of God.
> It follows that such a person lives in ardent longing[109] for the enlightenment of
>   knowledge, to the point of sensing it in the very feeling of the bones, no
>   longer knowing the self but entirely changed by God.
> Such a one is in this life and not in it: for [while] still in one's own body, by
>   the movement of the soul, through love, one moves out[110] ceaselessly toward
>   God.
> Unyieldingly the heart burns[111] with an intense desire[112] to be joined to God
>   through the fire of love,[113] once it has abandoned (ekstas) love of self for love
>   of God.
> "For while we are beside ourselves for God," says [the Apostle], "we are self-
>   controlled for you." (2 Cor. 5.13)[114]

Diadochus combines an Evagrian emphasis on knowledge with the Pseudo-Macarian themes of love, fire and ecstasy. This interplay of the two traditions is precisely what one finds in Cassian's teaching on prayer. The parallels between Diadochus' elucidation of the various "dispositions" (diatheseis) of prayer in the Holy Spirit and Cassian's analysis of "compunctions" suggest that Cassian had a soulmate in this near contemporary.

Compunction

Cassian's interest in the experience of prayer emerges most obviously in an intriguing analysis of the relationship between compunction (conpunctio) and fiery prayer (Conf. 9.26–27).[115] This overview leads naturally to the topic of tears, the mark of compunction (*Conf.* 9.28–30).[116] In these few chapters of *Conference* 9, Cassian reviews the kinds of spiritual experience characteristic of different stages of the monastic life. He notes the challenge posed both by the diversity of such experiences and their adventitious nature. Our difficulty in understanding his descriptions of *excessus mentis* and fiery prayer mirrors his own struggle to articulate what is essentially an indefinable and inexpressible experience. Cassian is trailblazing here, for he is the first spiritual theologian to undertake such a comprehensive analysis. The result is brief and occasionally obscure, but his insights were not lost.[117] A hundred years later the spiritual theology of the *Rule of Benedict* showed the influence of Cassian's teaching.[118] A half century after Benedict, Gregory the Great, the great doctor of contemplation and compunction, outlined four kinds of *conpunctio* ranging as broadly as Cassian's.[119]

Typically in Cassian's writings *conpunctio* means "sorrow" or "repentance," understood either as a state of being (typical in monastic literature)[120] or as a moment of conversion or conviction (its normal meaning in Christian texts).[121] In this section of *Conference* 9, however, it is used also for the sudden exaltation of heart that leads to wordless prayer (*Conf.* 9.26–27).[122] By broadening the normal range of meanings for *conpunctio* Cassian does not, however, sever its link with repentance and sorrow. He complements his analysis of causes and modes of *conpunctio* with a study of the spiritual significance of tears, the first such analysis in the Christian tradition. Tears are the most common form of spiritual experience, encompassing both keen sorrow and deep joy. The anchor point for both *conpunctio* and tears is sorrow, for the recognition of sinfulness is the basis for progress in the Christian life. Repentance is itself an experience of divine grace, as are fiery prayer or *excessus mentis*. All people, even (and most acutely) the saints, pass their days in awareness of sin; the spiritual exhilaration of *excessus mentis* arises from the *conpunctio* of sorrow and always returns to it. By placing all kinds of spiritual experience under the label of *conpunctio* Cassian situates these phenomena within the Christian understanding of human existence.[123]

Background

Cassian's choice of *conpunctio* as a generic label for intense spiritual experience seems surprising, but it actually harks back to the biblical use of the word. *Conpunctio* and its parent verb *conpungere* literally mean "piercing, puncturing" or even "goading," though they were most frequently used in a figurative rather than physical sense.[124] In biblical usage *conpunctio* and *conpungere* translated the Greek *katanyxis*, used in the Septuagint for temporary physical or spiritual trance,[125] and the verbal form *katanyssesthai*, denoting remorse or conviction.[126] Neither of these words is attested before the Septuagint. Greek biblical usage, then, suggests phenomena related both to "ecstatic" experiences and to feelings of sorrow.[127] The opening for the later Christian spiritualities of compunction came through Acts 2:37, in which the verbs *katanyssesthai* and *conpungere* describe the powerful effect on its hearers of Peter's speech on Pentecost.[128]

Origen is the founder of the spirituality of compunction.[129] He read the Greek text of Psalm 4:5 ("Be angry and do not sin; on your beds be conscious of [*katanygēte*] what you say in your hearts")[130] in terms of another biblical theme, *penthos/penthein* ("mourning"), which normally described ordinary forms of grief but was extended in some texts to mean an abiding state of penitential sorrow or to denote a group of people especially beloved of God.[131] The latter meaning is most evident in Matthew's beatitude, "blessed are those who mourn, for they shall be comforted" (Matt. 5:4). In the Greek East after Origen the notion of Christian *katanyxis* or *penthos* was developed further; the words became more or less interchangeable. Cassian's mentor John Chrysostom wrote an exhortation for monks on *katanyxis* emphasizing gratitude for divine providence.[132] In the West the narrower meaning of repentant sorrow prevailed, with *conpunctio* used synonymously with *luctus*, the Latin translation of *penthos*.[133]

The monastic movements recognized compunction as a fundamental aspect of their life.[134] When asked by a monk "What must I do?" Poemen replied: "When Abraham came into the promised land, he bought himself a tomb, and by means of that tomb he inherited the land." Poemen then explained that the "tomb" is "a place of weeping and of sorrow *(penthos)*."[135] Macarius the Egyptian warned his monks to weep now before they went to the place where their tears would burn their bodies.[136] For early monks, sorrow for sins and prayer for God's mercy shaped their entire lives: compunction *(penthos/katanyxis)* and tears were the monk's "daily food."[137] Monks such as Arsenius, whose constant flow of tears wore a groove into his chest, were considered icons of compunction.[138]

Weeping for sins was seen not as a phase of the monastic life but as a way to characterize the whole of it;[139] compunction merited its own book in the Systematic Collections of *Apophthegmata*.[140] Tears freed the monk from sins and built up the virtues; like all ascetical disciplines, they were never left behind.[141] Thus Jerome's dictum, "it is not the task of the monk to teach but to mourn."[142] Compunction and tears were seen as gifts of grace,[143] though some sayings recommend that tears be fostered in whatever way possible.[144]

Evagrius was heir to the traditional emphasis on compunction and tears.[145] He comments that "*[penthos]* fills those living in it with spiritual goods."[146] *Penthos* is a synonym for the monk's initial emphasis on the *praktikē* and is oriented toward the goal of "pure prayer."[147] In the opening chapters of *On Prayer*, Evagrius writes about "prayer with tears," which is clearly inferior to the pure or imageless prayer to which the treatise is primarily devoted.[148] The initial stages of *apatheia* are accompanied by "compunction *(katanyxis)*, tears, and an infinite longing for God."[149] Perfect *apatheia* is not marked by such experiences. Therefore, tears are not mentioned in the *Gnostikos* or *Chapters on Knowledge*; other texts place tears within the *praktikē*, or associate them with the kind of prayer characteristic of the *praktikē*.[150] In two elementary works, the "Instruction" *(Protrepticus)* and "Exhortation" *(Paraeneticus)*, Evagrius advises that one begin prayer by forcing tears and feeling contrite, "lay[ing] the foundations of repentance."[151] Tears fight accidie, pride, and other bad thoughts.[152] Evagrius cautions that many who have wept for their sins have forgotten the real point of their weeping and lost their minds in an excess of pride.[153] For Evagrius, tears are transitional, like images and thoughts during prayer.

The teaching of the Pseudo-Macarian texts parallels that of the Egyptian desert literature. Tears are the ascetic's delight and bread, *penthos* is sweetness and repose.[154] The experience of *katanyxis* can be stirred by grace through prayer[155] or by hearing the word of God.[156] Tears, repentance, and prayer are always closely associated.[157] *Penthos* is joyful as well as sorrowful,[158] cleansing the heart with tearful prayers and opening the door of the bridal chamber; tears wash away our darkness and enable the light of the Savior to shine in our hearts.[159] One finds the typical Pseudo-Macarian emphasis on the Holy Spirit, who both prays and weeps with us (see Rom. 8:26).[160] The fire of the Spirit is mingled with the virtue of weeping (and the other virtues) to make them fruitful.[161]

In the West the theme of compunction did not have the theological prominence it had in the East.[162] An emphasis on repentance and tears, of course, can be found in many texts simply because they are a part of the Christian landscape. Cassian's emphasis on compunction, however, is unusual, and Gregory the Great will be the first major Latin theologian of compunction. In the East the classical theologians of compunction will be John Climacus and Isaac of Nineveh in the seventh century and Symeon the New Theologian in the tenth–eleventh centuries. All these later theologians profited from the work of earlier writers like Cassian (for the Latins) or his near contemporary Diadochus (for the Greeks) who broadened the scope and explored the phenomenology of compunction.

Cassian's Analysis of Compunction and Tears

COMPUNCTION

Cassian's *conpunctio* is a multivalent term, signifying both state and event. He hands on the traditional understanding of *katanyxis/penthos* as an abiding virtue of the monastic life, thereby adhering to the tradition of Egyptian desert monasticism.[163] By including various episodes of spiritual experience such as *excessus mentis* and fiery prayer, Cassian prefigures later theologians like Gregory the Great and Isaac of Nineveh. Cassian's analysis of the causes, processes, and forms of *conpunctio* echoes several of his earlier schematizations of the spiritual life.[164] Particularly relevant is the discussion between Germanus and Abba Daniel in *Conference* 4 on spiritual moods and the visitations of grace, in which Germanus contrasts exuberant experiences of pure prayer with periods of dejection and distraction (*Conf.* 4.2–5).

There is no indication that Cassian regards his examples as exceptional or particularly noteworthy.[165] The first section of his analysis, on the causes of *conpunctio*, is unremarkable (*Conf.* 9.26). From the "innumerable" ways by which the mind is "stirred up" (*excitari*) by God's grace, Cassian chooses four. He had already observed that "keenness of spirit" and "pure and devout prayers" can be given to anyone at any time (*Conf.* 9.15.3), so it is no surprise that the range of causes spans both preliminary and advanced stages of the monastic life. Singing psalms or hearing another singer's beautiful voice can prompt fiery prayer. Cassian is recalling the very first description of ecstatic prayer back in the *Institutes* (*Inst.* 2.10.1) and anticipating the claim in *Conference* 10 that continual *meditatio* of a single psalm verse can prepare for fiery prayer (*Conf.* 10.11.6). The next (rather self-advertising) cause of compunction is listening to a spiritual conference from a wise elder.[166] News of a death can also touch one deeply; this example would remind the reader of the opening chapter of *Conference* 6, in which John and Germanus are distressed by the murder of some monks at Tekoa in Palestine. Finally, there is recollection of one's own negligence, the traditional cause of "compunction."

None of those causes of compunction would seem out of place in any monastic text. The next section of Cassian's analysis, however, on the mechanisms and manifestations of *conpunctio*, is extraordinary. When this brief chapter is taken with its kindred descriptions of *excessus mentis* and fiery prayer, it is clear that Cassian has established a firm place for mystical experience in the Latin monastic tradition. I shall examine it alongside a similar passage from Diadochus. Both writers grapple with the reality and elusiveness of intense spiritual experience, and do so at similar stages of development with respect to the literary sources.

Cassian gives us three scenarios:

> But how and in what forms these compunctions arise in the inmost recesses of
>   the soul is a thing of no little difficulty to search out.
> Frequently, through ineffable joy and quickening (*alacritas*) of spirit, the fruit of
>   salutary compunction [167] emerges and bursts forth in shouts owing to the
>   greatness of unbearable joy; the delightfulness of heart and of exultation is
>   loud enough to reach the neighbor's cell.
> Sometimes, however, the mind is hidden in such great silence within the
>   solitude of profound quiet that the dazzlement (*stupor*) of sudden
>   illumination entirely confines (*includat*) all sound of the voice; the awe-
>   struck (*adtonitus*) spirit contains within itself all thoughts (*sensus*) [168] or lets
>   them go and pours forth its desires to God with unutterable sighs (*gemitibus
>   inenarrabilibus*).[169]
> Sometimes, however, the mind prays with such abundance of compunction
>   (*conpunctio*) and grief (*dolor*) that it cannot express anything except by the
>   escape (*evaporatio*) of tears. (*Conf.* 9.27)

Cassian does not rank these experiences. The first two are analogous to *excessus mentis* or fiery prayer, that is, sudden interruptions of a normal state by extraordinary feelings; the third returns to the baseline of normal compunction.

In the first example compunction suddenly yields to joy, manifested in shouts loud enough to be heard by one's monastic neighbors. Is it a kind of glossolalia? An uncontrollable urge to whoop? Cassian does not tell us. The joy itself is "ineffable," but the "clamoring" heard by the neighbors may be a particularly heartfelt psalmody or cry in prayer.[170]

The closest parallel to this experience is the passage in *Conference* 4 in which Germanus describes spiritual exultation:

> Sometimes as we sat in the cell we were filled with such quickening of heart
>   (*alacritas cordis*) and abundance of most sacred thoughts (*sensus*) [171]
> that neither speech nor thought (*sensus*) was adequate;
> pure and ready prayer was offered, and the mind full of spiritual fruits could
>   feel its powerful and light (*leves*) [172] prayers going to God even when praying
>   while asleep. (*Conf.* 4.2)

A couple of (brief) chapters later Abba Daniel describes this experience as a *conpunctio* given by God to stir one from sloth. There are also frequent but sudden visitations in which one is filled with supernatural fragrances and the mind is caught up in delight, rapt in an *excessus spiritus* that makes it forget that one still dwells in the flesh (*Conf.* 4.5). The vocabulary for both Germanus' and Daniel's descriptions is that of Cassian's many evocations of ecstatic prayer, though only the first is described as a *conpunctio*.

Diadochus associates exultation with psalmody rather than with the highest ⌐ form of prayer (which he calls "prayer in the Holy Spirit"). He writes:

> Whenever the soul is in abundance of its natural fruits[173] it does its psalmody
>   in a louder voice and wants to pray vocally. . . . That disposition is
>   accompanied by an imaginative[174] joy. . . .
> When we are weighed down by great despair, it is necessary to raise the voice a
>   little for the psalmody, striking up the sounds of the soul with the joy of
>   hope, until that heavy cloud is dissolved by the winds of song.[175]

Diadochus describes the interplay of exuberant joy and vocal prayer: joy raises the voice, and raising the voice stirs up joy. Cassian's description, however, emphasizes the sudden, uncontrollable nature of joy, while Diadochus depicts a more "natural" (*physikos*) disposition more subject to human control.

Cassian's second kind of "compunction" differs from the first in that it arises from and remains in profound silence.[176] Cassian indicates no precondition besides *taciturnitas* for this "amazement of sudden illumination." These few lines are among the most mysterious that Cassian wrote. Does the silent *stupor* have any relation to the explosive joy of the first example? Do these first two kinds of *conpunctio* with their ecstatic, adventitious quality have any link with the third, which belongs to the normal ambient of compunction and is expressed nonverbally through tears?

Diadochus' parallel description reads like a commentary on Cassian's text. This material intercalates with Diadochus' text on loud and joyful psalmody just quoted and describes a "spiritual" experience contrasted with the "natural" one:[177]

> When [the soul] is energized by the Holy Spirit, it sings and prays with all
>   relaxation and sweetness in the solitude of the heart. . . . This [disposition is
>   accompanied by] spiritual tears and, after them, a kind of strong desire that
>   loves silence;[178] for the memory[179] remains fervent because of the restraint
>   of the voice, and prepares the heart to bear only ideas that are entirely tearful
>   and soothing.
> Thus one sees the seeds of prayer sown in the earth of the heart with tears, in
>   hope of the joy of the harvest.[180]

Diadochus' distinction between "natural joy" and "energizing by the Holy Spirit" and his linking the first to psalmody and the second to silent prayer of the heart situates his examples of intense experience within an explicitly theological framework. Cassian is content simply to list his examples, all of which are the free work of grace. It is the reality of grace that matters to him, not the theological explanation for it. For neither Cassian nor Diadochus can words express the experience of being touched by God; prayer withdraws into the heart and leaves human language behind. Diadochus concurs with Cassian's emphasis on divine intervention, solitude, and restraint of the voice; for both writers, tears begin and accompany the transition from sorrow to joy.

TEARS

Cassian's analysis of *conpunctio* modulates into the first etiology of tears known in Christian spiritual literature.[181] Germanus notes a typical progression: remembrance of sins produces tears, followed by the "ineffable joy" of the Lord's "visitation."[182] This process cannot, however, be triggered at will. Simply remembering one's sins guarantees neither tears nor "visitation." In a vivid simile Germanus notes that his eyes are often like "the hardest flints" even when he earnestly desires to weep (*Conf.* 9.28.2). Tears, like "fiery prayer," are beyond human control. Nonetheless, the recollection of sins can often be an occasion for the gift of tears, which is certainly more common than the always elusive ecstatic prayer.

Cassian suggests four reasons for tears. The first, third, and fourth are somehow related to sorrow for sin, and the second is akin to the ecstatic experiences mentioned in chapter 27 of *Conference* 9.[183] Cassian is drawing back into a narrower and more typical understanding of *conpunctio* of the kind amply illustrated in the *Apophthegmata* and other texts. Tears are caused by recollection of one's own sins, as Germanus had already noted (see *Conf.* 20.7).[184] The second cause is contemplation of future glory, which produces even more tears than does sorrow for past and present sins. The fruits of such contemplation are "unbearable joy" (*intolerantia gaudii*, see *Conf.* 9.27) and "tremendous liveliness" (*alacritatis inmensitas*).[185] The tone and vocabulary are those of the descriptions of ecstatic prayer and of the first form of spiritual experience described in *Conference* 9. The second and third causes of tears, fear of hell and consideration of judgment,[186] were noted earlier in *Conference* 9 as suitable dispositions for prayer (*Conf.* 9.15). Both of these can produce "keenness of spirit" (*spiritus alacritas*), though sorrow and fear are more suited to beginners, and contemplating God's blessings in ineffable joy belongs to the "pure in heart" (*Conf.* 9.15.3). The fourth reason for tears is the sorrow of the righteous for the sins of others. Because the examples given are Samuel, Jeremiah and Jesus, surely this weeping belongs to the pure in heart.[187] Cassian quotes Matthew 5:3, "blessed are the poor in spirit," anticipating the centrality of that particular beatitude to Cassian's teaching on unceasing prayer in the next conference (*Conf.* 10.11.1).

Gregory the Great's schema of four kinds of *conpunctio* in the *Moral Teachings on Job* owes much to Cassian's teaching on tears. Gregory's model consists of compunction arising from: (1) remembrance of one's past sins (*ubi fuit*); (2) consideration of God's judgment (*ubi erit*); (3) acknowledgment of the ills of the present age (*ubi est*); (4) contemplation of the good things of the heavenly homeland (*ubi non est*).[188] Later in the same work he simplifies and revises his model, outlining a fearful compunction based on awareness of one's sins and a wholly joyful compunction arising from regarding heavenly joy.[189] This simpler schema is the one Gregory himself seems to prefer.[190] Gregory associates compunction so closely with contemplation that in practice they become synonymous;[191] as P. Régamey notes, Gregory, like Cassian, includes under the heading of "compunction" spiritual states that are quite elevated and beyond sorrow.[192] While the influence of Augustine on Gregory's thought is often noted, here one finds Greg-ory developing Cassian's teaching on *conpunctio*, another example of how Cas-sian's bridging of East and West brought so much to later Latin monastic tradi-tion.[193]

The study of spiritual experience in *Conference* 9 concludes with Cassian's caution against artificially inducing tears. The basic premise is familiar: human effort can never produce the flow of tears possible with divine grace (*Conf.* 9.30.1). A sparse diet of forced tears cannot sustain unceasing prayer (*Conf.* 9.30.2). Cas-sian concedes some benefit in the practice for those still advancing toward "love of virtue" (which Cassian will identify in *Conf.* 11.6.1 as the highest motivation for seeking perfection), but he warns against trying too hard. Forced tears are pointless for those who have already made some progress in the monastic life. There is always a risk in trying too hard to weep, for the possibility of despair lurks here as in all ascetical practices. Such despair inevitably results in departure from the monastic life.[194]

Cassian returns to the problem of induced tears in *Conference* 20, where Germanus asks if he should be calling to mind his sins in order to generate "tears of confession." The reply sidesteps the issue of tears, noting simply that mind-fulness of the past is necessary until God grants forgetfulness of sins and removes the "thorns of conscience from the inmost parts of the soul" (*Conf.* 20.6–7.2).[195] But one does not cease weeping: tears continue, though changed from tears about past failures to tears in anticipation of future beatitude (*Conf.* 20.8.11).[196] In *Con-ference* 23, Cassian notes that even the saints must continue to shed tears of peni-tence, for purity of heart is a fragile state in this life (*Conf.* 23.10.1).[197] A monk proficient in unceasing prayer and feeding continually on the "highest and most sublime *sacramenta* of the Bible" still sings the psalms "with deep compunction of heart" (*Conf.* 10.11.4). The monk progresses from fear to love and then to a "more sublime fear" lest the God who has loved and forgiven so much should be disappointed (*Conf.* 11.13).

Again Diadochus can help elucidate Cassian's analysis of the interplay of compunction and tears. Diadochus mentions tears of sorrow for sin and confes-sion (*exomologēsis*) of sins[198] but also a "pleasant sadness" and "tears without grief" that succeed penitential tears.[199] Prayer in the Holy Spirit brings "spiritual tears"[200] and in the silence of contemplation the mind is occupied with "tearful" thoughts.[201] Diadochus offers a more coherent synthesis along lines similar to Cassian's. His progressive categories are much closer to Cassian's teaching than to Evagrius'. They are without clear parallels in the writings of Pseudo-Macarius, though broadly compatible with the Pseudo-Macarian approach to spiritual expe-rience. Once more one is left with the striking affinity between Cassian and Dia-dochus, schooled in the same traditions and devoted to the same endeavor of voicing the ineffable touch of God.

Teacher of Prayer

Cassian's teaching on the interplay of Bible, prayer, and experience is the very heart of his monastic theology. It is from this heart that he continues to nourish and to challenge those who find him to be a spiritual guide. The centrality of Christ in both reading and praying the Bible, the call to deeper awareness of the divine presence in the biblical text and in daily experience, the simplification of prayer to a handful of words and then beyond words to a fiery silence are themes more remarkable and even provocative in our day than they were in his. For the historian of theology Cassian's relationship to his sources is a fascinating and finally frustrating problem. We simply cannot know where and how he found much of what he teaches us; the balance between experience and text remains his secret. However it happened, the achievement remains: once more he stands across the divide of language and custom to bring the best of the eastern Christian world to the hungry monks of the western one. In the end his importance is greatest not to the historical theologians who puzzle over his thought but to those of both East and West who recognize in him the great charism of Teacher.

Afterword

THIS BOOK BEGAN WITH MANY QUESTIONS about who John Cassian was; I end it with questions about who he is for us. These last observations are framed particularly in terms of Cassian's significance for monastic men and women today.

Most fundamental is Cassian's reminder that the essence of the monastic life lies in the intention and orientation with which it is lived rather than its structures and disciplines. Spending years outside of purely monastic environments and writing for monks who might find themselves called to service beyond the monastery, Cassian asserts that the core of the monastic vocation is the monk's belief in heaven. Such eschatological faith brings the freedom of engagement on which monastic life for the world must be based. Such faith enabled monks like Cassian to do whatever they were called on to do, monastic and pastoral, as if it mattered absolutely, while knowing that from another perspective it mattered not at all. This teacher of asceticism reminded his readers at every turn that disciplines are always provisional. Secondary even now to the law of love for others, they will be finally dissolved in the perfect love of God.

Cassian reminds one, too, that every aspect of human existence has a role in the reintegrative process he calls "purity of heart," "perfect chastity," or "unceasing prayer." He was no dualist: the most intimate and private realms of bodily and sexual experience were drawn into the project of transformation through grace. His biology is problematic, and his psychology is not ours, but his confidence that we go to God as whole persons, body and soul, never one without the other, shames the prudery that we so often mask with affected openness and selective honesties. Cassian's achievement can encourage those modern Christians willing to undertake the massive challenge of fashioning a theology of sexuality that takes full account of both human experience and grace.

For Cassian the Christian and monastic world was always shaped by the Bible read, meditated, and prayed. He accepted the authority of the Bible in a way we find unacceptably absolute, while living under that authority with a confident ease of interpretation. Here, again, his answers are not ours, but he challenges modern readers to ask themselves what they really understand or believe about the role of the Bible in the Christian life. He challenges those who follow the monastic way really to base their lives on the *lectio divina* they profess to be their spiritual nourishment.

Cassian's theology of prayer is of a piece with his eschatological orientation, his integrative view of the human person, and his spiritual understanding of the Bible. All come to bear on the practice and experience of prayer. Eluding our conventional labels of apophatic and kataphatic mysticism, Cassian vigorously criticizes self-invented comforts and crutches in prayer while reminding his readers that the truest prayer can rock one from top to bottom with tears of compunction and spiritual exhilaration. His ability to conceive of the spiritual life in complex terms calls us to do the same.

There is no question that Cassian remains a teacher of the monastic life. More precisely, he forms a link in the succession of monastic teachers continuing to this day. His achievement is unique in scope but has never been definitive: nor did he not suffer the illusion that such finality was possible. He leaves us humbled, wondering how his heirs will rise to the challenge he met so impressively.

Cassian on Monastic Egypt

Lower Egypt: Monasticism in the Delta

Cassian wrote three accounts of his and Germanus' early days in Egypt (*Inst.* 5.36–38, *Conf.* 11.1–4, *Conf.* 18.1).[1] Only at the beginning of *Conference* 11 does he describe their actual arrival in Egypt at Thennesus and subsequent visit to Panephysis. Cassian had set the first ten *Conferences* in Scetis (and Kellia, in the case of Theodore, *Conf.* 6), and he opened the second set with a change of scenery. He writes in the preface to *Conferences* 11–17 that he wishes "to make known the reason for our journey" through *Conferences* by "the three fathers living in another desert whom we saw first" (*Conf. Pref.* 2 2).

Panephysis

Of the three hermits visited by Cassian and Germanus while in the vicinity of Panephysis, Chaeremon (*Conf.* 11–13) is described as very old (more than a centenarian), bent over with age, and no longer willing to serve as an elder for monastic disciples. He could be the same as the Chaeremon of Scetis, of whom a story is preserved in the *Apophthegmata*, or the Chaeremon "the ascetic" mentioned by Palladius.[2]

Nesteros (*Conf.* 14–15) is even more obscure; Cassian offers no personal information other than that he lived six miles from Abba Joseph's cell (*Conf.* 15.10.5). The *Alphabetical Collection* of *Apophthegmata* contains two sets of sayings attributed to monks named Nisteros (spelled Νιστερῶς or Νισθερῶς in Greek, while Cassian spells the name "Nesteros"), one about "Nisteros"[3] and the other about "Nisteros the Cenobite."[4] The "Nisteros" sayings describe him as a "friend" of Antony the Great,[5] and contain an exchange between Nisteros and a Joseph,[6] conceivably the Joseph of Panephysis also mentioned by Cassian. Hans-Oskar Weber suggests, quite plausibly, that one of the sayings is the source for Cassian's *Conference* 14.4.[7]

Joseph of Panephysis (*Conf.* 16–17), says Cassian, came from an illustrious family in Thmuis and was himself a leading figure (*primarius*) of the town. There are several sayings of Joseph of Panephysis in the *Alphabetical Collection* of *Apophthegmata*, including references to encounters with Poemen that suggest a young Poemen still in his early days of learning the monastic life.[8]

Cassian also refers to a Paul of Panephysis in *Conference* 7.26–27.[9] This Paul, an anchorite, can be distinguished from Paul the cenobitic abbot in *Conference* 19.1; Cassian associates him with Abba Archebius of Panephysis (see *Conf.* 11.2.1). Paul lived an overly rigid asceticism that led to a breakdown; he was subsequently tended by women, whom he had previously scorned in his hypervigilance about chastity. There is no other historical trace of this Paul.

Diolcos

At the end of book 5 of the *Institutes*, Cassian wishes to include the example of the monks of Diolcos, and especially of one named Archebius, in his catalog of monks who illustrate the virtues to be highlighted in the second part of the *Institutes*. The chapter opens: "when we beginners had just come *(admodum venissemus)* from the monasteries of Palestine to the town of Egypt that is called Diolcos" *(Inst.* 5.36.1). It would be natural to infer that this passage is about their initial arrival in Egypt, were it not for other indications *(Conf.* 11.1 and 18.1) that Thennesus and then Panephysis, in the eastern Delta, were in fact the first ports of call.[10] Diolcos may perhaps best be understood as a stopping point on the way to Scetis.

Ambiguities in the Delta

There are some difficulties in Cassian's descriptions of monasteries in the Delta. First is the puzzle of the monk or monks named "Archebius." Is Cassian careless, describing one and the same person with conflicting information? The evidence suggests that he really is referring to two different people. The locations differ (Diolcos versus Panephysis), and the way of life and chronology differ (one was a monk entirely separated from "the world" for fifty years; the other was a monk for thirty-seven years before becoming a bishop).[11] Cassian's story about Archebius of Diolcos in *Inst.* 5.37 has affinities with other edifying stories in the desert tradition,[12] and the account of *Inst.* 5.37 with its clearly anchoritic setting sits uneasily with *Inst.* 5.38 and its more cenobitic atmosphere. The Archebius of book 5 of the *Institutes* seems to be a vehicle for various edifying tales, while Bishop Archebius of Panephysis in *Conference* 11 takes a more active role in Cassian's narrative.

Second, it remains unclear whether the monastery of Abba Paul,[13] the setting of *Conference* 19, is to be located in Diolcos or Panephysis. The first words of *Conference* 19 have been taken by some to suggest a return to Panephysis,[14] though this location is by no means clear from the text itself. *Conference* 18 is set in Diolcos and *Conference* 20 in Panephysis, but there is no indication of where to place Abba Paul's cenobium described in *Conference* 19, nor any geographical sequence within the whole set of *Conferences* 18–24.[15]

Abba John, a monk of Paul's cenobium, is assigned *Conference* 19. He is perhaps the same monk as John, "father of monasteries" in Diolcos, mentioned by the author of the *History of the Monks in Egypt*.[16] The prominence of John in *Conference* 19 makes it credible that he would have later succeeded Paul as superior of the cenobium; although Cassian refers to him as a "very old man," the visit recorded in the *History of the Monks in Egypt* was only about a decade after Cassian's arrival in Egypt.[17]

Two other references to "Abba John" are probably about John of Diolcos. In book 5 of the *Institutes* Cassian records two sayings of an Abba John who is superior of a "large cenobium of many brothers" (*Inst.* 5.27–28); the setting fits that of *Conference* 19, and the dying words recorded in chapter 28 match the tenor of the teaching in *Conference* 19.[18] In *Conference* 14 Cassian mentions an Abba John who presided over a "large cenobium" in the vicinity of Thmuis (*Conf.* 14.4.2).[19] Cassian describes him as "aglow with apostolic signs": might this be an allusion to the healing powers ascribed to John of Diolcos in the *History of the Monks of Egypt?* Thmuis was close enough to Diolcos and sufficiently prominent that it could have been used as a general geographical referent.[20]

Abba Abraham, to whom Cassian attributes *Conference* 24, should also be included among the anchorites of Diolcos. Cassian does not explicitly locate him at Diolcos, but the topographical references agree with those of the *Institutes*.[21] Abraham's comparison of the monks of the "desert of Calamus or Porphyry" with those of Scetis (*Conf.* 24.4.2) distinguishes his own location from both those places. Abraham "the simple" of *Conference* 15.4–5 is probably someone else, an anchorite "from the desert" (Nitria/the Cells or Scetis) who would go to "Egypt" to help at harvest time.[22] It is impossible on the basis of the evidence to relate either of Cassian's Abrahams to the various ones known from other sources.

Scetis

Cassian sets several of the *Conferences* in Scetis and relates many stories about its famous monks. His descriptions generally conform to what is known about these monks from other sources, and he is often himself the source of important information that has become part of the received tradition about these monks.

The prosopography of Scetis (as of the whole of monastic Egypt) is notoriously difficult. The usual historical challenges of fragmentary or lost evidence are compounded by the extraordinary mobility of ancient monks. It was not unusual for them to live in several places during their monastic careers. They might change locale in pursuit of a monastic elder, to shun fame, to practice detachment, or to escape what they perceived to be the degeneration of a particular group. Often a move was prompted by external forces, such as the expulsion of Athanasian monks from Egypt in the 370s, the diaspora after the condemnation of Origenism in 400, the devastation of Scetis by nomadic marauders in 407–8. Furthermore, monks with the same name were often confused in the literary sources (the most famous example is that of Macarius the Alexandrian and Macarius the Egyptian). In the *Alphabetical Collection* of the *Apophthegmata*, sayings of several different monks of the same name were often gathered together under a single heading (here the most obvious example is Poemen).

In *Conferences* 1–10 Cassian uses monks of Scetis as oracles of monastic teaching he considers (and presumed they would have considered) to be traditional. The formulations, of course, must not be assumed to have been theirs. The Scetic matrix of the *Conferences*, however, can contain historically reliable material even if the theological content is Cassian's own synthesis of many sources.

Cassian's references to Abbas Moses and Paphnutius were discussed in chapter 1. Here I will consider the other monks of Scetis to whom Cassian attributes *Conferences*.

Conferences 4–8: *Daniel, Sarapion, and Serenus*

Abba Daniel of *Conference* 4, says Cassian, was designated by Paphnutius to succeed him as presbyter of their congregation in Scetis but predeceased him (*Conf.* 4.1).[23] Sarapion (*Conf.* 5), mentioned elsewhere in the *Conferences*, emerges as a seasoned, humble monk with unsophisticated theological views.[24] Cassian's description of Serenus (*Conf.* 7–8) as "a mirror of his name" and the attribution to him of a *Conference* on stability amidst trials may seem too conveniently apposite, though he is mentioned again later as an example of extraordinary chastity (*Conf.* 12.7.6), and one of the sayings of "Serenus" in the *Alphabetical Collection* is about constancy when away from the cell.[25]

Conferences 9–10: *Isaac*

There are various mentions in the literature of Isaacs with Scetic links. Cassian's Isaac is perhaps the anchorite of Scetis mentioned in Ammon's letter to Theophilus of Alexandria.[26] An Isaac who was a disciple of Serenus (perhaps Cassian's Serenus), accompanied his elder on a visit to Poemen,[27] and there is an Isaac associated with Poemen in the *Alphabetical Collection*.[28] The possibility of identifying these Isaacs with Cassian's depends at least in part on resolving the chronological questions about Poemen.[29] The Serenus–Isaac link in the saying from the Systematic Collection is noteworthy in light of Cassian's juxtaposition of Serenus' *Conferences* 7–8 and Isaac's *Conferences* 9–10. Isaac's description of Antony as *quem . . . novimus* (*Conf.* 9.31) could derive from a youthful visit with Serenus to Antony at Pispir, where they met Antony's disciple Poemen.

In his *Dialogue on the Life of John Chrysostom*, Palladius includes "Isaac, disciple of Macarius" among the Egyptian monks seeking refuge in Constantinople.[30] This Isaac had memorized the entire Bible; Cassian's Isaac is portrayed as an expert on the relationship between unceasing prayer and the interpretation of Scripture (see *Conf.* 10.10–11). Palladius also notes Isaac's ability to handle perilous "horned snakes" without danger;[31] Cassian's Isaac states that use of the prayer formula from Ps. 69(70):2 enables one to become an "exterminator of deadly serpents" (*Conf.* 10.11.4).[32]

Could Cassian's "Isaac" be the presbyter of Kellia known from the *Apophthegmata*?[33] Cassian does include a *Conference* from Theodore of Kellia among those attributed to monks of Scetis (*Conf.* 6), and it is not impossible that *Conferences* 9–10 are also from there. The theology of these *Conferences* is clearly allied with that of the Evagrian circle at Kellia; while the insertion of the story of the reception at Scetis of Theophilus' Festal Letter of 399 (*Conf.* 10.2–3) between Isaac's two *Conferences* suggests that Isaac, too, was at Scetis, the text does not explicitly state as much. Cassian had good reasons for obscuring any links with Kellia and the Evagrian teaching propounded there.

Conferences 21–23: Theonas

Cassian attributes *Conferences* 21–23 to a Theonas, often assumed to be a monk in the Delta,[34] perhaps because *Conferences* 19–20, as well as *Conference* 24, are set there. However, the last set of *Conferences* is not presented as a geographical unity like *Conferences* 1–10 (Scetis) and *Conferences* 11–17 (Panephysis). Nor is there an itinerary to be traced through these last *Conferences*. *Conference* 18 opens with the departure from Panephysis to visit "the further regions of Egypt" (*ulteriores Aegypti partes*), which in this instance probably means the monasteries of Diolcos,[35] and *Conference* 19 is probably set in Diolcos.[36] But in *Conference* 20 the setting is again Panephysis, home of Pinufius, and that conference ends with a look toward Scetis.[37]

Conferences 21–23 have no explicit links with those that precede or follow, apart from that closing reference to Scetis at the end of *Conference* 20. There is no geographical reference in them that fixes Theonas' location, though the milieu seems to be anchoritic. In *Conferences* 21–23, Cassian's Theonas speaks about the *monasterium* rather than the *coenobium*; *monasterium* is an inclusive label used for both anchoritic and cenobitic dwellings.[38] There are references to "solitude" suggestive of anchoritic life.[39] In *Conference* 2.11 Moses describes an incident at Scetis with his own elder, named Theonas.[40] The *Apophthegmata* by or about Theonas suggest an anchorite with links to Scetis.[41]

Cassian tells us that as a young married man, Theonas had brought an offering to Abba John, who "presided over the *diaconia*," that is, the material goods of the monastic group used both for their own support and for the needs of the poor.[42] On that occasion Abba John spoke about the virtue of free offering to those who had brought tithes and first fruits.[43] Theonas was so moved by the exhortation that he left his wife (without her consent) and fled to the monastery, where he was later "elected" to the *dispensatio diaconiae* after the death of John and of his immediate successor Elias (*Conf.* 21.9.7).[44] Theonas' mentor, Abba John of the *dispensatio diaconiae*, is probably the Abba John who was steward (*oeconomus*) of Scetis at the time of Paphnutius; this Abba John is recorded by Cassian as receiving a gift of figs on behalf of the monks (*Inst.* 5.40.1).[45] The Elias named as John's immediate successor to the post (*Conf.* 21.9.7) is probably "Elias of the ministry (*diakonia*)" mentioned in the *Alphabetical Collection*, though that saying provides no geographical information.[46] The evidence seems to converge on Scetis, rather than either Panephysis or Diolcos, as Theonas' monastic home.

Other Monks of Scetis

One of the sayings of Macarius the Egyptian quoted by Cassian (*Inst.* 5.41) is found also in Evagrius' *Praktikos*, perhaps Cassian's source for it.[47] The story of Macarius raising someone from the dead to refute a Eunomian heretic (*Conf.* 15.3) can be found in somewhat different versions in the *Lausiac History* and in the Latin version of the *History of the Monks in Egypt*.[48] Cassian also uses a saying and two stories of Macarius that are not found anywhere else.[49]

Cassian has two stories about Apollo; one is also found in the chapter on fornication in the *Systematic Collection* of *Apophthegmata* (*Conf.* 2.13).[50] The other (*Conf.* 24.9), also found among the *Apophthegmata*, is about Apollo's way of dealing with family ties.[51] The tradition knows several monks with this name; it is likely that Cassian's Apollo is the "Apollo of Scetis" found in one of the sayings.[52]

Cassian relates the story of Heron, who had an exemplary asceticism but no discernment and fell prey to fatal delusions about his own powers (*Conf.* 2.5). Heron's story has certain affinities with a story Palladius preserves about someone of the same name who was from Kellia; Abba Moses, who tells the story in *Conference* 2, describes Heron as living for fifty years "in this desert." It seems likely that Cassian and Palladius are telling versions of the same story and that the geograpical significance of "in this desert" should not be pressed.[53]

Paphnutius' predecessor as presbyter, the famous Isidore,[54] appears in a story about envy and humility (*Conf.* 18.15–16) also found in the Greek *Systematic Collection*.[55]

Paesius[56] is featured in one story along with "John, superior *(praepositus)* of a large monastery of many brethren" (*Inst.* 5.27),[57] but one learns nothing of historical interest about Paesius from the story, except that he lived "in a vast desert," a description typical of Scetis.[58]

By the time of Cassian's stay in Scetis, Paul, formerly of the "Porphyrion desert" (see the next section), was in residence at Scetis, where Cassian consulted him about accidie (*Inst.* 10.25).

Moses, Calamus, and the "Desert of Calamus or Porphyry"

Cassian's references to "Calamus" have been a source of confusion to his readers and the basis for seriously questioning Cassian's historical reliability. Calamus, Cassian writes, was the home of Abba Moses.[59] Cassian also refers, once, to a desert of "Calamus or Porphyry" (*Conf.* 24.4) associated with nobody in particular. Finally, he writes of the "Porphyrion" desert, home of Abba Paul until he went to Scetis, where Cassian and Germanus consulted him about their struggles against accidie.[60]

Jean-Claude Guy thought that Cassian was confused about Abba Moses, thinking there were two of them: Moses of Scetis, to whom *Conferences* 1–2 are attributed, and another Moses who lived in the eastern or Porphyrion desert.[61] Guy supposed that when Cassian wrote "Calamus" he meant a site in the Porphyrion desert. By associating a Moses with both Scetis and Calamus, Guy concludes, Cassian was dividing into two monks the single Abba Moses even though Cassian's own descriptions combine to form a picture of the famous Nubian. Cassian, suggests Guy, must not have understood what he was writing about. Such an error about a significant figure makes Cassian's claim to have known Moses suspect and casts doubt on Cassian's historical reliability generally.

In fact, Cassian knew but one Moses,[62] and his geographical references make perfect sense. The Calamus of Moses was in Scetis, while the "desert of Calamus or Porphyry" and the "Porphyrion desert" were the same place, in the eastern desert. Cassian had not split one Moses into two, but Guy had read Cassian's remarks about two different places called Calamus as if they were about the same place and then concluded that the problem lay with Cassian's inaccurate knowledge and reporting.

In *Conference* 3, Cassian mentions Moses' history as a repentant murderer and locates him in Calamus, which he describes as "a place in this desert that is called Calamus."[63] Since this *Conference* follows the two attributed to Moses, which were clearly set in Scetis, and describes Moses of Calamus as having attained the "supreme heights of perfection," there can be little doubt that Cassian is still referring to the Moses of *Conferences* 1–2. The second link with Calamus, in *Conference* 7, describes Moses' home as "a place in this solitude that is called Calamus," a description very much like the one in *Conference* 3.[64] The next chapter of *Conference* 7 refers to Moses as "in this desert" (*in hac heremo*), again clearly a reference to Scetis, the site of the *Conference* (*Conf.* 7.27).[65] This region of Scetis is manifestly a different place than the "desert of Calamus or Porphyry" described in *Conference* 24.4.

When one considers the meaning of "Calamus" it is no surprise that there were two monastic sites known to Cassian with the same name, taken from the Greek καλαμός, "reed."[66] It is a common place-name in ancient texts, generally in the form "Calamon" (καλαμῶν) or "reed-bed." At least two other Calamons are known in Egypt, in addition to Cassian's two (which are unknown from other texts).[67]

Moses' Calamus was perhaps the same place known as Petra to which he retired on the recommendation of Macarius the Great.[68] Cassian is quite clear that Moses' Calamus was in Scetis. Scetis was—and still is—a region of marshy areas, including one in view of the site H. G. Evelyn-White identified as Moses' "Petra." A place known as Calamus would be unremarkable in such terrain;[69] E. Amélineau quotes the fifteenth-century Arab writer Al-Maqrizi's description of the papyrus industry at Wadi Al-Natrun.[70] When it comes to place-names, in Egypt or anywhere else, "Rock" and "Reed" are about as generic as one can get.[71] One cannot exclude the possibility of a certain monastic humor that led Moses' brothers to dub his home "Reed" in honor of his namesake's hiding place.[72]

The desert of "Calamus or Porphyry" of *Conference* 24.4, with which Cassian associates no particular figure, is surely the Porphyrion desert of book 10 of the *Institutes*, the *Mons Porphyrites* (modern Jabal Abu Dukhkhan) in the eastern desert, so called from the porphyry stone quarried there (*Inst.* 10.24).[73] In *Conference* 24.4, Abba Abraham refers to the "vast solitude" of the desert of Calamus or Porphyry, which requires seven or eight days' journey to reach. Because the labor there is agricultural, the monks are not accustomed to staying within the monastic enclosure and practicing stillness as is done at Scetis and at Abraham's own "squalid" location at Diolcos.[74] The mention of agriculture indicates the presence of water, probably a spring as at Antony's Inner Mountain;[75] this could explain the alternative name "Calamus."

Secondhand Tales

Despite the intention to visit "even the remotest desert of the Thebaid" (*Conf.* 11.1), we have neither claim nor evidence that Cassian actually visited the Pachomian monks of Upper Egypt,[76] the sites associated with Saint Antony at Pispir or at the Inner Mountain, or Lycopolis, home of the famous hermit John. Antony himself had been dead for thirty years; Cassian knew the *Life of Antony* and the traditions from which it was drawn,[77] as well as the oral tradition about Antony that contributed to the *Apophthegmata*.[78] Samuel Rubenson has noted parallels with the *Letters* of Antony.[79] Antony is credited with two sayings on prayer that are found nowhere else (*Conf.* 9.31);[80] these may well have come from Evagrian circles and been attributed to Antony. As the great exemplar of the solitary life, material attributed to him could be presented as authoritative monastic doctrine.[81] Cassian includes Paul (probably Jerome's "Paul the Theban") in such statements.[82] John of Lycopolis was a recluse in the Thebaid, an area unvisited by Cassian and Germanus. John plays much the same role as Antony, that of a model to be invoked for illustrative purposes.[83]

Monks Unknown from Other Sources

Finally, there are Egyptian monks whom Cassian names in edifying (or unedifying) stories but who are otherwise unknown. Cassian's Patermuthius (*Inst.* 4.27–28) bears no resemblance to the one described in the *History of the Monks in Egypt*,[84] but Cassian appears to have modelled his story of the monk who preferred monastic obedience to his paternal duties on a story also found in the *Alphabetical Collection*, though attributed there to Sisoes.[85] Three other monks— Andronicus (possessed by a demon, freed by holy communion, *Conf.* 7.30.3), Benjamin (disobedient and departed from the monastic life, *Conf.* 2.24), and Machetes (who stayed awake during spiritual conversation but became narcoleptic when talk turned to gossip, *Inst.* 5.29)—are unknown from other sources.

Notes

Chapter 1

1. *Conf. Pref.* 1 6. All references to Cassian's works are to the edition of Petschenig in CSEL 13 and 17. References are to work (*Inst., Conf., De Inc.*), book or *Conf.* number, chapter, and (where necessary) section. In the interest of economy of citation page numbers have been omitted.

2. See Chadwick, *John Cassian* (1950 ed.), 6.

3. Noted by Guy, *Jean Cassien*, 12.

4. "John Cassian on John Cassian," 432. I find more recoverable biographical and historical data in Cassian's writings, however, than Frank allows.

5. The best walk-throughs are in Marrou, "Jean Cassien à Marseille," 5–17; Chadwick, *John Cassian* (1950 ed.), 190–98; Cappuyns, "Cassien," 1320–22. For pre-twentieth-century scholarship, Cuper's review in the *Acta Sanctorum* is lucid and judicious.

6. Iohannes: *Inst.* 5.35, *Conf.* 14.9.4.

7. Cappuyns suggests that Cassian used Iohannes anachronistically in *Inst.* and *Conf.* in memory of John Chrysostom, whom he met only after leaving Egypt ("Cassien," 1319). Marrou thinks Iohannes was his given name and Cassianus was an ethnic name used to link him to a certain district near Histria in Scythia Minor ("La patrie de Jean Cassien," 595–96).

8. See *TLL Onomasticon* 2, cols. 238–39. John Cassian is no. 15 of the entries in *DHGE*. Pauly's *Realencyclopädie* devotes almost one hundred pages to the name Cassius and its derivatives.

9. However, Marrou notes inscriptional evidence in support of the Balkan hypothesis ("La patrie de Jean Cassien"); see further, Coman, "Le patrimoine de l'oecuménisme," 63–65.

10. The chronology is constructed backward from the hints we have: in 403–04 he was working with John Chrysostom; it is likely he left Egypt in 400 as a result of the Origenist crisis (we know he was there as late as 399); he spent several years in Egypt and in his early days there he could still be described as youthful; he spent only a few years in Bethlehem; he entered the monastery in Bethlehem very probably before Jerome's community was founded in 386; he was very young when he entered; thus a birthdate in the early 360s makes sense. The details of this chronology will be explored hereafter. For a schematic overview of suggested chronologies, see Summa, *Geistliche Unterscheidung bei Johannes Cassian*, 5 n. 10.

11. Zelzer notes that the generic nature of this description renders it useless for local-ization ("*Cassianus natione Scytha*," 164); in combination with the comment about cold weather, it has been read as referring both to Gaul (e.g., Cappuyns, "Cassien," 1321) and to the Dobrudja, as Chadwick notes in *John Cassian* (1950 ed.), 195.

12. The parallel with Cassian's characterization of Gaul as cold and frozen in *Conf. Pref.* 2 is adduced as an argument in favor of Gaul as his birthplace; see, for example, Cappuyns, "Cassien," 1321. See note 13.

13. This description would fit the Arianism of the Goths in Scythia Minor. Coman quotes Dionysius Exiguus' words, "Scythia quae frigoribus simul et barbaris probatur esse terribilis" (*Praefatio Dionysii Exigui ad Joannem et Leontium*, CCL 85, p. 55, in Coman, "Les 'Scythes' Jean Cassien et Denys le Petit," 29 n.3).

14. Cappuyns suggests this statement echoes that in *Conf. Pref.* 3 about the scarcity of anchorites in Gaul ("Cassien," 1321). Coman notes the emerging monastic presence in the Dobrudja ("Le patrimoine de l'oecuménisme," 65–66 and 75).

15. Frank suggests that Cassian alludes to information known to his audience in Gaul—that not only was Cassian's sister with him in Marseilles but that they were natives, living in monasteries established by Cassian from their family wealth ("John Cassian on John Cassian," 422–25).

16. Abel, *Studien zu dem gallischen Presbyter Johannes Cassianus*, 11–12; followed by Cappuyns, "Cassien," 1321, and Frank, "John Cassian on John Cassian," 422.

17. *De vir. inlustr.* 62 (p. 82.7).

18. Scetis: most notably Petschenig, "Prolegomena" (CSEL 17, pp. iv–v); Gibson, "Prolegomena," 183–84; Abel, *Studien zu dem gallischen Presbyter Johannes Cassianus*, 13; revived by Zelzer, "*Cassianus natione Scytha*" and Frank, "John Cassian on John Cassian," 425–26. Scythia Minor: argued vigorously by Marrou, "Jean Cassien à Marseille," 5–17, and "La patrie de Jean Cassien," *passim*, following the lead of Tillemont, *Mémoires pour servir à l'histoire ecclésiastique des six premiers siècles*, 14: 739–40; Cuper, *Acta Sanctorum*, 462A–64A; Zahn, "Neuere Beiträge zur Geschichte des apostolischen Symbolums," 29–33; Mer-kle, "Cassian kein Syrer" (Merkle rebuts Hoch's suggestion that Cassian was born near Bethlehem); Schwartz, "Cassian und Nestorius," 1–2, and "Lebensdaten Cassians," 1–4. At the conclusion of his thorough review of the arguments in the 1950 edition of *John Cas-sian*, Chadwick inclined toward the Dobrudja (p. 198); the much shorter discussion in the 1968 edition (p. 9) simply notes Marrou's "La patrie de Jean Cassien." Pichery followed Marrou (introduction to *Jean Cassien*, 8–9), as did Guy (*Jean Cassien*, 14–15). See also Coman's helpful "Le patrimoine de l'oecuménisme chrétien du quatrième au cinquième siècles en Scythe-Mineure (Dobrudja)," especially 63–66, and "Les 'Scythes' Jean Cassien et Denys le Petit," 27–31; Damian's "Some Critical Considerations and New Arguments" summarizes earlier debates.

19. Athens: mentioned in the first lesson for the feast of Saint Cassian in the sixteenth-century breviary from Saint Victor in Marseilles, as in Cuper, *Acta Sanctorum*, 460B; see his efforts to resolve the contradiction with the same office's hymn, which mentions *natione Scythicus* (p. 461AB). Palestine: Hoch, "Zur Heimat des Johannes Cassianus" (near Bethlehem) and Ménager, "La patrie de Cassien" (Scythopolis), following Bulteau's sug-gestion in the seventeenth century (as in Cuper, *Acta Sanctorum*, 461B). Sert: Thibaut, *L'ancienne liturgie gallicane*, 103–10.

20. Photius writes: Ῥώμην λαχόντος πατρίδα, "belonging to a Roman family/lin-eage" (*Bibliotheca* cod. 197, as in Petschenig, CSEL 17, p. xcvii). Marrou, "Jean Cassien à Marseille," 9. Note Cuper's argument that Photius uses "Roman" in the narrow sense of someone from the imperial capital, that is, Constantinople. Since Scythia Minor, as part of the ecclesiastical province of Thrace, was under the patriarchal jurisdiction of Constan-

tinople, Cassian as a native of Scythia could by extension be described as a "Roman" (Cuper, *Acta Sanctorum*, 463A–64A).

21. For details of the Greek tradition of Cassian's works, see the section on Legacy later in this chapter.

22. See Coman, "Le patrimoine de l'oecuménisme chrétien du quatrième au cinquième siècles en Scythe-Mineure (Dobrudja)," 69–78, and "Les 'Scythes' Jean Cassien et Denys le Petit," 38–46, emphasizing the parallel with Dionysius Exiguus.

23. See Paucker, "Die Latinität des Johannes Cassianus"; Abel, *Studien zu dem gallischen Presbyter Johannes Cassianus*, 15–17 (though the arguments about dialect are by no means definitive); Marrou, "Jean Cassien à Marseille," 8. Tillemont, however, thought Cassian probably learned Latin from westerners living in Bethlehem, and considered Cassian's Latin style to be "very obscure and not very Latin" (*Mémoires pour servir à l'histoire ecclésiastique des six premiers siècles*, 14:159 and 176). Cassian's own remarks about his education in *Conf.* 14.12 do not indicate whether he learned his profane literature in Latin, Greek or both; elsewhere he quotes Cicero, Virgil, and Persius (all in *De Inc.*, though he mentions Virgil in *Inst.* 12.19) but no Greek classical authors (see Abel, *Studien zu dem gallischen Presbyter Johannes Cassianus*, 24–25).

24. See *Conf.* 16.1, on conversing with Abba Joseph in Greek; *Inst.* 5.39 about another monk in Egypt who knew only Latin; *Conf. Pref.* 1 6 on translating what he had heard in Egypt into Latin for the benefit of his readers. On Cassian's Greek, see Courcelle, *Late Latin Writers and Their Greek Sources*, 227, and Stewart, "From λόγος to *verbum*," with a review of all instances in which he actually uses Greek words.

25. Many of his Latin biblical quotations are clearly based on the Septuagint (LXX) he had memorized as a young monk, and he cited the actual Greek of the LXX and New Testament several times; see chapter 2 and Stewart, "From λόγος to *verbum*," 15–17 (to the list of quotations from the LXX in n. 85 must be added Eccl. 5:3 as in *Conf.* 9.12.1). In *De Inc.* he refers to several Greek theological texts.

26. There were Greek cities along the western shore of the Black Sea and Latin cities inland and along the Danube (see Popescu, "Zur Geschichte der Stadt in Kleinskythien"). On the implications for Cassian, see Zahn, "Neuere Beiträge zur Geschichte des apostolischen Symbolums," 31–33; Marrou, "La patrie de Jean Cassien," 593–95; Coman, "Le patrimoine de l'oecuménisme chrétien du quatrième au cinquième siècles en Scythe-Mineure (Dobrudja)," 76–77 and 81–83; Damian, "Some Critical Considerations," 261–64.

27. For culture and monastic life in Scythia Minor in this period, with an emphasis on Dionysius Exiguus, see Coman, "Le patrimoine de l'oecuménisme chrétien du quatrième au cinquième siècles en Scythe-Mineure (Dobrudja)" and "Les 'Scythes' Jean Cassien et Denys le Petit," *passim*; less thorough is Damian, "Some Critical Considerations and New Arguments," 266–72. On Dionysius, see Berschin, *Greek Letters and the Latin Middle Ages*, 79–81. Zelzer argues that Cassiodorus' note about Dionysius (*monachus Scytha natione*, *Div. litt.* 1.23 [col. 1137B]) refers to Dionysius' links with Egypt, not Scythia Minor, in the same way that Zelzer claims Gennadius' *natione Scytha* refers to Cassian's sojourn in Scetis ("*Cassianus natione Scytha*," 167–68). However, Dionysius' *Praefatio ad Iohannem et Leontium* 1 (p. 55.3–4), noted earlier, refers both to the cold weather in Scythia and to Dionysius' being a native of the region: despite the cool desert nights, one would hardly describe Scetis as "beset by cold weather"!

28. See, for example, Loseby, "Marseille," *passim*.

29. Since Cassian says nothing about having met Jerome in Bethlehem, it is presumed that he and Germanus had left for Egypt before Jerome settled there in 386.

30. We know from *Conf.* 16.1 that they were friends rather than blood brothers; *Conf.*

24 witnesses to their common homeland; *Conf.* 1.1 and 16.1 state that Germanus and Cassian were together from the outset of their monastic lives, both in the cenobium (Bethlehem) and in the desert (Egypt); *Conf.* 17 is about their shared dilemma about returning or not to Bethlehem.

31. See the section on "Constantinople and Rome."

32. In *Inst.* 4.21 he mentions the desert regions near the Dead Sea; in *Conf.* 6.1–2 he speaks more specifically of the area near Tekoa, though the incident described there seems to date not from their own time in Palestine but to have happened while they were in Egypt.

33. *Hist. Laus.* 36 (p. 107.1–2); see Epiphanios, *Enarr. Syr.* (col. 264B). Noted by Schiwietz, *Das morgenländische Mönchtum*, 2.153–54, and Bagatti, *Gli antichi edifici sacri di Betlemme*, 236–37.

34. *Inst. Pref.* 5 and *De Inc.* 7.26.1–2. On Cassian and Jerome, see Driver's "From Palestinian Ignorance to Egyptian Wisdom."

35. See Kelly's summary of the evidence in *Jerome*, 130–34.

36. Frank is not convinced: he thinks Cassian and Germanus may well have arrived after 386 and been in Jerome's community ("John Cassian on John Cassian," 428–29).

37. Kelly, *Jerome*, 134.

38. Cassian knew much of the Greek Bible by heart; he doubtless learned it in the course of his monastic *meditatio* and liturgical prayer (see chapter 2). This deep familiarity was probably rooted in diligent study and memorization as a young monk in Bethlehem. Presumably he and Germanus spoke Greek with Abba Pinufius in Bethlehem, and certainly used Greek with the monks they met in Egypt (*Conf.* 16.1). Cassian gives us no hint of an experience of Latin monasticism in Palestine.

39. *Inst.* 3.4. See Taft, *Liturgy of the Hours*, 191–209 on this new office, not to be confused with the liturgical hour of Prime.

40. See *Conf.* 11.1 and 5; *Conf.* 17.2, 17.5, 17.7, 18.1.4, 18.3, 18.16.15. See Driver, "From Palestinian Ignorance to Egyptian Wisdom."

41. *Inst. Pref.* 4: (re. the eastern monks) *a pueritia nostra inter eosdem constituti; Inst.* 3.4.1: *[Iesus Christus] dignatus nostram quoque adhuc in religione teneram et lactantem infantiam sua gratia confirmavit; Conf.* 11.1: while *in coenobio Syriae consistentes post prima fidei rudimenta* they went to Egypt; *Conf.* 11.5: having learned *de Bethleemitici coenobii rudimentis; Conf.* 17.7, the monks of Bethlehem *qui nos docuerunt a parvulis.*

42. *Inst.* 4.31; *Conf.* 20.1.5. Chadwick is bothered by this doublet, but unnecessarily so (*John Cassian*, 41).

43. *Conf.* 17.2.2: *ut vel cursim liceret nobis huius provinciae sanctos ac monasteria circuire;* 17.5.3: *ut postquam velocissimo reditu iuris iurandi fuerit inpleta condicio, haec denuo loca celeri repetamus recursu.*

44. *Conf.* 20.2.1: *post non longum tempus.*

45. *Conf.* 14.9.4: *aetas . . . adulescentior.*

46. See Chadwick, *John Cassian*, 20; Frank, "John Cassian on John Cassian," 427.

47. *Inst.* 2.5 and *Conf.* 18. 5–8. See the remarks of Vogüé in "Monachisme et Église dans la pensée de Cassien," 214–22.

48. See the analysis in chapter 5.

49. Most notably by Guy, who remarked: "sa documentation en ce domaine est souvent fantaisiste" (*Les Apophtegmes des Pères*, 1:44); see "Cassien, historien du monachisme?" and his more recent comments in "Cassian, Saint John," 461–64. Nonetheless Guy ended up basing much of the prosopographical section of *Les Apophtegmes des Pères* (1:46–73) on the same "fanciful" evidence. Frank is cautious in "John Cassian on John Cassian."

For a more positive view of Cassian's trustworthiness, see Butler, *Lausiac History*, 1:203–8 (though he goes too far, as in his acceptance of *Conf.* 10.1–3 as accurate reporting); Chadwick, *John Cassian*, 18–22; Devos, "Saint Jean Cassien," 73.

50. See Weber's *Die Stellung des Johannes Cassianus zur ausserpachomianischen Mönchstradition* for parallels between Cassian and contemporary monastic literature and an attempt to identify when Cassian was dependent on, independent of, or the source for other texts.

51. See the appendix for an analysis of prosopographical and geographical information not covered in this chapter.

52. Petschenig, CSEL 13, p. 499 n., noted by Chadwick, *John Cassian*, 15–18. Chadwick suggests that this manuscript evidence may call into question the assumption that Cassian spent several years in Egypt; Frank finds the suggestion attractive ("John Cassian on John Cassian," 430).

53. See the appendix for Cassian's secondhand tales about places and people he never visited.

54. Cappuyns is among those who does so ("Cassien," 1323–25) though Chadwick is cautious (*John Cassian*, 15), and Frank is skeptical ("John Cassian on John Cassian," 427–28). Rousseau, writing about the next phase of Cassian's life, notes the importance of unearthing whatever historical information can be found (*Ascetics, Authority, and the Church*, 170–71).

55. On Thennesus, see Amélineau, *La Géographie de l'Égypte*, 507–8, and Maspero and Wiet, *Matériaux pour servir à la géographie de l'Égypte*, 60–61.

56. Cassian's writings are the only extant texts that refer to Archebius. LeQuien uses *Conf.* 11.2 to place Archebius between Philip, who attended the Council of Nicea in 325, and Ammonius, who was at the Council of Ephesus in 431 (*Oriens Christianus*, 2:547C); Fedalto follows LeQuien (*Hierarchia Ecclesiastica Orientalis*, 2:607). Bishop Archebius is probably not the same person as the Archebius mentioned in *Conf.* 7.26 as having been an associate of Paul, anchorite at Panephysis: see the appendix.

57. On Panephysis, see Coquin and Martin, "Monasteries in the Daqahliyyah Province," 1648. The ancient town was on the site of modern al-Manzalah, or somewhat farther north, depending on how one interprets the various (and contradictory) data about the town's location with respect to Lake Manzalah; Cassian describes the town's destruction by flooding and the consequent transformation of agricultural land into salt marshes, which would indicate that the ancient town may have been north of the present site, in the area now covered by Lake Manzalah. See Amélineau, *La géographie de l'Égypte*, 64–65 and 301 (on Panephysis) and Maspero and Weit, *Matériaux pour servir à la géographie de l'Égypte*, 35–36 (on Lake Manzalah).

58. *Conf.* 11.3; see *Conf.* 7.26. A bishop of Panephysis is recorded as late as the Council of Ephesus. Cassian's observation about the compatibility of monastic asceticism with episcopal service was surely meant to console (and to challenge) monk-bishops in Gaul.

59. Bagnall notes that bilingualism was probably rather widespread among monks, at least in the Delta (*Egypt in Late Antiquity*, 244–45).

60. *Conf.* 19.1 may suggest that Cassian and Germanus returned to Panephysis to see Abba Paul's monastery after their visit to Diolcos, though this is not certain.

61. On Diolcos and the uncertainty shrouding its exact location, see Coquin and Martin, "Diolkos," 908, and their article "Monasteries in the Gharbiyyah Province," 1651–52. In any case it was on the coast, at a mouth of the Nile itself or of a tributary, on the site of modern Dumyat (also known as Damietta) or a few miles to the west. Cassian's topographical description in *Conf.* 18.1.1–2 corresponds to that of *Inst.* 5.36.1–2 with the

mention of river, sea, and mountains. Other mentions of Diolcos in early monastic literature contain similar details. See Sozomen, *Hist. eccl.* 6.29.7–8 (pp. 279.23–80.5), on Diolcos and its two famous monasteries under Piamun and John. Other texts refer to travel
by boat to the "mountains" of the area; see *Apoph. Anon.* Nau 614 (p. 261), *Hist. mon.*
Epil. 8 (p. 137.31–35), and especially *Anon.* Nau 459 (p. 154) on the female sightseer who
moors her boat at "the mountain of the monks" and sits up on the hill above the river,
creating something of a sensation.

62. "When we beginners had scarcely come *(admodum venissemus)* from the monasteries of Palestine to the town of Egypt that is called Diolcos" *(Inst.* 5.36.1). It would be
natural to understand this statement as a reference to their initial arrival in Egypt, were it
not for the clear indications in *Conf.* 11.1 and *Conf.* 18.1 that Thennesus and then Panephysis, in the eastern Delta, were in fact the first ports of call.

63. Latin *monasterium,* an example of Cassian's inclusive use of the term for the
dwelling-place of both anchorites and cenobites. According to *Inst.* 5.36, the anchorites of
Diolcos had begun in the cenobium and then proceeded to solitude; however, it is unclear
whether and for how long Archebius was a cenobite.

64. His monastic detachment was not absolute, for he paid off family debts with the
proceeds from his manual labor: see Cassian's skeptical view in *Conf.* 4.20.1 and *Conf.* 24
of depending on one's relatives for financial support.

65. For John, see the appendix.

66. Piamun is known from *Hist. mon.* 25 (p. 134) and Sozomen, *Hist. eccl.* 6.29.7–8
(pp. 279.23–280.5). Both clearly refer to Cassian's Piamun, though Cassian does not relate
their story of Piamun's visions during the eucharist.

67. This term was actually the invention of the Master in one of the great satirical
passages of monastic literature *(Reg. Mag.* 1.13–74, pp. 332–46), severely abbreviated by
Benedict *(Reg. Ben.* 1.10–11, pp. 438–40).

68. The area is still home to four Coptic monasteries. On Scetis see Amélineau, *La
géographie de l'Égypte,* 433–52, and Maspero and Weit, *Matériaux pour servir à la géographie de l'Égypte,* 226–27, though they assumed that Nitria and Scetis were both at Wadi al-
Natrun; Bousset, "Das Mönchtum der sketischen Wüste"; Evelyn-White's important *The
Monasteries of the Wâdi 'n Natrûn,* 2:60–144; Guy, "Le Centre monastique de Scété" (see
pp. 144–46 on Cassian) and the section of the same title in *Les Apophtegmes des Pères,*
1:35–46; Giamberardini and Gelsi, "Scete"; Cody, "Scetis," 2102–6; Gould, *The Desert Fathers on Monastic Community,* 9–17.

69. On the hearsay character of much early writing on Scetis, see Guy's two articles
just cited. Although the author of *Hist. mon.* mentions Scetis *(Hist. mon.* 23.1, pp. 130–31),
the information is secondhand; Rufinus' Latin translation draws on a more informed tradition *(Hist. mon. [Ruf.]* 29.2, p. 370). Palladius' eyewitness account is the first, published
around 419–20, just before Cassian's; see especially *Hist. Laus.* 23 and 26 (pp. 75.6–8 and
81.15–17) and Guy's analysis in "Le centre monastique de Scété," 142–44.

70. *Conf. Pref.* 1 2 and 7; *Conf.* 1.1, 3.1.1, 10.2.3, 18.15.1 and 18.16.15. See Guy's analysis
in "Le centre monastique de Scété," 145–46.

71. *Conf.* 1–10 follow this plan (though *Conf.* 6 is located at Kellia; see next note);
Conf. 21–23 also are set in Scetis (see the appendix). On the relationship between the
Institutes and the *Conferences,* see chapter 2.

72. *Conf.* 6 is attributed to Theodore, a monk of Kellia, even though in both *Conf.
Pref.* 1 and *Conf. Pref.* 2, Cassian assigns *Conf.* 1–10 to monks of Scetis *(Conf. Pref.* 1 2, has
. . . *decem conlationes summorum patrum, id est anachoretarum qui in heremo Sciti mora-
bantur; Conf. Pref.* 2 2, decem conlationes in Scitiotica heremo commorantium patrum).
The second statement is particularly significant, since it was written *after Conf.* 6.

73. Cassian was not the only ancient writer who referred to "Scetis" in such an inclusive manner; see Evelyn-White, *Monasteries of the Wâdi 'n Natrûn*, 2.30, and Guy, "Le centre monastique," *passim*. For example, Evagrius described himself as ἐν τῇ Σκίτει καθεζομένῳ (*Prak. Prol. 1, p. 482.2*).

74. *Conf.* 3.1.1, 10.2.3; see 18.15.1. Paphnutius' Origenist leanings are inferred from his criticism of Anthropomorphism (*Conf.* 10.2–3); corollary information from other sources supports viewing him as a monastic Origenist like Antony the Great (as demonstrated by Antony's letters).

75. On his ties to the monastery in Bethlehem, see *Inst.* 3.4.1 and 4.31 *(nostrum monasterium); Conf.* 17.30.2 *(coenobium nostrum)*.

76. *Conf.* 17.30.2: *remeavimus.* Gibson suggests that their first visit to Scetis came *after* the return to Bethlehem, but this deduction does not seem to fit the text ("Prolegomena," 86). This is the passage Chadwick noted is missing from one of the oldest manuscripts and may have been a later addition; see note 52.

77. Cassian's comments match in broad outline the picture of Moses in Palladius' *Hist. Laus.* 19 (pp. 58.14–62.15) and the sayings (eighteen of them in *Apoph. Alph.* Moses cols. 281B–89C). There are some ambiguities, however: Cassian never mentions Moses' blackness, the point of several of the *Apoph.*; his geographical references are confusing (see the appendix on the desert of Calamus); he does not mention Moses' murder by the Saracens (*Alph.* Moses 10, col. 283BC); *Conf.* 2.2.1 could be taken to suggest that as a child Moses knew Antony in the Thebaid (although it need not be taken so literally). On the other hand, Cassian knew Moses' criminal history (*Conf.* 3.5.2) and linked him to Macarius the Great in an otherwise unknown story (*Conf.* 7.27). It may be that Cassian thought Moses' race to be of no particular import; he may not have known of Moses' murder in 406/7, some years after Cassian had left Egypt. Butler distinguishes four or possibly five different monks with the name of Moses (*Lausiac History*, 2:197–98), though more recent work has found a greater coherence among the various traditions (see Sauget, "Mosè," and Devos, "Saint John Cassian"). For Guy's claim that Cassian mistakenly thought there were two different monks named Moses, one of Scetis and the other of "Calamus" near the Red Sea, see the appendix. For a collection of sources (though without Cassian's evidence), see Wicker, "Ethiopian Moses"; Wimbush analyzes the stories in "Ascetic Behavior and Color-ful Language."

78. See also *Conf.* 1 and 2 *passim*, 3.5.2, 7.26–27, 19.9.

79. *Conf.* 3.5.2, *in loco istius heremi qui Calamus nuncupatur; Conf.* 7.26.2, *qui habitavit locum huius solitudinis qui Calamus nuncupatur,* followed in 7.27 by a story of an encounter between Moses and Macarius. Moses' Calamus is a different location from the Calamus mentioned in *Conf.* 24.4 as another name for the Porphyrion desert; see the appendix.

80. See *Alph.* Macarius the Egyptian 22 (col. 272B) and Moses 13 (col. 283A). As Guy points out, this "Petra" must be distinguished from the one near Clysma associated with Sisoes (*Alph.* Gerontios [col. 153AB], Sisoes 23 and 33 [cols. 400C and 404A]); it is also clearly not the Petra of Troë associated with Arsenius, which was near Memphis (*Alph.* Arsenius 32, 34, 42 [cols. 100B, 101B, 108A]); Evelyn-White seems to confuse Arsenius' Petra with Moses' (*Monasteries of the Wâdi 'n Natrûn*, 2:124). Amélineau sifts the data on sites within Scetis and suggests that the "Petra" of Moses is the same as the "Rock of Macarius," at the southeastern end of Wadi al-Natrun (*La géographie de l'Égypte*, 442 and 447–48), but this site does not seem isolated enough to match the indications in the sayings. Evelyn-White suggests that the "Rock of Sheit" (modern Karet el Muluk), some fifteen kilometers farther up the wadi, is the correct site for Petra (see *Monasteries of the Wâdi 'n Natrûn*, 2:37–38, 2:304, 3:4, and 3:29). The remoteness of the site and its proximity to Deir al-

Baramus, a present-day monastery in Wadi al-Natrun, support Evelyn-White's suggestion; the monks of Deir al-Baramus claim to have the relics of both Isidore and Moses (and perhaps Paphnutius as well), and believe that a site under excavation fifty meters beyond the present inner monastic enclosure was the ancient "monastery of Moses."

81. Paphnutius has six sayings in *Apoph. Alph.* (cols. 377C–380D; no. 6 is in *Alph. Supp.*, p. 31); there is a story about him among the sayings of Macarius the Egyptian (no. 37, cols. 277D–80A); see also the saying in *Boh.*, p. 178. Some confusion exists about whether Cassian's Paphnutius "the Bubal" (Βούβαλος, a desert buffalo or antelope; see Sophocles, *Greek Lexicon*, 313b) is the same person as the Paphnutius Kephalas described by Palladius in *Hist. Laus.* 47 (pp. 137.3–142.10) and generally associated with Nitria (though Melania meets someone at Nitria in 373 whom Palladius refers to as "Paphnutius of Scetis," *Hist. Laus.* 46.2, p. 134.13). Butler argued that Cassian and Palladius were describing the same person and adduced parallels between Paphnutius' address on the perils of monastic life in *Hist. Laus.* 47 and the remarks in *Conf.* 3.20, attributed by Cassian to Paphnutius (*Lausiac History*, 2:224–25). Evelyn-White (*Monasteries of the Wâdi 'n Natrûn*, 2:120–22) and Guy (*Les Apophtegmes des Pères*, 1:59 n.4) agree with Butler. Guillaumont lays out the evidence with care and tact ("Paphnutius of Scetis, Saint," 1884–85). See also Sauget, "Pafnuzio," 26–28.

82. See *Inst.* 5.40; *Conf.* 2.5.4, 3.1–4, 4.1.1–2, 10.2–3, 15.10, 18.15–16, 19.9.1.

83. *Conf.* 3.1.2–3 and *Conf.* 18.15.1. See Florovsky, "Theophilus of Alexandria and Apa Aphou of Pemdje," 104–5 and 128–29.

84. See Evelyn-White's summary of the evidence in *Monasteries of the Wâdi 'n Natrûn*, 2.120–21.

85. His anti-Anthropomorphitism supports identifying Cassian's Paphnutius Bubalis with the Paphnutius Kephalas of Palladius and some of the sayings.

86. *Lausiac History*, 1:206–08. Butler thinks the vividness an argument for the historicity of Cassian's account; I argue in chapter 5 that Cassian's narrative is a literary construction, though certainly based on a genuine controversy and perhaps an actual event.

87. See the appendix for information on all these monks.

88. *Conf.* 15.3: *qui habitationem Scitioticae solitudinis primus invenit*; see *Hist. mon.* 23.1 (p. 130), confusing the two Macarii and referring to Macarius of Alexandria as ὃς εἰς τὴν Σκῆτιν πρῶτος μοναστήριον ἔπηξεν; see Evelyn-White, *Monasteries of the Wâdi 'n Natrûn*, 2.65.

89. See Guillaumont, "Macaire l'Égyptien ou le Grand" and "Macarius the Egyptian, Saint"; Bunge, "Evagre le Pontique et les deux Macaire"; Guy, *Les Apophtegmes des Pères*, 1:47–49. On confusion between Macarius the Great and Macarius the Alexandrian, see Guillaumont, "Le problème des deux Macaire." Cassian alludes to Macarius the Alexandrian in *Conf.* 19.9.1, when Abba John acclaims the anchoritic purity of Abba Moses, Paphnutius, and "the two Macarii." The "Abba Macarius" of *Conf.* 14.4.2, praised by Abba Nesteros for the his guest house in Alexandria, is identified by Butler as the Macarius of Palladius' *Hist. Laus.* 6.5 (see *Lausiac History*, 2:194).

90. See Bunge, "Évagre le Pontique et les deux Macaire" and Guillaumont, "Le problème des deux Macaire," 49–52.

91. According to Palladius, Macarius died a year before he himself arrived in the desert, which was ca. 390 (*Hist. Laus.* 17, p. 47.19–21). Perhaps the phrase *beatus Macarius* in *Inst.* 5.41 and *Conf.* 15.3 can be taken to refer to Macarius' death. Guillaumont assumes that Cassian and Germanus arrived in Scetis after the death of Macarius, but he provides no reason for his conclusion: perhaps it is the lack of any mention of a meeting ("Macaire l'Égyptien ou le Grand," 12). Cappuyns ("Cassien," 1324) and others have taken *Conf.* 14.4.2 as referring to the death of Macarius the Great; this passage, however, refers to

Macarius the Hosteller. It may be that Cassian was cautious about highlighting Macarius too much, given the links they both shared with Evagrius.

92. In *Conf.* 17.30.2 Cassian refers to the "frequent letters" he and Germanus sent back to Bethlehem; presumably they received this news from Bethlehem by letter.

93. For an overview, see Guillaumont et al., "Kellia." On the history of Kellia, see Guillaumont, "Histoire du site des Kellia d'après les documents écrits" and "Histoire des moines aux Kellia." Kellia is of particular interest to modern scholars because it is at least partially accessible to archeological exploration (unlike Nitria, located in a region now heavily settled); on the site itself, see Daumas, "Origine des fouilles, Description du site."

94. *Conf.* 6.1.2: *singularem in conversatione actuali; Inst.* 5.33: *summa sanctitate et scientia . . . non solum in actuali vita, sed etiam notitia scripturarum.*

95. As noted earlier. Frank finds setting *Conf.* 6 in Kellia to be problematic; he seems to suggest that Cassian may not have visited Kellia at all ("John Cassian on John Cassian," 427–28). I think Cassian was at Kellia but had good reasons to be somewhat reserved about his contacts there because of controversy over Evagrius.

96. A Roman mile was about fifteen hundred meters. At its maximum, the distance from Scetis to Kellia is about sixty-five kilometers; Palladius' forty miles ($\sigma\eta\mu\epsilon\widehat{\iota}\alpha$) is therefore quite accurate (*Hist. Laus.* 26, p. 81.16–17). Kellia is approximately eighteen kilometers south of Nitria; *Apoph. Alph.* Antony 34 (col. 88A) accurately measures it as twelve miles ($\sigma\eta\mu\epsilon\widehat{\iota}\alpha$), and Rufinus has Kellia "about ten miles away" (*Hist. mon.* [*Ruf.*] 22.2.1 [p. 358]). Guy takes the discrepancies between Cassian's and other ancient reckonings of the distance to be an indication of his unreliability in geographical matters ("Jean Cassien, historien du monachisme égyptien?" 370). Chitty notes that Kellia covered a large expanse, with cells located as far as three or four miles from the church and from each other, making these discrepancies less worrisome (*The Desert a City*, 29–30). Even Guy does not, however, question the fact of Cassian's visit. It is noteworthy that Cassian does not seem to be depending on any literary sources for his distances!

97. Kellia lay between Scetis and Nitria.

98. The story about Heron (*Conf.* 2.5) may derive from Kellia; see the appendix.

99. Except for the phrase "the two Macarii" in *Conf.* 19.9.1.

100. Cappuyns suggested that Abraham, to whom *Conf.* 24 is attributed, was from either Nitria or Kellia, since in *Conf.* 24.4.2 he refers both to the desert of Calamus/Porphyry and to Scetis as being other than his own "squalid" district ("Cassien," 1323). See the appendix for the suggestion that Abraham was a monk from the Delta region near Diolcos.

101. The story in *Inst.* 5.32.1 about "a brother from Pontus" is probably about Evagrius, but neither name nor monastic location is provided.

102. Theological aspects of both the controversy and Cassian's reporting of it will be of concern in chapter 5. Although the history is known from several ancient accounts and has been well studied by modern scholars, many questions remain. See Socrates, *Hist. eccl.* 6.7–23 (cols. 684A–736A), *passim*; Sozomen, *Hist. eccl.* 8.11–28 (pp. 363.26–389.12), *passim*; Palladius, *Dial.* 6–8 (pp. 126–180), *passim*. For a brief and readable modern summary, see Chitty, *The Desert a City*, 57–61; for thorough and valuable studies of the historical and theological dimensions of the controversy, see Dechow, *Dogma and Mysticism*, *passim*; Clark, *The Origenist Controversy*, 42–84, 105–21; Vogüé, *Histoire littéraire du mouvement monastique dans l'antiquité*, 3:80–90.

103. See Jerome, *Ep.* 92.1.3 (CSEL 55, p. 148.9–11).

104. See the accounts in Palladius, *Dial.* 7 (pp. 140–54), *passim*; Socrates, *Hist. eccl.* 6.7 (col. 688BC); Sozomen, *Hist. eccl.* 8.13 (pp. 366.13–367.10); Kelly, *Golden Mouth*, 191–202.

105. *De Inc.* 7.31.1; he also alludes to the priesthood in *Inst.* 12.20 *(ordinis mei gradus).* Gennadius thought it worth noting that Cassian was *Constantinopolim a Iohanne Magno episcopo diaconus ordinatus (De vir. inlustr.* 62, p. 82.7–8).

106. This phrase may be simply a figure for membership in the church and thus citizenship in the true homeland of heaven.

107. They also confirm that Germanus actually existed and was not a character invented by Cassian for literary purposes.

108. *Dial.* 8 (pp. 170.164–172.167); see the same information in Chrysostom's letter to Innocent (in Malingrey's edition of *Dial.*, p. 74.66–68). See Kelly's account of the Synod in *Golden Mouth*, 211–27, especially 220.

109. *Dial.* 3 (p. 76.83–86).

110. See Malingrey's chronology in SC 342, p. 38.

111. *Dial.* 3 (pp. 76.90–78.95).

112. Tillemont, *Mémoires pour servir à l'histoire ecclésiastique des six premiers siècles,* 14:173. Gibson, "Prolegomena," 188; Cabrol, "Cassien," 2349; followed by Chadwick, *John Cassian,* 31–32, and Kelly, *Golden Mouth,* 252.

113. See Cappuyns, "Cassien," 1325–26, and Malingrey in SC 341, p. 77 n.5.

114. Innocent, *Ep.* 7 (col. 501B [Lat.] and 502B [Gk.]), included by Sozomen in *Hist. eccl.* 8.26.8 (p. 385.14–15).

115. Palladius, *Dial.* 4 (pp. 84.1–86.9). It cannot be proven that the letter by Innocent mentioned in *Dial.* 4 is the same as the one preserved as Innocent's *Ep.* 7, for Palladius says nothing about the letter's content or its addressee. Innocent's *Ep.* 7 itself is silent about how it is being sent.

116. Rousseau, *Ascetics, Authority, and the Church,* 173, following Marrou, "Jean Cassien à Marseille," 18, and Griffe, "Cassien a-t-il été prêtre d'Antioche?" 241.

117. *Dial.* 4 (pp. 84.1–92.68). Marrou ("Jean Cassien à Marseille," 18) claims that Germanus and Cassian, as Chrysostom's envoys to Innocent, must have been the couriers for Innocent's reply. The mission to Constantinople, however, was on a much larger scale than that of Germanus and Cassian to Rome and was working through many channels in Chrysostom's behalf.

118. A spirited argument by Marrou: "extrêmement vraisemblable," "comment douter," and so on. The only evidence he adduces is Palladius' note that the priests from the delegation to Constantinople were packed off to Arabia and Palestine; surely, Marrou says, Cassian was among them. Cassian's cenobitic instincts, Marrou suggests, would have led him back to his monastery in Bethlehem ("Jean Cassien à Marseille," 18–19). Rousseau thinks it unlikely, given Cassian's criticisms of the community in *Conf.* 17.5–7 *(Ascetics, Authority, and the Church,* 173).

119. Gennadius refers to Cassian as *apud Massiliam presbyter (De vir. inlustr.* 52, p. 82.8–9). For the suggestion that he was ordained to the priesthood in Rome rather than Marseilles, see Cappuyns, "Cassien," 1326; Chadwick, *John Cassian,* 32; Jenal, *Itala Ascetica,* 1.74; Frank, "John Cassian on John Cassian," 419–20.

120. Rousseau notes that Leo would have been too young at the time *(Ascetics, Authority and the Church,* 173); for this reason, Cappuyns has Cassian in Rome until 415–17 ("Cassien," 1326). Frank takes a cautious and balanced view, suggesting that the relationship with Leo should not be overemphasized but that Cassian must have been in Rome long enough to have made his mark, at least until 410 or 411 ("John Cassian on John Cassian," 421).

121. *Ep.* 19–20, cols. 540–43.

122. Tillemont, *Mémoires pour servir à l'histoire ecclésiastique des six premiers siècles,* 10:653 and 14:174.

123. See Coustant's commentary on Innocent's *Ep.* 19 (*S. Innocentii Papae Epistolae et decreta*, col. 541C) and Cappuyns, "Cassien," 1326.

124. Griffe, "Cassien a-t-il été prêtre d'Antioche?" *passim* and *La Gaule chrétienne*, 3:342. Schwartz contends that Innocent's letters suggest that "Cassianus" is a presbyter of Antioch sent to Rome as Alexander's envoy but is not John Cassian ("Cassian und Nestorius," 2 n. 1).

125. So Cappuyns, "Cassien," 1326. Marrou rejects the whole hypothesis, though on different grounds ("Jean Cassien à Marseille," 18–19).

126. Cappuyns accepts the plausibility of such a role for Cassian in Rome even though it cannot be proven: "que Cassien . . . ait été consulté au sujet d'une affaire qui concernait précisément l'archevêque martyr, faut-il s'étonner?" ("Cassien," 1326). He does not accept the argument that Cassian was in Antioch. Frank is skeptical of the whole scenario ("John Cassian on John Cassian," 420–21).

127. *De Inc.* 6.5.3–6.1, noted by Rousseau, *Ascetics, Authority, and the Church*, 174–75.

128. The passage accuses him of betraying the noble church of Antioch, which had produced both him and the saintly Chrysostom.

129. Twice he refers to Germanus as *sanctus* (*Conf.* 1.1 and 17.3), perhaps an allusion to his death, though with no indication of when it may have occurred.

130. For the early history, see Rivet, *Gallia Narbonensis*, 9–53; for an overview, see Guyon, "Marseille."

131. On Marseilles in Cassian's time, see Loseby, "Marseille," 180–81; on trade with the East, see especially pp. 172–73.

132. Cappuyns, "Cassien," 1326.

133. The evidence for Lazarus' return to Gaul was an epitaph (now lost) in the crypt of Saint Victor at Marseilles; Marrou interpreted it to be that of a bishop named Lazarus, whom he then identified as Lazarus of Aix (see the different interpretation of Leclercq, "Marseille," cols. 2254–55). See Marrou, "Jean Cassien à Marseille," 21–26, and "Le fondateur de Saint-Victor," 298–99, accepted by Griffe, *La Gaule chrétienne*, 3:342–43; see Rousseau, *Ascetics, Authority and the Church*, 174–75, and "Cassian: Monastery and World," 74 n. 23, where he refers to "the disputed but still attractive view of H. I. Marrou."

134. Castor was bishop by 419 and died before Cassian wrote the first set of *Conferences* (see *Conf. Pref.* 1 2); see Duchesne, *Fastes épiscopaux de l'ancienne Gaule*, 1:282, citing the letter of Pope Boniface I addressed to bishops of Gaul, including Castor, in 419 (ed. *Regesta pontificum romanorum*, Jaffé, p. 53, no. 349).

135. See Chadwick, *John Cassian*, 33–35, and Nürnberg, *Askese als sozialer Impuls*, 34–35.

136. On Proculus, see Leclercq, "Marseille," cols. 2217–18; Palanque, *Le diocèse de Marseille*, 17–22.

137. *Ep.* 125.20.2 (CSEL 56, p. 141.3–8). See Driver, "The Development of Jerome's Views on the Ascetic Life," 59–62, on Jerome and Rusticus.

138. On Rusticus and early monastic life in Marseilles, see most recently Atsma, "Die christlichen Inschriften Galliens," 10–17. Atsma argues persuasively on chronological grounds that Rusticus could not have been a monk of Cassian's monastery.

139. Gennadius, *De vir. inlustr.* 52 (p. 82.9–10). See Guyon, "Marseille," 131–32.

140. See Leclercq, "Marseille," cols. 2238–43; Benoit, *L'Abbaye de Saint-Victor*, 7–68, and "Le martyrium rupestre"; Palanque, *Le diocèse de Marseille*, 22–25. New excavation in the 1970s revealed the extent of the burial complex at Saint Victor; see Archimbaud, "Les fouilles de Saint-Victor" and "Saint-Victor de Marseille."

141. On Cassian's relics and the cult in Marseilles, see Cuper, *Acta Sanctorum*, 459E–461A. For the crypt, see Leclercq, "Marseille," cols. 2274–76. The monastery became Bene-

dictine in 977 and was secularized in 1739; the cloister and other buildings were destroyed in the Revolution, though the church survived. For the later history, see Amargier, *Un Âge d'or*. On the sarcophagus associated with Cassian, see Drocourt-Dubreuil, *Saint-Victor de Marseille*, 59–62.

142. Atsma, "Die christlichen Inschriften Galliens," 33–37. He suggests that the letter of Gregory the Great to the abbess of Saint Cassian is not about a new monastery seeking canonical establishment, but about an old one—perhaps recently renamed—seeking confirmation of privileges. See Gregory, *Ep.* 7.12 (pp. 454–55; *PL* 77.866–67).

143. *V. Caes.* 1.35 (p. 310.5–8).

144. Cassian's situation in Gaul is best explored by Rousseau, *Ascetics, Authority, and the Church*, 169–234, and "Cassian: Monastery and World." The latter explores Cassian's network of contacts and has recent bibliography.

145. "Cassian: Monastery and World," 69.

146. See note 134.

147. Cassian does not suggest that he and Jerome ever met; one can infer that Cassian left Bethlehem before Jerome arrived in 386 unless this silence is diplomatic: Jerome was famous for his anti-Origenism and died in 419, about the time Cassian wrote the *Institutes*. Driver has suggested that Cassian was in fact writing against conceptions of monasticism fostered by Jerome; see "From Palestinian Ignorance to Egyptian Wisdom."

148. Fontaine takes it in the broader sense ("L'ascétisme chrétien dans la littérature gallo-romaine d'Hilaire à Cassien," 110 n.56).

149. Prinz notes the significance of "das Vorbild des Orients" for the monks of Provence (*Frühes Mönchtum im Frankenreich*, 94–101 and 471).

150. Fontaine prefers to see Cassian's project not as a rejection of the earlier model but as a critique and reform pursuing its "logical development" ("L'ascétisme chrétien dans la littérature gallo-romaine d'Hilaire à Cassien," 105–13). See also Leyser's "*Lectio divina, oratio pura*" on Cassian's distinctive contribution in terms of cenobitic monasticism in Gaul.

151. Rousseau notes that Cassian "may have been disturbed by Hilary, Martin, Sulpitius" but suggests that it is impossible to discover the extent of Cassian's familiarity with them or his precise views about them (*Ascetics, Authority, and the Church*, 182). I would take a more definite line. See Nora Chadwick's comments in *Poetry and Letters in Early Christian Gaul*, 231–32, and Vogüé in "Les débuts de Lérins," 11. Fontaine notes that the contrast between Cassian's and Sulpitius' approaches may not be as absolute as it first appears ("L'ascétisme chrétien dans la littérature gallo-romaine d'Hilaire à Cassien," 111–12).

152. Adalbert de Vogüé has reminded me of this further twist.

153. Included in the critique here are the monks of Lérins; see Vogüé's comments in *Césaire d'Arles: Oeuvres monastiques I*, pp. 114–17.

154. It was a central issue in the criticism of Euchite and Messalian ascetics (see Stewart, *Working the Earth of the Heart*, 20–24, 45–46, 50–51, 62–63). Treatises such as Nilus' *On Voluntary Poverty* and Augustine's *On the Work of Monks* were devoted largely to defending the necessity of manual labor.

155. See Sulpitius' *V. Mart.* 10.6 (p. 274) and Fontaine's commentary in SC 134, pp. 676–79; *V. Mart.* 10.8 (p. 274). Fontaine notes that a camel-hair garment, imported from Egypt, would have been a "snobisme ascétique" of the kind condemned by many later writers (SC 134, pp. 681–82). Fontaine wonders why Cassian never mentions the camel-hair garment, but does not note this reference in *Inst.* 1.3. Vogüé argues in pt. 1, vol. 4 of *Histoire littéraire du mouvement monastique dans l'antiquité* that rather than being monas-

tic snobbery, the camel-hair garments of Martin's monks are an early witness that camels were raised in late antique Gaul, a surprising fact for which there is later evidence.

156. *Ep.* 22.34 (CSEL 54, pp. 196.16–197.13).

157. Vogüé notes that Cassian's praise of Honoratus in *Conf. Pref.* 2 1 may be attributable in part to the emphasis on manual labor at Lérins as depicted in the *RIVP* ("Les débuts de la vie monastique à Lérins," 37).

158. Therefore Cassian notes that because Leontius is united to Castor by *germanitatis affectus*, Cassian's debt owed to Castor now devolves on Leontius by right of inheritance (*Conf. Pref. 1* 3).

159. See Pricoco, *L'isola dei santi*, 33–34.

160. Vogüé, *Les Règles des saints Pères* (SC 297, pp. 148–49).

161. *Conf. Pref.* 2 2. The location of Helladius' episcopal see is uncertain. Chadwick suggested that he was bishop of Arles before Honoratus (see "Euladius of Arles"). Chadwick's argument is based on a manuscript of Prosper of Aquitaine's letter to Augustine about the Pelagian controversy in Gaul (preserved as Augustine's *Ep.* 225) which names "Elladius" as bishop of Arles at the time of Prosper's letter (the more common reading is "Hilarius"). Chadwick suggests that Elladius is to be preferred on the principle of *lectio difficilior*, noting that "Euladius" occurs in a late-ninth-century list of Arlesian bishops ("Euladius of Arles," 203–4). Behind Chadwick's interest in Helladius lay his wonder that Prosper's letter makes no mention of Cassian or of *Conf.* 13, which Chadwick reads as a response to Augustine's *De correptione et gratia* and which Prosper would later savage in his *Contra collatorem*. If Helladius was bishop of Arles when Prosper wrote to Augustine, then Honoratus could not have become bishop of Arles until 427–28 (his death is traditionally dated 430). Thus *Conf.* 13 could be dated later than previously thought, namely *after* Prosper's letter, and interpreted as a concretization of the general disquiet Prosper notes in his letter to Augustine.

Chadwick's suggestion was accepted by Griffe (*La Gaule chrétienne*, 2:240–41) and Pricoco (*L'isola dei santi*, 36 and 43; *Storia letteraria e storia ecclesiastica*, 64 n. 167). Labrousse (*Saint Honorat*, 15) and Jacob, editor of the *Life* of Hilary of Arles (SC 404, pp. 28–29), accept it; Valentin, editor of the *Life* of Honoratus for SC, considers it plausible (SC 235, p. 22). Rousseau thinks Chadwick was probably right ("Cassian: Monastery and World," 70). On the other hand, Cappuyns rejects it, noting that the ninth-century list cited by Chadwick included several bishops not of Arles; the "Euladius" named there, while probably a scribal contraction of "episcopus Helladius" and referring to Cassian's Helladius, included him as Honoratus' colleague, not as his predecessor. Cappuyns also has problems with dating *Conf.* 13 so late ("Cassien," 1331). Markus agrees. He sees *Conf.* 13 as a product of Cassian's concerns not so much about Augustine as about Pelagianism ca. 425–26, though with awareness of Augustine's position ("The Legacy of Pelagius" and *The End of Ancient Christianity*, 177–79). Weaver agrees with Markus (*Divine Grace and Human Agency*, 94–96). I incline to Markus' view about *Conf.* 13; about "Helladius of Arles" we may never know.

162. See Rousseau's "Cassian: Monastery and World" for the Lerinian connection. Prinz notes the divide between the monasticism of western Gaul and that of Cassian and Lérins; the basic issue was the idealization by the latter of eastern models, particularly those of Egypt (*Frühes Mönchtum im Frankenreich*, 90–101). The standard work on Lérins is Pricoco's *L'isola dei santi*; for chronological and prosopographical analysis, see pp. 30–59. In *Les Règles des saints Pères* Vogüé links a series of early Latin monastic rules to Lérins and supplements Pricoco's chronology and prosopography. Klingshirn provides a helpful summary (*Caesarius of Arles*, 23–29); Nouailhat surveys the early history of Lérins

in *Saints et patrons*; Kasper's *Theologie und Askese* studies Lerinian spirituality and challenges some of Vogüé's conclusions (though see Vogüé's criticisms of Kasper's work in "Les débuts de la vie monastique à Lérins").

163. According to the traditional reckoning he became bishop of Arles in 426; Chadwick's suggestion (see note 161) would delay his election to early 428. On Cassian and Honoratus, see Rousseau, "Cassian: Monastery and World," 70–72. On cenobitic life under Honoratus and the significance of Cassian's dedication, see Vogüé, "Les débuts de la vie monastique à Lérins," 19–22.

164. Before 441. Eucherius was married and had children; his whole family embraced the monastic life. See Pricoco, *L'isola dei santi*, 44–46, and Rousseau, "Cassian: Monastery and Church," 72–73.

165. Vogüé notes Eucherius' attraction to Egyptian anchoritic life (*Les Règles des saints Pères*, SC 297, pp. 126–27 and 254–55). See chapter 2 for more about Cassian's motives.

166. Now lost; see note 222.

167. The modern Îles d'Hyères, Ratonneau, and Pomègue; see Vogüé, *Les Règles des saints Pères* (SC 297, p. 110 n. 59).

168. Vogüé notes the significance of this combination of forms of monastic life ("Les débuts de la vie monastique à Lérins," 15–16), correcting Kasper's misinterpretation of *Conf. Pref.* 3. Later both cenobitic and anchoritic ways of life would be found also at Lérins; see *Reg. Patr.* 30 (SC 297, p. 280; see pp. 103–06) and Vogüé's additional remarks in "Les débuts de la vie monastique à Lérins," 40–41.

169. See Vogüé in *Les Règles des saints Pères* (SC 297, p. 256 n. 30).

170. The literature on Pelagianism and Semi-Pelagianism is immense; for overviews and further bibliography, see Nuvolone and Solignac, "Pélage"; Solignac, "Semipélagiens"; and Tibiletti's review of the secondary literature in "Rassegna di studi e testi sui 'Semipelagiani'." Amann's "Semi-Pélagiens" remains helpful. For recent assessments, see Markus, "The Legacy of Pelagius" and Weaver, *Divine Grace and Human Agency*. On the monks of Gaul, see Tibiletti, *Pagine monastiche provenzali*.

171. See Solignac, "Semipélagiens," 556–57, for the name.

172. This point was made by Rébillard in "*Quasi funambuli*," 209; see Markus, "The Legacy of Pelagius," 221–22, on the influence of Augustine at Lérins despite the adherence of the monks there to the traditional pre-Augustinian teaching of Cassian and others.

173. Even so, Cassian makes no reference to Augustine's monastic writings, and his remarks on Augustine in *De Inc.* 7.27.1 are markedly less effusive than those about the other western authorities he is quoting: he identifies Augustine simply as "priest of Hippo Regius."

174. *Const. Sirm.* 6 (pp. 911–12; the essentials are also in *PL* 45.1751).

175. Pricoco, however, takes pains to dissociate Lérins from anti-Augustinianism; see *Storia letteraria e storia ecclesiastica*, 59–67. He questions the tendency to magnify the significance and extent of Semi-Pelagianism in Gaul, and he focuses particularly on the work of Gennadius (see pp. 47–58).

176. However, *Conf.* 13 may have been as late as 428 if one follows Chadwick's suggestion, noted above. Chadwick's concern was to establish the following sequence of events: Augustine's *De corr. et grat.* arrives in Marseilles; Cassian responds with *Conf.* 13; Prosper writes to Augustine. The interplay of these events remains unclear.

177. This view is held by both Markus (*The End of Ancient Christianity*, 177–79) and Rousseau ("Cassian: Monastery and World," 82–83). Amann had made the same point: "tout l'ensemble de cette littérature ascétique était composée avant l'apparition du *Correptione et gratia* d'Augustin. Mais Cassien avait certainement eu connaissance d'autres

ouvrages du maître africain" ("Semi-Pélagiens," 1803). Markus also notes that the kind of study required to establish the relationship between *Conf.* 13 and the other texts remains to be done; see Rébillard's observations about Cassian's awareness of the key biblical texts used in the Pelagian controversy and the difficulty of ascertaining just how he gained his familiarity with them (though probably from reading Augustine and Jerome: "*Quasi funambuli,*" 209). Weaver follows Markus' dating (*Divine Grace and Human Agency,* 96–97). Chadwick read *Conf.* 13 as a response to *De corr. et grat.*; hence he sought to push Honoratus' move to Arles to a later date, thereby providing a window for Cassian to have read *De corr. et grat.* before writing *Conf.* 13 ("Euladius of Arles"; *John Cassian* [1st ed.], 112–34, *passim*; in the 2nd ed. he takes a less certain position).

178. Markus notes the close ties between *Conf.* 12 and 13 (*The End of Ancient Christianity,* 178); the connection between chastity and grace is even more pervasive, as will be seen in chapter 4.

179. Prosper's *Ep. ad Ruf.* is in PL 51.77A–90A; the quotation is from sec. 4 (PL 51.80A).

180. Prosper's *Ep. ad Aug.* is preserved with Augustine's own letters as *Ep.* 225 (CSEL 57, pp. 454–68; also published in PL 51.67–74). The quotation is from *Ep.* 225.2 (p. 455.12). Weaver dates Prosper's *Ep. ad Ruf.* to 426 and *Ep. ad Aug.* to 429 (*Divine Grace and Human Agency,* 97) while Amann dates the latter to 428 (along with Hilary's letter to Augustine; "Semi-Pélagiens," 1809). Amann takes the unusual position of dating *Ep. ad Ruf.* after *Ep. ad Aug.* ("Semi-Pélagiens," 1815–16).

181. *Ep. ad Aug.* (Augustine, *Ep.* 225.2–3), CSEL 57, pp. 456 and 459.

182. Preserved among Augustine's letters as *Ep.* 226 (CSEL 57, pp. 468–81). The quotation is from *Ep.* 226.2 (p. 469.4–5).

183. *Ep.* 226.9 (CSEL 57, p. 478.15–17).

184. Cassian's allies would have included Hilary of Arles (or, if Chadwick is correct, Helladius), named in Prosper's letter to Augustine as a bishop who agrees with Augustine on every issue except these (*Ep. ad Aug.* [Augustine, *Ep.* 225.9], CSEL 57, p. 467.12–17).

185. *Ep. ad Ruf.* 4 (PL 51.80). Cappuyns ("Le premier représentant de l'augustinisme médiéval," 311 nn. 5 and 7; "Cassien," 1343) and Chadwick (*John Cassian,* 129) doubt that Prosper had actually read *Conf.* 13; Amann ("Semi-Pélagiens," 1815) and Weaver (*Divine Grace and Human Agency,* 97) take the opposite view.

186. See Amann, "Semi-Pélagiens," 1818; Chadwick, *John Cassian,* 130–32; Markus, "Chronicle and Theology," 36–37; Weaver, *Divine Grace and Human Agency,* 120 n.10.

187. Celestine's letter is published in PL 50.528–30; the second half (cols. 531–37) is a later addition, probably by Prosper. See Amann's remarks about the text in "Semi-Pélagiens," 1818–19 and 1828–30.

188. See Markus, "The Legacy of Pelagius," 218.

189. PL 51.215–76. The dating is due to Prosper's reference to Sixtus, who became pope in 432 (*C. coll.* 21.4, col. 273C).

190. Especially in *C. coll.* 2.1 (*quem non dubium est illis omnibus in sanctarum Scripturarum studio praestare; vir . . . sacerdotalis, qui disputandi usu inter eos,* col. 217B–18A) and 2.5 (*doctor catholicus,* col. 221A); is this the requisite deference noted earlier by Hilary? Or simply the respect owed an opponent approaching the end of his days?

191. See *Conf.* 13.7 and 11–12.

192. This fact is noted by Cappuyns in "Le premier représentant de l'augustinisme médiéval," 321–22.

193. See Chadwick, *John Cassian,* 133–34; Weaver, *Divine Grace and Human Agency,* 121–31. Gennadius, though not impartial, judged it defamatory (*De vir. inlustr.* 85, p. 90.21–25).

194. See Markus, "Chronicle and Theology," 36–37.

195. For the intervening period, see Amann, "Semi-Pélagiens," 1819–42; Markus, "The Legacy of Pelagius," 219–27; Weaver, *Divine Grace and Human Agency*, 131–225. On the Council of Orange, see Amann, "Semi-Pélagiens," 1842–49; Klingshirn, *Caesarius of Arles*, 140–43; Weaver, *Divine Grace and Human Agency*, 225–32.

196. Nevertheless, Gennadius describes him as *sanctus* (*De vir. inlustr.* 64, p. 83.13), and Gregory the Great refers to *sanctus Cassianus* in his letter to an abbess in Marseilles (*Ep.* 7.12, p. 454.22; *PL* 77.866–67). Marseilles has kept Cassian's feast on July 23. In the east, where his monastic writings have always been respected and Semi-Pelagianism is a cipher, his feast is February 29. See Cuper in *Acta Sanctorum*, 458A–60A, Cappuyns' summary in "Cassien," 1328, and Chadwick, *John Cassian*, 158–61. Loorits suspects that the February 29 date was fixed in an era when tensions between East and West meant that Cassian, regarded as a "Roman" despite his eastern training, was suspect: thus, Loorits says, he was robbed of "three-quarters of his saintliness" (*Der Heilige Kassian*, 132). Loorits' book is a fascinating study of the legends that developed in eastern Europe and Russia about this leap-year observance: typically they claim that Cassian was punished by God for having led a delegation of other saints jealous of the attention Saint Nicholas got on his feast day!

197. The entry (among the "Books Not To Be Received") reads: *opuscula Cassiani presbyteri Galliarum apocrypha* (*Decr. Gel.* 5.7, p. 56; *PL* 59.163B). See Cuper's analysis in *Acta Sanctorum*, 482B; Olphe-Galliard, "Cassien," 268; Cappuyns, "Cassien," 1345–46; Chadwick, *John Cassian*, 150–52.

198. On the title, see Cappuyns, "Cassien," 1332.

199. We do not know the date of Leo's birth; he was elected bishop of Rome in 440 and died in 461, suggesting a birthdate ca. 390.

200. *De Inc. Pref.* 2: *a te . . . conpellor;* 3: *pareo obsecrationi tuae, pareo iussioni;* 4: *amor Iesu Christi domini mei praecepit, qui hoc ipsum etiam in te iubet* and *me enim, sive par sim tuo imperio sive non sim, ipsa aliquatenus oboedientiae ratio atque humilitatis excusat;* 5: *ora et obsecra, ne imperitia mea periclitetur electio tua . . . ego per oboedientiae veniam bene pareo, tu tamen per inconsiderantiam iudicii male imperasse videaris.*

201. As noted by Chadwick, *John Cassian*, 142.

202. Codina, *El aspecto cristologico en la espiritualidad de Juan Casiano*, 126, following Brand, *Le De Incarnatione Domini de Jean Cassien*, 55.

203. On the historical context and documents available to Cassian, see Schwartz, "Cassian und Nestorius," 1–17; Amann, "L'affaire Nestorius vue de Rome," pt. 2, pp. 225–44, and "Nestorius," 98–101; Vannier, "Jean Cassien a-t-il fait oeuvre de théologien dans le *De incarnatione domini?*"

204. See Amann's remarks in "L'affaire Nestorius vue de Rome," pt. 2, pp. 229–32 and 237–38, and Grillmeier, *Christ in Christian Tradition*, 1:468–71.

205. See Amann, "Nestorius," 98–99; Plagnieux suggests that a more fundamental link between Pelagianism and Christology was made by Augustine and transmitted to Cassian through Prosper of Aquitaine ("Le grief de complicité entre erreurs nestorienne et pélagienne").

206. See Leporius' *Libellus emendationis* in CCL 63, pp. 111–23, and the biographical material on pp. 97–98. On Cassian's use of Leporius, see Amann, "Leporius," 434–40, and "L'affaire Nestorius vue de Rome," pt. 2; De Beer, "Une tessère d'orthodoxie," 146.

207. Thus Amann in "L'affaire Nestorius vue de Rome," pt. 2, pp. 228–230; see De Beer, "Une tessère d'orthodoxie," 155–59.

208. *De Inc.* 1.4.2: *a nobis admonitus, a deo emendatus.* We know that the bishops of Gaul, and especially of Marseilles, were involved in calling Leporius to account; was Cassian simply associating himself with their actions?

209. The most thorough analysis is that of Brand in *Le De Incarnatione Domini de Jean Cassien*, which I have not been able to consult; fortunately, Brand's conclusions are cited abundantly by subsequent writers. Codina devotes the second half (pp. 119–80) of *El aspecto cristologico en la espiritualidad de Juan Casiano* to *De Incarnatione*.

210. "Jean Cassien a-t-il fait oeuvre de théologien dans le *De incarnatione domini?*" 125.

211. *De Inc.* 1.2.4–3.6; in Cassian's remark that Leporius was *a nobis admonitus, a deo emendatus* (*De Inc.* 1.4.2) the plural may refer to the collective human effort to persuade Leporius before God actually reformed him as well as to Cassian's own involvement in the case. On the theological theme, see Codina, *El aspecto cristologico en la espiritualidad de Juan Casiano*, 153–71.

212. "L'influence de Jean Chrysostome." Cassian concludes the whole treatise with his praise of John (*De Inc.* 7.30–31).

213. Amann, "L'affaire Nestorius vue de Rome," pt. 2, pp. 242–44, and "Nestorius," 100–101; Chadwick, *John Cassian* (1950 ed.) 157; Grillmeier, *Christ in Christian Tradition*, 1:468–71; Vannier, "Jean Cassien a-t-il fait oeuvre de théologien dans le *De incarnatione domini?*" 128–30.

214. "L'affaire Nestorius vue de Rome," pt. 2, pp. 237–38.

215. "Cassian: Monastery and World," 84.

216. Though he also admits that he had not quite arrived there yet: *absolutis dudum collationum spiritalium libellis . . . cogitaram et propemodum constitueram post illum proditae inscientiae pudorem ita me in portu silentii collocare* (*De Inc.* Pref. 1).

217. This point is underscored by Codina (*El aspecto christologico en la espiritualidad de Juan Casiano*, 122–23, 127, and 185) and by Rousseau ("Cassian: Monastery and World," 85, developing themes in *Ascetics, Authority, and the Church*, 227–31).

218. In the 1950 edition of *John Cassian* Chadwick balances his harsh critique of *De Incarnatione* with a section, "The Monk and Christ," that draws out the significance of that work for Cassian's piety in a most helpful way. Unfortunately, when Chadwick moderated his criticisms in the 1968 edition he also dropped this section. Codina disputes Brand's argument that *De Incarnatione* represents a shift from the more psychological and intellectualist Christology of the *Institutes* and *Conferences* (*El aspecto cristologico en la espiritualidad de Juan Casiano*, 185–94); Codina argues (correctly, I think) that *De Incarnatione* makes explicit the profoundly Christocentric nature of Cassian's monastic theology.

219. The entry for Cassian in Prosper's *Chronicon* for 433 has long been considered suspect (thus *PL* 51.596CD); Mommsen places it among the fifteenth-century interpolations (as in *Chronica Minora*, 1:499; see Cappuyns, "Cassien," 1327–28).

220. For overviews, see Chadwick, *John Cassian*, 148–62; Cappuyns, "Cassien," 1343–47; Olphe-Galliard, "Cassien," 267–74.

221. *Form. Pref.*, citing the basic definitions of *Conf.* 14.1, 14.4 and 8.

222. See Gennadius, *De vir. inlustr.* 64 (p. 83.13–15). The fragments of a ninth-century manuscript in Paderborn were thought by Honselmann to be from Eucherius' lost epitome ("Bruchstücke von Auszügen aus Werkens Cassians"); Vogüé thinks they are from another abridgment ("Un morceau célèbre de Cassien parmi des extraits d'Évagre," 12 n. 24). The material in *PL* 50.867D–94A is in fact a Latin translation of the *Greek* epitome; see Honselmann, "Bruchstücke von Auszügen aus Werken Cassians," 303–4.

223. *Common.* 2.5 (p. 149). The Christological arguments of Cassian's *De Incarnatione* shaped Vincent's thought, as is evident in the notes to the CCL edition. On Vincent, see Rousseau, "Cassian: Monastery and World," 76–77; Weaver, *Divine Grace and Human Agency*, 157–60.

224. See Weaver, *Divine Grace and Human Agency*, 162–80.

225. See Ferrandus' *V. Fulg.* 12 (col. 128C), as noted by Olphe-Galliard, "Cassien," 267. Fulgentius got as far as Syracuse, only to be told by the bishop that the monks of Egypt were schismatics (since the refusal of the Egyptian church to accept the Council of Chalcedon in 451) and that to visit them would mean depriving himself of the eucharist. Fulgentius did not pursue his quest (col. 129CD).

226. *De vir. inlustr.* 64 (p. 82.13–31).

227. *Div. litt.* 29, col. 1144B.

228. Recently edited by Ledoyen; see also Vogüé, "La "Regula Cassiani"."

229. Cassiodorus refers to Cassian as *facundissimus* in *Expos. in Ps.* 69:2 (p. 624) and *Expos. in Ps.* 141 (p. 1274); *eloquentissimus* in the preface to *Div. litt.* (col. 1108C).

230. He refers to the story in *Inst.* 5.33 about the role of prayer in the interpretation of Scripture (cited, however, as *in quinto Collationum . . . volumine*: *Div. litt.* Pref., col. 1108C); he praises *Conf.* 9–10 (*Expos. in Ps.* 141, p. 1274), particularly Cassian's choice of Ps. 69(70):1 as a text for frequent meditation (*Conf.* 10.10, cited in *Expos. in Ps.* 69:2, p. 624). Cassiodorus also notes Cassian's teaching on the eight principal faults (*Div. litt.* 29, col. 1144A), especially that on accidie (*Expos. in Ps.* 118:28, p. 1072). Finally, he mentions Cassian's condemnation of "certain kinds of monks" (an allusion to *Conf.* 18.7–8, *Div. litt.* 29, col. 1144B).

231. *Div. litt.* 29 (col. 1144A).

232. See Vogüé's analysis in *Césaire d'Arles: Oeuvres monastiques I*, 45–47.

233. For example, for the influence of Cassian on the sermons for monks, see Courreau in Vogüé and Courreau, *Césaire d'Arles: Oeuvres monastiques II*, 45–46. See also the index on pp. 268–71. A later copyist even added a section from *Inst.* 4 to one of Caesarius' letters; see Vogüé's "Une interpolation inspirée de Cassien dans un texte monastique de Césaire d'Arles."

234. *Reg. Mag.* 10, adapted in *Reg. Ben.* 7; see Vogüé, "Cassien, le Maître et Benoît" and "De Cassien au Maître et à Eugippe." For an overview of Cassian's influence on the Master, see Vogüé's edition of *Reg. Mag.*, *passim*, and his study *Community and Abbot in the Rule of Saint Benedict*. In Vogüé's many articles on both *Reg. Mag.* and *Reg. Ben.*, Cassian figures prominently.

235. On Benedict's famous recommendation that his monks read the *Institutes* and *Conferences* (*Reg. Ben.* 42.3 and 5 [p. 584], 73.5 [p. 672]), see Vogüé, "Les mentions des oeuvres de Cassien chez saint Benoît et ses contemporains." On Cassian's influence on Benedict independently of the Master, see, for example, Kardong, "Benedict's Use of Cassianic Formulae for Spiritual Progress" and the bibliography there.

236. See Vogüé's notes to *Reg. Ben.* 20.3–5 in *La Règle de Saint Benoît*, 537–38 or any major commentary such as Kardong's *Benedict's Rule*.

237. See Olphe-Galliard, "Cassien," 269; Cappuyns, "Cassien," 1346–47; Gillet, introduction to *Grégoire le Grand*, 89–102.

238. Photius in his *Bibliotheca* cod. 197 describes three epitomes: *Inst.* 1–4, *Inst.* 5–12, *Conf.* 1–2 and 7. Petschenig prints Photius' description and an analysis of Greek MSS in CSEL 17, pp. xcv–civ. The Greek epitome of *Inst.* is in *PG* 28.849C–905B. Dyovouniotis published a Greek version of *Conf.* 1–2 and 7–8 from a tenth–century manuscript; a description can be found in *Byzantinische Zeitschrift* 22 (1913):578–79. Besides the articles of Marsili and Vogüé cited in note 241, see Bardenhewer, *Geschichte der altkirchlichen Literatur*, 4.563–64, and Dekkers, "Les traductions grecques des écrits patristiques latins," 213–14.

239. Cassian has eight sayings in *Alph.* (cols. 244A–45D): the first is the same as *Inst.* 5.24; the second is not from Cassian, though see *V. Patr.* 3.24 (col. 753AD); the third is the same as *Inst.* 5.25; the fourth, *Inst.* 5.27; the fifth, *Inst.* 5.28; the sixth, *Inst.* 5.29 and 31; the seventh, *Inst.* 7.19; the eighth is not from Cassian.

240. And, as Chadwick notes, the Greek abridgment of Cassian's works is included in the *Philokalia*; Cassian is the only Latin author to be found there ("Cassianus," 656).

241. On Evagrius, see Vogüé, "Un morceau célèbre de Cassien parmi des extraits d'Évagre"; for Nilus, see Marsili, "Résumé de Cassien sous le nom de saint Nil."

242. See *The Desert a City*, 134–36, on prayer: "much here is reminiscent of Cassian, whose works may well have been known to the Old Men [Barsanuphius and John]—they were early translated into Greek." He refers to *Ep.* 71 (ed. Schoinas, pp. 67–68 [no. 140 of Regnault's trans., p. 126]) and 74 (ed. Schoinas, pp. 68–69 [no. 143 of Regnault's trans., pp. 127–28]). If Chitty is right, these passages would be our only witness to a Greek translation of *Conf.* 9.

243. See their edition of *Instr.*, p. 41, and the entries for Cassian in the index of ancient authors, p. 540.

244. *Scala parad.* 4 (col. 717B) on the origins of discernment, citing *Conf.* 2.10: ὡς καὶ τῷ μεγάλῳ Κασσιανῷ ἐν τῷ Περὶ διακρίσεως αὐτοῦ λόγῳ πεφιλοσόφηται κάλ-λιστα τε καὶ ὑψηλότατα. See Archimandrite Sophrony on correspondences between Cassian and Climacus ("De la nécessité des trois renoncements chez St. Cassien le Romain et St. Jean Climaque"); although none of the Greek versions we possess include anything other than *Conf.* 1–2 and 7–8, this article suggests that Climacus had read other *Conferences*.

245. *Sacra parallela* 1.23 (*PG* 95.1212B–13C) on accidie; 9.5 on sadness (*PG* 96.25C–28A).

246. This question is posed by Rousseau ("Cassian: Monastery and World," 77–86, developing themes in *Ascetics, Authority, and the Church*, 199–234).

247. Rousseau suggests as much in both *Ascetics, Authority and the Church* and "Cassian: Monastery and World"; see also Leyser's "*Lectio divina, oratio pura*," on Cassian's development of a cenobitic model of sanctity susceptible to a variety of institutional interpretations.

Chapter 2

1. As I will show in chapter 5, Cassian presents the four in various sequences within *Conf.* 14.

2. See *Inst. Pref.* 3, *Conf. Pref.* 1 3, *Conf. Pref.* 2 1.

3. In *De Incarnatione* his polemics are open, though even there he never names Nestorius, the object of his attack.

4. Though Markus has questioned (I think rightly) whether *Conf.* 13 really is a reply to Augustine; it could very well be addressed to the Pelagians. See Markus, *The End of Ancient Christianity*, 177–78. *Conf.* 23 can be seen as a response to Jerome's *Ep.* 133 to Ctesiphon (CSEL 56, pp. 241–60), a critique of Evagrian teaching on *apatheia*. On Cassian's response to Jerome more generally, see Driver, "From Palestinian Ignorance to Egyptian Wisdom."

5. For structural analysis of Cassian's monastic writings, see Leroy, "Les préfaces des écrits monastiques de Jean Cassien"; Vogüé, "Pour comprendre Cassien"; and Pristas, *The Theological Anthropology of John Cassian*. Chadwick questions the present form of some of the texts (*John Cassian*, 38–50), though many of his concerns seem to have been superseded by the kind of structural analysis done by Vogüé and Pristas.

6. *Instituta monasteriorum: Inst. Pref.* 3, 7, 8, 9; *Inst.* 1.1.1, 5.1; *Conf.* 3.1.2. *Instituta coenobiorum: Inst.* 4.19.1, 5.36.1; *Conf. Pref.* 1 1; *Conf. Pref.* 2 2; *Conf.* 19.2.4. *Instituta seniorum: Inst.* 2.3.3, 2.3.5 (*seniorum institutio . . . instituta patrum*), 2.5.2 (*instituta mai-*

orum), 8.10.1; *Conf.* 2.15.3, 14.9.4; *Conf. Pref.* 3 3; *Conf.* 18.2.1 *(instituta magistrorum)*, 24.12.1. See *instituta sanctorum* (*Conf.* 18.1.3, 20.4.2).

7. For example, *Conf.* 2.15.3, 3.1.2, 14.9.4, 24.12.1.

8. For the clearest cases, see *Conf. Pref.* 1 3, 5, 7 *(ad conlationes eorum et instituta)*, *Conf.* 2.13.3, 2.15.3, 10.1; *Conf. Pref.* 2 1; *Conf.* 16.1, 19.6.3.

9. Cassian frequently refers to the *regula monasteriorum* or *seniorum* or similar (*Inst. Pref.* 8–9; *Inst.* 1.1.1, 1.2.3, 3.1, 4.6, 4.33, 4.39.2, 4.41.1, 5.36.1, 7.10, 7.31, 12.27.2; *Conf.* 1.20.7, 4.19.4, 18.11.3, 19.2.2, 19.14.6, 20.2.2, 21.22.6). By this term he means not a written charter like the "Rule" of Saint Benedict, but "teaching" or "norm." This intention is evident in the use of the plural *regulae* to describe "rules" of monasteries (*Inst. Pref.* 7, *Inst.* 1.2.4, 2.2.1, 2.3.5, 3.4.3, 4.1, 4.15.2), and in the references to specific kinds of rules, for example, the "rule of fasting" (see *Inst.* 2.18, 3.10, 5.5.1, 5.23.2, 5.24) or of obedience (*Inst.* 4.10), vigils (*Inst.* 7.10), or discernment (*Conf.* 18.7.3, 19.14.6). On the emergence of the Latin rules, see the extensive work of Vogüé; "*Sub regula vel abbate*" can serve as an introduction.

10. Most often *disciplina coenobii/coenobiorum/monasterii* (*Inst.* 4.3.1, 4.4, 5.36.1, 7.9.2, 7.30, 12.30; *Conf.* 5.8.3; *Conf. Pref.* 3 1; *Conf.* 18.5.1, 18.7.3, 18.7.8, 19.2.1, 19.8.4, 19.11.1) or *disciplina anachoretica/anachoreseos/anachoretarum* (*Conf.* 11.2.1; *Conf. Pref.* 3 2–3; *Conf.* 18.7.8, 18.11.1, 19.2.4, 19.3.1, 19.6.2, 19.8.4, 24.11.1, 24.19.4; see *Inst.* 2.9.3).

11. The word *praeceptum* usually means "commandment," in the biblical sense. For the monastic use meaning "teaching" or "instruction," see *Inst.* 4.10, 7.9.1; *Conf. Pref.* 2 1; *Conf.* 14.7.2, 16.1, 17.13; *Conf. Pref.* 3 3 (twice); *Conf.* 18.2.1, 19.8.2, 20.1.1, 20.2.2, 24.26.19.

12. For *instituta* with *regula*: *Inst. Pref.* 7 (plural), 8 and 9 (singular); *Inst.* 1.1.1, 1.2.4; *Conf.* 18.2.2. With *doctrina*: *Conf. Pref.* 1 3 *(institutum atque doctrina)*; *Conf.* 2.13.3, 2.15.3, 3.1.2. With *praecepta*: *Conf.* 16.1, *Conf. Pref.* 3 3, *Conf.* 18.2.1. On Latin monastic terminology, see Vogüé, *Histoire littéraire, passim*.

13. See *Conf.* 9.1.1, 20.1.1, 20.2.2; for other uses of *institutio* where *instituta* would be expected, see *Inst.* 2.3.5, 2.9.3, 4.13, 7.18 and *Conf.* 21.12.2. For the normal use of *institutio* for a program of instruction or formation, see, for example, *Inst.* 2.3.5, 4.1, 4.2.1, 4.6, 4.7, 4.23, 4.33, 4.41.3, 7.10, 7.31, 10.2.1, 10.7.8, 10.11, 12.13; *Conf.* 2.10.2, 2.11.7, 2.14, 2.15.1, 2.26.4, 24.8.3, 24.13.5–6.

14. See Frank, "Johannes Cassian, *De institutis coenobiorum.*"

15. Rom. 15:26; see *Inst.* 7.17.1–3, 10.8.3. See *Conf.* 1.20.6, also about money, or *Conf.* 23.3.2, about gemstones.

16. See *Inst.* 5.29, 5.31, 12.27.2–4; *Conf.* 2.5.2, 2.15.3, 16.12.

17. As Cassian almost always uses *conlatio* in this way, references are unnecessary.

18. Only *Conference* 15 contains no questions from either Germanus or John. On these genres, see Hermann and Bardy, "Dialog"; Dörrie and Dörries, "Erotapokriseis"; Hoffmann, *Der Dialog bei den christlichen Schriftstellern*; Voss, *Der Dialog in der frühchristlichen Literatur*; Blowers, *Exegesis and Spiritual Pedagogy*, 36–52 (40–42 on Cassian); Frank, "Fiktive Mündlichkeit."

19. See Nora Chadwick on Cassian's use of the dialogue compared to Sulpitius'; she observes fairly that Cassian cannot match Sulpitius' clever use of the format (*Poetry and Letters in Early Christian Gaul*, 230–33).

20. Seventy questions are attributed to Germanus, only one (*Conf.* 14.12) to John.

21. Sixteen begin with a question or problem presented by both monks (*Conf.* 1–7, 10–11, 14, 16, 18–19, 21, 23–24). Three open with a question from Germanus (*Conf.* 8, 13, 20); the most interesting of these is *Conf.* 13, where Germanus is troubled by the suggestion that human efforts do not play the greater part in the acquisition of chastity. *Conf.* 9 is presented as part of a much longer discourse; *Conf.* 17 opens with a conversation between John and Germanus that sets up the problem to be considered by the elder. In the re-

maining three cases an elder gives an additional conference and there is no need either for setting the stage or introducing the topic with a question (*Conf.* 12, 15, 22).

22. See Burton-Christie, *The Word in the Desert*, 77–79.

23. Those that begin each set (*Conf.* 1, 11, 18), as well as *Conf.* 6, which is introduced with the story of monks murdered by nomads in Palestine, and *Conf.* 17, which opens with a conversation between John and Germanus about their broken promise to the community in Bethlehem. Both *Conf.* 10 and 21 begin with lengthy stories of obvious theological and monastic import, the first about the Anthropomorphite controversy of 399, the second about chastity.

24. *Inst.* 1.1.1: *quorum interiorum cultum consequenter tunc poterimus exponere*, a reference explained by the distinction in *Inst.* 2 between physical postures and inner dispositions in prayer.

25. *Inst.* 2.1, 2.9.1, 2.18, 5.4.3.

26. "Les préfaces des écrits monastiques de Jean Cassien," 167.

27. See *Conf. Pref.* 1 2, "the institutes of the cenobites and the remedies of the eight principal faults," and 5, "cenobia . . . and the actual [Cassian's translation of the Greek πρακτική] life."

28. *Conf. Pref.* 1 5: "the exterior and visible way of life (*cultus*) of the monks"; *Inst.* 1.1.1: "the habit of the monk . . . outer wear"; *Inst.* 2.9.3: "the dress and clothing of the outer person" and "the observance of the outer person and the *institutio* of the cenobia."

29. *Inst. Pref.* 8: "correction of our ways (*morum*) and the fulfillment of the perfect life"; *Conf. Pref.* 1 5: "the ousting of carnal faults."

30. *Inst.* 2.9.3: "the life and teaching of the anchorites"; *Conf. Pref.* 1 2: "these ten *Conferences* of the greatest fathers, that is of the anchorites who dwell in the desert of Scetis"; *Conf. Pref.* 1 4: "*anachoresis* . . . contemplation of God, a greater and higher act."

31. *Inst.* 1.1.1: "the inner life"; *Inst.* 2.9.3: "the discipline of the inner [person] and perfection of heart"; *Conf. Pref.* 1 5: "the invisible conduct (*habitus*) of the inner person" and "the insight of divine purity . . . the height of perfection"; *Conf.* 18.1.3: "instruction on the perfect life."

32. See Markus' argument that in the course of writing the various sets of *Conferences* Cassian gradually erased the differences between cenobitic ("active") and anchoritic ("contemplative") ways of life (*The End of Ancient Christianity*, 181–97). Evidence suggests, however, that Cassian was using these labels allegorically from the outset, though it is true that his support for the cenobitic way of life becomes more explicit in the final set of *Conferences*. For a perceptive analysis of the cenobitic and anchoritic labels, see Driver, *The Reading of Egyptian Monastic Culture in John Cassian*.

33. *Inst.* 5.4.3: "that there can be one goal (*finis*) of our religion but various professions that lead to God will be more fully explained in the *Conferences* of the elders"; see *Conf.* 14.4.

34. *Inst.* 2.1, 2.9.1; *Conf. Pref.* 1 5.

35. *Inst.* 2.9.1: "the condition (*status*) of the inner person . . . and edifice of the [inner person's] prayers"; *Inst.* 2.9.3: "the nature (*qualitas*) of prayer . . . in what way (*qualiter*) spiritual sacrifices should be offered."

36. *Inst.* 2.1: "how to pray without ceasing, according to the meaning of the Apostle"; *Inst.* 2.9.1: "the nature (*qualitas*) and unceasingness of [canonical] prayers"; *Conf. Pref.* 1 5: "the unceasingness of perpetual prayer commanded by the Apostle"; *Conf.* 9.1: "the perpetual and incessant unceasingness of prayer."

37. See *Inst.* 2.18. He raises the issue again in *Inst.* 3.9–12, but the promised discussion of the reason for the practice does not in fact appear until *Conf.* 21.

38. See Leroy, "Les préfaces des écrits monastiques de Jean Cassien," 162–70.

39. See chapter 7.

40. See the discussion in chapter 3.

41. See Vogüé's note of other correspondences having to do with the eight principal faults ("Pour comprendre Cassien," 253).

42. On the intricate (and careful) structure of *Inst.* 5, see Pristas, *The Theological Anthropology of John Cassian*, 34–44, 74–75; for analysis of content and for the prospective quality of *Inst.* 5, see Driver, *The Reading of Egyptian Monastic Culture in John Cassian*, 146–57.

43. *Inst.* 5.4–5, on discernment: see *Conf.* 2; *Inst.* 5.4.3, on one end and various ways to it: see *Conf.* 14.4–5, *Conf.* 18–19; *Inst.* 5.10, on the instability of the mind: see, e.g., *Conf.* 1.17–18; *Inst.* 5.10, on the enemy creeping into the heart: see *Conf.* 1.22.2; *Inst.* 5.14.4, on contemplating heavenly beatitude even now: see, e.g., *Conf.* 1.10.5; *Inst.* 5.15–17, on the "mark" or "target": see *Conf.* 1.5; *Inst.* 5.21–22, on the "inner fast" from anger leading to purity of heart: see *Conf.* 1.7; *Inst.* 5.22, on pursuing the goal of purity of heart indefatiga-bly: see *Conf.* 1.2.3; *Inst.* 5.24–26, on the demands of charity greater than fasting: see *Conf.* 17.21–24, 28–30; *Inst.* 5.32.1, on distraction from contemplation of divine things in purity of heart: see *Conf.* 1 etc.; *Inst.* 5.33–34, on proper interpretation of the Bible: see *Conf.* 14.

44. See *Inst.* 8.16–19; *Conf.* 18.4–6, *Conf.* 19 *passim*.

45. *Inst. Pref.* 8: *propositum siquidem mihi est non de mirabilibus dei, sed de correctione morum nostrorum et consummatione vitae perfectae secundum ea, quae a senioribus nostris accepimus, pauca disserere. Conf.* 18.1.3: *non enim de mirabilibus dei, sed de institutis studi-isque sanctorum quaedam quae reminisci possibile est nos spopondimus memoriae tradituros, ut necessarium tantum perfectae vitae instructionem, non inutilem absque ulla emendatione vitiorum ac supervacuam admirationem legentibus praeberemus.*

46. Two were mentioned earlier: fasting and kneeling on Sundays and during the Fifty Days of Easter (*Inst.* 2.18) are explained finally in *Conf.* 21; the idea that various forms of monastic life lead to a common Christian end (*Inst.* 5.4.3) is addressed in *Conf.* 14.4, 18–19 *passim*.

47. *Facundissimus* in *Expos. Ps.* 69 (col. 492D) and *Expos. Ps.* 141 (col. 1009B); *elo-quentissimus* in the preface to *Div. litt.* (col. 1108C).

48. Paucker, "Die Latinität des Johannes Cassianus," 391; Abel, *Studien zu dem gal-lischen Presbyter Johannes Cassianus*, 15–17; Courcelle assumed Latin was Cassian's native language (*Late Latin Writers and Their Greek Sources*, 227). Tillemont did not, figuring that Cassian had learned Latin in Bethlehem and noting that Cassian's literary style is "fort obscur et peu Latin" (*Mémoires pour servir à l'histoire ecclésiastique des six premiers siècles*, 14:176).

49. Prinz, *Frühes Mönchtum im Frankenreich*, 471 and 479–80.

50. On Cassian's use of Greek, see Stewart, "From λόγος to *verbum*."

51. *Gastrimargia* (γαστριμαργία) for gluttony, *filargyria* (φιλαργυρία) for avarice, *acedia* (ἀκηδία) for listlessness, *cenodoxia* (κενοδοξία) for vainglory.

52. *Inst.* 8.10; *Conf.* 7.4.2.

53. Gen. 3:1 (*Conf.* 8.10.1), Job 15:15 (*Conf.* 23.8.2), Isa. 66:2 (*Inst.* 12.31).

54. Matt. 5:22 as in *Inst.* 8.21; in general, *Inst.* 1.2.1.

55. LXX: Exod. 18:21 (*Conf.* 7.5.2), Ps. 115:9 (*Conf.* 9.12.1), Ps. 145:8b (*Conf.* 3.15.3), Eccl. 5:3 (*Conf.* 9.12.1), Sir. 5:3 (*Conf.* 9.12.1), Wis. 9:15 (*Conf.* 7.4.2). Greek NT: Matt. 6:11 (*Conf.* 9.21.1), Phil. 3:14 (*Conf.* 1.5.3), 1 Tim. 6:20 (*Conf.* 14.16.4).

56. As in his interpretation of Judg. 3:15 in *Conf.* 6.10.1; of the story of Martha and Mary (Luke 10:38–42, as in *Conf.* 1.8), using a textual variant unknown in the extant Latin tradition; his commentary on alternative Latin translations of the Greek ἐπιούσιον from the Lord's Prayer (*Conf.* 9.21).

57. Ciacconius lists hundreds of examples (pp. 699–718) and Petschenig indicates more than a hundred (pp. 392–400).

58. He almost always cited Proverbs and Ecclesiastes in a form approximating that of the LXX; with Job and Song of Songs he did so about half the time, with Wisdom somewhat less than half the time. He also prefers to cite some of the minor prophets (Joel, Jonah, Habbakkuk, Haggai, Zachariah) in a form close to that of the LXX.

59. See Abel, *Studien zu dem gallischen Presbyter Johannes Cassianus*, 23–31; Cappuyns, "Cassien," 1334; Courcelle, *Late Latin Writers and Their Greek Sources*, 228–29; Djuth, "Cassian's Use of the Figure *Via Regia* in *Collatio II* 'On Discretion'."

60. See Neuhausen, "Zu Cassians Traktat De amicitia (Coll. 16)," 186.

61. For overviews, see Olphe-Galliard, "Cassien," 223–27; Cappuyns, "Cassien," 1334–36; Courcelle, *Late Latin Writers and Their Greek Sources*, 227–31; Weber, *Die Stellung des Johannes Cassianus zur ausserpachomianischen Mönchstradition*; Marsili, *Giovanni Cassiano ed Evagrio Pontico*. Vogüé's "Les sources des quatre premiers livres des Institutions de Jean Cassien" is a foretaste of pt. 1, volume 6 of his *Histoire littéraire du mouvement monastique dans l'antiquité*, largely devoted to Cassian. Our knowledge of Cassian's intellectual background should be considerably enriched by Vogüé's investigations. See also the specialized studies indicated hereafter.

62. See *De Inc.* 7.24–30: Hilary, Ambrose, Jerome, Rufinus, Augustine; Gregory of Nazianzus, Athanasius, John Chrysostom. Despite Cassian's devotion to Chrysostom, his influence on Cassian's spiritual theology remains unclear.

63. See Vogüé's "Les sources des quatre premiers livres des Institutions de Jean Cassien," 245–47 and *passim*. As Vogüé notes, Cassian relies on Rufinus' translation of Basil's *Asc. parv.*, though there are hints of an acquaintance with the Greek text of *Reg. fus.* (see p. 300).

64. Jerome's *Ep.* 22.34–37 (CSEL 54, pp. 196.10–202.17) was the basis for Cassian's description of the kinds of monks in *Conf.* 18.4–7, though Vogüé notes that *Inst.* 4.10 and 4.17 seem closer to Jerome's indications in *Ep.* 22.35.1–2 (pp. 197.14–198.3) than to his Pachomian translations ("Les sources des quatre premiers livres des Institutions de Jean Cassien," 293–94). *Ep.* 22 turns up again in *De Inc.* 7.26.1. Jerome's *Ep.* 133 is the (unacknowledged) reason for Cassian's denial in *Conf.* 23 that monks can achieve a sinless state. See Driver, "From Palestinian Ignorance to Egyptian Wisdom."

65. See the appendix.

66. For Hermas, see *Conf.* 8.17.1 and 13.12.7. For Irenaeus, see Olphe-Galliard, "Les sources de la Conférence XI de Cassien," 296–98. For Cyprian and Tertullian, see Vogüé's "Les sources des quatre premiers livres des Institutions de Jean Cassien," 281–83; for Eusebius via Rufinus, see pp. 268–71.

67. For example, *Inst.* 5.4.2 on the monk as a "wise bee" (*apis prudentissima*): see Athanasius, *V. Ant.* 3.4 (p. 136.17), σοφὴ μέλισσα. Cassian follows Evagrius of Antioch's translation exactly (col. 844C), while the earlier anonymous Latin version translates the Greek literally as *sapiens illa apis* (p. 75). For Cassian's knowledge of traditions about Antony, see the appendix.

68. Vogüé, "Les sources des quatre premiers livres des Institutions de Jean Cassien," 303.

69. On Basil, see note 63; for Pachomius, see "Les sources des quatre premiers livres des Institutions de Jean Cassien," 274.

70. See, for example, Butler, *Lausiac History*, 2:224–25, and Vogüé, "Les sources des quatre premiers livres des Institutions de Jean Cassien," 293.

71. This knowledge is indicated implicitly by his rebuttal of them and explicitly as noted by Vogüé, "Les sources des quatre premiers livres des Institutions de Jean Cassien," 304–6.

72. See Vogüé, "Les sources des quatre premiers livres des Institutions de Jean Cassien," 273, 285, 288; Ramsey, "John Cassian, Student of Augustine?"; the discussion in chapters 1 and 4 of this study of Cassian's involvement in controversy about Augustine's views on grace. Duchrow suggested reverse influence, claiming that in the preface to *De doctrina christiana* (written, he proposes, in 426/27 with the later part of the work) Augustine was rebutting some of Cassian's views on the charismatic interpretation of Scripture ("Zum Prolog von Augustins *De Doctrina christiana*"). In the introduction to his edition of *De doctr.*, Green is cautious about the dating and skeptical of the parallels adduced between Cassian's ideas and those criticized by Augustine (pp. xiii–xiv).

73. Weber, building on Bousset's work in *Apophthegmata* (71–75), analyzes this material in *Die Stellung des Johannes Cassianus zur ausserpachomianischen Mönchstradition*.

74. See Ménager, "Cassien et Clément d'Alexandrie" and Olphe-Galliard, "Les sources de la Conférence XI de Cassien"; both wrote before Marsili's *Giovanni Cassiano ed Evagrio Pontico* demonstrated Cassian's dependence on Evagrius. See Vogüé, "Les sources des quatre premiers livres des Institutions de Jean Cassien," 279–80. Cassian does seem to depend on Clement for the distinction between τέλος and σκοπός (see chapter 3).

75. The first description is that of Courcelle (*Late Latin Writers and Their Greek Sources*, 229); Olphe-Galliard describes Cassian as "ni plagiaire, ni compilateur" but a "bon vulgarisateur" ("Cassien," 266). McGinn (*The Foundations of Mysticism*, 218–19) follows Chadwick's more nuanced view (*John Cassian*, 92–93), similar to that of Cappuyns ("Cassien," 1336).

76. Kemmer's two major works are *Charisma Maximum* and "Gregorius Nyssenus estne inter fontes Joannis Cassiani numerandus?"

77. See chapter 1.

78. *Reg. Ben.* 64.19 (p. 652). Modern editors suggest *Inst.* 2.12 and *Conf.* 2.4.4 as possible sources.

79. See the rather arch comments of A. Salles, whose 1929 thesis on Cassian was quoted by Olphe-Galliard: "A particular difficulty *(gêne)* is imposed on us by the manifest inadequacy of the vocabulary used in the *Conferences*. We don't mean simply the imprecision of a stammering kind of discourse, or the summary character of analyses that have barely been sketched out; the imprecision comes from the words themselves, which drift vaguely from one meaning to another" ("Vie contemplative et vie active d'après Cassien," 256 n. 18).

80. See Hadot's remarks about the unsystematic nature of ancient philosophical instruction in "Spiritual Exercises," 104–6.

81. See Harl, "Le guetteur et la cible: Les deux sens de *Skopos* dans la langue religieuse des chrétiens," especially pp. 454–58. I am indebted to Fr. Boniface Ramsey for this reference. See also Marsili, *Giovanni Cassiano ed Evagrio Pontico*, 38–39; Groves, "Mundicia cordis," 314–16; Kardong, "Aiming for the Mark"; Sheridan, "Models and Images," 114–16.

82. Evagrius used σκοπός in its ordinary sense of "purpose" or "aim," but not as a technical term or paired with τέλος.

83. See *Conf.* 3.15.3, 4.6.2, 7.4.2, 7.5.2, 9.12.1, 9.21.1, 14.16.4.

84. This famous Nubian ex-brigand would hardly have known the Latin Bible, which Cassian tells us was a useless curiosity in monastic Egypt (see *Inst.* 5.39).

85. This tendency is evident throughout the first several chapters of *Conf.* 1 and also in *Conf.* 2.26.4 (a summary of *Conf.* 1). *Destinatio* is used in a similar way in *Conf.* 10.7.3 (with *finis* as a synonym, though see 10.7.2 where *finis* has its eschatological meaning), 17.12.3 and 4, 17.14.1 and 3, 17.17.4, and 24.3.1. *Scopos* does occur one more time, along

with *destinatio*, in reference to the imperative to show God a "clean" heart (*Conf.* 17.14.3).

86. For *finis* as "end," see *Conf.* 1.2, 1.4, 1.5, 1.7, all *passim*; 1.11.1, 2.26.4 summarizing *Conf.* 1. For *finis* as a monastic "goal" or "purpose," see *Inst.* 5.4.3, 5.22, 6.14, 6.20, 12.13, 12.23; *Conf.* 9.2.1–2, 9.7.4, 9.31, 10.7.2–3, 11.14, 12.8.3, 12.16.3, 18.4.3, 19.4.3, 19.7, 19.8.3–4, 23.10.2.

87. Used even in *Conf.* 1.1 and 1.19.1. But see also *Inst.* 1.2.1, 4.23, 4.40, 5.4.1, 6.7.2; *Conf.* 3.2.1, 10.8.5, 11.2.1, 13.6.3, 14.4.1, 14.5.1, 16–17 *passim*, 18.1.3, 18.7.4, 18.7.6, 18.13.1, 18.14.2–3, 19.3.2–3, 19.5.2, 19.14.2, 20.1.3, 21.13.3, 21.32.2, 21.34, 23.2.1, 23.5.7, 23.6.5, 24.1.2, 24.2.2, 24.8.1, 24.8.5, 24.9.1, 24.10. An adjectival form is used in *Conf.* 17.14.3 with *destinatio* to define *scopos*, the only time this word is used outside of *Conf.* 1.

88. See the discussion of these themes in Chapter 3, and see passages such as *Conf.* 20.10, *studendum nobis est, ut virtutum potius adpetitu* [i.e., purity of heart] *et desiderio regni caelorum quam noxiis vitiorum recordationibus.*

89. *Certissima norma* (*Conf.* 24.6.1), *index veritatis* (*Conf.* 24.6.2).

Chapter 3

1. 1 Cor. 15:28, a text of great significance for Cassian's magnificent description of the human end in *Conf.* 10.7. As noted in chapter 6, the same biblical text was central to Origen's vision of the final restoration of all things in Christ.

2. See the discussion of this distinction in chapter 2.

3. Examples are unceasing prayer (*Conf.* 10.8), chastity (*Conf.* 12.8.3–4), interpreting the Bible "spiritually" (*Conf.* 14.1–4), and various forms of monastic life (*Conf.* 18.2–4). In terms of the model proposed by Thurman ("Tibetan Buddhist Perspectives on Asceticism," 109), Cassian is using examples of "mundane relative" and "mundane ultimate" asceticism to illustrate his argument for "spiritual relative" (*scopos*, purity of heart) and "spiritual ultimate" (*telos*, kingdom of heaven) asceticism.

4. *Conf.* 1.2.3–1.3; see *Inst.* 12.12, *Conf.* 20.10. Cassian uses "reign of God" and "reign of heaven" synonymously. Any preference for one or the other can usually be explained by the biblical passage being quoted or interpreted at that point.

5. See the discussion later in this chapter on "the reign of God is within you."

6. See the discussion later in this chapter on "Blessed are the pure in heart, for they shall see God."

7. See *Inst.* 4.43. Because *Inst.* 5–12 form the separate treatise on the eight principal faults, *Conf.* 1 resumes the discussion begun in *Inst.* 4. The final lines of the first set of *Conferences* return to the theme of purity of heart (*Conf.* 10.14.3).

8. The most thorough study remains that of Juana Raasch, "The Monastic Concept of Purity of Heart and its Sources." See also Colombás, *El monacato primitivo*, 2.287–90; Regnault, "The Beatitudes in the *Apophthegmata Patrum*," 36–39; the useful and concise summary in Groves, "Mundicia cordis," 308–14. For Origen's teaching, see Crouzel, *Origène et la "connaissance mystique"*, 430–32.

9. *The Habit of Being*, 126.

10. Occurring more than fifty times: eleven in *Inst.*, forty in *Conf.*

11. These two phrases are used in exactly the same way as *puritas cordis*, and they will be incorporated into the analysis of purity of heart. See note 12 on Evagrius.

12. See *Gnost.* 49 (pp. 190–91); for this chapter, as for so much of *Gnost.*, one depends on the Syriac version, the original Greek being no longer extant. Frankenberg is probably correct in assuming that σκοπός underlies the Syriac *nīšā* (*Gnost.* [*Syr.*], p. 552.27). See *Prak.* 78 (pp. 666–67) and *Gnost.* 2 (pp. 90–91) for a similar statement about the purpose of the πρακτική.

13. For the definition, see *Schol. in Ps.* 15:9 (*PG* 12.1216A): "it is customary in Scripture to have καρδία instead of νοῦς." Philo and Clement had made a similar equation, but Origen did so more consistently and determinatively; see p. 3 of Raasch, "The Monastic Concept of Purity of Heart," on Philo, Clement, and Origen. On the "heart" in early Christian literature, see Guillaumont, "Les sens des noms du coeur dans l'antiquité" and "Le "coeur" chez les spirituels grecs à l'époque ancienne."

14. Much has been written on the subject; see, for example, the Guillaumonts' introduction to *Prak.* (SC 170, pp. 98–112); Bell, "Apatheia: the Convergence of Byzantine and Cistercian Spirituality"; Tibiletti, "Giovanni Cassiano," 365–68; Bunge, *Evagrios Pontikos: Briefe aus der Wüste*, 118–25, and the commentary on *Prak.* 57–70 in *Evagrios Pontikos: Praktikos oder der Mönch*, 189–213; McGinn, *Foundations of Mysticism*, 105–6 and 151–52.

15. *Ep.* 133 to Ctesiphon (CSEL 56, pp. 241–60; see sec. 3.5–6, p. 246). Cassian was aware of Jerome's critique; *Conf.* 23 can be taken as a reply to Jerome's letter.

16. He quotes the text only three times: *Inst.* 8.20.1, here at *Conf.* 1.10.5, *Conf.* 14.9.1. He alludes to it in *Conf.* 11.12.2. Almost a hundred other biblical texts are cited as often as this one. He has a general discussion of all the beatitudes in *Conf.* 11.12.2; cites Matt. 5:3 ("poor in spirit") four times (*Conf.* 3.9.1, 9.29.4, 10.11.1, 21.5.2), Matt. 5:4 ("meek") once (*Conf.* 12.6.1). See Regnault's comments on the scarcity of Matt. 5:8 in the *Apophthegmata* ("The Beatitudes in the *Apophthegmata Patrum*," 37).

17. He cites two other texts referring to a clean or pure heart, Ps. 50(51):12 (*Conf.* 13.9.4) and Prov. 20:9 (*Conf.* 23.17.1).

18. In *Conference* 1 he quotes the beatitude only in his summary statement, following the Latin versions, which use *mundus* ("clean") instead of *purus* (*Conf.* 1.10.5). Cassian uses *cor mundum* in *Inst.* 5.21.5, and he describes it as the *scopos* or *destinatio* of the monastic life in *Conf.* 17.14.3. He also uses nouns and verbs related to *mundus* when he describes the process of purification for heart and mind, though these are less frequent than words related to *purus/puritas*. For *emundare* and *mundare*, see, for example, *Inst.* 6.2, 7.12; *Conf.* 5.14.2, 9.30.1, 10.6.4, 11.9.5, 14.8.3, 14.9.1. For *emundatio*, see, for example, *Inst.* 5.34; *Conf.* 1.10.1, 1.10.5, 4.19.2, 5.14.4, 6.11.1, 9.3.2, 21.36.4. On the early Cisterican writers who prized Cassian's teaching but used *munditia cordis* rather than *puritas cordis*, see Groves, "Mundicia cordis," 318–31.

19. For an overview, see Raasch, "The Monastic Concept of Purity of Heart," *passim*. For Origen, see Rahner, "Le début d'une doctrine des cinq sens spirituels," 127 n. 101. For Evagrius, see, for example, *De orat.*, *passim*, on "pure prayer" (καθαρὰ προσευχή); *Prak.* 23 (p. 554.7) and 42 (p.596.3–4): καθαρὰ . . . ἡ εὐχή/προσευχή; 49 (p. 612.6): νοῦς . . . καθαρός; and see 100 (p. 710.4): διὰ τῶν ἁγίων μυστηρίων καθαρίζοντας; *Gnost.* 3 (p. 90): οἱ ἀκάθαρτοι contrasted with οἱ καθαροί (see *Schol. in Prov.* 72, p. 168); *Schol. in Prov.* 31 (p. 124): νοῦς καθαρός; 63 (p. 154): τοῖς δὲ ἀπαθέσι καὶ καθαροῖς; 93.1 (p. 192): οἱ λογισμοί . . . οἱ μὲν καθαροί . . . οἱ δὲ ἀκάθαρτοι; 153 (p. 248.20–21): διαφόραι . . . καθαραὶ καταστάσεις; *Schol. in Ps.* 65:20 (*PG* 12.1504A) on pure heart and pure prayer. See Gregory of Nyssa, *De beat.* 6 (p. 144.2–4): καθαρότης γὰρ καὶ ἀπάθεια καὶ κακοῦ παντὸς ἀλλοτρίωσις ἡ θεότης ἐστίν.

20. Nonetheless, the Vulgate consistently translates καθαρίζω and καθαρός with *mundare* and *mundus* or related words. Only in 1–2 Tim. does one find καθαρός translated *purus* (1 Tim. 1:5, 3:9; 2 Tim. 1:3, 2:22); Cassian does not quote these texts.

21. On Cassian's teaching, see Olphe-Galliard, "La pureté de coeur d'après Cassien"; Raasch, "The Monastic Concept of Purity of Heart and Its Sources," p. 5; Groves, "Mundicia cordis," 314–18; Kardong, "John Cassian's Evaluation of Monastic Practices," 92–96.

22. For Evagrius' teaching, see the Guillaumonts' introduction to *Prak.*, SC 170, pp. 98–112, and Joest, "Die Bedeutung von Akedia und Apatheia bei Evagrios Pontikos."

23. For example, *Inst.* 4.43, 5.7, 5.22, 8.22, 12.15.2, 12.24; *Conf.* 1.4.3, 1.7.4, 2.26.4, 3.10.5, 4.12.1, 4.12.4, 5.27, 10.14.3, 12.5.4, 12.5.5, 12.6.7, 12.7.3, 12.8.5, 12.12.1, 13.5.2, 14.4.1, 17.14.3, 19.14.7, 21.36, 22.3.4.

24. Love: *Inst.* 4.43; *Conf.* 1.6.3, 1.7.2, 1.10.5, 20.12.4, 21.17.1. Contemplation: *Inst.* 2.12.2, 5.32.1; *Conf.* 1.10.5, 1.15.3, 9.15.3. Spiritual knowledge: *Inst.* 1.11, 5.33; *Conf.* 1.14, 14.9.3, 14.9.7, 14.15. Prayer: *Conf.* 9.8.1. Chastity: *Conf.* 12.7.4, 12.8.1. Union with God: *Conf.* 2.2.2. Beatitude: *Conf.* 22.6.9.

25. See *Inst.* 12.24, *Conf.* 1.10.5, 11, *passim*, 22.3.4.

26. *Inst.* 9.1; *Conf.* 4.4.1, 12.6.7–9, 19.6.6.

27. *Inst.* 5.34; *Conf.* 1.15.3, 9.8.1, 15.9, 15.10.4, 21.22.1, 21.22.3.

28. See the Guillaumonts' introduction to *Prak.*, in SC 170, pp. 108–11.

29. See chapter 2 for Cassian's play on the Greek and Latin texts.

30. See, for example, Rahner, "Le début d'une doctrine des cinq sens spirituels," 127 n. 101, and McGinn, *Foundations of Mysticism*, 118–30.

31. See *Prak.* Prol. 8 (p. 492.49–51) and 81 (p. 670), though see 84 (p. 674); see the Guillaumonts' remarks in the introduction to *Prak.* in SC 170, pp. 111–12. Cassian seems to follow Evagrius with a similar statement about purity of heart and love in *Inst.* 4.43, when he describes the stages of monastic life from fear of the Lord to purity of heart and "the perfection of apostolic love." See *Conf.* 20.12.4 and 21.17 on "apostolic love."

32. See *Prak.*, Prol. 8 (p. 492.49–51) and the Guillaumonts' commentary (SC 170, pp.103, 109–112). On the role of ἀγάπη, see *Prak.* 38 (p. 586), 81 (p. 670), 84 (p. 674); *Gnost.* 47 (p. 184); *Keph. gnost.* 3.35 (p. 111); *Ad mon.* 3 (p. 45). The relationship between love and knowledge in Evagrius' thought is ambiguous; his general tendency is to posit knowledge of God as the ultimate goal, which then suggests that love is a means toward knowledge. Bunge has argued that Evagrius does not exalt γνῶσις over ἀγάπη, but sees love as the organizing principle for *all* stages of the spiritual life. See, for example, *Evagrios Pontikos: Briefe aus der Wüste*, 129–39, and Joest's summary in "Die Bedeutung von Akedia und Apatheia bei Evagrios Pontikos," 41–45.

33. See *Conf.* 10.7 and *Conf.* 14, *passim*.

34. See Kardong, "John Cassian's Evaluation of Monastic Practices," 93–95.

35. *Conf.* 1.7.4 and 19.12.2–3; see 16.15–20.

36. See Evagrius, *Ep.* 28, noting that one who has asceticism (Syr. ʿānwāyūtā) without long-suffering and love is like the foolish virgins who had lamps without oil (p. 584 [Syr.] and p. 585 [Gk. retroversion]).

37. For example, *Apoph. Alph.* Joseph of Panephysis 1 (col. 228AC), Moses 5 (col. 284BC), Matoes 6 (col. 292A). Marsili (*Giovanni Cassiano ed Evagrio Pontico*, 88–89) and Weber (*Die Stellung des Johannes Cassianus zur ausserpachomianischen Mönchstradition*, 74–75) suggest Evagrius, *Rerum mon. rat.* 10 (cols. 1261D–6A) as the source for *Inst.* 5.24, though Weber admits that it is impossible to tell if the dependence is literary or mediated by oral transmission either by Evagrius himself or by others. Since the only elements common to Evagrius' and Cassian's discussions are the importance of fulfilling the commandment of love (Evagrius: νόμον ἀγάπης πεπλήρωκας, Cassian: *opus . . . caritatis inpleri exigit praecepti necessitas*) and the possibility of having to eat more than once a day if guests come (up to three times in Evagrius, six times in a story Cassian relates), it would seem that Cassian may simply be relating a tradition valued also by Evagrius but not unique to him.

38. *Inst.* 5.24–26; see *Conf.* 2.26, 17.21–24, 21.14, 24.20. Note his conclusion that a monk truly afire with divine love will attract ever-increasing numbers of visitors who must be received kindly (*Conf.* 24.19.1). Summa analyzes these passages in *Geistliche Unterscheidung bei Johannes Cassian*, 154–56.

39. This issue underlies the discussion of discernment in *Conf.* 2, the difference between the second and third renunciations in *Conf.* 3.10, the comparison of physical continence and "integrity of mind" (i.e., chastity) in *Conf.* 12.2 and 4, the reprise of 1 Cor. 13 in *Conf.* 15.2, the relativization of ascetical undertakings and promises in *Conf.* 17, the exposure of false humility in *Conf.* 18.11, the comparison of fasting to love in *Conf.* 21.13–20, the confusion of purity of heart with outward disciplines in *Conf.* 22.3.4, and the probing of motives for anchoritic withdrawal "back home" in *Conf.* 24.18–21.

40. Olphe-Galliard suggests a parallel between *Conf.* 11.6.1 and Basil's prologue to *Reg. fus.* (col. 896); see "Les sources de la Conférence XI de Cassien," 292. The progression from fear to love was already suggested in the signs of humility outlined in *Inst.* 4.39.3, which were the source for the twelve steps of humility found in the *Rule of the Master* (*Reg. Mag.* 10) and adopted by Benedict (*Reg. Ben.* 7). For Cassian, humility is a fundamental virtue, secured by obedience and allowing one to move on to purity of heart; for the Master and for Benedict, humility is the summit of monastic perfection, analogous to Cassian's "purity of heart." The twelfth step of humility in *Reg. Mag.* 10.82–86 (vol. 1, pp. 436–38) and *Reg. Ben.* 7.62–66 (p. 488) is the classic description for the western monastic tradition of the monk who is "pure of heart."

41. See "perfection of heart" (*Conf.* 11.10), "integrity of heart" (*Conf.* 11.14).

42. *Corporales exercitationes* versus *principalia mandata*. In *Inst.* 5.24 the contrast is between the "free-will offering" (*voluntarii muneris oblatio*) of fasting and the "imperative of the commandment" (*praecepti necessitas*) to fulfill a work of love.

43. See Golìnski, "Doctrina Cassiani de mendacio officioso"; Ramsey, "Two Traditions on Lying and Deception in the Ancient Church" and "John Cassian: Student of Augustine?" 7–8; Fleming, *The Helpful Lie: the Moral Reasoning of Augustine and John Cassian.*

44. See *Inst.* 10.2.4, *Conf.* 1.20.4–5, 24.13. See Evagrius, *De orat.* 10 (col. 1169B) and *Rerum mon. rat.* 3 (col. 1253CD, citing Martha and Mary); and see *Ep.* 7 (p. 572.5–10 [Syr.], p. 573.5–11 [Gk. retroversion]), 41 (p. 594.1–8 [Syr.], p. 593.48–595.8 [Gk. retroversion]).

45. See note 13 on Evagrius' use of νοῦς and καρδία. Ordinarily Cassian makes no distinction between these words, though when working from biblical texts he tends to favor *cor* and when following Evagrius more closely he tends to use *mens*. Cassian also uses *anima/animus*, "soul," in the same way as *mens* and *cor*. Where the "soul" properly understood is the subject, such as *Conf.* 1.14 and *Conf.* 24.15, he uses *anima*. For Cassian *anima* and *animus* are basically synonymous, though he uses *anima* more frequently and tends to prefer it for definitions of perfection and other qualities. See Wrzol, "Die Psychologie des Johannes Cassianus," p. 2, pp. 428–30.

46. Cassian uses *tranquillitas* alone about twenty times; *t. mentis* occurs six times (*Inst.* 5.32.2, *Conf.* 1.7.4, 9.2.1, 9.6.5, 18.16.4, 19.11.2); *t. cordis* occurs five times (*Conf.* 11.9.2, 12.11.3, 15.10.3, 16.22.3, 19.6.5; see *Conf.* 12.7.3), *t. animae* occurs twice, once along with *cordis* (*Conf.* 19.6.5) and once as synonymous with *puritas cordis* (*Conf.* 19.14.7). The adjective *tranquillus* is used in this way at *Inst.* 9.1 and 12.33.1; *Conf.* 12.6.5, 12.7.3, 16.26.2, 16.27.3, 19.5.1. The superlative form *tranquillissimus* is used at *Conf.* 7.2.3 and 24.3.2, but with no apparent difference in meaning.

47. *Stabilitas mentis, Conf.* 7.6.3, 19.6.5; *s. boni, Conf.* 11.8.3; *s. cogitationum, Conf.* 10.10.12; *s. cordis, Conf.* 10.10.8; *s. humilitatis, Conf.* 18.13.1; *s. iustitiae, Conf.* 22.13.6; *s. puritatis, Conf.* 7.3.1; *s. sensuum, Conf.* 22.7.1. The adjective *stabilis* is used in this way at *Conf.* 7.3.2, 7.23.1, 9.2.1, 10.14.1, 16.24, 18.13.1, 19.14.5, 23.3.4; for the adverbial form *stabiliter*, see *Conf.* 10.8.5, 10.12, 12.4.4, 12.6.3, 14.16.6, 23.9.1.

48. *Firmitas* alone, *Conf.* 14.10.2; *f. puritatis*, *Conf.* 7.3.1, 19.16.5; *f. animae*, *Conf.* 10.14.1; *f. pacis*, *Conf.* 12.10.2; *f. patientiae*, *Conf.* 19.11.1; *f. recti consilii*, *Inst.* 8.22; *f. sanctarum cogitationum*, *Conf.* 9.7.2. For the adjective *firmus* see *Inst.* 4.8, 7.31; *Conf.* 1.20.7, 2.2.1, 7.3.2, 9.2.1, 11.8.3, 12.6.6, 18.16.1. The superlative form *firmissimus* is in *Inst.* 5.17.1; *Conf.* 12.11.1, 15.7.2. For the participle *firmatus*, see *Inst.* 3.5.2; *Conf.* 10.11.1. For the adverb *firme*, see *Inst.* 9.7; for *firmiter*, see *Conf.* 3.18.1; for *firmissime*, see *Inst.* 12.32.1.; 12.33.2; *Conf.* 10.8.3.

49. *Patientia* is used dozens of times, describing a virtue often linked to humility; some of these occurrences are synonymous with purity of heart, while others are not so specifically associated with the achievement of perfection. For *patientia cordis*, see *Inst.* 6.23 and *Conf.* 12.6.1, 18.13.1; *animi*, *Conf.* 18.14.5. The participial form *patiens* is used at *Inst.* 8.18, 9.11; *Conf.* 3.7.10, 9.12.2, 18.13.2. *Patienter* is used in a more general sense.

50. *Constantia* is often described as a particular virtue: see *Inst.* 4.3.1, 4.27.3; *Conf.* 4.6.3, 6.9.3, 7.5.1, 9.7.2, 9.23.1, 10.10.13, 14.16.7, 17.8.4, 18.15.2, 18.16.1, 24.8.5. *Constantia mentis*: *Inst.* 5.9, *Conf.* 4.4.2, 19.11.1; *c. cordis*, *Inst.* 9.1; *c. desiderii*, *Conf.* 4.6.3; *c. fidei*, *Conf.* 13.14.4; *c. patientiae*, *Inst.* 4.39.2. The one relevant use of *constanter* is at *Conf.* 19.14.5.

51. *Immobilitas* occurs once (*Conf.* 18.16.1), though the adjective *immobilis* is used four times (*Conf.* 1.8.1, 6.14.2, 18.13.1, 19.9.2). Relevant uses of the adjective *inmobiliter* are at *Conf.* 6.14.1, 6.16.3, 9.2.3, 10.8.4, 10.12, 10.13.3, 11.7.6, 17.27, 19.4.5, 24.6.3.

52. *Integritas* is often used as a synonym for *castitas*, "chastity," which for Cassian is itself a synonymn for purity of heart, perfection, and so on; for this use, see *Inst.* 6.4.1, 6.8, 6.18 (thrice), 6.20, 12.10; *Conf.* 4.16, 12.4.3 (twice), 12.6.8, 12.10.1, 13.6.1, 21.23.3, 21.33.3, 21.36.3, 22.3.6, 22.5.1. Other occurrences of the word are not so explicitly associated with chastity, though of course there would be an implicit association; these are in *Inst.* only: *Inst.* 5.6, 5.7, 5.9, 5.14, 6.2, 12.11.2, 12.13, 12.20. The most frequent construction is *integritas mentis* (*Inst.* 4.24.2, 5.9, 5.10, 6.4.1, 6.16; *Conf.* 12.2.5, 21.23.2), followed by *i. cordis* (*Inst.* 6.19; *Conf.* 4.15.2, 11.14, 19.16.3), *i. pacis* (*Conf.* 16.3.5) and *i. puritatis* (*Conf.* 4.15.1). For the adjective *integer*, see *Inst.* 6.22; *Conf.* 1.7.2, 1.21.2, 7.5.6, 8.3.6, 8.24.3, 10.14.3, 17.17.3, 17.19.8, 19.9.1, 20.7.2, 21.25.1, 23.17.3.

53. For *Conf.* 3.3–4 on three calls, see Antony's *Ep.* 1 (noted by Rubenson, *The Letters of St. Antony*, 85–86 n. 5; text on pp. 197–98); for *Conf.* 3.6 on the three renunciations, see Evagrius, *Keph. gnost.* 1.78–80 (pp. 53–55; noted by Marsili, *Giovanni Cassiano ed Evagrio Pontico*, 94–95). Note that Evagrius' third renunciation is of ignorance, while Cassian's is about the move from present, earthly realities to invisible, future ones, as in *Inst.* 4.35 and elsewhere.

54. *Conf.* 3.10.5–6; see 3.7.3.

55. I take *militare domino coeperimus* to mean "we will begin to serve the Lord" rather than "no longer [be] at war with the Lord" as does Gibson, *The Works of John Cassian*, 322.

56. *Conf.* 20.5.2–3. For Cassian, such fantasies indicate either spiritual immaturity or theological error. See *Inst.* 6.7.2, 6.10; *Conf.* 3.7.3, 9.3.3, 10.5, 10.11.6, 14.12; and see the discussion of erotic images in chapter 4 and of false images of God in chapter 5.

57. See the discussion in chapter 5.

58. See *Inst.* 11.18 (united to *theoria divina*); *Conf.* 1.11.2 (God), 1.12 (God), 1.13.1 (Christ), 2.2.2 (God), 3.1.2 (Lord), 7.6.1 (Lord), 7.6.4 (Christ), 10.7.2 (Father with Son), 14.4.1 (God), 19.8.4 (Christ), 23.5.2 (God), 23.5.7 (Christ), 23.11.1 (God), 23.16.2 (God and Christ). These passages use the verbs *adhaerere, cohaerere, copulari, inhaerere*, and *uniri*, often in combination. Codina notes Cassian's Christocentrism in *El aspecto cristologico en la espiritualidad de Juan Casiano*, 85–90. See the discussion in chapter 5.

59. Thus the explicit equation later in *Conf.* 1.13.1: *inhaerere quidem deo iugiter et contemplationi eius . . . inseparabiliter copulari*; see the discussion later in this chapter on "beatitude" and in chapters 5–6 on *Conf.* 9–10.

60. *Theoria* occurs three times in this *Conf.*: 1.8.2, 1.8.3, 1.12; the adjective *theoretica* occurs at 1.1. There is no verbal form used in Cassian's works, as there was no Latinization of the Greek verb θεωρέω either by him or others. *Contemplatio* is, not surprisingly, the more common word, occurring twelve times in *Conf.* 1 and dozens of times thereafter: *Conf.* 1.2.2, 1.4.3, 1.6, 1.8.2–3 (thrice), 1.10.5, 1.13 (twice), 1.15.1, 1.15.3, 1.22.2. The verbal form *contemplari* is relatively less common but still frequent.

61. For overviews, see Hausherr et al., "Contemplation" (the Greek Christian tradition); Olphe-Galliard, "Contemplation" (the Latin Christian tradition of Augustine and Cassian); McGinn, *The Foundations of Mysticism*, 100–130; Špidlík, *Spirituality of the Christian East*, 327–49. For Origen, Crouzel's *Origène et la "connaissance mystique"* is fundamental: for the vocabulary of contemplation, see especially pp. 375–82. See the section hereafter on "beatitude" for further bibliography.

62. "Eyes of the heart" (*oculi cordis*), *Inst.* 5.34 and 8.6; *Conf.* 1.13.2, 3.7.4, 14.9.7, 23.6.5; "eyes of the soul" (*oculi animae*), *Inst.* 4.35 and 5.2.3; *Conf.* 5.15.4; "eye of the mind" (*oculus mentis*), *Inst.* 8.1.1; "eyes of the inner person" (*oculi interioris hominis*), *Conf.* 7.21.4; "spiritual eyes" (*spiritales oculi*), *Conf.* 5.16.6. Often he uses "eyes" in a way that clearly refers not to physical sight but to considering spiritual goals or realities, as when describing the goal of the monastic life in *Conf.* 1.5.4, the eight faults outlined in *Conf.* 5.27.2, the ineffable gifts of God in *Conf.* 9.14, and the divinity of Christ in *Conf.* 10.6.2. Cassian does not elaborate a doctrine of "spiritual senses," faculties of the soul corresponding to the physical organs of the body, as do Origen and Evagrius (see Rahner, "Le début d'une doctrine des cinq sens spirituels"; Canévet, "Sens spirituel"; Stewart, *Working the Earth of the Heart*, 119–21 and 133–37). Cassian uses the word *sensus* for physical sensation, for the meaning or "sense" of a text, or for the faculty of understanding (see the English expression, "someone with good sense"). The phrase *sensus spiritalis* for Cassian refers to the spiritual interpretation of the Bible, not to the "eyes" or "ears" of the soul (though *Inst.* 10.4 and *Conf. Pref.* 1 seem to be exceptions). He also mentions "spiritual fragrance" in *Conf.* 4.5, 14.13.3, 20.9.1.

63. The occurrences of these adjectives are so many and so frequent that, as with *purus*, it becomes pointless to list them all.

64. See *Conf. Pref.* 1 5, *Conf.* 5.23.2, 12.11.2; *De Inc.* 7.9. This interpretation appears to have originated with Philo and been adopted by Origen. On this theme, see Rubenson, *The Letters of St. Antony*, 41, 69 (with references to Philo and Origen) and 169; Sheridan's "Jacob and Israel" is the most thorough treatment.

65. See Reypens, "Dieu (connaissance mystique)," 886–89.

66. For an overview, see Hausherr et al. "Contemplation," 1767–72 and 1779–83; Camelot, "Gnose chrétienne"; McGinn, *The Foundations of Mysticism*, 89–130. For Clement, see *Strom.*, *passim*, especially 7.3 (pp. 10–16); Camelot, *Foi et gnose*; Völker, *Der wahre Gnostiker nach Clemens Alexandrinus*; Guillaumont, "Le gnostique chez Clément d'Alexandrie et chez Évagre le Pontique." On Origen, see Völker, *Das Vollkommenheitsideal des Origenes*, 84; Crouzel, *Origène et la "connaissance mystique,"* *passim*, and *Origen*, 119. For Evagrius, note the titles of the second and third volumes of his foundational trilogy: the *Gnostikos* and *Kephalaia gnostica*, "The Knowing One" and "Chapters on Knowledge." His assumptions are in, for example, *Prak.* 3 (p. 500) and *Gnost.* 1–3 (pp. 88–90). See Hausherr, "Ignorance infinie" and his reprise in "Ignorance infinie ou science infinie?"; A. and C. Guillaumont, introductions to *Prak.*, SC 170, pp. 102–4, 109–12, and to *Gnost.*,

SC 356, pp. 24–33; Géhin's introduction to *Schol. in Prov.*, SC 340, pp. 37–44. See Guillaumont, "Le gnostique chez Clément d'Alexandrie et chez Évagre le Pontique."

67. See, for example, *Inst.* 5.33–34 and *Conf.* 14.16. This issue will be discussed in chapter 5.

68. The principal loci are Origen's *Hom. in Luc.* fr. 171 [formerly fr. 39] (p. 298) and *Comm. in Iohann.* fr. 80 (p. 547). In the first, Origen contrasts Martha's literalist, bodily, "Judaic" interpretation of the Law with Mary's devotion to "contemplation alone and spiritual [matters]," applying the story to ways of interpreting the Bible. Evagrius' use of the story in *Rerum mon. rat.* 3 (col. 1253 CD) is about the dangers of hospitality. On Origen, see Crouzel, *Origène et la "connaissance mystique"*, 434–38; on the history of exegesis of the text, see Csányi, *"Optima pars,"* especially pp. 33 (Evagrius) and 59–65 (Cassian, though see note 131); the Guillaumonts' introduction to *Prak.*, SC 170, pp. 43–48; Solignac and Donnat, "Marthe et Marie"; Constable, "The Interpretation of Mary and Martha." Augustine saw Martha and Mary as types of the church, present and eschatological; see Bonnardière, "Marthe et Marie."

69. Cassian describes contemplation as both *summum bonum* (*Conf.* 1.7.4, foreshadowing the Martha and Mary story; 1.8.3, 1.13.1, 9.6.4–5, 23.5.3, 23.5.7, 23.10.2, 23.15.5, 23.19.1) and *principale bonum* (*Conf.* 1.8.2, 23.11.1 [see *Conf.* 1.8.1], 23.15.5).

70. Origen had praised Mary's devotion to θεωρία μόνη (*Hom. in Luc.*, fr. 171 (p. 298.21). A similar phrase is also found in *Conf.* 9.18, describing the higher stage of prayer that *contemplatione dei solius et caritatis ardore formatur*.

71. *Conf.* 1.8.3, 23.5.5.

72. See *Conf.* 23.3.4. The literature on the philosophical background is immense; any basic study would indicate the key texts. The articles by Lilla, "Neoplatonism" and "Platonism and the Fathers," are dense but comprehensive. For a more discursive treatment, see McGinn, *The Foundations of Mysticism*, 46–47, 58–59.

73. For overviews and bibliography, see McGinn's *The Foundations of Mysticism*, 114–18 (Origen) and 147–57 (Evagrius), as well as standard works such as Crouzel, *Origen*, 205–18 and 235–66, and Guillaumont, *Les 'Képhalaia gnostica' d'Évagre le Pontique*, 102–19. On Evagrius, see more recently Bunge, *"Mysterium Unitatis."* Here as elsewhere, Bunge argues that Evagrius' teaching—even in its most speculative aspects—is firmly rooted both in both Christian and monastic tradition; see his "Origenismus-Gnostizismus." For a helpful overview of Bunge's work, see O'Laughlin, "New Questions Concerning the Origenism of Evagrius."

74. The most helpful overviews are P. Hadot, "Ancient Spiritual Exercies and 'Christian Philosophy'," especially pp. 136–38, and "La division des parties de la philosophie"; and McGinn, "Asceticism and Mysticism in Late Antiquity," 62–68. See the useful summaries of sources in the Guillaumonts' introduction to Evagrius' *Prak.*, SC 170, pp. 38–56; Viller, "Aux sources de la spiritualité de saint Maxime"; Rahner, "Le début d'une doctrine des cinq sens spirituels," 126–41 (though many of the scholia on the Psalms Rahner finds most interesting are by Evagrius rather than by Origen); Solignac's "Vie active, vie contemplative, vie mixte," 592–602; Géhin's introduction to Evagrius' *Schol. in Prov.* (SC 340, pp. 27–31).

75. The order varied, especially in the placement of λογικός (*logikos*), often listed first. By the first century CE, the order had stabilized into the sequence ἠθικός (*ēthikos*), φυσικός (*physikos*), and ἐποπτικός (*epoptikos*), the last a Platonic term that replaced the Stoic λογικός. See P. Hadot, "Les divisions des parties de la philosophie dans l'Antiquité," 208–12 and 218–21, and "Philosophie, discours philosophique, et divisions de la philosophie chez les stoïciens."

76. See the Guillaumont's introduction to *Prak.*, SC 170, pp. 40–48; P. Hadot, "Les divisions des parties de la philosophie dans l'Antiquité," 213–21; McGinn, "Asceticism and Mysticism in Late Antiquity," 61.

77. See the Prologue to *Comm. in Cant.* (p. 75). See Crouzel, *Origène et la "connaissance mystique,"* 50–54. Note that Porphyry applied the Stoic schema to Plotinus' *Enneads* (P. Hadot, "Les divisions des parties de la philosophie dans l'Antiquité," 219).

78. See the prologue to *Prak.* (p. 492.54–57), describing the plan for Evagrius' basic monastic writings, which we know as: (1) *Praktikos*; (2a) *Gnostikos*; and (2b) *Kephalaia Gnostica*, "the Knowing Chapters."

79. This scheme is most famously presented in *Prak.* 2 (p. 498): Χριστιανισμός ἐστι δόγμα τοῦ Σωτῆρος ἡμῶν Χριστοῦ ἐκ πρακτικῆς καὶ φυσικῆς καὶ θεολογικῆς συνεστός. See *Gnost.* 12–13 (pp. 106–7), 18 (p. 117), 20 (pp. 119–21), 49 (p. 191).

80. See Géhin's observation that Evagrius applied the model systematically to interpretation of the Bible. Clement had used it as one possible device; Origen had applied it to the three Solomonic texts of Proverbs, Ecclesiastes, and Song of Songs (see Géhin's introduction to *Schol. in Prov.*, SC 340, pp. 29–30).

81. See *Gnost.* 37 (p. 158) on the need to persevere in fasting to maintain *apatheia*.

82. See *Hist. mon.* 8.8 (p. 49) for Apollo's skill at determining whether a monk should concentrate on *praktikē* or *theōrētikē*.

83. Πρακτική ἐστι μέθοδος πνευματικὴ τὸ παθητικὸν μέρος τῆς ψυχῆς ἐκκαθαίρουσα, *Prak.* 78 (p. 666).

84. The threefold pattern associated with Proverbs, Ecclesiastes, and Song of Songs does appear, however, in *Conf.* 3.6.4, with respect to the "three renunciations." See Olphe-Galliard, "Vie contemplative et vie active d'après Cassien."

85. *Conf.* 14.1.3: *id est actualis, quae emendatione morum et vitiorum purgatione perficitur.*

86. *Conf.* 14.9.2, 14.9.5; see *Conf.* 5.21.3. For the background, see the Stoic sources noted by the Guillaumonts in their introduction to *Prak.*, SC 170, p. 38 n.1. The most important Christian use of the tripartite moral/natural/rational scheme is Origen's in *Comm. in Cant.* Prol. (p. 75).

87. Cassian normally translates *praktikos* with the late Latin *actualis*, a better equivalent than *activus*, which is too suggestive of "action" rather than "practice, exercise." See Solignac, "Vie active, vie contemplative, vie mixte," 601.

88. See *Conf.* 14.1.3, 14.2–4, 14.16.3, 15.2.2, and cf. 21.36.4. See P. Hadot, "Spiritual Exercises," 100–01.

89. The word was derived from *actus*, "deed," but could not produce its own substantive form as readily as the Greek πρακτικός, which became simply τὸ πρακτικόν or ἡ πρακτική.

90. *Conf.* 10.3.1, 14.3.1, 14.9.2, 14.9.4, 21.34.4.

91. *Inst.* 5.33, *Conf. Pref.* 1 4, *Conf.* 8.3.6. Note that this phrase is the only way *actualis* is used in *Inst.*

92. *Conf.* 6.1.2.

93. *Opus: Conf.* 1.8.3; *operatio: Conf.* 1.10.5.

94. *Conf.* 14.9.5.

95. *Conf.* 14.8.6.

96. *Conf.* 10.9.1.

97. *Conf.* 23.5.5.

98. *Conf.* 14.8.3.

99. *Conf.* 14.16.3.

100. *Conf.* 1.1.

101. *Conf.* 14.4.1–3; see 14.8.1 and 24.8.3.

102. *Inst.* 6.1, 6.18; *Conf.* 1.14.1, 14.8–17, *passim.*

103. See *Inst.* 5.2.2, 5.34, 6.18; *Conf.* 6.3.1, 11.13.2, 14.9.5, 14.13.4, 14.16.2.

104. He is more willing to use the adjectival *theoreticus* than *theoria*, and does so several times in *Conf.* 14; see *Conf.* 14.2 (twice, with *scientia*), 14.8.3 *(disciplina),* 14.9.2 *(puritas).* In *Conf.* 14, he uses *contemplatio* only once; otherwise he uses the Greek or *scientia spiritalis.* He does, however, use forms of the verb *contemplari* (*Conf.* 14.1.3, 14.9.7; 14.11.3 is in a very different context). This usage is probably owing to his explicit use in *Conf.* 14 of the Origenist/Evagrian system, though it is noteworthy that he prefers the more traditional θεωρητική *(theōrētikē)* to Evagrius' γνωστική *(gnōstikē)* or θεολογική *(theologikē).* For Cassian's role in establishing *contemplatio* as a technical term, see Stewart, "From λόγος to *verbum,*" 20. On spiritual knowledge, see chapter 5.

105. *Conf.* 14.1.3: *quae in contemplatione divinarum rerum et sacratissimorum sensuum cognitione consistit.*

106. The one other occurrence of *scientia dei* is in *Conf.* 23.15.2, where it is related to baptism and probably used simply as a term for the Christian life.

107. In *Conf.* 1.8.3 the verb is *pascatur*, in *Conf.* 10.11.2 it is *saginari*. In *Conf.* 10.11.2, the knowledge of God is described as *multiforma*, related to the various spiritual meanings of scripture. For other examples of "feeding" on spiritual realities, see *Conf.* 6.10.2, 8.3.4, 9.3.4, 10.11.4.

108. Origen, *De princ.* 2.11.7 (p. 192), for example; Evagrius, *Prak.* 56 (pp. 630–32); see *Keph. gnost.* 2.32 (p. 73), 2.88 (p. 95), 3.4 (p. 99).

109. See P. Hadot, "Les divisions des parties de la philosophie dans l'Antiquité," *passim;* "Spiritual Exercises," 97–99; "La physique comme exercice spirituel," *passim*, and "Marcus Aurelius," *passim.*

110. For Clement, see *Strom.* 7.11 (pp. 43.29–44.32). For Origen, see, for example, *De Princ.* 1.1.6 (pp. 20.24–21.9); and see Crouzel, *Origène et la "connaissance mystique,"* 50–54, 104–7 and *Origen*, 101–2. For Evagrius, see, for example, *Prak.* 1–3 (pp. 498–500), 84 (p. 674); *Keph. gnost.* 3.57 (p. 121); *Ep. Mel.*, *passim.*

111. See also *De princ.* 1.1.9, using the notion of spiritual senses to explain the meaning of Matt. 5:8 (pp. 26–27).

112. See especially *De princ.* 2.11.6–7 (pp. 189–92) and Crouzel, *Origène et la "connaissance mystique,"* 465–68.

113. See *Prak.* Prol. 50 (p. 494), 1–2 (p. 498; see *Schol. in Prov.* 2, p. 90), 84 (p. 674), 89.11–20. (pp. 684–88), 92 (p. 694); *Gnost.* 13.2 (p. 106), 22 (p. 122), 48–49 (pp. 186–91); *Keph. gnost., passim.* See also the references that follow. For overviews, see the Guillaumonts' introduction to *Prak.*, SC 170, pp. 110–12, as well as the commentary on the passages just listed; Driscoll's remarkably cogent summary in *The "Ad monachos" of Evagrius Ponticus*, 6–23; McGinn, *The Foundations of Mysticism*, 150–57; Rahner, "Le début d'une doctrine des cinq sens spirituels," *passim*, especially pp. 137–41 for Evagrius, although many of the scholia on the Psalms that Rahner attributes to Origen earlier in the article were actually by Evagrius.

114. A Stoic concept, the term was also used in this way by Origen, and it was translated by Rufinus as *ratio*; see Crouzel, *Origène et la "connaissance mystique,"* 54–61. The translation of λόγοι as *raisons d'être* is Géhin's in his introduction to *Schol. in Prov.*, SC 340, pp. 43–44; on λόγοι, see also Špidlík, *Spirituality of the Christian East*, 330–31, and Guillaumont, "La vie gnostique selon Évagre le Pontique," 467–68.

115. See *Ep. Mel.* 1–4 (Syr.: Frankenberg, 612–14; Eng.: Parmentier, 8–11), and Parmentier's commentary on this part of the letter, with references to other Evagrian texts ("Evagrius of Pontus' 'Letter to Melania' I," 21–23).

116. See *Prak.* 92 (p. 694); the saying is not in *Apoph. Alph.* but is found in Socrates, *Hist. eccl.* 4.23 (col. 516C) and in *Apoph. Syst. (Latin)* (col. 1018BC) and *Apoph. Pasch.* 84.3 (p. 308).

117. *Schol. in Eccles.* 15 (pp. 80–82). See the similar theme in *Keph. gnost.* 5.54–57 (p. 201).

118. See, for example, *Gnost.* 48 (with the Guillaumonts' commentary, p. 188); *Keph. gnost.* 1.27 (p. 29), 1.70 (p. 51), 6.43 (p. 235), 6.59 (p. 243), 6.75 (p. 249); *Schol. in Prov.* 2–3 (pp. 90–92), 88 (pp. 186–88), 104 (p. 202); *Schol. in Eccles.* 1 (p. 58); *Schol. in Ps.* 138:16 (ed. Pitra, p. 344 [PG 12.1661C]).

119. See the explanations of judgment and providence in *Schol. in Ps.* 138:14–16 (ed. Pitra, p. 344, PG 12.1661CD) and *Keph. gnost.* 6.43 (p. 235) and 6.59 (p. 243).

120. See, for example, *De orat.* 56–57 (cols. 1177D–80A); Cassian notes the same danger in *Conf.* 10.1–6, as explained in chapter 5.

121. See the discussion of this theme in chapter 4.

122. Though, as Driscoll notes, Evagrius did not use the phrase "double creation" (*The "Ad monachos" of Evagrius Ponticus*, 8–10). Marsili (*Giovanni Cassiano ed Evagrio Pontico*, 123–25) follows Bousset (*Apophthegmata*, 310) in suggesting that in *Conf.* 1.8.3 (*theoria . . . quae prius in paucorum servabatur consideratione sanctorum* and *sanctorum actus ac ministeria mirifica*) Cassian is referring to a contemplation of the angels and of their heavenly "liturgy" or service, that is, Evagrius' "contemplation of incorporeal beings." However, this conclusion seems to be founded on misconceptions about both Evagrius and Cassian. First, Evagrius' category of "incorporeal" was not meant to distinguish angels from humans; in his theology, angels, humans, and demons all have some sort of body in their fallen state but are also "incorporeal" when considered in their unfallen, essential state. The passages of *Keph. gnost.* (5.4 and 7) quoted by Marsili to support the identification of the "incorporeal beings" with the angels are from the less accurate of the two Syriac versions of the text; the better version identified and edited by Guillaumont does not sustain the point. Second, Cassian's parallel statement in *Conf.* 1.15.1 is clearly about human saints (*quando scilicet quae cum sanctis suis per singulas generationes egerit mente purissima perlustramus*). Although Cassian does refer to the blessedness of angels (*Inst.* 12.15.2, *Conf.* 13.13.3), he never refers to angels as "saints," while he often does so with respect to humans.

123. *Conf.* 7.10, 7.13.1–2, 10.3.3. See Tibiletti, "Giovanni Cassiano," 363, and Colish, *The Stoic Tradition from Antiquity to the Early Middle Ages*, 2.122.

124. Cassian: *paucis vero opus est aut etiam uno. Maria bonam partem elegit, quae non auferetur ab ea.* For the first part, Codex Sinaiticus and Codex Beza read: ὀλίγων δέ ἐστιν χρεία ἢ ἑνός, as against the standard text, ἑνὸς δὲ ἐστιν χρεία (see Aland et. al., *Novum Testamentum Graece*, p. 194), and the Vulgate's *porro unum est necessarium*. Origen clearly witnesses to the same tradition, and he is perhaps Cassian's source, for he compares the phrase ὀλίγων ἐστιν to the phrase ἑνὸς ἐστι χρεία (*Hom. in Luc.*, fr. 171, p. 298.14–15); the only mention of the story in Evagrius' extant works (see note 68) follows the standard text. For the second part (*Maria . . . ab ea*), Cassian follows the whole Greek tradition of referring to Mary's choosing τὴν ἀγαθὴν μερίδα ("the good portion") rather than the Vulgate's translation *optimam partem* ("the best part"). Actually, the superlative would have better suited Cassian's point. Jerome uses the same text as Cassian in *Ep.* 22.24.5 (CSEL 54, p. 178) without any commentary.

125. *Conf.* 1.8.3. In *Conf.* 23.3, comparing the "many" to the "one," he condenses what was said in *Conf.* 1.8 about "many" and "few" into one category.

126. This is the point made in *Conf.* 9 about preparation for prayer and quality of prayer and in *Conf.* 14 about *praktikē* and *theōrētikē*.

127. *Mirabilia mysteriorum*, probably a reference to the sacraments. Elsewhere Cassian uses *mysteria* for what lies hidden in the Scriptures, seen only by those who have eyes to see (*Conf.* 8.3.1, 10.11.2, 14.8.3, 21.25.1), as well as for the eucharist (though usually as *sacrosancta mysteria: Inst.* 1.9.2, 3.3.9; *Conf.* 22.4, 22.6.1, 22.8, 23.21.2) and (in the singular) for the Passion of Jesus (*Conf.* 22.13.4).

128. See the use of Rom. 1:20 in *Conf.* 23.3.2–3, on seeing the invisible things of God through the things of this world. In *Conf.* 8.21.4–7, working with the text of Wis. 7:17–21 (LXX), Cassian writes about the "natural knowledge" that enabled the descendants of Abel (until Noah) to understand the workings of natural creation.

129. *Conf.* 1.7.2–3, 1.8.3, 23.3.1.

130. *Conf.* 1.7.4: when tranquillity is disturbed, works (here ascetical) are to be avoided as harmful (*ut noxium*); *Conf.* 23.3.2: all the "merits of holiness" are cheap (*vilia*) in comparison to the contemplation to which they lead.

131. For this view, see, for example, Csányi, "*Optima pars*," 59–64. For a judicious assessment of Cassian's philosophical assumptions and difficulties, see Colish, *The Stoic Tradition from Antiquity to the Early Middle Ages*, 2.114–22, especially 119–20.

132. Lukewarmness (*tepor*) is Cassian's characterization of inaction or lack of spiritual fervor; see, for example, *Conf.* 4.12, 4.17–19.

133. The examples are: anchoritic life, cenobitic life, hospitality, care of the sick, intercession for others, teaching, almsgiving.

134. *Republic* 514A–17A (ed. Burnet, vol. 4); the significance is noted by Dillon, "Rejecting the Body, Refining the Body," 83.

135. Other examples are Abbas Or and Apollo in *Hist. mon.* 2.2–3 (pp. 35–36) and 8.3–8 (pp. 47–49).

136. Gal. 5:17; 1 Cor. 15:53, 15:44; most important, 1 Tim. 4:8.

137. See *Conf.* 11.12.7 for the same point.

138. See *Conf.* 14.1–2; Nesteros is the speaker in both *Conf.* 14 and 15.

139. For examples, see Liddell and Scott, *A Greek-English Lexicon*, pp. 1073b–74a, and Lampe, *A Patristic Greek Lexicon*, 823ab.

140. Baert provides the key Platonic texts and traces their influence in "Le thème de la vision de Dieu." See also Lossky, *The Vision of God*, and McGinn's chapter on "Mystical Elements in Early Greek Christianity" in *The Foundations of Mysticism*, 84–130, *passim*. For the Alexandrians, see, for example, Clement, *Strom.* 7.3.13 (p. 10); Origen, *De princ.* 1.1.9 (pp. 26–27). Cassian uses the actual phrase *visio dei* only once, in his overview of Matthew's beatitudes (*Conf.* 11.12.2); a few times he uses *conspectus dei*, which usually means "in the sight of God," to refer to human vision of God (*Conf.* 14.2, 23.5.7, 23.10.1; see 23.13.2). Nonetheless, as noted earlier, his writings are full of references to seeing God or spiritual realities.

141. *Quaest. in Exod.* 2.51 (p. 99).

142. This explication was most thorough in Origen's doctrine of the "spiritual senses," as noted earlier in this chapter. See also Reypens, "Dieu (Connaissance mystique)," 886–87.

143. Μακάριος occurs twenty-six times in the Psalms, twelve times in Sirach, and thirty-five times elsewhere in LXX; thirteen times in Matthew, twelve times in Luke, and twenty times elsewhere in the Greek NT. Μακαριότης, "beatitude," is found only at 4 Macc. 4:12. The Latin follows a similar pattern, though *beatitudo* (rather than *beatus*) is used five times to translate the Greek μακάριος or μακαρισμός.

144. *Adv. haer.* 4.20.7 (p. 648.180–81).

145. For example, Origen ends book 2 of *De princ.* with Matt. 5:8: *In omnibus autem cibus hic intellegendus est theoria et intellectus dei, habens mensuras proprias et conpetentes*

huic naturae, quae facta est et creata; quas mensuras singulos quosque incipientium "videre deum," id est intellegere per "puritatem cordis," conpetit observare (*De princ.* 2.11.7, p. 192.11–14); see Crouzel, *Origène et la "connaissance mystique,"* 375–82, 430–32. See also Gregory of Nyssa's homily on Matt. 5:8 (*De beat.* 6, pp. 136–48) and Regnault's survey of *Apoph.* in "The Beatitudes in the *Apophthegmata Patrum.*"

146. Occasionally he also uses the word as a title or attribute of someone (e.g., *Conf.* 3.5.2, 10.4.1, 10.8.1, 17.5.1, 19.13.2, 24.7, 24.18). The many occurrences of the adjective *beatus* are almost all of this type, for example, *beatus David, beatus apostolus*. The very few other exceptions are quotations from the evangelical Beatitudes and from a handful of Old Testament texts.

147. For example, *De orat.* 117–23 (col. 1193AC); *Keph. gnost.* 3.82 (p. 132), 3.86–88 (pp. 132–35); *Ad mon.* 92 (cf. 21) (pp. 62 and 49); *Schol. in Ps.* 123:7 (PG 12.1637C), 143.15 (PG 12.1672C).

148. *Schol. in Eccles.* 55 (p. 156). See *Prak.*, Prol. 8 (p. 492) and ch. 24 (p. 556); *Ep. fid.* 7, three times (pp. 98–99); *Schol. in Ps.* 5:11 (ed. Pitra, p. 455); no. 41 of the *Paraenesis*, which was inspired by Evagrius, even if not actually written by him (p. 132 [Syr.] and 162 [French]).

149. For example, *Ep. fid.* 12 (p. 110); *Ep.* 56 (p. 604.6–10 [Syr.], p. 605.8–13 [Gk. retroversion]); *Schol. in Ps.* 68:29 (PG 12.1517AB), 118:1 (PG 12.1588C).

150. For example, *Ad mon.* 8 (p. 46), 131 (p. 69), 133 (p. 70); *Schol. in Prov.* 199 (p. 294), 247 (p. 342), 291 (pp. 382–84), 328 (p. 418); *Ep.* 12 (p. 574.18–25 [Syr.], p. 575.23–33 [Gk. retroversion]); *Paraenet.* (p. 558.24–26 [Syr.], p. 559.32–35 [Gk. retroversion]); see *Schol. in Ps.* 65:20 (PG 12.1504A) on purity of heart and pure prayer. He also cites Heb. 12:14 ("strive . . . for the holiness without which no one will see God") in *Gnost.* 13 (p. 107).

151. Ἵνα καθαροὶ γενόμενοι ἴδωσι τὸν θεόν· τοῦτο γάρ ἐστι τὸ μακάριον τέλος ὅπερ πάσῃ λογικῇ φύσει τετήρηται, Schol. in Prov. 136 (p. 232). See *De orat.* 150 (col. 1200A) and Hausherr's comments in *Les leçons d'un contemplatif*, 181–83.

152. *Conf.* 15.2.3, 15.9.

153. *Inst.* 6.15.2, 12.11.1; *Conf.* 22.6.7.

154. *Conf.* 9.6.5 and 19.5.1. On the angelic life as a model for the monk, see Evagrius, *Ep.* 57 (p. 606.1–23 [Syr.], p. 607.1–32 [Gk. retroversion]), *De orat.* 113 (col. 1192D), *Keph. gnost.* 4.38 (p. 153). Frank's ΑΓΓΕΛΙΚΟΣ ΒΙΟΣ explores aspects of this theme.

155. See, for example, *Inst.* 12.4.2–3, 12.11.1 and 3, 12.12, 12.15.2; *Conf.* 6.16.1, 8.7.1, 8.10.1, 12.11.1.

156. See *Inst.* 5.14.4, 9.10, 9.13, 12.12, 12.15.2; *Conf.* 1.8.3, 10.6.4, 10.7.3, 23.5.1, 23.8.1, 23.11.2, 23.15.4, 23.15.6.

157. For example, *Conf.* 10.6.4: *similitudo . . . beatitudinis*, 10.7.3: *imago futurae beatitudinis*. See Olphe-Galliard, "Vie contemplative et vie active d'après Cassien," 287–88.

158. See Codina, *El aspecto cristologico en la espiritualidad de Juan Casiano*, 76–77 and 83–84.

159. He uses the beatitude in a similar way in *Inst.* 8.20.1, where it is referred to as the *divinum praemium*, "divine reward."

160. *Conf.* 23.5.1 (see 1.13.1) and 23.15.6. For *vera beatitudo* see also *Conf.* 1.13.4.

161. Cassian uses the adjective *caelestis* frequently, often in the phrase *sacramenta caelestia*, to refer to the hidden mysteries of heaven.

162. See, for example, *Inst.* 4.35 and *Conf.* 9.4.1–3.

163. In contrast, vivid pictures are found in the sacred texts of other religions, for example Sura 56 of the *Qur'an*. Apocalyptic literature, of course, is devoted to eschatological description, though not particularly of the joys of heaven. The Syriac tradition is the

major exception, perhaps best illustrated by Ephrem's hymns *On Paradise* (see Daniélou, "Terre et Paradis chez les Pères de l'Église"). In Greek tradition the *Visio Sancti Pauli* is an unusually graphic description of paradise; in Latin translation it had a great influence in the West, as on the descriptions of paradise in *Reg. Mag.* 3.83–94 (vol. 1, pp. 372–74), 10.92–117 (vol. 1, pp. 438–44), 90.17–27 (vol. 2, pp. 380–84), though Benedict omits each of these in the parallel chapters of *Reg. Ben.* Frank notes that the literature of Egyptian monasticism often characterized monastic life as a return to, or anticipation of, paradise (*ΑΓΓΕΛΙΚΟΣ ΒΙΟΣ*, 106–19), though the literature did not speculate about heaven per se. Among Latin writers, Prudentius stands out for his poetic imaginings of paradise, as noted by Daley, *The Hope of the Early Church*, 158. Ciccarese identifies the principal early sources that inspired medieval Latin writers in their imaginative descriptions of the afterlife (see "Vision").

164. See *Conf.* 9.19, interpreting the petition "Your kingdom come" of the Lord's Prayer as a prayer that Christ may supplant the devil's reign in the heart. See Evagrius: "if our interior is occupied by demons, it is said for good reason that the Philistines occupy the promised land" (*Keph. gnost.* 5.30, p. 189; the same text can be found as *Schol. in Ps.* 134:12 [*PG* 12.1653C]).

165. See *Conf.* 5.24 for a similar point, though in *Conf.* 5.19 Cassian nuances the possibility of total elimination of faults by admitting that gluttony cannot be entirely uprooted since it arises from a natural and necessary human function. See the next section and also chapter 4 for Cassian's teaching on the possibility of perfect chastity.

166. On this theme in Origen's writings, see the examples in Rahner, "Le début d'une doctrine des cinq sens spirituels," 121–22, 126–27, with some of Evagrius' *Schol. in Ps.* mixed in among the examples Rahner thought were by Origen. For Evagrius, see *Schol. in Prov.* 7.5–6 (p. 96), 116.3–4 (p. 214), 332.1–2 (p. 420); *Schol. in Eccl.* 27.3–4 (p. 102), 54.2–4 (pp. 155–56); *Schol. in Ps.* 10:8 (*PG* 12.1193D, especially close to Cassian's point), 13.7 (*PG* 12.1205D), 32.8 (*PG* 12.1305B), 45.7 (*PG* 12.1433CD), 67.19 (*PG* 12.1508D), 76.11 (*PG* 12.1540B), 78.11 (ed. Pitra, p. 102), 88.49 (*PG* 12.1549CD), 112.7 (*PG* 12.1572C), 113.4 (*PG* 12.1572D), 120.8 (*PG* 12.1632C), 121.4–5 (ed. Pitra, p. 319), 125.1 (*PG* 12.1640C), 138.11 (*PG* 12.1661B), 149.6 (*PG* 12.1681B). Géhin discusses the theme with respect to *Schol. in Prov.* in his introduction, SC 340, pp. 37–42.

167. *Mentis intuitu consideremus statum illum, in quo degunt caelestes supernaeque virtutes quae vere in regno dei sunt* (*Conf.* 1.13.3). See Evagrius, *Schol. in Ps.* 10:8 (*PG* 12.1193D), contrasting the reign of the devil among the vicious and ignorant with the presence of "holy powers" among the virtuous and knowledgeable.

168. See *Conf.* 12.6.1–6 for Cassian's classic discussion of anger, patience, and chastity; he returns to the topic in *Conf.* 16. *Inst.* 8 is entirely devoted to the *vitium* of anger. For the link between anger and lust, patience and chastity, see chapter 4.

169. Athanasius, *V. Ant.* 20.4 (p. 188). Marx notes that here Athanasius changes the Lucan text in the same way Evagrius does, so that "reign of God" becomes "reign of heaven" ("Incessant Prayer in the *Vita Antonii*," 126–27). See note 172.

170. See Frank, *ΑΓΓΕΛΙΚΟΣ ΒΙΟΣ*, 92; Raasch, "The Monastic Concept of Purity of Heart and Its Sources," p. 4, pp. 288–92.

171. See Origen's *Comm. in Matt.* 10.14 (pp. 17–18) for the explanation: Origen understands "reign of heaven" to mean the spiritual instruction brought by Jesus, and thus he claims that the phrase "the reign of God is within you" really means that the "reign of heaven," that is, the revelation by the Logos, is "within you."

172. The distinction is in *Prak.* 2–3 (pp. 498–503, with references to other texts and commentary by the Guillaumonts). For Luke 17:21, see *Schol. in Eccl.* 15 (pp. 82–85, with references and commentary by Géhin); *Keph. gnost.* 5.30 (p. 189); *Ep. fid.* 12 (p. 110); *Ep.*

15 (p. 576.3 [Syr.], p. 577.3 [Gk. retroversion]). See *Schol. in Ps.* 9:37–38 (ed. Pitra, p. 464); *Schol. in Ps.* 10:16 (PG 12.1196 BC). See P. Hadot's remarks linking this distinction to that between *praktikē* and *theōrētikē*, "Ancient Spiritual Exercises and 'Christian Philosophy'," 136–38.

173. *Conf.* 7.6.2–4, quoting Eph. 4:13.

174. *Conf.* 7.1, 12.7.6.

175. *Conf.* 22.7 and 13–14; *Conf.* 23, *passim.*

176. *Inst.* 12.15; *Conf.* 23.6.2.

177. See *Conf.* 1.13, 6.14.2, 7.3–8, 9.4–7, 10.12–14, 23.5.3, 23.8.1, 23.16, 23.18–19.

178. *Conf.* 11.9.6, 18.13.4, 20.12.2, 22.7–9, 23.17.

179. *Conf.* 2.2.3, 15.10.

180. *Conf.* 10.6.4 and 7.3. See chapter 5 for the significance of 1 Cor. 15:28 for Origen and Cassian.

181. Cassian uses *arras* twice (*Conf.* 7.6.4, 10.7.3), and *subarratum* once (*Conf.* 7.6.4). The first is a direct equivalent for ἀρραβών, while the second is a neuter perfect participle from a derivative verb, *subarro.*

182. For a brief discussion of the Semitic background, see Stewart, *Working the Earth of the Heart*, 200–202. The word ἀρραβών appears in both the LXX (Gen. 38:17–18, 38:20) and the Greek NT (2 Cor. 1:22 and 5:5; Eph. 1:14). In the Vulgate it is usually translated *pignus* (a word Cassian uses only once, when quoting Ezek. 33:13–16 at *Conf.* 17.25.16); the exception is Gen. 38:17–18, where the transliterated form *arrabon* is used. Cassian cites none of the biblical texts that use ἀρραβών.

183. A letter attributed to Sulpitius uses *subarro* in the context of betrothal (*Ep. App.* 2.12, p. 241.22). Both earlier and contemporary writers used *arras* with its financial meaning of a "down payment" or "pledge"; see *TLL* 2.631–33, citing Pliny, the Latin version of Irenaeus, and Augustine. Tertullian and Jerome seem to have preferred *arrabo* or *arrabonem.*

184. See Lampe, *A Patristic Greek Lexicon*, 229ab.

185. See 1 Cor. 12:12–27, Rom. 12:4–5. The allusion in *Conf.* 7.6.4 is within a meditation on Eph. 4:13, a verse that does not mention the body of Christ though it is part of a discussion that parallels 1 Cor. 12 and Rom. 12.

Chapter 4

1. See Kardong, "John Cassian's Teaching on Perfect Chastity," 253–56; Russell, "John Cassian on a Delicate Subject," 2–3.

2. In *Inst.* 5.9–11, chastity is related to disciplined intake of food and drink; *Inst.* 12.9–23, a lengthy discussion of grace, centers on the issue of chastity; *Conf.* 4.15–20 is about the desires of the flesh; *Conf.* 5.4–6 is about gluttony and fornication, while *Conf.* 5.11–12 recapitulates *Inst.* 6 and discusses the relationship between fornication and vainglory; *Conf.* 7.1–2 describes the supernatural chastity of Abba Serenus; *Conf.* 14.16 prescribes the elimination of "carnal vices" as a precondition for "spiritual knowledge"; *Conf.* 15.10 relates Paphnutius' discovery that he was not entirely free of sexual desires; *Conf.* 21, *passim*, discusses marriage and celibacy.

3. See, for example, *Conf.* 21.36.1–2, citing Rom. 2:28–29.

4. *Inst.* 6.18, *Conf.* 13.4–5. See Clement of Alexandria's comparison of pagan and Christian ἐγκράτεια in *Strom.* 3.7 (p. 222).

5. *Inst.* 12.19; *Conf.* 14.9.7, 14.16.6. See *Conf.* 21.36.1, where he returns to this point.

6. *Conf.* 12.1.1, 21.33.3. See the section on "Worldly Knowledge and Spiritual Knowledge" in chapter 5.

7. See Foucault, "The Battle for Chastity," 23–24, on Cassian's link between chastity and "techniques of self-analysis" such as discernment of thoughts.

8. The generic use is best illustrated in Pinufius' address on mortification (*Inst.* 4.32–43) and in the title of *Conf.* 4, *De concupiscentia carnis ac spiritus.*

9. See, for example, *Timaeus* 89e–90d (ed. Burnet, vol. 4).

10. See especially *Prak.* 86 and 89 (pp. 676 and 680–88). See the Guillaumonts' commentary there and in the introduction to *Prak.*, SC 170, pp. 106–7.

11. *Conf.* 24.15–17. See the models in *Inst.* 5 and *Conf.* 5.

12. *Conf.* 23.14–15, Theonas playing Rom. 8:2 against Germanus' use of Rom. 7:19. Among minor offenses, Cassian had previously included nocturnal emissions (*Conf.* 20.12.2). *Conf.* 22 explores how these can occur without sinful complicity of the will.

13. *Conf.* 24.8.4, *insita . . . in naturam*; see 24.8.5 on how *sanctae conversationis antiquitas* leads *naturaliter* to firmness of purpose.

14. Especially *Inst.* 12.9–23 and *Conf.* 13, *passim*. See the discussion that follows.

15. *Conf.* 1.14.8, 3.15.1, 5.21.3, 5.24.2, 7.4.3, 7.11, 8.21, *passim*, 8.23–24, *passim*, 13.9.5, 13.12, *passim*, 16.2.2, 20.4.3, 23.2.2.

16. *Inst.* 4.39.3, 5.34; *Conf.* 9.3–4, *passim*, 10.11.6, 14.3.1, 23.2.2, 24.8.4–5.

17. *Inst.* 7.1, 7.30, 8.18.2, 12.4.2–3; *Conf.* 2.13.11, 4.7.1, 4.11.2, 5.3–4, 5.6.4, 5.19.1, 5.21.1, 11.9.4, 12.12.3, 20.12.3, 21.9.1, 22.14, 22.15.3, 23.3.4, 23.11.1, 23.11.3, 23.13.1, 23.14.1, 23.15.7, 23.19.1.

18. *Inst.* 6.6 (*ultra naturam*); *Conf.* 7.1, 12.8.6, 19.8.2 (all *supra naturam*); *Conf.* 12.5.2 (*naturam . . . suam vincant*).

19. *Inst.* 6.9, 6.12.

20. *Conf.* 22.12.1. See *Conf.* 13.7.3, where Cassian writes of *originale vel actuale peccatum*, "the first explicit assertion in Cassian of an 'original sin' which affects all" (Pristas, *The Theological Anthropology of John Cassian*, 283). See the section on marriage later in this chapter.

21. *Conf.* 22.11–12; see *Conf.* 5.5. In *De Inc.* Cassian critiques the Pelagian assumption that we can share in Christ's sinlessness by virtue of shared humanity (*De Inc.* 1.3, 5.1–4, 6.14).

22. *Conf.* 5.5, 5.6.4.

23. On the eight principal faults, see the Guillaumonts' introduction to Evagrius' *Prak.*, SC 170, pp. 63–93. The key Evagrian material is *Prak.* 6–33, pp. 506–77, with commentary; see Bunge's commentary in *Evagrios Pontikos: Praktikos oder der Mönch*, 79–140. Cassian transmits Evagrius' system to the Latin West, where it is then transformed by Gregory the Great into the famous seven deadly sins; see Gillet's introduction to *Mor. in Iob*, SC 32bis, pp. 89–93.

24. He relates the two in *Inst.* 5, *passim*; *Conf.* 2.22.2, 5.3–4, 5.6.3, 22.3.7–8, 22.6.2, 22.6.4–5.

25. As in *Inst.* 5.11.2, 7.21, 7.23–26; *Conf.* 1.4.2, 1.20.3, 5.8.3, 23.12.4, 24.2.2.

26. *Inst.* 7.1, *Conf.* 5.8.

27. *Conf.* 5.4; see *Inst.* 6.1–2.

28. *Inst.* 5.11.1; see 5.20.

29. *Reg. fus.* 18 (col. 965C).

30. *De vit.* (col. 1141C) and *De octo spir. mal.* 4 (col. 1148C); see *Antirr.* 10 (p. 486 [Syr.], p. 487 [Gk. retroversion]). See Clement, *Paedag.* 2.9 (sec. 81.1–2, pp. 206–7); *Apoph. Alph.* Antony 22 (col. 84AB) and Antony's *Ep.* (*Lat.*) 1.4 (PG 40.979AB) on the natural movements of the body caused by food and drink; *Apoph. Anon.* Nau 94 (p. 401), 183 (p. 271, *Syst.* [*Gk.*] 5.36, pp. 274–76), 592/54 (p. 228); Isaiah, *Log.* 7 (Gk.: 7.8, p. 47; ed. Regnault and Broc, 7.19, p. 89) and *Log.* 29 (Gk.: 29.3, p. 200; Regnault and Broc 29.32, p. 269).

31. See Evagrius, *Prak.* 23 (p. 554) and *De orat.* 27 (cols. 1172D–73A). In *Antirr.* 22, however, Evagrius identifies anger as a counterforce to lust (pp. 486–88 [Syr.], p. 489 [Gk. retroversion]).

32. *Conf.* 5.12.1–4; see *Conf.* 7.19.2 on the incompatibility of vainglory and the lust for fornication. See Evagrius, *Prak.* 58 (pp. 636–38), who adds that the ability to play vainglory off against fornication is a sign of approaching *apatheia*.

33. *Conf.* 4.15.1; see *Conf.* 12.4.3–4, 12.6.7, 22.6.2.

34. *Conf.* 21.33.2, 22.6.7.

35. See *Conf.* 5.11.4–5 and *Conf.* 12.2–3.

36. See *TLL*, 5.1126, ll. 56–83; *Oxford Latin Dictionary*, 724c-725a. The word *fornicatio* appears frequently in the Vulgate.

37. See *Apoph. Syst.* (*Gk.*) 5.51 (p. 304), where fornication (πορνεία) is defined as committing sin with the body; "uncleanness" (ἀκαθαρσία) is a subheading describing caressing of the body, laughter, and "(over)familiarity" (παρρησία).

38. *Conf.* 5.11.4; see *Conf.* 12.2.2–3 on Col. 3:5, with a narrower definition of *fornicatio* as intercourse and a similar interpretation of *inmunditia* with the added note that it can be while awake or asleep.

39. See the section on "Disciplines of Continence" later in this chapter for the link between water, demons, and lust.

40. *Conf.* 4.19.4, 21.33.3 (see 22.6.7).

41. On this theme, see Cloke, *"This Female Man of God,"* 121–33.

42. See the story of Amoun of Nitria as in *Hist. Laus.* 8 (pp. 27–28).

43. See Brown, *The Body and Society*, 266–71; Rader, *Breaking Boundaries*, 62–71; Elm, *Virgins of God*, 48–51.

44. See Gregory of Nyssa's remarks in *De virg.* 3–4 (pp. 256–77).

45. See the appendix for Theonas.

46. This renunciation is a theme in *Conf.* 11—where obedience out of fear yields to action based on love—and throughout the rest of *Conf.* 21.

47. The text suggests that he did not envisage celibate cohabitation: Theonas refers to the "fragile and uncertain condition of human nature," which makes it dangerous to be involved any longer in "carnal desires and works" (*Conf.* 21.9.1).

48. See most conveniently Brown's *The Body and Society*.

49. In this respect Abba Abraham's negative remarks about marriage in *Conference* 24 seem discordant; it is noteworthy that this *Conference* seems to have a more explicit disciplinary agenda than the others.

50. See Ward, *Harlots of the Desert*.

51. See Stewart, "The Portrayal of Women in the Stories and Sayings of the Desert."

52. See Evagrius, *Rerum mon. rat.* 1–2 (cols. 1252D-53C) on marriage and monks.

53. This "simple and natural stirring" is described in *Inst.* 7.3 and *Conf.* 7.2.1.

54. *Conf.* 12.9, 12.11.4–5.

55. *Inst.* 3.5.1, 6.20 and 22; *Conf.* 12.7.7, 12.8.2 and 12.8.5, 22.3, 22.5.2, 22.6.2, 22.6.5. See Philoxenos, *Hom.* 13 (pp. 586–87), developing Evagrius' teaching on images and emissions and noting that emissions occur even without dreams, owing to the "superfluity" of the "material of lust."

56. *Medulla*, used in this sense in *Conf.* 2.23.1, 12.10.2, 22.3.2, 22.6.7.

57. On theories of the genesis of semen, see Jacquart and Thomasset, *Sexuality and Medicine in the Middle Ages*, 52–60; Rousselle, *Porneia*, 171–73; Russell, "John Cassian on a Delicate Subject," 4. On orgasmic dreams as understood by ancient medical writers, see Pigeaud, "Le rêve érotique dans l'Antiquité gréco-romaine." The most thorough ancient discussion of nocturnal emissions is in book 5 of Caelius Aurelianus' Latin translation of

the Greek *Chronic Diseases* of Soranus of Ephesus, a second-century physician who studied in Alexandria and practiced in Rome (pp. 958–63). See the section later in this chapter on "Body and Soul" for similarities and differences between Soranus' and Cassian's teaching. The date of translation is unknown, perhaps the fifth century (see Drabkin's edition of Caelius' translation, xi, though see Pigeaud, "Le rêve érotique dans l'Antiquité gréco-romaine," 20 n.1); whether or not Cassian knew the text in either Greek or Latin form, it represents the state of medical knowledge in his day. The link with Alexandria is, of course, significant in light of Cassian's own Egyptian formation. On the issue to which Cassian refers, Kinsey observes, "we are . . . almost completely in the dark as to the possibility of a biologic mechanism that could force nocturnal emissions when other sexual outlets were insufficient" (*Sexual Behavior in the Human Male*, 528).

58. *Inst.* 7.3.1; *Conf.* 4.15.1, 7.2.1, 12.7.3, 12.12.3, 22.3.5–6, 22.6.7. Kinsey doubted that emissions ever occur without accompanying dreams, but noted the possibility (*Sexual Behavior in the Human Male*, 518). See Antony, who as the first of three reasons for the "motion" of the body that produces nocturnal orgasm listed a "passionless" movement (κίνησις) that is natural; the other two causes are food and drink, which heat up the blood, and demonic attack (*Apoph. Alph.* Antony 22, col. 84AB, and *Ep.* [*Lat.*] 1.4, col. 979AB; see Vivian, " 'Everything Made by God is Good'," 80–84). Cassian also wrote about "pure and simple" sleep, that is, without erotic dreams (*Inst.* 3.5.1). Evagrius had noted the "simple movement" of the memory in sleep as it converses with saints; this movement is caused either by oneself or by "holy powers," as opposed to demonic interference via images "impressed and sketched" on the ruling faculty (ἡγεμονικόν, *De mal. cog.* 4, col. 1204D).

59. For the views of other writers on this question, see the discussion later in this chapter on nocturnal emissions.

60. See, for example, *Inst.* 5.10; *Conf.* 12.2.3, 13.5 *passim*, 21.36.1, 22.6.9–10.

61. *Conf.* 12.5.1 and 12.10.3. Cassian's assumption that eunuchs did not experience sexual arousal is not strictly accurate; see Rousselle, *Porneia*, 121–28. Cassian's disparagement of eunuchs is noteworthy in light of the tradition that Origen had castrated himself.

62. See *Inst.* 6.2, *Conf.* 23.1.5, and the discussion in Brakke, *Athanasius and the Politics of Asceticism*, 93–95.

63. *Conf.* 4.15.1, 12.4.4, 12.6.7. See *Hist. Laus.* 47 (pp. 138–39) on pride leading to the withdrawal of grace and a fall into impurity.

64. An even more bizarre aspect of this story is the exegesis of 2 Chr. 24:25 in the light of Rom. 1:26–28 to suggest that Joash was raped by Syrian soldiers (*Inst.* 12.21). The Vulgate's description of the way the soldiers left Joash *in languoribus magnis* is interpreted in this way: *Vides quam flagitiosis ac sordidis passionibus tradi mereatur superbia. Qui enim elatus adrogantia ut Deum se passus est adorari, "traditur" secundum Apostolum "in passiones ignominiae" et "in reprobum sensum, ut patiatur ea quae non convenit"* (*Inst.* 12.21.2).

65. The distinction is introduced in *Inst.* 6.4 and returns in *Conf.* 11 and 12.

66. *Continentia*, like its Greek analogue, ἐγκράτεια, can be used in a broader sense to include other (primarily physical) disciplines such as control of the diet. Thus, in *Inst.* 5 and *Conf.* 2, *continentia* is the virtue opposed to gluttony. In *Conf.* 5 *continentia* can mean dietary discipline and/or sexual restraint. In discussions of chastity, *continentia* means sexual discipline. As noted earlier, Cassian links gluttony and fornication, so that *continentia* can apply to sex and *concupiscentia* can apply to food. On ἐγκράτεια see Lampe, *A Patristic Greek Lexicon*, 402–3.

67. Cassian uses the words *castitas* and *castimonia* interchangeably, with a preference for the former (*Inst.*: 17 versus 5; *Conf.*: 68 versus 30). In the *Institutes* he uses *integritas* as a third synonym (eighteen times with this meaning; once referring to obedience); he uses it less frequently in *Conf.* (10 times).

68. The distinction Cassian makes between ἐγκρατής and ἀγνός is not philological. In Greek usage, ἐγκρατής/ἐγκράτεια is the more general term, referring to various disciplines though also applied specifically to sexual continence, and ἀγνός/ἀγνεία is the specific term for chastity (see Lampe, A Patristic Greek Lexicon, 20–21). Evagrius does not use this distinction; usually for him, ἐγκράτεια is the virtue opposed to gluttony and σωφροσύνη the virtue opposed to lust. See De vit. (col. 1141C), De octo spir. mal. 4 (cols. 1148C–49B), Schol. in Ps. 22:3 (PG 12.1260C), and Schol. in Ps. 45:2 (PG 12.1433B) for examples; see also Prak. 89 and the Guillaumonts' commentary (pp. 680–88). For a general discussion of ἐγκράτεια in Evagrius see Viller, "Aux sources de la spiritualité de saint Maxime," 173–74. When commenting on Ps. 18:10 (ὁ φόβος κυρίου ἀγνός), Evagrius' scholion is general enough that ἀγνεία could mean "purity" rather than "chastity" (PG 12.1245A).

69. Cassian is working with Ps. 75:2–3; the same image is found frequently in Evagrius' writings, often related to Exod. 24:10; see Cap. cogn. 25 (p. 61); Keph. gnost. 5.39 (p. 192; note that the image is missing from the better Syriac version on p. 193); De mal. cog. 18 (col. 1221B); Ep. 39 (p. 592 [Syr.], p. 593 [Gk. retroversion]); Schol. in Ps. 25:8 (Pitra, p. 483); Schol. in Ps. 36:11 (Pitra, p. 10 and PG 12.1317B); Schol in Ps. 67:6 (Pitra, p. 82 and PG 12.1505D); Schol in Ps. 75:2 (PG 12.1536C); Schol. in Ps. 78:7 (Pitra, p. 131); Schol. in Ps. 92:4–5 (Pitra, p. 175); Schol. in Ps. 131:5 (PG 12.1649C); in Schol. in Ps. 133:1 (PG 12.1652C), the θεωρητικοί are in the house of God, while the πρακτικοί are in the courts of the house of God. On the theme of "place of God" in Evagrius' thought, see Bunge, Das Geistgebet, 67–68 and 80–82, and Guillaumont, "La vision de l'intellect par lui-même dans la mystique évagrienne," 258–60.

70. Conf. Pref. 1 5, Conf. 5.23.2, 12.11.2; De Inc. 7.9. As noted in chapter 3, this interpretation appears to have originated with Philo and been adopted by Origen.

71. See Cassian's anagogical interpretation of Jerusalem/Zion in Conf. 14.8.3–4.

72. See Inst. 5.10, 6.1, 6.23.

73. Inst. 6.1, 6.3; Conf. 4.12.4, 22.3.6.

74. On fasting, see the general studies of Musurillo, "The Problem of Ascetical Fasting," and Vuillaume, "Le jeûne dans la tradition monastique ancienne et aujourd'hui."

75. Conf. 12.15.2, 13.6.2. For more general prescriptions about food and drink, see Inst. 5.9, 5.11, 5.14.3, 6.1, 6.23; Conf. 4.12.4, 5.4.3, 12.4.1, 12.11.5, 22.3.2. Rousselle analyzes Cassian's recommendations in "Abstinence et continence dans les monastères de Gaule méridionale," 242–46.

76. Inst. 6.20 and 22; Conf. 12.7.7, 12.8.2 and 5, 22.3, 22.5.2, 22.6.2, 22.6.5. See Rousselle, "Abstinence et continence dans les monastères de Gaule méridionale," 248–49.

77. Inst. 5.11.1; see 5.20.

78. See Palladius, Hist. Laus. 11 (p. 34) on Ammonius' diet of uncooked foods (ὠμοφαγία), in which he persevered until his death, and Moses' subsistence on dried bread as an antidote to lust (Hist. Laus. 19, p. 60). See note 80 on Evagrius. Rousselle devotes an entire chapter to monastic diets in Porneia, 160–78.

79. See the Guillaumonts' commentary on Prak. 17 (p. 545) noting Hippocrates and Philo. See also Jacquart and Thomasset, Sexuality and Medicine in the Middle Ages, 119–20, 148–49; Rousselle, Porneia, 18–19, 172–75; Vivian, " 'Everything Made by God Is Good'," 93–94.

80. The diet damaged his digestive system, and toward the end of his life he had to begin eating cooked foods again (Hist. Laus. 38, pp. 120 and 122). For his recommendation of dried foods, see Prak. 91 (p. 692). The harsh diet helped nonetheless, for Palladius quotes Evagrius as claiming that in the last three years of his life he was not tempted by lust (Hist. Laus. 38, p. 122).

81. *Prak.* 17 (p. 542; n.b. the commentary); *Ad mon.* 102 (p. 63); *Antirr.* 41, 48, 55 (pp. 490 and 492 [Syr.], 491 and 493 [Gk. retroversion]); *De mal. cog.* 24 (col. 1228BC). He finds a biblical basis in *Schol. in Prov.* 227 on Prov. 21:19, citing several other texts (p. 322); see 380 (p. 472). Note his point in *Antirr.* 22 that while anger is born from fire, lust is born from water (pp. 486–88 [Syr.], 487 [Gk. retroversion]). See *Hist. mon.* 20.16 (p. 123), citing Evagrius on the way demons seek out moist places (based on Matt. 12.43, about the unclean spirit unable to find rest in a waterless place); Rufinus' Latin version is more developed on the link between too much water and *phantasiae* (*Hist. mon.* [*Ruf.*] 27.7.4, p. 364). See *Apoph. Syr.* Bu II.656 (Syr.: pp. 946–47 [no. 44]; Eng.: pp. 316–17), presenting Evagrius' teaching as passed on by Jerome!

82. See *Inst.* 5.7, 5.14.3; *Conf.* 21.22. As noted already, Cassian was aware of the need to train the conscience in discernment; see *Conf.* 12.8.1–2.

83. *Inst.* 5.9 and 6.23; *Conf.* 21.23.

84. Summa uses fasting to illustrate Cassian's understanding of *discretio*: see *Geistliche Unterscheidung bei Johannes Cassian,* 143–56.

85. See Rousselle, "Abstinence et continence dans les monastères de Gaule méridionale," 252–53, and *Porneia,* especially 175–78; Brown, *The Body and Society,* 218–24.

86. Rousselle, for instance, calculates the value of the celebratory meal described in *Conf.* 8.1 as about one thousand calories ("Abstinence et continence dans les monastères de Gaule méridionale," 250–52, and *Porneia,* 175). See also Dembinska, "Diet: A Comparison of Food Consumption between Some Eastern and Western Monasteries in the fourth–twelfth Centuries," 431–45.

87. Rousselle states in *Porneia,* 176–77, that Cassian's program is for a novice who can thereby "achieve almost perfect chastity."

88. *Extractus a cunctis confabulationibus otiosis et mortificatus ab omni ira ac sollicitudine curaque mundana* (*Conf.* 12.15.2).

89. *Non amplius quam sex mensibus perfectionem istius inpossibilem sibi non esse cognoscet* (*Conf.* 12.15.2).

90. See *Antirr.* 2.30 and 2.55 (pp. 488 and 492 [Syr.], 489 and 493 [Gk. retroversion]) for Evagrius' recommendation of sackcloth as an aid in the struggle against lust. Cassian dislikes sackcloth because he thinks it is ostentatiously ascetic, as perhaps it was in Gaul (*Inst.* 1.2.3–4).

91. See *Inst.* 6.7.2. The practice is mentioned by Caelius Aurelianus in *On Chronic Diseases* 7 (sec. 84, p. 960). Rousselle (*Porneia,* 170) and Brakke (*Athanasius and the Politics of Asceticism,* 95) confuse Cassian's description of athletes with his prescriptions for monks. Weber (*Die Stellung des Johannes Cassianus in der ausserpachomianischen Mönchstradition,* 90) suggests a shared source or parallel tradition to Palladius' description of Ammonius (*Hist. Laus.* 11, pp. 33–34), who applied a hot iron whenever his desire was stirred up. The athletic and medical background is more plausible, however, given that Cassian writes about cool lead rather than hot iron!

92. *Hist. Laus.* 38 (p. 121).

93. *Inst.* 6.1–2; *Conf.* 4.12.4, 5.4.3, 5.4.6, 12.4.1, 12.6.6, 13.6.2. See Evagrius, *Antirr.* 2.41, 2.55, 2.57 (pp. 490 and 492 [Syr.], 491 and 493 [Gk. retroversion]).

94. *Conf.* 1.18.2, 5.4.6.

95. See *Inst.* 10.8.2 and *Conf.* 5.4.3–6; see also *Inst.* 5.11.2 and *Conf.* 15.8, 24.16.

96. See, for example, *Conf.* 4.12.4, 12.11.2, 14.13.7.

97. See *Conf.* 14.10.4 on biblical *meditatio* during the night. See Evagrius, *Antirr.* 2.15, 2.19, 2.52, 2.53 (pp. 486 and 492 [Syr.] and 487 and 493 [Gk. retroversion]) for references to visions at night (without reference to dreams). One recalls the vivid nocturnal visions of Antony and other desert monks that are not described as dreams; see, for example, *Hist.*

mon. 1.51–52 (p. 30) for John of Lycopolis' story about a monk who became proud about his ascetical achievement, was then tempted by evil thoughts "of the world," and on the third night simulated intercourse with an imaginary woman; see Evagrius' allusion to the same story in *Antirr.* 2.36 (p. 490 [Syr.] and 491 [Gk. retroversion]). Erotic dreams are discussed later in this chapter.

98. *Inst.* 2.13.1, 3.5.1.

99. *Inst.* 6.3; *Conf.* 4.12.4, 5.4.3, 5.4.5–6, 12.15, 13.6.2. On this theme, see Rousselle, *Porneia,* 147–52, and Russell, "John Cassian on a Delicate Subject," 10–11.

100. See *Inst.* 6.3 and *Conf.* 5.4.6; cf. *Conf.* 18.16 and 19.10–14 on those who withdraw into solitude without having dealt with their (other) faults in community.

101. See Stewart, "The Portrayal of Women in the Sayings and Stories of the Desert" for stories about encounters between monks and women.

102. *Conf.* 5.4.5–6 and 19.16.3; see *Inst.* 6.3 and *Hist. mon.* 1.36 (p. 22).

103. The principal texts are usefully gathered and discussed by Rousselle, *Porneia,* 147–49 and 155–57. See also Stewart, "The Portrayal of Women in the Stories and Sayings of the Desert" and, on boys, *Apoph. Alph.* Isaac of the Cells 5 (col. 225AB) and Poemen 176 (col. 365A), *Alph. Supp.* Carion 1 (p. 26), *Anon.* Nau 125 (p. 403), 412 (p. 138), 533 (p. 196), 542–45 (p. 199), 592/64 (pp. 230–31).

104. See Evagrius, *Prak.* 96 (p. 702), and see the commentary and other references (p. 703).

105. For Evagrius on avoiding actual encounters with women, see the rather snide *De octo spir. mal.* 4–5 (cols. 1148C–49D), tracing the stages by which seemingly innocent contact degenerates into licentious behavior. The largest collection of texts about memory and fantasy is in book 2 of *Antirr.* (pp. 484–95), devoted entirely to "thoughts" of lust. See also, for example, *Prak.* 23 (p. 554) on anger and fornication as ways of "darkening" the soul and stirring up images (τὰ εἴδωλα φαντάζομενος) at time of prayer; *Ad virg.* 6 (p. 146) on εἴδωλα of men in the nun's soul at time of prayer; numerous texts from *De orat.*: 45 (col. 1176D), 46 (col. 1176D), 49 (col. 1177AB), 63 (col. 1180D), 68 (col. 1181B), 90 (col. 1188A), 91 (col. 1188A), 92 (col. 1188B). In *De octo spir. mal.* 6 (cols. 1149D–52D), he notes that the real test comes not during actual encounters but in the recollection of them; when the memory of a woman becomes ἀπαθῶς, then one is nearing the borders of chastity.

106. *Gnost.* 11 (p. 105). See *Rerum mon. rat.* 5–7 (cols. 1256C–60B) for counsel about boys, solitude, and socializing.

107. *Conf.* 19.16.3; see 19.12.3.

108. See Evagrius, *Schol. in Ps.* 145:8 (PG 12.1676A): it is not women or money or business in themselves that hinder salvation, but the passions of lust and avarice, which blind the νοῦς.

109. See *Conf.* 24 on the need to break from familial attachments. On this theme in Cassian's thought, see Borias, "Le moine et sa famille," 195–203.

110. *Inst.* 8.16–19, *Conf.* 1.6, 19.10–14; See *Conf.* 16.15–20.

111. See *Conf.* 2.9–13. On this central theme in the Egyptian monastic tradition, see Hausherr, *Spiritual Direction in the Early Christian East;* Stewart, "The Desert Fathers on Radical Honesty about the Self"; Gould, *The Desert Fathers on Monastic Community,* 26–87. For a different perspective, see Brakke's comments on the social significance of the ascetical process of transparency before others and before God ("The Problematization of Nocturnal Emissions in Early Christian Syria, Egypt, and Gaul," 450–55).

112. See Fiske, "Cassian and Monastic Friendship"; Neuhausen, "Zu Cassians Traktat *De amicitia* (Coll. 16)"; McGuire, *Friendship and Community,* 77–82.

113. Neuhausen notes that Cassian departs from Cicero, who had emphasized the danger of false flattery; although Cassian mentions that problem in *Conf.* 16.18.4–5, he emphasizes anger and sadness far more: "spielen Schmeichelei und verwandte Untugenden in der 16. Collatio keine wesentliche Rolle; Cassian sieht vielmehr im 'Zorn' (*ira, iracundia, furor*) und in der 'Traurigkeit' *(tristitia)* die größten Gefahren für die Verwirklichung seines Ideals der Freundschaft" ("Zu Cassians Traktat *De amicitia* [Coll. 16]," 204–5). Cassian's emphasis on anger is part of his translation of Cicero's views into an ascetical/monastic context.

114. Neuhausen notes Cassian's revaluing of the pre-Christian (Ciceronian) understanding of *amicitia* in Christian theological terms so that the supreme value is not *amicitia* itself but *caritas* ("Zu Cassians Traktat *De amicitia* (Coll. 16)," 215–18). Munz notes the significance of this move for Cassian's monastic theology ("John Cassian," 17–18). Fiske notes the social implications; she challenges the idea that Cassian devalues human relationships in his theology while suggesting that his thought remains only partially developed ("Cassian and Monastic Friendship," 204–5).

115. *Schol. in Ps.* 43:11 (PG 12.1421D): προστασσόμεθα φεύγειν μέν τὴν πορνείαν, τὴν δὲ φιλοξενίαν διώκειν.

116. See *Gnost.* 46 and the Guillaumonts' commentary (pp. 182–84).

117. The best example in Cassian's writings is Abba John, the speaker in *Conf.* 19: after thirty years as a cenobite he went into solitude for twenty years, then returned to the cenobium when the toing and froing of the anchoritic life proved too distracting. Antony, of course, after twenty years of strict solitude began a ministry to both monks and laity; Pachomius, after his anchoritic formation, established the *koinonia* as a way to bring others to God. For other examples of anchorites who later undertook formational work in semi-anchoritic or near-cenobitic communities, see Abbas Or and Apollo in *Hist. mon.* 2.2–3 and 8.3–8 (pp. 35–36 and 47–49).

118. It seems better to translate *vigilans* as "while awake" rather than more narrowly as "while keeping vigil."

119. Foucault, "Battle for Chastity," 19, suggests that Cassian means by this phrase that "the mind is no longer troubled by physical reactions over which the will has no control." This interpretation seems, however, more accurate for the fourth stage. Cassian does not mention the *mens* in his description of the first stage. The contrast between the first and fourth stages seems to lie in the role of fantasy, which is resisted in the first stage and completely absent in the fourth. See Evagrius, *Antirr.* 2.23, 2.25, 2.63 (pp. 488 and 494 [Syr.], 489 and 495 [Gk. retroversion]).

120. Cassian uses *inmunditia*, "uncleanness," as a synonymn for both masturbation and nocturnal emissions, as in *Conf.* 5.11.4, 12.2.2–3, 13.5.2. Clearly he ruled out masturbation as an acceptable form of sexual release.

121. The text reads *ne femineo vel tenuiter ad concupiscentiam moveatur aspectu*; it seems to suggest actual encounter with a woman, though it could also be referring to memory. The source for Cassian's first three stages may well be Evagrius' *De octo spir. mal.* 6 (cols. 1149D-52D), on the power of both actually seeing and remembering a woman.

122. See *Inst.* 7.3.1; *Conf.* 4.15.1, 7.1–2, 12.7.3, 12.12.3, 22.3.5–6, 22.6.7.

123. See the discussion later in this chapter of nocturnal emissions for parallels in the work of other writers.

124. See Palladius, *Hist. Laus.* 29 (p. 85) on Elias' dream of the angels castrating him to take away his passions. *Apoph. Alph.* Longinus 5 (col. 257B) seems to suggest that the chaste monk should expect emissions to cease: just as a woman ceases to menstruate when she becomes pregnant, so the soul's "flowing passions," which are "from its lower [parts],"

cease when it conceives the Holy Spirit. The soul still "held back" by emissions is not *apathēs* (ἀπαθής). This claim is followed by the cryptic dictum, "give blood and receive the Spirit," also found in Dorotheus, *Instr.* 104 (p. 338).

125. See *Inst.* 6.5–6, 12.10–13; *Conf.* 4.15.2, 7.1, 11.9.2, 12.4.1–4, 12.5.4, 12.6.3–9, 12.8.6, 12.11.2, 12.12, *passim*, 12.13.2–3, 12.15.2–3, 12.16.1, 13, *passim*, 21.32.3, 21.33.3, 22.6.2, 22.6.4, 22.6.7, 22.7.1, 22.13.7.

126. See Haag, "A Precarious Balance: Flesh and Spirit in Cassian's Works," and Pristas, *The Theological Anthropology of John Cassian*, 198–209.

127. Cassian returns to the image of a scale in *Conf.* 21.22.1, where the monk's "reasonable examination of mind" and "purity of heart" weighs abstinence against indulgence; in *Conf.* 21.22.3, by a "true judgment of conscience," the monk weighs "purity of soul" against "bodily strength" to determine what is ascetically possible.

128. In addition to the general studies of the Semi-Pelagian controversy cited in chapter 1, on Cassian see Hoch, *Lehre des Johannes Cassianus von Natur und Gnade*; Wrzol, "Die Psychologie des Johannes Cassianus," pt. 3, pp. 87–96; Kemmer, *Charisma Maximum*, 38–41; Amann, "Semi-Pélagiens," 1802–8; Munz, "John Cassian," 15–17; Chadwick, *John Cassian*, 110–36, an overview in broad strokes; Tibiletti, "Giovanni Cassiano" and *Pagine monastiche provenzali*, 33–38; Macqueen, "John Cassian on Grace and Free Will," an illuminating effort to read Cassian on his own terms; Markus, *End of Ancient Christianity*, 177–79; Pristas, *The Theological Anthropology of John Cassian*, 271–341, for a sensitive reading of *Conf.* 13 (see especially pp. 315–18, the summary of *Conf.* 13.11–14); Weaver, *Divine Grace and Human Agency*, 71–116.

129. See Prosper's *Contra collatorem*; analysis in Amann, "Semi-Pélagiens," 1825–27, and Weaver, *Divine Grace and Human Agency*, 121–31.

130. *Bonarum voluntatum . . . principia* and *consummatio virtutum* (*Conf.* 13.9.5).

131. See *De Inc.* 1.3, 5.1–4, 6.14.

132. *John Cassian*, 126; see 127–28.

133. See Ladner, *The Idea of Reform*, 404–9, and Markus' very important points in "The Legacy of Pelagius" and *The End of Ancient Christianity*, 177–79. See also the discussion of means and end in chapter 3.

134. See Jaeger, *Two Rediscovered Works of Ancient Christian Literature*, 88–98, followed by Ladner, *The Idea of Reform*, 404 (though Ladner still seems to read Cassian through Prosper); Chadwick, *John Cassian*, 110–16; Colish, *The Stoic Tradition from Antiquity to the Early Middle Ages*, 116; Burns, "Grace: The Augustinian Foundation," 331–33; On the endurance of the eastern perspective in Provence after the Pelagian controversy, see Markus, "The Legacy of Pelagius," 221–22, and Zananiri, "La controverse sur la prédestination au Ve siècle."

135. See Markus, "The Legacy of Pelagius," 216, on the irrelevance of the controversy to the eastern churches.

136. Cassian also briefly takes up the issue in *Conf.* 3.11–19 (on this, see Wrzol, "Die Psychologie des Johannes Cassianus," pt. 3, pp. 83–87). Prosper's attack, however, was directed against *Conf.* 13. In their commentaries on *Inst.* 12, Gazet (*PL* 49.272) and Guy (SC 109, p. 463 n.1) preferred the approach taken in *Inst.* 12 to that of *Conf.* 13. Macqueen sees a unity of thought between *Conf.* 13 and the other loci in Cassian's work ("John Cassian on Grace and Free Will," 20–25).

137. *Inst.* 12.10. Cassian also reiterates the "fragility of the flesh," another way of describing the same reality: see *Inst.* 12.15.2, 12.17.4, 12.18.

138. *Inst.* 12.13–14, 12.16.

139. For example, *Conf.* 3.19.1 and *Conf.* 13.3.

140. *John Cassian*, 119.

141. *Inst.* 12.13, 12.15.1, 12.19.

142. This interest, evident already in *Inst.* 12.15.1–2, has its final development in *Conf.* 23.

143. See Macqueen's remark: "admittedly, his discussion of the topic—scattered through many works—is deficient in the method and precision appropriate to a formal treatise on theology" ("John Cassian on Grace and Free Will," 24). Kemmer makes the same point in *Charisma Maximum*, 39.

144. At least, he eschews it until the *De Incarnatione*. See Chadwick on this point (*John Cassian*, 119–20).

145. *Inst.* 12.18; *Conf.* 13.11.1–5, 13.18.5.

146. Guy asks in his commentary on *Inst.* 12.15.1, "faut-il y voir un des premiers témoignages historiques de la scission entre dogme et spiritualité?" (*Jean Cassien. Institutions cénobitiques*, p. 470 n.1). Pristas has a more nuanced view in *The Theological Anthropology of John Cassian*, 163–64.

147. This echoes *Conf.* 3.11, a question from Germanus about the scope of free will given God's initiation and completion of salvation. The focus there, however, is not specifically on chastity.

148. *Conf.* 13.3.5; see *Conf.* 3.19.1.

149. *Conf.* 13.6.3; see *Inst.* 12.11–14.

150. Note Pristas' summary: "Cassian affirms a qualified natural capacity for good. The pagans, by refraining from immoral behavior, are doing good inasmuch as they restrain their evil impulses. There is no question here, however, of acts tending toward salvation" (*The Theological Anthropology of John Cassian*, 276). See Diadochus, *Cap. gnost.* 74 (pp. 132.24–133.8) on the Greek philosophers who thought they could achieve by discipline what can be obtained only by the gift of "eternal and really true wisdom" by the Holy Spirit.

151. Tibiletti notes the Stoic background of the *scintilla* within ("Giovanni Cassiano," 370–73); see Basil, *Asc. parv.* 2.16–17 (p. 11).

152. *Conf.* 13.8.3, 13.18.2.

153. See *Inst.* 12.16, 12.18, 12.23; *Conf.* 3.19.1.

154. *Conf.* 13.9.4–5; see *Inst.* 12.14.2.

155. See Macqueen, "John Cassian on Grace and Free Will," 12–13, 17, 19.

156. See Pristas, *The Theological Anthropology of John Cassian*, 289–93 and 349–50.

157. This position is a clear criticism of Augustine and his followers; as Amann notes, for Cassian "il ne faut pas généraliser" about the modes of grace ("Sémi-Pélagiens," 1807). See Kemmer, *Charisma Maximum*, 46.

158. Spinelli, "Teologia e 'teoria'," uses *Conf.* 14 on *praktikē* and *theōrētikē* as a way to resolve the contradictory biblical witnesses found in *Conf.* 13.

159. See *Conf.* 23.11 for *semina virtutum*. The image is Stoic; see Tibiletti, "Giovanni Cassiano," 360–62, 372–73. Evagrius used it in *Prak.* 57 (p. 634, with commentary on pp. 635–36).

160. See Rufinus' Latin version of the early *Asc. parv.* (pp. 9–25) and the similar passage in the later *Reg. fus.* (cols. 908B–16C). For the *semina virtutum* see *Asc. parv.* 2.63 (pp. 63–64). Prosper's summary of Cassian's position in *C. coll.* 20 (cols. 269C–70B) caricatures this optimistic anthropology. Tibiletti gathers background material in *Pagine monastiche provenzali*, 8–24.

161. See *Conf.* 13.13, 13.18.5. See Wrzol's summary ("Die Psychologie des Johannes Cassianus," pt. 3, pp. 93–96) and Macqueen's arguments for similarities with Augustine's teaching ("John Cassian on Grace and Free Will," 18–19).

162. Chadwick notes that Cassian is matching Augustine (in *De correptione et gratia*) biblical text for text (*John Cassian*, 122).

163. *Conf.* 3.19.1, 13.11.1, 13.17.1.

164. 1 Cor. 15:10, *Conf.* 13.13.4–5.

165. *Sed absoluta plane pronuntiamus sententia etiam exuberare gratiam dei et transgredi humanae interdum infidelitatis angustias* (*Conf.* 13.16.1).

166. *Inst.* 12.18 and *Conf.* 13.15.2, 13.17.1, 13.18.2. It is in this context that one must interpret Cassian's suggestions that God "compels" or "draws" even the unwilling to salvation in Christ: *nolentes invitosque conpellere, Conf.* 13.17.1; *ignorantes nos atque invitos adtrahit, Conf.* 13.17.2; *nolentes resistentesque pertrahere, Conf.* 13.18.2; see the similar words used about Paul in *Conf.* 13.15.2, *invitum ac repugnantem adtrahit Paulum.*

167. Grace is given to those *non semper resistentes nec perseveranter inviti* (*Conf.* 13.18.3).

168. *Conf.* 13.14.9; see *Conf.* 3.12.4. Cassian compares God's providence to a mother's care in *Conf.* 13.17.4. On the general theme of testing, see *Conf.* 4.6.

169. Ramsey (*John Cassian. The Conferences*, 498) has noted Pseudo-Macarius' *Coll. III* 27.3 (pp. 320–22); the text is also found in *Coll. II* 46.3 (p. 302). See *Coll. I* 6.5.1 (vol. 1, p. 88), also found in *Coll. II* 27.11 (p. 224).

170. Antony's trial in Athanasius, *V. Ant.* 9–10 ends with a dialogue between Antony and God. Antony: "Where were you? Why didn't you appear at the outset, to end my sufferings?" God: "Antony, I was there, but I was waiting to see your struggle. Because you endured and were not defeated, I will be your defender forever, and I shall make you famous everywhere" (p. 164).

171. See especially the *De instituto christiano*, as analyzed by Jaeger in *Two Rediscovered Works of Ancient Christian Literature*, 92–109. Although Jaeger wrote before Staats' demonstration that Gregory based his treatise on Pseudo-Macarius' *Epistola magna* (see Staats' edition), the portions he analyzes are Gregory's own material. The Pseudo-Macarian text, while making similar points, contains a less philosophical vocabulary than Gregory's.

172. *Conf.* 13.17.2; see *Inst.* 12.16 and 18.

173. See *The Theological Anthropology of John Cassian*, 326–29.

174. See Jaeger, *Two Rediscovered Works of Early Christian Literature*, 88–89.

175. *John Cassian*, 116 and 120. See Amann's summation, "Telle est cette fameuse conférence XIII, où la multiplicité des détails, la finesse même de certaines analyses psychologiques, n'arrivent pas à masquer l'incertitude de la pensée métaphysique" ("Sémi-Pélagiens," 1808).

176. *The Theological Anthropology of John Cassian*, 337.

177. This term is the commonly used euphemism for orgasm during erotic dreams.

178. Kinsey studies the phenomenon of nocturnal emissions in his famous report, *Sexual Behavior in the Human Male*; he is skeptical about the assumptions made by religious writers that nocturnal emissions function as an alternative sexual outlet for the celibate. He also noted the need for scientific study of celibates (pp. 527–29). See Sipe, *A Secret World*, 146–49, for a psychotherapist's evaluation of celibacy and nocturnal emissions; he, too, does not consider emissions to be an alternative form of sexual release.

179. See Pigeaud, "Le rêve érotique dans l'Antiquité gréco-romaine" for the Classical sources.

180. The concern was, like so many sexual issues, framed largely in terms of ritual impurity. See *Conf.* 22.5.5 with its use of Lev. 7:19–20 (LXX), about eating of the Temple sacrifice by the impure, and Deut. 23:10–11, on nocturnal pollution. See Evagrius, *Prak.* 55 (p. 628); *Hist. mon.* 16.1 and 20.1–4 (pp. 112 and 118–19), and the Latin version collated by Schulz-Flügel in "The Function of Apophthegmata in *Vitae* and *Itineraria*," 290 n. 28;

Basil, *Reg. brev.* 22 and 309 (cols. 1097C and 1301C–04A); *Reg. Mag.* 11.119 (vol. 2, pp. 30–32). The best survey is Brakke, "The Problematization of Nocturnal Emissions in Early Christian Syria, Egypt and Gaul." For medieval attitudes, see Browe, *Beiträge zur Sexualethik des Mittelalters,* 80–113, and Payer, *Sex and the Penitentials,* 49–52. Refoulé surveys Christian authors in "Rêves et vie spirituelle d'après Évagre le Pontique"; for erotic dreams and emissions, see pp. 488–93. See Brakke's summary of Egyptian episcopal views in *Athanasius and the Politics of Asceticism,* 90–96.

181. The *Letter to Ammoun,* which takes a wise pastoral approach and shifts "blame" for such dreams from the scrupulous monk to the devil. See Vivian, " 'Everything Made by God Is Good,' " for an analysis and translation of this text.

182. Evagrius, *Prak.* 55 (p. 628), claims that τοῦ σώματος φυσικαὶ κινήσεις without images (ἀνείδωλοι) are the sign of a soul in good health, while with images (εἰδώλων) they indicate bad health; and *Cap.* 6 (col. 1265A), that nocturnal emission (γονόῤῥοια) is a disorder of the rational part of the soul, corrected by spiritual teaching. In *Hist. mon.* 20.1–3 (p. 119), there is to be no communion for those who pondered an image in the night lest they had a (possibly orgasmic) dream after doing so; it is clear that the problem was the dreams, not the emissions (γονόῤῥοιαι), which can be purely natural and involuntary, thus not sinful. Rufinus' Latin version specifies that even dreams caused by an "abundance of natural humor" are a bar to communion: again, it is the dream rather than the emission that is problematic (*Hist. Mon. [Ruf.]* 20.4, pp. 354–55). See *Apoph. Anon.* Nau 605 (p. 259), which takes the less severe view that emissions even when accompanied by a fantasy are not culpable if one remains distant from the "thought," presumably meaning that one does not entertain it when awake.

183. The best example is Athanasius, who though writing for monks in his *Letter to Ammoun,* is intent on reducing anxiety about their dreams and emissions; he describes emission as φυσική τις ἔκκρισις, comparing it to excrement, spit, and nasal secretions as being entirely natural and not remotely sinful (pp. 63–65). Nemesius of Emesa, writing ca. 400, considered genital activity during sleep to be outside the realm of reason (thus disagreeing with Evagrius), which meant that emissions, even in dreams indicating a desire for sexual intercourse, were not a moral problem (*De nat. hom.* 25, col. 700A). The *Didascalia* rejects the contention that emissions are ritually impure (Syr. ch. 26 [pp. 255 and 259], Lat. 56 and 59–60 [pp. 91 and 95–96]).

184. *Inst.* 6.3, 6.11, 6.13.1; *Conf.* 5.4.5–6. On Cassian's teaching about dreams, see Wrzol, "Die Psychologie des Johannes Cassianus," 441–49.

185. See Caelius Aurelianus, *On Chronic Diseases* 5.7 (p. 960). Tertullian saw three sources as the inducers of dreams: demons, God, and the soul itself *ex intentione circumstantiarum* (*De anima* 47.1–3, p. 853). This teaching is very much like Cassian's on the three sources of thoughts in *Conf.* 1.19, thought by Ramsey to come from Origen, *De princ.* 3.2.4 (*John Cassian. The Conferences,* 72). See Basil, *Reg. brev.* 22 (col. 1097C) and *Hom. in martyrem Julittam* 4 (col. 244D); Augustine, *Confess.* 10.30.41–42 (vol. 1, p. 135) and *De Gen. ad litt.* 12.15 (pp. 400–401).

186. For example, *Prak.* 55 (p. 628), *De mal. cog.* 4 (cols. 1204C–5B), *Antirr.* 2.15, 2.19, 2.34, 2.52, 2.60 (pp. 486–92). See Refoulé, "Rêves et vie spirituelle d'après Évagre le Pontique," and Miller, "Dreaming the Body," 290 on Evagrius' differences from the Cappadocian Gregories.

187. *Conf.* 19.16.3; see *Conf.* 12.7.3 on no longer being disturbed by such texts. See Benedict's prescription in *Reg. Ben.* 42.4 (p. 584) that the Heptateuch and the Books of Kings not be read in the evening lest the subject matter disturb those of "weak understanding." See Vogüé's commentary on this text in *La Règle de Saint Benoît,* 5.711–12.

188. *Inst.* 2.13.1, 3.5.1, 6.7.2, 6.11; *Conf.* 2.23.1, 4.15.2, 12.4.3, 12.6.7, 12.7.4–5, 22.3.4–5, 23.7.2.

189. *Inst.* 6.10; *Conf.* 12.7.4, 12.16.2. Kelly (*Jerome*, 157–58 and 314 n.24) notes that Jerome, commenting on Ps. 14(15) initially taught that the holy are preserved from sin even while asleep (*Tract. in Ps. [ser. alt.]*, pp. 375–77), which followed Origen's line of thought whereby one of supreme chastity is no longer subject to emissions (*Comm. in Ps.* 15:7, *PG* 12.1213D–16A); later Jerome condemned this view (*Ep.* 133.3, CSEL 56, p. 247.15–17).

190. See Pigeaud, "Le rêve érotique dans l'Antiquité gréco-romaine"; Jacquart and Thomasset, *Sexuality and Medicine in the Middle Ages*, 150–52. See Soranus' view, based on the Greek term for nocturnal emissions, ὀνειρωγμός (ὄνειρος, "dream" + ῥωγμός, "wheezing"); in Caelius' Latin translation, ὀνειρωγμός is *somnus venerius*, "sexual dream," defined as a *seminis lapsus* prompted by "empty visions" in which the dreamer imagines himself to be copulating (*On Chronic Diseases* 5.7, p. 958). Women, too, of course, have erotic dreams and can experience orgasm during them; ancient writers, believing in female "sperm" and its ejaculation during orgasm, wrote of female ὀνειρωγμός. For the intellectual constructs of women's bodies that passed as anatomical knowledge in antiquity, see Rousselle, *Porneia*, 24–46 (on "female sperm," see pp. 26–32) and Jacquart and Thomasset, *Sexuality and Medicine in the Middle Ages*, *passim* (on female sperm, especially pp. 61–71).

191. *Conf.* 12.7.7 (as a postscript) and 22.6.5. In *Inst.* 6.23 he links nocturnal fantasies to overconsumption of food, the cause of emissions as well. For the same view, see *Hist. mon.* 20.3 (p. 119). Clement claimed that an excess of food plunges the rational faculty of the soul (λογιστικόν) into senselessness (ἀναισθησία), seizes the visual faculty, (διορατικόν) and fills the mind (διανοία) with a multitude of images (*Paed.* 2.9, [sec. 81.1–2, pp. 206–7]). Evagrius notes that *enkrateia* (ἐγκράτεια) stops the flow of evil desires, probably an allusion to emissions (*Gnost.* 47, p. 184).

192. See Hippocrates, *De genitura* 1.3, as cited by Pigeaud, "Le rêve érotique dans l'Antiquité gréco-romaine," 13: the cause of ejaculation is the "humor" itself, aroused for whatever reason; the fantasy of intercourse is generated by the state of the humor, which resembles that in real intercourse. Diogenes of Oenoanda underscored the "reality" of the visions, while Lucretius took a mediating position (Pigeaud, 16–19).

193. For *inlusio* as fantasy, see *Inst.* 2.13.1, 3.5.1 (though this example is ambiguous), 6.10 (also ambiguous), 6.11, 6.23; *Conf.* 12.7.4, 12.7.7, 12.16.2, 22.3.6 (first occurrence), 22.6.2 (second occurrence), 22.6.5, 22.6.6. For *inlusio* as the emission itself, see *Inst.* 6.10 (ambiguous); *Conf.* 4.15.2, 22.3.6 (second occurrence), 22.4, 22.6.2, 22.6.4. The latter is most common in *Conf.* 22, where the emphasis is on the psychology of shame exploited by the devil.

194. See Vivian, " 'Everything Made by God Is Good,' " 88–90.

195. *Confess.* 10.30.41–42 (vol. 1, p. 135); Augustine does not regard such emissions to be morally culpable. See *De Gen. ad litt.* 12.15 (pp. 400–401): emissions occur without sin for those who are chaste during their waking hours; Augustine is reluctant to concede that either fantasies or natural physical reactions cease during sleep, though he admits that sometimes the soul's merits due to chastity are manifest even in sleep. See Brakke's analysis in "The Problematization of Nocturnal Emissions in Early Christian Syria, Egypt, and Gaul," 455–57. On the difference between Augustine and Cassian on this point, see Brown, *The Body and Society*, 420–23.

196. *Inst.* 6.20, 6.22; *Conf.* 2.23.1, 12.8.5, 12.16.2. Note, however, that in *Conf.* 20.12.2 he places *somnii pollutio* among the unavoidable minor sins of day-to-day living. This change fits with the tendency in the final set of *Conferences* to backtrack from the claims made for ascetical perfection in *Conf.* 1–10 and 11–17.

197. *Conf.* 12.11.4, 12.12.3, 12.16.2 (though even this nonprurient *conmotio* is due to "carelessness" of the mind; see *Conf.* 20.12.2).

198. *Conf.* 21.35; see 22.2, 22.3.6.

199. See *Apoph. Anon.* Nau 80 (p. 398); *Apoph. Dial.* 26–27 (p. 181).

200. Timothy of Alexandria, writing in 381 about whether a layman who has had an impure dream (ὀνειρασθείς) can go to communion, replies that if there was an underlying desire for a woman, he may not go; if there was not, then Satan was testing him in order to hinder communion with the divine mysteries, and he ought to commune (*Quaest.* 12, pp. 247–48). See Pseudo-Justin's view that erotic dreams (there is no mention of emissions) are caused by demons to deter people from communion, and that the dreamer cannot be held responsible for them (*Quaest.* 21, col. 1268; the author was thought by Quasten to be Theodoret, *Patrology* 3.548–49).

201. Clement notes that "[the Lord] commands that [the Gnostic] keep conduct by night like that done in the day, pure and unstained" (ἀλλὰ καὶ τῆς νυκτὸς τὴν πολιτείαν, ὡς ἐν ἡμέρᾳ ἐνεργουμένην, καθαρὰν καὶ ἀκηλίδωτον διαφυλάττειν προστάττει, *Strom.* 4.22, [sec. 139.4, p. 310]). See *Strom.* 6.9 (sec. 79.1, p. 471) and *Strom.* 7.12 (sec. 77.3, p. 55 and sec. 78.5, p. 56). Brakke interprets Cassian's emphasis on transparency in terms of boundaries of the self in monastic community, "The Problematization of Nocturnal Emissions in Early Christian Syria, Egypt, and Gaul," 448–55.

202. On the kidneys as the source of semen, see Jacquart and Thomasset, *Sexuality and Medicine in the Middle Ages*, 13. Origen's *Comm. in Ps.* 15:7 (PG 12.1213D–16A), noted earlier, compares the physical kidneys, which are the source of seed, to the spiritual kidneys, which are the source of deeds and "true contemplations"; in the truly chaste person, the physical (αἰσθητοί) kidneys hold back the flow of bodily seed at night (ἕως καὶ τῆς νυκτὸς ἐπεχόμενοι σώφρονος λογισμοῦ τὰς σωματικὰς ἐκρεῖν γονάς). Evagrius interpreted other references to the kidneys in the Psalms to mean the empassioned part of the soul: *Schol. in Ps.* 25:2 (PG 12.1273A), *Schol. in Ps.* 72:21 (PG 12.1528C).

203. *Inst.* 6.3; *Conf.* 11.8.2, 12.11.2, 12.12.6–7, 12.13.1.

204. *Conf.* 12.12.2 and 12.12.6; see chapter 7.

205. *Conf.* 14.10.4, 14.11, *passim*, 14.14.2, 14.16.2, 14.16.7–8.

206. The phrase is Michel Foucault's title for the first section of vol. 1 of his *History of Sexuality*.

Chapter 5

1. *Claritas*, which Cassian uses several times to describe the radiance of Christ (*Conf.* 3.7.2, 10.6.2–3, 19.14.6), divine realities and their contemplation (*Conf.* 9.29.2, 23.4.4, 23.13.2), virginity (*Conf.* 22.6.9), and holy people (*Conf.* 3.1.1, *Conf. Pref.* 2 1). The closest parallel to this particular text is *Conf.* 19.14.6, where one is cautioned against losing, through anger, the *veri atque aeterni luminis claritas*, almost exactly the same phrase as in *Conf.* 9.31.

2. *In excessu mentis frequenter orante cum solis ortus coepisset infundi, audierimus eum in fervore spiritus proclamantem: quid me inpedis, sol, qui ad hoc iam oreris, ut me ab huius veri luminis abstrahas claritate?* (*Conf.* 9.31). See *Apoph. Alph.* Arsenius 30 on his practice of praying with hands upraised from sundown on Saturday to dawn on Sunday.

3. Like that at the beginning of this chapter, this saying of Antony is unknown from other sources, though there are parallels in Evagrius and Diadochus.

4. *Lausiac History*, 1:208.

5. It should be remembered that although Cassian describes Sarapion as an Anthropomorphite, he never describes his own circle as Origenist, nor indeed does he ever cite Origen by name.

6. Note that Theophilus had engineered the destruction of the Serapeum in Alexandria; see Clark, *The Origenist Controversy*, 53–56.

7. Φωτεινός is derived from φῶς, "light."

8. Age: *antiquissimae districtionis* (*Conf.* 10.3.1), *tantae antiquitatis* (10.3.4), *per quinquaginta annos in hac heremo* (10.4.1), *consuetudine erroris antiqui* (10.5.1). Inexperience or simplicity: *inperitia* (10.3.1), *inperitia . . . simplicitate rusticitatis errantem* (10.3.4), *ignorantiae huius vitio* (10.4.1), *hominem simplicissimum . . . rusticitatis vitio* (10.5.1), *inperitia seu rusticitate* (10.5.2). And then the diagnosis: *in errore pristino perdurare, qui non recenti sicut putatis daemonum inlusione, sed ignorantia pristinae gentilitatis infertur dum secundum consuetudinem erroris illius, quo daemonas hominum figura compositos excolebant* (10.5.1).

9. *Ita est in oratione senex mente confusus, eo quod illam anthropomorphon imaginem deitatis, quam proponere sibi in oratione consueuerat, aboleri de suo corde sentiret, ut in amarissimos fletus crebrosque singultus repente prorumpens in terramque prostratus* (*Conf.* 10.3.4).

10. Sarapion: *Heu me miserum! tulerunt a me deum meum, et quem nunc teneam non habeo vel quem adorem aut interpellem iam nescio* (*Conf.* 10.3.5). Mary Magdalene's reply when asked why she is weeping: *Quia tulerunt Dominum meum: et nescio ubi posuerunt eum* (John 20:13; Cassian never quotes this text).

11. Cassian tells a similar story about Heron, a monk who lived fifty years of the strictest asceticism, only to be fatally deceived by an "angel of Satan" because he lacked discernment. This story, like that about Sarapion, is presented as a recent occurrence in the circle of Paphnutius and as personally known to John and Germanus (*Conf.* 2.5). Palladius has a somewhat similar story about a monk of the same name whom he locates at the Cells (*Hist. Laus.* 26, pp. 81–82).

12. Cassian makes it clear that Sarapion and those like him have not actually been "polluted by pagan superstition" (*gentilicia superstitione polluti*, *Conf.* 10.5.2) but through a misunderstanding of the bibical text have fallen into the same trap. See Clark, *The Origenist Controversy*, 52–58, on the significance of charges of paganism in light of Theophilus' policy of destroying pagan temples.

13. Recent scholarship suggests that Cassian's emphasis on anthropomorphism exaggerates the significance of that strand of the larger controversy; see, for example, Gould, "The Image of God," especially pp. 549–51, and Clark, *The Origenist Controversy*, 44.

14. Their major critic in the 370s was Epiphanius, and concern for the issue is evident in the *Life of Aphou*, which Florovsky and Gould value as an important source (Florovsky, "The Anthropomorphites in the Egyptian Desert," and "Theophilus of Alexandria and Apa Aphou of Pemdje"; Gould, "The Image of God"). On the debates over the image of God in human beings, see also Dechow, *Dogma and Mysticism in Early Christianity*, 302–15; Clark, *The Origenist Controversy*, 71–75, 101–4. Cassian's handling of this question is in the Origenist/Evagrian tradition, suggesting that one "receives," "attains," or "bears" the image and likeness of God in the perfection of love, synonymous for Cassian with purity of heart and perfect chastity (*Conf.* 11.6.3, 11.7.3, 11.9.2–3, 11.14). He does not state that the image was lost in the Fall, nor does he seem interested in ontological issues. His focus, rather, is ascetical and moral, and he writes about worthiness to be accounted a child of God and to bear the image. Thus he says that Adam lost the "divine glory" (*Inst.* 12.5), and that the image was profaned (*violata*, *Conf.* 5.6.1; see *De Inc.* 7.6). Nonetheless, he could be interpreted as sailing rather close to the positions attacked by Epiphanius and others. See Cod-

ina, *El aspecto cristologico en la espiritualidad de Juan Casiano*, 39–46, for Cassian's teaching.

15. According to his *Life*, Aphou was successful; as is known from other sources, Theophilus reversed himself on the entire Origenist issue. For Aphou's interview with Theophilus, see Drioton, "La discussion d'un moine anthropomorphite audien avec le patriarche Théophile d'Alexandrie en l'année 399," 96–115 (Coptic and French); Florovsky, "Theophilus of Alexandria and Apa Aphou of Pemdje," 112–17 (English).

16. The name had been in circulation at least since Origen's time and was applied to those making a bodily interpretation of Gen. 1:26; see Lampe, *A Patristic Greek Lexicon*, 140ab. As a name for a group of Egyptian monks resistant to Origenism, it was used in the fifth-century accounts of Socrates, Sozomen, and Palladius; see Clark, *The Origenist Controversy*, 44–49. Whether such a group actually existed or would have recognized itself as believing what Cassian and others attribute to them is a central question in recent scholarship on the Egyptian phase of the Origenist controversy.

17. See Florovsky, "The Anthropomorphites of the Egyptian Desert," 91–94, and especially Golitzin, "The Vision of God and the Form of Glory," on theological shifts after Nicea: Sarapion and Photinus stand on either side of a revisioning of divine glory made necessary by Nicene Christology. Regnault notes of the desert tradition generally, "Le Dieu dont se souviennent les Pères du désert est ordinairement le Christ," and affirms with Codina (*El aspecto cristologico en la espiritualidad de Juan Casiano*, 99) that Cassian understands the formula of unceasing prayer from Ps. 69(70), "God, come to my assistance," to be addressed to Christ ("La prière continuelle 'monologistos' dans les Apophtegmes des Pères," 491).

18. See Florovsky's comments on Cassian and Origen in "The Anthropomorphites of the Egyptian Desert," 91–94, though he takes a dim view of Origen's influence.

19. See the similar view of Jerome as in, for example, *Comm. in Hierem.* 6.48 (p. 344.10).

20. *Inst.* 8.3: *secundum vilem litterae sonum; Conf.* 10.3.3: *secundum humilem litterae sonum*. See *secundum litteram* in *Inst.* 8.3 and 8.4.1 and *non nuda significatione verborum* in *Conf.* 23.2.1.

21. *Inst.* 8.4.5. See also *Conf.* 5.18.1, 5.19.3, 6.10.1, 18.6.3, 18.16.8, 21.20.2.

22. *Conf.* 10.3.3. See also *Inst.* 1.8.1; *Conf.* 1.20.2, 3.15, 6.17.2, 11.3.1, 14.11.2, 16.3.5.

23. *Inst.* 8.3: *liniamenta membrorum, quae tamquam de homine figurali et conposito describuntur; 8.4.5: omnia quae de deo humana significatione figuraliter in scripturis dicta. Conf.* 10.2.2: *negans deum humanae figurae conpositione formatum;* 10.3.3: *humana conpositio ac similitudin[is];* 10.5.2: *liniamentis nostris et humana figuratione conposita [sc. divinitatis substantia]*.

24. *Inst.* 8.3, *Conf.* 10.5.3.

25. *Inst.* 8.4.1, *Conf.* 10.5.3.

26. *Inst.* 8.4.5, *Conf.* 10.4.1.

27. *Inst.* 8.4: *invisibilis, ineffabilis, inconprehensibilis, inaestimabilis, simplex et inconpositus. Conf.* 10.3.3: *[maiestas] inmensa, incomprehensibilis, invisibilis; [natura] incorporea, inconposita, simplex. Conf.* 10.5.1: *[maiestas] inconprehensibilis, ineffabilis. Conf.* 10.5.2: *[substantia divinitatis] inmensa, simplex.*

28. Again one sees the seminal role of *Inst.* 5.

29. *Summa sanctitate et scientia praeditu[s] non solum in actuali vita, sed etiam notitia scripturarum (Inst.* 5.33).

30. *Inst.* 5.33: *praeditum non solum in actuali vita* (Theodore); *Conf.* 10.3.1: *in actuali disciplina per omnia consummatus* (Sarapion).

31. On Theodore: *[notitiam scripturarum] quam ei non tam studium lectionis vel lit-*

teratura mundi contulerat . . . siquidem vix ipsius quoque Graecae linguae perpauca verba vel intellegere posset vel proloqui (*Inst.* 5.33). On Sarapion: *cuius inperitia super praedicti dogmatis opinione* (*Conf.* 10.3.1), *inperitia sola et simplicitate rusticitatis erran[s]* (*Conf.* 10.3.4), *ignorantiae huius vitio* (*Conf.* 10.4.1), *hom[o] simplicissimu[s] . . . rusticitatis vitio* (*Conf.* 10.5.1), *inperitia seu rusticitate faciente contractus est* (*Conf.* 10.5.2). Given Sarapion's Egyptian name and "rusticity," he probably knew little Greek. See *De Inc.* 3.15.2 on Thomas' recognition of Christ's divinity even though he was *homo . . . rusticus et imperitus, dialecticae artis nescius, philosophicae disputationis ignarus.*

32. *Inst.* 5.33: *summa sanctitas et scientia* (Theodore); *Conf.* 10.3.2: *diaconus summae scientiae* (Photinus).

33. *Inst.* 5.34, on those who are not pure in heart and come up with *errores* and opinions that are *contraria . . . fidei; Conf.* 10.3.2–3 and 10.5.3 on Catholic faith versus error.

34. For *scientia* and the Bible, see *Conf.* 10.11.2 and *Conf.* 14, *passim;* for *sacramenta,* see *Conf.* 10.11.4, 14.1.3, 14.3.1, 14.8.2, 14.9.7, 14.17.2–3.

35. *Conf.* 14.7, 15.10.

36. *V. Ant.* 72–73 (pp. 320–24); see 20.4–9 (pp. 188–92) on the pagans who cross the sea to learn letters while Christians find the reign of God within themselves. The point is analogous to Evagrius' (see note 37).

37. *Gnost.* 4 (p. 92, with references to other texts); see Viller, "Aux sources de la spiritualité de S. Maxime," 242 n. 126.

38. *Gnost.* 45 (p. 178). The text continues, characterizing the "worthy" as those who could see the light of the intellect when at prayer. For this Evagrian way of describing spiritual vision, see the section on "Seeing and Knowing Christ" later in this chapter.

39. Evagrius uses the term for Christian knowledge generally, without applying it specifically to biblical interpretation; *pneumatikos* ($\pi\nu\epsilon\nu\mu\alpha\tau\iota\kappa\acute{o}\varsigma$) is simply a modifier of the nearly ubiquitous *gnōsis* ($\gamma\nu\tilde{\omega}\sigma\iota\varsigma$); see its generic use in, for example, *Gnost.* 47 (p. 184), *Schol. in Prov.* 1 (p. 90), 104 (p. 202), 153 (p. 248), 310 (pp. 400–02), 354 (p. 444); *Schol. in Eccl.* 31 (p. 110) and 44 (p. 140).

40. Even *spiritalis scientia* is not always specifically about the Bible; in *Inst.* 6.1 it is linked to continual *meditatio;* in *Inst.* 6.18, Cassian notes it is impossible without chastity; and see *Conf.* 1.14.1, the reign of God is possessed through practice of the virtues in purity of heart and spiritual knowledge. For the similar *vera scientia,* see *Inst.* 5.2.2, 5.34 (Theodore and biblical insight), 6.18; *Conf.* 6.3.1, 11.13.2, 14.9.5, 14.13.4, 14.16.2 (these last three are synonymous with *spiritalis scientia* as it is used in *Conf.* 14).

41. See Codina's remarks on Cassian's Christological understanding of the *sacramenta divina* hidden in the Bible (*El aspecto cristologico en la espiritualidad de Juan Casiano,* 113–15).

42. For Clement, see, for example, *Strom.* 5, *passim.* Mondésert, *Clément d'Alexandrie,* 65–162, provides a thorough overview of Clement's teaching on biblical interpretation; see Camelot, *Foi et gnose,* 71–90. The starting point for understanding Origen's theory of interpretation is *De princ.* 4.1–3. See the analysis of this text by Crouzel and Simonetti in their edition (SC 269, pp. 151–234), as well as Harl's edition and commentary on various texts on biblical interpretation preserved in the Cappadocian catena known as the *Philocalia* (SC 302). Other key texts are the Prologue to *Comm. in Cant.* and *Hom. in Num.* 27. For a brief overview of early Christian exegesis, see Simonetti, *Biblical Interpretation on the Early Church,* with basic bibliography.

43. *Conf.* 14.1–8, 14.9–11, 14.12–19.

44. See chapter 3 for the history of these divisions of human experience. For the

relationship between Evagrius' broader schema and his exegesis, see Driscoll, *The "Ad monachos" of Evagrius Ponticus,* 19–20.

45. See chapter 3 for Cassian's translations of the Evagrian schemata.

46. *The "Ad monachos" of Evagrius Ponticus,* 20. See the Guillaumonts' introduction to *Gnost.* (*SC* 356, pp. 29–30).

47. This work is to be understood with respect to the eight principal faults outlined in *Inst.* 5–12 and *Conf.* 5; see *Conf.* 14.3.

48. *Conf.* 14.2; see 14.9.2, 14.14–16. Cassian does allow, perhaps as an expression of his own modesty, that God does sometimes grant the grace of spiritual teaching to someone not of irreproachable life *(conversatio)* for the sake of benefitting others (*Conf.* 14.19).

49. *Professiones studiaque, Conf.* 14.4.1.

50. *Conf.* 14.8.1. Evagrius' interpretation of the same text according to his own schema, *Schol. in Prov.* 247 (p. 342).

51. The standard account both of Cassian's relation to Origen and the later development of his scheme are De Lubac's "On an Old Distich: The Doctrine of the 'Fourfold Sense' in Scripture" and also the relevant section of *Exégèse médiévale* (1:187–219). Although these two studies overlap somewhat, they have different orientations, and both should be read.

52. Four are obtained by adding "historical" to the three "spiritual" senses.

53. See Codina's summary of Cassian's four senses, *El aspecto cristologico en la espiritualidad de Juan Casiano,* 105–15.

54. The literal and allegorical meanings could pertain to different aspects, as Evagrius notes in *Gnost.* 18 (pp. 119–21).

55. See, for example, Origen, *De princ.* 4.2.6 (pp. 318–26) and Evagrius, *Schol. in Prov.* 270 (p. 364).

56. See Géhin's "Exégèse évagrienne" in the introduction to *Schol. in Prov.* (SC 340, pp. 26–32; esp. 30); Bunge, " 'Der mystische Sinn der Schrift,' " 138–39. Bunge notes Evagrius' advice to the *gnōstikos* (γνωστικός), the monastic teacher, to avoid allegorizing merely for effect (*Gnost.* 34, p. 153). The result might be amusement for the hearers without any edification.

57. Evagrius simply quotes Paul's spiritual interpretation of Jerusalem in *Schol. in Ps.* 118:18 (*PG* 12.1591B).

58. For allegory he uses: 1 Cor. 10:1–4, Paul interpreting Exodus allegorically; for tropology: 1 Cor. 11:13, on whether women should pray with heads uncovered; for anagogy: 1 Thess. 4:12–15, an explicitly eschatological text; for history: the parainetical passages 1 Cor 15:3–5 and Gal. 4:4–5, with the *Shema* as a third example (Deut. 6:4–5, also cited in *Conf.* 8.3.4 as an example of a text that is profitable in its literal meaning).

59. *Conf.* 14.8.1: *historia/ tropologia—allegoria—anagōgē; Conf.* 14.8.2–3: *historia/allegoria—anagōgē—tropologia; Conf.* 14.8.4–5, following 1 Cor. 14:6: *allegoria—tropologia—anagōgē/historia.* De Lubac suggests that the difference between the first two series has to do with questions about the place of *tropologia:* is it ethical in a general human sense and thus to be placed before the theological interpretations (*Conf.* 14.8.1), or is it a specifically Christian moral application of a text, in which case it should follow the theological interpretations (*Conf.* 14.8.2–3)? The first model is based on the tripartite division of philosophy that influenced Origen's model of the historical, moral, and allegorical senses (alluded to by Cassian in *Conf.* 3.6.4); the second was also from Origen, and Cassian displays both. De Lubac describes them and the resolution of the two schemata in the Latin West after Cassian (*Exégèse médiévale,* 1:192–219).

60. In addition to the examples studied in this chapter, see the way he uses Phil. 3:13–14 in *Inst.* 5.17.2 and *Conf.* 1.5.2–4 on the *scopos* of monastic life; the interpretation of

Martha and Mary (Luke 10:40–42) in *Conf.* 1.8; the extended play on the apocryphal command by Jesus that his followers be "wise moneychangers" in *Conf.* 1.20–22 (see the discussion in Stewart, "From λόγος to *verbum*," 17); "the war between flesh and spirit" (Gal. 5:17) in *Conf.* 4.7–17; the application of the "seven nations" of Deut. 7:1–2 to the eight principal faults in *Conf.* 5.16–19; the ambidextrous man of Judg. 3:15 (LXX) applied to the mastery of both spiritual and carnal challenges in *Conf.* 6.10; the interpretation of four kinds of prayer (1 Tim. 2:1) and the Lord's Prayer in *Conf.* 9.9–24; the series of interpretations in *Conf.* 13 and 16; the extended meditation on Rom. 7 throughout *Conf.* 23.

61. See *Conf.* 14.9.7, 14.10, 14.13.7; see *Conf.* 10.10.14–15, 10.11.4–6.

62. See the Guillaumonts' introduction to their edition of *Gnost.* (SC 356, pp. 24–42), and the notes that follow, indicating thematic parallels between *Gnost.* and *Conf.* 14. On *Conf.* 14 as outlining a training program for teachers of asceticism, see also Leyser, "*Lectio divina, oratio pura.*"

63. See Miquel, "Un homme d'expérience."

64. *Inst. Pref.* 4–5; see *Conf. Pref* 1 7, *Conf. Pref.* 3 3.

65. *Conf. Pref.* 1 6, *Conf. Pref.* 2 1.

66. See *Gnost.* 32–33 (pp. 148–50).

67. See *Gnost.* 22 (p. 122).

68. See *Gnost.* 24 and 34 (pp. 126 and 153).

69. *Conf.* 14.9.2–7, 14.16.4–9.

70. *Conf.* 14.17.2; see *Inst. Pref.* 5 on the obligation of hearers to put into practice what they have heard. On this theme, see *Gnost.* 12–15, 23, 25–26, 29, 31, 35–36 (pp. 106–12, 124–25, 128–31, 142, 146, 154–55) on adapting teaching according to the needs and progress of the students.

71. Of course the prefaces to *Inst.* and to the three sets of *Conf.* are full of standard apologies for the unworthiness of the writer.

72. *De Inc.* 6.6.5, 7.6–9. See Codina, *El aspecto cristologico en la espiritualidad de Juan Casiano*, 188–89.

73. *Deum totius potentiae ac maiestatis ad inanimam materiam et figmenta insensibilia transtulisti* (*De Inc.* 6.7.3).

74. See Codina, *El aspecto cristologico en la espiritualidad de Juan Casiano*, 184–91.

75. See Codina, *El aspecto cristologico en la espiritualidad de Juan Casiano*, 89: "la oración cuyo objeto es la visión de Jesús glorioso, cuyo cuerpo no impide la transparencia de la divinidad. Esta oración pura anticipa la beatitud celeste, es la theoría."

76. *Conf.* 10.6 and 1.15.3; see *Conf.* 9.8.2 and 9.15.3. The narrower focus in *Conf.* 10 is consistent with the Christological emphasis of *Conf.* 9–10.

77. Cassian writes that they are "held back by a kind of Judaic weakness," that is, they cannot accept the divinity of Christ. For a similar phrase, see *Conf.* 1.20.2, 8.7.

78. The positive use of *imago* is significant: while there are images created by human imagination that are fatal to prayer (See *Conf.* 3.7.3, 9.3.3, 10.5.1, 10.11.6, 14.12), there can also be an image of God that is revealed by God. Cassian uses the Genesis text to contrast the image of God in the soul with images stamped on the coins worshipped by the covetous (*Inst.* 7.7.6), to defend the immortality of the soul (*Conf.* 1.14.8), to contrast the perfect image and likeness of God in the human Jesus with the "profaned" (*violata*) image of Adam (*Conf.* 5.6.1; see *Inst.* 12.5 on Adam's "lost glory"), and to compare human beings to the swine into which Jesus cast the demonic spirits (*Conf.* 7.22.1). His most extended discussion of the theological implications of Gen. 1:26 is in *Conf.* 11, where acquiring the highest kind of love is described as "receiving" (*Conf.* 11.6.3, 11.7.3), "arriving at" (*Conf.* 11.9.2), "bearing" (*Conf.* 11.9.3), or "ascending to" (*Conf.* 11.14) the image and likeness of

God. There the image and likeness is equated with adoption as a child of God, developing themes introduced in *Inst.* 4.39 and *Conf.* 9.18.

79. Beyer ("Die Lichtlehre der Mönche des vierzehnten und des vierten Jahrhunderts," 504–7), notes the importance of the Transfiguration in Pseudo-Macarius' writings; note that the Psuedo–Macarian text I will cite in chapter 7 includes a visionary experience related to the Transfiguration (*Coll. II* 8.3 [p. 79.29–34], *Coll. I* 4.9.2 [vol. 1, p. 50.28–51.4]). See also the vision of Christ's face in formless light described by Symeon the New Theologian (*Catech.* 36.8 [SC 113, p. 344]). I owe this reference to H. Alfeyev.

80. See *Comm. in Matt.* 12.37 (pp. 152–53; for the quotation, see p. 153.23–25).

81. *Comm. in Matt.* 12.36 (p. 152.9–14).

82. See Hausherr's comment about Evagrius' *De orat.* 115: the humanity of Christ "n'est pas la félicité dernière . . . En tant que Logos seulement, le Christ est Lui aussi la félicité dernière, dans l'unité de la Sainte Trinité" (*Les leçons d'un contemplatif*, 147).

83. *V. Pach. Boh.* 82, trans. Veilleux, *Pachomian Koinonia*, 1.107 (Bohairic text in Lefort, p. 90). The significance of this parallel was pointed out to me several years ago by Victor Kenney, formerly of Mount Saviour Monastery.

84. *De Inc.* 3.1–2, 5.1.1, 6.14.1. See Codina, *El aspecto cristologico en la espiritualidad de Juan Casiano*, 153–58.

85. See especially *Conf.* 11.6–10; see Codina, *El aspecto cristologico en la espiritualidad de Juan Casiano*, 47–67.

86. *De orat.* 120 (col. 1193B); see *Ad virg.* (p. 148). On "imageless" prayer, see, for example, *De orat.* 66–70 (col. 1181AC) and 114–17 (cols. 1192D–93A); *Schol. in Ps.* 140:2 (Pitra, p. 348). For commentary, see Hausherr in *Les leçons d'un contemplatif*, 93–103 and 144–53; Bunge, *Das Geistgebet*, 68–73 and 78–80; Clark, *The Origenist Controversy*, 66–71, see also 77–84.

87. See Bunge, *Das Geistgebet*, 68–73, 78–83, 106–7.

88. See Gould, "The Image of God," 557 n. 51, suggesting that Cassian's description of encounter with Christ in prayer is contrary to the teaching of both Evagrius and *Apoph.*

89. *De orat.* 115 (col. 1192D).

90. See the section of chapter 3 on "A Continuum of Contemplations."

91. See, for example, *Prak.* 64 (p. 648); *Gnost.* 45 (p. 178); *Cap. cogn.* 1 and 3 (p. 51); *De orat.* 73 (col. 1184A, though note Hausherr's emendations in "Le *Traité de l'oraison* d'Évagre le Pontique (Pseudo Nil)," 122). On "light of the Holy Trinity," see *Antirr.* Prol. (p. 474.11 [Syr.], p. 475.9 [Gk. retroversion]); *De mal. cog.* 42 (Muyldermans, 55); *Cap. cogn.* 3 and 17 (pp. 51 and 53). For other references and commentary, see Beyer, "Die Lichtlehre der Mönche des vierzehnten und des vierten Jahrhunderts," 474–91; Guillaumont, "La vision de l'intellect par lui-même" and "Les visions mystiques dans le monachisme oriental chrétien," 124–27. Clark, *The Origenist Controversy*, 70–71, suggests that Evagrius never satisfactorily explains just what this light is; Hausherr, commenting on *De orat.* 114, had suggested that seeing the "light of one's own mind" and "seeing God" are effectively synonymous (*Les leçons d'un contemplatif*, 144–46). It would be more precise to argue, as have most later writers, that the "light of one's own mind" is the reflection of the light of the Trinity, a vision as "in a mirror." See also Refoulé, "La christologie d'Évagre," 256–62; Guillaumont's commentary on *Gnost.* 45 (pp. 180–81); Bunge, *Das Geistgebet*, 68–73 and 81–83.

92. See, for example, *Antirr.* 7.31 (pp. 534–35.21–27 [Syr.], p. 535.23–28 [Gk. retroversion]) and *De orat.* 116 (col. 1193A) on the insidious effects of vainglory on prayer.

93. See *De orat.* 55–57 (cols. 1177D–80A).

94. See *De orat.* 67 (col. 1181AB).

95. See *De orat.* 66 (col. 1181A), 68 (col. 1181B), 72 (col. 1181D), and 117 and 119 (col. 1193AB); Bunge provides commentary and other references in *Das Geistgebet*, 69 and 80. P. Hadot, "Spiritual Exercises," 101, and Guillaumont, "La vision de l'intellect par lui-même," 261, both note the similar theme in Plotinus, *Enn.* 5.3.17 (vol. 5, p. 134), 6.7.33 (vol. 7, pp. 188–90), and 6.9.10 (vol. 7, p. 340).

96. Principally in "The 'Spiritual Prayer' " and the similar arguments of the last chapter of *Das Geistgebet*, 88–109, and in "*Mysterium Unitatis*."

97. In *De Inc.* 6.17–23. Cassian demonstrates a robust but unremarkable trinitarian orthodoxy.

98. In *De Inc.* 3.7.5 he writes that the glory and majesty of Father and Son are inseparable; to be drawn into the divine nature in Christ is to be drawn into the glory of both Father and Son, as Cassian describes in *Conf.* 10.7.

99. See Codina, *El aspecto christologico en la espiritualidad de Juan Casiano*, 193–94.

100. It is not always clear, for example, how he understands the relationship between "Word" (λόγος) and "Christ," and consequently the relationship made possible by Christ between the believer and the trinitarian God. See especially *Ep. fid.* 7 (pp. 98–102); Refoulé, "La christologie d'Évagre;" Kline, "The Christology of Evagrius and the Parent System of Origen."

101. The locus classicus in Origen is *De princ.* 3.6; see also *Comm. in Iohann.* 20.7. Both Origen's and Evagrius' trinitarian theology and Christology are complex and controverted topics. Refoulé explores particularly the links between Evagrius and Origen in "La christologie d'Évagre." Bunge has argued vigorously in defense of Evagrius' trinitarianism. See "The 'Spiritual Prayer'," especially 198–204; *Das Geistgebet*, 88–109; "*Mysterium Unitatis*," *passim*. Bunge suggests a distinction between Evagrius' protological/eschatological emphasis on unity and his "economic" emphasis on Father, Son, and Spirit, as indeed one sees in *Ep. fid.* 7 (see note 102); Cassian avoids this kind of approach.

102. See, for example, *Ep. fid.* 7, *passim* (pp. 98–102). See Codina, *El aspecto cristologico en la espiritualidad de Juan Casiano*, 78–90; Bunge, "The 'Spiritual Prayer'," 199–202; *Das Geistgebet*, 103–9; "*Mysterium Unitatis*," especially 465–66.

103. See especially *Prak.* 2–3 (pp. 498–500) and *Ep. Fid.* 7 (p. 100.22–24); see also *De orat.* 115 (cols. 1192D–93A) and Hausherr's commentary (*Les leçons d'un contemplatif*, 147–49).

104. The view of Kline ("The Christology of Evagrius and the Parent System of Origen") and Bunge (as in notes 96, 101–2).

105. See Guillaumont, *Les Képhalaia Gnostica d'Évagre le Pontique*, 124–72 and 303–32, and Refoulé, "La christologie d'Évagre," especially 228–33 and 251–66. Codina follows Guillaumont in considering Evagrius' Christology to be problematic (*El aspecto cristologico en la espiritualidad de Juan Casiano* , 78–79).

106. See, for example, the fourth discourse from the *Book of the Holy Hierotheos* (pp. 110*–20*); on Stephen, see Blum, "Vereinigung und Vermischung."

107. Codina compares Cassian to Evagrius on these points in *El aspecto cristologico en la espiritualidad de Juan Casiano*, 183–84.

108. Codina, *El aspecto cristologico en la espiritualidad de Juan Casiano*, 90.

109. See Codina, *El aspecto cristologico en la espiritualidad de Juan Casiano*, 103–4: "Ver a Christo no se opone a la visión del Padre, pues Christo es el único que nos lo puede revelar, y la humanidad de Christo, asumida por el Verbo, tiene un valor y significado perenne."

110. Cassian calls this the *supplicatio perfecta* in *Conf.* 9.17.3. On Evagrius' use of the text, cf. Bunge, "*Mysterium Unitatis*," 464–66.

111. None of these Johannine texts is used elsewhere by Cassian.

112. The Pauline text contributes the refrain of *omnis,* "all," which Cassian uses to great effect throughout the chapter.

113. In *De princ.* 3.6.1, Origen quotes John 17:24 and 17:21 and 1 Cor. 15:28 (p. 281.1–5); then in 3.6.3 he takes off on 1 Cor. 15:28: *Per singulos autem "omnia" erit hoc modo, ut quidquid rationabilis mens, expurgata omni vitiorum faece atque omni penitus abstersa nube malitiae, vel sentire vel intellegere vel cogitare potest, "omnia" deus sit nec ultra iam aliquid aliud nisi deum sentiat, deum cogitet, deum videat, deum teneat, omnis motus sui deus modus et mensura sit* (p. 283.15–20).

114. *Inst.* 5.4.2–3; *Conf.* 1.13.6 and 7.6.4.

Chapter 6

1. The literature on unceasing prayer is vast. Major studies are: Marx, *Incessant Prayer in Ancient Monastic Literature;* Hausherr, "Comment priaient les Pères" (an overview), "La prière perpétuelle du chrétien" (emphasis on Basil), and *The Name of Jesus* (on monologistic prayer); Regnault, "La prière continuelle 'monologistos' dans les Apophtegmes des Pères"; Guillaumont, "Le problème de la prière continuelle dans le monachisme ancien"; McDonnell, "Prayer in Ancient Western Tradition"; Taft, *The Liturgy of the Hours in East and West,* 66–72. See also the articles by Vogüé cited in notes 6 and 14.

2. See Taft's fine summary in *The Liturgy of the Hours in East and West,* 66–72.

3. Cassian uses this phrase, or variants of it, throughout *Inst.* 2 and 3, as well as once each in *Inst.* 4.1, *Conf. Pref.* 1 5, and *Conf.* 10.10.8.

4. These are synonyms, as Cassian explains in *Inst.* 2.10.1. He uses the words interchangeably throughout both *Inst.* and *Conf.,* preferring the Latin to the Greek in *Inst.* but the Greek to the Latin in *Conf.* He often describes a conference as occurring just before or just after the time for prayer; using the Greek term authenticates the Egyptian setting. See, for example, *Conf.* 1.23.4, 8.16.1, 9.36.3, 10.10.8, 13.1, 15.1.1, 17.3, 20.2.2, 22.1.1 (though see *Conf.* 2.26.3 and 8.1.1 for *sollemnitas* used in such a way, and *Conf.* 13.1.1 for both *synaxis* and *sollemnitas*). *Sollemnitas* can also mean "festival," as in its modern Roman Catholic liturgical usage (see *Conf.* 2.5.3, 10.2.1, 19.1.1, 21.20.3, 21.23.1–4, 22.1.1), or refer to the celebration of Sunday (*Conf.* 7.34.2, 18.15.3, 19.4.2).

5. On the use of *synaxis* and *meletē* in both communal and individual contexts, see Taft, *The Liturgy of the Hours in East and West,* 71.

6. For the distinction between "psalmody" and "prayer," see, for example, Bunge, *Das Geistgebet,* 13–43, and Vogüé, *La Règle de Saint Benoît,* 7:209–14 (Eng. trans.: *The Rule of Saint Benedict, a Doctrinal and Spiritual Commentary,* 142–44). Debate on this issue has been complicated by strong feelings about interpretation of the liturgical code of *Reg. Ben.;* Gribomont argued against Vogüé's analysis by appealing to Basil ("The Commentaries of Adalbert de Vogüé and the Great Monastic Tradition," 238–40), to which Vogüé responded in "Twenty-Five Years of Benedictine Hermeneutics—An Examination of Conscience," 438–39. See also McDonnell, "Prayer in Ancient Western Tradition," 46–56, for a balanced view. The dispute about Basil and Benedict need not affect our interpretation of Cassian, whose teaching on this point is comparatively clear.

7. See *Inst.* 2.T, 2.1, 2.2.2, 2.5.4–5, 2.7.1–2, 2.8, 2.10.1, 2.11.1, 2.13.1, 2.13.3, 3.T, 3.3.1, 3.4.1–2, 3.7.2, 3.11, 3.12 (where *sola oratio* means prayer without a preceding psalm), 4.1; see *Conf.* 7.23.1, 9.26.1, 13.1, 17.3, 23.6.2, 23.7.2, 23.16.1.

8. Thus *Inst.* 2.10.2–3 and *Conf.* 9.36.1 on the brevity of *oratio* in the *synaxis* and elsewhere; see *Reg. Ben.* 20.4–5 (pp. 536–38).

9. Palestine and the West also knew the office of Prime, an additional morning office; Cassian's references to this "innovation" have generated considerable controversy among

liturgical historians trying to understand just what he was describing. See Taft, *The Liturgy of the Hours in East and West*, 76–80 and 96–100.

10. On Basil, see *Reg. fus.* 37 (cols. 1009C–16C).

11. On Gaul, see Taft, *The Liturgy of the Hours in East and West*, 96–100.

12. See *Inst.* 2.12.2 and 3.2.

13. See Bunge's helpful interpretation of key texts in *Das Geistgebet*, 31–38; he published a French version of the same material in " 'Priez sans cesse': aux origines de la prière hésychaste."

14. See Vogüé's sketch of this development in *La Règle de Saint Benoît*, 5:580–88 and 7:213–21 (Eng. trans. of the latter in *The Rule of Saint Benedict, a Doctrinal and Spiritual Commentary*, 144–49).

15. See Veilleux's comments on how the distinction between communal and "private" prayer was not the same for early monks as it is for modern ones (*La liturgie dans le cénobitisme pachômien au quatrième siècle*, 315–23).

16. For general overviews, see Bacht, " 'Meditatio' in den ältesten Mönchsquellen," and Burton-Christie, *The Word in the Desert*, 122–29.

17. See Liddell and Scott, *A Greek-English Lexicon*, 1096b, and Lampe, *A Patristic Greek Lexicon*, 840b–41a, for μελέτη and its verbal form μελετάω.

18. See P. Hadot, "Spiritual Exercises," 84–86 (Stoic), 87–89 (Epicurean), 96–97 (Platonic); "Ancient Spiritual Exercises and 'Christian Philosophy,' " 133–34, on the links between philosophical and monastic "meditation"; "Reflections on the Idea of the 'Cultivation of the Self' " and "Un dialogue interrompu avec Michel Foucault," on self-transcendence. Ilsetraut Hadot provides greater detail in her *Seneca und die griechisch-römische Tradition der Seelenleitung*, 55–61. Both Pierre and Ilsetraut Hadot acknowledge their debt to Rabbow's seminal work, *Seelenführung*; on meditation, see especially pp. 23–150 of Rabbow's book.

19. See Severus, "Das Wort 'Meditari' im Sprachgebrauch der Heiligen Schrift."

20. See Graham, *Beyond the Written Word*, 30–35; on the significance of the voice and exercise of it in the classical world, see Rousselle, "Parole et inspiration."

21. " 'Meditatio' in den ältesten Mönchsquellen," 371 (*Das Vermächtnis des Ursprungs*, 261).

22. See *Apoph. Alph.* Ammonas 1 (col. 120A), though the sense is ambiguous; more certain are Achilles 5 (col. 126A), Apollo 2 (col. 136A), John Colobos 35 (col. 216C), Joseph of Panephysis 7 (col. 229CD), Poemen 168 (col. 361C); *Anon.* Nau 127 (p. 103), Nau 168 (p. 54), Nau 184 (p. 271), Nau 274 (p. 371), Nau 366 (pp. 138–39), Nau 408 (p. 136), Nau 572 (p. 208), Nau 645 (p. 289); *Syst. (Gk.)* 5.53 (p. 308.11).

23. See, for example, *Apoph. Anon.* Nau 487 (p. 165), 522 (p. 192), 531 (p. 196), 548 (p. 200), 592/51 (p. 227); *Syst. (Gk.)* 3.55 (p. 180).

24. See *Apoph. Alph.* Jean Colobos 35 (col. 216C) and Joseph of Panephysis 7 (col. 229CD).

25. Associated with psalmody: *Apoph.* Regnault, SPT J741 (p. 47); *Syst. (Gk.)* 5.5.3 (p. 308); see *Alph.* Poemen 168 (col. 361C). Distinct from psalmody (probably meaning "canonical" psalmody): *Alph.* John Colobos 35 (col. 216C), Nau 168 (p. 54).

26. *Apoph. Alph.* Joseph of Panephysis 7 (col. 229CD).

27. *Apoph. Anon.* Nau 168 (p. 54).

28. See Lampe, *A Patristic Greek Lexicon*, 209b.

29. For Antony, see *Athanasius, V. Ant.* 55.3 (p. 282) on psalmody and learning the scriptures by heart (ἀποστηθίζειν); see also 44.2 (p. 254), "devotion to Scripture (φιλολογούντων)." There are two references to "meditating" a particular biblical verse, though the meaning seems to be "reflect on" rather than "recite" (*V. Ant.* 19.2, p. 186; 55.4, p. 282). See

Bacht's analysis in " 'Meditatio' in den ältesten Mönchsquellen," 368 (*Das Vermächtnis des Ursprungs*, 257). See *Hist. mon.* 2.5 (p. 37) on the illiterate Abba Or, who was given the divine charism of reciting the Scriptures from memory (τὰς γραφὰς ἔξωθεν ἀπεστήθιζεν) as well as suddenly being able to read (see *Hist. mon. [Ruf.]* 2.7, p. 277, which omits the first gift); Patermuthius also claimed the gift of memorization and recitation (*Hist. mon.* 10.7, p. 78: the sentence is very similar to the one describing Or's gift; *Hist. mon. [Ruf.]* 9.2.10, p. 313, keeps this one: *ut omnes paene scripturas memoriter teneret*). Apollo's disciples spent the night in the desert reciting from memory (*Hist. mon.* 8.50, p. 67: ἀποστηθίζοντες τὰς γραφὰς; see *Hist. mon. [Ruf.]* 7.14.2, p. 303: *scripturas divinas memoriter recolentes*).

30. Palladius claims six million lines (μυριάδαι ἑξακοσίαι); see *Hist. Laus.* 11.4 (p. 34.5–8). Palladius also mentions a young monk called Mark who had memorized the whole Bible (*Hist. Laus.* 18.25, p. 56.8–9), describes Heron's manic recitation (*Hist. Laus.* 26.3, pp. 81.19–82.3), and praises the Tabennesiotes for their learning the Bible by heart (*Hist. Laus.* 32.12, p. 96.4–5). On Palladius and the Bible, see Meyer, "Lectio divina in Palladius" and "Palladius and the Study of Scripture."

31. In his writings μελέτη/μελετάω kept their older meanings of "exercise" or "ponder." See, for example, *Prak.* 52 (p. 618), and *Gnost.* 45 (p. 178), where he claims to quote Basil the Great; *Schol. in Prov.* 263 (p. 358).

32. See *Prak.* 15 and 69 (pp. 536–38 and 654) and *De orat.* 82–85 (col. 1185AB). See Hausherr, *Les leçons d'un contemplatif*, 115–20; Guillaumont in the commentary to *Prak.* 69 (p. 654); Bunge, *Das Geistgebet*, 13–28, explains the place of psalmody in the Evagrian schema. For psalmody distinguished from "prayer," see *Paraenet.* (p. 560.15–16 [Syr.], 561.22–23 [Gk. retroversion]).

33. See Veilleux, *La liturgie dans le cénobitisme pachômien au quatrième siècle*, 262–75, for an overview of the significance of the Bible in the Pachomian tradition; pp. 265–69 are about memorization and recitation. See also Bacht, " 'Meditatio' in den ältesten Mönchsquellen," and Graham, *Beyond the Written Word*, 126–40.

34. This so-called Gallican Psalter is the one quoted by Cassian. On Jerome's translation of the Psalms, see Severus, "Das Wort 'Meditari' im Sprachgebrauch der Heiligen Schrift," *passim*.

35. Evident from the Greek fragments of *Praec.* provided by Boon in an appendix to *Pachomiana Latina* (pp. 169–82). While the Coptic fragments of *Praec.* do not include the relevant texts, the Coptic text of Horsiesios' *Regulae* edited by Lefort shows that μελετάω was a loan word and was likely to have been in the Coptic *Praec.* as well. For *meditatio* and its verbal form *meditor/meditari*, see *Oxford Latin Dictionary*, 1090a–b.

36. The "Rules" are a hodgepodge of prescriptions from a Greek-speaking monastery of the Delta affiliated with the Coptic Pachomian houses of Upper Egypt. Jerome's Latin translation is the only complete version. There are Coptic fragments of about a third of *Praec.* and Greek excerpts taken from the Greek version Jerome knew. Comparison of Jerome's Latin with the Coptic original suggests an accurate tradition. See Veilleux, Introduction to *Pachomian Koinonia* 2.7–9, and Rousseau, *Pachomius*, 48–53.

37. *Praec.* 3 (p. 14), 28 (p. 20); see Horsiesios, *Reg.* 13 and 14 (p. 85.33 and p. 86.15).

38. *Praec.* 59–60 (pp. 31–32). See 116 (p. 44), which mentions chanting psalms and other texts while working (*de psalmis et de scripturis aliquid decantabunt*); the Coptic and Greek fragments have μελετάω.

39. *Praec.* 36–37 (p. 22). The "dessert" was the *tragēmatia* that Cassian calls *trogalia* in *Conf.* 8.1.2, consisting of dried or candied fruits. For this and other culinary terms, see Stewart, "From λόγος to *verbum*," 12–13.

40. See *Praec.* 6 (p. 14), 13 (p. 16), 16–17 (p. 17). On the Pachomian *synaxis*, see Veilleux, *La liturgie dans le cénobitisme pachômien au quatrième siècle*, 279–315, and Taft,

The Liturgy of the Hours in East and West, 62–66. Both Veilleux and Taft caution against reading the Pachomian texts too much in terms of Cassian's descriptions of various practices he attributes to the Tabennesiotes.

41. *Praec.* 139–40 (pp. 49–50). See the maxim "Let us be wealthy in texts learned by heart" (Horsiesios, *Reg.* 16, p.86.28, as translated by Veilleux, *Pachomian Koinonia* 2.202).

42. Horsiesios, *Lib.* 51 (p. 143.19–20), trans. Veilleux, *Pachomian Koinonia,* 3.210.

43. Cassian follows Jerome in translating μελέτη with *meditatio,* while the Lerinian tradition of the *Second Rule of the Fathers* and the *Rule of Macarius* use the form *medite.* These rules are dated by Vogüé to ca. 426–28 and 500, respectively *(Les Règles des saints Pères,* pp. 26–28 and 247–66 for 2 *Reg. Patr.*; pp. 32–34 and 339–56 for *Reg. Mac.).* For *medite,* see 2 *Reg. Patr.* 11 (p. 276) and 22–24 (p. 278); *Reg. Mac.* 10 (p. 376). Despite the influence of both Jerome and Cassian, the noun *meditatio* is not used in the rules associated with Lérins, and it appears only in later rules such as Caesarius' *Rule for Nuns* and the *Rule of the Master* (see Vogüé, "Les deux fonctions de la méditation dans les Règles monastiques anciennes").

44. Horsiesios, *Reg.* 8–10 (pp. 83–85). See the simpler *Praec.* 4–5 of Pachomius (p. 14). See Taft's overview and cautions, *The Liturgy of the Hours in East and West,* 62–65. Veilleux notes the absence of "psalm-prayers" or collects, which Cassian seems to have known (see *La liturgie dans le cénobitisme pachômien au quatrième siècle,* 308–9; Cassian, *Inst.* 2.7.3, 2.10.2).

45. *Inst.* 2.7.1–3; see 2.10.1–2.

46. *V. Pach. boh.* 34 (p. 37; trans. Veilleux, *Pachomian Koinonia* 1.58).

47. *Apoph. Alph.* Antony 1 (col. 76AB).

48. *Hist. Laus.* 20 (p. 63.13–14) and 38 (p. 120.11). See Bunge's commentary on these and similar examples of anchoritic μελέτη/*meditatio* and prayer in *Das Geistgebet,* 31–38 (published in *SM* as "'Priez sans cesse': aux origines de la prière hésychaste").

49. See *V. Pach. boh.* 10 (p. 85); *V. Pach. gr.* 1 6 (p. 4), *V. Pach. gr.* 2 and *V. Pach. lat.* (pp. 96–97). The Coptic and Greek texts use μελέτη; the Latin has *meditatio.* See Bacht, "'Meditatio' in den ältesten Mönchsquellen," 364–65 (*Das Vermächtnis des Ursprungs,* 250–53), for other texts from the *V. Pach.* and their handling in the versions.

50. Against temptation in general: *Apoph. Alph.* Amoun 3 (col. 128D; see *Anon.* Nau 293 [p. 377]), *Alph.* Elias 7 (cols. 184D–85A); *Anon.* Nau 167 (p. 54; see Nau 184 [pp. 271–72]), Nau 621 (pp. 267–68); *Anon.* Nau 574 (pp. 208–09) for an insincere (and ineffectual) prayer. For specific situations: after committing bodily sins, *Anon.* Nau 592/22 (p. 220); Sarah's prayer lasting thirteen years against lust, *Alph.* Sarah 1 (col. 420B); against sins of the tongue, *Alph.* Sisoes 5 (col. 393A); in preparation for receiving guests, *Anon.* Nau 592/9 (p. 218); against vainglory, *Alph.* Pambo 1 (col. 368BC), *Anon.* Nau 592/33 (p. 223); against stubbornness and self-will, *Anon.* Nau 504 (p. 182: "Lord, send me an illness, for when I am well I disobey you"). On the role of the Bible in battle against demons, see Colombás, "La Biblia, panoplia del monje" (pt. 4 of "La Biblia en la espiritualidad del monacato primitivo," *Yermo* 2[1964]: 3–14.

51. *Apoph. Anon.* Nau 184 (p. 272, *Syst.* [*Gk.*] 5.37 [pp. 276–78]).

52. See *De orat.* 98 (col. 1189A), and see *De mal. cog.* 34 (ch. 67 of the edition of *Prak.* in *PG* 40.1241B).

53. The text is organized in eight chapters corresponding to the eight principal faults; in each chapter there is a list of approximately sixty "thoughts" with a biblical verse provided as a response to each. See O'Laughlin's helpful and sensitive overview in "The Bible, the Demons and the Desert: Evaluating the *Antirrheticus* of Evagrius Ponticus."

54. The best overviews are: Hausherr, "Comment priaient les Pères," 284–90, and *The Name of Jesus,* especially pp. 191–240; Regnault, "La prière continuelle 'monologistos' dans

les Apophtegmes des Pères," a concise and systematic survey. See also his "La prière de Jésus dans quelques apophtegmes conservés en arabe."

55. *Apoph. Alph.* Apollo 2 (cols. 133C–36A), Lucius (col. 253BC), Macarius the Great 19 (two formulae, one a general prayer for doing God's will, another for use in time of danger, col. 269C; see Barsanuphius' commentary on Macarius' formulae in *Ep.* 140 [no. 71 in Schoinas, pp. 67–68]), Paul the Great 2 (col. 381C); *Anon.* Nau 403 (p. 133), Nau 524 (p. 193), Nau 583 (pp. 211–12); *Syr.* Bu II 386 (Serapion of Thmuis' formula: "Lord, teach me to do your will" taught to newcomers [Bedjan, p. 836; Budge, p. 2.231]). See Pseudo-Macarius, *Coll. I* 6.3.3 (p. 85), on the use of the formula "I beseech, I beseech you, Lord" when walking, eating, and drinking, without ever letting up (μηδέποτε ἀργήσῃς). The point being made is that one can pray in any circumstance, not only when "bending the knee."

56. See Hausherr, *The Name of Jesus*, 220–29, and see the introduction to Diadochus' works by Des Places in SC 5bis, pp. 49–52. On the remembrance of God, see Hausherr's "Comment priaient les Pères," 55–58, and *The Name of Jesus*, 158–65; see Rousseau on the importance of this theme for Basil (*Basil of Caesarea*, 225–28).

57. Diadochus, *Cap. gnost.* 59 and 61 (pp. 119–21); note that ch. 60 is one of the texts discussed in chapter 7 of this study with respect to tears. See Cassian's teaching that unceasing repetition of the formula can bring one to "invisible and celestial contemplations *(theoriae)*" and dispose one for the "ineffable flame *(ardor)* of prayer" (*Conf.* 10.10.14).

58. See ch. 10 of *The Life of Dositheos*, preserved among Dorotheus' writings (SC 92, p. 138); the editors note that Hausherr's interpretation in *The Name of Jesus* (pp. 267–70) depended on a defective manuscript tradition, but in fact the difference is slight. See Regnault, "La prière de Jésus dans quelques apophtegmes conservés en arabe."

59. See Hausherr, *The Name of Jesus*, pp. 265–308 (on Climacus, see pp. 280–86), and his earlier "La méthode d'oraison hésychaste"; Ware provides a good overview of Climacus' teaching on prayer (introduction to *The Ladder of Divine Ascent*, 44–54), understanding it to be closer to the Byzantine practice of the Jesus Prayer than Hausherr allows.

60. For an overview of the role played by the Bible in Cassian's teaching, see Bauer, "Die Heilige Schrift bei den Mönchen des christlichen Altertums."

61. *Inst.* 2.12–14, 3.2; *Conf.* 1.2.3, 1.7.2, 1.17.2, 5.14.1, 6.10.3, 17.28.1, 21.14.2.

62. See *Inst.* 3.2, 4.12, 6.1; *Conf.* 1.17.2, 1.18.2, 7.4.2, 7.24, 10.8.4, 10.10.2, 10.11.3, 10.12, 14.10.2 and 4; note the need to choose texts carefully lest they hurt rather than help: *Conf.* 19.16.3.

63. On the significance of voice, see note 20 and also Burton-Christie, *The Word in the Desert*, 123.

64. *Conf.* 1.2.3, 1.17.2, 14.13.1, 17.28.1, 21.14.2, 24.12.1.

65. As Cassian indicates in *Conf.* 1.17.2, 14.10.2, 14.10.4, *lectio* is preparation for *meditatio*.

66. *Inst.* 6.7.1, 10.3.

67. Cassian is perhaps quoting Evagrius, *Prak.* 15 (p. 536.1–2), which lists reading (ἀνάγνωσις), vigil (ἀγρυπνία), and prayer (προσευχή).

68. *Inst.* 2.5.2, 2.12.3, 2.14, 2.15.1. See *Reg. Hors.* 17 (pp. 86.27–87.3).

69. *Inst.* 2.14, 3.5.2; cf. 6.13.2.

70. *Conf.* 10.13.2, 14.12, 23.5.9, 23.7.2, 23.16.1. See the vivid tale of distractions at the communal synaxis contained in *Hist. mon.* (*Ruf.*) 29.4.1–13 (pp. 371–73).

71. *Inst.* 2.10.1–3 (see *Conf.* 9.36.1 on prayer in general); on the wandering mind, see *Conf.* 10.13.2, 23.6.2, 23.7.2, 23.16.1.

72. *Mens mobilis semper ac vaga* (*Conf.* 10.13.2). For *mens mobilis*, see *Conf.* 7.4.2, 7.7, 9.4.1, 14.7.1; for *mens vaga*, see *Inst.* 5.10, *Conf.* 10.8.5 (*vagus animus*) and 10.14.1.

73. *Conf.* 14.10.4; see *Inst.* 6.1, *continuata meditatio scripturarum, huicque fuerit scientia spiritalis adiuncta.*

74. See *Apoph. Anon.* Nau 184 (pp. 271–72), describing a monk's lack of comprehension of the words he recited and Poemen's assurance that the words nonetheless had their effect on the demons.

75. See *Inst.* 9.13; *Conf.* 3.7.3, 9.4.2, 19.4.1. In *Conf.* 10 the *meditatio* of the one verse from Ps. 69(70) is a springboard for ecstatic experience; see *Conf.* 10.11, *passim.*

76. *Conf.* 10.11.4–6, 14.10.2, 14.14.7.

77. *Quamobrem quales orantes volumus inveniri, tales nos ante orationis tempus praeparare debemus.* See *Conf* 12.8.5–6, the monk "the same in bed as at prayer." The theme is a common one in the *Apoph.* and in Evagrius' writings; see *Apoph. Anon.* Nau 96: "Prayer is the mirror of the monk" (p. 401); Evagrius' *De orat.*, *passim*, and *Ep.* 25 (p. 582.11–13 [Syr.], p. 583.15–18 [Gk. retroversion]).

78. See Origen's *De orat.* 8.1–9.1 (pp. 316–18).

79. *Conf.* 1.10.5, 1.13, 7.6.4; see 10.6.4 and 10.7.3; and see the discussion at the end of chapter 3.

80. See Hausherr, "Comment priaient les Pères," 50–55.

81. *Conf.* 9.3.4, cf. 9.6.5. The same quotation had appeared in *Inst.* 8.13 with respect to the way anger destroys prayer.

82. See *Conf.* 1.8.3, feeding only on the beauty and knowledge of God (the same word, *pascatur*, is used); 6.10.2, being fed by *(pascitur)* spiritual contemplations; 10.11.2, being nourished *(saginari)* "on sublimer and still more sacred mysteries" in prayer; 10.11.4, being fed by *(pascetur)* the pastures of the "mountains of the prophets and apostles."

83. *Similitudo, Conf.* 9.6.5. On acquiring a "likeness" of heavenly beatitude, see *Conf.* 10.6.4; for acquiring the "image and likeness" of God in the third stage of love, *Conf.* 11.7.3–4, 11.9.2–3, 11.14; on becoming a likeness of the biblical word assiduously meditated, *Conf.* 14.10.2.

84. See *Inst.* 6.1, 8.13, 8.18.1, 9.1; *Conf.* 2.22.2, 4.2, 4.4.2, 6.10.2, 9.3.1 and 4, 9.4.3, 9.6.5, 9.8.2, 9.12.2, 9.15, 9.26.1, 10.5.3, 10.6, 10.11.6, 23.7.1. For Evagrius, see *Prak.* 23 (καθαρὰ εὐχή, p. 554) and 42 (καθαρὰ προσευχή, p. 596); *Schol. in Ps.* 65:20 (PG 12.1504A); although he makes the same point throughout *De orat.*, especially with respect to "spiritual" or "true" prayer, he uses the term "pure prayer" to describe imageless prayer. See *Schol. in Ps.* 85:1 (ed. Pitra, 148), where he writes that it is natural for the "pure intellect" (καθαρὸς νοῦς) to praise God.

85. See *Conf.* 2.22.2, 4.2. Philip Rousseau has pointed out to me the importance of the spatial/cosmological imagery used in Cassian's descriptions of prayer.

86. *Conf.* 9.3.4; see *Conf.* 1.22.2. Pachomius' disciple Theodore records of Cornelios that "he has purified his heart to such a point that in the *synaxis* he has no idle thought during the whole *synaxis*" (*V. Pach. boh.* 91, p. 107; trans. Veilleux, *Pachomian Koinonia,* 1.122).

87. *Conf.* 9.3.3. Cautions about anger and sadness, which are particular threats to prayer, can be found in *Inst.* 8.13–14 (anger), and 9.1 and 9.11 (sadness). The point is much stronger in the writings of Evagrius, especially throughout *De orat.* See chapter 4 for Cassian's teaching on lust and the perdurance in the mind of erotic images.

88. *Per intuitum sacramentorum caelestium (Conf.* 9.7.1).

89. See the discussion in chapter 5. As noted there, Evagrius thought of pure prayer primarily in terms of freedom from images of any kind; see, for example, *De orat.* 67, 70, 72 (all about praying purely [καθαρῶς], col. 1181B–D), 97 (καθαρὰ προσευχή, p, col. 1188D); *Schol in Ps.* 140:2 (ed. Pitra, 348).

90. It opens and closes the set: *Conf.* 1.4.4, 1.5.4, 1.12–13, 1.16–18; *Conf.* 9.3.3–4, 9.4,

9.6.5, 9.7, 10.14.2. Cassian had also devoted the whole of *Conf.* 7 to the issue, after introducing it in *Conf.* 6.13. The passage in *Conf.* 10.14.2 is similar to one in the *Epistola magna* of Pseudo-Macarius. Cassian: *numquam vero orat, quisquis etiam flexis genibus evagatione cordis qualicumque distrahitur.* Pseudo-Macarius: μή . . . ἐμπληροφορούμενος εἰς τὴν σωματικὴν μόνον γονυκλισίαν τοῦ νοὸς ἐν συγχύσει ἢ ρεμβασμῷ καθεστῶτος (*Ep. mag.* 9.7, pp. 151.65–152.66–67).

91. *Conf.* 23.10, 23.17–19, 24.3.

92. This metaphor was used in *Inst.* 2.9.1 when Cassian outlined his plans for further teaching on prayer in the *Conf.* On the theme of laying a proper foundation for building a tower of virtues or for attaining the heights of perfection, see also *Inst.* 4.2, 6.18, 12.26, 12.31; *Conf.* 6.17.1–2, 15.7.2, 18.13.1, 18.15.8, 19.2.1. For a similar metaphor, see Evagrius, *Protrep.* (p. 554.3–5 [Syr.], p. 555.3–7 [Gk. retroversion]). The theme of the "heights" or "pinnacle" of perfection is common in Cassian's writings. *Perfectionis excelsa fastigia, Conf.* 10.8.2–3; see *Conf.* 2.4.4, 9.2.3. *Culmen perfectionis,* see *Inst.* 4.8, 5.28, 7.5, 7.13, 10.24; *Conf. Pref.* 1 5, 2.4.4, 2.24.2, 3.22.4, 4.19.4, 9.2.3, 9.7.4, 20.12.3, 21.33.1, 22.15.2. *Culmen virtutum,* see *Inst.* 4.23, 12.24; *Conf.* 18.15.7, 22.7.2. *Culmen caritatis,* see *Inst.* 12.32.1 and *Conf.* 3.7.8.

93. See *Prak.* 15 (p. 536), with references to other sources.

94. *Conf.* 10.14.2; see *Inst.* 2.14, the clearest statement. He returns to the point in *Inst.* 7 and 10, *passim,* and *Conf.* 4.12.4.

95. Note that Cassian had used *status* in the previous chapter to refer to prayer itself (*Conf.* 9.7.3).

96. *Secundum mensuram namque puritatis, in quam mens unaquaeque proficit et qualitatem status in quo vel . . . inclinatur vel . . . renovatur* (*Conf.* 9.8.2); see *Conf.* 1.15.3: *pro qualitate vitae ac puritate cordis* and *Conf.* 7.2.3: *de qualitate cogitationum nostrarum et interioris hominis statu tranquillissima conpellatione quaesisset vel quid nobis ad eius puritatem tanti temporis heremi habitatio contulisset.*

97. The moods: lively, sad, despairing, invigorated by spiritual progress, depressed by assaults by demons. States of conscience: asking forgiveness of sins, praying for grace or virtue or the elimination of a fault (*vitium*), feelings of compunction when considering hell or future judgment, being stirred by hope of future rewards.

98. See Origen, *De orat.* 14 (pp. 330–33); Evagrius (see note 100); Ambrose, *De inst. virg.* 2.8–9 (cols. 307B–8A); Augustine, *Ep.* 149.2.12–16 (CSEL 44, pp. 359–63); see Gregory of Nyssa, *De orat. dom.* 2 (pp. 21.15–15) on εὐχή and προσευχή.

99. Origen, *De orat.* 14.2 (pp. 330–31).

100. At least not on extant material. In one text Evagrius defines εὐχή, προσευχή, δέησις, ἔντευξις (*Cap. cogn.* 26–29, p. 53, there numbered 16–19), while 1 Tim. 2:1 features: δέησις, προσευχή, ἔντευξις, εὐχαριστία (all in the plural). Thus, only three of his four kinds of prayer are from 1 Tim. 2:1. See Marsili, *Giovanni Cassiano ed Evagrio Pontico,* 98, and Weber, *Die Stellung des Johannes Cassianus zur ausserpachomianischen Mönchstradition,* 50–51. In another text, Evagrius defines δέησις and προσευχή (*Schol. in Ps.*60.2 [ed. Pitra, 68]), but these definitions are neither particularly striking nor relevant for Cassian's interpretation. On Evagrius' understanding of προσευχή, see Messana, "Le definizioni di προσευχή nel *De oratione* de Evagrio Pontico." Cassian's commentary on εὐχή is much more extensive than Evagrius', and Evagrius says nothing at all about εὐχαριστία, which for Cassian was the most important of the four.

101. See Evagrius: δέησίς ἐστιν ὁμιλία νοῦ πρὸς Θεὸν μεθ᾽ ἱκεσίας, βοήθειαν ἢ αἴτησιν ἀγαθῶν περιέχουσα ("supplication is the conversation of the mind with God, accompanied by entreaty, and involving assistance of or request for good things," *Cap. cogn.* 31, p. 53 [there no. 18]). The first part of the phrase is from Clement, *Strom.* 7.39.6 (p. 30.15–16) and appears also in Evagrius' *De orat.* 3 (col. 1168C).

102. Cassian rather tortuously defines *oratio* as "vow" by reverting to the Greek εὐχή, which can mean either "prayer" or "vow" (although 1 Tim. 2:1 actually reads προσευχάς, "prayers," and there is no manuscript evidence for εὐχάς). He then traces the use of the word through the Septuagint and finds that the Latin version of these texts (Ps. 115:9 and 14, Eccl. 5:3) uses *votum*, "vow." Though strained, it does allow him to follow Origen, who distinguished between two kinds of εὐχή (*De orat.* 3.2–4, pp. 304–07), and Evagrius, who distinguished between εὐχή and προσευχή. Evagrius' definition reads: εὐχή ἐστιν ὑπόσχεσις ἀγαθῶν ἑκούσιος, "prayer is a voluntary promise of good things," that is, a vow (*Cap. cogn.* 29 [p. 53, there no. 16, reading εὐχή for ψυχή], as noted in Marsili, *Giovanni Cassiano ed Evagrio Pontico*, 98, and Weber, *Die Stellung des Johannes Cassianus zur ausserpachomianischen Mönchstradition*, 51–52). Although Evagrius does comment on προσευχή, the word used in 1 Tim. 2:1, Cassian borrows instead his definition of εὐχή because it suits his purpose better.

103. See *Conf.* 9.29.3 on weeping for the sins of others. Note that Evagrius defined intercession as prayer for others by someone advanced (ὑπὸ μείζονος), for whom such prayer would not be a dangerous distraction (*Cap. cogn.* 33, p. 53 [there no. 19]); see Hausherr's remarks in *Les leçons d'un contemplatif*, 58–60. See Ammonas, *Ep. Syr.* 8 (p. 588.1–4) on prayer for others being possible for those who have migrated to heaven while still living in the body.

104. The actual phrase *inmobilis patientia* occurs in *Conf.* 12.6.3 (associated with chastity, as here) and in 19.11.1 (see similar usage at 19.14.5).

105. *Ferventissimae . . . preces ignitaeque* and *purae ac ferventissimae supplicationes* (*Conf.* 9.15.1), *purae intentaeque preces* (*Conf.* 9.15.3). As noted earlier, the idea of "pure prayer" seems to be inspired both by an ascetical reading of 1 Tim. 2:8 ("lifting up pure hands," see *Conf.* 9.3.4) and by the understanding of purity as a state of focused intention (see chapter 3). See *Inst.* 2.13.2 (*orationum nostrarum puritas*), 8.18.1 (*contemplatio purissima*); *Conf.* 2.22.2 (*preces purae levesque*), 4.2 (*oratio pura*), 6.10.2 (*orationes purius atque alacrius emittit*), 9.3.1 (*fervore ac puritate qua debet emitti possit oratio*), 9.6.5 (*purissima ac sincerissima . . . oratio*), 10.5.3 (*orationis purissima qualitas*).

106. Although Cassian mentions both "pure" (*Conf.* 9.15.1 and 3) and "purest" (*Conf.* 9.6.5, see 10.5.3) prayer, the distinction should not be pressed.

107. Four kinds of prayer (*Conf.* 9.9–17) to Lord's Prayer (9.18–24) to single verse as prayer formula (10.10–11).

108. See the move from *Conf.* 9.15.2 to *Conf.* 9.25–26 and then to *Conf.* 10.7.

109. Published by Lagarde in 1886. Hausherr included J. Simon's French translation of the Bohairic original in "Le *Traité de l'oraison* d'Évagre le Pontique," 88–89; see also p. 68 for background information. A slightly revised version was included in *Les leçons d'un contemplatif*, 83–84, without attribution to Simon. Unfortunately, Simon's translation was quite free, omitting and obscuring some key Evagrian terminology.

110. See Origen, *De orat.* 22.5 (p. 349) on living as if in heaven, praying "Our Father" constantly, and Evagrius' statement that one who loves God "converses" with God as with a father (*De orat.* 54, col. 1177D). Cassian, however, differs from both in his emphasis on ecstatic prayer.

111. Here he quotes Matt. 25:34 as he did in *Conf.* 1.9, though without the following verse on works of charity.

112. See Evagrius, *Schol. in Ps.* 108:7 (ed. Pitra, 222), where praying for earthly rather than heavenly things changes prayer into sin. Ramsey notes a parallel with Augustine's teaching on the Lord's Prayer (*Ep.* 130.12.22–23 [CSEL 44, pp. 65–67], cited in "John Cassian: Student of Augustine," 13–14).

113. In addition to the topics of preparation for prayer and the kinds of prayer, Cassian addresses intense spiritual experience (*Conf.* 9.25–31; see chapter 7), the efficacy of prayer (*Conf.* 9.32–34) and the importance of silent, brief prayer (*Conf.* 9.35–36). For an analysis of the structure of *Conf.* 9–10, see Stewart, "John Cassian on Unceasing Prayer."

114. *Ars seu disciplina: Conf.* 1.2.1, 1.4.1, 2.11.7, 2.26.4, 12.8.3, 12.15.1, 14.1.2, 19.5.2, 21.15.1.

115. *Deo iugiter inhaerere,* see *Conf.* 1.12, *deo valeat cohaerere* and *Conf.* 1.13, *inhaerere . . . deo iugiter;* also *Conf.* 1.8.1, 23.5.2.

116. *Theoriae spiritales* (*Conf.* 10.8.5); the plural use of *theoria* is also found in *Conf.* 3.7.3, 6.10.2, 19.4.1, 19.6.4.

117. The word is used in *Inst.* 1.3 to mean "regulation" or "control" of behavior; in *Conf.* 9.18.2, 9.22.1, and 9.25 for the "Our Father"; in 14.7.1 for a "model" for imitation; in 16.22.2, *perfectionis evangelicae formula,* for Jesus' command to turn the other cheek; in 19.8.1, in defining the purpose of cenobitic or anchoritic life; in 23.18.1, for the "Our Father."

118. *Qua meditatione teneatur vel cogitetur deus . . . qua deus mente concipiatur vel perpetuo teneatur* (*Conf.* 10.8.4).

119. See Antony's dictum that "perfect prayer" transcends every kind of self-awareness (*Conf.* 9.31).

120. *Conf.* 10.9; see *Inst.* 7.13.

121. Elsewhere Cassian suggests other formulae for prayer, though without presenting them as "methods" or universally applicable phrases. See, for example, *Conf.* 3.12.2, 12.6.6. These would be more akin to the "antirrhetic," occasional, prayers as described in texts from the Egyptian desert tradition.

122. The theme of perseverance in *memoria dei* returns in *Conf.* 23.7.3, 23.9.1, 23.13.1; cf. 24.6.1.

123. See Codina, *El aspecto cristologico en la espiritualidad de Juan Casiano,* 97–101, on the Christological orientation of the formula; Regnault follows Codina in this ("La prière continuelle 'monologistos' dans les Apophtegmes des Pères," 491).

124. This point is also made by Leyser, *"Lectio divina, oratio pura,"* 91–95.

125. See *Conf.* 1.15.3, 1.17.2, 3.8.2, 4.12.2, 6 and 7, *passim,* 9.6.4, 9.7.3–4, 9.8.1–2.

126. *Conf.* 10.10.3–11; see Diadochus, *Cap. gnost.* 61 (p. 120) on the power of the repeated name of Jesus against anger, hangovers, discouragement, and the general effects of the passions.

127. *Conf.* 10.10.13; see *Conf.* 4.2.3, 9.28.1.

128. *Conf.* 10.10.11; see *Conf.* 9.8.

129. *Conf.* 10.10.12 and 14.

130. See *Conf.* 12.6.6, on the monk's need to "repeat frequently" *(frequenter . . . repetendus),* with tears and sighs, Ps. 37(38):7–8, "I am miserable and afflicted" in order to obtain the "peace" of chastity; see *Conf.* 18.16.12, on "constantly" *(iugiter)* imploring the divine assistance.

131. Evagrius writes about this paradox in *Ep.* 11, where knowledge of God makes the poor rich (p. 574.16–18 [Syr.], p. 575.20–22 [Gk. retroversion]); see also *Ep.* 43, where knowledge is wealth of the soul and ignorance is poverty (p. 596.7–9 [Syr.], p. 597.6–8 [Gk. retroversion]) and *Schol. in Ps.* 24:16, where one must do everything for the sake of the knowledge of God (PG 12.1272C). For Cassian, knowledge of God is to be found in the spiritual meaning of the Bible.

132. *Conf.* 10.11.4, *pascetur in propheticis atque apostolicis montibus . . . iugi pascuo vegetatus;* see *Conf.* 1.8.3, *solius dei iam pulchritudine scientiaque pascatur,* and 9.3.4, *iugi omnipotentis dei contemplatione pascatur.*

133. See Prov. 30:26 and Ps. 103(104):18. (For this use of *sacramenta*, see *Conf.* 8.3.2, 10.11.4, 14.8.2, 14.9.7, 14.17.2–3, 17.19.4, 21.28.2, and see the discussion of *Conf.* 1.19 in chapter 3.) Ramsey (*John Cassian. The Conferences*, 392) notes that Cassian was not the first to be intrigued by the hedgehog and the deer in Ps. 103 (104); Jerome, *Tract. in Ps.* (pp. 185–86) and Augustine, *Enarr. in Ps.* 103, Serm. 3.18 (p. 1515–16). Evagrius uses Ps. 17(18):34 in comparing the soul freed from encumbrances of flesh and thoughts to the agile deer at home in the mountains (*Ep. fid.* 12, p. 112.33–34); his commentary on Ps. 17:32–34 notes that the *praktikē* provides the agility, while *theōria* raises one up to the heights (*Schol. in Ps.* 17, PG 12.1236D–37A). See *Schol. in Prov.* 341 (p. 430) on the "grass of the mountains" in Prov. 27:25 representing knowledge of the "holy powers" (angels).

134. See *Conf.* 23.2.1, on understanding Rom. 7:18–25 by exploring the feelings and insight that underlay Paul's words.

135. *Magistris adfectibus*; see *Conf.* 23.2.1: *sententias deo inspirante . . . conprehendere poterimus, cum eorum a quibus promulgatae sunt statum ac meritum perpendentes non verbo, sed experimentis parem induerimus adfectum.*

136. Codina notes, "Casiano en esto ha sido una vez más el puente de unión entre occidente y oriente. La 'oración a Jesús' entra pues en occidente a través de los escritos de Casiano, antes de que llegue el '*relato del peregrino ruso*'. Casiano es el primer peregrino que cuenta a los latinos los secretos de la oración continua de los orientales" (*El aspecto cristologico en la espiritualidad de Juan Casiano*, 100).

137. *Reg. Ben.* 17.3 (p. 526), 18.1 (p. 528), 35.17 (p. 568). For commentary, see Vogüé, *La Règle de Saint Benoît*, 5:535–38 and 6:1029–30.

138. Leyser makes a similar point (from a different perspective) in "Lectio divina, oratio pura."

139. See *Reg. Ben.* 42.3 and 5 (p. 584); 73.5 (p. 672).

Chapter 7

1. Such prayer is discussed once in the *Inst.* (*Inst.* 2.10.1) and throughout the *Conf.*: see *Conf.* 3.7.3, 4.2, 4.5 (see 4.19.4), 6.10.2, 9.14–15, 9.25–29, 10.10.12, 10.11.6, 12.12.6, 19.4.1, 19.5.1, 19.6.4–5.

2. See, for example, the analyses by Butler, *Benedictine Monachism*, 78–82; Olphe-Galliard, "Cassien (Jean)," 1928–29; Kirchmeyer, "Extase chez les Pères de l'Église," 2109–10; Bouyer, *The Spirituality of the New Testament and the Fathers*, 506–10; Špidlík, *La spiritualité de l'orient chrétien*. Vol. 2, *La prière*, 281–82. Völker compares Cassian's teaching on experience of prayer with that of John Climacus in *Scala Paradisi*, 240–44 (throughout that section of his book, Völker works with Cassian's teaching on prayer).

3. It should be noted that *Conf.* 9.31, which consists of the two sayings on prayer attributed to Antony, contains distinctive terminology. For example, "true prayer" (*oratio vera*), an Evagrian term, is used by Cassian only twice elsewhere (*Conf.* 10.9.2 and 23.18.2). The phrase "end of prayer" (*finis orationis*) occurs one other time (*Conf.* 9.2.2), though it resembles other uses of *finis*. Nor is "perfect prayer" (*oratio perfecta*) a typical term; Cassian uses it only once elsewhere, describing the Lord's Prayer (*Conf.* 23.18.1), though he does write about "perfection of prayer" (*perfectio orationis, Conf.* 9.2.1, 10.9.3).

4. *Schol. in Ps.* 126:2 (PG 12.1644A): ὥσπερ ὑπνοῦντες οὐδ᾽ αὐτὸ τοῦτο γινώσκομεν, ὅτι ὑπνοῦμεν, οὕτω καὶ θεωροῦντες μηδ᾽ αὐτὸ τοῦτο γινώσκομεν, ὅτι ἐν θεωρίᾳ γεγόναμεν. See *De orat.* 120: μακάριός ἐστιν ὁ νοῦς, ὁ κατὰ τὸν καιρὸν τῆς προσευχῆς τελείαν ἀναισθησίαν κτησάμενος (col. 1193B), though this should be understood more in terms of eliminating thoughts and images during prayer. I thank Adalbert de Vogüé for his helpful suggestions about these texts.

5. On Diadochus, see the introduction by Des Places to his edition of Diadochus' works (SC 5bis, pp. 9–81), a slightly revised version of his article in *DSp* 3.817–834; Messana, "Diadoco di Fotica e la cultura cristiana in Epiro nel V secolo" and "San Diadoco di Fotica." See also Dörries, "Diadochus und Symeon"; Louth, *The Origins of the Christian Mystical Tradition*, 125–31. An affinity between Cassian and Diadochus was noticed as early as Reitzenstein's *Historia Monachorum und Historia Lausiaca*, but he noted only one point they shared: the highest form of prayer is silent (p. 135, comparing *Cap. gnost.* 8 and *Conf.* 9.25).

6. *Cap. gnost.* Preamble (p. 84.10–11): ὅρος τῆς ἐπιγνώσεως· ἀγνοεῖν ἑαυτὸν ἐν τῷ ἐκστῆναι Θεῷ.

7. Elsewhere in his writings *conpunctio* has its usual meaning of "sorrow" and is always used in the singular.

8. For the classic exposition of this way of viewing the eastern tradition, see Hausherr, "Les grands courants de la spiritualité orientale." His schema of major currents can be a useful device but needs nuancing when actually applied to specific writers and texts.

9. See Kemmer, *Charisma Maximum*, on parallels with the *Liber graduum* and with Pseudo-Macarian texts; see the criticisms by Hausherr (*OCP* 6 [1940] 247–49), Capelle (*RHE* 39 [1943], 471–72), and Chadwick (*John Cassian*, 1st ed., 148 n.7; omitted in the 2nd ed.). Kemmer's subsequent "Gregorius Nyssenus est-ne inter fontes Iohannis Cassiani?" trying to show Cassian's dependence on Gregory of Nyssa's *De instituto christiano*, actually forms a sequel to *Charisma Maximum*, for Staats has since demonstrated that Gregory's treatise was based on the *Epistola magna* of Pseudo-Macarius.

10. Kemmer was quite prepared to ascribe to Cassian what he thought were "Messalian" tenets. As Hausherr noted, however, these same elements also characterized the teaching of the major spiritual writers of the Alexandrian tradition (review of Kemmer, *Charisma Maximum*, 248–49).

11. For the Messalian controversy and the role of the Pseudo-Macarian writings in it, see Stewart, *Working the Earth of the Heart*.

12. Olphe-Galliard, "Contemplation," 1926; Hausherr makes the same point in his review of Kemmer, *Charisma Maximum* (p. 249). Kirchmeyer, however, dealt with the problem by claiming that Cassian's teaching on ecstatic prayer is sufficiently paralleled in the Egyptian desert literature to make recourse to the Pseudo-Macarian texts unnecessary ("Extase chez les Pères de l'Église," 2109). As I will show later in this chapter, Kirchmeyer's position is only partly sustainable.

13. Kemmer, for instance, devotes slightly over two pages to the topic (*Charisma Maximum*, 106–8).

14. On Diadochus and Evagrius, see Reitzenstein, *Historia Monachorum und Historia Lausiaca*; see Draguet, "L'Histoire Lausiaque', une oeuvre écrite dans l'esprit d'Évagre," *passim*. Des Places notes the similarities between Cassian and Diadochus with respect to Evagrius; see his introduction to Diadochus, *Capita Gnostica*, SC 5bis, p. 11.

15. Diadochus borrowed heavily from the Pseudo-Macarian vocabulary of "spiritual sensation" typified by words such as αἴσθησις, πεῖρα, and πληροφορία, as well as by a variety of words having to do with spiritual sensation; see Stewart, *Working the Earth of the Heart*, 96–157. As Des Places notes, "cette langue n'est ni celle d'Évagre ni celle d'aucun auteur ascétique se rattachant à Origène" (introduction to Diadochus, *Capita Gnostica*, p. 60). Because of his demonstrable borrowing from the Pseudo-Macarian writings, Diadochus was more directly suspected of Messalianism than was Cassian; see Des Places, "Diadoque de Photicé," and Dörries, "Diadochos und Symeon," both with bibliography.

16. Dörr (*Diadochus von Photike und die Messalianer*, 64n.) thinks it unlikely that Diadochus could read Latin, yet he notes thematic (and even stylistic) parallels with Au-

gustine and Leo the Great; he suggests as an explanation the regular traffic between Rome and the province of Epirus, in which Photike was located (Diadochus' see was near the present-day border between Albania and Greece). Victor of Vita's *History of the Vandal Persecution* (written in 486) names a "Diadocus" as the teacher of Eugenios, bishop of Carthage from 481 to 505; Marrou suggests that Diadochus of Photike had been among the notables of Epirus captured by the Vandals between 467 and 474 and taken to Carthage ("Diadoque de Photiké et Victor de Vita"). If indeed he was in Carthage he could have come across Cassian's writings. Des Places (introduction to Diadochus, *Capita Gnostica*, SC 5bis, pp. 9–10) seems open to the hypothesis, while Courtois (*Victor de Vita et son oeuvre*, 21) and Dörries ("Diadochus und Symeon," 421–22) firmly reject it. Solignac argues that Eugenios was indeed the student of Diadochus of Photike, though not in Carthage: Eugenios, claims Solignac, was himself of eastern origin. It was he, not Diadochus, who came to Carthage from the East ("Victor de Vita," 548). It is conceivable that Diadochus learned of Cassian's work in some other way; later Cassian enjoyed a certain popularity in the East, and at least portions of his work were translated into Greek (see chapter 1).

17. Holm provides an overview of modern methodologies and research in "Ecstasy Research in the Twentieth Century." For various approaches, see Graef, "Ekstase"; Wißmann, "Ekstase"; Sharma, "Ecstasy"; Hof, "Ectasy and Mysticism"; Jones, "Mysticism, Human and Divine"; Poloma, "The Sociological Context of Religious Experience," 167–70; Špidlík, *La spiritualité de l'orient chrétien. Vol. 2, La prière*, 230–38. The most thorough general study is Arbman's *Ecstasy or Religious Trance*; see 1:291–334 and 353–415 on intellectual vision, especially of light, and 2:300–360 on ecstatic feeling and experience (Cassian is mentioned briefly on p. 304). Guibert's brief discussion in *The Theology of the Spiritual Life*, 353–55, contains a helpful definition of ecstasy emphasizing the paradox of spiritual concentration and loss of external sense activity.

18. On this reserve among early Christian writers, see Kirchmeyer, "Extase chez les Pères de l'Église"; Špidlík, *The Spirituality of the Christian East*, 339–40; Graef, "Ekstase," 789–90; the discussion later in this chapter.

19. For an example of twentieth-century reservations, see Hausherr's "Mystique extatique," *passim*. Hausherr tries to restrict the label "ecstasy" to certain descriptions within the Christian Neo-Platonic tradition that meet three criteria: 1) the experience involves the intellect, not just the senses or general awareness (French: *conscience*); 2) it is a going out (*sortie*) of the intellect beyond itself, its laws, and its limits; 3) the going out is an ascent in which the intellect, now beyond its own limits, enters into contact with God. If any criterion is not met, claims Hausherr, the experience is a ravishment, a suspension of the senses, an acute form of perception, or madness, but not a religious ecstasy ("Mystique extatique," 1863). Useful as a way to categorize certain forms of ecstasy, Hausherr's definition is too narrow to be of use when considering Cassian's descriptions, which cross the lines Hausherr tries to draw so clearly. Butler's comments on Cassian's teaching on prayer in *Benedictine Monachism*, 81–82, evidence a concern to distinguish Cassian's "pure prayer" from deliberately induced trances, visionary experiences, and "quietism."

20. See, e.g., Poulain, *The Graces of Interior Prayer*, 243–82.

21. Rahner and Viller note, "Wir möchten wünschen, daβ er sich über die Natur dieses erhabeneren Gebetes ausführlicher ausgesprochen hätte" (*Aszese und Mystik*, 192).

22. *Ad illum praecelsiorum . . . statum* and *gradu eminentiore perducit* (*Conf.* 9.25).

23. The relevant passages are: *Inst.* 2.10.1; *Conf.* 3.7.3, 4.2, 4.5, 6.10.2, 9.14, 9.15.1, 9.15.2, 9.15.3, 9.25, 9.26.1, 9.27, 9.28.1, 9.29.2, 10.10.12, 10.11.6, 12.12.6, 19.4.1, 19.5.1, 19.6.4–5.

24. See "pure and light prayers" (*Conf.* 2.22.2), "pure and ready (*prompta*) prayer" (*Conf.* 4.2), "purer and livelier (*alacrius*) prayers" (*Conf.* 6.10.2), "fervor and purity with

which one should pray" (*Conf.* 9.3.1), "pure and intent *(intentas)* prayers *(preces)*" (*Conf.* 9.15.3), "pure and most fervent" (*Conf.* 9.26.1), "purest of prayer" (*Conf.* 10.5.3). See note 3 for "true prayer."

25. Spiritalis: *Conf.* 3.7.3, 4.2, 6.10.2, 10.10.12, 19.4.1. Invisibilis: *Conf.* 3.7.3, 6.10.2.

26. These words are synonymous with *oratio* in these descriptions. Theoria: *Conf.* 3.7.3, 6.10.2, 19.4.1. Meditatio: *Conf.* 3.7.3, 19.4.1. Contemplatio: *Conf.* 9.29.2.

27. Excessus mentis: *Inst.* 2.10.1, and see 3.3.4 and 3.3.7 on Peter; *Conf.* 6.10.2, 9.31, 10.10.12, 19.4.2; excessus cordis: *Conf.* 10.11.6, 12.12.6; excessus spiritus: *Conf.* 4.5; excessus without specification: *Conf.* 3.7.3, 19.4.1, 19.5.1–2. In other contexts, Cassian uses *excessus* in a nonecstatic or even negative sense, reflecting a traditional ambivalence about language suggestive of *ekstasis*: as "amazement" at God's mercy: *Conf.* 1.15.2; as dangerous imbalance of mind or imprudence: *Conf.* 2.2.4, 2.16.1, 4.2, 4.12.6, 7.26.4, 22.3.1, 22.3.5.

28. *Conf.* 3.7.3 *(rapiatur)*, 4.5 *(rapiatur)*, 9.15.1 *(raptantur)*, 19.4.1 *(raptum)*, 19.5.1 *(rapiebamur)*; see 9.26.2. This word also is used negatively in other places: see *Conf.* 4.2 (with *excessus*), as a negative counterpart to the positive ecstasy described a few lines earlier; also *Conf.* 9.4.1, 12.4.3, 16.27.1, 21.33.2, 23.8.2, 24.16.

29. *Conf.* 9.27: adtonitus spiritus; 19.6.4: adtonita anima.

30. *Conf.* 3.7.3, 4.5, 6.10.2, 9.14, 9.15.3, 9.25, 10.10.12, 19.4.1, 19.5.1. On the spiritual senses, see chapter 3.

31. *Inst.* 2.10.1 *(ignita mens in semet ipsa non praevalet continere)*, *Conf.* 9.15.1, 9.15.2, 9.26.1, 9.27a, 9.27b, 9.28, 10.11.6, 12.12.6; see *Conf.* 9.25 on the "return" of the mind to its normal state and *Conf.* 9.31, Antony's observation that it is not "perfect prayer" when monks are aware *(intellegit)* of themselves or that they are praying.

32. *Conf.* 4.2, 6.10.2, 9.29.2.

33. The word is almost always used with this sense; see *Inst.* 9.1, *Conf.* 4.2, 4.4.1, 6.10.2, 9.15.3, 9.27, 9.29.2, 10.10.12, 10.11.4, 10.11.6, 11.12.5, 12.12.6, 19.6.5. For a negative *alacritas*, see *Conf.* 13.8.1.

34. *Conf.* 4.2, 10.10.12. The word is used elsewhere to describe the abundance of grace or virtue: *Inst.* 6.18; *Conf.* 4.12.1, 13.16.1, 16.14.4.

35. Occurrences in this context are *Conf.* 4.2, 9.14, 9.15.3, 9.27, 9.28.1, 9.29.2, 10.10.12, 12.12.6.

36. *Conf.* 4.2 *(ut [alacritatem] non dicam sermo subsequi, sed ne ipse quidem sensus occurreret)*, 9.15.1 *([oratio quae] in ore hominum nec comprehendi nec exprimi potest)*, 9.15.2 *(ineffabiles . . . preces . . . quanta non dicam ore percurrere)*, 9.25 *(nullo non dicam sono vocis nec linguae motu nec ulla verborum pronuntiatione distinguitur . . . non humanis atque angustis designat eloquiis)*, 10.11.6 *([oratio] nulla vocis, nulla verborum prosecutione distinguitur)*, 9.27 *(silentio mens intra secretum profundae taciturnitatis absconditur, ut omnem penitus sonum vocis stupor subitae inluminationis includat)*. With these can be compared the practical injunction of *Conf.* 9.35.3 urging silent prayer both out of respect for others and to avoid being overheard (and subsequently attacked) by demons.

37. *Inst.* 2.10.1; *Conf.* 9.15.2, 9.27, 10.11.6; see 16.13 quoting Rom. 8:26–27. Normally, however, this word is associated with contrition or tears (e.g., *Conf.* 1.23.2, 12.6.6) sometimes linked with prayer in such states *(Inst.* 6.17; *Conf.* 2.13.7); see the discussion of *conpunctio* later in this chapter.

38. *Inst.* 2.10.1; *Conf.* 4.2, 9.14, 9.15.2–3, 9.25 (twice), 9.27, 9.28.1, 10.11.6, 12.12.6, 19.6.5. See *Conf.* 17.24.3 on the *ineffabilia verba* heard by Paul when he was "caught up" to heaven (2 Cor 12:4, though the Vulgate has *arcana verba*). For *ineffabilis* applied to God or to divine qualities, see *Conf.* 1.15.2, 9.22.1, 10.5.1, 12.12.1, 17.25.14.

39. *Conf.* 9.15.2, 9.27, 10.11.6; see 16.13, quoting Rom. 8:26–27.

40. *Conf.* 10.11.6; see 1.23.1 on the effects of Abba Moses' conference, which fired an

ardor inexplebilis in his two hearers: in this regard, see Cassian's claim that an elder's conference can be a cause of compunction (*Conf.* 9.26.2).

41. *Conf.* 3.7.3: *nec intuendis praetereuntium imaginibus occupetur, sed ne adiacentes quidem moles et ingentes materias obiectas oculis carnis aspiciat. Conf.* 10.11.6: *oratio . . . quae non solum nullius imaginis occupatur intuitu.*

42. *Ardor: Conf.* 6.10.2, 19.5.1. *Fervor/ferveo: Inst.* 2.10.1; *Conf.* 9.15.1, 9.27, 9.29.2, 12.12.6. *Flamma/inflammatus: Conf.* 9.15.2, 9.26.1. *Ignis/ignitus: Inst.* 2.10.1; *Conf.* 9.15.1 (twice), 9.25, 10.11.6, 12.12.6 (see *Conf.* 4.19.4 and 19.5.2). *Successus: Inst.* 2.10.1; *Conf.* 6.10.2, 9.26.1.

43. Thus Bouyer, "This prayer of fire is clearly a theme that fascinated Cassian. He returns to it often and cannot, it seems, finish speaking of its ineffable nature" (*The Spirituality of the New Testament and the Fathers,* 508).

44. *Inluminatio: Conf.* 9.27. *Inlustratio/inlustratus: Conf.* 9.25, 10.10.12. *Lumen: Conf.* 9.25.

45. See Beyer, "Die Lichtlehre der Mönche des vierzehnten und des vierten Jahrhunderts," *passim.*

46. *Conf.* 9.25: *illa ignea ac perpaucis cognita vel experta . . . oratio; Conf.* 10.10.14: *perpaucis expertus . . . orationis ardor.*

47. *Conf.* 9.25: *in illo brevissimo temporis puncto.*

48. *Conf.* 19.4.1–2. It should be noted that *Conf.* 19.4–6 has a different character from the other descriptions of ecstatic experience. Although the passage about Abba John refers to the "ecstatic" move out of ordinary experience, the emphasis of these chapters is on "contemplation" (associated with the anchoritic life) rather than "prayer." Thus one does not find in them the "fiery" language characteristic of the descriptions of ecstatic prayer. *Conf.* 19.5.1 refers to the *ardor animi* with which one seeks the angelic life of contemplation in solitude, but the phrase is more akin to the language Cassian uses to describe desire for or dedication to the monastic life than it is to the descriptions of ardent prayer.

49. See *Inst.* 2.10.1 and *Conf.* 9.26.

50. See De Goedt, "L'extase dans la Bible" (covering both Old and New Testaments) and André, "Ecstatic Prophecy."

51. See Ringgren, "Ecstasy," 280a.

52. Judg. 14:6, 14:19, 15:14: ἥλατο . . . πνεῦμα κυρίου (Codex Vaticanus), κατηύθυνεν. . . πνεῦμα κυρίου (Codex Alexandrinus); *irruit . . . spiritus domini* (Vulgate).

53. 1 Sam. (LXX: 1 Kgs.) 10:6: ἐφαλεῖται ἐπὶ σὲ πνεῦμα κυρίου, καὶ προφητεύσεις μετ' αὐτῶν καὶ στραφήσῃ εἰς ἄνδρα ἄλλον (LXX), *insiliet in te spiritus domini, et prophetabis cum eis, et mutaberis in virum alium* (Vulgate); 1 Sam. (LXX: 1 Kgs.) 10:10: ἥλατο ἐπ' αὐτὸν πνεῦμα θεοῦ, καὶ ἐπροφήτευσεν μέσῳ αὐτῶν (LXX), *insiluit super eum spiritus domini, et prophetavit in medio eorum* (Vulgate).

54. 1 Sam. (LXX: 1 Kgs.) 19:20: ἐγενήθη ἐπὶ τοὺς ἀγγέλους τοῦ Σαουλ πνεῦμα θεοῦ and 19:23: ἐγενήθη καὶ ἐπ' αὐτῷ πνενεῦμα θεοῦ (LXX); *factus est etiam Spiritus Domini in illis* and *factus est etiam super eum Spiritus Domini* (Vulgate).

55. De Goedt points to Isa. 21:3–4; Ezek. 1:28–2:2, 3:22–24, 8:1–9:11, 37:1–14, 40:1–42:2, 43:3, 44:4; Dan. 8 and 10 as the clearest cases ("L'extase dans la Bible," 2080–82).

56. De Goedt, "L'extase dans la Bible," 2074.

57. Usually describing reactions to horrible or fearful events, or the events themselves (Gen. 27:33; Num. 13:32; 1 Sam. 11:17; 2 Kgs. 4:13; 2 Chr. 14:13, 15:5, 17:10, 20:29, 29:8; Odes 4:14 [Hab. 3:14]; Zech. 14:13; Jer. 5:30; Ezek. 26:16, 27:35, 32:10; Dan. 7:28, 10:7). It can also mean insanity or stupidity (Deut. 28:28, Prov. 26:10, Zech. 12:4). More neutrally, it means "sleep" or "stupor" (Gen. 2:21, 15:12). One of the Psalms (30[31]) is attributed to David "in ecstasy," but there the word means "alarm" or "bewilderment" (see v. 23, and also Ps. 115:2 [116:11]). Another psalm has a mysterious allusion to Benjamin, "youngest of the tribes,"

"in ecstasy" (ἐν ἐκστάσει) but it seems to mean "standing out" or "in the lead" (Ps. 67[68]:28). All of these uses of ἔκστασις in the Psalms are translated as *excessus mentis* in the Gallican Psalter, Jerome's revision of the Old Latin on the basis of the LXX.

58. Mark 5:42, 16:8; Luke 5:26; Acts 3:10.

59. Rev. 1:10, 4:2, 17:3, 21:10: ἐν πνεύματι, *in spiritu*.

60. Gk: ἐξέστημεν; Vulg.: *mente excedimus*.

61. For example, Ambrose, Augustine, and Pseudo-Macarius, as in notes 72, 74, 102–03. See Harl's comments on the passage in "Le langage de l'expérience religieuse chez les Pères grecs," 9–10. One of the best examples of the use of this and other biblical models is by Nilus of Ancyra in *De vol. paup.* 27 (col. 1004AB). For Hausherr's reluctance to describe Paul's experience as "ecstatic," see "Mystique extatique," col. 1868.

62. Gk.: ἁρπαγέντα, Lat.: *raptus est*.

63. Gk.: ἡρπάγη, Lat.: *raptus est*.

64. Gk.: ἄρρητα ῥήματα, Lat.: *arcana verba*.

65. The two "ecstatic" texts Cassian actually quotes are used to make other points: Acts 10:10 (*Inst.* 3.3.4 and 7) and 2 Cor. 12:2–4 (*Conf.* 17.24.3).

66. See Kirchmeyer, "Extase chez les Pères de l'Église," and the overview and bibliography in McGinn, *The Foundations of Mysticism*, 44 and 52–53; Louth, *The Origins of the Christian Mystical Tradition*, 13–14 (Plato) and 47–51 (Plotinus) is very helpful. On Plotinus, see Jansen, "Das mystische Erlebnis bei Plotin," Corrigan, "Solitary Mysticisms," and especially P. Hadot, *Plotinus*, 23–34.

67. See Giversen, "L'expérience mystique chez Philon"; Louth, *The Origins of the Christian Mystical Tradition*, 33–35; McGinn, *The Foundations of Mysticism*, 39; there is a useful selection of relevant texts in English in Winston, *Philo of Alexandria*, 164–74.

68. Clement's mystical theology has been interpreted in many and often contradictory ways, as noted by Völker (*Der wahre Gnostiker nach Clemens Alexandrinus*, 427–32), though it is clear that he was resistant to the idea of ecstatic prayer. For Origen, the locus classicus is *Hom. in Num.* 27.12 (p. 275.17–22); for other references, with a cautious assessment, see Kirchmeyer, "Extase chez les Pères de l'Église," 2094–97. Hausherr concedes ecstatic experience to Origen but not the label, since Origen himself does not use the word ("Mystique extatique," 1862–63 and 1868). When Origen does use the word, it signifies insanity. See, e.g., his late work *C. Celsum* 1.67 (SC 132, p. 266), 3.24 (SC 136, p. 56), 4.19 (SC 136, p. 228), 7.3 SC 150, p. 20). In this last text he speaks directly to the issue of prophetic inspiration, criticizing the ecstasy and frenzy of a Greek prophetess which cannot, he claims, be the work of the Holy Spirit because of the subject's loss of self-control. See also Völker, *Das Vollkommenheitsideal des Origenes*, 134–44; Louth, *The Origins of the Christian Mystical Tradition*, 72; McGinn, *The Foundations of Mysticism*, 128. Harl's remarkable "Le langage de l'expérience religieuse chez les Pères grecs" is an important contribution to the study of how religious emotion was communicated by Clement, Origen, Basil, and Gregory of Nyssa. Although her focus is not specifically on ecstatic language, her remarks on Origen particularly (pp. 13–16) are most helpful in understanding his appeal to experience. Coakley's "Why Three?" links Origen's hesitations about ecstasy to his theology of the Holy Spirit, prayer, and sexuality (see pp. 40–45).

69. On Gregory, see Daniélou, "Mystique de la ténèbre chez Grégoire de Nysse," 1876–82, and Kirchmeyer, "Extase chez les Pères de l'Église," 2099; Louth, *The Origins of the Christian Mystical Tradition*, 80–84 and 96–97; Völker's analysis in *Gregor von Nyssa als Mystiker*, 202–15, emphasizing Gregory's links to Origen. On Pseudo-Dionysius, see Roques, "Contemplation, extase et ténèbre chez le Pseudo-Denys" and Kirchmeyer, "Extase chez les Pères de l'Église," 2101; Louth, *The Origins of the Christian Mystical Tradition*, 175–78; Völker, *Kontemplation und Ekstase bei Pseudo-Dionysius Areopagita*, 197–217.

70. See Völker, *Maximus Konfessor als Meister des geistlichen Lebens*, especially 351–65; Krivocheine, *In the Light of Christ*, especially 339–49.

71. *De anima* 45.3 (p. 849), 47.4 (p. 853).

72. *Confess.* 9.10.24–25 (pp. 113–14). See Quinn, "Mysticism in the Confessiones," 266–71; Van Fleteren, "Mysticism in the Confessiones," 311–22; more generally, see Bonner, "Augustine and Mysticism." For Ambrose, see especially the commentary on 2 Cor. 12 in *De Isaac vel anima* 4.11 (pp. 650–51); see McGinn, *The Foundations of Mysticism*, 205–6.

73. See, for example, *De Gen. ad litt.* 12.5 and 26 (pp. 386 and 419–20, noted by Butler, *Western Mysticism*, 71–78, who gives other references). See Olphe-Galliard, "La contemplation dans la littérature chrétienne latine"; Williams, *The Wound of Knowledge*, 86–89; Louth, *The Origins of the Christian Mystical Tradition*, 137–40 and 148–49; McGinn, *The Foundations of Mysticism*, 253–55.

74. See *Liber de vid. Deo* (*Ep.* 147) 31 (CSEL 44, pp. 305–6); see *De Gen. ad litt.* 12.34 (p. 432), both analyzed by Butler, *Western Mysticism*, 71–83; see Teske, "St. Augustine and the Vision of God," 293–98; Van Fleteren, "Mysticism in the Confessiones," 322–27.

75. For general overviews, see Holze, *Erfahrung und Theologie im frühen Mönchtum*, 150–53; Leloir, *Désert et communion*, 225–28 (using the Armenian version of *Apoph.*); Völker, *Scala Paradisi*, 241–42; Gould, *The Desert Fathers on Monastic Community*, 177–82, on "ecstasy"; Guillaumont, "Les visions mystiques dans le monachisme oriental chrétien."

76. *Apoph. Alph.* Arsenius 30 (col. 97C), Bessarion 4 (col. 140AB), John Colobos 23 (col. 212D), Silvanus 3 (col. 409A, *ἐν ἐκστάσει*), Tithoes 6 (col. 428CD, *ἐν ἐκστάσει*); *Anon.* Nau 629 (p. 274); *Hist. Laus.* 1.3 (pp. 15.24–16.1), 17.5 (p. 44.25–27).

77. *Alph.* John Colobos 14 (col. 208CD, *ἐν ἐκστάσει*), Poemen 144 (col. 357B, *ἐν ἐκστάσει*), Silvanus 2 (col. 408CD, *ἐν ἐκστάσει*); *Anon.* Nau 211 (pp. 280–82, *ἐν ἐκστάσει*), 598 (pp. 253–54, *ἐν ἐκστάσει*), 622 (p. 268, *ἐν ἐκστάσει*), 630 (p. 274); Palladius, *Hist. Laus.* 29.4 (p. 85.14).

78. See Athanasius, *V. Ant.* 82.3–13 (pp. 344.7–350.2); *Apoph. Anon.* Nau 135 (pp. 47–48, *ἐν ἐκστάσει*), 254 (p. 366, *ἐν ἐκστάσει*); Palladius, *Hist. Laus.* 38.4–7, Evagrius' vision while in an "ecstasy" (pp. 117.16–119.9).

79. *Apoph. Alph.* Antony 37 (col. 88B, *ἔκστασις φρενῶν*); Palladius, *Hist. Laus.* 18.3 (p. 48.22) and 39.1 (p. 123.7–8). See Canivet's "Erreurs de spiritualité et troubles psychiques" on a sixth-century monastic text about mental illness and spiritual instability.

80. Leloir provides a useful overview based on the Armenian *Apoph.* (which are largely to be found in the extant Greek sayings listed in notes 81–84) in *Désert et communion*, 226–28; see also Edsman, *Le Baptême de Feu*, 154–62.

81. *Apoph. Alph.* Arsenius 27 (col. 96BC), Joseph of Panephysis 7 (col. 229CD; cf. 6, col. 229C); *Anon.* Nau 639 (p. 277; see *Alph.* Theodore of Pherme 25, col. 193AB: because Theodore could not become a pillar of fire at the altar, he did not serve as a deacon); QRT 15 (Regnault, *SPT*, p. 112); see *Alph.* Pambo 12 (col. 372A) and Silvanus 12 (col. 412C) about the radiant faces of these monks. Joseph Hazzaya used the story about Arsenius in interpreting Evagrius' *Keph. gnost.* 1.11, as analyzed by Guillaumont in "De l'eschatologie à la mystique," 191–92.

82. See *Apoph. Alph.* Isaiah 4 (col. 181 AB), Macarius the Great 33 (col. 277AB); *Anon.* Nau 567 (p. 207). Sulpitius reports that Martin was seen to have fire coming from his head when celebrating the eucharist (*Dial.* 2.2.1, pp. 181–82). Leroy's "La splendeur corporelle des saints" studies this phenomenon in medieval and modern hagiography.

83. *Apoph. Anon.* Nau 36 (p. 66); *Syr.* Bu 1.135 (Syr.: Bedjan, p. 488, no. 128; E.T.: Budge, 2.30–31); a saying attributed to Ammonas compared prayer to standing on fire (*PO* 11, p. 422.11–13); *Alph. Suppl.* James 2 (p. 25).

84. *Apoph. Alph.* Horsisios 2 (col. 316CD), Sisoes 9 (col. 393BC); *Gk. Syst.* 11.52 (Arm. II 203 in Regnault, *SPN*, p. 265); *Boh.*, p. 41.11 and p. 195.1, especially interesting with its description of the heart "ardent and boiling in the Spirit, in the heavenly fire full of exultation" (Regnault in *SPT*, p. 188, rightly corrects Amélineau's translation of the Coptic ΠΙΧΡΩΜ from "foi" to "feu"). Ammonas writes frequently of God-given "fervor" for the monastic life (Gk.: θέρμη/θερμότης, Syr.: *ratīḥūtā/rathā*); see *Ep. Syr.* 3.2 (p. 574.6–7), *Ep. Gk.* 6.2 (p. 451.6–7), *Ep. Syr.* 3.4 (p. 576.7–10)/*Ep. Gk.* 2.3 (p. 437.10–13), *Ep. Syr.* 4.2 (pp. 579.10–580.1)/*Ep. Gk.* 3.2 (p. 440.3), *Ep. Syr.* 10.2 (p. 595.4–5 and p. 596.3–7) and 10.3 (pp. 596.11–597.2 and p. 598.3–4), *Ep. Syr.* 11.2 (p. 600.6–10)/*Ep. Gk.* 5.3 (p. 448.3–6); *Ep. Gk.* 8 (ed. Marriot, pp. 47–48); see *Ep. Syr.* 8 (p. 586.8–9), which reads *mawhabtā*, "gift," while the Georgian and Arabic read "fire." I thank Samuel Rubenson for suggesting that I look for these themes in the writings of Ammonas.

85. *Apoph. Alph.* Syncletica 1 (col. 421AB).

86. See the section on Evagrius by Hausherr [Lemaître], Roques, and Viller in "Contemplation. A III.1," 1775–85, especially 1784, Olphe-Galliard's "La contemplation dans la littérature chrétienne latine," 1921–29, esp. 1928–29; Kirchmeyer's "Extase chez les Pères de l'Église," cols. 2099–101 (on Evagrius) and 2109–110 (on Cassian). Hausherr deals with the question of "ecstatic" language in Evagrius' work in "Ignorance infinie" (esp. pp. 357–60), as do Draguet, "L'Histoire Lausiaque', une oeuvre écrite dans l'esprit d'Évagre," 348–50, and Bunge, *Das Geistgebet*, 74–87. See the Guillaumonts' introduction to *Prak.*, SC 170, pp. 103, 109–12.

87. For example, *Prak.* 61 and 66 (pp. 642 and 650); *De orat.* 35 (col. 1173D), 46 (col. 1176D), 52 (col. 1177C).

88. See Hausherr, "Ignorance infinie," 358–59, and *Les leçons d'un contemplatif*, 153. Golitzin provides helpful nuancing in *Et introibo ad altare Dei*, 338–40, though he concludes: "True, there seems to be no ecstasy, no enraptured transcending of creaturely limits in Evagrius' scheme of things, and here we must admit a difference between the Areopagite and—perhaps even more so—the Nyssene" (p. 339).

89. See *Prak.* 14 (p. 534.6–7), *De mal. cog.* 22 (ed. Muyldermans, 47), *Cap.* 9 (col. 1265B), *Schol. in Prov.* 323 (p. 414). Note too Evagrius' concern that excessive weeping for one's sins could lead to insanity (*De orat.* 8, col. 1169A); see Driscoll, "Penthos and Tears in Evagrius Ponticus," 152.

90. *Das Geistgebet*, 76.

91. See *Prak.* 57 (p. 634), *De orat.* 52 (col. 1177C), 61 (col. 1180C), 118 (col. 1193A); the most striking is *De orat.* 52: κατάστασίς ἐστι προσευχῆς ἕξις ἀπαθὴς, ἔρωτι ἀκροτάτῳ εἰς ὕψος νοητὸν ἁρπάζουσα τὸν φιλόσοφον, καὶ πνευματικὸν νοῦν. The other two texts use πόθος rather than ἔρως.

92. The first was included in Frankenberg's Syriac edition of *Cap. cogn.* as *Keph. gnost.* 7.30 (p. 454 [Syr.] and 455 [Gk. retroversion]). The Greek original, *Cap. cogn.* 17 (p. 53) reads: προσευχή ἐστι κατάστασις νοῦ, φθαρτικὴ παντὸς ἐπιγείου νοήματος· ὑπὸ φωτὸς μόνου γινομένη τῆς ἁγίας Τριάδος. The Syriac translation added the words *byad taḥrā metpasaqā*, "by separation," which Frankenberg retroverted as δι' ἐκστάσεως. The second text adduced (*Keph. gnost.* 3.88), suggesting that one can be caught up into "limitless unknowing" (like the saying of Antony in Cassian's *Conf.* 9.31), puzzled commentators (e.g., Hausherr in "Ignorance infinie") until it was corrected to "limitless knowledge" on the basis of the previously unknown version published by Guillaumont (p. 135). Despite Guillaumont's edition, Hausherr maintained ("Ignorance infinie ou science infinie?") that "unknowing" was the preferred reading, though his actual interpretation of the text had shifted in the twenty years since his original article.

93. See the discussion of this theme in chapter 5.

94. See "La vision de l'intellect par lui-même dans la mystique évagrienne," especially 260–61. See chapter 5 for references to Evagrius and to modern studies.

95. See *Antirr.* 4.48–49 (p. 508.20–23 [Syr.], 509 [Gk. retroversion]), *De mal. cog.* 26 (ed. Muyldermans, 51).

96. *Cap. cogn.* 6 (Muyldermans, 51, there no. 4), the pure mind as a "censer" (θυμιατήριον); *De orat.* 94 (col. 1188BC), devoting oneself ἐμπύρως to colloquy with God; *De orat.* 111 (col. 1192C), demons are unable to lead a monk's mind away from "fiery" (ἐμπύρος) prayer.

97. *De orat.* 111 (col. 1192C).

98. See *Conf.* 3.7.3, 6.10.2, 9.15.3, 10.10.12, 19.4.1, 19.5.1. See note 48 on the distinctive traits of the passage from *Conf.* 19.4–5.

99. Olphe-Galliard follows a more purely Evagrian interpretation of Cassian's teaching than is suggested here; see "La science spirituelle d'après Cassien," 149–50, and the similar "Cassien (Jean)," 264. McGinn disputes Olphe-Galliard's internalized understanding of *excessus mentis* (*The Foundations of Mysticism*, 224 n. 169).

100. For an overview of both, see Stewart, *Working the Earth of the Heart*, 70–92.

101. For example, *Coll.* I 50.2.2 (vol. 2, p. 127.3); *Coll.* II 4.7 and 12–15 (pp. 32.110–25 and pp. 36.180–38.244); 7.1 (pp. 70.1–71.19); 8.1 (pp. 76.1–77.14), 46.3–4 (p. 302.50–53). For the *Liber graduum*, see cols. 336.3, 340.12–348.5, 349.19–352.3, 353.24–356.5, 356.8–15.

102. The contrast between "this" world (κόσμος) or age (αἰών) and "that" one (heaven) is a common theme in the Pseudo-Macarian texts.

103. *Coll.* II 8.1 (p. 77.7–14). See *Coll.* II 8.3–5 (pp. 78.25–83.75), especially 8.4 (p. 80.48–50): νυκτὸς καὶ ἡμέρας εἰς τὰ τέλεια μέτρα ἔστηκεν, ὧν ἐλεύθερος καὶ καθαρός, πάντοτε αἰχμάλωτος καὶ μετέωρος. Despite the mention of "night and day" the point is that although the experience of ecstasy is real, it is not permanent; see also 8.5 (pp. 82.68–83.75), on the abiding presence of sin even though one abides in grace. See Dörries' commentary on this material in *Die Theologie des Makarios/Symeon*, 294–302.

104. *Coll.* II 8.2 (p. 78.20–24). See 8.5 (p. 82.64–66): ἔστι γὰρ καιρός, ὅτε πλέον ἐξάπτει καὶ παρακαλεῖ καὶ ἀναπαύει· ἔστι καιρός, ὅτι ὑποστέλλεται καὶ στυγνάζει, ὡς αὐτὴ ἡ χάρις οἰκονομεῖ πρὸς τὸ συμφέρον τῷ ἀνθρώπῳ.

105. See, for example, *Coll.* I 8.4.5 (vol. 1, p. 123.4–8), 33.4.5 (vol. 2, pp. 32.25–33.5), 35.1.8 (p. 43.23–31), 63.4.5 (p. 215.14–22); *Coll.* II 7.1 (p. 71.17–19), 9.9 (pp. 87.90–88.97), 11.1 (pp. 96.1–97.13), 25.9–10 (pp. 204.126–205.158), 40.7 (p. 278.85–88), 43.1–3 (pp. 283.1–287.55); *Coll.* III 26.4.1 (p. 302.5–9).

106. For example, *Coll.* I 29.1.7–8 (vol. 1, p. 261.18–26), *Coll.* II 10.2 (p. 93.21–22), 10.4 (p. 95.51–60), 40.2 (p. 276.21–24).

107. *Coll.* II 8.3 (p. 79.35–41).

108. Gk: ἐν αἰσθήσει καρδίας. The word αἴσθησις is part of the distinctive Pseudo-Macarian terminology adopted by Diadochus. See Stewart, *Working the Earth of the Heart*, 116–38, for the background and for Diadochus' use of the word.

109. Gk: ἐν ἔρωτί τινι σφοδρῷ. Evagrius uses a similar phrase in *De orat.* 52 (col. 1177C), a rare instance of this kind of language in his writings.

110. Gk: ἐκδημεῖ. See the definition of hope that prefaces *Cap. gnost.*: ἐκδημία τοῦ νοῦ ἐν ἀγάπῃ πρὸς τὰ ἐλπιζόμενα (p. 84.4–5); see 91 on the soul moving out (ἐκβῆναι) from the body toward the Lord in unutterable joy and love (p. 152.12–14). See Evagrius, *De orat.* 46 (col. 1176D) and Hausherr, "Ignorance infinie," 357.

111. Gk: καιόμενος. See *Cap. gnost.* 15 (p. 92.9–10) on the soul inflamed (ἀναζωπυροῦσα) by the heat (θέρμη) of the love of God; 34 (p. 104.8–9) on the love from the Holy Spirit which "inflames" (ἐκκαίει) the soul with the love of God so that it wants to be

joined ineffably (ἀλαλήτως ἐγκολλᾶσθαι) to the sweetness of divine longing (πόθος); 67 (p. 127.17–18) on theology as an illuminating fire of transformation; 74 (p. 133.3–8) on the "heat" (θέρμη) the Holy Spirit creates in the heart, leading to desire (πόθος) for God.

112. Gk. ἀνάγκη τινὶ πόθου> See Evagrius, *Prak.* 57 (p. 634.5) and *De orat.* 118 (col. 1193A) for πόθος.

113. See *Cap. gnost.* 32 (p. 102.4) on the "warm memory of God" that joins the soul to God's love.

114. *Cap. gnost.* 14 (p. 91.8–20).

115. On compunction, the standard work remains Hausherr, *Penthos*, though the book is showing its age. For useful overviews and penetrating analysis, see especially Pegon, "Componction"; Régamey, "La componction du coeur" (particularly good on Cassian); Petersen, *The Dialogues of Gregory the Great*, 160–65; Chryssavgis, *Ascent to Heaven*, 125–61, focused on John Climacus but with abundant references to earlier tradition. See Gómez, "Compunctio lacrymarum," and Guibert, "La componction du coeur." For works related specifically to monastic compunction, see notes 133–34.

116. On tears, see in addition to the works on compunction just cited, Lot-Borodine, "Le mystère du 'don des larmes' dans l'Orient chrétien" and Adnès, "Larmes." For a modern study on the value of tears in the spiritual life (inspired particularly by Isaac of Nineveh), see Ross, *The Fountain and the Furnace.*

117. However, as Régamey notes, Cassian's teaching on compunction had less impact on medieval tradition than one might have expected; he notes the same for the best aspects of Gregory's teaching, claiming that Gregory's "less interesting" texts on compunction were the most popular ("La componction du coeur," pt. 1, p. 12). This fact probably says more about later perspectives on compunction than about the merits of Cassian's work. Kasper notes that among the Lerinian monastic writers only Eucherius understood *conpunctio* in terms similar to Cassian's (*Theologie und Askese*, 72).

118. See *Reg. Ben.* 4.57 (p. 460), 20.3 (p. 536), 49.4 (p. 606), 52.4 (p. 610).

119. See note 193 for Gregory's parallels with Cassian on the theme of compunction.

120. See especially *Inst.* 4.43, 5.14.1, 5.14.2, 8.9.1, 12.15.1, 12.27.5; *Conf.* 1.17.2, 10.10.11, 10.11.4, 19.14.5, 20.6.1, 21.30.2.

121. *Conf.* 1.19.1, 2.11.3, 2.17.2, 3.4.1, 3.4.2, 4.5, 6.9.4, 9.15.1, 9.28.1.2, 10.10.11, 14.12, 16.15, 19.16.2, 20.1.4, 20.6.1, 20.10, 21.30.2, 22.1.3, 23.7.2. For Cassian the verb *conpungere* means "to be sorry for sins" or "to move deeply" (*Inst.* 8.9 [quoting Ps. 4:5], 12.18, 12.27.6; *Conf.* 2.11.3, 3.2.2, 3.5.1, 3.22.4, 4.15.2, 4.19.4, 9.8.3, 9.11, 9.15.3, 9.29.1, 9.33, 11.5, 11.7.2, 21.8.1, 22.7.3) or even "to be disturbed by thoughts/temptations" (*Conf.* 3.4.4, 5.5, 10.10.9, 23.6.5, 23.13.1). His description in *Inst.* 9.10–12 of a salutary *tristitia* (see 2 Cor. 7:10) arising from penance or desire for perfection or heaven anticipates Gregory the Great's teaching in *Mor. in Iob* 23.41 (pp. 1175–76).

122. At the end of *Conf.* 9.27 and in 9.28 it reverts to its usual meaning.

123. See the similar observation of Régamey: "en somme, pour Cassien, la componction est toute douleur que l'âme éprouve dans le drame de sa solitude avec Dieu, depuis le premier dépouillement de sa conversion quand la crainte de Dieu la frappe, jusqu'aux plus insignes faveurs de l'union" ("La componction du coeur," pt.1, p. 15).

124. See *TLL* 3.2171–72 (*compunctio*) and 2172–75 (*compungo*).

125. Ps. 59(60):5 (Vulgate: *conpunctio*) and Isa. 29:10 (Vulgate: *sopor*, translating from the Hebrew though cited in Vulgate Rom. 11:8 as *conpunctio*, following the "Gallican Psalter" based on the LXX). See the summaries by Pegon ("Componction," 1312–13), Guibert ("La componction du coeur," 226), Régamey ("La componction du coeur," pt. 1, pp. 5–9), and Harl ("Les origines grecques du mot et de la notion de componction dans la Septante et chez ses commentateurs," esp. 4–11).

126. On the LXX, see Harl, "Les origines grecques du mot et de la notion de compunction dans la Septante et chez ses commentateurs." This verb (in both active and passive forms) has the same literal meaning as *conpungere* but like the Latin verb tends to be used psychologically or morally. See Gen. 27:38 and 34:7; Lev. 10:3; 3 Kgs. 20:27 and 20:29; Ps. 4:4, 29(30):12, 34(35):15, 108(109):16; Sir. 12:12, 14:1, 20:21, 47:20; Isa. 6:5 and 47:5. Of these, the texts from the Psalms are translated with *conpunctio* (Ps. 59[60]:5) or *conpungere* (Ps. 4:4, 29[30]:12, 34[35]:15), and additionally Jud. 16:14 translating κατακεντεῖν, "to prick or goad." The Vetus Latina includes two more uses of *conpungere*, Zech. 12:10 (for ὀδυνᾶιν, "to cause pain") and John 19:37 (for ἐκκεντεῖν, "to pierce").

127. Harl, "Les origines grecques du mot et de la notion de componction dans la Septante et chez ses commentateurs," 19.

128. Gk: κατενυγήσαν τὴν καρδίαν; Lat.: *conpuncti sunt corde*.

129. See Pegon, "Componction," 1313, and Harl, "Les origines grecques du mot et de la notion de componction dans la Septante et chez ses commentateurs," *passim*.

130. The text Origen and other early Christian commentators knew differed slightly from that in Rahlfs' edition of LXX. Origen knew the text ὀργίζεσθε καὶ μὴ ἁμαρτάνετε· ἃ λέγετε ἐν ταῖς καρδίαις ὑμῶν, ἐπὶ ταῖς κοίταις ὑμῶν κατανύγητε. Rahlfs has: ὀργίζεσθε καὶ μὴ ἁμαρτάνετε· λέγετε ἐν ταῖς καρδίαις ὑμῶν καὶ ἐπὶ ταῖς κοίταις ὑμῶν κατανύγητε. The relative pronoun beginning the second clause of Origen's text was the opening for his interpretation. See Harl's observations in "Les origines grecques du mot et de la notion de componction dans la Septante et chez ses commentateurs," 11–13.

131. Origen's commentary on Ps. 4:5 can be found in *Comm. in Ps.*, PG 12.1144B–45B. For οἱ πενθοῦντες, see Isa. 61:1 and Sir. 48:24.

132. *De compunctione*, actually two treatises with distinct addressees preserved together. Chrysostom's treatises do not contain anything like Cassian's teaching on ecstatic compunction.

133. See Pegon, "Componction," 1314. Hausherr (*Penthos*, 10) suggests that in the monastic tradition πένθος (and its Latin equivalent, *luctus*) is more frequent in earlier texts like the *Apophthegmata*, while κατάνυξις (and *conpunctio*) became the more common term in later texts (in the case of *conpunctio*, because of Cassian's use of the word). Harl suggests that in nonmonastic circles *penthos* became the dominant term ("Les origines grecques du mot et de la notion de componction dans la Septante et chez ses commentateurs," 3 n. 1).

134. Besides the works cited in note 115, see also Colombás, *El monacato primitivo*, 2:112–15, 163–69, 341–43; McEntire, *The Doctrine of Compunction in Medieval England*, 11–34; Miquel, *Lexique du désert*, 219–32; Holze, *Erfahrung und Theologie*, 229–38.

135. *Apoph. Alph.* Poemen 50 (col. 333B).

136. *Apoph. Alph.* Macarius 34 (col. 277BC).

137. *Apoph. Anon.* Nau 592/5 (p. 217). See *Alph.* Poemen 26, 39, and 72 (cols. 328D–29A, 332B, 340BC) for other classic statements of the need to mourn and weep; note the straightforward reasoning found in *Anon.* Nau 140 (p. 49): because human beings carry malice everywhere they go, they should carry tears and compunction also.

138. *Alph.* Arsenius 41 (col. 105C). According to the next saying, his eyelashes had fallen out from weeping (Arsenius 42, col. 108A).

139. See *Apoph. Anon.* Nau 561 (p. 205), on the way that tears have become necessary despite God's original creation of human beings for joy rather than sorrow; see Nau 582 (pp. 210–11) on compunction and tears as a *goal*.

140. *Syst.* (*Gk.*): bk. 3, with fifty-six sayings (pp. 1480–82); *Syst.* (*Lat.*): bk. 3, with twenty-seven sayings (cols. 860C–64C); a section of *Anon.* is headed "On Compunction" (περὶ κατανύξεως), starting with Nau 519 (p. 190).

141. *Apoph. Pasch. (br.)* 38.1 (col. 1055CD), quoting Antony.

142. *Monachus . . . non doctoris habet, sed plangentis officium, Contra Vig.* 15 (PL 23.367A), quoted by Gómez, "Compunctio lacrymarum," 247.

143. See *Apoph. Anon.* Nau 592/35 (p. 223) on compunction as a gift that can be taken away if gloried in; Nau 592/42 (p. 225) on the gift of compunction as a possible sign of one's approaching death; Nau 592/63 (p. 230) compunction as God's gift compensating for the renunciation of material things. Nau 521 (pp. 191–92) refers to two brothers at Nitria who had the "gift of compunction and tears." On the adventitious nature of tears, see *Anon.* Nau 142 (p. 49) on a tormented brother unable to cry, who was reminded that Israel had to wait forty years to enter the promised land; Nau 537 (pp. 197–98) compares the fickleness of tears to rain, in that both must be used whenever they happen to fall; Nau 540 (p. 199) speaks of tears "coming from on high" to purify body and soul. An ascetical text probably of the fourth century contains the first extant reference to the "gift of tears" (Pseudo-Athanasius, *De virg.*, col. 272C). The text was wrongly attributed to Athanasius; its geographical provenance is uncertain. See Brakke, "The Authenticity of the Ascetic Athanasiana," 44–47.

144. Thus *Apoph. Anon.* Nau 548 (pp. 200–201), advises one to force tears by any means that work, and having done so, then to turn one's thoughts in an appropriate direction; Nau 592/1–2 (pp. 215–17) comments on the value of forcing tears; two sayings from the Sinai MS 448, also found in Hyperechios' *Paraenesis*, refer to "pressing the heart" to make tears flow during vigils (J 666 [Regnault, *SPD*, p. 41, no. 17], Hyperechios, *Parain.* 85 [col. 1481BC]).

145. See Driscoll's very helpful "Penthos and Tears in Evagrius Ponticus," situating Evagrius' teaching on *penthos* and tears within the broader scope of his theology.

146. This comment is in a scholion on the text "[*penthos*] is the end of every human being" (Eccl. 7:2), *Schol. in Eccl.* 55 (p. 156). See Driscoll's analysis of this text in "Penthos and Tears in Evagrius Ponticus," 160–61.

147. Especially evident in *De orat.* See Driscoll, "Penthos and Tears in Evagrius Ponticus," 148–53.

148. *De orat.* 5–8 (cols. 1168D–69B). See Hausherr's remark: "les larmes et la pénitence conviennent surtout dans les débuts, comme plus tard la charité et la joie" (*Les leçons d'un contemplatif,* 19). See *Schol. in Ps.* 6:7 (ed. Pitra, p.457) and 38.13 (ed. Pitra, p. 33), and *Ad virg.* 25 (p. 148) on prayer with tears. Evagrius also notes that weeping (κλαυθμός) nourishes the soul better than anything else, and then comments, "blessed are those weeping now, for they shall laugh" (*Schol. in Ps.* 41:4 [PG 12.1416C]).

149. *Prak.* 57 (p. 634). See *De orat.* 5 (col. 1168D) on praying for the gift of tears at the outset of prayer to "soften" the soul, and on the inferior stage of *apatheia* characterized by humility, compunction (κατάνυξις), tears, and "infinite desire" (πόθος) for God; he also notes that someone tempted by pride after attaining *apatheia* should remember old faults for the sake of humility (*Prak.* 33, pp. 574–76). For more texts and analysis, see Driscoll, "Penthos and Tears in Evagrius Ponticus," *passim.*

150. See *Prak.* 90 (p. 690), *Schol. in Ps.* 125:5–6 (PG 12.1641AB); see *Sent. aliae* 14 (p. liv, no. 62). Cf. *Inst. Suppl.* 7 (p. 201), *De orat.* 5–8 (cols. 1168D–69B).

151. *Protrep.* (p. 554.27–29 [Syr.], p. 555.37–41 [Gk. retroversion]) and *Paraenet.* (p. 560.13–14 [Syr.], p. 561.18–20 [Gk. retroversion]); see Hausherr, *Penthos,* 83–84.

152. On accidie, see *Prak.* 27 (p. 562.1–3), *Ad virg.* 39 (p. 149), *Ad mon.* 56 (p. 55), *Inst.* (col. 1236A), *Antirr.* 6.10 (p. 522.32–35 [Syr.], p. 523.26–29 [Gk. retroversion]), and 6.19 (p. 524.20–22 [Syr.], p. 525.24–25 [Gk. retroversion]); on pride, see *Antirr.* 12.21 (p. 540.12–13 [Syr.], p. 541.12–14 [Gk. retroversion]); on tears as a weapon against the incursion of bad thoughts during psalmody, see *Paraenet.* (p. 560.15–16 [Syr.], p. 561.21–23 [Gk. retrover-

sion]) and *De mal. cog.* 34 (no. 67 of Migne's ed. of *Prak.* in *PG* 40.1241B). See also Driscoll, "Penthos and Tears in Evagrius Ponticus," 154–59.

153. *De orat.* 8 (col. 1169B).

154. *Coll. II* 15.26 (p. 143.366–67) and 15.36 (p. 149.516–17). See *Coll. III* 6.3.3 (p. 110. 36–39) and 6.4.2 (p. 112.20–114.23) on continual weeping.

155. *Coll. II* 27.16 (p. 226.226–28); the "wise ascetic" described here later fell from grace through vainglory.

156. *Coll. II* 27.20 (p. 229.293–97).

157. *Coll. I* 8.1.4 (vol. 1, p. 119.9–11); *Coll. II* 11.14 (p. 105.219–21), 16.2 (p. 159.22–24), 16.11 (p. 164.153–59); *Coll. III* 10.3.3 (p. 160.24–25).

158. *Coll. I* 5.2.3 (vol. 1, p. 76.10–12).

159. *Coll. I* 7.18.8 (vol. 1, p. 116.14–16) and 7.18.5 (p. 115.13–18).

160. *Coll. I* 63.1.4 (vol. 2, p. 207.18–20).

161. *Coll. I* 63.1.6 (vol. 2, p. 208.21–25) and 63.4.5 (p. 215.14–19).

162. See Pegon, "Componction," 1314–15; Régamey, "La componction du coeur," pt. 1, pp. 9–11.

163. See especially *Inst.* 4.43, 5.14.1–2, 8.9, 12.15.1, 12.27.5; *Conf.* 1.17.2, 10.10.11, 10.11.4, 19.14.5, 20.6.1, 21.30.2; see the other instances of *conpunctio* cited earlier with reference to specific situations.

164. See, for example, his analyses on the origins of thoughts (*Conf.* 1.19), the different moods experienced by a monk (*Conf.* 4.2–3), the various "qualities" of prayer (*Conf.* 9.8).

165. Note Lot-Borodine's observation: "Ce qui l'intéresse, ce n'est pas l'évolution ou genèse spirituelle du charisme qui nous frappe, nous, c'est son caractère d'imprévisibilité . . . sa nature fulgurante de *Spiritus flat ubi vult*" ("Le mystère du 'don des larmes' dans l'Orient chrétien," 82). The same is true of *Conf.* 4.2–5, where the point is precisely the sovereignty of the Holy Spirit.

166. Illustrated previously in *Conf.* 1.23.1, 3.2.2, 3.22.4, and later in *Conf.* 21.8.1. See a remark of Diadochus: ὁ πνευματικὸς λόγος τὴν νοερὰν αἴσθησιν πληροφορεῖ· ἐνεργείᾳ γὰρ ἀγάπης ἐκ τοῦ Θεοῦ φέρεται, διόπερ καὶ ἀβασάνιστος ἡμῶν νοῦς διαμένει ἐν τοῖς τῆς θεολογίας κινήμασιω (*Cap. cogn.* 7, p. 87) and *Apoph. Anon.* Nau 553 (p. 203) declaring that reading dogmatic treatises dries up compunction, while reading the lives and words of the elders illumines the soul. (Regnault [SPA, 203, also notes the addition in the *Synagoge* of Paul Euergetinos: "by filling it with spiritual tears".)

167. The phrase *saluberrima conpunctio* occurs four other times in Cassian's works, always with the usual meaning of sorrow for sins leading to conversion or amendment (*Inst.* 8.9; *Conf.* 1.19.1, 3.4.1, 6.9.4). To these can be added *salubris conpunctio* (*Conf.* 23.7.2) and *salutaris conpunctio* (*Inst.* 4.43; *Conf.* 2.17.2, 20.6.1).

168. It is difficult to know exactly what Cassian means here by *sensus*: faculties? feelings? thoughts?

169. This phrase from Rom. 8:26 is found in Cassian's descriptions of ecstatic prayer in *Conf.* 9.15.2, 9.27, 10.11.6.

170. He describes this feeling as "unbearable joy" (*intolerabile gaudium*) that bursts out in "shouts" (*clamores*). He rarely uses the word *intolerabilis* in a positive way; usually it means "unbearable" in the dire sense. The two parallels would be the "unbearable zeal" forcing the psalmist to speak out (*Conf.* 7.31.2) and the "unbearable, burning fervor of spirit" giving rise to silent but fiery prayer (*Inst.* 2.10.1).

171. See *Conf.* 4.5: *abundantia spiritalium cogitationum*.

172. See *Conf.* 9.4 on the lightness of the soul and its prayers.

173. These fruits are human rather than divine: see *Cap. gnost.* 34 (p. 104.4–13) and 74 (p. 133.9–11) on "natural love" compared with "spiritual love."

174. Earlier he refers to an "initial joy" that is "not without share in imagination"; between this initial joy and "consummate" joy there is a passage through "God-loving sorrow and tears without grief (*Cap. gnost.* 60 [p. 120.1–5]). For Diadochus, φαντασία is not necessarily a bad word: see *Cap. gnost.* 37 (p. 106.16–19), where the pure mind beset by a bad dream wakes up the body "in the imagination" (πεφαντασμένως) to stop the dream, and the discussion of angels in *Vis.* 27 (pp. 177.25–78.12), where it is evident that the "imagination" is a faculty of perception and self-conceptualization. Nonetheless, following Evagrius, Diadochus writes of contemplation "beyond images" (πάσης φαντασίας ἐκτός, *Cap. gnost.* 68 [p. 128.18–19]; see 59 [p. 119.8–9] and 70 [p. 130.8–10]).

175. Gk.: ὅταν ἐν εὐθηνίᾳ ᾖ ἡ ψυχὴ τῶν φυσικῶν αὐτῆς καρπῶν, μεγαλοφωνότερον καὶ τὴν ψαλμῳδίαν ποιεῖται καὶ φωνῇ μᾶλλον θέλει προσεύχεσθαι. . . . ἕπεται δὲ ἐκείνη μὲν τῇ διαθέσει χαρὰ πεφαντασμένη. . . . Πλὴν ὅτε ὑπὸ πολλῆς δυσθυμίας βαρούμεθα, δεῖ ὀλίγον μείζονι τῇ ποιεῖσθαι ἡμᾶς τὴν ψαλμῳδίαν τῇ τῆς ἐλπίδος χαρᾷ τοὺς φθόγγους τῆς ψυχῆς ἀνακρούοντας, ἄχρις οὗ τὸ νέφος ἐκεῖνο τὸ βαρὺ ὑπὸ τῶν ἀνέμων τοῦ μέλους διαλυθῇ (*Cap. gnost.* 73 [p. 132.1–4, 6–7, 13–16]).

176. In *Inst.* 2.10.1 the "ineffable sigh" is clearly silent; in *Conf.* 9.15.2 the Holy Spirit is interpolating "unutterable sighs" that are presumably silent; the "unutterable sighs" of *Conf.* 10.11.6 are soundless *(nulla vocis, nulla verborum).* Cassian's emphasis throughout *Conf.* 9 and 10 on moving beyond image and word would indicate silence.

177. Messana ("Le definizioni di προσευχή nel *De oratione* di Evagrio Pontico," 85–86) reads this text in Evagrian terms as the movement from "psalmody" (ψαλμῳδία) to "prayer" (προσευχή); note, however, that Diadochus is clothing the Evagrian framework in his characteristically vivid experiential language derived from Pseudo-Macarius.

178. Θυμηδία τις φιλήσυχος. See *Cap. gnost.* 87 (p. 147.1–3) on desolation leading to fear of God, tears of confession (ἐξομολογήσεως), and great desire for the best kind of silence (τῆς καλλίστης σιωπῆς πολλὴν ἐπιθυμίαν). See *Cap. gnost.* 9 (p. 88.17–21) on the link between knowledge of God and silence.

179. Probably to be understood in terms of Diadochus' teaching on the "remembrance of God" (μνήμη τοῦ Θεοῦ); see Des Places' introduction to *Capita Gnostica*, SC 5bis, p. 49.

180. Gk.: ὅτε δὲ ὑπὸ τοῦ ἁγίου πνεύματος ἐνεργεῖται, μετὰ πάσης ἀνέσεως καὶ ἡδύτητος ψάλλει καὶ εὔχεται ἐν μόνῃ τῇ καρδίᾳ. . . . ταύτῃ δὲ πνευματικὸν δάκρυον καὶ μετὰ ταῦτα θυμηδία τις φιλήσυχος· θερμὴ γὰρ ἡ μνήμη διὰ τὴν τῆς φωνῆς μένουσα συμμετρίαν δακρυώδεις τινὰς καὶ ἠπίους ἐννοίας τὴν καρδίαν πάντως παρασκευάζει φέρειν. ὅθεν ὄντως ἔστιν ἰδεῖν τὰ σπέρματα τῆς εὐχῆς μετὰ δακρύων ἐν τῇ γῇ τῆς καρδίας διὰ τὴν ἐλπίδα τῆς τοῦ θερισμοῦ ἐνσπειρόμενα χαρᾶς (*Cap. gnost.* 73 [p. 132.4–6, 7–12]). On silence and illumination by the Holy Spirit, see *Cap. gnost.* 8 (pp. 87.18–88.5): οὔτε ἀφώτιστον ὄντα δεῖ ἐπιβάλλειν τοῖς πνευματικοῖς θεωρήμασιν, οὔτε μὴν πλουσίως καταλαμπόμενον ὑπὸ τῆς χρηστότητος τοῦ ἁγίου πνεύματος ἐπὶ τὸ λέγειν ἔρχεσθαι. ὅπου μὲν γὰρ πενία, φέρει τὴν ἄγνοιαν· ὅπου δὲ πλοῦτος, οὐ συγχωρεῖ τὸ λέγειν. μεθύουσα γὰρ τότε ἡ ψυχὴ τῇ ἀγάπῃ τοῦ θεοῦ σιγώσῃ φωνῇ θέλει κατατρυφᾶν τῆς δόξης τοῦ κυρίου (*Cap. gnost.* 8, pp. 87–88).

181. See Adnès, "Larmes," 295.

182. *Frequenter enim recordatione delictorum meorum obortis lacrimis ita sum hoc ineffabili ut praefatus es gaudio visitante domino vegetatus (Conf.* 9.28.1). *Visitatio* or the verb *visitare* is used several other times for the presence or intervention of grace, healing, and so on; see *Inst.* 12.16 and 18; *Conf.* 1.13.5 (quoting Isa. 60:17–20), 1.19.1, 3.19.4, 4.4.1, 4.4.2, 4.5, 6.11.6, 10.10.12, 13.15.2. For similar schemata, see Lot-Borodine, "Le mystère du 'don des larmes' dans l'Orient chrétien," 77–82 and 104–9.

183. Elsewhere Cassian links tears to: significant moments of decision such as joining

a monastery or asking a monastic elder for spiritual help (*Inst.* 4.36.2; *Conf.* 1.1, 1.23.2, 15.4, 20.1.3, 24.1.4); prayers of various kinds, either for particular intentions (*Conf.* 2.13.7; cf. 18.15.5) or for deliverance from the passions (*Inst.* 5.14.2; *Conf.* 7.2.2).

184. For other examples of tears of sorrow, see *Conf.* 2.11.3, 7.3.2, 9.27, 16.17, 17.25.10 (quoting 4 Kgs. 20.3), 18.16.7, 20.6.1, 20.7.1, 20.7.3 (quoting Ps. 41[42]:4 and Jer. 31:16), 20.8.2, 22.13.5, 23.10.

185. See *Conf.* 20.8.11, on the shift from tears for old sins to weeping with *spes futurorum . . . gaudiorum . . . ex aeternae illius laetitiae alacritate.*

186. See *Inst.* 10.12; *Conf.* 9.8.3, 9.15.3, 9.19. For fear of judgment combined with desire for the kingdom, reward, and so on, see *Inst.* 6.4.2; *Conf.* 4.2, 7.5.5, 11.6.1, 11.7.4, 11.8.1. *Conf.* 11.6 distinguishes between fear of hell and desire for the kingdom of heaven.

187. See Evagrius, *De orat.* 39 (col. 1176B) and *Cap. cogn.* 19 (p. 53); Palladius, *Hist. Laus.* 71.4 (p. 168.10–11).

188. *Mor. in Iob.* 23.41 (p. 1175).

189. *Mor. in Iob.* 24.10 (pp. 1194–95).

190. Régamey, "La componction du coeur," pt. 2, p. 67.

191. See Gillet, "Doctrine spirituelle," introduction to *Grégoire le Grand*, SC 32bis, p. 78. Gillet's discussion on compunction in *Mor. in Iob* is quite helpful; see pp. 72–79.

192. "La componction du coeur," pt. 2, p. 75.

193. Although Gillet cites Cassian as a source for Gregory's ascetical teaching (notably the eight principal faults), he does not mention the affinities between the two on compunction; introduction to *Grégoire le Grand*, SC 32bis, pp. 89–102. Régamey notes that Cassian's texts "exposent, quant à l'essentiel, la doctrine que reprendra saint Grégoire" ("La componction du coeur," pt. 1, p. 12); Straw (*Gregory the Great*, 23 n.) and Petersen (*The Dialogues of Gregory the Great*, 160–165) credit Cassian as the main influence on Gregory's doctrine of compunction. McGinn notes Cassian's role but suggests that Fulgentius of Ruspe was perhaps a more significant influence (*The Growth of Mysticism*, p. 48 n. 11).

194. See *Conf.* 1.20.3 and *Conf.* 2, *passim*.

195. Note the link with the literal meaning of *conpunctio*. The image of thorns is used only in *Conf.* 9 and 20 (*Conf.* 9.29.1, 9.33, 20.7.2). He also writes about brambles growing in the heart and weeded out by ascetical labor (*Conf.* 3.10.5, 4.3, 23.11.3, 23.13.1, 23.15.7), and of thorns being consumed in a fire (*Conf.* 21.33.3). In *Conf.* 9.29.1, Cassian quotes Ps. 6:7, used again in *Conf.* 20.6.

196. See Diadochus, *Cap. gnost.* 27 (p. 98.20–21) on the way that one sees one's sins more clearly as one advances in purity and 100 (p. 162.4–5) on the assurance of pardon of sins given ἐν δακρύῳ ἀγάπης.

197. Diadochus ends *Cap. gnost.* with a caution very much like that of *Conf.* 23 about not presuming sinlessness; he notes that human beings cannot avoid human failings (οὐ γὰρ ἔστιν ἄνθρωπον ὄντα μὴ πταίειν ἀνθρώπινα), and thus even the advanced must confess their sins and await the tears of love that signify pardon (*Cap. gnost.* 100, p. 162.3–5).

198. *Cap. gnost.* 27 (p. 98.20–21) and 87 (p. 146.23–147.3); see 73 (p. 132.10–12) on prayer sown with tears producing a harvest of joy.

199. *Cap. gnost.* 37 (p. 106.20–22) and 60 (p. 120.4–5); see 100 (p. 162.4–5) on the "tears of love" that signify assurance (πληροφορία) of pardon after confession.

200. *Cap. gnost.* 73 (p. 132.7–8).

201. *Cap. gnost.* 68 (p. 127.18–20) and 73 (p. 132.8–10).

Appendix

1. Each of these is at the start of a new section of the writings: *Inst.* 5 begins the treatise on the eight principal faults; *Conf.* 11 is the first of the second installment of *Conferences* and *Conf.* 18 the first of the third installment.

2. *Alph.* Chaeremon (col. 436C); *Hist. Laus.* 47.4 (p. 137.11–14), about Chaeremon's dying while seated at work. Butler identifies Palladius' Chaeremon with Cassian's (*Lausiac History,* 2.225 n. 90). Regnault suggests that all these texts refer to the same person, who lived in Scetis and then moved to the Delta (Regnault, *SPAlph.,* 322); Sauget assumes the same ("Cheremone," 1186). One must always keep in mind the mobility of the early monks: for various reasons of their own or because of external circumstances, it was quite common for Egyptian monks to live in several locales over the course of their monastic careers.

3. This set has five sayings (cols. 305C–8C); Regnault suggests that the last of these must belong to some other Nisteros, as it refers to Arsenius in the past tense (*SPAlph.,* 209). It is possible, however, that the story is about the fourth-century Arsenius of Scetis rather than Arsenius the Great, who lived in the following century; see Guy's *Les Apophtegmes des Pères,* 1:54–55. *Alph. Suppl.* contains a saying about a Nisteros who lived at Raïthou in the Sinai (p. 27).

4. This set has two sayings (cols. 308D–9A). These sayings mention Poemen, and one of the stories about Poemen and Anoub (*Alph.* Poemen 131, col. 356A) refers to Nisteros. However, Cassian's Nisteros is not a cenobite.

5. *Alph.* Nisteros 2 (cols. 305D–8A). The Ethiopian collection contains two sayings of a Nisteros who was a disciple of Abba Paul; if this was Paul the Simple, Antony's disciple, then a relationship with Antony would have been possible (*Eth.* 13.25 and 13.74, pp. 293 and 306). The second saying is about interior tranquillity; see *Conf.* 14.10–14 and 15.10.

6. *Alph.* Nisteros 3 (col. 308AB).

7. *Alph.* Nisteros 2 (col. 305D–8A), as in Weber, *Die Stellung des Johannes Cassianus,* 110–11. The saying is in the Latin version at *Syst. (Lat.)* 1.11 (col. 856BC).

8. *Alph.* Joseph of Panephysis 2 and 3 (cols. 228C–29A); similarly, his encounters with Abba Lot, Joseph of Panephysis 6 and 7 (cols. 229CD). Among the sayings of Poemen are several that mention an Abba Joseph, who seems to be a disciple: *Alph.* Poemen 21 (col. 328A), 31 (col. 329C), 61 (col. 336D), 112 (col. 349C–52A), 144 (col. 357B). This could be another "Joseph," for the name is (not surprisingly) frequent in the *Apophthegmata:* see *Alph.* Antony 17 (col. 80D), Agathon 25 (col. 116BC), Theodore of Pherme 19 (col. 192B), Nisteros 3 (col. 308AB), Sisoes 22 (col. 400C); *Anon.* Nau 412 (and perhaps also 413, p. 138); *Syr.* Bu II.256 (Syr.: pp. 792–98 [no. 253]; Eng.: pp. 206–10); *Eth.* Coll. 13.83 (p. 309). On the various Josephs, see Sauget, "Giuseppe." There is also a story about Eulogius, follower of John Chrysostom, who visited Joseph (*Alph.* Eulogius the Priest, cols. 169C–72A).

9. Note that Gibson's translation (p. 371) is misleading: the reference to Calamus applies to Abba Moses only.

10. Amélineau is misleading here, scrambling the references somewhat (*La géographie de l'Égypte,* 147).

11. For a brief assessment of the evidence, see Albers, "Eine patristische Frage."

12. See, for example, the stories about Ammonius in *Hist. mon.* 20.9 (p. 121), and *Hist. mon. (Ruf.)* 23.3.6–7 (p. 361). I thank Adalbert de Vogüé for these suggestions.

13. Not to be confused with the anchorite Paul of Panephysis, of whom a story is told in *Conf.* 7.26.2–4.

14. *Post dies admodum paucos maioris doctrinae desiderio pertrahente rursus ad abbatis Pauli coenobium . . . perreximus* (*Conf.* 19.1.1). See Cappuyns, "Cassien," 1323; Guy, "Jean Cassien, historien du monachisme égyptien?" 367; Chitty, *The Desert a City*, 62 n. 48.

15. See also the discussion in the next section on the possibility that the Theonas of *Conf.* 21–23 was a monk of Scetis.

16. John is mentioned, along with Piamun, as a famous monk of Diolcos. See *Hist. mon.* 25 on Piamun and 26 on John (pp. 135–36); picked up by Sozomen, *Hist. eccl.* 6.29.7–8 (pp. 279.23–280.5). Gazet, seventeenth-century editor and commentator on Cassian's works, made this suggestion (*Commentarius, PL* 50.1126C–28C). Cassian's Abba Piamun is an anchorite; in fact Cassian describes him as his first teacher on the solitary life (*Conf.* 18.16.15). *Hist. mon.* 25–26 identifies Piamun as an anchorite and John as "father of monasteries"; Sozomen describes both John and Piamun as presiding over "monasteries." The words μοναστήριον or *monasterium* could describe both a hermitage and a cenobium.

17. Presuming Cassian's arrival to have been ca. 385 and the visit described in the *Hist. mon.* to have been in 394.

18. The deathbed stories also appear in *Alph.* Cassian 4–5 (cols. 244C-45A); *Inst.* 5.27 appears in *Syst.* (*Gk.*) 4.26 (pp. 1.196–98) with Paesius' name changed to Arsenius; *Inst.* 5.28 is in *Syst.* (*Lat.*) 1.10 (col. 856AB). The question of possible sources and parallels for this material is complex. Sulpitius, *Dial.* 1.12.1 (p. 163), has a version of the first story (*Inst.* 5.27) set in the Thebaid. He does not give the name of the two monks, and he describes them as having lived together in the monastery for forty years. Bousset thought both Cassian and Sulpitius had a written source for this story (*Apophthegmata*, 75 n.3), against Butler who saw it as an oral tradition heard by both Cassian and Postumian in Egypt (*Lausiac History*, 1:212–13).

As for the second story, *Inst.* 5.28, Rousseau considers it to be an oral tradition Cassian cites from memory, though Rousseau identifies the subject as John of Lycopolis (*Ascetics, Authority, and the Church*, 255). Rousseau's earlier reference to "John the Coenobite" is more likely (*Ascetics and Authority*, 24). Cassian knew of John of Lycopolis (see *Inst.* 4.23–27, *Conf.* 1.21 and *Conf.* 24.26.16–17); no extant tradition about him includes this story, even though his death is mentioned in *Hist. mon.* 1.65 (p. 35). If Cassian is correct in linking the Abba John of *Inst.* 5.27 to the story in *Inst.* 5.28, the description of him as superior of a large cenobium certainly excludes John of Lycopolis, who lived in reclusion (see *Hist. mon.* 1 and Palladius, *Hist. Laus.* 35).

19. I suggest in the next section that John the cenobite of *Conf.* 14.4.2 is not the same as the Abba John of *Conf.* 14.7, a monk of Scetis.

20. See Gazet's notes in *Commentarius, PL* 50.957CD and 1127C.

21. Compare *Conf.* 24.2.3, 24.10.1 and 24.12.4 with *Inst.* 5.36 on Diolcos and *Conf.* 7.26.2 and 11.3 on Panephysis: the description echoes that of Diolcos in the emphasis on hauling water a great distance from river to monastery. In any case it is clearly about a site in the Delta region.

22. Gazet thinks that the Abraham of *Conf.* 15.4–5 is the same as that of *Conf.* 24 (*Commentarius, PL* 50.1279–81), while Brandi is more cautious ("Abramo il Semplice"). I would be more definite that they are not the same person.

23. Daniel is not known from any other source. His early death suggests that he cannot be Daniel the Pharanite, who appears in *Apoph. Alph.* as someone who left Scetis in 407–8 because of the devastating raids by marauders (see *Alph.* Daniel 1, col. 153B).

24. See *Conf.* 2.11, on Sarapion's manifestation of conscience to Abba Theonas; *Conf.* 5.1 on Sarapion's discernment; *Conf.* 18.11 on his insights on true humility. This last story appears as *Apoph. Alph.* Serapion 4 (cols. 416D–17A; in *Alph.* the name is spelled with a

Greek ε, though Butler notes that the proper spelling is with α, *Lausiac History*, 2:213). The story certainly matches the characterization of Sarapion as *gratia discretionis ornatus* (*Conf.* 5.1), though Guy notes that in four manuscripts the saying is attributed to Sarapion of Thmuis (*Recherches sur la tradition grecque des Apophthegmata Patrum*, 34). Guy is unsure whether or not to identify Cassian's Sarapion with the old man of *Conf.* 10.3 ("Cassian, Saint John," 462; *Les Apophtegmes des Pères*, 1:71); the sympathetic portrayal of Sarapion in *Conf.* 2, 5, and 18 suggests not (Guillaumont, "Sarapion," 2094–95). Palladius mentions a Sarapion of Nitria (*Hist. Laus.* 7 and 46, pp. 25.12 and 134.12–13); Sozomen has a Serapion of Scetis in *Hist. eccl.* 6.30.1 (p. 284.14), probably the same monk mentioned earlier in *Hist. eccl.* 3.14.4 (p. 118.23). Palladius' Sarapion and Sozomen's Serapion are probably the same person; Guillaumont doubts they are Cassian's Sarapion of *Conf.* 5 ("Sarapion," 2094), though I would not press the distinction between Nitria and Scetis too much. See Butler's notes on the various Sarapions in *Lausiac History*, 2:213–15.

25. *Apoph. Alph.* Serenus 1 (col. 417B). Serenus is also mentioned in *Syst. (Gk.)* 10.73, preserved in Evergetinos, *Synagoge* 4.38.3 (Regnault, SPN, 196), where he goes with his disciple Isaac to see Poemen. See the discussion immediately following on chronological issues about Cassian's Isaac of Scetis.

26. *Ep. Ammon* 35 (p. 157), noted by Evelyn-White, *Monasteries of the Wâdi 'n Natrûn*, 2:95. Goehring, however, thinks that Ammon's Isaac is Isaac of the Cells (p. 294).

27. *Syst. (Gk.)* 10.73 (PE 4.38.3 as in Regnault, SPN, 196).

28. *Alph.* Poemen 107, 141, 144, 184 (cols. 348C, 357A, 357C, 368A).

29. Chitty and Guy distinguish the Poemen at Pispir in the later part of the fourth century from the one who left Scetis after the devastation of 407–8 and lived until after the death of Arsenius (ca. 449). According to this suggestion, Poemen of Pispir is the one mentioned in *Apoph. Alph.* Antony 4 (col. 77A), Amoun 2 (col. 128CD), and Macarius the Egyptian 25 (col. 272D). The vast number of other sayings attributed to Poemen in *Alph.* and elsewhere would belong to the later Poemen and, perhaps, to others as well (see Chitty, *The Desert a City*, 69–71; Regnault, *SPAlph.*, 220; Guy, *Les Apophtegmes des Pères*, 1:48 and 77–79). On this basis, one could then associate the saying from *Syst. (Gk.)* with Poemen of Pispir and with Cassian's Serenus and Isaac, and the sayings from *Alph.* with the later Poemen and another Isaac. More recently, however, Regnault has questioned Chitty's hypothesis and claimed a single Poemen whose chronological ambiguities remain unresolved ("Poemen, Saint," 1983). For a more skeptical perspective, see Frank, "Abbas Poimen."

30. Palladius, *Dial.* 17 (p. 340, ll. 101–7), suggested by Evelyn-White (*Monasteries of the Wâdi 'n Natrûn*, 2:172 n.1); Regnault thinks Palladius' Isaac was Isaac of Kellia (see note 33).

31. Gk.: κεράστας ὄφεις, *Dial.* 17 (p. 340, l. 104).

32. Latin: *virulentorum serpentium exterminator.* Behind Palladius' description is probably Mk. 16:18 on the believer's ability to handle snakes; Cassian's is closer to Lk. 10:19, where Jesus gives the Seventy authority to tread on snakes and scorpions (are these Cassian's "horned snakes"?).

33. Twelve sayings in *Alph.* (cols. 224B–28A). Regnault has suggested that Palladius' Isaac is Isaac of Kellia and distinct from Isaac of Scetis ("Isaac, Saint," 1304), though earlier Regnault had been less definite (*SPAlph.*, 139).

34. Petschenig suggested Panephysis (CSEL 17, pp. 421 and 434); Marrou suggested Diolcos ("L'origine orientale des diaconies romaines," *Mélanges Archéologiques* 57 [1940]: 95–142, here at p. 134, as in Sternberg, "Der vermeintliche Ursprung der westlichen Diakonien in Ägypten," 175). Cappuyns situates *Conf.* 21–23 at Scetis, while noting the common

assumption that all in the last set belong to monks of the Delta; unfortunately he does not provide evidence for his own decision ("Cassien," 1323). He wrongly suggests that *Conf.* 24 belongs at Scetis or Nitria/Cells.

35. It is difficult to know if Cassian uses "Aegyptus" here narrowly to mean the Delta region (as opposed to the desert or the Thebaid) or more broadly; we have no evidence that in fact he did reach the Thebaid. See *Conf.* 10.2.3 for an example of "monasteries of Egypt" versus "those dwelling in Scetis."

36. See the preceding discussion.

37. *Tamen fama Scitioticae solitudinis invitatos . . . [Pinufius nos] emisit (Conf.* 20.12.4).

38. See *Conf.* 18.10 for definitions of these two words. For *monasterium* applied to anchorites, see, for example, *Conf.* 1.20.5, 2.7.1, 2.13.6 (about Apollo), 3.1.2 (Paphnutius), 3.5.2 (Moses), 4.20.4, 4.21.1, 5.11.2, 6.1.3, 8.18.2 (Antony). In the set of *Conf.* 18–24, *coenobium* occurs twenty-three times in *Conf.* 18, twenty-five times in *Conf.* 19, four times in *Conf.* 20, twice in *Conf.* 24. Similarly, the phrase *cunctorum seniorum coetus*, used in *Conf.* 21.1.2, occurs elsewhere only with reference to anchorites (*Conf.* 4.20.1, 5.1, 11.2.1, 19.14.3). Leroy assumed Theonas was a cenobite, perhaps because of the term *monasterium* ("Les préfaces des écrits monastiques de Jean Cassien," 174).

39. *Conf.* 21.14.2: *solitudinis remotio; Conf.* 23.5.8: *solitudinis secreta.*

40. Guy in *Les Apophtegmes des Pères*, 1:63, does not commit himself on the question of whether Theonas of *Conf.* 2 and *Conf.* 21–23 could be the same.

41. See *Alph.* Theodore of Pherme 18 (col. 192AB) and Poemen 151 (col. 360AB), both quoting Theonas. Regnault notes that the one saying under the name of Theonas has affinities with the teaching of *Conf.* 23, though Regnault assumes that this Theonas was a monk at Panephysis (*SPAlph.*, 116). A story attributed to Theonas in the manuscript Sinai 448 is about Abba Marcellus, who ended up in Nitria (Regnault, *SPT*, 46–47). The Theonas described in *Hist. mon.* 6 (pp. 43–45), a solitary near Oxyrhynchus, is clearly another person altogether.

42. *Cunctorum seniorum coetus, Conf.* 21.1.2. On the meaning of *diaconia* in this context, see Sternberg, "Der vermeintliche Ursprung der westlichen Diakonien in Ägypten," 185–90. I owe this reference to Ramsey's *John Cassian. The Conferences*, 658–59.

43. *Decimas vel primitias frugum suarum*, perhaps indicating a harvest-time act of piety (*Conf.* 21.1.3). See Sternberg, "Der vermeintliche Ursprung der westlichen Diakonien in Ägypten," 176–85.

44. The story is similar to one told by John of Thmuis in *Conf.* 14.7, though in that story the donor of firstfruits is unnamed, has been living chastely with his wife, and evidently does not become a monk. There are similarities with *Alph.* Eucharistos (cols. 168D–69C), though Cassian's version seems earlier (cf. Weber, *Die Stellung des Johannes Cassianus zur ausserpachomianischen Mönchstradition*, 35–38). The differences between the stories suggest that the one in *Conf.* 21 was not a reworking of the one in *Conf.* 14.

45. John is described in *Inst.* 5.40.1 in this way: *qui dispensationem ipsius ecclesiae temporibus beati Pafnutii presbyteri ab eodem sibi creditam gubernabat.* Guy vacillates on this point; first he identifies the John of *Inst.* 5.40 with the one of *Conf.* 21.1 and then suggests that the John of *Conf.* 21 might be John of Thmuis ("Cassian, Saint John," 462b). Sternberg concludes that the John of *Inst.* 5.40 is the same as the one in *Conf.* 21 and places Theonas among the monks of Scetis ("Der vermeintliche Ursprung der westlichen Diakonien in Ägypten," 175–76).

46. Greek: ὁ ἀββᾶς Ἡλίας τῆς διακονίας, *Alph.* Elias 3 (col. 184B). Guy distinguishes him from the Elias of the previous saying (*Alph.* Elias 2, col. 184AB), who had been at Scetis but then went to "Egypt," perhaps after the devastation of Scetis in 407–8.

Guy thinks that *Alph.* Elias 3 is about Cassian's Elias (*Les Apophtegmes des Pères*, 1:65–66).

47. See the commentary by A. and C. Guillaumont on Evagrius' *Prak.* 29 (SC 171, pp. 566–69); they note that Cassian actually names Macarius, whereas Evagrius refers to "our master" (ἡμῶν διδάσκαλος). Either Cassian supplied the name from what he knew of Evagrius' relationship with Macarius or he had another source. On Macarius and Evagrius, see Bunge, "Évagre le Pontique et les deux Macaire," especially 333–47.

48. Palladius, *Hist.Laus.* 17.11 (p. 46.17–19) and *Hist. mon.* (*Ruf.*) 28.4 (pp. 367–68); Weber notes the clearer parallel with the P manuscript of Palladius as published by Preuschen, *Palladius und Rufinus*, 124–30; Weber does not establish the priority of Cassian over Palladius or vice versa (Weber, *Die Stellung des Johannes Cassianus zur ausserpachomianischen Mönchstradition*, 93–96).

49. *Conf.* 5.12.3, a saying about fasting and vainglory; *Conf.* 7.27, the story about Moses' surliness with Macarius; *Conf.* 24.13, a morality tale about a barber's freedom from care about material things.

50. The first is found in both Latin and Greek collections. Weber thinks *Syst.* (*Lat.*) 5.4 (cols. 874B–75C) is the original text, though perhaps not in its present state (Weber, *Die Stellung des Johannes Cassianus zur ausserpachomianischen Mönchstradition*, 32–35); the Greek in *Syst.* (*Gk.*) 5.4 (p. 1:242) begins Εἶπεν ἀββᾶ Κασιανός even though it is far closer to its parallel in *Syst.* (*Lat.*) than to Cassian's text!

51. No. 7 in the appendix to *Apoph. V. Patr.* published in PL 74.379 as a supplement to Palladius' *Hist. Laus.*; Weber does not find any basis for establishing the priority of one version over the other (*Die Stellung des Johannes Cassianus zur ausserpachomianischen Mönchstradition*, 98–99).

52. See *Alph.* Apollo 2 (cols. 133C–36B) on his horrifying background. Guy identifies him as Cassian's Apollo (*Les Apophtegmes des Pères*, 1:64–65).

53. Palladius, *Hist. Laus.* 26 (pp. 81.1–82.18). Heron is mentioned again in Ch. 47.4 (p. 137.18). Butler found the inconsistencies between Cassian's and Palladius' stories sufficient to make it doubtful that they were about the same person (*Lausiac History*, 2:202), while Weber sees the two versions as somehow related (*Die Stellung des Johannes Cassianus zur ausserpachomianischen Mönchstradition*, 89–90), a plausible conclusion for a story that serves as an object lesson. Guy mentions the two versions (*Les Apophtegmes des Pères*, 1:56–57) without drawing a conclusion.

54. Isidore has nine sayings in *Apoph. Alph.* (cols. 220B–21C). On him, see Sauget, "Isidoro," and Guy, *Les Apophtegmes des Pères*, 1:57–59.

55. Bousset suggests that a story preserved by Evergetinos (*Apoph. P. E.* 2.46.6) is the source for Cassian's version (*Apophthegmata*, 73) but Weber thinks that the stories are too different for one to be the source for the other (*Die Stellung des Johannes Cassianus zur ausserpachomianischen Mönchstradition*, 87–88). Evergetinos labels the story as from the *Gerontikon*, and it is only since Guy's recovery of *Syst.* (*Gk.*) that it can be identified as *Syst.* (*Gk.*) 16.29 (Regnault, *SPN*, 180–81). Guy links the Greek text to Cassian's story without specifying their relationship (*Recherches sur la tradition grecque des Apophthegmata Patrum*, 171).

56. See Guy, *Les Apophtegmes des Pères*, 1:52–53.

57. The story appears in *Apoph. Alph.* as Cassian 4 (cols. 244C–45A) and in *Syst.* (*Gk.*) 4.26 (pp. 196–98), where Paesius' name is changed to Arsenius. Guy notes that Cassian's version "a plus de chance d'être exact" (*Les Apophtegmes des Pères*, 1:197 n.1). The same story is used by Sulpitius, *Dial.* 1.12.1 (p. 163), though he places it in a cenobium.

58. See Guy's remarks in "Le centre monastique de Scété," 139–40; the word πανέ-

ρημος is used in monastic literature to describe the great desert embracing both Scetis and Nitria/Cells; see Lampe's *A Patristic Greek Lexicon*, 1002a.

59. *Conf.* 3.5.2, 7.26.

60. *Inst.* 10.24–25. He is not the same as the Paul of Panephysis described in *Conf.* 7.26.2 along with Moses of Calamus. It is conceivable that the Paul of *Inst.* 10.24–25 is the Paul of Pherme of the *Apoph.* and *Hist. Laus.*, though this attribution is problematic: Palladius describes Paul as living at Pherme, on the edge of Scetis, devoting himself to unceasing prayer to the exclusion of any work (*Hist. Laus.* 20, p. 62). The point of Cassian's story about Paul in *Inst.* 10.24 is that he so prized the ascetical value of manual labor that he worked even when he did not need to.

61. Guy, "Jean Cassien, historien du monachisme égyptien?" 370–71 and *Les Apophtegmes des Pères*, 1:68, followed by Sauget, "Mosè," 652.

62. See Devos, "Saint Jean Cassien et Saint Moïse l'Éthiopien."

63. *Conf.* 3.5.2: *in loco istius heremi qui Calamus nuncupatur.*

64. *Conf.* 7.26.2: *locus huius solitudinis qui Calamus nuncupatur.*

65. Gibson's translation (p. 371) misconstrues the Latin to suggest that both Paul of Panephysis and Moses lived in Calamus; if one compounded such an error by thinking that Paul of Panephysis (*Conf.* 7.26) and Paul of the Porphyrion desert (*Inst.* 10.24–25) were the same person, then Guy's conclusion would make sense, for Moses would seem to be placed by Cassian in the Porphyrion desert.

66. Liddell and Scott, *A Greek-English Lexicon*, 865b–66a; Sophocles, *Greek Lexicon of the Roman and Byzantine Periods*, 621a.

67. In Egypt there were: (1) the monastic site in the Thebaid associated with Abba Sisoes ("Calamon of Arsinöe," *Alph.* Sisoes 32–33 [cols. 401D–4A], 48 [col. 405C]) and with Samuel of Calamon (see Amélineau, *La geographie de l'Égypte*, 388–89; Maspero and Weit, *Matériaux pour servir à la géographie de l'Égypte*, 151; Alcock, "Samū'īl of Qalamūn, Saint"; (2) a village in the western oasis of Dakhlah that bears the name al-Qalamun to this day and may have had monks associated with it (Amélineau, *La géographie de l'Égypte*, 290; Coquin, "Monasteries of the Western Desert," 1658). In Palestine there was the famous semi–anchoritic *laura* of Calamon at Ain Hajla near the Jordan. Pauly's *Realencyclopädie* lists four other places in Palestine, Phoenicia, and Syria with the name "Calamos/Calamon" (3:1.1329).

68. See *Apoph. Alph.* Macarius the Egyptian 22 (col. 272B) and Moses 13 (col. 283A).

69. See Evelyn-White, *Monasteries of the Wâdi 'n Natrûn*, 2:37–38. Coquin and Martin cite the suggestion of Daumas that a site at Jabal Khashm al-Qu'ud, 30 kilometers west of Scetis, may be Cassian's "Calamus" ("Jabal Khashm al-Qu'ud," 1316). Chitty prefers to identify this site with that of Pherme, noting Toussant's discovery at Jabal Khashm al-Qu'ud of an amphora stopper featuring a cross and the name Paul, as in "Paul of Pherme" (*The Desert a City*, 68), while Regnault thinks that this is the site of the Petra of Moses, perhaps following De Cosson (noted by Coquin and Martin in "Jabal Khashm al-Qu'ud," 1316).

70. *La géographie de l'Égypte*, 444.

71. Pauly, *Realencyclopädie*, 19:1, lists eight different sites called Petra in the ancient Mediterranean world; for "Calamon," see note 67.

72. The LXX of Exod. 2:3 and 5 actually refers to τὸ ἕλος, "marshy area," while the Vulgate reads *in carecto* (v. 3) and *in papyrione* (v. 5).

73. See *Palladius, Hist. Laus.* 34.3 (p. 98.16) on Piterium of Porphyrites; *Hist. Laus.* 36.2 (p. 107.4–5), relates that Posidonius the Theban lived for a year at Porphyrites; see Palladius' *Dial.* 17, ll. 79–85, on Hierax, who withdrew to the Porphyrite mountain, stayed there four years, and then went to Nitria for twenty-five more. See also Pauly, *Realencyclo-*

pädie, 32:1.313–14; Amélineau, *La géographie de l'Égypte*, 362; Coquin, "Monasteries of the Eastern Desert."

74. However, in *Inst.* 10.24 Cassian notes that Abba Paul exhausted the employment possibilities in the Porphyrion desert!

75. Athanasius, *V. Ant.* 49.7 (p. 268.28–30).

76. He refers to the Pachomian or "Tabbennesiote" monks in *Inst.* 2.3, 2.4, 4.1, and 4.30, but with no suggestion of having visited them. In *Inst.* 4.23 he notes that Lyco (i.e., Lycopolis) is a town in the Thebaid, but again there is no claim of a visit there. Even so, Tillemont presumed that he had made it to Upper Egypt (*Mémoires pour servir à l'histoire ecclésiastique des six premiers siècles*, 14:171).

77. Four instances: (1) *Inst.* 5.4 on the image of the wise bee: see Athanasius, *V. Ant.* 3.4 (p. 136) and the discussion in Weber, *Die Stellung des Johannes Cassianus zur ausserpachomianischen Mönchstradition*, 81–82; (2) *Conf.* 3.4.2: the story of Antony's call: see *V. Ant.* 2.3 (p. 132); (3) *Conf.* 8.18–19: Antony and the philosophers; see *V. Ant.* 73 (pp. 322–24), which Weber thinks comes from the same tradition as Cassian's story (p. 98); (4) *Conf.* 24.11: the story of Antony and a monk who was financially supported by his family so that he did not need to work: see *V. Ant.* 3.6 (p. 138), which Weber suggests is a modification by Athanasius of a tradition known also to Cassian (pp. 97–98).

78. *Conf.* 2.2–4: a discourse by Antony on discernment; see *Alph.* Antony 8 (col. 77B) as noted by Weber, *Die Stellung des Johannes Cassianus zur ausserpachomianischen Mönchstradition*, 42–44, with additional material from Evagrius (Marsili, *Giovanni Cassiano ed Evagrio Pontico*, 94).

79. *Conf.* 3.3–4: on the three calls: see Antony *Ep.* 1 (Rubenson, *The Letters of St. Antony*, 85–86 n. 5). Rubenson notes that Cassian and Antony are the only early monastic writers to follow Philo and Origen in interpreting "Israel" to mean "one who sees God" (p. 169; see pp. 41 and 69).

80. See the discussion in chapter 5.

81. See *Conf.* 14.4 and *Conf.* 18.5.4 and 18.6.1, where Antony is invoked as the model for the solitary life.

82. See *Conf.* 18.5.4 and 18.6.1, where Paul and Antony are mentioned together, with Paul first. On Paul, see Guillaumont and Kuhn, "Paul of Thebes, Saint."

83. John appears three times: (1) *Inst.* 4.23–27: the story in *Inst.* 4.24 is similar to *Apoph. Alph.* John Colobos 1 (col. 204C), while a version closer to Cassian's is in Sulpitius' *Dial.* 1.19 (pp. 171–72); see Weber, *Die Stellung des Johannes Cassianus zur ausserpachomianischen Mönchstradition*, 111–12; on *Inst.* 4.23–27 generally, see Vogüé, "Les sources des quatre premiers livres des Institutions de Jean Cassien," 303–6); (2) *Conf.* 1.21 (a story unique to Cassian); (3) *Conf.* 24.26.16–17 (see *Hist. mon.* 1.1–2, pp. 9–10 and Palladius, *Hist. Laus.* 35.2, pp. 100.16–101.3). On John, see Sauget, "Giovanni di Licopoli," though the material from *Conf.* is not included.

84. *Hist. mon.* 10.3–24 (pp. 76–85), *Hist. mon. (Ruf.)* 9.2–6 (pp. 311–18).

85. *Alph.* Sisoes 10 (cols. 393C–96A), where the abba is Sisoes and the obedient disciple is unnamed; Cassian names the disciple (Patermuthius) but not the abba. Vogüé suggests that "Patermuthius" was used by Cassian for its appropriateness, like Rufinus' version of the name in *Hist. mon. (Ruf.)* 9.2.1 as *nomine Pater Mutius* (p. 311); Cassian's Patermuthius suffers his trial of obedience in silence (Vogüé, "Les sources des quatre premier livres des Institutions de Jean Cassien," 306–7). On Cassian's use of the story in *Alph.* Sisoes 10, see Weber, *Die Stellung des Johannes Cassianus zur ausserpachomianischen Mönchstradition*, 38–40.

Bibliography

Bibliographical Note:

Because of the abundance and constant appearance of translations of primary sources, I
have generally not included translations in this bibliography. The references in the notes
should allow fairly easy location of texts in the various translations available. Where English translations of secondary sources exist, however, references are to the translations.

Abbreviations

ABR   American Benedictine Review
BSanc   Bibliotheca Sanctorum
CC   Collectanea cisterciensia
CCL   Corpus christianorum, series latina
CE   Coptic Encyclopedia
CRAI   Comptes rendus de l'Académie des Inscriptions et Belles-Lettres
CSCO   Corpus scriptorum christianorum orientalium
CSEL   Corpus scriptorum ecclesiasticorum latinorum
CSS   Cistercian Studies Series
DACL   Dictionnaire d'archéologie chrétienne et de liturgie
DHGE   Dictionnaire d'histoire et de géographie ecclésiastique
DIP   Dizionario degli Istituti di Perfezione
DSp   Dictionnaire de spiritualité
DTC   Dictionnaire de théologie catholique
EEC   Encyclopedia of the Early Church
FZPT   Freiburger Zeitschrift für Philosophie und Theologie
JEH   Journal of Ecclesiastical History
JTS   Journal of Theological Studies
LTK   Lexikon für Theologie und Kirche
OCA   Orientalia christiana analecta
OCP   Orientalia christiana periodica
PG   Migne, Patrologia graeca
PL   Migne, Patrologia latina
PO   Patrologia orientalis
RAC   Reallexikon für Antike und Christentum
RAM   Revue d'ascétique et de mystique

RB   *Revue bénédictine*
REA   *Revue des études augustiniennes*
ROC   *Revue de l'Orient chrétien*
RSR   *Revue des sciences religieuses*
RTAM   *Recherches de théologie ancienne et médiévale*
SA   Studia Anselmiana
SC   Sources chrétiennes
SM   *Studia Monastica*
SP   *Studia Patristica*
TLL   *Thesaurus Linguae Latinae*
TRE   *Theologische Realenzyklopädie*
TU   Texte und Untersuchungen
ZKG   *Zeitschrift für Kirchengeschichte*

Primary Sources

Ambrose. *De institutione virginis (De inst. virg.).* PL 16.305–54.
————. *De Isaac vel anima.* Ed. Karl Schenkl. *Sancti Ambrosii opera.* CSEL 32.1, pp. 641–
    700. Vienna: Tempsky, 1897.
Ammon. *Epistola (Ep. Ammon).* Ed. James E. Goehring. *The Letter of Ammon and Pa-
    chomian Monasticism.* Patristische Texte und Studien 27. Berlin: De Gruyter, 1986.
Ammonas. *Epistolae.* Syriac version *(Ep. Syr.).* Ed. Michael Kmoskó. *Ammoni Eremitae
    epistolae,* 567–616. PO 10. Paris: Firmin-Didot, 1915. Greek version *(Ep. Gk.):* (1) ed.
    François Nau, *Ammonas, successeur de Saint Antoine: textes grecs et syriaques,* 432–54.
    PO 11. Paris: Firmin-Didot, 1915; (2) ed. G. Marriot, *Harvard Theological Studies* 5
    (1918):47–48, published as *Hom.* 57 of (Pseudo-)Macarius.
Antony the Great. *Epistolae (Ep.).* Latin version *(Ep. (Lat.)).* PG 40.977–1000. English
    trans. Samuel Rubenson. *The Letters of St. Anthony: Monasticism and the Making of
    a Saint,* 197–231. Minneapolis: Fortress, 1995. For information on the versions and
    textual problems, see Rubenson, 15–34.
Apophthegmata Patrum (Apoph.).
Abbreviations
    Alph.   Alphabetical Collection, PG 65.72A–440D.
    Alph. Suppl.   Jean-Claude Guy, ed. *Recherches sur la tradition grecque des Apoph-
                       thegmata Patrum.* 2nd ed. Subsidia hagiographica 36. Brussels: So-
                       ciété des Bollandistes, 1984.
    Anon.   Anonymous Collection. References to Nau 1–400 are to the edition
                       of François Nau: Nau 1–132 in *ROC* 12 (1907); Nau 133–215 in *ROC*
                       13 (1908); Nau 216–97 in *ROC* 14 (1909); Nau 298–358 in *ROC* 17
                       (1912); Nau 359–400 in *ROC* 18 (1913). French trans.: Regnault,
                       SPA. References to Nau 401–670 are to Regnault's translation in
                       SPA.
    Boh.   Bohairic text and French trans., Émile Amélineau. *Histoire des
                       monastères de la Basse-Égypte. Vies des Saints Paul, Antoine, Ma-
                       caire, Maxime et Domèce, Jean le Nain, et autres.* Monuments pour
                       servir à l'histoire de l'Égypte chrétienne. Annales du Musée Gui-
                       met 25. Paris: Leroux, 1894. Following Regnault's system, references
                       are to page and line number where the saying begins.
    Dial.   Jean-Claude Guy, "Un dialogue monastique inédit." *RAM* 33
                       (1957):171–88.

Eth.	French trans. in Regnault, *SPN*, 287–338.
Pasch.	Latin collection of Paschasius of Dumium. Ed. José Geraldes Freire. *A versão latina por Pascásio de Dume dos Apophthegmata Patrum.* Vol. 1, pp. 99–340. Coimbra: Instituo de Estudos Classicos, 1971.
Pasch. (br.)	*Vitae Patrum*, book 7. PL 73.1025A–62C.
P.E.	The Συναγωγή of Paul Evergetinos as in Regnault, *SPN*.
Regnault, *SPA*	Trans. Lucien Regnault. *Les sentences des Pères du désert: Série des anonymes.* Spiritualité orientale 43. Solesmes-Bellefontaine: Abbayes, 1985.
Regnault, *SPAlph.*	Lucien Regnault. *Les sentences des Pères du désert: Collection alphabétique.* Solesmes: Abbaye, 1981.
Regnault, *SPD*	Trans. Lucien Regnault, Jean Dion, and Guy Oury. *Les sentences des Pères du désert: Recueil de Pélage et Jean.* Solesmes: Abbaye, 1966.
Regnault, *SPN*	Trans. Lucien Regnault et al. *Les sentences des Pères du désert: Nouveau recueil. Apophtegmes inédits ou peu connus.* 2nd ed. Solesmes: Abbaye, 1977.
Regnault, *SPT*	Trans. Lucien Regnault. *Les sentences des Pères du désert: Troisième recueil et tables.* Solesmes: Abbaye, 1976.
Syr.	Syriac version. Ed. Paul Bedjan. *Paradisus patrum.* Vol. 7 of *Acta martyrum et sanctorum.* Paris: Harassowitz, 1897. Reprint, Hildesheim: Olms, 1968. English trans. Ernest A. Wallis-Budge. *The Paradise of the Fathers.* 2 vols. London: Chatto and Windus, 1907; reprint, Seattle: St. Nectarios Press, 1978. The numbering follows that of Budge and Regnault.
Syst. (Gk.)	Greek Systematic Collection. Ed. and French trans. Jean-Claude Guy. *Les Apophtegmes des Pères I: Collection systématique (books 1–9).* SC 387. Paris: Cerf, 1993. For books 10–21, see the key in Regnault, *SPT*, 291–301, and the translations in Regnault, *SPT*, 65–121.
Syst. (Lat.)	Latin Systematic Collection. *Vitae Patrum (V. Patr.).* Books 5–6. PL 73.855A–1022B.
V. Patr.	*Vitae Patrum*, PL 73.

Athanasius. *Letter to Ammoun.* Ed. Périclès-Pierre Joannou. *Fonti. Fascicolo XI: Discipline générale antique (quatrième–neuvième siècles).* Vol. 2, *Les canons des Pères grecs,* 63–71. Grottaferrata: Tipografia Italo-Orientale S. Nilo, 1963.

———. *Vita Antonii (V. Ant.).* Ed. and French trans. G. J. M. Bartelink. *Athanase d'Alexandrie: Vie d'Antoine.* SC 400. Paris: Cerf, 1994.

———. *Vita Antonii.* Anonymous Latin version. Ed. H. Hoppenbrouwers. *La plus ancienne version latine de la vie de S. Antoine.* Latinitas Christianorum primaeva; studia ad sermonem Latinum Christianum pertinentia 14. Nijmegen: Dekker and Van de Vegt, 1960.

———. *Vita Antonii.* Latin version of Evagrius of Antioch. PG 26.837–976.

Athanasius, Pseudo-. *De virginitate (De virg.).* PG 28.251–82.

Augustine. *Confessiones (Confess.).* Ed. James J. O'Donnell. *Augustine: Confessions.* Vol. 1, introduction and text. Oxford: Clarendon Press, 1992.

———. *De correptione et gratia (De corr. et grat.).* PL 44.915–46.

———. *De doctrina christiana (De doctr.).* Ed. and English trans. R. P. H. Green. Oxford Early Christian Texts. Oxford: Clarendon, 1995.

————. *De dono perseverantiae (De don. pers.)*. PL 45.993–1034.

————. *De Genesi ad litteram (De Gen. ad litt.)*. Ed. Joseph Zycha. CSEL 28. Vienna: Tempsky, 1894.

————. *De gratia et libero arbitrio (De grat. et lib. arb.)*. PL 44.881–912.

————. *De praedestinatione sanctorum (De praed. sanct.)*. PL 44.959–92.

————. *Enarrationes in Psalmos (Enarr. in Ps.)*. Ed. E. Dekkers and J. Fraipont. CCL 38–40. Turnhout: Brepols, 1956.

————. *Epistolae (Ep.)*. Ed. A. Goldbacher. CSEL 34/1–2, 44, 57, 58. Vienna: Tempsky, 1895–1923.

Barsanuphius and John of Gaza. *Epistolae (Ep.)*. Ed. Nicodemus of the Holy Mountain. Venice, 1816. Reprinted with corrections by Soterios N. Schoinas, Βίβλος ψυχωφελεστάτη περιέχουσα ἀποκρίσεις, διαφόροις ὑποθέεοιν ἀνηκούσας συγγραφεῖσα μὲν παρὰ τῶν ὁσίων καὶ θεοφόρων πατέρων ἡμῶν Βαρσανουφίου καὶ Ἰωάννου. Volos (Greece): Hagioreitike Bibliotheke, 1960. Partial ed. and English trans. (*Ep.* 1–124) Derwas J. Chitty. *Barsanuphius and John: Questions and Answers.* PO 31.3. Paris: Firmin-Didot, 1966. Complete French trans.: Lucien Regnault, Philippe Lemaire, and Bernard Outtier. *Barsanuphe et Jean de Gaza: Correspondance.* Solesmes: Abbaye Saint-Pierre, 1971. The numbering follows that of Regnault et al.; references are also provided to the edition by Schoinas, and a key to systems of numerotation may be found in Regnault et al., 542–43.

Basil of Caesarea. *Asceticon parvum (Asc. parv.)*. Ed. Klaus Zelzer. *Basili Regula a Rufino latine versa.* CSEL 86. Vienna: Hoelder-Pichler-Tempsky, 1986.

————. *Hom. in martyrem Julittam.* PG 31.237A–61A.

————. *Regulae brevius tractatae (Reg. brev.)*. PG 31.1080A–1305B.

————. *Regulae fusius tractatae (Reg. fus.)*. PG 31.889–1052.

Benedict of Aniane. *Concordia regularum (Conc. reg.)*. PL 103.713–1380.

Bible. Vulgate version, *Biblia Sacra iuxta Vulgatam Clementinam.* Ed. Alberto Colunga and Laurentio Turrado. Bibliotheca de autores cristianos 14. Madrid: BAC, 1977.

————. Greek New Testament. Ed. K. Aland et al. *Novum Testamentum Graece.* 27th ed. Stuttgart: Deutsche Bibelgesellschaft, 1993.

————. Old Latin version of the Gospels. Ed. Adolf Jülicher, Walter Matzkow, and Kurt Aland. *Itala. Das Neue Testament in altlateinischer Überlieferung.* 2nd ed. Berlin: De Gruyter, 1970–.

————. Septuagint (LXX). Ed. Alfred Rahlfs. *Septuaginta.* 7th ed. Stuttgart: Deutsche Bibelgesellschaft, 1962.

Caelius Aurelianus. *On Acute Diseases and On Chronic Diseases.* Ed. and English trans. I. E. Drabkin. Chicago: University of Chicago Press, 1950.

Caesarius of Arles. *Regula ad virgines (Reg. virg.)*. Ed. and French trans. Adalbert de Vogüé and Joël Courreau. *Césaire d'Arles: Oeuvres monastiques. Tome 1: Oeuvres pour les moniales.* SC 345. Paris: Cerf, 1988.

————. *Sermones.* Ed. Germain Morin. CCL 103–4. Turnhout: Brepols, 1953.

————. *Vita Caesarii (V. Caes.)*. Ed. Germain Morin. *Sancti Caesarii episcopi arelatensis Opera omnia.* Vol. 2, pp. 293–345. Maredsous: Abbaye, 1942.

Cassian, John. *De Incarnatione domini libri VII (De Inc.)*. Ed. Michael Petschenig. CSEL 17. Vienna: Tempsky, 1888.

————. *De institutis coenobiorum et de octo principalium vitiorum remediis libri XII (Inst.)*. Ed. Michael Petschenig. CSEL 17. Vienna: Tempsky, 1888. Ed. and French trans. Jean–Claude Guy. *Jean Cassien. Institutions cénobitiques.* SC 109. Paris: Cerf, 1965.

————. *Conlationes XXIIII (Conf.)*. Ed. Michael Petschenig. CSEL 13. Vienna: Geroldus, 1886.

————. *Ioannis Cassiani Eremitae de institutis renuntiantium Libri XII. Collationes Sanctorum Patrum XXIIII. Adiectae sunt quarundum obscurarum dictionum interpretationes ordine alphabeti dispositae: et observationes in loca ambigua et minus tuta, etc.* Ed. Petrus Ciaconnius. Rome, 1588.

Cassiodorus. *Expositio Psalmorum (Expos. in Ps.).* Ed. Marcus Adriaen. CCL 97–98. Turnhout: Brepols, 1958.

————. *Institutiones divinarum litterarum (Div. litt.).* PL 70.1105D–50C.

Celestine I, Pope. *Epistola ad episcopos galliarum. (Ep.).* PL 50.528–30.

Clement of Alexandria. *Paedagogus (Paed.).* Ed. Otto Stählin, rev. L. Früchtel and Ursula Treu. GCS *Clemens Alexandrinus* 1. Berlin: Akademie Verlag, 1972.

————. *Stromateis (Strom.).* Ed. Otto Stählin, rev. L. Früchtel and Ursula Treu. GCS *Clemens Alexandrinus* 2 (books 1–6). Berlin: Akademie Verlag, 1960. *Clemens Alexandrinus* 3 (book 7). Berlin: Akademie Verlag, 1970.

Constitutiones Sirmondianae (Const. Sirm.). Ed. Theodor Mommsen. *Theodosiani Libri XVI cum Constitutionibus Sirmondianis.* Vol. 1, pt. 2, pp. 907–21. Berlin: Weidmann, 1905.

Decretum Gelasianum (Dec. Gel.). Ed. Ernst von Dobschütz. *Das Decretum Gelasianum de libris recipiendis et non recipiendis.* TU 38 pt. 4. Leipzig: Hinrichs, 1912. Also in *PL* 59.157A–64B.

Diadochus of Photike. *Capita gnostica (Cap. gnost.).* Ed. and French trans. Édouard des Places. *Diadoque de Photicé: Oeuvres spirituelles*, pp. 84–163. SC 5bis. Paris: Cerf, 1976.

————. *Visio (Vis.).* Ed. des Places in *Diadoque de Photicé: Oeuvres spirituelles*, pp. 169–79.

Didascalia Apostolorum. Syriac version. Ed. and trans. Arthur Vööbus. CSCO 401 and 407 (text), 402 and 408 (English trans.). Louvain: Secrétariat du CSCO, 1979. Latin version. Ed. Erik Tidner. *Didascaliae Apostolorum Canonum Ecclesiasticorum Traditionis Apostolicae Versiones Latinae.* TU 75. Berlin: Akademie Verlag, 1963.

Dionysius Exiguus. *Praefatio ad Ioannem et Leontium*, in *Scriptores Illyrici minores*, pp. 55–56. CCL 85. Turnhout: Brepols, 1972.

Dorotheus of Gaza. *Instructions (Instr.).* Ed. and French trans. Lucien Regnault and Jacques de Préville. *Dorothée de Gaza: Oeuvres spirituelles.* SC 92. Paris: Cerf, 1963.

Epiphanios Hagiopolites. *Enarratio Syriae (Enarr. Syr.).* PG 120.260C–72D.

Eucherius of Lyons. *Formulae spiritalis intellegentiae (Form.).* Ed. Karl Wotke. *Sancti Eucherii Lugdunensis Opera Omnia*, pp. 3–62. CSEL 31. Vienna: Tempsky, 1894.

Evagrius Ponticus. *Ad monachos (Ad mon.).* Ed. Hugo Gressmann. "Nonnenspiegel und Mönchsspiegel des Euagrios Pontikos," pp. 153–65. TU 39, pt. 4. Leipzig, 1939. Greek text and English trans. in Jeremy Driscoll, *The "Ad monachos" of Evagrius Ponticus: Its Structure and a Select Commentary.* SA 104. Rome: Abbazia S. Paolo, 1991. References are to Driscoll's text.

————. *Ad virgines (Ad virg.).* Ed. Hugo Gressmann. "Nonnenspiegel und Mönchsspiegel des Euagrios Pontikos," pp. 146–51. TU 39, pt. 4. Leipzig, 1939.

————. *Antirrhetikos (Antirr.).* Syriac version and Greek retroversion. Wilhelm Frankenberg, *Euagrius Ponticus*, pp. 472–545. Abhandlungen der königlichen Gesellschaft der Wissenschaften zu Göttingen, Philologisch-historische Klasse, Neue Folge 13.2. Berlin: 1912.

————. *Capita cognoscitiva (Cap. cogn.*; sometimes known as *Skemmata*). Ed. J. Muyldermans. "Evagriana," *Le Muséon* 44 (1931): 51–57. Syriac version and Greek retroversion. Ed. Wilhelm Frankenberg. *Euagrius Ponticus*, pp. 422–71. Abhandlungen der königlichen Gesellschaft der Wissenschaften zu Göttingen, Philologisch–historische Klasse, Neue Folge 13.2. Berlin: 1912.

————. *Capitula XXXIII: Definitiones passionum animae rationalis (Cap.)*. PG 40.1264D–68B.

————. *Epistola ad Melaniam (Ep. Mel.)*. Syriac version and Greek retroversion of part 1. Wilhelm Frankenberg. *Euagrius Ponticus*, pp. 610 (last line)–19. Abhandlungen der königlichen Gesellschaft der Wissenschaften zu Göttingen, Philologisch-historische Klasse, Neue Folge 13.2. Berlin: 1912. English trans. and commentary by Martin Parmentier. "Evagrius of Pontus' 'Letter to Melania' 1," *Bijdragen, tijdschrift voor filosofie en theologie* 46 (1985):8–21. Syriac text and French trans. of part 2. Ed. Gösta Vitestam, *Seconde partie du traité, qui passe sous le nom de «La grande lettre d'Évagre le Pontique à Mélanie l'Ancienne»*. Scripta minora regiae societatis humaniorum litterarum lundensis. Lund: CWK Gleerup, 1964.

————. *Epistola fidei (Ep. fid.)*. Ed. and Italian trans. as Pseudo-Basil, *Ep*. 8 by Marcella Forlin Patrucco. *Basilio di Cesarea: Le lettere*, vol. 1, pp. 84–112. Corona Patrum. Turin: Società Editrice Internazionale, 1983.

————. *Epistolae*. Syriac version and Greek retroversion. Ed. Wilhelm Frankenberg. *Euagrius Ponticus*, pp. 562–635. Abhandlungen der königlichen Gesellschaft der Wissenschaften zu Göttingen, Philologisch–historische Klasse, Neue Folge 13.2. Berlin: 1912. German translation. Gabriel Bunge. *Briefe aus der Wüste*. Sophia 24. Trier: Paulinus–Verlag, 1986.

————. *Expositio in orationem dominicam (Expos. in orat. dom.)*. Ed. Paul Anton de Lagarde. *Catenae in Evangelia aegyptiacae quae supersunt*, 13. Göttingen: Dieterich, 1886.

————. *Gnostikos (Gnost.)*. Greek fragments and French trans.. Antoine and Claire Guillaumont. *Évagre le Pontique: Le Gnostique*. SC 356. Paris: Cerf, 1989. Syriac version (*Gnost. [Syr.]*) and Greek retroversion. Ed. Wilhelm Frankenberg. *Euagrius Ponticus*, pp. 546–53. Abhandlungen der königlichen Gesellschaft der Wissenschaften zu Göttingen, Philologisch–historische Klasse, Neue Folge 13.2. Berlin: 1912.

————. *Institutio (Inst.)*. PG 79.1236A–40B. Supplement (*Inst. Suppl.*) in J. Muyldermans, "Evagriana," *Le Muséon* 51 (1938):200–3.

————. *Kephalaia gnostica (Keph. gnost.)*. Ed. and French trans. Antoine Guillaumont. *Les Six Centuries des "Kephalaia gnostica" d'Évagre le Pontique. Édition critique de la version syriaque commune et édition d'une nouvelle version syriaque, intégrale, avec une double traduction française*. PO 28. Paris: Firmin-Didot, 1958.

————. *De malignis cogitationibus (De mal. cog.)*. PG 79.1200D–33A, PG 40.1236C–44B, and J. Muyldermans, *À travers la tradition manuscrite d'Évagre le Pontique. Essai sur les manuscrits grecs conservés à la Bibliothèque Nationale de Paris*, 47–60. Bibliothèque du Muséon. Paris: Bureaux du Muséon, 1932. See table in SC 170, p. 419, for numerotation.

————. *De octo spiritibus malitiae (De octo spir. mal.)*. PG 79.1145A–64D.

————. *De oratione (De orat.)*. PG 79.1165A–1200C. Numbering follows that of PG.

————. *Paraenesis*. Syriac text and French trans. J. Muyldermans. *Evagriana Syriaca. Textes inédits du British Museum et de la Vaticane*, pp. 131–33 (Syriac), 160–63 (French). Bibliothèque du Muséon, 31. Louvain, 1952.

————. *Paraeneticus (Paraenet.)*. Syriac version and Greek retroversion. Wilhelm Frankenberg. *Euagrius Ponticus*, pp. 556 (last line)–562.11. Abhandlungen der königlichen Gesellschaft der Wissenschaften zu Göttingen, Philologisch-historische Klasse, Neue Folge 13.2. Berlin: 1912.

————. *Praktikos (Prak.)*. Greek text and French trans. Antoine and Claire Guillaumont. *Évagre le Pontique: Traité pratique ou le moine*. SC 170–71. Paris: Cerf, 1971.

————. *Protrepticus (Protrep.)*. Syriac version and Greek retroversion. Wilhelm Frankenberg. *Euagrius Ponticus*, pp. 554–57. Abhandlungen der königlichen Gesellschaft der Wissenschaften zu Göttingen, Philologisch-historische Klasse, Neue Folge 13.2. Berlin: 1912.

————. *Rerum monachalium rationes (Rerum mon. rat.)*. PG 40.1252D–64C.

————. *Scholia in Ecclesiasten (Schol. in Eccl.)*. Greek text and French trans. Paul Géhin. *Évagre le Pontique: Scholies à l'Ecclésiaste*. SC 397. Paris: Cerf, 1993.

————. *Scholia in Proverbia (Schol. in Prov.)*. Greek text and French trans. Paul Géhin. *Évagre le Pontique: Scholies aux Proverbes*. SC 340. Paris: Cerf, 1987.

————. *Scholia in Psalmos (Schol. in Ps.)*. Greek text. PG 12.1054–1686, PG 27.60–545, and Jean Baptiste Pitra. *Analecta Sacra*. Vol. 2 (Frascati, 1884), pp. 444–483 (Pss. 1–25) and vol. 3 (Paris, 1883), pp. 1–364 (Pss. 26–150). The key to disentangling these texts from those of Origen and Athanasius with which they were preserved is provided by Marie-Josèphe Rondeau, "Le commentaire sur les Psaumes d'Évagre le Pontique," *OCP* 26 (1960):329–48. References are to the psalm and verse as in the editions, then to the edition (PG or Pitra) and column or page.

————. *Sententiae aliae (Sent. aliae)*. Ed. Anton Elter. *Evagrii Pontici sententiae*. In *Index scholarum quae summis auspiciis regis augustissimi Guilelmi II imperatoris germanici in Universitate Fridericia Guilelmia Rhenana per menses hibernos a. 1892–1893 a die XV m. octobris publice privatimque habebuntur*, pp. 53–54. Bonn: Georg, 1891.

————. *De vitiis quae opposita sunt virtutibus (De vit.)*. PG 79.1140B–44D.

Ferrandus. *Vita Fulgentii (V. Fulg.)*. PL 65.117B–150D.

Gennadius of Marseilles. *De viris inlustribus (De vir. inlustr.)*. Ed. Ernest Cushing Richardson. TU 14, pt. 1. Leipzig: Hinrichs, 1896.

Gregory of Nyssa. *De Beatitudinibus (De Beat.)*. Ed. John F. Callahan. *Gregorius Nysseni Opera*. Vol. 7, pt. 2. Leiden: Brill, 1992.

————. *De instituto christiano (De inst. christ.)*. Ed. Reinhart Staats. *Makarios-Symeon: Epistola Magna. Eine messalianische Mönchsregel und ihre Umschrift in Gregors von Nyssa 'De instituto christiano'*. Abhandlungen der Akademie der Wissenschaften in Göttingen, Philologisch-historische Klasse, 3. Folge, 134. Göttingen, 1984.

————. *De oratione dominica (De orat. dom.)*. Ed. John F. Callahan. *Gregorius Nysseni Opera*. Vol. 7, pt. 2. Leiden: Brill, 1992.

————. *On Virginity (De virg.)*. Ed. J. P. Cavarnos. *Gregorius Nysseni Opera*. Vol. 8, pt. 1. Leiden: Brill, 1952.

Gregory the Great. *Epistolae (Ep.)*. Ed. Paul Ewald. *Gregorii I Papae Registrum Epistolarum*. Monumenta Germaniae Historica: Epistolarum 1–2. Berlin: Weidmann, 1887.

————. *Moralia in Iob. (Mor. in Iob)*. Ed. Marcus Adriaen. CCL 143, 143A, 143B. Turnhout: Brepols, 1979–85.

Hilary of Arles. *Vita S. Honorati (V. Hon.)*. Ed. and French trans. Marie-Denise Valentin. *Hilaire d'Arles: Vie de saint Honorat*. SC 235. Paris: Cerf, 1977.

Hilary of Marseilles. *Epistola ad Augustinum (Ep. ad Aug.)*. Preserved as Augustine, *Ep.* 226. CSEL 57, pp. 468–81.

Historia monachorum in Aegypto (Hist. mon.). Ed. André-Jean Festugière. Subsidia hagiographica 53. Brussels: Société des Bollandistes, 1961.

————. *(Hist. mon. [Ruf.])*, Latin version by Rufinus of Aquileia. Ed. Eva Schulz-Flügel. *Tyrannus Rufinus. Historia monachorum sive De vita sanctorum patrum*. Patristische Texte und Studien 34. Berlin: De Gruyter, 1990.

Honoratus of Marseilles. *Vita S. Hilarii Episcopi Arelatensis (V. Hil.)*. Ed. and French trans. Paul-André Jacob. *Honorat de Marseille: La vie d'Hilaire d'Arles*. SC 404. Paris: Cerf, 1995.

Horsiesios. *Liber (Lib.)*. Latin version. Ed. Amand Boon. *Pachomiana Latina. Règle et épitres de S. Pachome. Épitre de S. Théodore et "Liber" de S. Orsiesius*, 109–47. Bibliothèque de la Revue d'histoire ecclésiastique 7. Louvain: RHE, 1932.

———. *Regulae (Reg)*. Ed. and French trans. L. Th. Lefort. *Oeuvres de S. Pachome et de ses disciples*. CSCO 159, pp. 82–89 (Coptic); CSCO 160, pp. 81–99 (French trans.). Louvain: L. Durbecq, 1956. The numbering is that of Veilleux in *Pachomian Koinonia*, 2.197–220.

Hyperechios. *Paraenesis (Paraen.)*. PG 79.1473–89.

Innocent I, Pope. *Epistolae (Ep.)*. Ed. Pierre Coustant. PL 20. 463–608.

Irenaeus. *Adversus haereses (Adv. haer.)*. Book 4. Ed. and French trans. Adelin Rousseau et al. *Irénée de Lyon: Contre les hérésies*. SC 100. Paris: Cerf, 1965.

Isaiah of Scetis. *Logoi (Log.)*. Ed. Augustinos Monachos. Τοῦ ὁσίου πατρὸς ἡμῶν ἀββᾶ Ἡσαΐου. Jerusalem, 1911. French trans. by Lucien Regnault and Hervé de Broc. *Abbé d'Isaïe. Recueil ascétique*. Spiritualité orientale 7bis. Bégrolles-en-Mauges, France: Abbaye de Bellefontaine, 1976.

Jerome. *Commentarium in Hieremiam (Comm. in Hierem.)*. Ed. Marcus Adriaen. CCL 74. Turnhout: Brepols, 1960.

———. *Epistolae (Ep.)*. Ed. Isidore Hilberg. *Sancti Eusebii Hieronymi Epistulae*. CSEL 55–56. Vienna: Tempsky, 1910–18.

———. *Tractatus in librum Psalmorum. (Tract. in Ps.)*. Ed. Germain Morin. *Opera Homiletica*, pp. 1–352. 2nd ed. CCL 78. Turnhout: Brepols, 1958.

———. *Tractatuum in Psalmos series altera (Tract. in Ps. [ser. alt.])*. Ed. Germain Morin. *Opera Homiletica*, pp. 353–447. 2nd ed. CCL 78. Turnhout: Brepols, 1958.

———. *Vita Pauli Primi Eremitae*. PL 23.17A–28C.

John Chrysostom. *De compunctione*. PG 47.393–422.

John Climacus. *Scala paradisi (Scala parad.)*. PG 88.632A–1164D.

John Damascene. *Sacra parallela*. PG 95.1041A–1588A and 96.9A–441A.

Justin, Pseudo-. *Quaestiones et responsiones ad orthodoxos (Quaest.)*. PG 6.1249A–1400D.

Leporius. *Libellus emendationis*. Ed. Roland Demeulenaere. *Foebadius, Victricius, Leporius, Vincentius Lerinensis, Evagrius, Ruricius: Collectanea*, pp. 111–23. CCL 64. Turnhout: Brepols, 1985.

Liber graduum (Lib. grad.). Ed. and Latin trans. Michael Kmoskó. *Patrologia syriaca* 1.3. Paris: Firmin-Didot, 1926.

Macarius, Pseudo-. *Homiliae (Hom.)*. Collection I *(Coll. I)*. Ed. H. Berthold. *Makarios/ Symeon: Reden und Briefe. Die Sammlung I des Vaticanus Graecus 694 (B)*. 2 vols. GCS. Berlin: Akademie Verlag, 1973.

———. *Homiliae (Hom.)*. Collection II *(Coll. II)*. Ed. Hermann Dörries, E. Klostermann, and M. Kroeger. *Die 50 geistlichen Homilien des Makarios*. Patristische Texte und Studien 4. Berlin: Walter de Gruyter, 1964.

———. *Homiliae (Hom.)*. Collection III *(Coll. III)*. Ed. and French trans. Vincent Desprez. *Pseudo-Macaire: Oeuvres spirituelles, I*. SC 275. Paris: Cerf, 1980.

———. *Epistola magna (Ep. mag.)*. Ed. Reinhart Staats. *Makarios-Symeon: Epistola Magna. Eine messalianische Mönchsregel und ihre Umschrift in Gregors von Nyssa 'De instituto christiano'*. Abhandlungen der Akademie der Wissenschaften in Göttingen, Philologisch-historische Klasse, Dritte Folge, 134. Göttingen, 1984.

Nilus of Ancyra. *De voluntaria paupertate (De vol. paup.)*. PG 79.968C–1060D.

Nemesius of Emesa. *De natura hominis (De nat. hom.)*. PG 40.504A–817A.

Origen. *Commentarii in Canticum (Comm. in Cant.)*. Ed. W. A. Baehrens. GCS *Origenes Werke* 8. Leipzig: Hinrichs, 1925.

———. *Commentarii in Iohannem (Comm. in Iohann.)*. Ed. E. Preuschen. GCS *Origenes Werke* 4. Leipzig: Hinrichs, 1903.

————. *Commentarii in Matthaeum (Comm. in Matt.)*. Ed. E. Klostermann and E. Benz. GCS *Origenes Werke* 10. Leipzig: Hinrichs, 1935.

————. *Commentarii in Psalmos (Comm. in Ps.)*. PG 12.1054–1686 and Jean Baptiste Pitra. *Analecta Sacra.* Vol. 2 (Frascati, 1884), pp. 444–83 (Pss. 1–25) and vol. 3 (Paris, 1883), pp. 1–364 (Pss. 26–150). Included with these texts are Evagrius' *Schol. in Ps.*, listed in Marie-Josèphe Rondeau, "Le commentaire sur les Psaumes d'Évagre le Pontique," *OCP* 26 (1960):329–48. References are to the psalm and verse as in the editions, then to the edition (*PG* or Pitra) and column or page.

————. *Contra Celsum (C. Celsum)*. Ed. and French trans. Marcel Borret. SC 132, 136, 147, 150, 227. Paris: Cerf, 1967–76.

————. *Homiliae in Lucam (Hom. in Luc.)*. Ed. Max Rauer. GCS *Origenes Werke* 9. 2nd ed. Berlin: Akademie Verlag, 1959.

————. *Homiliae in Numeros (Hom. in Num.)*. Ed. W. A. Baehrens. GCS *Origenes Werke* 7.2. Leipzig: Hinrichs, 1921.

————. *Philocalia*. Ed., French trans., and notes by Marguerite Harl. *Origène: Philocalie 1–20 Sur les Écritures.* SC 302. Paris: Cerf, 1983.

————. *De principiis (De princ.)*. Ed. P. Koetschau. GCS *Origenes Werke* 5. Leipzig: Hinrichs, 1913. Ed. and French trans. Henri Crouzel et Manlio Simonetti. *Origène: Traité des principes.* SC 252–253, 268–269, 312. Paris: Cerf, 1978–84.

Pachomius. *Praecepta (Praec.)*. Latin text. Ed. Amand Boon. *Pachomiana Latina. Règle et épitres de S. Pachôme. Épître de S. Théodore et "Liber" de S. Orsiesius,* 13–52. Bibliothèque de la Revue d'histoire ecclésiastique 7. Louvain: RHE, 1932. Coptic fragments and Greek *excerpta*. Ed. L. Th. Lefort. In Boon, *Pachomiana Latina*, pp. 155–82.

————. *Vita Pachomii bohairica (V. Pach. boh.)*. Ed. and French trans. L. Th. Lefort. *S. Pachomii vita Bohairice scripta.* CSCO 89 and 107. Louvain: L. Durbecq, 1952–53. English trans. Armand Veilleux. *Pachomian Koinonia I: The Life of Saint Pachomius.* CSS 45. Kalamazoo: Cistercian Publications, 1980.

————. *Vita Pachomii graeca prima (V. Pach. gr. 1)* and *secunda (V. Pach. gr. 2)*. Ed. François Halkin. *Sancti Pachomii vitae Graecae.* Subsidia hagiographica 19. Brussels: Société des Bollandistes, 1932.

————. *Vita Pachomii latina (V. Pach. lat.)*. Ed. H. Van Cranenburgh. *La vie latine de Saint Pachome.* Subsidia hagiographica 46. Brussels: Société des Bollandistes, 1969.

Palladius. *Dialogus de vita Iohannis Chrysostomi (Dial.)*. Ed. and French trans. Anne-Marie Malingrey and Philippe Leclercq. *Palladios: Dialogue sur la vie de Jean Chrysostome.* SC 341–42. Paris: Cerf, 1988.

————. *Historia Lausiaca (Hist. Laus.)*. Ed. Cuthbert Butler. *The Lausiac History of Palladius.* Vol. 2. Texts and Studies 6. Cambridge: Cambridge University Press, 1904. Section numbers as in Robert Meyer, *Palladius: The Lausiac History.* Ancient Christian Writers 34. Westminster, Md.: Newman Press, 1965.

Philo. *Quaestiones et solutiones in Exodum (Quaest. in Exod.)*. English trans. from the Armenian version by Ralph Marcus. *Philo with an English Translation.* Suppl. 2, 2–176. Loeb Classical Library. Cambridge: Harvard University Press, 1953.

Philoxenos of Mabbug. *Homiliae (Hom.)*. Ed. and English trans. E. A. Wallis Budge. *The Discourses of Philoxenus Bishop of Mabbôgh, A.D. 485–519.* London: Asher, 1894.

Plato. *Republic (Rep.)*. In *Platonis Opera*, vol. 4. Ed. John Burnet. Oxford Classical Texts. 5 vols. Oxford: Clarendon, 1900–07; reprint 1973.

————. *Timaeus (Tim.)*. In *Platonis Opera*, vol. 4. Ed. John Burnet. Oxford Classical Texts. 5 vols. Oxford: Clarendon, 1900–07; reprint 1973.

Plotinus. *Enneads (Enn.)*. Ed. and English trans. A. H. Armstrong. Loeb Classical Library. 7 vols. Cambridge: Harvard University Press, 1966–88.

Prosper of Aquitaine. *Contra collatorem (C. coll.)*. PL 51.215–76.

———. *Epistola ad Augustinum (Ep. ad Aug.)*. Preserved as Augustine, *Ep.* 225. CSEL 57, pp. 454–67.

———. *Epistola ad Rufinum (Ep. ad Ruf.)*. PL 51.77A–90A.

Regesta pontificum romanorum. Ed. Philippe Jaffé. *Regesta pontificum romanorum ab condita ecclesia ad annum post Christum natum 1594*. 2nd ed. Wilhelm Wattenbach et al. Leipzig: Veit, 1885.

Regula Benedicti (Reg. Ben.). Ed. and French trans. Adalbert de Vogüé and Jean Neufville. *La Règle de Saint Benoît*. Vols. 1–2. SC 181–82. Paris: Cerf, 1972.

Regula Cassiani. Ed. Henri Ledoyen. *RB* 94 (1984):170–94.

Regula Magistri (Reg. Mag.). Ed. and French trans. Adalbert de Vogüé. *La Règle du Maître*. SC 105–7. Paris: Cerf, 1964–65.

Regula Sanctorum Patrum Serapionis, Macharii, Pafnutii et alterius Macharii (RIVP). Ed. and French trans. Adalbert de Vogüé. *Les Règles des Saints Pères*, pp. 180–205. SC 297. Paris: Cerf, 1982.

Regula Sancti Macharii (Reg. Mac.). Ed. and French trans. Adalbert de Vogüé. *Les Règles des Saints Pères*, pp. 372–89. SC 297. Paris: Cerf, 1982.

Regula Sanctorum Patrum secunda (Reg. Patr.). Ed. and French trans. Adalbert de Vogüé. *Les Règles des Saints Pères*, pp. 274–83. SC 297. Paris: Cerf, 1982.

Socrates Scholasticus. *Historia ecclesiastica (Hist. eccl.)*. PG 67.33A–841B.

Sozomen. *Historia ecclesiastica (Hist. eccl.)*. Ed. Joseph Bidez. GCS. Berlin: Akademie-Verlag, 1960.

Stephen Bar Sudaili. *Book of the Holy Hierotheos*. Ed. and trans. F. S. Marsh. London: Text and Translation Society, 1927.

Sulpitius Severus. *Epistolae (Ep.)*. Ed. Karl Halm. *Sulpicii Severi: Libri qui supersunt*, pp. 138–51. CSEL 1. Vienna: Geroldus, 1866. *Ep. App.* (letters of uncertain authorship attributed to Sulpitius), pp. 219–56.

———. *Vita Martini (V. Mart.)*. Ed. and French trans. Jacques Fontaine. *Sulpice Sévère: Vie de Saint Martin*. SC 133–35. Paris: Cerf, 1967–69.

———. *Dialogi (Dial.)*. Ed. Karl Halm. *Sulpicii Severi: Libri qui supersunt*, pp. 152–216. CSEL 1. Vienna: Geroldus, 1866.

Symeon the New Theologian. *Catechetical Discourses (Catech.)*. Ed. and French trans. Basile Krivocheine. *Symeon le Nouveau Théologien: Catéchèses*. SC 96, 104, 113. Paris: Cerf, 1963–65.

Tertullian. *De anima*. Ed. J. H. Waszink. *Tertullianus: Opera*. Part 2: *Opera Montanistica*, pp. 781–869. CCL 2. Turnhout: Brepols, 1954.

Timothy of Alexandria. *Quaestiones (Quaest)*. Ed. Périclès-Pierre Joannou. *Fonti. Fascicolo XI: Discipline générale antique (quatrième–neuvième siècles)*. Vol. 2, *Les canons des Pères grecs*, 240–58. Grottaferrata: Tipografia Italo-Orientale S. Nilo, 1963.

Vincent of Lérins. *Commonitorium (Comm.)*. Ed. Roland Demeulenaere. *Foebadius, Victricius, Leporius, Vincentius Lerinensis, Evagrius, Ruricius: Collectanea*, pp. 147–95. CCL 64. Turnhout: Brepols, 1985.

Secondary Sources

Abel, Otto. *Studien zu dem gallischen Presbyter Johannes Cassianus*. Munich: Wolf, 1904.

Adnès, Pierre. "Larmes." *DSp*, 9:287–303.

Albers, Bruno. "Eine patristische Frage." *Studien und Mitteilungen zur Geschichte des Benediktinerordens und seiner Zweige* 4 (1914):345–47.

Alcock, Anthony. "Samū'īl of Qalamūn, Saint." *CE*, 2092–93.

Amann, Émile. "L'Affaire Nestorius vue de Rome." *RSR* 23 (1949):3–37, 207–44; 24 (1950):28–52, 235–65.

———. "Leporius." *DTC*, 9:434–40.

———. "Nestorius." *DTC*, 11:76–157.

———. "Semi-Pélagiens." *DTC*, 14:1796–1850.

Amargier, Paul. *Un Âge d'or du monachisme: Saint-Victor de Marseille (990–1090)*. Marseille: Tacussel, 1990.

Amélineau, Émile. *La géographie de l'Égypte à l'époque Copte*. Paris, 1893.

André, Gunnel. "Ecstatic Prophecy in the Old Testament." In *Religious Ecstasy. Based on Papers read at the Symposium on Religious Ecstasy held at Åbo, Finland, on the 26th–28th of August 1981*, pp. 187–200. Ed. Nils H. Holm. Scripta Instituti Donneriani Aboensis 11. Stockholm: Almquist and Wiksell, 1982.

Arbman, Ernst. *Ecstasy or Religious Trance, in the Experience of the Ecstatics and from the Psychological Point of View*. 3 vols. Stockholm: Svenska Bokförlaget/Norstedts, 1963–70.

Archimbaud, Gabrielle Demians d'. "Les fouilles de Saint-Victor de Marseille." *CRAI* (1971):87–117.

———. "Saint-Victor de Marseille: Fouilles récentes et nouvelles interprétations architecturales." *CRAI* (1974):313–46.

Atsma, Hartmut. "Die christlichen Inschriften Galliens als Quelle für Klösterbewohner bis zum Ende des 6. Jahrhunderts." *Francia* 4 (1976):1–57.

Bacht, Heinrich. "'Meditatio' in den ältesten Mönchsquellen." *Geist und Leben* 28 (1955):360–73. Reprint, *Das Vermächtnis des Ursprungs. Studien zum frühen Mönchtum*. Vol. 1, pp. 244–64. Würzburg: Echter, 1972.

Baert, Edward. "Le thème de la vision de Dieu chez S. Justin, Clément d'Alexandrie et S. Grégoire de Nysse." *FZPT* 12 (1965):439–97.

Bagatti, Bellarmino. *Gli antichi edifici sacri di Betlemme. In seguito agli scavi e restauri praticati dalla Custodia di Terra Santa (1948–51)*. Publicazioni dello Studium Biblicum Franciscanum 9. Jerusalem: Tipografia dei PP. Francescani, 1952.

Bagnall, Roger S. *Egypt in Late Antiquity*. Princeton: Princeton University Press, 1993.

Bardenhewer, Otto. *Geschichte der altkirchlichen Literatur*. Vol. 4, *Das fünfte Jahrhundert mit Einschluss der syrischen Literatur des vierten Jahrhunderts*. Freiburg im Breisgau: Herder, 1924.

Bauer, Franz. "Die Heilige Schrift bei den Mönchen des christlichen Altertums." *Theologie und Glaube* 17 (1925):512–32.

Bell, David N. "Apatheia: the Convergence of Byzantine and Cistercian Spirituality." *Cîteaux* 38 (1987):141–63.

Benoit, Fernand. *L'Abbaye de Saint-Victor et l'Église de la Major à Marseille*. 2nd ed. Paris: Laurens, 1966.

———. "Le *martyrium* rupestre de l'abbaye Saint-Victor." *CRAI* (1966):110–26.

Berschin, Walter. *Greek Letters and the Latin Middle Ages*. Rev. and expanded ed. Trans. Jerold C. Frakes from *Griechisch-lateinisches Mittelalter. Von Hieronymus zu Nikolaus von Kues*. Berne and Munich: A. Francke Verlag, 1980.

Beyer, Hans-Veit. "Die Lichtlehre der Mönche des vierzehnten und des vierten Jahrhunderts, erörtert am Beispiel des Gregorios Sinaïtes, des Euagrios Pontikos und des Pseudo-Makarios/Symeon." *Jarhrbuch der österreichischen Byzantinistik* 31 (1981):473–512.

Blaise, Albert. *Dictionnaire latin-français des auteurs chrétiens*. Strasbourg: Le latin chrétien, 1954.

Blowers, Paul M. *Exegesis and Spiritual Pedagogy in Maximus the Confessor: An Investiga-*

tion of the Quaestiones ad Thalassium. Christianity and Judaism in Antiquity 7. Notre Dame, Ind.: University of Notre Dame Press, 1991.

Blum, G. G. "Vereinigung und Vermischung: Zwei Grundmotive christlich-orientalischer Mystik." *Oriens Christianus* 63 (1979):41–60.

Bonnardière, A.-M. la. "Marthe et Marie, figures de l'Église d'après saint Augustin." *La Vie Spirituelle* 86 (1952):404–27.

Bonner, Gerald. "Augustine and Mysticism." In *Augustine: Mystic and Mystagogue*, pp. 113–57. Ed. Frederick Van Fleteren, Joseph C. Schnaubelt, and Joseph Reino. Collectanea Augustiniana. New York: Peter Lang, 1994.

———. *Church and Faith in the Patristic Tradition: Augustine, Pelagianism, and Early Christian Northumbria.* Variorum Collected Studies Series. Aldershot: Variorum, 1996.

Borias, André. "Le moine et sa famille." *CC* 40 (1978):81–110, 195–217.

Bousset, Wilhelm. *Apophthegmata. Studien zur Geschichte des ältesten Mönchtums.* Tübingen: Mohr, 1923.

———. "Das Mönchtum der sketischen Wüste." *ZKG* 42 (1926):1–41.

Bouyer, Louis. *The Spirituality of the New Testament and the Fathers.* Vol. 1 of *A History of Christian Spirituality.* London: Burns and Oates, 1963. Reprint, New York: Seabury, 1982. Trans. Mary P. Ryan from *La spiritualité du Nouveau Testament et des Pères.* Paris: Montaigne, 1960.

Brakke, David. *Athanasius and the Politics of Asceticism.* Oxford Early Christian Studies. Oxford: Clarendon Press, 1995.

———. "The Authenticity of the Ascetic Athanasiana." *Orientalia* 63 (1994):17–56.

———. "The Problematization of Nocturnal Emissions in Early Christian Syria, Egypt, and Gaul." *Journal of Early Christian Studies* 3 (1995):419–60.

Brand, Charles. "Le *De Incarnatione Domini* de Jean Cassien." Contribution à l'étude de la christologie en Occident à la veille du Concile d'Ephèse. Doctoral diss., University of Strasbourg, 1954.

Brandi, Maria Vittoria. "Abramo il Semplice." *BSanc*, 1:121.

Browe, Peter. *Beiträge zur Sexualethik des Mittelalters.* Breslauer Studien zur historischen Theologie 23. Breslau: Müller und Seiffert, 1932.

Brown, Peter. *The Body and Society. Men, Women and Sexual Renunciation in Early Christianity.* New York: Columbia University Press, 1988.

Bunge, Gabriel. "Évagre le Pontique et les deux Macaire." *Irénikon* 56 (1983):215–27, 323–60.

———. *Evagrios Pontikos: Briefe aus der Wüste.* Sophia 24. Trier: Paulinus-Verlag, 1986.

———. *Evagrios Pontikos: Praktikos oder der Mönch, Hundert Kapitel über das geistliche Leben.* Köln: Luthe-Verlag, 1989.

———. *Das Geistgebet. Studien zum Traktat De oratione des Evagrios Pontikos.* Köln: Luthe-Verlag, 1987.

———. "*Mysterium unitatis.* Der Gedanke der Einheit von Schöpfer und Geschöpf in der evagrianischen Mystik." *FZPT* 36 (1989):449–69.

———. " 'Der mystische Sinn der Schrift': Anlässlich der Veröffentlichung der Scholien zum Ecclesiasten des Evagrios Pontikos." *SM* 36 (1994):135–46.

———. "Origenismus-Gnostizismus. Zum geistgeschichtlichen Standort des Evagrios Pontikos." *Vigiliae Christianae* 40 (1986):24–54.

———. " 'Priez sans cesse': aux origines de la prière hésychaste." *SM* 30 (1988):7–16.

———. "The 'Spiritual Prayer': On the Trinitarian Mysticism of Evagrius of Pontus." *Monastic Studies* 17 (1987):191–208.

Burns, J. Patout. "Grace: The Augustinian Foundation." In *Christian Spirituality: Origins to the Twelfth Century*, edited by Bernard McGinn and John Meyendorff. *World Spirituality: An Encyclopedic History of the Religious Quest*. Vol. 16, pp. 331–49. New York: Crossroad, 1989.

Burton-Christie, Douglas. *The Word in the Desert: Scripture and the Quest for Holiness in Early Christian Monasticism*. New York: Oxford University Press, 1993.

Butler, Cuthbert. *Benedictine Monachism. Studies in Benedictine Life and Rule*. London: Longmans, Green and Co., 1919.

————. *The Lausiac History of Palladius*. Vol. 1, A Critical Discussion together with notes on Early Egyptian Monasticism. Vol. 2, The Greek Text Edited with Introduction and Notes. Text and Studies 6. Cambridge: Cambridge University Press, 1898 and 1904.

————. *Western Mysticism*. New York: Dutton, 1924.

Cabrol, Fernand. "Cassien." *DACL*, 2:2348–57.

Camelot, Pierre-Thomas. *Foi et gnose: Introduction à l'étude de la connaissance mystique chez Clément d'Alexandrie*. Études de théologie et d'histoire de la spiritualité 3. Paris: J. Vrin, 1945.

————. "Gnose chrétienne." *DSp*, 6:509–23.

Canévet, Mariette. "Sens spirituels." *DSp*, 14:598–617.

Canivet, Pierre. "Erreurs de spiritualité et troubles psychiques. À propos d'un passage de la *Vie de S. Théodose* par Théodore de Petra (530)." *RSR* 50 (1962):161–205.

Cappuyns, M. "Cassien." *DHGE*, 11:1319–48.

————. "Le premier représentant de l'augustinisme médiéval, Prosper d'Aquitaine." *RTAM* 1 (1929):309–37.

Chadwick, Nora K. *Poetry and Letters in Early Christian Gaul*. London: Bowes and Bowes, 1955.

Chadwick, Owen. "Cassianus." *TRE*, 7:650–57.

————. "Euladius of Arles." *JTS* 46 (1945):200–205.

————. *John Cassian. A Study in Primitive Monasticism*. Cambridge: Cambridge University Press, 1950. 2nd ed. 1968.

Chéné, Jean. "Les origines de la controverse semi-pélagienne." *L'Année théologique augustinienne* 14 (1953):56–109.

Chitty, Derwas J. *The Desert a City: An Introduction to the Study of Egyptian and Palestinian Monasticism under the Christian Empire*. Oxford: Blackwell, 1966.

Chryssavgis, John. *Ascent to Heaven: The Theology of the Human Person according to Saint John of the Ladder*. Brookline, Mass.: Holy Cross Orthodox Press, 1989.

Ciccarese, Maria Pia. "Vision." *EEC*, 872b–73a.

Clark, Elizabeth A. *The Origenist Controversy. The Cultural Construction of an Early Christian Debate*. Princeton: Princeton University Press, 1992.

Cloke, Gillian. *"This Female Man of God": Women and Spiritual Power in the Patristic Age, AD 350–450*. London: Routledge, 1995.

Coakley, Sarah. "Why Three? Some Further Reflections on the Origins of the Doctrine of the Trinity." In *The Making and Remaking of Christian Doctrine. Essays in Honour of Maurice Wiles*, pp. 29–56. Ed. Sarah Coakley and David A. Pailin. Oxford: Clarendon Press, 1993.

Codina, Victor. *El aspecto cristologico en la espiritualidad de Juan Casiano*. OCA 175. Rome: Pontificium Institutum Orientalium Studiorum, 1966.

Cody, Aelred. "Scetis." *CE*, 2102–6.

Colish, Marcia L. *The Stoic Tradition from Antiquity to the Early Middle Ages*. 2 vols. Leiden: Brill, 1985.

Colombás, García M. "La Biblia en la espiritualidad del monacato primitivo." *Yermo* 1 (1963):3–20, 149–70, 271–86; 2 (1964):3–14, 113–29.

———. *El monacato primitivo.* Vol 1., *Hombres, hechos, costumbres, instituciones.* Vol. 2, *La espiritualidad.* Biblioteca de autores cristianos 351, 376. Madrid: BAC, 1974–75.

Coman, Jean. "Le patrimoine de l'oecuménisme chrétien du quatrième au cinquième siècles en Scythe-Mineure (Dobrudja)." *Contacts* 22 (1970):61–85.

———. "Les 'Scythes' Jean Cassien et Denys le Petit." *Kleronomia* 7 (1975):27–46.

Constable, Giles. "The Interpretation of Mary and Martha." In *Three Studies in Medieval Religious and Social Thought,* pp. 1–141. Cambridge: Cambridge University Press, 1995.

Coquin, René-Georges and Maurice Martin. "Diolkos." *CE,* 908.

———. "Jabal Khashm al-Qu'ûd." *CE,* 1315–16.

———. "Monasteries in the Daqahliyyah Province." *CE,* 1648–49.

———. "Monasteries of the Eastern Desert." *CE,* 1649–50.

———. "Monasteries of the Western Desert." *CE,* 1658–59.

Corrigan, Kevin. "Ecstasy and Ectasy in Some Early Pagan and Christian Mystical Writings." In *Greek and Medieval Studies in Honor of Leo Sweeney, S.J.,* pp. 27–38. Ed. William J. Carroll and John J. Furlong. New York: Peter Lang, 1994.

———. " 'Solitary' Mysticism in Plotinus, Proclus, Gregory of Nyssa, and Pseudo-Dionysius." *Journal of Religion* 76 (1996):28–42.

Courcelle, Pierre. *Late Latin Writers and Their Greek Sources.* Cambridge: Harvard University Press, 1969. Trans. Harry E. Wedeck from *Les lettres grecques en Occident de Macrobe à Cassiodore.* 2nd ed. Paris: Boccard, 1948.

Courreau, Joël and Adalbert de Vogüé. *Césaire d'Arles: Oeuvres monastiques* II. SC 398. Paris: Cerf, 1994.

Courtois, C. *Victor de Vita et son oeuvre.* Algiers: Direction de l'Intérieur et des Beaux–Arts—Service des Antiquités, 1954.

Coustant, Pierre. *S. Innocentii Papae Epistolae et decreta.* Excerpted in *PL* 20.463–608 from *Epistolae romanorum pontificum, et quae ad eos scriptae sunt a S. Clemente I. usque ad Innocentium III. Tomus 1, ab anno Christi 67 ad annum 440.* Paris: L.D. Delatour, 1721.

Cristiani, Léon. *Jean Cassien.* 2 vols. Figures monastiques. Abbaye S. Wandrille: Éditions de Fontenelle, 1946.

Crouzel, Henri. *Origen.* Trans. A. S. Worrall. San Francisco: Harper and Row, 1989.

———. *Origène et la "connaissance mystique."* Museum Lessianum section théologique 56. Toulouse: Desclée de Brouwer, 1961.

Csányi, Daniel A. "*Optima pars.* Die Auslegungsgeschichte von Luk 10, 38–42 bei den Kirchenvätern der ersten vier Jahrhunderte." *SM* 2 (1960):5–78.

Cuper, Guillaume. "De Sancto Joanne Cassiano Abbate Massiliae in Gallia." In *Acta Sanctorum Iulii.* Vol. 5, pp. 458–82. Paris: Palmé, 1868.

Daley, Brian E. *The Hope of the Early Church: a Handbook of Patristic Eschatology.* Cambridge: Cambridge University Press, 1991.

Damian, Theodor. "Some Critical Considerations and New Arguments Reviewing the Problem of St. John Cassian's Birthplace." *OCP* 57 (1991):257–80.

Daniélou, Jean. "Mystique de la ténèbre chez Grégoire de Nysse." *DSp,* 2:1872–85.

———. "Terre et Paradis chez les Pères de l'Église." *Eranos-Jahrbuch* (1953):433–72.

Daumas, F. "Origine des fouilles, description du site." In *Kellia I. Kom 219: Fouilles exécutées en 1964 et 1965.* Vol. 1, pp. vii–xviii. Ed. F. Daumas and Antoine Guillaumont. Fouilles de l'Institut Français d'Archéologie Orientale du Caire 28. Cairo: IFAO, 1969.

De Beer, Francis. "Une tessère d'orthodoxie. Le 'Libellus emendationis' de Leporius (vers 418–21)." *REA* 10 (1964):145–83.

Dechow, Jon F. *Dogma and Mysticism in Early Christianity: Epiphanius of Cyprus and the Legacy of Origen.* North American Patristic Society Patristic Monograph Series 13. Macon, Ga.: Mercer University Press, 1988.

De Goedt, M. "L'extase dans la Bible." *DSp,* 4:2072–87.

Dekkers, Eligius. "Les traductions grecques des écrits patristiques latins." *Sacris Erudiri* 5 (1953):193–233.

De Lubac, Henri. *Exégèse médiévale: Les quatres sens de l'Écriture.* 3 vols. Théologie 41–42, 59. Paris: Aubier, 1959–64.

———. "On an Old Distich: The Doctrine of the 'Fourfold Sense' in Scripture." In *Theological Fragments,* pp. 109–27. San Francisco: Ignatius, 1989. Trans. Rebecca Howell Balinski from *Théologies d'occasion.* Paris: Desclée de Brouwer, 1984.

Dembinska, M. "Diet: A Comparison of Food Consumption between Some Eastern and Western Monasteries in the Fourth–Twelfth Centuries." *Byzantion* 55 (1985):431–62.

Des Places, Édouard. "Diadoque de Photicé." *DSp,* 3:817–834.

———. "Diadoque de Photicé et le Messalianisme." In *Kyriakon. Festschrift Johannes Quasten,* pp. 591–605. Ed. Patrick Granfield and Josef A. Jungmann. Münster: Aschendorff, 1970.

Devos, Paul. "Saint Jean Cassien et Saint Moïse l'Éthiopien." *Analecta Bollandiana* 103 (1985):61–73.

Dillon, John M. "Rejecting the Body, Refining the Body: Some Remarks on the Development of Platonist Asceticism." In *Asceticism,* pp. 80–87. Ed. Vincent L. Wimbush and Richard Valantasis. New York: Oxford University Press, 1995.

Djuth, Marianne. "Cassian's Use of the Figure *Via Regia* in *Collatio* II 'On Discretion'." In *SP* 30, pp. 166–74. Leuven: Peeters, 1996.

Dörr, Friedrich. *Diadochus von Photike und die Messalianer: Ein Kampf zwischen wahrer und falscher Mystik im fünften Jahrhundert.* Freiburger theologische Studien 47. Freiburg im Breisgau: Herder, 1937.

Dörrie, Heinrich and Hermann Dörries. "Erotapokriseis." *RAC,* 6:342–70.

Dörries, Hermann. "Diadochus und Symeon." In *Wort und Stunde.* Vol. 1, pp. 352–422. Göttingen, 1966.

———. *Die Theologie des Makarios/Symeon.* Abhandlungen der Akademie der Wissenschaften in Göttingen, Philologisch-historische Klasse, 3. Folge, 103. Göttingen: Vandenhoeck und Ruprecht, 1978.

Drabkin, I. E. *Caelius Aurelianus: On Acute Diseases and On Chronic Diseases.* Chicago: University of Chicago Press, 1950.

Draguet, R. "L''Histoire Lausiaque', une oeuvre écrite dans l'esprit d'Évagre." *RHE* 41 (1946):321–46.

Drioton, Étienne. "La discussion d'un moine anthropomorphite audien avec le patriarche Théophile d'Alexandrie en l'année 399." *ROC* 20 (1915–17):92–128.

Driscoll, Jeremy. *The "Ad monachos" of Evagrius Ponticus: Its Structure and a Select Commentary.* SA 104. Rome: Pontificio Ateneo S. Anselmo, 1991.

———. "Penthos and Tears in Evagrius Ponticus." *SM* 36 (1994):147–64.

Driver, Steven D. "The Development of Jerome's Views on the Ascetic Life." *RTAM* 62 (1995):44–70.

———. "From Palestinian Ignorance to Egyptian Wisdom: Cassian's Challenge to Jerome's Monastic Teaching." *ABR* 48 (1997).

———. "The Reading of Egyptian Monastic Culture in John Cassian." Ph.D. diss., University of Toronto, 1994.

Drocourt-Dubreuil, Geneviève. *Saint-Victor de Marseille: Art funéraire et prière des morts aux temps paléochrétiens (quatrième–cinquième siècles)*. Paris: De Boccard, 1989.

Duchrow, Ulrich. "Zum Prolog von Augustins De Doctrina christiana." *Vigiliae Christianae* 17 (1963):165–72.

Duchesne, Louis. *Fastes épiscopaux de l'ancienne Gaule*. Vol. 1, *Provinces du Sud-est*. Paris: Fontemoing, 1907.

Dyovouniotis, K. J. "'Ιωάννου Κασσιανοῦ Διαλέξεις πατέρων." 'Εκκλησιαστικὸς Φάρος 6 (1913):51–65, 161–76, 225–43.

Edsman, Carl-Martin. *Le Baptême de Feu*. Acta Seminarii Neotestamentici Upsaliensis 9. Leipzig: Alfred Lorentz, 1940.

Elm, Susanna. *Virgins of God: The Making of Asceticism in Late Antiquity*. Oxford Classical Monographs. Oxford: Clarendon Press, 1994.

Evelyn-White, Hugh Gerard. *The Monasteries of the Wâdi 'n Natrûn*. 3 vols. New York: Metropolitan Museum of Art, 1932–33.

Fedalto, Giorgio. *Hierarchia Ecclesiastica Orientalis. Series episcoporum ecclesiarum christianorum orientalium*. Vol. 2, *Patriarchatus Alexandrinus, Antiochenus, Hierosolymitanus*. Padua: Messagero, 1988.

Fiske, Adele. "Cassian and Monastic Friendship." *ABR* 12 (1961):190–205.

Fleming, Julia. "The Helpful Lie: the Moral Reasoning of Augustine and John Cassian." Ph.D. diss., Catholic University of America, 1993.

Florovsky, Georges. "The Anthropomorphites in the Egyptian Desert." In *Aspects of Church History*, pp. 89–96. Vol. 4 of *Collected Works*. Belmont, Mass.: Nordland, 1975.

———. "Theophilus of Alexandria and Apa Aphou of Pemdje." In *Aspects of Church History*, pp. 97–129. Vol. 4 of *Collected Works*. Belmont, Mass.: Nordland, 1975.

Fontaine, Jacques. "L'ascétisme chrétien dans la littérature gallo-romaine d'Hilaire à Cassien." In *La Gallia Romana*, 87–115. Problemi Attuali di Scienza e di Cultura, Quaderno 158. Rome: Accademia Nazionale dei Lincei, 1973.

Foucault, Michel. "The Battle for Chastity." In *Michel Foucault. Politics, Philosophy and Culture: Interviews and Other Writings 1977–1984*, pp. 228–41. Ed. Lawrence D. Kritzman, trans. Alan Sheridan et al. New York: Routledge, 1988.

———. *The History of Sexuality*. 3 vols. New York: Random House, 1978–86. Trans. Robert Hurley from *Histoire de la sexualité*. Paris: Gallimard, 1976–84.

Frank, Karl Suso. "Abbas Poimen—Versuch über die Apophthegmata Patrum." *Münchener Theologische Zeitschrift* 40 (1989):337–47.

———. *ΑΓΓΕΛΙΚΟΣ ΒΙΟΣ: begriffsanalytische und begriffsgeschichtliche Untersuchung zum 'engelgleichen Leben' im frühen Mönchtum*. Beiträge zur Geschichte des alten Mönchtums und des Benediktinerordens 26. Münster: Aschendorff, 1964.

———. "Fiktive Mündlichkeit als Grundstruktur der monastischen Literatur." In *SP* 25, pp. 356–75. Leuven: Peeters, 1993.

———. "Johannes Cassian, De institutis coenobiorum. Normativer Erzähltext, präskriptiver Regeltext und appellative Du-Anrede." In *Dialogische Strukturen. Dialogic Structures. Festschrift für Willi Erzgräber*, pp. 7–16. Ed. Thomas Kühn and Ursula Schaefer. Tübingen: Gunter Narr, 1996.

———. "John Cassian on John Cassian." In *SP* 30, pp. 418–33. Leuven: Peeters, 1996.

Gazet, Alardus. *Commentarius* from *Cassiani Opera Omnia*. Douai, 1616. Reprinted in *PL* 49.55C–476C and 50.477A–1328D.

Giamberardini, G., and D. Gelsi. "Scete." *DIP*, 8:1023–30.

Gibson, Edgar C. S. "Prolegomena." *The Works of John Cassian*. Select Library of Nicene and Post-Nicene Fathers, 2nd series, vol. 11. Reprint, Grand Rapids, Mich.: Eerdmans, 1982.

Gillet, Robert. Introduction to *Grégoire le Grand: Morales sur Job*, pp. 7–109. SC 32bis. Paris: Cerf, 1975.

Giversen, Soren. "L'expérience mystique chez Philon." In *Mysticism. Based on Papers Read at the Symposium on Mysticism Held at Åbo on the 7th–9th September, 1968*, pp. 91–98. Ed. Sven S. Hartman and Carl-Martin Edsman. Stockholm: Almquist and Wiksell, 1970.

Golìnski, Z. "Doctrina Cassiani de mendacio officioso." *Collectanea Theologica* 17 (1936):491–503.

Golitzin, Alexander. *Et introibo ad altare Dei: The Mystagogy of Dionysius Areopagita, with Special Reference to Its Predecessors in the Eastern Christian Tradition*. Analecta Vlatadon 59. Thessaloniki: Patriarchal Institute for Patristic Studies, 1994.

———. "The Vision of God and the Form of Glory: Some Thoughts on the Anthropomorphites." Unpublished paper presented at the annual meeting of the North American Patristics Society, 1996.

Gómez, Alberto. "Compunctio lacrymarum. Doctrina de la compunción en el monacato latino de los siglos IV–VI." *Collectanea Ordinis Cisterciensium Reformatorum* 23 (1961):232–53.

Gould, Graham. *The Desert Fathers on Monastic Community*. Oxford Early Christian Studies. Oxford: Clarendon Press, 1993.

———. "The Image of God and the Anthropomorphite Controversy in Fourth Century Monasticism." In *Origeniana Quinta. Papers of the Fifth International Origen Congress, Boston College, 14–18 August 1989*, 549–57. Ed. Robert J. Daly. Bibliotheca Ephemeridum Theologicarum Lovaniensium 105. Leuven: University Press, 1992.

Graef, Hilda. "Ekstase." *LTK*, 3:788–91.

Graham, William A. *Beyond the Written Word: Oral Aspects of Scripture in the History of Religion*. Cambridge: Cambridge University Press, 1987.

Gribomont, Jean. "The Commentaries of Adalbert de Vogüé and the Great Monastic Tradition." *ABR* 36 (1985):229–52. Trans. Terrence Kardong from "Les commentaires d'Adalbert de Vogüé et la grande tradition monastique." In *Commentaria in S. Regulam I*, 109–43. SA 84. Rome: Pontificio Ateneo San Anselmo, 1982.

Griffe, Élie. "Cassien a-t-il été prêtre d'Antioche?" *Bulletin de littérature ecclésiastique* 55 (1954):240–44.

———. *La Gaule chrétienne à l'époque romaine*. 2nd ed. 3 vols. Paris: Letouzey et Ané, 1964–66.

Grillmeier, Aloys. *Christ in Christian Tradition*. Vol. 1, *From the Apostolic Age to Chalcedon (AD 451)*. 2nd. ed. London: Mowbrays, 1975. Trans. John Bowden from *Jesus der Christus im Glauben der Kirche*. Freiburg im Breisgau: Herder, 1979.

Groves, Nicholas. "*Mundicia cordis*. A Study of the Theme of Purity of Heart in Hugh of Pontigny and the Fathers of the Undivided Church." In *One Yet Two: Monastic Tradition East and West. Orthodox-Cistercian Symposium, Oxford University, 26 August–1 September, 1973*, pp. 304–31. Ed. M. Basil Pennington. CSS 29. Kalamazoo: Cistercian Publications, 1976.

Guibert, Joseph de. "La componction du coeur." *RAM* 15 (1934):225–40.

———. *The Theology of the Spiritual Life*. New York: Sheed and Ward, 1953. Trans. Paul Barrett from *Theologia spiritualis ascetica et mystica*. 3rd. ed. Rome: Gregorian University Press, 1946.

Guillaumont, Antoine. *Aux origines du monachisme chrétien: Pour une phénoménologie du monachisme*. Spiritualité orientale 30. Bégrolles-en-Mauges: Abbaye de Bellefontaine, 1979.

———. "Le 'coeur' chez les spirituels grecs à l'époque ancienne." *DSp*, 2:2281–88.

———. "De l'eschatologie à la mystique: histoire d'une sentence d'Évagre." In *Mémorial du cinquantenaire, 1914–1964: École des langues orientales anciennes de l'Institut Catholique de Paris*, pp. 187–92. Institut Catholique Travaux 10. Paris: Bloud et Gay, 1964.

———. "Le gnostique chez Clément d'Alexandrie et chez Évagre le Pontique." In *Alexandrina. Mélanges offerts à Claude Mondésert SJ*, pp. 195–201. Paris: Cerf, 1987.

———. "Histoire des moines aux Kellia." *Orientalia Lovaniensia Periodica* 8 (1977):187–203.

———. "Histoire du site des Kellia d'après les documents écrits." In *Kellia I. Kom 219: Fouilles exécutées en 1964 et 1965*. Vol. 1, pp. 1–15. Ed. F. Daumas and Antoine Guillaumont. Fouilles de l'Institut Français d'Archéologie Orientale du Caire 28. Cairo: IFAO, 1969.

———. *Les Képhalaia gnostica d'Évagre le Pontique et l'histoire de l'origénisme chez les grecs et chez les syriens*. Patristica Sorbonensia 5. Paris: Éditions du Seuil, 1962.

———. "Macaire l'Égyptien ou le Grand." *DSp*, 10:11–13.

———. "Macarius the Egyptian, Saint." *CE*, 1491.

———. "Paphnutius of Scetis, Saint." *CE*, 1884–85.

———. "Le problème de la prière continuelle dans le monachisme ancien." In *L'expérience de la prière dans les grandes religions. Actes du colloque de Louvain-la Neuve et Liège (22–23 novembre 1978)*, pp. 285–94. Ed. Henri Limet and Julien Ries. Homo Religiosus 5. Louvain-la-Neuve: Centre d'Histoire des Religions, 1980.

———. "Le problème des deux Macaire dans les *Apophthegmata Patrum*." *Irénikon* 48 (1975):41–59.

———. "Sarapion." *CE*, 2094–95.

———. "Les sens des noms du coeur dans l'antiquité." In *Le coeur*, pp. 41–81. Les études carmélitaines. Paris: Desclée de Brouwer, 1950.

———. "La vie gnostique selon Évagre le Pontique." *Annuaire du Collège de France* 80 (1979–80): 467–70.

———. "La vision de l'intellect par lui-même dans la mystique évagrienne." *Mélanges de l'Université Saint-Joseph* 50 (1984):255–62.

———. "Les visions mystiques dans le monachisme oriental chrétien." In *Les visions mystiques. Colloque organisé par le Secrétariat d'État à la Culture, Paris, 17–18 mars 1976*, pp. 116–27. *Nouvelles de l'Institut Catholique de Paris* (février 1977). Reprint, *Aux origines du monachisme chrétien*, pp. 36–47.

Guillaumont, Antoine, et al. "Kellia." *CE*, 1396–1410.

Guillaumont, Antoine, and K. H. Kuhn. "Paul of Thebes, Saint." *CE*, 1925–26.

Guy, Jean-Claude. *Les Apophtegmes des Pères. Collection systématique*. SC 387. Paris: Cerf, 1993.

———. "Cassian, Saint John." *CE*, 461–64.

———. "Le Centre monastique de Scété dans la littérature du cinquième siècle." *OCP* 30 (1964):129–47.

———. "Jean Cassien, historien du monachisme égyptien?." In *SP* 8 (TU 93), pp. 363–72. Berlin: Akademie Verlag, 1966.

———. *Jean Cassien. Institutions cénobitiques*. SC 109. Paris: Cerf, 1965.

———. *Jean Cassien: Vie et doctrine spirituelle*. Collection Théologie, Pastorale et Spiritualité 9. Paris: Lethilleux, 1961.

———. *Recherches sur la tradition grecque des Apophthegmata Patrum*. 2nd ed. Subsidia hagiographica 36. Brussels: Société des Bollandistes, 1984.

Guyon, Jean. "Marseille." In *Topographie chrétienne des cités de la Gaule des origines au milieu du VIIIe siècle*. Ed. Nancy Gauthier and Jean-Charles Picard. Vol. 3, *Provinces ecclésiastiques de Vienne et d'Arles. Viennensis et Alpes Graiae et Poeninae*, pp. 121–33. Ed. Jacques Biarne et al. Paris: De Boccard, 1986.

Haag, Modestus. "A Precarious Balance: Flesh and Spirit in Cassian's Works." *ABR* 19 (1968):180–92.

Hadot, Ilsetraut. *Seneca und die griechisch-römische Tradition der Seelenleitung.* Quellen und Studien zur Geschichte der Philosophie 13. Berlin: De Gruyter, 1969.

Hadot, Pierre. "Ancient Spiritual Exercises and 'Christian Philosophy'." In *Philosophy as a Way of Life,* 126–44. Trans. from "Exercices spirituels et 'philosophie chrétienne'." In *Exercices spirituels et philosophie antique,* 59–76.

———. "Un dialogue interrompu avec Michel Foucault. Convergences et divergences." In *Exercices spirituels et philosophie antique,* 229–33.

———. "Les divisions des parties de la philosophie dans l'Antiquité." *Museum Helveticum* 36 (1979):201–23.

———. *Exercices spirituels et philosophie antique,* 2nd ed. Paris: Études Augustiniennes, 1987.

———. "Marcus Aurelius." In *Philosophy as a Way of Life,* 179–205.

———. "Philosophie, discours philosophique, et divisions de la philosophie chez les stoïciens." *Revue Internationale de Philosophie* 178 (1991):205–19.

———. *Philosophy as a Way of Life: Spiritual Exercises from Socrates to Foucault.* Ed. Arnold I. Davidson, trans. Michael Chase. Oxford/ Cambridge, MA: Blackwell: 1995.

———. "La physique comme exercice spirituel ou pessimisme et optimisme chez Marc Aurèle." In *Exercices spirituels et philosophie antique,* 119–33.

———. *Plotinus, or, the Simplicity of Vision.* Chicago: University of Chicago Press, 1993. Trans. Michael Chase from *Plotin ou la Simplicité du regard.* 2nd ed. Paris: Études Augustiniennes, 1971.

———. "Reflections on the Idea of the 'Cultivation of the Self'." In *Philosophy as a Way of Life,* 206–13. Trans. from *Michel Foucault philosophe.* Ed. François Ewald. Paris: Éditions du Seuil, 1989.

———. "Spiritual Exercises." In *Philosophy as a Way of Life,* 81–125. Trans. from "Exercices spirituels." *Annuaire de la Ve Section de l'École Pratique des Hautes Études* 84 (1977):25–70. Reprinted in *Exercices spirituels et philosophie antique,* pp. 13–58.

Harl, Marguerite. "Le guetteur et la cible: Les deux sens de *Skopos* dans la langue religieuse des chrétiens." *Revue des études grecques* 74 (1961):450–68.

———. "Le langage de l'expérience religieuse chez les Pères grecs." *Rivista di storia e letteratura religiosa* 15 (1977):5–34.

———. "Les origines grecques du mot et de la notion de componction dans la Septante et chez ses commentateurs." *REA* 32 (1986):3–21.

Hartman, Sven S., and Carl-Martin Edsman. *Mysticism. Based on Papers read at the Symposium on Mysticism held at Åbo on the 7th–9th September, 1968.* Stockholm: Almquist and Wiksell, 1970.

Hausherr, Irénée. "Comment priaient les Pères." *RAM* 32 (1956):33–58, 284–96.

———. [J.Lemaitre]. "Contemplation. A III.2." *DSp,* 2:1787–1801.

———. "Les grands courants de la spiritualité orientale." *OCP* 1 (1936):114–38.

———. *Hésychasme et prière.* OCA 176. Rome: Pontificum Institutum Orientalium Studiorum, 1966.

———. "Ignorance infinie." *OCP* 5 (1936):351–62.

———. "Ignorance infinie ou science infinie?" *OCP* 25 (1959):44–52.

———. *Les leçons d'un contemplatif. Le Traité de l'oraison d'Évagre le Pontique.* Paris: Beauchesne, 1960. Revision of "Le *Traité de l'oraison* d'Évagre le Pontique (Pseudo Nil)."

———. *La méthode d'oraison hésychaste.* Orientalia Christiana, vol. 9:2, no. 36. Rome: Pontificium Institutum Orientalium Studiorum, 1927.

———. "Mystique extatique." In "Contemplation. A III.3." *DSp,* 2:1862–67.

————. *The Name of Jesus*. CSS 44. Kalamazoo: Cistercian, 1978. Trans. Charles Cummings from *Noms du Christ et voies d'oraison*. OCA 157. Rome: Pontificium Institutum Orientalium Studiorum, 1960.

————. *Penthos: The Doctrine of Compunction in the Christian East*. CSS 53. Kalamazoo: Cistercian Publications, 1982. Trans. Anselm Hufstader from *Penthos: La doctrine de la componction dans l'Orient chrétien*. OCA 132. Rome: Pontificium Institutum Orientalium Studiorum, 1944.

————. "La prière perpétuelle du chrétien." In *Laïcat et sainteté, II: Sainteté et vie dans le siècle*, pp. 111–66. Rome: Herder, 1965. Reprinted in *Hésychasme et prière*, 255–306.

————. Review of Alfons Kemmer, *Charisma Maximum*. OCP 6 (1940):248–49.

————. *Spiritual Direction in the Early Christian East*. CSS 116. Kalamazoo: Cistercian Publications, 1990. Trans. Anthony P. Gythiel from *Direction spirituelle en Orient autrefois*. OCA 144. Rome: Pontificium Institutum Orientalium Studiorum, 1955.

————. "Le *Traité de l'oraison* d'Évagre le Pontique (Pseudo Nil)." RAM 15 (1934):36–93, 113–70.

Hausherr, Irene [J.Lemaitre], R. Roques, and M. Viller. "Contemplation. A III.1." *DSp*, 2:1762–87

Hermann, Alfred and Gustave Bardy. "Dialog." RAC, 3:928–55.

Hoch, Alexander. *Lehre des Johannes Cassianus von Natur und Gnade: Ein Beitrag zur Geschichte des Gnadenstreits im 5. Jahrhundert*. Freiburg im Breisgau: Herder, 1895.

————. "Zur Heimat des Johannes Cassianus." *Theologisches Quartalschrift* 82 (1900):43–69.

Hof, Hans. "Ecstasy and Mysticism." In *Religious Ecstasy. Based on Papers read at the Symposium on Religious Ecstasy held at Åbo, Finland, on the 26th–28th of August 1981*, pp. 240–52. Ed. Nils H. Holm. Scripta Instituti Donneriani Aboensis 11. Stockholm: Almquist and Wiksell, 1982.

Hoffmann, Manfred. *Der Dialog bei den christlichen Schriftstellern der ersten vier Jahrhunderte*. TU 96. Berlin: Akademie Verlag, 1966.

Holm, Nils H. "Ecstasy Research in the Twentieth Century." In *Religious Ecstasy*, 7–26.

————, ed. *Religious Ecstasy. Based on Papers read at the Symposium on Religious Ecstasy held at Åbo, Finland, on the 26th–28th of August 1981*. Scripta Instituti Donneriani Aboensis 11. Stockholm: Almquist and Wiksell, 1982.

Holze, Heinrich. *Erfahrung und Theologie im frühen Mönchtum. Untersuchungen zu einer Theologie des monastischen Lebens bei den ägyptischen Mönchsvätern, Johannes Cassian und Benedikt von Nursia*. Forschungen zur Kirchen- und Dogmengeschichte 48. Göttingen: Vandenhoeck und Ruprecht, 1992.

Honselmann, Klemens. "Bruchstücke von Auszügen aus Werken Cassians—Reste einer verlorenen Schrift des Eucherius von Lyon?" *Theologie und Glaube* 51 (1961):300–304.

Jacquart, Danielle, and Claude Thomasset. *Sexuality and Medicine in the Middle Ages*. Princeton: Princeton University Press, 1988. Trans. Matthew Adamson from *Sexualité et savoir médical au Moyen-Âge*. Paris: Presses Universitaires de France, 1985.

Jaeger, Werner. *Two Rediscovered Works of Ancient Christian Literature: Gregory of Nyssa and Macarius*. Leiden: Brill, 1954.

Jansen, H. Ludin. "Das mystische Erlebnis bei Plotin." In *Mysticism. Based on Papers read at the Symposium on Mysticism held at Åbo on the 7th–9th September, 1968*, pp. 99–105. Ed. Sven S. Hartman and Carl-Martin Edsman. Stockholm: Almquist and Wiksell, 1970.

Jenal, Georg. *Italia ascetica atque monastica: Das Asketen- und Mönchtum in Italien von den Anfängen bis zur Zeit der Langobarden (ca. 150/250–604)*. Monographien zur Geschichte des Mittelalters 39. Stuttgart: A. Hiersemann, 1995.

Joest, Christoph. "Die Bedeutung von Akedia und Apatheia bei Evagrios Pontikos." *SM* 35 (1993):7–53.

Jones, Cheslyn. "Mysticism, Human and Divine." In *The Study of Spirituality*, pp. 17–24. Ed. Cheslyn Jones, Geoffrey Wainwright, and Edward Yarnold. London: SPCK, 1986.

Kardong, Terrence. "Aiming for the Mark: Cassian's Metaphor for the Monastic Quest." *Cistercian Studies* 22 (1987):213–21.

————. *Benedict's Rule: A Translation and Commentary*. Collegeville, Minn.: Liturgical Press, 1996.

————. "Benedict's Use of Cassianic Formulae for Spiritual Progress." *SM* 34 (1992):233–52.

————. "John Cassian's Evaluation of Monastic Practices." *ABR* 43 (1992):82–105.

————. "John Cassian's Teaching on Perfect Chastity." *ABR* 30 (1979):249–63.

Kasper, Clemens. *Theologie und Askese: Die spiritualität des Inselmönchtums von Lérins im 5. Jahrhundert*. Beiträge zur Geschichte des Alten Mönchtums und das Benediktinertums 40. Münster: Aschendorff, 1991.

Kelly, J. N. D. *Golden Mouth: The Story of John Chrysostom—Ascetic, Preacher, Bishop*. London: Duckworth, 1995.

————. *Jerome: His Life, Writings, and Controversies*. New York: Harper and Row, 1975. Reprint, Westminster, Md.: Christian Classics, 1980.

Kemmer, Alfons. *Charisma Maximum: Untersuchung zu Cassians Vollkommenheitslehre und seiner Stellung zum Messalianismus*. Leuven: Ceuterick, 1938.

————. "Gregorius Nyssenus estne inter fontes Joannis Cassiani numerandus?" *OCP* 21 (1955):451–66.

Kinsey, Alfred C., Wardell B. Pomeroy, and Clyde E. Martin. *Sexual Behavior in the Human Male*. Philadelphia: W. B. Saunders, 1948.

Kirchmeyer, J. "Extase chez les Pères de l'Église." *DSp*, 4:2087–2113.

Kline, Francis. "The Christology of Evagrius and the Parent System of Origen." *Cistercian Studies* 20 (1985):155–83.

Klingshirn, William E. *Caesarius of Arles: The Making of a Christian Community in Late Antique Gaul*. Cambridge: Cambridge University Press, 1994.

Krivocheine, Basil. *In the Light of Christ: Saint Symeon the New Theologian (949–1022). Life—Spirituality—Doctrine*. Crestwood, N.Y.: St Vladimir's Seminary Press, 1986. Trans. Anthony P. Gythiel from *Dans la lumière du Christ. Saint Syméon le Nouveau Théologien. Vie. Spiritualité. Doctrine*. Chevetogne (Belgium): Éditions de Chevetogne, 1980.

Labrousse, Mireille. *Saint Honorat: Fondateur de Lérins et évêque d'Arles*. Vie monastique 31. Bégrolles-en-Mauges: Abbaye de Bellefontaine, 1995.

Ladner, Gerhart B. *The Idea of Reform: Its Impact on Christian Thought and Action in the Age of the Fathers*. Cambridge: Harvard University Press, 1959.

Lampe, G. W. H. *A Patristic Greek Lexicon*. Oxford: Oxford University Press, 1961.

Leclercq, Henri. "Marseille." *DACL*, 10:2204–93.

Leloir, Louis. *Désert et communion: Témoignage des Pères du Désert recueillis à partir des Paterica arméniens*. Spiritualité orientale 26. Bégrolles-en-Mauges: Abbaye de Bellefontaine, 1978.

LeQuien, Michel. *Oriens christianus in quatuor patriarchatus digestus; quo exhibentur ecclesiae, patriarchae, caeterique praesules totius Orientis*. Paris: Typographia regia, 1740. Reprint, Graz: Akademische Druck- und Verlagsanstalt, 1958.

Leroy, Julien. "Le cénobitisme chez Cassien." *RAM* 43(1967):121–58.

————. "Les préfaces des écrits monastiques de Jean Cassien." *RAM* 42 (1966):157–80.

Leroy, Olivier. "La splendeur corporelle des saints." *Supplément à la "Vie spirituelle"* 45 (1935):65–85, 138–60, and 46 (1936):29–43.

Leyser, Conrad. "*Lectio divina, oratio pura*: Rhetoric and the Techniques of Asceticism in the 'Conferences' of John Cassian." In *Modelli di santità e modelli di comportamento: contrasti, intersezioni, complementarità,* pp. 79–105. Ed. Giulia Barone, Marina Caffiero, and Francesco Scorza Barcellona. Turin: Rosenberg e Sellier, 1994.

Liddell, Henry George, and Robert Scott, *A Greek-English Lexicon.* 9th ed. Oxford: Clarendon Press, 1940.

Lilla, Salvatore. "Neoplatonism." *EEC*, 585b–93a.

———. "Platonism and the Fathers." *EEC*, 689b–98b.

Loorits, Oskar. *Der Heilige Kassian und die Schaltjahrlegende.* Folklore Fellows Communications 149. Helsinki: Suomalainen Tiedeakatemia, 1954.

Loseby, S. T. "Marseille: A Late Antique Success Story?" *Journal of Roman Studies* 82 (1992):165–85.

Lossky, Vladimir. *The Vision of God.* Trans. Asheleigh Moorhouse. London: Faith Press, 1963. Reprint, Crestwood, N.Y.: St. Vladimir's Seminary Press, 1983.

Lot-Borodine, M. "Le mystère du 'don des larmes' dans l'Orient chrétien." *Supplément à la Vie Spirituelle* (septembre 1936):65–110.

Louth, Andrew. *The Origins of the Christian Mystical Tradition from Plato to Denys.* Oxford: Clarendon Press, 1981.

McDonnell, Kilian. "Prayer in Ancient Western Tradition." *Worship* 55 (1981):34–61.

McEntire, Sandra J. *The Doctrine of Compunction in Medieval England: Holy Tears.* Studies in Mediaeval Literature 8. Lewiston, N.Y.: E. Mellen Press, 1990.

McGinn, Bernard. "Asceticism and Mysticism in Late Antiquity." In *Asceticism,* pp. 62–68. Ed. Vincent L. Wimbush and Richard Valantasis. New York: Oxford University Press, 1995.

———. *The Foundations of Mysticism: Origins to the Fifth Century.* Vol. 1 of *The Presence of God: A History of Western Christian Mysticism.* New York: Crossroad, 1992.

———. *The Growth of Mysticism: Gregory the Great through the Twelfth Century.* Vol. 2 of *The Presence of God: A History of Western Christian Mysticism.* New York: Crossroad, 1994.

McGuire, Brian Patrick. *Friendship and Community: the Monastic Experience, 350–1250.* CSS 95. Kalamazoo: Cistercian, 1988.

Macqueen, D. J. "John Cassian on Grace and Free Will, with Particular Reference to *Institutio* XII and *Collatio* XIII." *RTAM* 44 (1977):5–28.

Markus, Robert A. "Chronicle and Theology: Prosper of Aquitaine." In *The Inheritance of Historiography,* pp. 31–43. Ed. Christopher Holdsworth and T. P. Wiseman. Exeter, 1986. Reprinted in *Sacred and Secular.*

———. *The End of Ancient Christianity.* Cambridge: Cambridge University Press, 1990.

———. "The Legacy of Pelagius: Orthodoxy, Heresy and Conciliation." In *The Making of Orthodoxy,* pp. 214–34. Ed. Rowan D. Williams. Cambridge: Cambridge University Press, 1989. Reprinted in *Sacred and Secular.*

———. *Sacred and Secular: Studies on Augustine and Latin Christianity.* Variorum Collected Studies Series. Aldershot: Variorum, 1994.

Marrou, Henri Irénée. "Diadoque de Photiké et Victor de Vita." *Revue des études anciennes* 45 (1943):225–32.

———. "Le fondateur de Saint-Victor à Marseille: Jean Cassien." *Provence historique* 16 (1966):297–308.

———. "Jean Cassien à Marseille." *Revue du moyen âge latin* 1 (1945):5–26.

———. "La patrie de Jean Cassien." *OCP* 13 (1947):588–96.

————. Review of Léon Cristiani, *Jean Cassien*. *Revue du moyen âge latin* 2 (1946):329–32.

Marsili, Salvatore. *Giovanni Cassiano ed Evagrio Pontico*. SA 5. Rome: Herder, 1936.

————. "Résumé de Cassien sous le nom de saint Nil." *RAM* 15 (1934):241–45.

Marx, Michael. *Incessant Prayer in Ancient Monastic Literature*. Rome: Facultas Theologica Sancti Anselmi de Urbe, 1946.

————. "Incessant Prayer in the *Vita Antonii*." In *Antonius Magnus Eremita, 356–1956. Studia ad antiquum monachismum spectantia*, pp. 108–35. Ed. Basil Steidle. SA 38. Rome: Orbis Catholicus/Herder, 1956.

Maspero, J., and G. Weit. *Matériaux pour servir à la géographie de l'Égypte*. Mémoires de l'Institut Français d'Archéologie Orientale 36. Cairo: IFAO, 1919.

Ménager, A. "Cassien et Clément d'Alexandrie." *La Vie Spirituelle* 9 (1924):138–52.

————. "La patrie de Cassien." *Échos d'Orient* 21 (1921):330–58.

Merkle, S. "Cassien kein Syrer." *Theologische Quartalschrift* 82 (1900):419–41.

Messana, Vincenzo. "Le definizioni di προσευχή nel *De oratione* di Evagrio Pontico." In *Oeconomus Gratiae: Studi per il 20 anniversario di episcopato di Alfredo M. Garsia*, pp. 69–87. Quaderni di Presenza Culturale 32. Caltanissetta: Edizioni del Seminario, 1995.

————. "Diadoco di Fotica e la cultura cristiana in Epiro nel V secolo." *Augustinianum* 19 (1979):151–66.

————. "San Diadoco di Fotica." In *Introduzione ai Padri della Chiesa. Secoli quarto e quinto*, pp. 425–42. Ed. G. Bosio, E. dal Covolo, and M. Maritano. Turin: Società Editrice Internazionale, 1995.

Meyer, Robert T. "Lectio divina in Palladius." In *Kyriakon: Festschrift Johannes Quasten*, pp. 580–84. Ed. Patrick Granfield and Josef A. Jungmann. Münster: Aschendorff, 1970.

————. "Palladius and the Study of Scripture." In *SP* 13, pp. 487–90. Berlin: Akademie Verlag, 1975.

Miller, Patricia Cox. "Dreaming the Body: An Aesthetics of Asceticism." In *Asceticism*, pp. 281–300. Ed. Vincent L. Wimbush and Richard Valantasis. New York: Oxford University Press, 1995.

Miquel, Pierre. *Lexique du désert. Étude de quelques mots-clés du vocabulaire monastique grec ancien*. Spiritualité orientale 44. Bégrolles-en-Mauges: Abbaye de Bellefontaine, 1986.

————. "Un homme d'expérience: Cassien." *CC* 30 (1968):131–46.

Mommsen, Theodor. *Chronica minora saec. IV., V., VI., VII.* 3 vols. Monumenta Germaniae historica 9, 11, 13. Berlin: Weidman, 1892–98.

Mondésert, Claude. *Clément d'Alexandrie: Introduction à l'étude de sa pensée religieuse à partir de l'Écriture*. Théologie 4. Paris: Aubier, 1944.

Munz, Peter. "John Cassian." *JEH* 11 (1960):1–22.

Musurillo, Herbert. "The Problem of Ascetical Fasting in the Greek Patristic Tradition." *Traditio* 12 (1956):1–64.

Neuhausen, Karl August. "Zu Cassians Traktat *De amicitia* (Coll. 16)." In *Studien zur Literatur der Spätantike*, pp. 181–218. Ed. Christian Gnilka and Willy Schetter. Antiquitas, Reihe 1, Band 23. Bonn: Habelt, 1975.

Nouailhat, René. *Saints et patrons. Les premiers moines de Lérins*. Annales Littéraires de l'Université de Besançon 382. Paris: Les Belles Lettres, 1988.

Nürnberg, Rosemarie. *Askese als sozialer Impuls*. Bonn: Borengässer, 1988.

Nuvolone, G., and Aimé Solignac. "Pélage." *DSp*, 12:2889–2942.

O'Connor, Flannery. *The Habit of Being: Letters*. Selected and ed. Sally Fitzgerald. New York: Farrar, Straus, Giroux, 1979.

O'Laughlin, Michael. "The Bible, the Demons and the Desert: Evaluating the *Antirrheticus* of Evagrius Ponticus." *SM* 34 (1992):201–15.

————. "New Questions Concerning the Origenism of Evagrius." In *Origeniana Quinta. Papers of the Fifth International Origen Congress, Boston College, 14–18 August 1989*, pp. 528–34. Ed. Robert J. Daly. Bibliotheca Ephemeridum Theologicarum Lovaniensium 105. Leuven: University Press/Peeters, 1992.

————. "Origenism in the Desert. Anthropology and Integration in Evagrius Ponticus." Th.D. diss., Harvard University, 1987.

Olphe-Galliard, Michel. "Cassien (Jean)." *DSp*, 2:214–76.

————. "La contemplation dans la littérature chrétienne latine." In "Contemplation," *DSp*, 2:1911–29.

————. "La pureté de coeur d'après Cassien." *RAM* 17 (1936):28–60.

————. "La science spirituelle d'après Cassien." *RAM* 18 (1937):141–60.

————. "Les sources de la Conférence XI de Cassien." *RAM* 16 (1935):289–98.

————. "Vie contemplative et vie active d'après Cassien." *RAM* 16 (1935):252–98.

Oxford Latin Dictionary. Ed. P. G. W. Glare. Oxford: Clarendon Press, 1982.

Palanque, Jean-Remy. *Le diocèse de Marseille*. Histoire des diocèses de France. Paris: Letouzey et Ané, 1967.

Parmentier, Martin. "Evagrius of Pontus' 'Letter to Melania' I." *Bijdragen, tijdschrift voor filosofie en theologie* 46 (1985):2–38.

Paucker, C. von. "Die Latinität des Johannes Cassianus." *Romanische Forschungen* 2 (1886):391–448.

Pauly, August Friedrich von. *Paulys real-Encyclopädie der classischen Altertumswissenschaft*. Rev. Georg Wissowa. Stuttgart: J. B. Metzler, 1894–1919.

Payer, Pierre J. *Sex and the Penitentials: The Development of a Sexual Code, 550–1150*. Toronto: University of Toronto Press, 1984.

Pegon, Joseph. "Componction." *DSp*, 2:1312–21.

Petersen, Joan M. *The Dialogues of Gregory the Great in Their Late Antique Cultural Background*. Studies and Texts 69. Toronto: Pontifical Institute of Mediaeval Studies, 1984.

Pichery, Eugène. Introduction to *Jean Cassien: Conférences*, pp. 7–72. SC 42, 54, 64. Paris: Cerf, 1955–59.

Pigeaud, J. "Le rêve érotique dans l'Antiquité gréco-romaine: l'oneirogmos." In *Rêve, sommeil et insomnie*, pp. 10–23. Littérature, Médecine, Société 3. Nantes: Université de Nantes, 1981.

Plagnieux, Jean. "Le grief de complicité entre erreurs nestorienne et pélagienne d'Augustin à Cassien par Prosper d'Aquitaine?" *REA* 2 (1956):391–402.

Poloma, Margaret M. "The Sociological Context of Religious Experience." In *Handbook of Religious Experience*, pp. 161–82. Ed. Ralph W. Hood Jr. Birmingham, Ala.: Religious Education Press, 1995.

Popescu, Emilian. "Zur Geschichte der Stadt in Kleinskythien in der Spätantike. Ein epigraphischer Beitrag." *Dacia: Revue d'archéologie et d'histoire ancienne* 19 (1975):173–82.

Poulain, Augustin. *The Graces of Interior Prayer*. Enlarged ed. London: Routledge and Kegan Paul, 1950. Trans. Leonora L. Yorke Smith and corrected to accord with the 10th. ed. of *Des grâces d'oraison*. Paris: Beauchesne, 1922.

Preuschen, Erwin. *Palladius und Rufinus: Ein Beitrag zur Quellenkunde des ältesten Monchtums: Texte und Untersuchungen*. Giessen: J. Rickersche Buchhandlung, 1897.

Pricoco, Salvatore. *L'isola dei santi: Il cenobio di Lerino e le origini del monachesimo gallico*. Rome: Edizioni dell'Ateneo and Bizzarri, 1978.

——. *Storia letteraria e storia ecclesiastica dal De viris inlustribus di Girolamo a Gennadio.* Quaderni del Siculorum Gymnasium 6. Catania: Facoltà di Lettere e Filosofia, Università di Catania, 1979.

Prinz, Friedrich. *Frühes Mönchtum im Frankenreich. Kultur und Gesellschaft in Gallien, den Rheinlanden und Bayern am Beispiel der monastischen Entwicklung (4. bis 8. Jahrhundert).* Munich: R. Oldenbourg, 1965.

Pristas, Lauren. "The Theological Anthropology of John Cassian." Ph.D. diss., Boston College, 1993.

Quasten, Johannes. *Patrology.* 3 vols. Westminster, Md.: Newman Press, 1950–1960.

Quinn, John M. "Mysticism in the Confessiones: Four Passages Reconsidered." In *Augustine: Mystic and Mystagogue*, pp. 252–86. Ed. Frederick Van Fleteren, Joseph C. Schnaubelt, and Joseph Reino. Collectanea Augustiniana. New York: Peter Lang, 1994.

Raasch, Juana. "The Monastic Concept of Purity of Heart and Its Sources." *Studia Monastica* 8 (1966):7–33, 183–213; 10 (1968):7–55; 11 (1969):269–314; 12 (1970):7–41.

Rabbow, Paul. *Seelenführung: Methodik der Exerzitien in der Antike.* München: Kösel, 1954.

Rader, Rosemary. *Breaking Boundaries: Male/Female Friendship in Early Christian Communities.* Ramsey, N.J.: Paulist Press, 1983.

Rahner, Karl. "Le début d'une doctrine des cinq sens spirituels." *RAM* 13 (1932):113–45.

Ramsey, Boniface. "John Cassian: Student of Augustine." *Cistercian Studies Quarterly* 28 (1993):5–15.

——. *John Cassian. The Conferences.* English trans. and commentary. Ancient Christian Writers 57. Mahwah, N.J.: Paulist, 1997.

——. "Two Traditions on Lying and Deception in the Ancient Church." *The Thomist* 49 (1985):504–33.

Rébillard, Eric. "*Quasi funambuli*: Cassien et la controverse pélagienne sur la perfection." *REA* 40 (1994):197–210.

Refoulé, F. "La Christologie d' Évagre et l'Origénisme." *OCP* 27 (1961):221–66.

——. "Rêves et vie spirituelle d'après Évagre le Pontique." *Supplément à La Vie spirituelle* 14 (1961):470–616.

Régamey, P. "La componction du coeur." *Supplément à La Vie spirituelle* 44 (juillet–août 1935):1–16; (septembre 1935):65–83; 45 (octobre 1935):8–21; (decembre 1935):86–99.

Regnault, Lucien. "The Beatitudes in the *Apophthegmata Patrum*." *Eastern Churches Review* 6 (1974):22–43. The French original was later published in *Les pères du désert à travers leurs apophtegmes*, pp. 155–84.

——. "Isaac, Saint." *CE*, 1304.

——. "Moses the Black, Saint." *CE*, 1681.

——. *Les pères du désert à travers leurs apophtegmes.* Solesmes: Abbaye, 1987.

——. "Poemen, Saint." *CE*, 1983–84.

——. "La prière continuelle 'monologistos' dans les Apophtegmes des Pères." *Irénikon* 48 (1974):467–93. Reprinted in *Les Pères du désert à travers leurs apophtegmes*, 113–39.

——. "La prière de Jésus dans quelques apophtegmes conservés en arabe." *Irénikon* 52 (1979):344–55. Reprinted in *Les Pères du désert à travers leurs apophtegmes*, pp. 142–52.

Reitzenstein, Richard. *Historia Monachorum und Historia Lausiaca: Eine Studie zur Geschichte des Mönchtums und der frühchristlichen Begriffe Gnostiker und Pneumatiker.* Göttingen: Vandenhoeck und Ruprecht, 1916.

Reypens, L. "Dieu (Connaissance mystique)." *DSp*, 3:883–929.

Ringgren, Helmer. "Ecstasy." *The Anchor Bible Dictionary*, 2:280–81. Ed. David Noel Freedman et al. New York: Doubleday, 1992.

Rivet, Albert Lionel Frederick. *Gallia Narbonensis, with a Chapter on Alpes Maritimae.* London: B. T. Batsford, 1988.

Roques, René. "Contemplation, extase et ténèbre chez le Pseudo-Denys." In "Contemplation," *DSp*, 2:1894–1911.

Ross, Maggie. *The Fountain and the Furnace: The Way of Tears and Fire.* New York: Paulist Press, 1987.

Rousseau, Philip. *Ascetics, Authority, and the Church in the Age of Jerome and Cassian.* Oxford Historical Monographs. Oxford: Oxford University Press, 1978.

———. *Basil of Caesarea.* The Transformation of the Classical Heritage 20. Berkeley: University of California Press, 1994.

———. "Cassian, Contemplation, and the Coenobitic Life." *JEH* 26 (1975):113–26.

———. "Cassian: Monastery and World." In *The Certainty of Doubt. Tributes to Peter Munz,* pp. 68–89. Ed. Miles Fairburn and W. H. Oliver. Wellington, New Zealand: Victoria University Press, 1995.

———. *Pachomius. The Making of a Community in Fourth-Century Egypt.* The Transformation of the Classical Heritage 6. Berkeley: University of California Press, 1985.

Rousselle, Aline. "Abstinence et continence dans les monastères de Gaule méridionale à la fin de l'antiquité et au début du moyen âge: étude d'un régime alimentaire et de sa fonction." In *Hommage à André Dupont (1897–1972). Études médiévales languedociennes,* pp. 239–54. Montpelier: Fédération Historique du Languedoc Méditerranéen et du Roussillon, 1974.

———. "Parole et inspiration: le travail de la voix dans le monde romain." *History and Philosophy of the Life Sciences* (1983):129–57.

———. *Porneia: On Desire and the Body in Antiquity.* Oxford: Blackwell, 1988. Trans. Felicia Pheasant from *Porneia: de la maîtrise du corps à la privation sensorielle.* Paris: Presses Universitaires de France, 1983.

Rubenson, Samuel. *The Letters of St. Antony: Monasticism and the Making of a Saint.* Studies in Antiquity and Christianity. Minneapolis: Fortress, 1995.

Russell, Kenneth C. "John Cassian on a Delicate Subject." *Cistercian Studies* 27 (1992):1–12.

Sauget, J.-M. "Cheremone." *BSanc*, 3:1186.

———. "Giovanni di Licopoli." *BSanc*, 6:818–22.

———. "Giuseppe." *BSanc*, 6:1303.

———. "Isidoro." *BSanc*, 7:957–59.

———. "Mosè." *BSanc*, 9:652–54.

———. "Pafnuzio." *BSanc*, 10:26–28.

Schiwietz, Stephan. *Das morgenländische Mönchtum.* 2 vols. Mainz: Kirchheim, 1904.

Schulz-Flügel, Eva. "The Function of Apophthegmata in *Vitae* and *Itineraria.*" In *SP* 18 pt. 2, pp. 281–91. Kalamazoo: Cistercian Publications, 1989.

Schwartz, Eduard. "Cassian und Nestorius." In *Konzilstudien. 1. Cassian und Nestorius. 2. Über echte und unechte Schriften des Bischofs Proklos von Konstantinopel,* pp. 1–17. Schriften der Wissenschaftlichen Gesellschaft in Strassburg 20. Heft. Strassburg: Trübner, 1914.

———. "Lebensdaten Cassians." *Zeitschrift für die neutestamentliche Wissenschaft* 38 (1939):1–11.

Severus, Emmanuel von. "Das Wort 'Meditari' im Sprachgebrauch der Heiligen Schrift." *Geist und Leben* 25 (1953):365–75.

Sharma, Arvind. "Ecstasy." In *Encyclopedia of Religion,* 5:11–17. Ed. Mircea Eliade. New York: Macmillan, 1987.

Sheridan, Mark. *Concordanza elettronica alle opere di Giovanni Cassiano.* Rome, 1990.

————. "Jacob and Israel: A Contribution to the History of an Interpretation." In *Mysterium Christi. Symbolgegenwart und theologische Bedeutung. Festschrift für Basil Studer,* pp. 219–41. SA 116. Rome, 1995.

————. "Models and Images of Spiritual Progress in the Works of John Cassian." In *Spiritual Progress: Studies in the Spirituality of Late Antiquity and Early Monasticism. Papers of the Symposium of the Monastic Institute Rome, Pontificio Ateneo Sant' Anselmo 14–15 May 1992,* pp. 101–25. Ed. Jeremy Driscoll and Mark Sheridan. SA 115. Rome: Pontificio Ateneo S. Anselmo, 1994.

Simonetti, Manlio. *Biblical Interpretation in the Early Church: An Historical Introduction to Patristic Exegesis.* Edinburgh: T. and T. Clark, 1994. Trans. John A. Hughes from *Profilo storico dell'esegesi patristica.* Rome, 1981.

Sipe, A. W. Richard. *A Secret World: Sexuality and the Search for Celibacy.* New York: Brunner/Mazel, 1990.

Solignac, Aimé. "Semipélagiens." *DSp,* 14:556–68.

————. "Victor de Vita." *DSp* 16:547–52.

————. "Vie active, vie contemplative, vie mixte." *DSp,* 16:592–623.

Solignac, Aimé, and Lin Donnat. "Marthe et Marie." *DSp,* 10:664–73.

Sophrony, Archimandrite. "De la nécessité des trois renoncements chez St. Cassien le Romain et St. Jean Climaque." In *SP* 5 (TU 80), pp. 393–400. Berlin: Akademie Verlag, 1962.

Sophocles, Evangelinus Apostolides. *Greek Lexicon of the Roman and Byzantine Periods.* Cambridge: Harvard University Press, 1914. Reprint, Hildesheim: Olms, 1983.

Špidlík, Tomás. *La spiritualité de l'orient chrétien.* Vol. 2, *La prière.* OCA 230. Rome: Pontificium Institutum Studiorum Orientalium, 1988.

————. *The Spirituality of the Christian East: A Systematic Handbook.* CSS 79. Kalamazoo: Cistercian Publications, 1986. Trans. Anthony P. Gythiel from *La spiritualité de l'orient chrétien,* Vol. 1, *Manuel Systématique.* OCA 206. Rome: Pontificium Institutum Studiorum Orientalium, 1978.

Spinelli. "Teologia e 'teoria' nella *Conlatio de Protectione Dei* di Giovanni Cassiano." *Benedictina* 31 (1984):23–35.

Sternberg, Thomas. "Der vermeintliche Ursprung der westlichen Diakonien in Ägypten und die *Conlationes* des Johannes Cassian." *Jahrbuch für Antike und Christentum* 31 (1988):173–209.

Stewart, Columba. "The Desert Fathers on Radical Honesty about the Self." *Sobornost* 12 (1990):25–39, 131–56. Reprinted in *Vox Benedictina* 8 (1991):7–53.

————. "From λόγος to *verbum.* John Cassian's Use of Greek in the Development of a Latin Monastic Vocabulary." In *The Joy of Learning and the Love of God. Studies in Honor of Jean Leclercq,* pp. 5–31. Ed. E. Rozanne Elder. CSS 160. Kalamazoo: Cistercian Publications, 1995.

————. "John Cassian on Unceasing Prayer." *Monastic Studies* 15 (1984):159–77.

————. "The Portrayal of Women in the Sayings and Stories of the Desert." *Vox Benedictina* 2 (1985):5–23.

————. *Working the Earth of the Heart: The Messalian Controversy in History, Texts, and Language to AD 431.* Oxford Theological Monographs. Oxford: Clarendon Press, 1991.

Straw, Carole. *Gregory the Great: Perfection in Imperfection.* Berkeley: University of California Press, 1988.

Summa, Gerd. *Geistliche Unterscheidung bei Johannes Cassian.* Studien zur systematischen und spirituellen Theologie 7. Würzburg: Echter, 1992.

Taft, Robert. *The Liturgy of the Hours in East and West: The Origins of the Divine Office and Its Meaning for Today.* Collegeville, Mn.: Liturgical Press, 1986.

Teske, Roland J. "St. Augustine and the Vision of God." In *Augustine: Mystic and Mystagogue*, pp. 287–308. Ed. Frederick Van Fleteren, Joseph C. Schnaubelt, and Joseph Reino. Collectanea Augustiniana. New York: Peter Lang, 1994.

Thesaurus Linguae Latinae. Leipzig: Teubner, 1900–.

Thibaut, Jean-Baptiste. *L'ancienne liturgie gallicane. Son origine et formation en Provence aux cinquième et sixième siècles sous l'influence de Cassien et de Saint Césaire d'Arles.* Paris: Maison de la Bonne Presse, 1929.

Thurman, Robert A. F. "Tibetan Buddhist Perspectives on Asceticism." In *Asceticism*, pp. 108–18. Ed. Vincent L. Wimbush and Richard Valantasis. New York: Oxford University Press, 1995.

Tibiletti, Carlo. "Giovanni Cassiano. Formazione e dottrina." *Augustinianum* 17 (1977):355–80.

———. *Pagine monastiche provenzali: Il monachesimo nella Gallia del quinto secolo.* Cultura cristiani antica. Rome: Borla, 1990.

———. "Rassegna di studi e testi sui 'Semipelagiani.' " *Augustinianum* 25 (1985):507–22.

Tillemont, Louis-Sébastien le Nain de. *Mémoires pour servir à l'histoire ecclésiastique des six premiers siècles.* 16 vols. Paris, 1701–12. Reprint, Venice, 1732.

Van Fleteren, Frederick. "Mysticism in the Confessiones—A Controversy Revisited." In *Augustine: Mystic and Mystagogue*, pp. 309–36. Ed. Frederick Van Fleteren, Joseph C. Schnaubelt, and Joseph Reino. Collectanea Augustiniana. New York: Peter Lang, 1994.

Vannier, Marie-Anne. "L'influence de Jean Chrysostome sur l'argumentation scripturaire du *De Incarnatione* de Jean Cassien." *RSR* 69 (1995):453–62.

———. "Jean Cassien a-t-il fait oeuvre de théologien dans le *De incarnatione domini?*" *RSR* 66 (1992):119–31. Reprint, *SP* 24, pp. 345–54. Leuven: Peeters, 1993.

Veilleux, Armand. *La liturgie dans le cénobitisme pachômien au quatrième siècle.* SA 57. Rome: Facultas Theologica Sancti Anselmi de Urbe, 1968.

———. *Pachomian Koinonia.* 3 vols. CSS 45–47. Kalamazoo: Cistercian Publications, 1980–82.

Viller, Marcel. "Aux sources de la spiritualité de saint Maxime." *RAM* 11 (1930):156–84, 239–68.

Viller, Marcel and Karl Rahner. *Aszese und Mystik in der Väterzeit. Ein Abriß.* Freiburg im Breisgau: Herder, 1939. Revision and translation of Viller's *La spiritualité des premiers siècles chrétiens.* Paris: Bloud et Gay, 1930.

Vivian, Tim. " 'Everything Made by God is Good.' " *Église et Théologie* 24 (1993):75–108.

Vogüé, Adalbert de. "De Cassien au Maître et à Eugippe: le titre du chapitre de l'humilité." *SM* 23 (1981):247–61.

———. "Cassien, le Maître et Benoît." In *Commandements du Seigneur et libération évangélique. Études monastiques proposées et discutées à Saint–Anselme, 15–17 février 1976*, pp. 223–35. Ed. Jean Gribomont. SA 70. Rome: Editrice Anselmiana, 1977.

———. *Community and Abbot in the Rule of Saint Benedict.* CSS 5/1–2. Spencer, Mass.: Cistercian Publications, 1979 and 1988. Trans. Charles Philippi and Ethel Rae Perkins from *La communauté et l'Abbé dans la Règle de Saint Benoît.* Paris: Desclée de Brouwer, 1961.

———. "Les débuts de la vie monastique à Lérins. Remarques sur un ouvrage récent." *Revue de l'histoire des religions* 88 (1993):5–53.

———. "Les deux fonctions de la méditation dans les Règles monastiques anciennes." *Revue d'histoire de la spiritualité* 51 (1975):3–16.

———. *Histoire littéraire du mouvement monastique dans l'antiquité.* Patrimoines christianisme. Paris: Cerf, 1991–.

————. "Une interpolation inspirée de Cassien dans un texte monastique de Césaire d'Arles." *SM* 25 (1983):217–21.

————. "Les mentions des oeuvres de Cassien chez Saint Benoît et ses contemporains." *SM* 20 (1978):275–85.

————. "Monachisme et Église dans la pensée de Cassien." In *Théologie de la vie monastique: Études sur la Tradition patristique*, pp. 213–40. Théologie 49. Paris: Aubier, 1961.

————. "Un morceau célèbre de Cassien parmi des extraits d'Évagre." *SM* 27 (1985):7–12.

————. "Pour comprendre Cassien. Un survol des Conférences." *CC* 39 (1979):250–72.

————. *Les Règles des saint Pères.* SC 297–98. Paris: Cerf, 1982.

————. "La 'Regula Cassiani': sa destination et ses rapports avec le monachisme fructuosien." *RB* 95 (1985):185–231.

————. "Les sources des quatre premiers livres des Institutions de Jean Cassien. Introduction aux recherches sur les anciennes règles monastiques latines." *SM* 27 (1985):241–311.

————. *The Rule of Saint Benedict, a Doctrinal and Spiritual Commentary.* CSS 54. Kalamazoo: Cistercian Publications, 1983. Trans. John Baptist Hasbrouck from *La Règle de Saint Benoît.* Vol. 7, *Commentaire doctrinal et spirituel.* Paris: Cerf, 1977.

————. "Sub regula vel abbate." In *Rule and Life: An Interdisciplinary Symposium*, pp. 21–64. CSS 12. Ed. M. Basil Pennington. Spencer, Mass.: Cistercian Publications, 1971. Trans. from "Sub regula vel abbate." *CC* 33 (1971):209–41.

————. "Twenty-Five Years of Benedictine Hermeneutics—An Examination of Conscience." *ABR* 36 (1985):402–52. Trans. John Baptist Hasbrouck from "Vingt-cinq ans d'herméneutique bénédictine." *Regula Benedicti Studia* 14/15 (1988):5–40.

Vogüé, Adalbert de, and Joël Courreau. *Césaire d'Arles: Oeuvres monastiques I-II.* SC 345 and 398. Paris: Cerf, 1988 and 1994.

Vogüé, Adalbert de, and Jean Neufville. *La Règle de Saint Benoît.* 7 vols. SC 181–86, 186a. Paris: Cerf, 1971–77.

Völker, Walther. *Gregor von Nyssa als Mystiker.* Wiesbaden: Franz Steiner, 1955.

————. *Kontemplation und Ekstase bei Pseudo-Dionysius Areopagita.* Wiesbaden: Franz Steiner, 1958.

————. *Maximus Konfessor als Meister des geistlichen Lebens.* Wiesbaden: Franz Steiner, 1965.

————. *Praxis und Theoria bei Symeon dem Neuen Theologen.* Wiesbaden: Franz Steiner, 1974.

————. *Scala Paradisi: Eine Studie zu Johannes Climacus und zugleich eine Vorstudie zu Symeon dem Neuen Theologen.* Wiesbaden: Franz Steiner, 1968.

————. *Das Vollkommenheitsideal des Origenes.* Tübingen: Mohr, 1931.

————. *Der wahre Gnostiker nach Clemens Alexandrinus.* Berlin: Akademie-Verlag, 1952.

Voss, Bernd Reiner. *Der Dialog in der frühchristlichen Literatur.* Studia et testimonia antiqua 9. München: Fink, 1970.

Vuillaume, Christophe. "Le jeûne dans la tradition monastique ancienne et aujourd'hui." *CC* 51 (1989):42–78.

Ward, Benedicta. *Harlots of the Desert: A Study of Repentance in Early Monastic Sources.* London: Mowbray, 1987.

Ware, Kallistos. Introduction to *John Climacus. The Ladder of Divine Ascent*, pp. 1–70. Trans. Colm Luibheid. Classics of Western Spirituality. New York: Paulist Press, 1982.

Weaver, Rebecca Harden. *Divine Grace and Human Economy: A Study of the Semi-*

Pelagian Controversy. North American Patristic Society Patristic Monograph Series 15. Macon, Ga.: Mercer University Press, 1996.

Weber, Hans-Oskar. *Die Stellung des Johannes Cassianus zur ausserpachomianischen Mönchstradition*. Münster: Aschendorff, 1961.

Wicker, Kathleen O'Brien. "Ethiopian Moses (Collected Sources)." In *Ascetic Behavior in Greco-Roman Antiquity: A Sourcebook*, pp. 329–48. Ed. Vincent L. Wimbush. Studies in Antiquity and Christianity. Minneapolis: Fortress, 1990.

Williams, Rowan. *The Wound of Knowledge: Christian Spirituality from the New Testament to St. John of the Cross*. London: Darton, Longman, and Todd, 1979.

Wimbush, Vincent L. "Ascetic Behavior and Color-ful Language: Stories about Ethiopian Moses." *Semeia* 58 (1992):81–92.

———, ed. *Ascetic Behavior in Greco-Roman Antiquity: A Sourcebook*. Studies in Antiquity and Christianity. Minneapolis: Fortress, 1990.

Winston, David. *Philo of Alexandria: The Contemplative Life, the Giants and Selections*. Classics of Western Spirituality. Ramsey, N.J.: Paulist Press, 1981.

Wißmann, Hans. "Ekstase." *TRE*, 9:488–91.

Wrzol, Ludwig. "Die Hauptsündenlehre des Johannes Cassianus und ihre historischen Quellen." *Divus Thomas* 37 (1923):385–404; 38 (1924):84–91.

———. "Die Psychologie des Johannes Cassianus." *Divus Thomas* 32 (1918):181–213, 425–56; 34 (1920):70–96; 36 (1922):269–94.

Zahn, Theodore. "Neuere Beiträge zur Geschichte des apostolischen Symbolums." *Neue kirchliche Zeitschrift* 7 (1896):16–33.

Zaniri, Marianne. "La controverse sur la prédestination au cinquième siècle: Augustin, Cassien et la tradition." In *Saint Augustin*, pp. 248–61. Ed. Patric Ranson. Les Dossiers H. Lausanne: L'Âge d'homme, 1988.

Zelzer, Klaus. "*Cassianus natione Scytha*, ein Südgallier." *Wiener Studien* 104 (1991):161–68.

Biblical Citations

Cassian's Writings

On the Incarnation of the Lord

Pref.

Books 1–7

Latin and Greek Words

General Index

Note: *References in the notes to authors and works listed in the bibliography may be found by locating the relevant subject in this index and consulting the notes to those pages of the main text.*

on "Elias of the ministry," 137
on hospitality, 44
on Isaac, 136
on Isidore, 138
on Joseph, 134
on Nesteros, 133
parallel with Cassian on Abba
Patermuthius, 140
and prosopography of Scetis, 135
on recitation of biblical texts, 102–03
and Scetis, 9–10;
on Serenus, 136
on Theonas, 137
Aramaic (language), 60
Arcadius, Emperor, 14
Archebius of Diolcos, 9, 134
Archebius of Panephysis, 8–9, 134
Arian controversy, 88
Aristotle, 50
Arles, 16
Arsenius, 124
asceticism
and biblical interpretation, 90–91
and chastity, 59, 62–84
and contemplation, 49–52
limited scope of, 55, 58
and *meditatio*, 104–05
and prayer, 106–07, 111
and purity of heart, 43–45, 47
and tears, 129
Athanasius, 23, 81, 90
Augustine
on concupiscence, 65
on ecstasy, 118–19
on erotic dreams, 82
influence on Cassian, 36
influence on Gregory the Great, 128
on the Lord's Prayer, 206 n.112
on lying, 45
on manual labor in the monastic life,
152 n.154
and monastic life in Hippo, 16
on nocturnal emissions, 190 n.195
and Pelagianism/ Semi-Pelagianism, 19–
23, 28, 63, 77–80
avarice, 66

Bacht, Heinrich, 102
Barsanuphius, 25
Basil

anthropology of, 80
Cassian's claim to supplement, 17
Cassian's knowledge of, 36
on chastity, 66
on day hours of liturgy, 101
on fear and love, 168 n.40
on knowledge, 90–91
on rememberance of God, 104
on virginity, 70
beatitude
biblical, 43, 55–56, 111–12, 124
heavenly, 53, 55–60, 96, 99, 129
Benedict of Aniane, 25
Benedict of Nursia
and Cassian's teaching on humility, 25,
168 n.40
and Cassian's teaching on prayer, 25,
116–17, 123
on evening reading, 189 n.187
on gyrovagues, 9
liturgical code, 199 n.6
recommendation of Cassian's writings,
25, 31, 158 n.235
use of Cassian's formula for unceasing
prayer, 113
Benjamin, 140
Bethlehem, 6–8, 14, 31, 33, 45–46
Bible
Cassian's use of, 35, 38, 80–81, 94
and chastity, 63, 74, 82
interpretation of, 11, 51, 53, 85–99, 105,
112–13 (*See also* knowledge,
spiritual)
versions of, 35, 38, 102
body, 69–71
Book of Steps (Liber graduum), 37, 115, 121
boys, 74
Bunge, Gabriel, 97, 120, 171 n.73
Butler, Cuthbert, 10, 86

Caesarius of Arles, 16, 21, 25
Calamon, 139
Calamus (area in Scetis), 10, 138–40
Cappadocia, 87
Carthage, Council of (418), 19
Cassian, John
bilingualism, 5–6, 36, 115, 144 n.38
birthplace, 4–6
chronology, 141 n.10
Conferences, 16, 18, 30–35, 40–41